THE EFFECTIVE DEPOSITION

Techniques and Strategies That Work

SIXTH EDITION

Carl W. Chamberlin

(Previous editions by Peter Toll Hoffman & David M. Malone)

NATIONAL INSTITUTE FOR TRIAL ADVOCACY

Address inquiries to:
Reprint Permission
National Institute for Trial Advocacy
325 W. South Boulder Rd., Ste. 1
Louisville, CO 80027–1130
Phone: (800) 225-6482
Email: permissions@nita.org

ISBN 978-1-60156-974-5
FBA 1974
eISBN 978-1-60156-975-2
eFBA 1975

Library of Congress Cataloging-in-Publication Data

Names: Chamberlin, Carl W., author.
Title: The effective deposition : techniques and strategies that work / Carl W. Chamberlin.
Description: Sixth edition. | Louisville, CO : The National Institute for Trial Advocacy, [2023] | Includes index.
Identifiers: LCCN 2022059087 (print) | LCCN 2022059088 (ebook) | ISBN 9781601569745 (paperback) | ISBN 9781601569752 (ebook)
Subjects: LCSH: Depositions--United States.
Classification: LCC KF8900 .M34 2023 (print) | LCC KF8900 (ebook) | DDC 347.73/72--dc23/eng/20230424
LC record available at https://lccn.loc.gov/2022059087
LC ebook record available at https://lccn.loc.gov/2022059088

The examples in this book use fictitious names and events. Any similarity to real cases or real persons, living or dead, is coincidental and not intended by the author. The views expressed in this book are those of the author and do not reflect the views of his employers, predict or imply the outcome of any case, or constitute legal advice.

SUSTAINABLE FORESTRY INITIATIVE
Certified Chain of Custody
At Least 10% Certified Forest Content
www.sfiprogram.org
SFI-01028

To my wife,

Nancy

CONTENTS

Contents

PART THREE: DEFENDING DEPOSITIONS

FOREWORD

Peter Toll Hoffman, author of all previous editions of *The Effective Deposition*, and David Malone, his co-author for all but the last edition, were recognized as two of the finest teachers of litigation skills in the country. So, too, was Professor Anthony J. Bocchino, who contributed to the Revised Third Edition. It is their work that established *The Effective Deposition* as the premier resource on depositions. Their insights and examples guided me during my deposition-taking days in private practice and have equipped me as I've taught deposition courses for the last few decades. It is an honor to follow in their footsteps as I assume the reins of *The Effective Deposition*.

Much has changed, of course, since the first edition of this book was published nearly fifty years ago. Indeed, much has changed since the most recent Fifth Edition was published in 2018. The nature of litigation has changed, technology has changed, and society has changed. Striving to keep pace, laws have changed as well. Change is what the Sixth Edition is all about.

Now more than ever, litigation is resolved not by trial but by summary judgment or negotiated settlement, based on evidence generated in depositions. Attorneys taking depositions must learn all the witness's information to best prepare case theories and attack what the witness might say in an affidavit or other evidentiary submission. They must know how to elicit critical admissions and decide which questioning approach will accomplish the deposition's purpose. Attorneys defending depositions must consider whether to follow conventional wisdom and prepare their witnesses not to volunteer information or to take a more modern approach and, through the right witness, reveal information that will establish triable factual issues or enhance the settlement value of the case. Whatever strategies the lawyers pursue, they must be implemented proficiently and efficiently.

Meanwhile, technological advances have altered depositions dramatically. Video depositions, once a high-end luxury, have become common—if not indispensable—in many practice areas, affecting witness preparation and the presentation of deposition testimony to the trier of fact. Increasingly sophisticated databases modify how lawyers get ready for the deposition. The tremendous increase in electronically stored information—from electronic communications to web pages to social media and ubiquitous video—change the format of deposition exhibits and the questions to ask about them. For many, real-time reporting and keystrokes on a laptop supplant court reporter "readbacks" and counsel's scrawled notes on a yellow pad. Videoconferencing allows depositions to occur among participants at multiple locations all over the world. When used well, technology can make depositions more efficient and deposition testimony more persuasive.

Societal change—including that wrought by a worldwide pandemic—has affected deposition practice too. Obstructionist defense tactics are tolerated less as a push for civility in the profession gains momentum. With international litigation proliferating and attorneys and parties becoming more diverse, counsel must appreciate a variety of perspectives. Clients are more sensitive than ever to soaring litigation costs. The grip of the pandemic, which convinced attorneys and clients to find new ways of doing things, normalized the remote deposition and changed forever how depositions can be conducted. And with these changes come challenges. While the remote deposition minimizes expense and travel burdens, it is fraught with risks and complexities as well. How can we do remotely what we once did face to face? This question—and the broader impact of technological advances—have resulted in an avalanche of new case law, statutes, and rules.

The Sixth Edition addresses these changes. It offers new material, extensive updates, and copious revisions to meet the challenges facing today's litigator. It expands the use of examples demonstrating the suggested skills and techniques. And it strives to meet the needs of the busy reader with new take-away checklists at the end of most chapters and electronic access to video demonstrations provided by the National Institute for Trial Advocacy.

As the originating authors of this book put it, each edition is a snapshot of deposition practice at a single point in time, seeking to be "of practical use to all attorneys who want to obtain the best results for their clients by mastering the facts and anticipating their opponents' proof." I hope this edition fulfills that tradition. And I hope it equips and inspires students and lawyers of every experience level to pursue . . . the effective deposition.

—C.W.C.

INTRODUCTION

There is no more important component of civil litigation than the deposition. No better tool exists for finding out what the opposing party did. No method better reveals what the opposing party does not want you to know. No discovery device better allows you to prepare your case for motion practice, arbitration, settlement negotiations, and trial. As recognized nearly three decades ago, "[d]epositions are the factual battleground where the vast majority of litigation actually takes place."[1] As observed fifteen years later: "More than 98% of all civil cases filed in the federal courts result in disposition by way of settlement or pretrial adjudication. Very often, these results turn on evidence obtained during depositions. Thus, depositions play an extremely important role in the American system of justice."[2]

Today's civil cases resolve overwhelmingly by motion or settlement rather than by trial, and the deposition has supplanted the courtroom as the crucible of truth. For the rare case that goes to trial, depositions show you what direct and cross-examination questions to ask, and deposition transcripts or video recordings deliver powerful evidence to the trier of fact. As the cost of litigation skyrockets, depositions must be conducted with efficiency and skill, and the need for *effective* depositions has never been greater.

The deposition concept is simple enough.[3] An attorney serves a notice or subpoena to require the witness's attendance and arranges for a court reporter to record what is said. During the deposition, the attorney sits across a table from the witness and (usually) the witness's attorney, or participants appear remotely on a screen via an online videoconference. The witness is placed under oath, the attorney questions the witness, the witness's attorney may interpose objections, and the witness answers. The proceedings may be videorecorded. The deposition transcript or recording can then be used to evaluate the client's case, to gain leverage in settlement negotiations, or to offer evidence in a summary judgment motion, arbitration, or—if it ever gets that far—at trial.

But too often, depositions go awry. Deposing attorneys enter the arena unprepared. Some fail to obtain critical information from the witness because they ask incorrect questions, or they ask questions incorrectly. Others extend the deposition needlessly by not knowing what facts must be elicited or believing they must chase down minutiae that will never make a difference to the outcome of the case. Questioners miss the witness's verbal or nonverbal clues. On the other side of the table, witnesses evade questions or lie. The defending attorney turns pale when the witness, inadequately counseled, volunteers incriminating information or undermines their credibility. The defending

---

1. Hall v. Clifton Precision, 150 F.R.D. 525, 531 (E.D. Pa. 1993).
2. GMAC Bank v. HTFC Corp., 248 F.R.D. 182, 185 (E.D. Pa. 2008).
3. This book focuses on the taking and defending of oral depositions (Fed. R. Civ. P. 30), as opposed to the far less common option of depositions upon written questions (Fed. R. Civ. P. 31).

attorney improperly coaches the witness, interferes with the proceedings, influences the testimony, or shuts it down altogether. Tempers flare. Discovery motions proliferate. Client costs increase. And testimony turns out to be unusable later in the litigation because counsel had not obtained recommended commitments from the witness at the beginning, entered into disfavored stipulations, left the deposition record unclear, neglected to lay evidentiary foundations, or forgot protocols or technical necessities for remote depositions. Much of this is considered to be just "the way it goes." How unfortunate. With some fine-tuning and redirection, all of it could have been addressed. Without much more effort, most of the problems could have been avoided.

So how, then, can we attain an *effective* deposition, from the perspective of both the deposing and the defending attorney? What techniques and strategies work in the real world, so the deposing attorney obtains needed information in a clear and usable form, while the defending attorney protects the witness and advances client interests commensurate with the rules? There is no one single answer, no one single approach, and no perfect deposition. But the following pages offer a collection of time-tested principles, skills, techniques, strategies, tips, considerations, and options wrought over the years by seasoned practitioners, judges, and advocacy experts from around the country, updated with the latest information to equip today's litigators.

Part One of the book explains the deposition rules and characteristics that create the foundation for an effective deposition. We will examine the laws that authorize and limit discovery generally and depositions in particular; the disparate purposes for taking a deposition; and how we can appreciate and exploit the advantages and disadvantages of depositions as a discovery device.

Part Two sets forth the skills, techniques, and strategies critical for taking and using depositions. To take and use a deposition effectively, you must:

- craft case theories and discovery plans that coordinate depositions with other discovery for maximum advantage;

- prepare for the deposition by strategically choosing lines of inquiry and potential exhibits, create a usable and flexible deposition outline, and anticipate issues that might arise;

- begin the deposition by avoiding unhelpful stipulations and eliciting commitments from the witness that set expectations, establish rapport with the witness, and undermine the witness's later attempts to wriggle out of their testimony;

- pursue an appropriate amount of background information and other preliminary inquiries of the witness;

- use the correct questioning method and techniques depending on the information you seek, including the funnel method to gather all the witness's information and assorted techniques for obtaining admissions and testing case theories;

- ask clear and concise questions, avoiding unnecessary words and language that gives the witness an out;

- listen to the witness, making sure they answered the question, following up as needed, and keeping the record clear;

- incorporate technology and strategy to gather, select, prepare, and use documents and electronically stored information in the deposition;

- get the witness to authenticate exhibits and lay an evidentiary foundation to ensure later use of the exhibits and testimony;

- deal with witnesses effectively by adopting a fitting style, handling prototype witness behaviors (forgetful, know-nothing, evasive, vague, lying, and combative), and responding to unfavorable testimony;

- deal successfully with the objecting, obnoxious, or obstructionist opposing counsel;

- conclude the deposition appropriately; and

- use deposition testimony in motions and at trial—in at least seven potential ways—for maximum impact.

Part Three then deals with effectiveness in defending depositions. To protect the witness's and client's interests and learn about the other side's case, you must:

- evaluate the deposition notice and seek protective orders;

- ethically prepare witnesses on deposition procedure and answering substantive questions, in a way that helps witnesses be more at ease, recall the preparation, and handle the questioning;

- employ the "one concept, three rules" guide to answering questions;

- reinforce deposition preparation and practice testimony in a mock deposition;

- make appropriate objections and instructions at the deposition and, if necessary, seek judicial intervention; and

- review the transcript or other recording of the deposition for accuracy and for potential use in motions and at trial.

Lastly, Part Four delves into greater detail regarding specific types of depositions: preservation depositions, depositions of organizations under Federal Rule of Civil Procedure 30(b)(6), depositions of expert witnesses, video depositions, and—the latest addition to the deposition world—remote depositions by videoconference.

Some readers may be deposition veterans looking for a refresher or a new tool for their deposition toolbelt. Others may have never taken a deposition before. This book welcomes both, combining basic information with the latest pros and cons of strategic and technological options. Some readers may practice primarily in federal court, which many chapters of this book use as a focal point; those who practice mostly in state court will find the same issues arise in their deposition practice too (with some variations in the rules, as the chapters point out). Overall, the essential skills and techniques of questioning and defending will apply regardless of the attorney's jurisdiction or practice area.

So use this book as it serves you best. You might read the chapters consecutively from the beginning of the book to the end; you might turn to a chapter on a topic of concern hours before your next deposition begins. After reading the skills, tips, and techniques, consider the example questions that have been provided to see how they might be applied in practice. As a summary or last-minute refresher, survey the checklists at the end of most chapters to have in mind the skills, techniques, and considerations covered by that chapter.

Video presentations are available to demonstrate the most critical skills discussed in this book. You can find these demonstrations at:

bit.ly/3NGHQCq

Password: NITAEffDep6

You can also use the following QR code to gain access to these video demonstrations.

But wait a minute. Is it really possible to conduct an effective deposition with little to no experience? Is it really possible to become more competent and confident even if you've been in the deposition trenches for years? Is it possible to prepare and defend a witness ethically and professionally without giving away the store? *Absolutely.* So let's get to it.

National Institute for Trial Advocacy

PART ONE

LAW AND PURPOSE

CHAPTER ONE

THE LAW OF TAKING AND DEFENDING DEPOSITIONS

You have to know the rules of the game,
and then you have to play better than anyone else.

—Albert Einstein

The young man knows the rules, but the
old man knows the exceptions.

—Oliver Wendell Holmes

A deposition will be more effective if you know the rules that authorize, limit, and control the deposition proceedings. While the specific rules are dictated by the law of the forum in which the lawsuit is pending, the issues they raise are common to depositions everywhere. Misunderstanding those rules can cost time and money, lead to embarrassment, and deprive the client of valuable deposition testimony.

In federal court, the rules governing depositions are found primarily in the Federal Rules of Civil Procedure ("FRCP" or "Rules"). To some extent, these rules may be supplemented by local rules of the relevant district court or orders issued by judges in the individual case. Judicial decisions interpreting the FRCP may vary a bit from jurisdiction to jurisdiction, but the best starting point is the language of the FRCP.

In state court, the rules governing depositions depend on the state. The majority of states have adopted rules akin to the FRCP, but variations abound; you must carefully check the laws that apply to the deposition at hand. While this book focuses on the FRCP, most of its advice also applies in some form to the FRCP's state counterparts.

> **In This Chapter:**
>
> - *A framework for discovery*
> - *Rules specific to depositions*
> - *Outline of the deposition procedure*

This chapter starts with the big-picture framework for discovery (Rule 26) and then examines the rules specific to depositions (Rules 30, 45).

1.1 Discovery Under the Federal Rules of Civil Procedure

Rules 26 through 37 of the FRCP address the discovery mechanisms available in federal litigation, including depositions, interrogatories, and requests for production of documents and electronically stored information (ESI). As relevant here, Rule 26(b) defines the scope of discovery generally, while Rule 26(c) allows a party from whom discovery is sought to seek an order barring or limiting that discovery. In addition, Rule 26(f) requires the parties to make initial disclosures of information before formal discovery begins, which impacts depositions as well.

1.1.1 Scope of Discovery

There is a limit to what can be sought in discovery and, therefore, to what a witness can be asked in a deposition. Rule 26(b)(1) states:

> Unless otherwise limited by court order, the scope of discovery is as follows: Parties may obtain discovery regarding any *nonprivileged* matter that is *relevant* to any party's claim or defense and *proportional* to the needs of the case, considering the importance of the issues at stake in the action, the amount in controversy, the parties' relative access to relevant information, the parties' resources, the importance of the discovery in resolving the issues, and whether the burden or expense of the proposed discovery outweighs its likely benefit. Information within the scope of discovery need not be admissible in evidence to be discoverable. (Emphasis added.)

In essence, whether a question can be asked at a deposition turns on whether it seeks information that is nonprivileged, relevant, and proportional to the needs of the case.

The first of these criteria—whether a matter is nonprivileged—is generally a question of state law in diversity cases, where state law supplies the substantive law applicable to the claims and defenses, while federal common law applies in federal question cases (Fed. R. Evid. 501). Privileges include those based on confidential communications arising in relationships of attorney-client, physician-patient, psychotherapist-patient, and the like. As a general matter, material that is privileged is not discoverable. We address objections and instructions not to answer on the ground of privilege in Chapter Eighteen.

The FRCP does not define "relevant to any party's claim or defense," but Federal Rule of Evidence 401 states that evidence is relevant if: "(a) it has any tendency to make a fact more or less probable than it would without the evidence" and "(b) the fact is of consequence in determining the action." In other words, discovery generally and depositions specifically may not inquire into matters that have no bearing on an element of a claim or defense or witness credibility (although, as we shall discuss, quite a bit of leeway is allowed on this point). Note that, other than the issue of relevance (and privilege), Rule 26(b)(1) makes clear that information does not need to be admissible in court to be discoverable.

> *Deposition questions must seek information that is:*
>
> - *nonprivileged,*
> - *relevant, and*
> - *proportional to the needs of the case.*

"Proportional to the needs of the case" is also not defined precisely by the FRCP, but Rule 26(b)(1) offers factors to consider:

> - the importance of the issues at stake in the action;
> - the amount in controversy;
> - the parties' relative access to relevant information;
> - the parties' resources;
> - the importance of the discovery in resolving the issues; and
> - whether the burden or expense of the proposed discovery outweighs its likely benefit.

You need not demonstrate proportionality in making a discovery request, and the party receiving the request cannot refuse to comply by merely making a boilerplate objection on proportionality grounds. In the deposition context, it is unlikely any single deposition question would be prohibited as disproportionate to case needs, but an unduly burdensome line of inquiry could be.

1.1.2 Protective Orders

Having suggested a broad scope of permissible discovery, the federal rules next confirm the power of the court to preclude discovery beyond those parameters. Rule 26(b)(2)(C)(iii) requires a judge, on a party's motion or on its own, to "limit the frequency or extent of discovery" if "the discovery is outside the scope permitted by Rule 26(b)(1)," which we just discussed.

Rule 26(b)(2)(C) provides two additional protections against discovery abuse. Rule 26(b)(2)(C)(i) permits the court to limit the frequency or extent of discovery otherwise permitted if "the discovery sought is *unreasonably cumulative or duplicative,* or can be obtained from *some other source* that is more convenient, less burdensome, or less expensive." (Emphasis added.) Rule 26(b)(2)(C)(ii) permits the court to limit otherwise proper discovery if "the party seeking discovery had ample opportunity to obtain the information by discovery in the action." In addition, the court may limit disclosure of work product under Rule 26(b)(3).

Protective orders can also be obtained to limit or prelude discovery under Rule 26(c) "to protect a party or person from annoyance, embarrassment, oppression, or undue burden or expense," including orders protecting "trade secret or other confidential research, development, or commercial information." We address protective orders further in section 16.2.

1.1.3   *Federal Disclosures, Discovery Conference, and Scheduling Order*

The FRCP require the parties to engage in a process early in the lawsuit that affects the course, content, and timing of discovery, including depositions. Although local rules and court orders may modify some aspects of the process, the key components are:

- **initial disclosures**, by which parties are required to exchange certain information and material (Rule 26(a)(1)(C));

- a **discovery planning conference** among the parties (Rule 26(f)(1)–(2)), which generally must be held before a party seeks formal discovery;

- a **discovery plan**, which is crafted by the parties after the planning conference and reported to the court (Rule 26(f)(3)); and

- a **scheduling order**, after the court's receipt of the report or after a scheduling conference (Rule 16(b)).

Let's look at these items more closely, because they affect how we can take and defend depositions.

Initial Disclosures

Under Rule 26(a)(1)(C), each party (unless the case is exempt) must provide to the other parties, without a discovery request, the identity of individuals likely to have discoverable information; a copy or description of documents, electronically stored information (ESI), and tangible things in its possession, custody, or control that it may use to support its case; a computation of damages; and any applicable insurance agreement. The deadline is generally fourteen days after the parties' Rule 26(f) conference, described below. Do not underestimate the value of these disclosures; they give you a head start on knowing what formal discovery to take and the information you need to obtain.[1]

Discovery Planning Conference Before Formal Discovery Occurs

Rule 26(d)(1) provides that "[a] party may not seek discovery from any source before the parties have conferred as required by Rule 26(f) [unless the case is exempted] or when authorized by these rules, by stipulation, or by court order." In other

> **Your initial disclosure checklist:**
>
> ✓ *The identity of individuals likely to have discoverable information.*
>
> ✓ *A copy or description of documents, electronically stored information (ESI), and tangible things in its possession, custody, or control that it may use to support its case.*
>
> ✓ *A computation of damages.*
>
> ✓ *Any applicable insurance agreement.*

words, schedule your discovery conference right away, because except in rare circumstances, you cannot notice a deposition, send interrogatories, serve requests for production, or conduct any other type of discovery authorized by the federal rules until the discovery conference has occurred.[2]

At the discovery planning conference, the parties are free to discuss any matters they choose, but Rule 26(f)(2) requires that they consider:

- the nature and basis of their claims;

- the possibilities for promptly settling or resolving the case;

- making or arranging for the initial disclosures required by Rule 26(a)(1); discussing any issues about preserving discoverable information; and

- developing the proposed discovery plan.

As a practical matter, other topics must be discussed at the conference. Rule 26(f)(3) contains a list of matters you must include in your discovery plan, including the subjects on which discovery may be needed (or limited), when discovery should be completed, claims of privilege, and other limitations on discovery. Since the discovery

---

1. Rule 26(a)(2) and (a)(3) require additional disclosures later in the case, regarding expert witnesses and evidence to be offered at trial. Under Rule 26(e)(1), all disclosures must be supplemented as the case proceeds.
2. Technically, under Rule 26(d)(2), a Rule 34 request for production of documents, ESI, or other tangible things can be "delivered" after twenty-one days following service of the summons and complaint but is deemed "served" at the Rule 26(f) conference.

plan results from the discovery planning conference, those items must be discussed at the conference too. Included in those topics may be consideration of the following:

- how many depositions are needed;

- what witnesses to depose;

- in what order to depose the witnesses;

- whether to place a limit shorter or longer than seven hours on the length of the depositions;

- whether any special rules, stipulations, or protective orders are necessary for the taking of the depositions, such as excluding other witnesses from the deposition room;

- whether to modify the time limits and content of the initial disclosures;

- whether to use other discovery devices, such as interrogatories, before depositions are taken;

- whether to waive the limitation on the number of interrogatories;

- what special orders, if any, are needed for the taking of discovery, such as a protective order concerning trade secrets;

- whether to pursue discovery in phases, either by witnesses or topics, to avoid duplicative discovery and to set the stage for any summary judgment motions;

- whether counsel should agree or be required to confer regularly to review and make suggestions for modifying the scheduling order.

Think about these topics before the planning conference. Additional concerns may come to mind depending on the case or circumstances. For example, the discovery conference and discovery plan may be used to identify the parties' positions and stipulations for conducting depositions remotely (*see* section 24.7) as well as matters regarding proportionality and burden arising out of the production of ESI. Even if counsel ultimately chooses not to raise an issue at the conference out of a desire to maintain flexibility in conducting discovery or worries about revealing litigation strategy, effective planning requires that attorneys at least consider the issues and whether they must be, or can best be, ironed out at the beginning of the case.

> *"Do not underestimate the value of initial disclosures; they give you a head start on knowing what formal discovery to take and the information you need to obtain."*

Unless shortened by local rule, hold the planning conference as soon as practicable, but not later than twenty-one days before a Rule 16(b) scheduling conference is set to be held or a scheduling order is due. The discovery planning conference may be conducted in any number of ways—face-to-face meetings, email discussions, or telephone conferences—but the court, if it chooses, can order the parties to attend the discovery planning conference in person.

Discovery Plan and Report of Conference to the Court

The discovery plan—the intended result of the discovery conference—must specify:

1) the changes that "should be made in the timing, form, or requirement" for the initial disclosures, "including a statement of when the initial disclosures were or will be made";

2) "the subjects on which discovery may be needed, when discovery should be completed, and whether discovery should be conducted in phases or be limited to or focused on particular issues";

3) "any issues about disclosure, discovery, or preservation of electronically stored information, including the form or forms in which it should be produced";

4) "any issues about claims of privilege or of protection as trial-preparation materials";

5) the changes that "should be made in the limitations on discovery imposed under these rules or by local rule, and what other limitations should be imposed"; and

6) any protective orders that the court should issue under Rule 26(c) or other order under Rule 16(b) and (c) affecting scheduling and discovery.[3]

The parties may also discuss other matters they might want included in the scheduling order even though not listed in Rule 26(f). They need not agree on each of the topics, but the proposed discovery plan should clearly set forth each side's position.

You are responsible for submitting the proposed discovery plan, in writing, to the court within fourteen days of the planning conference. Rule 26(f)(4)(B) allows the court to shorten the time for submitting the plan or allow counsel to report orally.

---

3. Fed. R. Evid. 26(f).

Scheduling Order

Unless the case is exempted under local rules, the court must issue a scheduling order under Rule 16(b) as soon as practicable and, unless there is good cause for delay, within the earlier of ninety days after any defendant has been served with the complaint or sixty days after any defendant has appeared (Rule 16(b)(2)). To help craft the order, the court will use the proposed discovery plan or report of the discovery planning conference.

> *Get to know your judge's clerks and administrative assistants. They are your best source for the answers you need. Treat them with respect as professionals and they will be happy to help you—disrespect them at your peril. More than one arrogant attorney has learned this lesson the hard way.*

Some judges routinely hold a scheduling conference with the attorneys before issuing the scheduling order; other judges hold a conference only when there are noted disagreements among counsel. (*See* Rule 16(b)(1).) The local rules or the court's website may indicate the judge's approach, but you will know for sure when you either receive notice of the time and place of the scheduling conference or the court issues a scheduling order without a scheduling conference. If the local rules are silent about the court's procedures, call the judge's case manager or clerk and ask what is expected of you and what you can expect from the judge.

The scheduling order sets forth deadlines for joining parties, amending pleadings, filing motions, and—most relevant here—the deadline to complete discovery. It may also modify the timing of initial disclosures, the extent of discovery, and the handling of ESI and issues of privilege. Depending on the type of case, the individual judge, and the results of the planning conference, the order may even contain detailed timetables and directives for conducting depositions. Although the parties may generally stipulate later to procedures governing or limiting discovery, the parties cannot extend the time for completing discovery, hearing a motion, or trial without court approval (Rule 29(b)).

The critical takeaway here is, early in the case, think carefully about the potential deponents, how the depositions will be conducted (remotely, in person, with or without video), the order of discovery, and the order and timing of the depositions, to avoid having the Rule 16(b) scheduling order preclude necessary discovery or dampen a strategic advantage.

1.2   The Deposition Rules (Rules 30 and 45)

Having discussed the parameters set forth in Rule 26, let's turn to the federal rules devoted to depositions specifically. We will revisit these concepts throughout the book, of course, but a survey of them now will give us a good foundation for what lies ahead. If your deposition will be governed by state law, determine how the jurisdiction handles each of the following issues.

1.2.1 Who Can Be Deposed

For the most part, you may depose anyone who has relevant information, regardless of whether they are a party to the litigation and whether an individual or an organization. Deponents may therefore include:

- parties to the case,
- agents and employees of the parties,
- former parties,
- nonparty witnesses,
- corporations and other entities, and
- in rare circumstances, even attorneys of the parties.

Depositions are usually taken of persons associated with the opposing party or a third party, but you may take a deposition of your own party or a friendly percipient or expert witness.

Notwithstanding the generally unlimited right to depose anyone who has relevant information, the courts have crafted some limitations that can be enforced by a protective order issued pursuant to Rule 26(c). Under the apex doctrine (*see* section 16.2), a court may protect high-ranking corporate executives from the burden of having their deposition taken if they have no unique personal knowledge of the matter in dispute, the information sought can be obtained from another witness, the information can be obtained through an alternative discovery method, or the deposition would impose severe hardship on the deponent.

Similarly, courts have restricted the ability to depose highly-placed government officials without a showing of extraordinary circumstances or a special need for the official's testimony. The rationale is to protect the official from the distraction of testifying and the loss of time from public duties, as well as to protect the governmental decision-making process. Like the apex doctrine, the restrictions on deposing high-ranking officials will not apply if the official has firsthand knowledge related to the claim being litigated and the information cannot be obtained from other sources.

In addition, courts have restricted the right to depose a witness who is so incapacitated that they are unable to answer questions or the questioning would threaten the witness's health. If the witness is incarcerated, a court order is required for their deposition (Rule 30(a)(2)(B)).

Depose high-ranking officials (corporate or government) if they have unique, firsthand knowledge that cannot be obtained from other sources.

Rule 30(b)(6) sets forth the unique procedure for deposing a corporation, part-nership, association, governmental agency, or other entity. Many times, you will suspect that employees or agents of these entities have valuable information relevant to the case, but you may not know the identity of the specific person in the organization with that information, or the information is held by more than one person in the organization, each knowing some pertinent aspect. While a series of individual depositions can be taken until all persons with relevant information have been identified and deposed, Rule 30(b)(6) offers an easier and more efficient method by which the entity is required to designate individuals to testify on its behalf. Rule 30(b)(6) depositions are referenced often in later chapters and are discussed extensively in Chapter Twenty-One.

1.2.2   Period for Depositions

As a basic rule, depositions may be taken after the Rule 26 discovery conference and before the discovery cutoff set forth in the Rule 16 scheduling order. As mentioned, Rule 26(d) generally precludes discovery, including depositions, until the parties have conferred to plan discovery pursuant to Rule 26(f). However, a deposition may be taken before the discovery conference by court order or by including in the deposition notice a certification, with supporting facts, that the witness is expected to leave the United States and be unavailable for examination in this country unless deposed before the parties have conferred (Rule 30(a)(2)(A)(iii)). (Note, however, that the deposition cannot be used in a pretrial motion or at trial against a party who shows that it was unable, despite the exercise of diligence, to obtain counsel to represent it at the deposition.)

1.2.3   Number of Depositions

Rule 30(a)(2)(A)(i) limits the parties to ten depositions per side unless the parties have stipulated in writing to a different number or the court has ordered otherwise. Note that the restriction is on the number of depositions per side, not per party. Therefore, a single plaintiff would be entitled to ten depositions, but three code-fendants would have ten depositions to share among them. If the deposition is of a corporation or other entity under Rule 30(b)(6), it is treated as a single deposition for purposes of Rule 30(a)(2)(A)(i), even if the entity designates more than one individual to testify on its behalf.

The discovery planning conference is usually where the parties discuss any desired departure from the rule limiting the number of depositions. If the parties cannot agree, the court can resolve the dispute in the Rule 16(b) scheduling order.

1.2.4   Length of Depositions

Rule 30(d)(1) imposes a seven-hour, one-day time limit for depositions. The seven hours must occur all on one day. Only actual deposition time is counted—not the time necessary for reasonable breaks and lunch. If the deposition is of a corporation or other entity under Rule 30(b)(6), each person designated by the entity to testify may be deposed for up to seven hours under Rule 30(d)(1).[4]

The parties may alter the time limit by stipulation, and the court may order a different time limit for a specific witness or for all the depositions in the case. The Advisory Committee Note to Rule 30 suggests some of the situations in which additional time might be permitted, such as where the witness needs an interpreter, the witness has not had enough time to review documents in advance or is taking excessively long to review them during the deposition, the examination reveals that documents have been requested but not produced and further examination is appropriate after their production, or the witness needs to be questioned by multiple parties. There may also be a need for additional time in expert witness depositions to allow full exploration of the expert's opinions and methodologies. In general, the court may allow more time to achieve fairness or if the deposition is impeded or delayed by a party or counsel.

1.2.5   Location of the Deposition

A deposition may be taken at any location on which the parties and the witness agree. If no agreement can be reached, the geographic location under the FRCP depends to a large extent on whether the witness is a party or nonparty.

Parties

Absent other controlling rules, the deposition of a party may be scheduled for any location, subject to the court's power under Rule 26(c)(1)(B) to grant a protective order designating a different place, usually due to undue burden or expense, or to shift travel costs to the deposing party to alleviate that burden.[5] Thus, for example, a party to litigation in San Francisco could receive a notice to attend a deposition in San Francisco, even though they live in New York.

The burden to apply for relief is on the person wishing to change the location from what is stated in the notice of deposition. (Usually, this is the deponent.) Some general guidelines have emerged delineating suitable locations for depositions, and some courts have adopted local rules on the subject. Typically, it will be reasonable for a plaintiff to depose an individual defendant where the defendant resides or is employed. A defendant may take the deposition of an

---

4. Adv. Comm. Note to 2000 Amendment to FRCP 30.
5. *E.g.*, Philadelphia Indem. Ins. Co. v. Fed. Ins. Co., 215 F.R.D. 492, 495 (E.D. Pa. 2003); Cadent Ltd. v. 3M Unitek Corp., 232 F.R.D. 625, 628 (C.D. Cal. 2002); Sec. & Exch. Comm'n v. Aly, 320 F.R.D. 116, 118 (S.D.N.Y. 2017). The burden of traveling to the deposition location or the location of the witness may be a basis for ordering that the deposition be held remotely. *See* Aly, 320 F.R.D. at 119–20; In re Terrorist Attacks on September 11, 2001, 337 F.R.D. 575, 577–80 (S.D.N.Y. 2020).

individual plaintiff where the plaintiff resides, is employed, or filed the
lawsuit. Corporations and other organizations are generally deposed
within the district containing their
principal place of business (or, if the
plaintiff, where it filed the lawsuit).
Corporate or organizational officers,
directors, or managing agents usu-

> *Thanks to the pandemic, many
> depositions are now taken
> remotely, doing away with
> the need for travel. Remote
> depositions are discussed in
> Chapter Twenty-Four.*

ally must be deposed either in the district of the organization's principal place of
business or where the individual witness lives or works. (By contrast, depositions
of rank-and-file employees or agents are treated as depositions of *non*party witnesses, compelled by subpoena, discussed below.) Again, however, these are not
hard and fast rules; the question will be whether the party seeking to move the
deposition to a location other than what was designated in the deposition notice
can demonstrate that the circumstances warrant it.

Nonparties

Because the attendance of nonparties at a deposition is compelled by a subpoena
under Rule 45, the place for a nonparty's deposition is generally restricted by Rule
45(c). Under Rule 45(c)(1)(A), the target of a deposition subpoena may be required
to physically attend only within 100 miles of where that person resides, is employed, or regularly transacts business in person.[6]

The deposing party may always arrange—with the consent of the witness or
their counsel—to have the witness's deposition taken at some place beyond the
reach of a subpoena. Many times, it is more efficient to agree to pay the witness's
expenses to come to another location than for the parties' attorneys to journey to
the witness.

Remote Depositions

When a deposition is conducted remotely, the deponent, the deponent's attorney,
the deposing attorney, and the court reporter may be in different physical locations.
Pursuant to Rule 30(b)(4), a remote deposition is deemed to take place where the
deponent is answering the questions.

---

6. Note that, if the deponent is an officer of a party and was served *by subpoena*, Rule 45(c)(1)(B)
allows the deposition to take place anywhere within the *state* where the person resides, is employed,
or regularly transacts business in person. *See* Advisory Committee Notes on Rule 45—2013
Amendment. Conceivably, that could require a resident of San Diego to testify hundreds of miles
away in Sacramento, or a resident of Houston to testify hundreds of miles away in El Paso. A court
is not required, however, to enforce the maximum geographical reach of a subpoena, and it may be
persuaded that the deposition should take place closer to the deponent's residence or workplace.

1.2.6 Recording the Deposition

Under Rule 30(b)(3)(A), the party taking the deposition must state in the notice of deposition the method of recording the testimony—stenographic (creating a written transcript), audio, or audiovisual—and bear the expense of the recording.

Under Rule 30(b)(3)(B), any other party, at its own expense and after giving notice to the witness and other parties, may designate a method of recording in addition to the method given in the deposition notice. So, for example, a party may decide to videorecord the deposition even if it had not been originally so noticed, as long as the party gives notice, makes the arrangements, and bears the cost.

In Chapter Twenty-Three, we discuss the details and relative advantages of recording a deposition by audiovisual means. Due to advances in technology, video depositions are less expensive and more common than ever, and they are particularly effective when played at trial as direct testimony or impeachment. For some practitioners, all depositions are recorded by audiovisual means unless there is a strategic reason not to.

While the parties are free to choose any recording method, keep Rule 32(c) in mind. Under that rule, unless the court orders otherwise, a party must provide a transcript of any deposition testimony the party offers at trial, even though it may also offer the testimony in an audio or audiovisual form. It is therefore prudent to notice and arrange for a stenographic recording of the deposition, even if it is recorded audiovisually, or arrange for a later transcription of the non-stenographic recording.

1.2.7 Court Reporter and Deposition Officer

Under Rule 28, depositions conducted in the United States and its territories and insular possessions may be taken before any person authorized to administer oaths, either by the laws of the United States or of the place in which the action is pending, or before a person appointed by the court in which the action is pending.[7]

In practice, the deposition is taken before a court reporter (stenographically recording the deposition) who is also a notary public (authorized to administer oaths). Thus, one person fulfills both functions, even though the rules permit the deposition officer and the person recording the testimony to be different people. The exception is video depositions, where the videographer recording the proceedings and the deposition officer (who can still be a court reporter) are typically separate individuals.

---

7. Special rules, contained in Rule 28(b), govern the taking of depositions in foreign countries.

As discussed in Chapter Twenty-Four on remote depositions, issues can arise where the deposition is conducted before a notary public who is not authorized to administer oaths in the relevant jurisdiction, or from a location other than where the deponent is answering the questions. As a general matter, these issues are resolved by local rule, court order, or stipulation, but make sure they are resolved before the deposition commences.

1.2.8 Scheduling the Deposition

The concept of "priority"—that the party first noticing the taking of a deposition has a right to complete the taking of that deposition before the opponent may take a deposition—has been abolished under the federal rules. Now, either party may notice and take a deposition even though a previously noticed deposition has not been completed.

As a matter of convenience and courtesy, most depositions are scheduled by agreement among counsel. By cooperating, you can avoid conflicts in the lawyers' and witness's schedules and avoid the expense of motions to reschedule the time for the deposition. Several courts, by local rule, require that before noticing a deposition, the parties attempt to arrive at a mutually agreeable date. Some courts prohibit scheduling a deposition for a time when opposing counsel is known to be unavailable.

Absent agreement to the contrary, the date set in the deposition notice (or subpoena for a nonparty deponent) will control, unless a party objects and moves for a protective order rescheduling the deposition or a nonparty moves to quash the subpoena or seeks similar relief.

1.2.9 Compelling the Attendance of Party Witnesses

The procedure for compelling a witness to attend the deposition depends on whether the witness is 1) a party, or an officer, managing agent, or director of a party; or 2) a nonparty. The first category of witness is discussed here; nonparty witnesses are discussed in the next section.

Under the federal rules, any party to the litigation may require an individual party to appear at a deposition by merely serving the party-deponent with a written notice of deposition that complies with Rule 30(b). Leave of court is not required unless the deposition would result in more than ten depositions taken, the deponent has already been deposed, the deposition is to be held before the onset of discovery under Rule 26(d), or the deponent is confined in prison (Rule 30(a)). If the deponent party is a corporation, partnership, association, governmental agency, or other entity, its attendance (through one or more representatives) is compelled by serving a notice pursuant to Rule 30(b)(6).

A party may also require an officer, director, or managing agent of a party to attend a deposition by serving a Rule 30(b)(1) notice of deposition, but the notice must name or adequately describe the witness and state that the witness is an officer, director, or managing agent.

Content of Rule 30(b)(1) notice. The notice must state the time and place for taking the deposition and, as mentioned, the method of recording. The notice must also include the name and address of each person to be examined if known or, if not known, a general description sufficient to identify the witness or the class or group to which the witness belongs. Under Rule 30(b)(4), when a deposition is to be conducted remotely by telephone or using a virtual platform, the deposition notice must disclose that intention as well.

Content of Rule 30(b)(6) notice. If the deposition is of a corporation or other entity pursuant to Rule 30(b)(6), the notice must comply with the requirements of Rule 30(b). However, instead of identifying the individual to testify, it will name the entity to be deposed and describe with reasonable particularity the matters for examination. (After a meet-and-confer process, the entity is obligated to designate one or more persons to testify on its behalf to information known or reasonably available to the entity. Rule 30(b)(6) depositions are discussed in Chapter Twenty-One.)

Reasonable notice. Unlike the deposition statutes in California and other states, Rule 30(b)(1) does not require the deposition notice to be served a specific number of days before the deposition. Instead, the rule requires "reasonable notice," which depends on the circumstances of the case (ten days is ordinarily deemed sufficient). Always check the local court rules and judge's orders to see if they provide for a minimum amount of notice.

Service of the notice. The party taking the deposition must serve a copy of the Rule 30(b) notice on the deponent and every party to the action. If the party is represented by an attorney, serve notice on the attorney. If the party is proceeding pro se, serve notice on the party. Service may be accomplished by the methods set forth in Rule 5 or as decreed by local rule or court order.

Retention of original. Like interrogatories, requests for production, and requests for admission, do not file deposition notices with the court until they are used in a proceeding, such as in a motion to compel or a request for a protective order.

1.2.10 Compelling the Attendance of Nonparty Witnesses

While a party can be compelled to attend a deposition merely by serving a notice of deposition under Rule 30(b), nonparties are required to attend only if they have been served with a subpoena under Rule 45. The subpoena is, in effect, an order from the court in which the action is pending.

Issuing the subpoena. There are two ways to issue the subpoena. One way is for the court clerk to sign and issue a blank subpoena to a party (or their attorney) on request, to be filled out by the party or attorney before service. The other way is for an attorney authorized to practice law in that court (including pro hac vice) to issue and sign the subpoena and then fill it out before service. Having the attorney issue the subpoena is easier—if nothing else, it avoids a trip to the clerk's office. Subpoena forms can be downloaded, filled out, and printed from www.uscourts.gov.

> ### *Subpoena-to-nonparty checklist:*
>
> ✓ *Issue the subpoena (court clerk or you may issue);*
> ✓ *Pay attention to the geographic reach of your subpoena—100-mile limit;*
> ✓ *Give reasonable notice;*
> ✓ *Work with the other attorney to set time for appearance;*
> ✓ *Serve the subpoena;*
> ✓ *Personal service required;*
> ✓ *Serve all parties to the action;*
> ✓ *Avoid undue burden and expense.*

Content of Rule 45 subpoenas. Besides the obvious—stating the name of the issuing court, the title of the action, and the civil action number—the subpoena must identify what it "command[s]" the person to whom it is directed to do, such as attend and testify at the deposition (and, if desired as discussed below, produce designated documents, electronically stored information (ESI), or tangible things in that person's possession, custody or control). The subpoena must also set out the text of Rule 45(d) and (e)—pertaining to protections to the subpoenaed party and duties in responding—and identify the method for recording the deposition testimony (Rule 45(a)(1)).

Reasonable notice. Rule 45 does not set a minimum number of days a subpoena must be served before the witness is to appear and testify at a deposition (or to produce documents, ESI, or other tangible things at the deposition). Perfect service a reasonable time before the deposition. The prudent approach may be to contact the witness's attorney in advance (or the witness, if unrepresented) to work out the time necessary to comply with the subpoena.

Serving the subpoena. Under Rule 45(b)(1), service of a subpoena generally requires delivering a copy to the person named in the subpoena along with the tender of a one-day witness attendance fee and statutory mileage. Personal service is required, absent a court order. Subpoenas directed to corporations require service on an officer or managing agent of the corporation. Again, it is often possible to work out the details of service by negotiating with the witness or witness's attorney.

In addition to serving the subpoena on the deponent, a notice of the deposition must still be served on each of the parties under Rule 30(b), along with a copy of the subpoena.

Geographic reach of the subpoena. As mentioned, subpoenas (except those requiring the inspection of premises) have a geographic limit: under Rule 45(c), the deposition and situs for producing documents must be within 100 miles of where the person resides, is employed, or regularly transacts business in person.

Avoiding undue burden or expense. The federal rules recognize that recipients of subpoenas are not parties to the litigation and, therefore, warrant a degree of protection. To this end, when issuing a subpoena, particularly for production of documents or ESI in addition to deposition testimony, consider carefully Rule 45(d)(1). As set forth in that rule, the "party or attorney responsible for issuing and serving a subpoena must take reasonable steps to avoid imposing undue burden or expense on a person subject to the subpoena," and the court in the district where compliance is commanded may impose sanctions on the party who fails to comply.

Responding to the subpoena. A person served with a subpoena has several responses available under Rule 45(d): comply with the subpoena; negotiate alternative compliance terms; object in writing on the grounds of privilege or other grounds to the person issuing the subpoena, by the earlier of the time specified for compliance or fourteen days after the subpoena is served; or, within that same time frame, file a motion to modify or quash the subpoena in the court for the jurisdiction in which compliance has been demanded.

1.2.11 *Compelling Production of Documents at the Deposition*

Generally, you will want to have documents, ESI, and other tangible evidence produced before the deposition, so you have time to become completely familiar with the materials before asking questions about them. Serve either a Rule 34 document request (for parties) or a Rule 45 subpoena (for nonparties) sufficiently in advance of the deposition to allow for the documents to be produced, copied, and reviewed before the deposition.

Sometimes, such as when time is short, you may choose to schedule the production of documents or other tangible items to occur at the deposition. The procedure for this again turns on whether the deponent is a party or a nonparty.

For party deponents, although nothing more than a notice of deposition is required to compel attendance at the deposition, the exclusive method for compelling the party to produce documents at the deposition is a request for production under Rule 34. As a result, while a deposition requires only reasonable notice, a deposition with production of documents requires thirty days' notice, based on the time allowed under Rule 34 for a response to the document demand.[8]

For nonparty deponents, a subpoena under Rule 45 is the only way to require production of documents as well as the attendance and testimony at the deposition. For these purposes, separate subpoenas may be issued—one requiring the subpoenaed witness to testify and one requiring the subpoenaed witness to produce documents and other tangible things. Alternatively, one subpoena can be issued requiring both attendance for testimony and production of tangible things. The latter route is usually easier, but there may be situations calling for multiple subpoenas: for example, a subpoena requiring a witness to testify at a deposition may be followed by a post-deposition subpoena directing the witness to produce documents identified at the deposition. Or, of course, a subpoena requiring production of documents may be served in advance of the deposition to allow counsel to review the documents, with a separate subpoena requiring attendance at a deposition if one is needed.

> *Obtain documents, ESI, and other tangible evidence produced before the deposition, so you have time to become completely familiar with the materials before asking questions about them.*

If a subpoena requires production of documents as well as attendance and testimony at the deposition, the items designated for production, as set out in the subpoena, must also be listed in the Rule 30(b) notice sent to the parties or in an attachment thereto (Rule 30(b)(2)). This is most easily accomplished by referring to the subpoena in the notice of deposition and attaching a copy of the subpoena.

Serve the subpoena, along with the notice of deposition, on all other parties to the action before serving the subpoena on the nonparty witness. This allows the parties to timely object or to serve their own subpoenas for additional materials. Rule 45 does not specify how much advance notice must be given to the other parties; what is reasonable notice will depend on the circumstances.

If the deposition is to be conducted remotely, whether the deponent is a party or a nonparty, consider how the witness will deliver the documents when not appearing physically for the deposition. One option is for the witness to email the documents at the outset of the deposition. A much more practical solution is to require the witness to produce the documents in advance of the deposition, allowing you to receive, print out (if needed), and review the documents, and then select and prepare the documents for use at the deposition.

---

8. Some state laws are different. *See, e.g.*, Cal. Code Civ. P. §§ 2025.280(a), 2025.220(a)(4), 2025.270(a) and (c).

1.2.12 Conducting the Deposition

The rules governing the deposition proceedings are relatively few; we highlight them here and expand on them in later chapters.

Deposition officer's required statements. Under Rule 30(b)(5), the deposition officer begins the deposition with a statement on the record that gives the officer's name and business address; the date, time, and place of the deposition; the name of the witness; and the identity of all persons present. The deposition officer administers the oath to the witness on the record. In a non-stenographic deposition, the officer recites the first three items at the beginning of each recorded unit. At the end of the deposition, the officer states on the record that the deposition is complete and recites any stipulations between counsel concerning the custody of the transcript or the recording (and the exhibits) or about any other pertinent matters.

Course of the examination. Examination and cross-examination of the deponent proceed as they would at trial as provided by the Federal Rules of Evidence. (Of course, the first examiner at a discovery deposition is normally the opposing party, so one does not normally think of that examination as "direct;" and the examination that may follow, perhaps by the attorney who will present the witness at trial, is not actually a "cross" examination. Some attorneys call these two examinations "the deposition" and the "follow-on examination.") Under Rule 30(c)(1), other witnesses cannot be excluded from the deposition room without first obtaining a stipulation or a protective order pursuant to Rule 26(c)(1)(e).

Objections. As discussed extensively in section 18.8, objections to some types of questions (such as those that challenge the form of a question) must be made at the deposition or will be deemed waived under Rule 32(d). The deposition officer notes on the record all objections made at the deposition to the evidence presented, the conduct of the deposition, the qualifications of the officer taking the deposition, or any other aspect of the proceedings. Nonetheless, the deposition proceeds with the testimony being taken "subject to any objections"—that is, the questions and answers continue unless the witness is instructed not to answer a question on permissible grounds (Rule 30(c)(2)).

> *Get to know your local deposition officers. Build a relationship with them and your depositions will run much more smoothly.*

Rule 30(c)(2) requires that any objection to evidence made during the deposition be stated concisely and in a nonargumentative and nonsuggestive manner. It also provides that a witness can be instructed not to answer a question only when necessary to preserve a privilege, to enforce a previous court order limiting the examination (e.g., "counsel may ask the witness about liability, but not damages"), or to seek an order limiting or terminating the deposition due to improper questioning or conduct. Objecting and instructing the witness as the witness's counsel is discussed further in section 18.8; dealing with objections and instructions as the deposing counsel is discussed further in Chapter Thirteen.

Exhibits. Any documents or other exhibits produced during the deposition are to be "marked" for identification (typically by the court reporter) and annexed to the deposition if any party requests it. Copies may be substituted for the originals if the parties had an opportunity to compare the copies with the originals, and the copies will thereafter serve as the originals (subject to court order, *see* Rule 30(f)(2)). In modern practice, documents may be exchanged and stored electronically, and electronic versions of documents are often used during the deposition. The marking, use, and annexation of exhibits in a remote deposition—where the court reporter, witness and counsel are in separate physical locations—must be thoroughly considered. Alternatives for accomplishing these tasks are discussed at length in Chapter Twenty-Four on remote depositions; techniques for handling and using exhibits are further discussed in Chapter Ten.

Written questions. A party may choose not to attend the deposition and instead serve written questions in a sealed envelope to the party taking the deposition. The party taking the deposition is required to transmit the questions to the deposition officer, who must ask the questions to the witness and record the answers verbatim. As a tactical matter, use such an approach only when the witness is willing to cooperate with the party submitting the questions, so that the questions and the answers may be considered in advance. The option is of little necessity if the party can attend the deposition remotely.

1.2.13   Post-Deposition Matters

The federal rules provide for the following after the deposition testimony concludes.

Witness reviews and signs. Under Rule 30(e)(1), the witness or party may request, before completion of the deposition, the opportunity to review, correct, and sign the deposition transcript; if so requested (as a practical matter, it always should be requested), the witness has thirty days after the transcript becomes available to review the deposition and make changes to the form and substance of the testimony, and to provide a signed statement of the reasons for the changes. If no changes are made, the witness is not required to sign anything. This is addressed further in sections 6.2.1 and 19.1.[9]

Certification by officer. Under Rule 30(f)(1), the deposition officer certifies that the witness was duly sworn by the officer and that the deposition accurately reflects

---

9. Some jurisdictions follow a different procedure, by which the court reporter notifies the deponent when the transcript is ready for reading, correcting, and signing unless the deponent and parties agreed otherwise on the record. *E.g.,* Cal. Code Civ. P. § 2025.520.

the witness's testimony. Under Rule 30(e)(2), the certificate also states whether a witness or one of the parties requested the witness to review the deposition; if so, the officer attaches any changes made by the witness to the questions or answers.

Sealing, delivery, and copies. Unless otherwise ordered by the court, the deposition officer seals the deposition in an envelope or package bearing the title of the action, marks it with the statement, "Deposition of [witness's name]," and promptly sends it to the attorney who arranged for the transcript or recording, normally the deposing attorney. The attorney is required to safely store the deposition and protect it from loss, destruction, tampering, or deterioration. Under Rule 30(f)(3), the officer retains a copy of the recording of a video or audio deposition or the notes of a stenographic deposition. When paid a reasonable charge, the officer furnishes copies of the deposition to any party requesting one.

CHAPTER TWO

PURPOSES OF DEPOSITIONS

*Efforts and courage are not enough without
purpose and direction.*

—John F. Kennedy

A deposition will be more effective if the deposing attorney understands the various purposes for depositions and keeps in mind the particular purpose that is fueling a given line of questioning. Many attorneys do not realize the broad goals that a deposition can accomplish; others fail to realize that the goal for an inquiry dictates the questioning techniques to use for best results.

In this chapter, we examine the primary purposes of depositions, grouping them into four categories:

1) Gathering information;

2) Obtaining admissions and testing theories;

3) Preserving testimony; and

4) Facilitating settlement.

These purposes are not mutually exclusive and often overlap. For example, you may primarily desire to

> **In This Chapter:**
>
> - Gathering information
> - Obtaining admissions and testing theories
> - Preserving testimony
> - Facilitating settlement

gather information from the witness but also hope to obtain admissions to support a motion and facilitate settlement. Sometimes the purposes conflict, as where an attorney wants to get the witness's full story to prepare for trial, but in so doing risks eliciting a barrage of excuses and bad facts that may preserve harmful testimony and muddy the waters for summary judgment. By knowing the purposes for depositions, and evaluating which purpose is most important for the inquiry into a specific topic, we can make intelligent adjustments to our questioning approach to get the most favorable results most efficiently. We revisit this exhaustively when we discuss questioning techniques in Chapters Eight and Nine, but for now, let's become familiar with each purpose.

2.1 Gathering Information

The most compelling reason for taking a deposition is to gather information—to find out as much as possible so you can best prepare your case. Depositions allow you to uncover information you do not already know, confirm the facts you think you know, develop your factual, legal, and persuasive theories for the case, and craft direct and cross-examinations for trial.

2.1.1 Finding Out What You Don't Know

Through interviews and other informal fact-gathering, you know what the client and friendly witnesses have to say about the events underlying the lawsuit. You can also learn about the facts from the pleadings, document discovery and, in federal court, mandatory initial disclosures under Rule 26. But many gaps will still pepper the timeline of events, and facts will remain unknown. Like a nineteenth-century explorer choosing a route by looking at the vacant areas on a map of a newly-discovered continent, you must seek to fill in the missing data to chart the best course for a case. And in litigation, you often must obtain information by deposing opposing parties (who cannot be interviewed without permission of their attorney) and third parties who choose not to cooperate or must be placed under oath.

What we don't know can hurt us. We must uncover the opposing party's story—what the opposing witnesses might say at trial or in a declaration supporting or opposing summary judgment. What is their version of what occurred? What documents, public information, and witnesses will they claim as corroboration? We must also find out what only they know. Where was the plaintiff going before the collision with your client's car? What was the employee thinking when she left with the drive containing the schematics? What happened at the meeting where your client claims the defendants fixed prices? And so on.

2.1.2 Confirming What You Think You Know

Taking a deposition also allows you to confirm—or try to confirm—the facts you have gleaned from informal fact gathering, initial disclosures and other discovery methods. Does the other side claim that the events happened just as your client says?

While opposing parties and their witnesses will have their own story, some facts may jive with what you learned from the client. If the opposing witnesses agree with your witnesses and a fact is confirmed, all counsel can have greater confidence that the issue is undisputed—one less issue for summary judgment or trial. If the witnesses disagree and the fact is not confirmed, you will recognize the dispute at the deposition, when there is still time to marshal further proof in favor of your client's version or to adjust your case with a different view of the facts. No one wants to discover at trial or summary judgment, when little can be done about it, that what you assumed to be undisputed is actually hotly contested.

2.1.3   Developing Case Theories

Finding out what you do not know, and confirming what you think you know, are not mindless pursuits of data. To the contrary, they are crucial tools for developing the three theories needed for favorable presentation of your case at summary judgment, arbitration, or trial: the factual theory (what happened in the case and why), the legal theory (what causes of action or defenses will lead you to victory), and the persuasive theory (why the trier of fact should want your client to prevail out of fairness).[1]

> *What we don't know* **can** *hurt us.*

During the discovery stage of litigation, the details of what happened in the case are typically undetermined, and you may be considering several different case theories. Factual disputes resolved one way will point to certain legal and persuasive theories, but resolved another way will point to different legal and persuasive theories. Through depositions and other discovery devices, you can decide which account of the facts is most likely to be accepted as true by the trier of fact and, in turn, what legal and persuasive theories are best supported.

To illustrate, let's take a typical personal injury case stemming from a car accident, in which the plaintiff claims that the defendant caused a collision—and the plaintiff's resulting injuries—by driving at an unsafe speed and failing to keep a proper lookout. The plaintiff's factual theory is that the defendant was speeding and not paying attention to the road just before the accident. During discovery, each side seeks admissions from the other side that support its legal, factual, and persuasive theories. Plaintiff's counsel, for example, will try to gain evidence of the defendant's speeding and failing to pay attention to the road (as well as evidence to support other causes of action and weaken the defendant's defenses). Counsel may learn that the defendant was not looking at the traffic in front of the vehicle at the time of the accident because they were texting for the prior half-block, but counsel might also find out that the defendant was driving at the legal speed limit. From this information, the plaintiff has found support for one case theory (failing to keep a proper lookout) but not the other (proceeding at an unsafe rate of speed) and, depending on other sources of evidence, may choose to abandon the unsafe speed theory. This in turn informs what legal theory to embrace (negligence) and what type of persuasive theory to pursue ("the defendant was too busy to care").

---

1. For a more complete discussion of developing these case theories, *see* section 4.1.

2.1.4 Developing Examinations for Trial or Arbitration

Gathering information during deposition not only helps you decide what case theories will lead to victory, it also points toward specific questions to ask at trial or arbitration, should the matter proceed that far.

For example, one of the cardinal rules of nearly all cross-examination at trial is never to ask a question to which you do not know the answer. Deposition is where you learn the answers to the questions you may want to ask at trial. Answers during the deposition that are favorable to your case indicate safe areas of inquiry during the later cross-examination; if the witness changes the answer at trial from what was given in the deposition, the deposition transcript is available for impeachment. On the other hand, if the answer to a deposition question was unfavorable, you know it is probably best to stay away from that question at trial.

Another rule of trial cross-examination is to ask only questions that ask for facts and do not contain characterizations or subjective terms. For instance, most trial lawyers would not ask a question on cross-examination of the opposing party such as, "Just before the accident, were you going very fast?" The answer to such a question at trial could well be "No"—either because the witness truly believes the car wasn't going "very" fast or because he simply doesn't want to admit it. Now you are stuck—unless you have other evidence showing how fast the opponent was going. Deposition is a safe place to ask such a question to see what the witness will say. If the witness agrees with the characterization in their deposition, you *can* ask them to characterize it that way at trial, too: if they answer "no" at trial, you can impeach them with their "yes" answer in the deposition transcript. If the witness does not agree with the characterization in the deposition, you can use the deposition to elicit the facts and bases for the witness refuting the characterization, and lock in the witness to that position. Thus, at deposition you might ask why the witness says they were not going too fast, get a response, and inquire into each reason for the witness's position. Those reasons may turn out to be illogical or otherwise subject to attack, and you can fashion a trial cross-examination or argument to demonstrate just that.

2.1.5 The Good, the Bad, and the Ugly

If the purpose of your deposition is to gather information, you need to gather *all* the information, whether it is helpful to your client's case or not. In other words, in finding out what you do not know and trying to confirm the "good" facts you think you know, you must be willing to risk that the witness will proclaim facts and theories that are seemingly "bad" or even "ugly" for your client's cause.

This is counter-intuitive for most newer attorneys and difficult for many, but it pays off. Encourage opposing witnesses to give you their best shot with all their reasoning and facts. Use open-ended questions (starting with "who," "what," "when," "where," "why," "how," or "explain"), which force the witness to articulate their positions. Resist the temptation to assume that you know how the witness would answer a question or that you understand the witness's answer. In the end, the good, the bad, and the ugly will give you the insight necessary to make your case theories more unassailable, and your case stronger, whether in a motion, in settlement discussions, or at trial.

2.2 Obtaining Admissions and Testing Theories

While the deposition purpose of gathering information seeks to find out everything the witness has to say, the deposition purpose of obtaining admissions seeks to get the witness to say only what you want.[2]

2.2.1 Admissions

Before the deposition, your review of documents and other sources of information may suggest that the witness will admit certain facts that directly help your case, contributing to your proof of claim or defense. In the deposition, typically through leading questions, you can induce the witness to concede these facts, which will provide evidence for use in a dispositive motion, arbitration, or trial. For example, in a breach of contract action the defendant may seek the plaintiff's admission that the plaintiff did not exercise a right of first refusal by the required date; if the defendant obtains this admission and submits the relevant portion of the deposition testimony as evidence, and the plaintiff cannot offer any contradictory evidence, the admission can lead to summary judgment and end the case.

Of course, you might elicit these helpful facts while pursuing the deposition purpose we discussed earlier—gathering all the witness's information—but that comes at a price. When eliciting all the witness's information, the helpful statements come in bits and pieces, scattered over dozens of pages in the transcript, interwoven with harmful statements. To be more useful for a summary judgment motion or at trial, force the witness to admit specific facts—and only those facts—in response to a flurry of leading questions that transpire in less than a minute on a single transcript page.

Put another way, the difference between obtaining admissions and getting the facts for the purpose of information-gathering is in how much you want the witness to talk. When your purpose is information-gathering, you want the witness to divulge all the witness's information, good and bad. When your purpose is obtaining admissions, you want the witness only to say "yes" to the specific facts

---

2. "Admission" is one of those terms that has several meanings in the law. It can be used in a limited way, to describe blockbuster confessions of liability or guilt, or in an evidentiary sense, to describe a statement by or on behalf of the opposing party that falls outside the scope of the hearsay rule (*see* Fed. R. Evid. 801(d)(2)). The term "admission" in this book is used in its colloquial sense— something said by a witness that supports your own case or weakens the opponent's case.

you need to win. This results in an easily citable and presentable segment for motions or evidence at trial (although it sacrifices hearing the witness's full side of the story).

Sometimes obtaining admissions and gathering information can be pursued together or consecutively. You might first find out everything the witness has to say by laboriously going through the events, and then follow up with more pointed questions to elicit the specific helpful facts you want the witness to admit in a discrete portion of the deposition. All of this is discussed more in Chapters Eight and Nine.

2.2.2   Theory Testing

Theory testing is like obtaining factual admissions, but on steroids. It is one thing to get the witness to admit specific facts that allow you to formulate your case theories and to use those admissions to support those theories in evidentiary motions or trial; it is even better to get the witness to agree in the deposition to the theory itself, confessing your version of what happened in the case and why. That is what theory testing is all about.

For example, let's say it would be helpful for the plaintiff in an accident case to get the defendant to admit in a deposition that the speed limit was 25 miles per hour, he was driving 45 miles per hour, it was raining, his car stereo was playing, and he was texting. It would be even more helpful to get the defendant to admit characterizations of those facts: he was driving faster than he was supposed to; he was driving too fast; there were many things competing for his attention; he was not fully focused on the

> *Good:* *"I was driving over the speed limit and texting."*
>
> *Better:* *"I was driving too fast and not paying attention to the road."*
>
> *Best:* *"I hit the plaintiff because I was going too fast and not paying attention."*

road. And it would be even better to get the defendant to admit your theory of what happened to cause the accident: he hit the plaintiff because he was going too fast and not paying attention.

By confronting the deponent with the theory ("you hit the plaintiff because you were going too fast"), you are testing that theory to see how the witness responds. If the witness agrees, you have obtained a blockbuster confession that deposing attorneys live for. If the witness does not agree, you can force the witness to list all the facts and reasons for the witness's disagreement, giving you time before motion practice or trial to find ways to shoot down the witness's facts and reasons.

Are these confessions possible to get? Well, at the risk of unduly disclosing your case theory, it's usually worth a try at a deposition. *See* Chapter Nine.

2.3 Preserving Testimony

A third purpose of depositions is to preserve what the witness has to say in an official, fixed format—such as a written transcript, a video recording, or both—so it can be used later in motions or at trial and the witness cannot change their story. While an informal, "off the record" interview can be enlightening, it is less likely to be admissible than a deposition, which can be used as direct evidence in support of a position in the case, a source for impeachment and witness control, and, if the witness later becomes unavailable, in lieu of live testimony at trial.

2.3.1 Direct Evidence

The deposition testimony of opposing parties, as well as the deposition testimony of witnesses containing statements attributable to opposing parties, are admissible at trial as substantive evidence when offered as a party statement (FRCP 32(a)(3); Fed. R. Evid. 801(d)(2)). In more limited circumstances, statements in the deposition testimony of your own witness might be admissible as a prior consistent statement (Fed. R. Evid. 801(d)(1)(B)).

While often not as persuasive or interesting as live testimony, deposition testimony can be a useful substitute—especially when presented by video, which allows the jurors to hear and see the witness giving the testimony helpful to your case. In addition, you may use admissible deposition excerpts in opening statements and admitted deposition excerpts in closing arguments.

Use deposition testimony to support or oppose summary judgment motions, limited to the extent the testimony would be admissible at trial (Rule 56(c)(1)(A)). To satisfy the deposition purpose of preserving testimony, make sure the record is clear and that evidentiary requirements for admission are satisfied.

2.3.2 Locked-In Testimony for Impeachment and Witness Control

Let's face it: not all witnesses at trial or in summary judgment proceedings are respectful of the oath to tell the truth. Some are out-and-out liars, while others, to be charitable, may have learned to see things differently since the deposition. In addition, witnesses may make mistakes or suffer imperfect recollection by the time of the summary judgment motion or trial. Depositions provide a control mechanism over these witnesses in three respects.

Use deposition transcripts to:

- *Present an opponent's statements;*
- *Impeach a lying witness;*
- *Discourage a tempted witness;*
- *Refresh a forgetful witness;*
- *Substitute for live testimony.*

First, if witnesses deviate from their prior deposition testimony, the deposition transcript or recording provides a means of punishing them through impeachment (at trial) or refuting and possibly precluding the statements in their declaration (for summary judgment).

Second, the mere fact that the deposition testimony has been preserved—and therefore the possibility of an embarrassing impeachment exists—may discourage the witness from offering untruthful testimony in the first place. Depositions freeze the witness's story so that any departure at trial or in declarations are made at the witness's peril.

Third, if any witness—friend or foe—forgets information at trial, the deposition transcript or recording can be used to refresh the witness's recollection.

> *Depositions freeze the witness's story so that any departure at trial or in declarations are made at the witness's peril.*

2.3.3   Substitute for Live Testimony of Unavailable Witness

If a witness is "unavailable" for trial for a specified reason—e.g., death, illness, being beyond the subpoena power of the court, or lack of memory—Rule 32(a)(4) and Federal Rule of Evidence 801(d) permit the use of the witness's deposition testimony as a substitute for their live testimony.

It can be critically important to take the deposition of a witness who is elderly, or who lives a great distance from the court, or who is potentially leaving the jurisdiction, particularly if the witness is your client or is "friendly" in the sense of being likely to testify favorably to your client's case. If they cannot testify at the trial, their evidence will most likely be lost unless their testimony has been preserved by deposition. Even when the goal is to resolve a case by dispositive motion, it may be prudent to depose the elderly, infirm, or transient witness to ensure that their favorable testimony will be available if they become unable to review and sign a declaration down the road.[3]

Preserving witness testimony can be a two-edged sword. For example, if counsel wants to learn all of what the witness has to say—good and bad—to prepare for trial, the deposition transcript or recording preserves not just the helpful testimony, but also the testimony harmful to the case. Having taken a thorough deposition of an opponent's witness, it is no fun to watch the opponent use the transcript at trial to present harmful testimony after the witness has become unavailable. Therefore,

---

3. Depositions to preserve testimony are covered in Chapter Twenty. *See also* Rule 27 (depositions to perpetuate testimony).

exercise caution in choosing the scope and manner of the deposition inquiries if you suspect that the deponent will be unavailable for trial.

2.4 Facilitating Settlement

The final purpose for depositions is to facilitate settlement. Depositions further this goal by permitting evaluation of the witness and attorney, opening lines of communication, presenting information to the opposing side, and exposing the witness firsthand to the nature of litigation.

2.4.1 Sizing Up the Witness and Opposing Attorney

A deposition allows each party and counsel to assess the witness's credibility, how well the witness testifies under pressure, and how the trier of fact will likely perceive the testimony. Does the witness appear sincere? Is the witness articulate, relatable, and believable? Is the witness invested in the outcome? Might the witness be a loose cannon or become flustered if cross-examined in front of a jury? How the witness behaves in the deposition can affect the settlement value of the case.

A case's settlement value can also be reflected in the opposing attorney's behavior. Does counsel seem confident in the witness, or does counsel cringe or attempt to derail the deposition when you pursue certain lines of inquiry? The perceived abilities of opposing counsel will factor in as well. Is counsel invested? Is counsel posturing? How well will they handle a trial? (And remember, the deponent's counsel is evaluating you too: Do you know the facts? Know how to ask questions? Have a grasp of the theories to pursue and how to get there through the questions and exhibits?)

2.4.2 Opening Lines of Communication

The deposition setting provides an opportunity for counsel to talk with each other about the case. A deposition may be the first time the two sides converse face-to-face (whether in person or remotely) while focused on the potential evidence and the merits of the litigation. Often, the deposition provides a relatively low-key way to raise the possibility of settlement.

A deposition can more likely spark a negotiated resolution if the parties are in attendance. A party who is being deposed can be affected by the deposition— sometimes toward settlement, sometimes away—but there is always the possibility that the presence of both the plaintiff and the defendant may facilitate a compromise.

2.4.3 Presenting Information to the Opponent

The information that surfaces in a deposition can, of course, help to persuade counsel and the parties that settlement is a good idea. The deposing attorney may confront the witness (and counsel) with damning evidence, perhaps unknown to the witness and opposing counsel, to persuade them of the futility of their case. Conversely, while witnesses are usually counseled by their attorney not to volunteer information, there may be instances where facts offered by the witness will show the deposing attorney that their client's case is not so great, either. In rare cases, you might even choose to bring out such information by questioning your own witness, following the deposing attorney's examination.

2.4.4   Exposing the Witness to the Realities of Litigation

Lastly, as a result of being rigorously examined during a deposition, a party or key witness may find the whole experience so unpleasant that they would rather settle the case than go through the experience again at trial. Similarly, a deposition may end up consuming so much of a party's or witness's time that the further demands of preparing for trial and the trial itself may not be an acceptable cost. While it is not ethical to take a witness's deposition to "punish" them, revelations about the nature of litigation are a frequent by-product of a deposition that is taken for other, legitimate reasons. Simply put, when confronted with the stark reality of litigation, parties may become more amenable to a swift and prudent resolution of the case.

CHAPTER THREE

ADVANTAGES AND DISADVANTAGES OF DEPOSITIONS

The world is ruled only by considerations of advantages.

—Friedrich von Schiller

Depositions will be more effective if you appreciate their advantages and disadvantages compared to informal fact-gathering and other discovery devices. Knowing these advantages and disadvantages helps you decide whether to depose a given witness. While the opposing party and key witnesses are almost always deposed, it may be a closer question for more peripheral witnesses. In addition, knowing the advantages and disadvantages of depositions helps you maximize the advantages—following up with the witness in real time with relatively little filtering by opposing counsel—and to minimize the disadvantages, particularly the limitations imposed by the witness's personal knowledge and the expense that depositions entail. In this chapter, we look at the advantages of depositions, and then their disadvantages.

In This Chapter: Pros and Cons of Depositions versus Other Formal Discovery (Interrogatories, Admissions)

Pros
- Information from nonparties
- Under oath and preserved on the record
- Unfiltered information
- Spontaneous answers
- Fewer obstructive objections
- Ability to follow up
- Opinions, mental impressions, and subjective details
- Quickly obtained
- Face to face

Cons
- No legal contentions
- Lapse of memory or lack of knowledge
- Gives the witness experience responding to questions
- Prompts opposing counsel to prepare the opponent's case
- Involves considerable expense
- Reveals theories

3.1 Advantages

A deposition is one of many ways a party can learn the facts of a case. Other ways include informal methods, such as interviews, online searches and investigations, and formal discovery devices such as interrogatories, requests or subpoenas for documents (as well as electronically stored information and tangible items), and requests for admission. While each method has its place, depositions are superior in several respects.

3.1.1 Information from Nonparties

When seeking information directly from persons and entities that are not parties to the litigation, the only available *formal* discovery device is the deposition. Interrogatories and document requests under the federal rules and typical state statutes can be served only on parties. Although documents, electronically stored information (ESI), and other tangible items of a nonparty witness can be obtained by service of a subpoena duces tecum (Rule 45(a)(1)), any information about that material must be obtained from a nonparty by deposition.

To obtain information from nonparties, therefore, the question is whether to depose the witness or to merely interview the witness informally. Generally, the interview option is available if the witness is not an opposing party or an employee of an opposing party.[1] However, nothing requires the nonparty to answer a lawyer's or investigator's questions; if the witness refuses to cooperate, the only way to get that person's story is through formal discovery, and the only available formal discovery device is a deposition. (Even when a nonparty witness *does* agree to be interviewed, a deposition has a specific advantage discussed in the next section.)

As to obtaining information from parties, a party can be compelled to respond to interrogatories and other formal discovery devices. The question is, therefore, whether to depose the party witness notwithstanding the availability of interrogatories, document requests, and the like. This question can be answered by considering the remaining advantages and disadvantages of depositions.

---

1. Ethics rules generally preclude an attorney from communicating with represented individuals. Specifically, ABA Model Rule 4.2 and corresponding state ethics rules forbid an attorney from communicating about a case with a person the lawyer knows to be represented by another lawyer in the matter, unless the other lawyer consents. The extent to which the prohibition applies to current and former employees of the represented opposing party turns on the law of the jurisdiction. *See, e.g.,* ABA Model Rule 4.2 [Comment 7]. Communicating with an unrepresented person is limited by ABA Model Rule 4.3 and its state counterparts.

3.1.2 *Under Oath and Preserved on the Record*

In a deposition, the witness takes an oath to tell the truth and the witness's statements are recorded in writing, on video, or both. The testimony is therefore fixed and can be readily used as evidence in motions practice or at trial. Moreover, the administration of the oath, the relative formality of the questioning, and the presence of the court reporter and opposing party at a deposition will often impress upon a witness the importance of telling the truth.

For these reasons, even if a nonparty is willing to talk informally, a deposition is ultimately the best tool to capture what the nonparty has to say. An informal interview is usually not recorded, and even if it is recorded, the interview is typically not provided under oath. Unless the interview leads to an affidavit or declaration signed under penalty of perjury, the conversation may not be admissible and is certainly less persuasive than a sworn statement. Furthermore, if you personally interview the witness, and the witness gives contrary testimony at trial, you could become a witness in the case.[2]

As for witnesses who are parties to the litigation, the oath-taking and formality of the deposition make it attractive. While a party's responses to interrogatories and document requests must be in writing and signed by the party under oath, the oath requirement does not seem to have the same effect as it has at a deposition. In the case of interrogatory answers, for example, the oath is frequently glossed over when signing the attorney-prepared responses. There is nothing like a witness having to raise their hand and commit to telling the truth in front of counsel and a court reporter at a deposition.

Relatedly, deposition testimony results in more powerful impeachment at trial if the witness changes their story. Impeaching a party witness with their interrogatory response is often unsatisfactory—the witness muddies the water with claims of not understanding the interrogatory, not knowing the significance of interrogatories, and thinking the oath merely meant the answers were read and their gist was generally accurate. Although such claims reflect an abrogation of the duties of the witness and counsel, jurors tend to side with a lay witness, at least to the extent they will not give much weight to the impeachment attempt. A deposition provides a much stronger source of impeachment because of the nature of the proceeding (particularly if the deposing attorney laid the proper groundwork by getting the witness commitments set forth in section 6.3).

---

2. You may want an investigator to interview the nonparty witness informally before noticing the nonparty's deposition, so you can get an idea of what the witness would say. If the testimony is going to be harmful, it is better not to preserve it in a deposition. If you are interested in the nonparty's documents, a subpoena duces tecum can be served to compel their production.

3.1.3   Unfiltered Information

A party's response to written discovery is made through their counsel. In responding to interrogatories, for example, the responding party's attorney usually obtains the necessary information from the client and then edits the answers to provide the least amount of usable information that is still responsive to the questions. What counsel serves as the interrogatory response therefore ends up bearing scant resemblance to the information originally given by the party.

At a deposition, on the other hand, the witness alone answers the questions. Defending counsel may influence the answer by carefully (or improperly) preparing the witness beforehand and by objecting, instructing, or giving advice during a break in the deposition, but to a large extent you will get the witness's own answers without opposing counsel's edits and filters. Deposing the opposing party and the opposing party's key witnesses thus offers a clear advantage over merely serving the party with interrogatories.

3.1.4   Spontaneous Answers

Depositions provide the opportunity to obtain a witness's response to questions without giving the witness a lot of time to reflect on the question and concoct an answer. Contrast this again with interrogatories, where a party and the party's attorney will have a minimum of thirty days to think how to phrase the response in the least damaging form. Of course, witnesses can rehearse answers to expected questions in a deposition, but your ability to attack a subject from several different angles means the witness will eventually have to answer spontaneously.

3.1.5   Fewer Obstructive Objections

Although the witness's attorney may well object to deposition questions, and depositions can indeed become contentious, counsel's objections generally do not excuse the witness from answering the question and are less likely to result in a blockage of information (*see* Rule 30). In the case of interrogatories, by contrast, some opposing counsel find it easier to object to an interrogatory than to answer it, forcing the attorney who propounded the interrogatory to live with a meaningless response or spend time and money bringing a motion to compel a better one.

3.1.6   Ability to Follow Up

When an answer to an interrogatory is evasive or does not provide the requested information, the only available options, other than accepting the response, is to negotiate with opposing counsel over providing a further answer, bring a motion to compel, or draft and send a new interrogatory that is better crafted to obtain the information (as long as you have not already exhausted the number of permissible interrogatories, *see* Rule 33(a)). These options take time, and none of them is foolproof.

Depositions, on the other hand, allow you to immediately ask follow-up questions until the area of inquiry is exhausted. For instance, you can quickly challenge evasive or nonresponsive answers and require the witness to answer:

Q: Where were you during the conversation with Mr. Mannix?

A: Most likely in our building at 123 Seminole Road.

Q: Most likely, or definitely?

A: Definitely.

Q: Where in the building?

A: On the fourteenth floor.

Q: Where on the fourteenth floor?

A: Do you mean at the beginning or the end of the conversation?

Q: Let's take both. Where were you at the beginning?

A: I was inside the office by the door.

Q: Where were you at the end of the conversation?

A: I was still by the door.

Q: Did you ever move away from the door during the conversation?

A: No.

Q: So you were by the door of your office on the fourteenth floor throughout the conversation.

A: Yes.

The ability to follow up is also important when the witness's answer or manner of answering suggests a new lead. For example, there may be something about the witness's facial expression when responding to the question, or a pause or hesitation in uttering the response, which shows there is more in the witness's mind than the witness's words suggest. Or sometimes the witness's phrasing of the answer will indicate that the witness is avoiding the question, like this:

Q: Did she say anything about the contract?

A: Not at that time.

Q: Was something said about the contract at another time?

A: Well, yes, later on.

Q: When?

A: At our meeting the next day.

Q: What was said?

A: The boss said we weren't going to honor the contract.

The ability to follow up on a witness's answers also allows you to attack a harmful answer:

Q: Were you paying attention to the car in front of you when you approached the light?

A: Yes, absolutely. I certainly was paying attention.

Q: Let's see. You told me a moment ago that you had seen a boy by the side of the road, correct?

A: Yes.

Q: You also told me that you were worried the boy was going to run out into the street?

A: Yes.

Q: So you were keeping your eyes on the boy in case he ran out in front of your car, true?

A: I guess so.

Q: When you were watching the boy to the side of you, you weren't watching the car in front of you, right?

A: Right.

Q: You told me that you noticed the car in front of you just before you ran into it?

A: Yes.

Q: Because you were paying attention to the boy, you weren't paying attention to the car in front of you?

A: Well, I mean . . . okay, yeah.

3.1.7   *Opinions, Mental Impressions, and Subjective Details*

Although interrogatories may suffice for discovering the opposing party's contentions, a list of supporting facts and documents, and contact information for witnesses, they do not usually elicit the party's opinions, mental impressions, and subjective information, which is often lost by the time the lawyer has edited (or drafted) the interrogatory response. For example, consider a typical interrogatory and the answer that might be given:

Interrogatory No. 22:   Please describe how the accident occurred.

Answer:	The defendant's automobile collided with the plaintiff's automobile.

Nor will it help to rephrase the interrogatory to state:

Interrogatory No. 22:	Please describe *in detail* how the accident occurred.
Answer:	The defendant's automobile collided very hard with the plaintiff's automobile.

Now compare this with a deposition:

Q: Please describe how the accident occurred.

A: Well, the other car hit me.

Q: Okay, let's back up. Where were you when you first saw the plaintiff's car?

A: I was east of the intersection of Kirby and Mattis.

Q: How far east?

A: About fifty feet.

Q: What lane were you in?

A: The curb lane.

Q: How fast were you going?

A: About fifteen miles per hour.

Q: Why were you going so slow?

A: The light looked like it was about to change.

Q: How did it look like it was about to change?

A: Well, it was yellow.

Q: How long had it been yellow?

A: A few seconds.

Q: What did you do when you saw the yellow light?

A: Well, I thought I'd better stop, so I put on the brakes.

Q: What were you thinking at the time?

A: I didn't want to run a red.

Q: Did you consider there were cars following behind you?

A: Well, no. I guess I was focused on the light.

Depositions are the only reliable discovery device for obtaining the details and subjective information lodged in the witness's mind.

3.1.8   Quickly Obtained

Depositions can be scheduled on "reasonable notice" under Rule 30(b)(1), usually satisfied by notice of seven to ten days, which corresponds roughly to the notice periods required by most states. By contrast, interrogatories need not be answered until a minimum of thirty days after service under Rule 33(b). When you need information quickly to prepare for a motion, other discovery, or settlement negotiations, depositions are the discovery method to use.

3.1.9   Face to Face

Depositions are the only formal discovery device that allows you to meet the opposing witnesses face to face, either in person or online during a remote deposition.

Face-to-face confrontation yields several benefits. It forces witnesses to tell their stories in front of opposing parties (or at least their attorneys) who know what occurred in the underlying events, which might lead the witness to be more truthful. It allows the witness, including the opposing party, to vent their frustrations and "be heard." It may give the party witness a bad taste for intensive questioning that will likely repeat at trial, making the party less inclined to proceed with the case. It allows counsel to observe nonverbal communications of the witness and opposing counsel—shrugs, grins, furrowed brows, tone of voice, and the like—which provide indispensable clues to their unspoken truths and concerns. You may invoke a stern manner that persuades a witness to back off from untruthful or harmful testimony, or a charm that induces the witness to concede facts. Finally, as discussed in the preceding chapter, face-to-face confrontation allows you to see how the witness would appear under similar questioning in front of a jury, to evaluate the abilities of opposing counsel, and to demonstrate trial prowess through incisive and penetrating examination, likeable personality, and command of the deposition room.

3.2   Disadvantages

Despite the many advantages of depositions as a discovery device, several drawbacks must also be considered.

3.2.1   Legal Contentions Not Discoverable

A party's legal contentions—that is, the legal theories asserted by their counsel in the case and the selection of facts supporting their claims for relief or defenses—are typically not discoverable in a deposition, because that information calls for a legal analysis by counsel. Instead, the information is obtained by interrogatories. Nonetheless, it is entirely appropriate to ask questions in a deposition about the *witness's* observations and conclusions and the facts the witness believes supports them.

3.2.2 Lapse of Memory or Lack of Knowledge

In most cases, a deposition witness is only required to answer questions based on their knowledge and recollection. If the witness claims a lapse of memory or lack of knowledge in response to a question, there is little that you can do besides trying to refresh the witness's recollection or find out who else might know. For instance, if you ask the president of the Widget Corporation how many widgets were sold in 2019 and the witness answers, "I don't recall" or "I don't know," you have no right to compel the witness to go look up the information (although it can't hurt to ask). By contrast, a party responding to interrogatories has an obligation to respond with all "available" information.[3]

There are, however, ways to prepare for this using other discovery devices. Serve a document request or third-party subpoena before the deposition to obtain the documents containing the necessary information, and then use the document as an exhibit in the deposition and refresh the witness's memory. Or seek the desired information in advance of the deposition by serving interrogatories, which reach both the memory and files of a party and the collective memory of an institutional party, requiring the party to take reasonable steps to provide the requested information. "I don't remember" will not suffice as an interrogatory response if the party can find the information with a reasonable amount of work, such as by checking records and conferring with employees. A further alternative exists where the opposing party is a corporation or other organization: schedule a Rule 30(b)(6) deposition, thereby requiring the organization to designate a witness who must be reasonably prepared, with the knowledge of the entire organization, to testify on the organization's behalf about identified matters (*see* Chapter Twenty-One). Coordinating depositions with other discovery is discussed in Chapter Four.

3.2.3 Gives the Witness Experience Responding to Questions

Inexperienced witnesses may become flustered, confused, or nervous when cross-examined at trial, which may cause the jurors not to believe them. A deposition, however, gives the witness practice answering questions, equipping the witness to be better prepared, more comfortable, and more effective in responding to similar questions at the trial.

---

3. Rule 33(b)(1)(B); Bryant v. Armstrong, 285 F.R.D. 596, 612 (S.D. Cal. 2012).

3.2.4   *Prompts Opposing Counsel to Prepare the Opponent's Case*

At times you may notice a defending attorney scribble down (or madly type on a laptop) every answer the witness gives in the deposition. This may be due to counsel's thoroughness or compulsive note-taking—a "skill" learned in law school. But sometimes it is because the defending attorney has not previously interviewed the witness or even considered the topic of inquiry. The witness's answers are as new to the defending attorney as to you, and the deposition is therefore helping the defending lawyer prepare their case. Even when opposing counsel *has* prepared the witness for deposition, it is often because the scheduled deposition forced the witness and the lawyer to prepare.

3.2.5   *Involves Considerable Expense*

Depositions cost money. The time of the court reporter and the preparation of transcripts are out-of-pocket expenses, as is the cost of a videographer and video editing for depositions recorded audiovisually. Attorney time preparing and taking the deposition must also be accounted for, either against the contingent fee or as billable hours. Preparing interrogatories and informal investigation entail much less time and expense.

Depositions become even more costly when travel is involved. Defendants and nonparty witnesses must normally be deposed close to their residence or work, and plaintiffs are usually deposed where they filed the litigation or near their residence or work. When litigation is national in scope, the costs of travelling to appear at depositions in person can be prohibitively high. By contrast, interrogatories, document requests and subpoenas, and requests for admission can be served by mail or, where permitted, electronically.

Of course, the travel costs of depositions can be avoided if the deposition is conducted by videoconference. The conclusion these days, therefore, may not be to forgo a distant deposition, but to hold it remotely as discussed in Chapter Twenty-Four. Similarly, technological advances have reduced other costs associated with depositions. The cost of video depositions has greatly decreased over the years, and the use of electronic exhibits relieves counsel (and the client) of the expense and resources needed to copy and transport hard copies.

3.2.6   *Reveals Theories*

Deposition questions often reveal the deposing attorney's legal, factual, and persuasive theories of the case. For instance, if the defendant's questions in a breach of contract case concern the plaintiff's efforts to exercise an option under the contract, the plaintiff's attorney can guess that this will be one of the defenses raised and will prepare the plaintiff's case accordingly.

In most instances, however, this is not much of a concern. Everyone involved in the litigation can anticipate from the pleadings and the facts what issues will be raised. Forgoing a deposition (or a line of inquiry during the deposition) just to conceal a theory forfeits the opportunity to learn how the opposing party will respond to it.

3.3   Conclusion

There is a place for other formal discovery devices such as interrogatories, document requests, and requests for admission, as well as informal interviews with third-party witnesses. But to obtain sworn, recorded information from nonparties and relatively unfiltered and spontaneous information from parties, the deposition is superior.

Moreover, you can make the most of a deposition by capitalizing on its advantages: exhaustively following up on the witness's answers, watching the witness for nonverbal cues, and obtaining the witness's mental impressions and characterizations. Conversely, counsel can minimize the potential disadvantages of a deposition by being ready to jog the witness's recollection if they cannot remember an answer, and being as efficient as possible to limit deposition expense and obtain the needed information in the allotted time.

PART TWO

TAKING AND USING DEPOSITIONS

CHAPTER FOUR

CASE ANALYSIS, DISCOVERY PLANNING, AND DEPOSITIONS

True genius resides in the capacity for evaluation of uncertain, hazardous, and conflicting information.

—Winston Churchill

Critical thinking is not something you do once with an issue and then drop it. It requires that we update our knowledge as new information comes in.

—Daniel Leviton

A deposition will be more effective if you position it favorably within the overall discovery plan of a well-analyzed case. By so doing, you will know the necessary factual inquiries to make of the deposition witness, while armed with the information and documents that will make those inquiries most meaningful.

This chapter discusses 1) case analysis techniques for creating an overall case theory based on the facts known to date; 2) crafting a discovery plan to obtain additional information to flesh out the case theory and prevail in the lawsuit; 3) coordinating depositions with other discovery devices to enhance their impact; 4) coordinating a deposition with other depositions; and 5) scheduling depositions for maximum advantage.

> **In This Chapter:**
>
> - Case analysis techniques
> - Crafting a discovery plan
> - Coordinating depositions with other discovery devices
> - Coordinating depositions with other depositions
> - Scheduling depositions for maximum advantage

4.1   Case Analysis to Create the Case Theory

Setting things up for an effective deposition starts with a case theory that explains why the client should prevail in the litigation. We touched on this idea in Chapter Two. Essentially, the case theory is comprised of three separate theories, each of which provides a way to view, evaluate, and advocate the case:

> 1) ***The factual theory*** describes what happened during the events underlying the litigation, including who did what to whom, when, where, how, and why.
>
> 2) ***The legal theory*** explains why the client is entitled to win under the law; that is, the plaintiff's claims for relief or causes of action, or the defendant's responses to those claims and its affirmative defenses.
>
> 3) ***The persuasive theory*** states why a party should prevail as a matter of fairness and justice, independent from the law; it appeals to the judge's or jury's sense of right and wrong by attributing reasonableness to your client, moral responsibility or blame to the opposing party, or both.

These theories look at the lawsuit from distinct vantage points. Collectively, they help you present the case in a way that is most compelling to the judge or jurors.

While the theories reflect three different perspectives, they are all intertwined. The factual theory dictates what legal theories are viable; the legal theories determine what facts may be relevant; and the persuasive theory is driven by the facts of what occurred and who the parties are.

Do not underestimate the value of formulating case theories. Early on, factual theory, legal theory, and persuasive theory organize the case information and suggest what facts must be obtained or confirmed in discovery, including in depositions. As new facts are discovered, the theories are adjusted and fine-tuned. As litigation continues, the theories indicate what motions to pursue and help assess the likelihood of victory and the value of the case. If the matter proceeds to trial, the theories suggest what questions to ask during jury voir dire, what prospective jurors to challenge, what to say in opening statements, the selection and order of witnesses, the content of direct and cross-examinations, and the arguments to make in closing.

You can—and must—have working theories from the beginning of the case to chart the plan for discovery and motions. A good starting point for those theories will come from the allegations and claims in the pleadings. The theories will evolve as new facts are learned during discovery and, indeed, up to the time of trial. So let's look more closely at the three types of case theories and how to develop them.

4.1.1   Factual Theory

The factual theory depicts what occurred in the events precipitating the lawsuit. It includes who the parties are, who did what to whom, and when, where, how, and why they did it. It may be illustrated in a chronology or list of facts, but it is ultimately more than that; the listed facts will be woven into a narrative or "story" that suggests motives, is believable and reasonable, and describes the evidence better than the stories of the other parties.

Develop the factual theory from the outset of the case. For plaintiffs, that means gathering as much information as possible from the client and other informal sources before filing the complaint. For defendants, it means gathering as much information as possible as soon as the complaint is served. This information—collected and analyzed before formal discovery—will help you craft written discovery requests (e.g., interrogatories, document demands), respond to discovery, decide who needs to be deposed, formulate fruitful lines of deposition questions, and challenge the witness's responses. Of course, information gleaned later in the case from discovery and otherwise will also be used to develop the factual theory; but the more you learn through informal means before conducting discovery, the better the discovery will be.

To begin developing the factual theory, tap into various sources of information and employ helpful tools to organize and understand it.

> *The factual theory, legal theory, and persuasive theory organize the case information and suggest what facts must be obtained or confirmed in discovery.*

Sources

Your client, client files, and ESI. Clients usually know the most about their own cases. After all, the lawsuit was brought because of what was done to the client, or by the client, and why. They know how the contract was negotiated, how the accident happened, how their rights came to be oppressed, and why they did what they did, including the reasonable steps and precautions they took. In business litigation, they know the industry and the applicable players and practices. They often know what witnesses will be best for their side and what witnesses are likely to appear for the other side. Interview your individual client, and the relevant employees of a client who is an organization, as soon as possible.

Obtain and review early on all the client's potentially relevant documents (including photographs and videos) and electronically stored information (including emails, texts, voicemails, and videos), which can involve a huge amount of data.

The time spent collecting and understanding this material will be invaluable when later addressing discovery demands and, in federal court, providing mandatory disclosures under Rule 26.

Nonparty witnesses. Interview unrepresented witnesses who are willing to talk informally about the events, at least by telephone. Not only will these individuals tell you what happened from their perspective, they will provide leads to other essential witnesses and documents. You might even request them to provide documents voluntarily, reenact what occurred, or (assuming their information is favorable to your client) record the statement in writing under penalty of perjury or by video.

To the extent allowed, contact even those witnesses you expect to be hostile—if the witness consents to an interview and discloses information harmful to your client, you might have one less deposition to take. There are, however, ethical constraints on interviewing people represented by an attorney or employees of an opposing party organization; carefully check the law in the relevant jurisdiction.

Public information. As we all know, the internet is a treasure trove of information. Google the parties in the case, potential witnesses, the locations of the events at issue, and the companies and industries involved. The resulting abundance of material must, of course, be scrutinized for accuracy. Social media searches unveil much additional information. Not to be forgotten, obtain public information held by government agencies with traditional requests under the Freedom of Information Act (5 U.S.C. § 552) and similar state laws (e.g., Cal. Govt. Code § 6252).

The scene. Visiting the scene of the underlying events always seems to spark questions for further investigation and puts raw factual data into context. In a personal injury case, visiting and photographing an accident scene will provide a better understanding of a witness's descriptions and explanations, and it may suggest an illustrative aid to use when taking a deposition. In a products liability case, seeing the factory where the product was manufactured can be helpful as well. In a construction case, visiting the job site may suggest a reason for a performance delay or failure alleged in the case.[1]

Experts. When the lawsuit involves matters requiring the assistance of an expert witness, hiring a consulting expert can help you understand the technical aspects of the case and identify the facts that need to be developed for expert opinions.

---

1. Informal witness interviews, internet searches, and site visits are low-cost and helpful and usually do not have to be revealed to the opponent if properly conducted by counsel (*see* Rule 26(b)(3)). There are, however, some drawbacks. In particular, the information may not be usable in court, and even if it can be, it may not seem as persuasive as testimony provided at a deposition. As suggested later in this chapter, following up to obtain admissible evidence of the facts through the formal discovery process—particularly depositions that force a witness to testify under oath and are recorded—will be an important part of preparing for motions and trial.

National Institute for Trial Advocacy

Experts can also provide crucial information concerning a relevant industry, a marketplace, or financial issues such as the measure of damages and lost profits.

Court filings. The pleadings and other filings in the case are an obvious source of facts and potential facts. A defendant's review of the allegations of the complaint, and the plaintiff's review of the answer and any counterclaim, discloses what the opposing party contends and what needs to be tested in discovery.

Initial disclosures. Absent a court order or exemption, parties litigating in federal district court must disclose, before formal discovery begins, basic information about the case as set forth in Rule 26(a). Specifically, each party must provide to all other parties the name and known address of each individual likely to have discoverable information; a copy or description of all documents and ESI in the party's possession, custody, or control that would support its claims or defenses; a computation of damages; and any applicable insurance agreement. The opposing party's disclosures offer a glimpse into the material available to the other side—at least the material helpful to the other side's case.

Tools

Information received from the foregoing sources will yield a lot of data. You must organize that data in a way that will help you put the data in context, develop a factual theory, and accommodate new information that comes in during discovery. Here are some possible tools for organizing the facts.

Chronologies and timelines. Making a chronological list of the facts you have uncovered and the events underlying the lawsuit, or creating a timeline of those facts and events (e.g., extending chronologically from left to right, with the earliest events on the left), will assist in explaining what happened in the case. A chronology or timeline is, in effect, a visual depiction of your factual theory.

Chronologies and timelines have several benefits. They list the facts you have been told to date, which you will need to question or confirm in discovery. They show the gaps between events that you need to fill and indicate additional information that you need to obtain. They suggest cause and effect relationships among the events, demonstrate who knew what when, and indicate potential motives for the parties' actions. And last but not least, they display any inconsistencies that must be resolved: for example, the story as told by one witness ("he was just outside his office at 7:00 p.m.") may conflict with documentary evidence or the stories told by others ("his parking lot ticket shows he picked up his car at 6:53 p.m. fifteen miles from the office").

To use the chronology or timeline to greatest advantage, look at the events it lists and ask yourself the following questions for each event:

- What happened exactly: where, how, for how long, with whom, why?
- What would a reasonable person have done in that situation?

- Who might have witnessed the event?

- What notes, photos, videos, or other documents might have recorded it?

- What conversations or actions did it prompt?

- How might this event have been caused by a prior event, and how might it have contributed to a later event?

- What facts are missing from the story?

- What was happening between one event and the other?

- Who might have a different opinion about what occurred, and what would make our client's account more believable?

Performing this exercise will let you know what facts you need to obtain through informal investigations and formal discovery. As you learn the additional facts and update the chronology and timeline accordingly, you continue to develop your factual theory.

While a simple chronology or timeline listing the dates and describing the events may suffice, you can create more sophisticated chronologies as well. For example, the chronology may have not only columns for the date (and time) of the event and for a description of the event (e.g., "meeting between Jones and Smith," "letter from X to Y," "site visit," "collision"), it may also have columns for supporting evidence (e.g., "X ltr to Y, Bates # 00001–00005;" "Adams Decl., ¶ 5") and individuals who have knowledge of the event (e.g., "Adams," "Smith," "Nguyen"). Then you can sort the information in various ways: for example, sort by date to get a pure chronology, or sort by witness to find all the topics known to the individual you are about to depose or examine at trial.

Relationship charts. A "relationship chart" is a visual representation of the interactions and potential interactions among the parties, witnesses, and organizations

Date/time	Event	Supporting Evidence	Person(s) with knowledge
10/12/2021	Purchase of car	Bill of sale	Client (owner)
11/15/2021	Client brings car to dealer for brake repair	Shop invoice Client's calendar	Client Shop foreman
1/15/2022 1:43 p.m.	Accident	Police report Photographs	Client Officer on the scene J. Zee, passenger Victory Munn, witness
1/15/2022 2:27 p.m.	Transport to hospital via ambulance	Ambulance bill	Client

in the litigation. To create the chart, identify all the parties and ancillary actors in the case. Then specify the relationships between any two of them with a connecting line, labeling the line with significant interrelating facts. (Think of the "perp charts" used on Chicago PD and other "procedurals" you see on television.) The relationship chart assists in explaining the parties' motives, and it can reveal the significance of ostensibly minor witnesses. For example, a witness who at first seems to play a minor role may turn out to possess, due to a relationship with a party or institution, case-changing information about why a contract was breached, why an employee was terminated, or why an automobile steering assembly was not repaired correctly.

RELATIONSHIP FLOWCHART

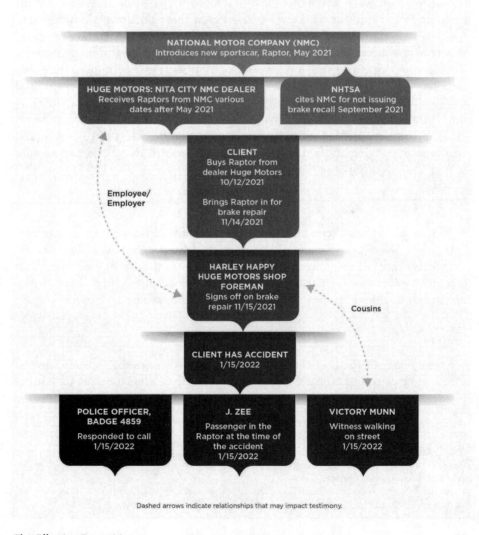

Dashed arrows indicate relationships that may impact testimony.

Combine timelines with relationship charts to introduce a chronological dimension for analyzing the actors' behaviors. The completed chart can suggest why things happened, who caused it to happen, and who would know about it. From these indications, you can think of additional questions for discovery generally and depositions specifically.

Document databases. Not too many years ago, documents received from clients and other parties were maintained in expanding file folders; documents that were produced in formal discovery would be manually stamped or affixed with a "Bates number"[2] and manually logged into a computer database, table, or word-processing document. That practice gave way to more and more sophisticated software for categorizing, analyzing, and retrieving all the documents in a case. Today, due in part to the proliferation of ESI and documents generally, most law firms have document management software that allows them to import or upload electronic documents (including PDF scans of hard copies) and assign those documents numbers and codes so they can be easily tracked and retrieved according to author, recipient, subject matter, date range, keywords, privilege, and the like. Appropriate software is critical for organizing and understanding ESI, such as electronic correspondence, business records, emails, voicemails, videos, photographs, social media, and websites, while preserving both their content and the metadata reflecting their creation.[3] The use of these software programs is largely outside the scope of this book; suffice to say they are vital to compiling and sorting the fruits of discovery, and helpful in identifying and retrieving the facts and documentary evidence relevant to your factual theory of the case.

4.1.2 Legal Theory

To state the obvious, legal theories are important because the outcomes of motions, trials, and even settlement negotiations are driven by the law. To further state the obvious, the facts we must pursue in discovery are those that will support (or negate) an element of the parties' claims for relief or defenses. Therefore, a critical step in case analysis is to identify the legal theories asserted by each party.

Sources

At the outset of the litigation, each party's legal theories can be found by examining the pleadings. The defendant will look to the claims for relief (or "causes of action" in California and other jurisdictions) that the plaintiff asserted in the

---

2. A "Bates number" is a number affixed to the bottom of a page to identify it. The term derives from the name of a machine that was invented to produce consecutive numbers each time the machine was pressed onto a piece of paper.
3. "Metadata" refers to data residing in electronic documents that reveals information about the document's origin and modification, including the date of creation and author.

complaint and will be cognizant of the affirmative defenses it eventually includes in its answer. The plaintiff will not only know the legal theories asserted in the complaint (presumably based on the plaintiff's factual theory at the time the complaint was filed) but will also look to the affirmative defenses alleged by the defendant. Both parties will consider legal theories set forth in any counterclaim, crossclaim, or third-party complaint filed thereafter.

For each legal theory, the elements of that theory must be identified—for example, duty, breach, proximate cause, and damage for a negligence claim. Sources for these elements include case law and the model jury instructions in the applicable jurisdiction.

After identifying the elements of each claim or defense, consider what facts support each element. Are there facts to support all the elements of all the claims? Then make sure you have admissible evidence of those facts, which you can obtain or confirm through discovery. Are there elements of a claim not supported by the facts as you know them? Then you need to obtain those facts through your client, discovery, or public sources.

While many lawyers perform this extensive research while drafting the pleadings and update it along the way, a surprising number wait until just before trial to determine with specificity what each party must prove, leaving no time to secure the necessary evidence. Finding out what must be proved or disproved while there is still an opportunity to obtain the evidence through discovery is obviously the better approach.

Tools

One way to keep track of the legal theories, as well as the known facts that support those theories and the facts still needed to establish them, is to make a "proof chart." Such a chart can be as simple as a large piece of butcher paper taped to the wall, with the elements of the claims and defenses written in one column and the corresponding facts listed in another column. Nowadays, the chart is more likely created using a computer spreadsheet or database program, which makes it easy to add new rows and columns of information, move the information around, and sort the information as needed.

In its most common form, the proof chart has four columns labeled across the top as "Supporting Facts," "Supporting Facts to Be Discovered," "Opposing Facts," and "Opposing Facts to Be Discovered." Once you insert the facts that you know in the appropriate column, it will be easy to see what additional facts are needed to prove (or refute) each element. The columns addressing the "Opposing Facts" force you to consider what the opposing party will try to prove. Information in the columns labeled "Supporting Facts to Be Discovered" and "Opposing Facts to Be Discovered" will help you create discovery requests and deposition outlines. The chart might look like this, in part:

	Supporting Facts	Supporting Facts to Be Discovered	Opposing Facts	Opposing Facts to Be Discovered
Representation	Jones and Smith heard	Was it said	Denial by defendant	Internal documents support
Reliance in Good Faith	No parts ordered	Plaintiff reserved parts		
Action Based on Representation	Smith told Marketing		No commission paid	

Update the chart as you receive new information, moving facts contained in the "To Be Discovered" column to the "Facts" column as discovery progresses. As you learn more facts, reassess your legal theories: you might jettison a theory or add a new one. Also assess your opponent's legal theories—calculate how to attack them, decide whether any are ripe for a dispositive motion, and determine your client's exposure. Once discovery is completed, review and evaluate each legal theory to make a final determination of its viability.

Like the chronology we discussed in section 4.1.1, the proof chart can be enhanced by adding more columns of information. As an example, for each fact listed under the element of a claim for relief, include in a separate column the evidence supporting that fact (e.g., "Smith ltr to Jackson, Bates #0001–0005") and in another column the witnesses who might be able to testify to that evidence ("Smith" or "Jackson"). You can then sort the database to readily find all topics relevant to a deponent and the corresponding documents.

4.1.3 Persuasive Theory

While the factual theory and legal theory may demonstrate to the judge and jurors that your client is legally entitled to a favorable ruling, the persuasive theory is what makes them want to rule in your client's favor. It appeals to their sense of fairness, justice, and reasonableness.

Sources

A persuasive theory may readily come to mind from the facts of a case, one that cries out for a particular result: for the plaintiff, it may be the severity of the plaintiff's suffering or the audacity of the defendant's actions or neglect; for the defense, it may be the manipulations and overreaching greed of the plaintiff, or the great extent to which the defendant took steps to avoid harm. But in other cases, we may need to give the persuasive theory more thought. What makes our client's position reasonable? Why is it just and fair for our client to prevail? From the client's view, what is unfair about what the other side did? If a compelling persuasive theory remains elusive, a brainstorming session—discussed next—may help.

Tools

Generically speaking, brainstorming is a powerful analytic process of encouraging a group of people—such as the client and litigation team—to engage in unrestricted thinking about facts involved in the case. One person acts as a facilitator or leader, who keeps the discussion flowing and ensures that everyone contributes. Normally, the facilitator refrains from offering ideas (so that others do not defer to them and eventually stop contributing).

A productive brainstorming session follows these rules: 1) there are no bad ideas—even if an idea seems off-base, it may provoke a good idea; 2) list all ideas before criticizing any of them, so as not to suppress contributions and to encourage thinking outside the box; 3) list the ideas on a white board or screenshare them for all participants to see; and 4) agree on a time limit for the discussion.

After explaining these rules, the facilitator asks the group to state the "good" facts in the case (that is, favoring your client) and the "bad" facts (favoring the opponent). After listing the facts, the group discusses and votes for the three best facts and the three worst facts. After the vote, use the best facts, tempered by the worst facts, to find a persuasive theory of how justice, fairness, and reasonableness favor the client. Use the worst facts to anticipate the opposing party's theories. One goal of discovery, including depositions, will be to confirm the good facts and discredit or explain away the bad facts.

4.1.4 Using Focus Groups to Develop Theories

Focus groups have become a fact of life in many types of litigation. While most commonly used after discovery is complete and the matter is being readied for trial, they can be used to develop factual and persuasive theories before and during discovery as well. Information about the parties, witnesses, and events is provided to a group of individuals who are representative of a potential jury pool and have had no exposure to the

Focus Groups Help:

- *Find holes in your theory.*
- *Highlight which issues jurors care about.*
- *Discover inferences you overlooked.*
- *Evaluate your witnesses.*
- *Identify hot-button traps.*
- *Run your appeals to justice and fairness through the "smell test."*

case. There are various approaches to the process, but these approaches share some core objectives:

- Identifying additional information a trier of fact would like to know;

- Alerting the lawyers to facts jurors would likely consider important;

- Identifying inferences that jurors might draw from the facts presented;

- Identifying witnesses from whom jurors would like to hear;

- Observing the impact of hot-button issues ("Once we found out he was a child molester, well . . ."); and

- Recognizing theories of justice, fairness, and reasonableness.

4.2 Crafting the Discovery Plan

From your factual, legal, and persuasive theories—and particularly your chronology and proof chart—you have a good idea of the facts you need to find out or confirm. The next step is to create a plan to get that information, considering your sources of information and available discovery devices.

By this point, you have already tapped the "friendly" or neutral sources of information discussed earlier in this chapter—your client, your client's documents and ESI, nonparty witnesses (to the extent permissible), internet searches and other public information, visits to the scene, experts, the pleadings, and (in federal court) mandatory initial disclosures under Rule 26. Although this informal fact-gathering can continue to the day of trial, formal discovery efforts will glean information from the opposing party, the opposing party's employees, and nonparties who have been unwilling to cooperate in informal interviews.

In addition, even if a nonparty witness has provided information informally, you may want to follow up with formal discovery to ensure its admissibility in the proceeding. For example, informal witness statements are usually not given under oath, notarized, or even in writing. Since opposing counsel was not present, such a statement would likely not be admissible if the witness later becomes unavailable for trial. Although informal witness statements might be used as impeachment if the witness changes their story at trial or in a declaration, they will not be as persuasive as statements recorded under oath. And while the mandatory disclosures give you a peek at the witnesses and documents on which the opposing party intends to rely, the opposing party is not required to identify witnesses or documents that would be harmful to its position. All of this must come from formal discovery—including depositions.

The formal discovery devices are well known, but we list the main ones here briefly:

- **Oral depositions:** to question an individual or an organization (through the organization's appointed representative), regardless of whether a party (Rule 30) or a nonparty (Rule 45(a)(1)), upon reasonable notice

- **Interrogatories:** to obtain the opinions and contentions of a party, the facts supporting those opinions and contentions, or other information such as the identity of witnesses and relevant documents, upon 30 days' notice; limited to 25 interrogatories without leave of court (Rule 33)

- **Requests for production:** to obtain copies or inspection of documents (including photos and videos), electronically stored information, and tangible things in the possession, custody, or control of a party (or to inspect the party's premises) within a reasonable time, along with a written response within 30 days (Rule 34)

- **Physical and mental examinations:** to obtain, by court order, a physical or mental examination by a licensed or certified examiner of a party whose mental or physical condition is in controversy (Rule 35)

- **Requests for admission:** to obtain the opposing party's admission of the truth of facts, the application of the facts, and genuineness of documents, upon 30 days' notice (Rule 36)

- **Subpoenas duces tecum:** to obtain documents, electronically stored information, and tangible things in the possession, custody, or control of nonparties (or to inspect the premises of nonparties), upon reasonable notice (Rule 45(a)(1); *see* Rule 34(c))

In state court, these and other discovery mechanisms may be available depending on your jurisdiction.

Decide which of these discovery devices to use, to whom to direct them, and the order in which to deploy them. Each discovery device has a potential place in the discovery plan, and the selection and ordering of the devices will vary depending on the nature of the case.

A common course of discovery in some practices goes like this:

1) serve interrogatories on parties to obtain their contentions, their factual support for those contentions, and the identity of relevant documents and witnesses;

2) serve document requests and subpoenas duces tecum to obtain relevant documents and electronically stored information;

3) serve requests for admission to narrow the issues and affirm the authenticity of documents; and then

4) take the depositions of the opposing party and additional witnesses, using the documents and other information obtained from informal fact-gathering and other discovery.

This course of discovery is not universal, however. Some attorneys forgo serving interrogatories and requests for admission because they expect not to get back any useful information, given the likelihood the opposing party's responses will be edited, sanitized, and manicured by opposing counsel. Some attorneys serve requests for admission last, in the belief that the opposing party is more likely to admit things when the bulk of discovery is completed and the facts and ultimate legal positions are better known. Others, in less document-intensive cases, may even start their discovery with a few depositions before opposing counsel has become familiar with the case.

4.3   Coordinating Depositions with Other Discovery

In creating the discovery plan, keep in mind how interrogatories, document requests, and requests for admission can be used to increase the effectiveness of the deposition.

4.3.1   *Using Interrogatories*

Interrogatories are useful deposition preparation tools for several reasons.

Identifying factual data and information that a witness is not likely to recall at the deposition. When you intend to question the witness about objective information in the hands of the opposing party—such as data, calculations, or other information that the witness will not likely remember—obtain this information before the deposition through interrogatories (or document production, discussed below).

Imagine, for example, what could happen in defense counsel's deposition of the plaintiff's employee in charge of purchasing:

> Q: Now, sir, please tell me the name of all vendors from whom the plaintiff purchases parts for use in manufacturing the electronic signs that are the subject of this action.
>
> A: Well, let's see. We purchase most of the circuit boards from Mitsubishi, but several of the more specialized ones come from AdvanCirc. The sign casings come from a small firm in town, Acucom, and we get some parts from jobbers.
>
> Q: Any other vendors?
>
> A: Oh, sure. We use over thirty vendors, but I can't remember them all right now.
>
> Q: Do you have a list of the various vendors?
>
> A: Yes, back at the office.

Q: Counsel, I suggest that you provide me with the list, we finish as much as we can today, and then continue the deposition tomorrow after I have a chance to review the list.

P's Atty: No. Give me a request in writing, and I will take it under advisement. But quite frankly, there's no need to drag out the deposition another day and cause further inconvenience and expense for my client. Depositions are limited to seven hours on one day. If you wanted a list of our vendors, you knew how to get it without waiting until the middle of this deposition. I'll resist any efforts to resume this deposition later.

The defendant's lawyer could have avoided the problem by serving the plaintiff, before the deposition, with interrogatories asking for the names of all vendors supplying parts for the signs.[4] The interrogatories could also ask for any other information that would be helpful in conducting the deposition, such as a description of the parts, the purchase price, quantities, and so on.

Identifying potential deposition witnesses and relevant documents. Interrogatories frequently ask for all witnesses who have knowledge of the facts—who attended an event or meeting, participated in a transaction, and so on. Similarly, interrogatories often ask a party to identify all documents referring to an event or resulting from a transaction. The primary purpose of such interrogatories is to learn of potential deposition witnesses and documents to request. While you can and should ask these same questions at the deposition, deponents many times do not have comprehensive knowledge or recall of other witnesses and documents. For instance, the plaintiff's president in our example may know who attended the meetings that they attended, but not know who attended other meetings when they were not present. Similarly, the defendant in a personal injury case may be unaware of witnesses to the accident who were only later located by their lawyer or a private investigator. The party answering the interrogatory must make reasonable inquiry of all of its employees and agents and conduct a reasonable search of all records.[5]

---

4. If the information had been sought by a discovery request before the deposition, and the information was not provided, further examination may be appropriate after the information is turned over. *See* Advisory Comm. Notes to Rule 30(d)(2).

5. Nat'l Fire Ins. Co. of Hartford v. Jose Trucking Corp., 264 F.R.D. 233, 238 (W.D.N.C. 2010) ("The answers to interrogatories must be responsive, full, complete and unevasive. The answering party cannot limit his answers to matters within his own knowledge and ignore information immediately available to him or under his control. If an appropriate interrogatory is propounded, the answering party will be required to give the information available to him, if any, through his attorney, investigators employed by him or on his behalf or other agents or representatives, whether personally known to the answering party or not. If the answering party lacks necessary information to make a full, fair and specific answer to an interrogatory, it should so state under oath and should set forth in detail the efforts made to obtain the information." (citations omitted)); Frontier-Kemper Constructors, Inc. v. Elk Run Coal Co., 246 F.R.D. 522, 529 (S.D. W.Va. 2007) (a party responding to interrogatories is under a "severe duty to make every effort to obtain the requested information").

Identifying who in an organization knows about a topic. In the breach of contract case example above, assume the defendant's attorney wants to inquire about the process the plaintiff used to decide what parts to purchase. The purchasing employee could respond with something like, "I am not sure. I think our president decided all that." Then, when the question is asked at the president's deposition, the answer could be, "No, it wasn't me. I'm pretty sure it was an outside designer." And so goes the game of "hot potato," increasing litigation expense and inconvenience. Sending an interrogatory that asks the process and responsibility for purchasing the parts, before the depositions, would avoid this difficulty.

Of course, you could also depose the organization under Rule 30(b)(6) to find out the information, by specifying in the deposition notice that the deposition will cover, among other topics, the process the plaintiff used in deciding what parts to purchase, thus requiring the organization to designate someone to testify on that topic on the organization's behalf. In fact, when the organization possessing the desired information is a nonparty, interrogatories cannot be used, so a Rule 30(b)(6) deposition is the way to go.

Narrowing the issues. Use interrogatories to ask about an opponent's opinions, contentions, and application of the law to the facts in the case. The opponent's response will help you narrow or clarify the issues. For example, in a negligence action, ask the plaintiff, by interrogatory, to identify the acts and omissions that allegedly constitute the defendant's negligence. In the breach of contract case described above, the defendant may ask in an interrogatory whether, for example, the plaintiff is claiming consequential damages as a result of the alleged breach. The answer to the interrogatory could eliminate an issue in dispute or, alternatively, inform the defendant of what it needs to defend against and identify topics for the ensuing deposition. Interrogatories can also ask a party to state all facts supporting its contentions, giving you a head start on areas of inquiry.

Interrogatories therefore have their place in preparing for depositions, but be mindful of their downsides. First, interrogatories—particularly those that ask for contentions and supporting facts—alert the opposing party and counsel to the topics on which there will be questions in a later deposition, allowing the witness and opposing lawyer to better prepare. As a practical matter, the witness and lawyer would likely anticipate those topics anyway, but this remains a consideration.

Second, using interrogatories to set up depositions delays the taking of the depositions, thereby allowing the opponent to seize the initiative and notice depositions first. Rule 33 gives the responding party thirty days after service to answer interrogatories, and courts often grant extensions of time. The interrogatory responses may be insufficient and filled with objections, requiring negotiation with opposing counsel or a motion to compel further responses, causing more expense and delay.

Therefore, where time is of the essence, an attorney may well forgo interrogatories or postpone them to later in the litigation, and commence taking at least some depositions as early as possible.

Third, absent a stipulation or good cause, some courts permit service on the opponent of only one set of a maximum twenty-five interrogatories (Rule 33(a)(1)). As a result, a party may want to delay serving interrogatories until most of the depositions have been taken, using interrogatories only to tie up any loose ends.

Finally, the usefulness of interrogatories is limited in other respects, as discussed in section 3.1. Interrogatories may be directed only to a party; they generally do not work well when asking about personal opinions, mental impressions, and subjective information of the individual witness; they require careful drafting; they draw many objections; and they result in answers that are drafted or filtered by opposing counsel.

Like much in litigation, no absolute rules dictate how to coordinate depositions with interrogatories. Consider and decide whether information must be obtained before taking a particular deposition and whether interrogatories are the best method of obtaining it.

4.3.2 Using Production Requests and Subpoenas Duces Tecum

Documents and ESI (including emails, voicemail, texts, social media, surveillance videos, and web pages) are key to an effective deposition. They are typically critical to the merits of the case, given how ubiquitous they are in recording events and how persuasive they can be to a judge or jurors. They help you formulate the case theory, prepare for the deposition, and decide what questions to ask. At the deposition, you will present key documents to the witness for interpretation or explanation; the witness may also authenticate the material so it can be used in evidentiary motions or trial. And documents and ESI can be used to refresh a deposition witness's recollection; instead of using interrogatories before the deposition to obtain data a witness would likely not remember, search for the data in documents that can be presented to the witness at the deposition for further inquiry.

While in some cases your client will have the relevant material already, in most cases you will need or want to obtain all the germane documents and ESI of the opposing party and the witness to be deposed. Documents and ESI in the possession, custody, or control of a party are obtained by service of a document request under Rule 34. Documents and ESI in the possession, custody, or control of a nonparty are obtained by service of a subpoena duces tecum under Rule 45. The opposing party's pleadings, initial disclosures, and responses to interrogatories and other discovery will help identify what documents and ESI to request, as will your client, consulting expert, and factual and legal theories.

Although you can request the deposition witness to bring documents to the deposition, obtaining the documents and ESI well before the deposition gives you time to review the material, check with other sources about the information it contains, and formulate questions about it. Getting the material before the deposition is particularly important in document-intensive litigation and cases involving substantial ESI. Conversely, waiting until the deposition to obtain the material creates a risk that you may not realize a needed area of questioning until after the deposition has concluded; this can be disastrous, since witnesses usually may be deposed only once (Rule 30(a)(2)(A)(ii)).

Like interrogatories, serve document requests far enough in advance of the deposition so as not to delay it. Under Rule 34, an opponent has thirty days to respond in writing to a production request and must produce the documents and ESI within a reasonable time. The opponent may resist responding, or resist producing the documents, by asking you or the court for extensions of time or by merely failing to comply until compelled to do so by the judge. Weeks can pass as you debate with opposing counsel over the documents to be produced, when they must be produced, and how to produce them, often resulting in motions practice. Moreover, to the extent you are interested in an organization's ESI, an early attempt to obtain the material is critical due to the time it usually takes to negotiate the scope and format of the data to be produced and the allocation of the cost of producing it.

In some instances, despite how helpful documents and ESI are to conducting a deposition, it can be better to proceed with at least some depositions, while reserving a right to resume them if later-obtained documents create a legitimate need (particularly if your opponent did not abide by its discovery obligations), rather than waiting months for the production to be complete. You might also obtain a scheduling order from the court pausing all depositions—including the opponents' depositions of your witnesses—until all responsive documents have been produced in response to your pending document requests.[6]

4.3.3   *Using Requests for Admission*

Requests for admission can impact a deposition by eliminating issues. If the responding party admits certain facts, the facts do not need to be proved and need not be belabored with the witness, saving deposition time and corresponding litigation costs. Requests for admission can be particularly useful to authenticate documents in the hands of nonparties, who might otherwise have to be deposed to obtain the necessary foundation for using the documents in motions or at trial.

There are two drawbacks of relying on requests for admissions. First, once again, they are time-consuming; the opposing party has thirty days to respond, and the

---

6. As an exception to the general rule that production requests should proceed depositions, a Rule 30(b)(6) deposition (or state court equivalent) is sometimes noticed as the first salvo in discovery—before production requests—to learn about the opposing party's ESI and document retention policies. With this information, counsel can craft better requests for the party's material.

court may grant an extension. Second, they rarely result in admissions of great value, leading some to question whether serving requests for admission is worth the time and expense. As an alternative, contact the opposing counsel to see if you can stipulate to certain facts, contentions, or the authenticity or admissibility of documents and ESI, thereby eliminating the need to prepare and serve formal requests for admission.

4.4   Coordinating Depositions with Other Depositions

Once you decide on the order in which to pursue discovery generally (e.g., interrogatories first, then requests to produce documents, followed by depositions and, possibly, requests for admissions), decide more specifically on the order of the depositions. While this order should turn on the circumstances of the case, we can identify factors to consider.

Is it necessary to obtain evidence from one witness before deposing another witness? To some, the process of building a case in litigation is like building a house: lay the foundation before putting up the walls. Obtaining informal and formal written discovery helps establish a foundation for deposing a witness, but you may still need to obtain evidence from another person to have the best foundation for taking the witness's deposition. For example, the defendant in a personal injury case who is challenging the extent and permanency of the plaintiff's injuries will probably want to depose the plaintiff about the injuries before deposing the plaintiff's medical expert about the plaintiff's prognosis. Likewise, in the breach-of-contract action described earlier, the defendant would generally want to find out from the purchasing agent what parts were necessary to manufacture the signs before questioning the bookkeeper about the manufacturing cost.

Should you depose key witnesses before minor witnesses? The general rule is to depose key witnesses (those heavily involved in the underlying events, such as the negotiator of a contract, the company's decision-makers, or the driver of the vehicle) before minor witnesses (bystanders and others tangentially involved in the events). This gives the key witnesses less time to study the facts and find opportunities to shore up defenses or spin their stories. Also, as a matter of human nature, if the key witnesses have an opportunity to review the deposition testimony of minor witnesses or to consider the topics covered in those earlier depositions (or are fed this information by their counsel), the key witnesses are more likely to adapt their stories to those of the minor witnesses. Minor witnesses, because they usually have less at stake, are less likely to spend the time and effort to conform their stories to the expected stories of the key witnesses.

There is an exception, however, if the client and you are unfamiliar with the facts giving rise to the dispute, the structure of an organization, or industry practices. When you need this type of background information, and it cannot be obtained from other discovery devices or informal fact-gathering, the information is often better learned from minor witnesses before proceeding to interrogate the more critical key witnesses.

Where a case has more than one key witness with similar knowledge, it may be wise to leave the deposition of one of them until close to the end of discovery. That way, if there are some unanswered questions after completing discovery of the other witnesses, there is still a key actor to question.

Should you depose low-ranking employees before high-ranking employees? There are two schools of thought here. One view is to depose low-ranking employees first, so you can obtain critical information that will help in taking the deposition of a high-ranking employee, who might be speaking for the company or may be a witness at trial. The other view is to depose the high-ranking employee first, before they have an opportunity to be briefed on the evidence and the theories in the lawsuit. Which approach to take will depend on the circumstances of the case.

Can you use Rule 30(b)(6) depositions to your advantage? Theoretically, you can take the deposition of an organization under Rule 30(b)(6), in addition to separate depositions of each of its individual officers, directors, and employees (subject, of course, to the limit on the number of depositions and the requirement that the deponent possess relevant information). Use a Rule 30(b)(6) deposition to obtain the collective knowledge of the organization on specified topics, laying the groundwork for future depositions of individual employees. The depositions of the individual employees can then focus on what each person knew of the events, using the information obtained from the Rule 30(b)(6) deposition.

Consider taking two Rule 30(b)(6) depositions, covering different topics: one deposition early in the case to understand the organization's structure and procedures (including the creation, storage, and retention of the organization's ESI and documents); and a second deposition at the end of discovery, to clean up loose ends, address unanswered questions, and clarify the factual record. (*See* Chapter Twenty-One.)

Should you always depose your opponents' witnesses first? If possible, depose the other side's key witnesses before the other side deposes your key witnesses, so you and your key witnesses gain the advantage of hearing the other side's claims and having more time to prepare. It does not always work out that way, however, due either to court order or to scheduling issues.

When should expert witnesses be deposed? Typically, expert witnesses are deposed after lay (percipient) witnesses. One reason, alluded to previously, is that this lets you learn the facts from the lay witnesses before considering the expert opinion that is supposedly based on those facts. Another reason is that court scheduling orders, and to some extent the FRCP and state counterparts, set it up this way. Under Rule 26(a), expert witnesses in most cases must provide a report of their opinions and the reasons for them, as well as any exhibits that support or summarize the opinions, the expert's qualifications, and the expert's compensation and experience testifying, ninety days before trial. An expert is not offered for deposition—and you do not want to depose an expert—until the expert provides the report (Rule 26(b)(4)(A)), which will help when preparing for the expert's deposition. Because the expert's report deadline is normally at or beyond the end of the period for other discovery, experts are normally the last witnesses to be deposed. Even for experts who need not provide a report or jurisdictions in which a report is not required, it makes sense to wait until the end of discovery so the expert has enough time to develop the opinions to be given at trial.

4.5   Scheduling the Deposition

Let's consider two aspects of scheduling depositions that can bring strategic advantage: timing and duration.[7]

4.5.1   *Timing*

Attorneys debate whether it is better to schedule depositions for as early as possible in the discovery period or toward the end. Scheduling them earlier in the case provides several benefits: you can obtain and preserve the witnesses' stories before memories fade (more than they already have), put the opponent on the defensive, question witnesses when they are likely less prepared, discover gaps and conflicts in the evidence while there is still time to resolve them, and develop evidence to facilitate a summary judgment motion or quick settlement of the case. As discussed previously in this chapter, however, holding depositions early in the case may turn out to be impossible to the extent interrogatories, document requests, and subpoenas duces tecum are served and disputes arise.

But there are also reasons not to conduct depositions early. Early depositions give your opponent more time to prepare for trial and to address any uncovered weakness or harmful testimony. A delay in conducting depositions may afford a chance of settling the matter before incurring the expense of deposition practice. A delay can also give time for adverse facts to change—the opposing plaintiff's medical condition may improve, or a terminated plaintiff may find new employment.

4.5.2   *Duration and Intervals*

A deposition should last as long as necessary to accommodate your good-faith purposes, subject to any time limitations set forth in the rules. Under Rule 30(d)(1), the deposition can last seven hours on one day, which can be modified by stipulation (Rule 29) or court order (*see* Rule 16, 26). Some depositions end up taking less than an hour; others, with the appropriate stipulation or court order, may legitimately last days or weeks. But depositions are an expensive form of discovery, and the longer

---

7. Other aspects of scheduling the deposition are discussed elsewhere in this book: the required form of written notice in Chapter One, and tasks for setting up the deposition in Chapter Five.

they go, the greater the expense for the client. Take every step to be as thorough as necessary in the deposition, but also as efficient as possible.

When the testimony is expected to be complex and extensive, and several parties' lawyers plan to question the witness, lengthy depositions are necessary. Before the deposition, or even during a deposition that unexpectedly goes awry or offers surprise testimony, you may request a stipulation or court order to extend the deposition to another day. Continuing the deposition to another day gives you an additional opportunity to analyze what the witness said. Of course, the longer the break between the sessions of a deposition, the more likely it is that the witness will also have time to reflect on the previous testimony and correct any errors or misstatements.

It is also common in complex cases for counsel to stipulate to longer depositions for experts and important senior executives. It can be efficient to stipulate that each side has, for example, three two-day depositions and one three-day deposition, with the remainder being one-day (seven hour) depositions. The stipulation could provide that once a two-day deposition is noticed, it is no longer available, no matter how long the deposition ultimately lasts. This would prevent the deposing attorney from forcing the other side into lengthy preparation for a multiday deposition, then rendering it useless by cutting the deposition short.

Should you schedule depositions back-to-back? It depends. The interval between depositions is often as much a function of the lawyers' and witnesses' calendars as it is of strategic planning. When you have the freedom to dictate the schedule, however, space the depositions only so far apart as needed for your review of the prior deposition testimony and preparation for the next deposition. The longer the break, the more thorough the opponent's preparation of the next witness will likely be. Not only will opposing counsel brief the witness about what occurred in the prior deposition, the witness may even read the prior deposition transcript. Short intervals—even taking several depositions on the same day—are more likely to produce unrehearsed testimony and place more pressure on the opposing attorney.

What about remote depositions? As with most of the topics in this book, we must add a caveat about depositions conducted online. While they reduce burden and cost by avoiding travel and allowing the witness and counsel to participate from their office or home, the online platform can easily result in "Zoom fatigue" for all involved. A few hours a day, with ample breaks, is suggested, which may justify a stipulation that a particular deposition be held over two consecutive days.

4.6 Final Caveat

One more caveat is in order. While it is worth considering how to best order depositions and manage their timing and intervals, these are relatively minor factors in how effective the deposition will be. Skirmishes with opposing counsel over these matters tend to be a waste of time. Much more critical to an effective deposition are the principles discussed in the chapters that follow.

CHECKLIST
CASE ANALYSIS, DISCOVERY PLANNING, AND DEPOSITIONS

✔ Create working cases theories—a factual theory, legal theory, and persuasive theory—to understand what information has been learned and to identify what information needs to be confirmed or obtained during discovery.

✔ Create an overall discovery plan to confirm and obtain that information, using informal discovery and formal discovery devices.

✔ Coordinate depositions with other discovery devices (e.g., interrogatories, document production requests, and requests for admission) so the responses received in written discovery can be used to take the deposition.

✔ Coordinate depositions with other depositions, ordering them so that information gleaned from earlier depositions enhances the effectiveness of later depositions.

✔ Schedule depositions with an eye to strategic timing.

CHAPTER FIVE

PREPARING TO TAKE THE DEPOSITION

By failing to prepare, you are preparing to fail.

—Benjamin Franklin

Give me six hours to chop down a tree and I will spend the first four sharpening the axe.

—Abraham Lincoln

A deposition will be more effective if you are well prepared. While Chapter Four discussed preparation in the sense of an overall case analysis and discovery plan that enhances the usefulness of depositions generally, this chapter addresses how to prepare for a specific deposition by performing the following tasks:

1) learn about the witness ahead of time;

2) craft a deposition outline by brainstorming topics and ordering them for maximum effect;

3) select and prepare exhibits;

4) plan how to use the outline with an aim for flexibility;

5) anticipate problem areas; and

6) make the tactical decisions and arrangements necessary for holding the deposition, including choices for the timing and method of recording the deposition, the selection of the court reporting service, service of adequate notices, and whether to use hard-copy or digital exhibits and real-time reporting.

5.1 Learn All You Can About the Witness

Usually, you will have a good idea of who the witness is because, after all, you decided to take the deposition. But it's worth giving the witness further thought. What exactly is the witness's relationship to the parties and other witnesses? What is the witness likely to know relevant to the case? What is the witness's involvement in the proceedings? What job responsibilities may shed light on what occurred? And what is the witness's personality and character—talkative, guarded, precise, biased, loyal, deceitful, begrudging?

In many cases, such as labor and employment lawsuits, landlord-tenant controversies, and some contract matters, your client may know the witness from past dealings and provide insight to the witness's background, activities, and personality. Searching social media and the internet often produces vital information. The pleadings, as well as depositions of other witnesses and interrogatory responses, may describe the witness's participation in the events underlying the litigation.

Another fruitful source of information resides in the documents (and ESI) assembled in the case. By the time of the deposition, you will have collected material from the client, from informal discovery of third parties, from mandatory initial disclosures (in federal court), and in response to document requests and subpoenas duces tecum. In anticipation of the deposition, pull and review all documents relating to the witness: documents in which their name appears; documents they produced; documents they authored; documents they received.

> **In This Chapter:**
> - *Investigating the witness*
> - *Crafting your outline*
> - *Selecting and preparing exhibits*
> - *Using your outline while remaining flexible*
> - *Anticipating problems*
> - *Making tactical decisions about the deposition logistics*

Search for pleadings or testimony in other litigation—even in criminal proceedings—that will provide a further wellspring of information about the witness. If the witness testified in deposition or at trial in previous litigation, review the testimony and ask the attorneys who deposed or cross-examined the witness for any insights they have about the person. If the witness has written any articles or books (as is very common with experts), have someone on the litigation team read them. If a witness has given speeches, webinars, podcasts, or seminars relating to the subject of the action, which sometimes happens with company executives in complex litigation, review these as well.

In a business case, knowing your witness also means becoming familiar with the witness's work and industry. Learn all you can about the organizational structure of the witness's company, the nomenclature used in the witness's field, and applicable industry standards. In technology-based intellectual property cases, have at least a basic understanding of the relevant technology; in medical cases, possess a basic understanding of the relevant science, best practices, and course of treatment. The client and a consulting expert will be helpful in this regard, and while you will not be a true expert in the witness's industry, equip yourself to ask intelligent questions and appear as a credible examiner.

Making these inquiries will give you a feel for what the witness will know about, the witness's experience, and how the witness will respond in the deposition. It will also suggest topics to cover with the witness—a calculation we address more extensively next.

5.2   Create the Deposition Outline

Most attorneys conduct depositions using an outline of topics from which they ask their questions. Your outline may be quite detailed and include subtopics, bullet points that prompt questions, and references to the documents to use as exhibits. Do not, however, set forth *in full* the questions to be asked, because that puts your focus on the outline and the next preordained question, rather than on the witness and their answers that may deserve follow-up inquiry. Even without the questions written in full, the outline reminds you of the facts to be obtained from the witness. The outline also provides a way of easily checking, before concluding the deposition, that you have covered all important areas. The outline is therefore a necessary and important tool, and preparing it requires careful thought.

No perfect method or formula exists for creating the deposition outline. The objective is to identify critical or useful topics for inquiry and ordering those topics, cognizant of the time limitations for the deposition. With practice, you will learn what outline style serves you best.

5.2.1   *Identifying Topics for the Deposition*

Selecting the topics is key, because you have only one shot at deposing the witness. Omitted areas of inquiry—even those coming to light for the first time after the deposition is over—will have to be explored through other means of discovery, because a court will rarely permit a second deposition of the same witness.[1]

For some witnesses, identifying the topics is easy. For a witness to a traffic accident, for example, there is one event to inquire about—the traffic accident. You may have subtopics (details of each car's travel, weather and visibility, statements

---

1. The exception is where the issue was not explored in the first deposition because of the opposing party's misconduct or wrongdoing.

overheard, etc.) and myriad individual questions pertaining to each of those topics, and you might also inquire about the witness's background and what they were doing before and after the collision, but the topics are obvious.

For other witnesses, particularly in complex civil litigation, the topics may be numerous and wide-ranging, from a summary of company regulations to contract drafts, numerous meetings, emails on various subjects, prior dealings with the other side, and the like. In an employment dispute, topics may include the plaintiff's hiring, the employment agreement, performance reviews, incidents of harassment, similar occurrences in the workplace, repercussions for conduct, emotional distress, lost wages, damages, and mitigation. Because of the seven-hour time limit in federal court or similar limit in state court, you may ultimately choose to pursue fewer than all the potential topics. The first step, however, is to figure out what topics the witness can discuss.

To generate a list of potential topics, or to double-check to make sure you've considered everything, think about the following (many of which overlap):

- Pleadings
- Legal theory and proof chart
- Factual theory and chronology
- Documents and ESI
- Previous discovery in the case
- Client
- Expert

Pleadings. The pleadings in the case are an obvious source of topics for the deposition. The complaint includes factual allegations of the relevant events, each of which can be a topic for inquiry with the witness. The pleadings also list the legal theories—the claims for relief and affirmative defenses—each of which is made up of elements presumably alleged in the pleading (and supplemented by your research into case law and model jury instructions). Knowing these elements helps you recognize which aspects of the witness's narrative of the events warrant more intense and detailed questioning.

In this regard, remember litigation is not just about proving the client's claim or defense—it is also about attacking or answering the opponent's claim or defense. That starts with examining the opponent's pleadings and continues with scrutinizing positions the opponent has taken in motions and settlement negotiations.

National Institute for Trial Advocacy

Give the same attention and diligence to researching the opposing party's legal and factual theories as you give to developing your client's own theories.[2]

Legal theory and proof chart. In Chapter Four we discussed proof charts, which list the facts that support or refute each element of each claim for relief or defense asserted in the case. A look at the chart shows what elements are lacking in evidence ("proof") as well as the facts you need to obtain or confirm. If the proof chart includes a column identifying persons who might know about these facts, it is easy to search the database for the person you are about to depose and come up with a rough list of all the topics of inquiry. (Even if your proof chart is not as robust—or if you you're not using a chart at all—you know the claims and defenses based on the pleadings, as discussed above.) What might the witness have to say about any of the elements of the asserted claims and defenses? Was there really a contract, a breach, and resulting damage? Was there really a hostile work environment? Was the invention truly novel?

> *Litigation is not just about proving the client's claim or defense—it is also about attacking or answering the opponent's claim or defense.*

Factual theory and chronology. In Chapter Four, we also discussed creating a chronology of the events in the case. The chronology will be more detailed and complete than the complaint because it reflects not only the plaintiff's allegations, but also the facts according to the defense, as updated throughout the litigation. If the chronology you created contains just a list of events, each event may be a topic for the deposition. If your chronology is in the form of a table that includes a column naming the individuals who would know about each event, the table can be sorted to identify all events associated with your witness and therefore many potential deposition topics.

Documents and ESI. The documents and electronically stored information in the case—letters, memos, reports, test results, receipts, order forms, notes, voice-mails, emails, texts, photos, videos, websites, social media—will suggest topics, or be topics, to include in the deposition outline. If there are relatively few documents,

---

2. One note about inquiring into allegations of a pleading at a deposition. The question, "What is your evidence for the allegation in Complaint Paragraph 4?" is usually not profitable. The answer will often devolve into quibbling about what constitutes "evidence," whether the question calls for a legal conclusion, whether the witness is responsible for their lawyer's choice of language, and so on. A better question is: "Do you believe that this allegation or response about control of the other car is accurate?" (Or, even better, pleadings and filings aside, "Do you believe that the driver of the other car was paying sufficient attention to controlling their car?"). Then follow up with: "Why?" For purposes of this chapter, the takeaway is that when you prepare to take a deposition, review the pleadings, note those portions that might be worthy of inquiry, and incorporate them into the deposition outline.

conduct a manual review. In a document-intensive case, use a document management system to pull the ones most useful: the documents you previously pulled to find out more about the witness that were specifically written to, from, or about that person; documents the witness might know about due to their role in the occurrence or the company; documents referring to the witness's actions; key documents that the witness should have known about; and documents pertaining to the areas you otherwise expect to cover in the deposition. Remember, you are not merely looking through the documents the other side produced, but all documents you have assembled in the case.

While the documents will suggest topics for the deposition, that does not mean that all the documents will be—or should be—used as exhibits in the deposition. For those documents you decide to use in light of their importance, the outline should refer to the document and the information to find out: what the document is; who created it; who received it; what the author meant by the words that appear in the document (or how the words were understood by the recipient); reasons for creating the documents (or actions it spurred); and any evidentiary foundation that might be necessary to use the document later as evidence. Merely confirming what is stated on a document, as opposed to what it means or how it was understood, is a poor use of deposition time because the document establishes its own content. (Questioning techniques regarding documents will be discussed in section 10.3.)

Previous discovery in the case. Prior depositions and written discovery responses may signal your opponent's theories and suggest areas for exploration at the deposition. You may also discover areas left out of the deposition you previously took of another witness, which can now be addressed with the upcoming witness.

Client. Your client is one of the best sources of information when preparing any portion of a lawsuit, including a deposition. Before deposing key witnesses, discuss with the client the other side's position and the facts that would have to be true to support it. The client will provide contrary facts or an explanation that you can test on the witness.

> *Give the same attention and diligence to researching the opposing party's legal and factual theories as you give to developing your client's own theories.*

Expert. Any expert you have retained can help identify areas for inquiry at the deposition too. While experts are commonly consulted to help prepare for the opposing expert's deposition, they can also suggest areas of inquiry for lay witnesses. The expert is in the best position to identify the facts that must be established to support the expert's opinions, as well as the factual assumptions on which the opposing expert's opinions must be based. These facts can be topics of questioning at the lay witnesses' depositions.

5.2.2 Prioritizing and Organizing the Topics

Once you have identified the potential topics, decide the order in which the outline will cover them. Typically, a deposition follows this pattern:

> - Stipulations and commitments (discussed in Chapter Six);
>
> - The witness's background, preparation for the deposition, and other preliminary matters (discussed in Chapter Seven);
>
> - To the extent applicable, questions about the witness's duties; the structure, policies, and procedures of an organization; and industry standards, as extensions of the witness's background (*see* Chapter Seven); and
>
> - The events, documents, and conversations relevant to the case—usually the bulk of the deposition (*see* Chapters Seven, Eight, and Nine).

Although this is the usual organization, strategic considerations may lead you to take another approach. It may be, for example, that right out of the gate you go after the witness on the most critical issue in the case, before asking about their background or preparation for the deposition, to catch them off guard.

But the biggest tasks in organizing the deposition are deciding how to cover everything within the time allowed and how to order the substantive topics—the events, documents, and conversations underlying the dispute—for maximum effect. Sometimes these tasks are straightforward because the topics are few. Other times you will need to make some choices.

Timing

Depending on the situation, you may have more potential inquiries of a key witness than you can cover within the time allotted for the deposition. Unless you obtain a stipulation or order extending the time limit, pare down the number of topics, or at least order them so you complete the most important ones before time is up. In deciding how to select and prioritize the topics, here are some considerations:

> - What *must* I get from this witness because there is no other source for the information?
>
> - What are the most important topics, given the disputed issues in the case?
>
> - What topics are most important given my purposes for the deposition (e.g., gathering information, gaining admissions for motions or trial, preserving testimony)?

> • Can I proceed through the topics chronologically and have enough time for the most important ones?
>
> • Should I save complex topics for the end of the deposition, to get admissions when the witness is more fatigued?
>
> • Should I put less important topics at the end, to make sure there is enough time for the critical ones?

The key is to assess the importance of each topic in light of the witness and the needs of the case. Then, as a default position, plan to proceed in the typical order and tackle the topics chronologically. If you expect time to be an issue, ask about the most important topics early, following with the lesser topics as time allows. If you believe time will not be an issue, and then an unexpected timing issue arises during the deposition, your pre-deposition assessment of the importance of each topic will help you decide what to cover with the time remaining.

Ordering Events, Documents, and Conversations

There is a reason to inquire about the events underlying the lawsuit as they happened chronologically or in some other orderly fashion until you have covered all the topics. It leads to complete coverage of the relevant issues and minimizes the chances of missing important information.

Some attorneys try a different approach, jumping randomly from one topic to a different, unrelated topic, and repeating the process until all their planned topics have been covered. Those who advocate this tactic—the "leapfrog" approach—argue that it keeps the witness off guard, prevents the witness from anticipating the deposing lawyer's goals, and reduces the opportunity for prevarication.

The random leapfrog approach is rarely a good idea. It does not keep the witness off guard, because a witness who is unsure about the direction of the questioning remains anxious, and the anxious witness remains on guard. Leapfrogging does little to mask the goals of the deposing lawyer, because any witness who has been prepared for the deposition by a half-decent attorney will know what topics will be covered. While leapfrogging does prevent the witness from anticipating what the next topic will be, once the leap occurs to the new topic, the questions on that new topic will be related to one another and build on the answers given, so the witness adjusts to the new topic and can, in fact, anticipate those questions. Furthermore, a witness's opportunity to prevaricate or hide information depends less on the order of the topics and more on the amount of time between the witness's last answer and the next question—the "pace" of the questioning. If, for example, the witness is motivated to shade the truth about whether a sales agreement included insurance for a shipment that has since been lost, his success in crafting a false answer depends more on how long he has to think about that answer than it does on whether the previous topic was changing the name of the business, the method of financing the sale, or the number of partners in the new operation.

It is not leapfrogging, but other techniques, that frustrate a witness's attempts to fabricate answers and anticipate questions: probing the witness's answers with follow-up questions, exhausting the witness's knowledge, coming back to topics to check the consistency of information given, and asking general questions before progressing to specifics.

Sometimes witnesses are surprised or lulled into blurting out truthful testimony harmful to them or an unguarded statement that would not have otherwise been obtained by a predictable progression through the topics.[3] But the leapfrog method is not the best way to accomplish this, given its major downside: leapfrogging makes it difficult to ensure you have exhausted the witness's knowledge. Because of the desire to "leap" or surprise and confound the witness, the deposing attorney often forsakes the opportunity to follow up on the witness's answers with more detailed questions. Moreover, by not moving chronologically or in some other logical order through the events, it is more difficult for the deposing attorney to gauge the accuracy and completeness of the testimony. A witness's description of events is easier to digest if we hear it chronologically, because life happens in chronological order: causes precede effects, and motivations beget actions. Taking events out of order robs us of the opportunity to assess the witness's account according to what we know about the usual sequence of human behavior.

As a final caveat against the leapfrog approach, it can result in confusing testimony. Witnesses remember events chronologically, and there may be more confusion (and more objections by opposing counsel) about which phone call you are addressing and what meeting you are referencing when you proceed in a haphazard manner.

That does not mean you should forgo altogether the chance to surprise or lull a witness into a spontaneous confession. While we disfavor the random leapfrog approach, your journey through the topics of the deposition does not have to proceed in exclusively chronological lockstep, or otherwise predictable order. You might slip in a couple of questions from an entirely different topic to catch the witness off guard. You might organize the topics chronologically except for one or two that

---

3. The impact of this is greater if the deposition is recorded by video. Unless it is a video deposition, there are no jurors to observe the witness's demeanor when, like Perry Mason, you leap to the crucial question: "Isn't it true that you never intended to buy the hammers?" and the witness, taken totally by surprise, stammers, "Why, I . . . I . . . I couldn't . . . I just couldn't; I never liked the hammers; I lied about wanting to buy them; I hated the hammers and everything they stood for." At the deposition, if the witness is momentarily speechless, with jaw dropping and eyes searching for help in the corners of the room, he may still recover and deliver a coherent answer (while the cold transcript reveals little of the witness's discomfort), no matter what the previous topic was.

you take out of order for some specific, strategic purpose, calculated to encourage the witness to answer one way rather than another on Topic B because of the information you elicited from them in Topic A. You might question on damages before inquiring about breach. Or there may be instances when you are not actually interested in learning the witness's full story of the events, but in disturbing the witness's linear analysis (e.g., the witness's progression from observation to hypothesis, to testing, to raw data, and to conclusion)—more typical of expert witness depositions. The takeaway, therefore, is that the default method for addressing issues is chronological, but you may stray from that if you have a specific reason to proceed otherwise, born of the facts of the case (as opposed to a blind hope that jumping around randomly is going to fool the witness).

5.3   Select and Prepare Documents for Use at the Deposition

You reviewed many documents in becoming familiar with the witness and generating potential topics for the deposition; use the most important of them as exhibits with the witness, inquiring about the documents' creation, receipt, content, and consequence. Sometimes it is important to learn that the witness knew of a document; other times it may be helpful to learn that the witness did not know of it. The witness may also establish an evidentiary foundation for the document's later use in a summary judgment motion or trial. Given how persuasive documents are to a trier of fact, it is critical to find out what the witness has to say about the key documents in the case.

Frequently, however, you will not have enough deposition time to ask the witness about all the emails, letters, reports, and other documents written or received by the witness or otherwise germane to the litigation. Indeed, given the likelihood that there will be far more documents than you have time to use—or need to use—carefully choose which ones are best. As with potential topics of the deposition, prioritize the documents that are most important based on a combination of their content (how key is the document to the case?) and the extent to which no other witness could testify as well about the document (e.g., the author, or the one who read the document and acted on it). You may conclude there are some "must use" documents, some "if I have time" documents (including documents to use only if there is time for the topic to which they relate), and some "just in case the witness can't remember" documents. Note them in your deposition outline under the topic to which they apply.

Once you decide which documents you want to use as exhibits, the next step is to decide how you will

> *Whatever organizing system you choose for your documents, adopt it early, include a cataloging protocol, communicate the system to everyone who will handle the documents, and follow it meticulously. Whether hard copy or electronic, documents stored without a consistent system are documents lost.*

use them at the deposition. Specifically, how you will get the exhibit in front of the witness and opposing counsel, and how you will get it to the court reporter, who needs to mark the document as an exhibit (if it has not been premarked) and include it with the deposition transcript.

Back in the day, I placed four copies of every exhibit I was potentially going to use in a file folder and label the folder lightly in pencil so I could tell what the document was but the nosy witness or opposing counsel could not. I put the folders in a banker's box and, entering the deposition room, plunked the box down on a chair next to me (enjoying the expression on the faces of the witness and counsel). When I came to the point in the deposition where I wanted to use one of the exhibits, I pulled out the file folder and handed one copy of the exhibit to the court reporter to mark as an exhibit and handed one to the witness. I also handed a copy to opposing counsel and retained one copy (with my notes) for questioning. It worked beautifully. And you can still do it that way for in-person depositions today.

In larger cases, with documents that are likely to be used as exhibits in multiple depositions, the parties may agree that certain exhibits will bear the same exhibit number for every deposition in the case, to avoid the confusion that otherwise results from the same document having multiple exhibit numbers ("Smith Decl. Ex. 2," "Martinez Decl. Ex. 18," etc.). In fact, the court's local rules may require counsel to meet and confer at the outset of the case regarding a sequential numbering system to be used for exhibits at depositions as well as for trial.[4] For further information, refer to sections 5.3 and 10.2.

Another decision to make is whether to use hard-copy (paper) exhibits or digital (electronic) exhibits. Section 10.2 discusses this in much greater length, but the choice may come down to the number of exhibits you are going to use, the extent to which the exhibits are currently in paper or electronic form, and the prevalence of electronically stored information in your exhibits (emails, video recordings, social media posts, webpages, chats, etc.).

Remote depositions add another wrinkle, since you cannot physically hand a hard-copy document to the court reporter, witness, or counsel, who are participating online from different locations. As we discuss further in section 24.7, there are three main approaches to getting exhibits to the witness: 1) email a password-protected file to the court reporter, opposing counsel, and the witness ahead of time (without giving the password to the witness or counsel until the deposition); 2) screenshare premarked exhibits as you need them during the deposition and send the "originals" to the court reporter later; or 3) use software that allows you to move documents into an online folder that the witness and counsel can view during the deposition, following up as needed with the court reporter.

---

4. *E.g.*, Local Rules of the United States District Court for the Northern District of California, rule 30-2 (requiring meet and confer as well as specific rules of internal numbering of documents).

Remember also that, whether the deposition is conducted in person or remotely, you can have a witness *create* an exhibit to explain their testimony. This can help pinpoint the witness's description of the areas of pain on a plaintiff's body or depiction of an intersection at which an accident occurred. At an in-person deposition, the witness can simply draw on a piece of paper you provide, marked as a deposition exhibit. At a remote deposition, the witness can be asked to use the "annotation" feature (or equivalent) on a screen-shared document.

5.4   Plan Your Use of the Outline at the Deposition

Having identified the topics and subtopics from the events listed on a chronology or inspired by a document or element of a claim or defense, the topics and subtopics can serve as the headings and subheadings on the deposition outline. Under the subheadings can be bullet points of the facts that need to be learned or confirmed from the witness—which you know from examining the chronology or proof chart—such as the details of each event (who, what, when, where, why, how), and the documents you will use as exhibits. With this basic organization, consider the following ways to make the deposition outline work better for you.

5.4.1   Choosing Printout or Laptop

Decide whether to print out the outline and use it at the deposition in hard-copy form, or to have the outline on a laptop. Choose whatever approach is more comfortable for you. The laptop makes it easier to rearrange the outline as you go, but a hard-copy approach eliminates having an obstacle—the laptop—between you and the witness and leads to better eye contact and more of a conversation between you and with witness. As we discuss later in this chapter, each method also comes with upsides and downsides in terms of taking notes.

Whichever approach you choose, use a font for your outline that is large enough so you can easily read it. Triple-space the outline (whether in paper or electronic format) so you can readily return to it after finishing an "improvisational" inquiry with the witness, and so you can jot notes on important things the witness says, add topics as ideas develop at the last moment or during the deposition, and flag items to which you would like to return later in the deposition.

5.4.2   Outlining Topics, Not Questions

We have been talking about outlines of topics, not lists of questions that are fully written out. This chapter deals with choosing the areas of inquiry before the deposition, which is different from (and a precursor to) framing specific questions to find out the information. We address question form in Chapters Eight and Nine.[5]

Moreover, as we alluded to earlier, if the outline consists only of written-out questions, in the deposition those preordained questions will soon become out of sync with the witness's testimony. By contrast, using an outline that contains topic headings, a few subtopic headings, and a bullet-point list of facts to inquire about under each subtopic, prompts you to ask the questions you had thought up during preparation, while leaving you focused enough on the witness's answers so you can ask follow-up questions that respond to what the witness has said. It is this conversational exploration of a witness's testimony that facilitates a deeper mining of the facts known to the witness.

An exception to the rule against writing out deposition questions arises when the evidentiary value of a witness's answer depends on the exact wording of the question. For example, in putting a hypothetical to an expert witness, it may be necessary to be very precise with the assumptions in the hypothetical and the nomenclature employed. In that situation, write out the question in advance rather than trying to pose the question extemporaneously during the deposition. Similarly, establishing an evidentiary foundation for an exhibit may require the use of operative buzzwords, such as the phrase "fair and accurate depiction" when laying the foundation for a photograph or the elements of the hearsay exception for records of a regularly conducted activity (*see* Chapter Eleven). You might write these questions out in advance too. Finally, in some cases particular words or phrases, such as "risk of loss" in a contract case, have legal significance or a specialized meaning within an industry.

Nevertheless, as a general rule, an outline composed of a list of topics and subtopics, with phrases or very brief bullet points rather than full written questions, is the best approach.

5.4.3 *Being Flexible Yet Prudent*

Listen carefully to the witness's answers. If they suggest a topic that is new and therefore not in the outline, or a topic that is elsewhere in the outline, decide whether to pursue it. While you do not want to be distracted from covering the

---

5. Here's a glimpse at the teachings of Chapter Eight: The headings of the outline—the topics and subtopics we've identified from the pleadings and documents in the case—will serve as "headlines" for our questioning in the deposition or silent markers for our own guidance; our initial questions in the information-gathering phase for each of those topics will start with "who," "what," "when," "where," "how," and "why," followed by questions designed to exhaust the witness's repository of information on the point, continuing with more probing and directive questions based on what the witness has said or known facts we want the witness to admit. It's not just that writing out the questions hampers the deposition; writing out the questions is usually unnecessary.

planned outline, neither do you want to miss important testimony by adhering too closely to the outline. You must therefore make a choice. If you choose to follow where the witness is taking you, hold your place in the outline and explore the new topic immediately, keeping in mind that you will have less time to cover what you planned. If you choose to forge ahead with your line of inquiry and not be diverted by the witness's new information, write the new information on your outline as a reminder to revisit the novel topic.

There are also times when the witness's answers tell you there is nothing to be gained by further exploring a topic. As topics are completed or abandoned, check them off on the outline and, before concluding the deposition, take a few moments during a break to review the outline and make sure there are no topics left.

5.5   Plan How to Keep Track of the Witness's Answers

Although the court reporter or videographer—or both—will record what the witness says in the deposition, take notes of any answers that will inform later parts of the questioning. For decades, a legal pad has sufficed in this regard. My practice was to take notes of the witness's answers directly on my outline, to the extent I needed to follow up (for example, if the witness's answer had several subparts that I didn't want to forget) or if there was a new name or date I wanted to remember. This approach still works, even though keystrokes on a laptop have largely replaced handwritten scrawls on a hard-copy document, and electronic notetaking today reigns supreme.

An upside to taking notes on a laptop is that it results in a document that is easier to edit, reorganize, annotate, file, and share than a hard-copy document. A downside, however, is that taking down information while typing leads us to look at the screen, while taking down notes on paper allows us to better focus on the witness. Whichever method you choose, never allow notetaking to interfere with your observation of the witness's nonverbal clues—gestures, frowns, etc.—that can be as meaningful as their words.

> **Creating and Using Your Outline:**
>
> - *Arrange topics in chronological/logical order;*
> - *use bullet points rather than questions;*
> - *cue the exhibits;*
> - *choose laptop or hard copy;*
> - *stay focused but flexible; and*
> - *jot critical notes quickly.*

A 2014 study found an interesting advantage of hard-copy notetaking over electronic notetaking: those who jot down notes by hand retained the content of the information better than those taking notes on a laptop.[6] The likely reason is that taking notes by hand forces us to reduce the information to a few words, while we are likely (and able) to take down a statement more verbatim when we type and therefore process it less. The moral of the story is that, whether notes are taken by hand on a hard-copy document or by typing on a laptop, write down just enough to keep things from slipping our mind, without taking our attention off the witness or slowing the pace of our questioning.

5.6   Decide Whether to Use Real-Time Reporting

In the early days of my practice, if you didn't hear what a witness said, you would have to ask the court reporter to read the answer back, and the court reporter would stop and locate the answer in their stenographic shorthand notes and read it aloud. This took time, and it was not the court reporter's favorite thing to do.

Real-time reporting solves that problem by displaying a draft transcript on a screen visible to counsel as the court reporter takes down what the witness is saying, allowing counsel to read as well as hear the answer. Essentially, the court reporter's stenotype is translated by a computer instantaneously into English and streamed to the laptop or tablet of any attorney who wants it. Each attorney can scroll to a prior answer and question, highlight testimony and flag it for follow-up, and conduct word searches. The ability to read a transcript of what the witness said before leaving the deposition is extremely helpful, if for no other reason than it saves you from the gut-wrenching experience of receiving a deposition transcript days after the deposition concluded and realizing the concessions you thought you had brilliantly elicited from the witness were not worded as you believed.

Why mention real-time reporting in this chapter on preparing for a deposition? Because if you don't decide you want it by the time you book the court reporter, you may be out of luck. As of this writing, not every court reporter is equipped to do it. If you do request real-time reporting, be ready to tell the court reporting service in advance about unusual terminology (technology, medical lingo, etc.), names, acronyms and other uncommon language that might arise in the testimony. This allows the court reporter to build a dictionary unique to the deposition, so the terms will be reported correctly in the real-time feed. Sending case materials, such as the complaint, the deposition notice (or subpoena) and even prior deposition transcripts may be helpful too. You may also be asked to identify who will be attending the deposition, so the court reporter can bring sufficient viewing equipment or prepare to transmit the real-time transcript to each attorney's electronic device.

I confess that I resisted real-time reporting when it first came out, because I feared it would interfere with my efforts to stay focused on the witness. As with

---

6. Pam A. Mueller, Daniel M. Oppenheimer, *The Pen is Mightier Than the Keyboard: Advantages of Longhand Over Laptop Note Taking*, 25 Psychological Science 1159–68 (2014).

notetaking, do not let a real-time feed or anything else keep you from observing the witness's demeanor, gestures, and expressions.

5.7   Anticipate Potential Problem Areas and Timing

After preparing your deposition outline and exhibits and deciding how to keep track of the testimony, think through or rehearse the deposition by using your outline, asking a question aloud, imagining how the witness might answer or what objection might be made, and continuing from question to question. (Attorneys newer to depositions will find this particularly useful; more seasoned attorneys may do this only for critical question areas.) Also practice how you will present the exhibits, especially if the deposition will be conducted remotely. For particularly important depositions, you may even roleplay your inquiry on a topic with a colleague or legal assistant playing the witness and opposing counsel.

This rehearsal process will help you to see if your questions are not worded well or if you need to reorder the topics. It will help you prepare for difficult areas of inquiry and suggest how to better organize your questions to increase the likelihood that the witness will give you the information you want.

For example, let's say you are going to depose your opponent's supervisory employee, and you want the supervisor to recall the details of a particular event. Having the witness first affirm their obligation to supervise and how good the witness is at supervising will make it more likely that the witness concedes knowledge and recollection of what occurred. If, on the other hand, you want to establish that the witness did not see what occurred, you would preface your questions with the wide range of responsibilities that the person has, the witness's inability to be everywhere at one time, and the like.

When rehearsing, take plenty of time "answering" your own questions as the witness. This will help you gauge the amount of time for each topic, so you can make sure you get to the most important ones in the deposition.

5.8   Plan to Be "Present"

Prepare diligently, but do not lose sleep over the sufficiency of your preparation; there will be some unexpected twist or turn in the deposition no matter how much time you spent crafting your outline. What matters most is listening closely to the witness, making sure you understand what the witness is saying, and following up on incomplete or interesting answers. Similarly, while keeping in mind the purposes of your deposition (whether to gain information, obtain admissions, preserve testimony, or test theories—*see* Chapter Two) and your factual, legal, and persuasive theories (*see* Chapter Four), simply engaging the witness in a conversation will do wonders.

The Fifth Edition of this book put it this way:

> No one has ever taken a perfect deposition. Fortunately, justice does not depend on perfection from lawyers or witnesses. From a full day of deposition testimony, perhaps twenty answers will have some value and some possible use at trial; of those twenty, perhaps five will be used; and experience shows that those five are most likely to have come in response to questions that were reactions to information provided by the witness that was unanticipated in the deposition outline

5.9 Make the Arrangements for the Deposition

Decide when, where, and how to hold the deposition, both to comply with the applicable rules and court orders and to gain tactical advantage.[7]

5.9.1 *When and Where (or Remotely)*

A key question is when and where the deposition will be held. After considering any limitations on timing and location in the Rule 16 scheduling order in federal court (or similar order in state court), decide what would be the best timing of the deposition in conjunction with other discovery in the case (*see* Chapter Four). For example, you will want to hold off on the deposition until you receive production of the documents you might use as exhibits. Similarly, the receipt of interrogatory answers may streamline the deposition, and taking one deposition before another may give you a strategic or practical advantage.

As to location, having the deposition in a conference room in your law office is generally best for in-person depositions, because you have your case materials and office support on your home turf. At times, however, you may have to go to the witness's location for an in-person deposition, particularly if the witness is a nonparty, since the deposition must occur within the geographical limitations of the subpoena (Rule 45(c)). Although it is not unheard of to take a deposition at the witness's kitchen table, the best alternative to your own conference room is a room at the court reporter's office.

Wherever the location, the room itself must be large enough to accommodate the witness, the attorneys, any parties or experts in attendance, the court reporter (and videographer if applicable) and all their gear. It should be in a quiet place and

---

7. This section addresses the tasks for a deposition taken in the United States. Depositions in foreign countries are governed by Rule 28(b), any applicable treaty, and the law of the foreign jurisdiction. Consider retaining local counsel and allow plenty of time to complete the arrangements.

have adequate lighting, particularly for video depositions. It also requires sufficient electrical outlets for the court reporter and videographer.

You may alternatively choose to conduct the deposition remotely on a platform such as Zoom or WebEx, thus reducing travel expenses for counsel and the witness and easing scheduling difficulties. If so, consider stipulations you may want to reach with opposing counsel about the security of the proceedings, the handling of exhibits, and other matters in a protocol discussed in Chapter Twenty-Four. Consider, also, the physical location of the participants, while understanding that each participant—the deposing attorney, the witness, the witness's attorney, and the court reporter—must have sufficient internet connectivity, lighting, and privacy.

Once you have decided the best location and date from your perspective, contact the witness's attorney to determine if agreement can be reached on the place and time of the deposition before sending out the deposition notice. In some jurisdictions, this is mandatory; in all jurisdictions, it is helpful.

5.9.2   Stenograph or Video (or Both)

Decide how you want the deposition to be recorded. The deposition can be recorded stenographically—that is, using a court reporter to take down what is said on the record at the deposition and transforming it into an official written transcript. An increasingly common option is also to record the deposition by video, which, among other things, enhances the use of the deposition testimony at trial (*see* Chapter Twenty-Three). Determining how the deposition will be recorded is important because it must be disclosed in your notice of deposition (Rule 30) and factored in with your arrangements with the court reporter service.

5.9.3   Court Reporting Service

Schedule the deposition with a court reporting service, including a videographer if applicable. Contact the service as early as possible. Be prepared to provide the following information: whether you want an in-person deposition or a remote deposition; how you want it recorded; the form of transcript (e.g., hard copy, condensed hard copy, PDF, etranscript); any need for an interpreter; how long the deposition is likely to last; whether you want real-time reporting; the notice of deposition or subpoena and, at least if you are ordering real-time reporting, case materials with party names and frequently used terms. For remote depositions, most court reporting services can host the videoconference and assist with the handling of exhibits.

5.9.4   Notice or Subpoena

Finally, serve a notice of the deposition as required by the Federal Rules of Civil Procedure or applicable state statute. For party witnesses (or officers, managing agents, and directors of a party), the federal rules require service of a notice of deposition, which must include the time and location of the deposition and the manner in which it will be recorded (Rule 30). For nonparty witnesses, you must serve a subpoena on the witness with similar information (Rule 45) and serve a Rule 30 notice on the parties' counsel with the subpoena attached. If you want the witness to bring documents to the deposition, the notice of deposition or subpoena must comply with the jurisdiction's rules. Make sure that the notice or subpoena, or both, are served enough days ahead of the deposition. Some court reporting services will arrange for service of the notice of deposition and any subpoenas as part of the services they provide.

CHECKLIST

PREPARING TO TAKE THE DEPOSITION

✔	Review the applicable Federal Rules of Civil Procedure or state statutes and relevant discovery orders.
✔	Learn about the proposed witness from the client, case materials, and documents.
✔	Review the pleadings, factual theory (chronology), legal theory (proof chart), persuasive theory, and documents to cover all possible topics of inquiry.
✔	Pare down, prioritize, and order the topics in an outline.
✔	Select and prepare the documents to use as exhibits at the deposition and annotate the deposition outline with references to the exhibits.
✔	Decide whether to use hard copy or electronic exhibits.
✔	Decide the best time and place for the deposition, including the possibility of a remote deposition.
✔	Decide whether to record the deposition stenographically, audiovisually, or both.
✔	Meet and confer with attorneys for the witness and the parties, as needed or required, regarding scheduling the deposition and establishing a protocol for a remote deposition.
✔	Schedule with the court reporting service and provide requested information.
✔	Timely and properly serve notice of the deposition (and subpoena a nonparty).
✔	Rehearse or think through the more difficult portions of the deposition for fine tuning and timing (and for remote depositions, use of the exhibits).
✔	Prepare to be flexible and responsive to the witness's answers while keeping the deposition purposes in mind.

CHAPTER SIX

BEGINNING THE DEPOSITION

A few strong instincts and a few plain rules
suffice us.

—William Wordsworth

A deposition will be more effective if, at the very beginning, you set the tone and expectations for the examination and make it difficult for the deponent to later wriggle out of their deposition testimony. In this chapter, we discuss 1) the deposition setup; 2) stipulations between counsel about how the deposition will proceed; and 3) commitments to obtain from the witness regarding the deposition ground rules.

6.1   The Deposition Setup

Many readers already know the material in this section on how the deposition room is set up, but we provide it anyway because so many newer attorneys ask us for this basic information during trainings. It also offers some tips on more recent developments with remote depositions.[1]

6.1.1   Where Do I Sit?

For in-person depositions that are recorded by a court reporter stenographically, without video, the typical setup is for the court reporter to sit at the end of a rectangular conference table, close to an electrical outlet. This placement of the court reporter ensures there is ample elbow space for typing shorthand, marking

> **In This Chapter:**
> - *The deposition setup*
> - *Stipulations between counsel*
> - *Commitments to obtain from the witness*

---

1. Less-experienced attorneys will also find it helpful to observe a couple of depositions before taking or defending one.

exhibits, and the like. The longer sides of the conference table, perpendicular to the court reporter, are used for the attorneys and the witness: the deposing attorney and perhaps a legal assistant or co-counsel on one side, and the witness and the witness's attorney(s) on the other side. Seat the witness closest to the court reporter to aid the reporter in taking down what the witness is saying. As the deposing attorney, sit directly across from the witness.

Some attorneys care strongly about which side of the table they are on and, therefore, which side of the table the witness is on. Some want the witness facing an outside window, with the idea that the witness may become distracted and miss a nuance in the deposing attorney's questions and agree with the cross-examination. Others prefer the witness to be on the side facing the door (i.e., with the back to the window), which subliminally communicates that the witness is "captive" and cannot slink out of the room without getting past the deposing attorney and the court reporter. This positioning may also make it easier for the deposing attorney to be handed messages or delivered documents from someone outside the room. But does any of this really make a difference? In my view, not enough to argue about, but all things being equal I would prefer to be the one closest to the door.

The court reporter may need access to the conference room about a half hour before the deposition is scheduled to begin, to set up their equipment and settle in. This is an excellent time to stop by, say hello, offer refreshments, and, if not already provided, drop off the deposition notice and a list of any nomenclature, names, or acronyms the court reporter might otherwise have trouble transcribing.

For **video** depositions, the setup is a little different. To ensure that the witness is adequately framed in the video, the witness sits at the short end of the conference table, the court reporter at a corner near the deponent, the videographer sets up across the table from the witness, and the attorneys sit on either side of the table. (This may vary a bit by jurisdiction.) For video depositions, the videographer may need to access the conference room up to an hour before the deposition is scheduled to begin.

For remote depositions, the key is for each person to be positioned so that the camera and lighting is in front of them, at an angle and distance from the camera that allows them to be framed akin to a news anchor or "talking head" on TV. More on the setup for remote depositions is found in Chapter Twenty-Four.

6.1.2   How Do I Start?

Although there are regional variations, and even variations among court reporters, the deposing counsel typically starts the deposition with the words "on the record" or "let's begin" or a simple nod of the head to the court reporter or videographer, any of which will prompt them to say the opening words required by the jurisdiction's rules. In a deposition recorded stenographically, the court reporter typically announces the date and time, the case name, and the deponent, asks counsel to identify themselves for the record, and administers the oath to the witness. If the deposition is being recorded by audiovisual means, the videographer announces similar information, and the deposition officer (usually the court reporter) then swears in the witness.

6.2 Attorney Stipulations

Shortly before or after the deposition begins, the subject of stipulations may come up. Sometimes you will raise the issue, sometimes opposing counsel will broach the subject, and sometimes the court reporter will ask, "Are there any stipulations?"

Under Rule 29, the parties may stipulate to nearly anything concerning depositions, provided the court's timetable is not breached.[2] This gives the parties the power to alter such things as:

- notice given;
- qualifications of the officer administering the oath;
- the method of recording;
- time and date;
- the length of the deposition;
- continuing the deposition for more than one day;
- where the deposition is held;
- the order of depositions;
- production of documents at the deposition;
- handling of exhibits at the deposition;
- preserving exhibits used at the deposition;
- forms and types of objections that must be made at the deposition;
- types of objections that need not be made at the deposition;
- preserving the deposition;

---

2. Rule 29 provides: "Unless the court orders otherwise, the parties may stipulate that:
   (a) a deposition may be taken before any person, at any time or place, on any notice, and in the manner specified—in which event it may be used in the same way as any other deposition; and
   (b) other procedures governing or limiting discovery be modified—but a stipulation extending the time for any form of discovery must have court approval if it would interfere with the time set for completing discovery, for hearing a motion, or for trial."

- reviewing and signing the deposition; and

- uses of the deposition.

This is not a complete list of all possible stipulations. Barring some local rule that commands otherwise, there is nothing preventing the attorneys from altering nearly any aspect of the procedure governing depositions or other discovery when it serves their clients' interests to do so.

Altering the procedures provided by the FRCP offers advantages and disadvantages to each side. The rules were carefully drafted to protect the interests of both the deposition taker and the deposition defender, as well as the interests of witnesses. Stipulations alter this carefully crafted balance. Nevertheless, it is sometimes in the interest of both sides to agree to change the procedures for the deposition, the steps leading up to it, or requirements after its completion.

We sound a strong note of caution at this point. While stipulations can be beneficial in the right case, never agree to a modification of the procedures imposed by the applicable rules or statutes without first carefully considering what is being gained and what is being given up in the stipulation. Only agree to a stipulation when it is clearly in your client's interest. If there is a default position to take, make it "just say no."

Let's look at some stipulations that are routinely proposed by one side or the other, noting the advantages and disadvantages for each side and whether the stipulation may be advisable in the right situation.

6.2.1 *"The Usual Stipulations"*

We will begin with a refrain that is frequently agreed to in many parts of the country, while being virtually unheard of in other areas—"The usual stipulations, counsel?"

The first thing to understand is that there is no universal agreement on what constitutes the "usual stipulations," and there is no obligation to agree to them. While the "usual stipulations" may stand as shorthand for a frequent agreement made in some regions of the country, state, or county, attorneys tend to have only a vague understanding of what is included.[3] Case law contains endless arguments about

---

3. In a few jurisdictions, the term "usual stipulations" refers to a specific set of stipulations that the court reporter prepares and shows to the parties at the beginning of the deposition. These jurisdictions are a distinct minority. Caution born of experience suggests that the attorney who is not certain what the "usual stipulations" are in the jurisdiction should specifically instruct the reporter that no stipulations have been agreed to. After making exactly that statement on his first trip to take a deposition in Des Moines, one of the original authors of this book was surprised to see two pages of stipulations show up in the written transcript, inserted automatically by the reporter. A telephone call brought a new transcript, without stipulations, to the hotel room door within a couple of hours.

National Institute for Trial Advocacy

the phrase; as one court has noted: "Everyone purports to know without asking the content of the 'usual stipulations' until a dispute arises; the ephemeral nature of the parties' understanding is then quite apparent."[4]

Because of the lack of agreement about the phrase's meaning, your first question in response to a proposal for the usual stipulations is, "What do you mean by the usual stipulations?" It may well be that the attorney proposing the stipulation has no idea what the phrase means and is only repeating what they have heard in other depositions. Custom is a powerful force and compels many attorneys to mimic what they have seen or heard other attorneys do, even though they have no understanding of why it was said or done.

If there are clearly defined "usual" stipulations in your jurisdiction—and you think they are beneficial after reading the next few pages of this book—confirm with the other lawyer(s) what they are and state them on the record to avoid later confusion or controversy. Never stipulate unless it is clear what you are stipulating to.

> *There is no universal agreement on what constitutes the "usual stipulations," and there is no obligation to agree to them.*

Be prepared. You will be strongly tempted to agree to the "usual stipulations" the first time an attorney proposes them to you. No one wants to appear clueless about proper procedures or custom or present themselves as an ignorant neophyte unaware of the meaning of a stipulation process with a long tradition among attorneys. This is especially true of newer lawyers, who fear they will be revealing their lack of experience if they ask what is meant by the usual stipulations. Do not be embarrassed to inquire. To display confidence, ask with a downward inflection in your voice. Alternatively, respond with "No, I stand with the Federal Rules of Civil Procedure" (or whatever rules or statutes govern your deposition).

6.2.2   Reserving Objections

Perhaps the most common deposition stipulation—and the one with the best claim to being part of the usual stipulations—takes varying forms. Depending on the area of the country in which the defender practices, it is usually phrased in one of these ways:

> "Let's reserve all objections until there is an attempt to use the deposition, or some portion thereof, at some later point in the proceedings."

> "Let's reserve all objections except for form."

---

4. United States v. Liquid Sugars, Inc., 158 F.R.D. 466, 473 n.8 (E.D. Cal. 1994).

"Let's reserve all objections except for form and foundation."

"Let's reserve all objections to form and foundation."

This type of stipulation is usually proposed by the defender, since all of its versions are to the defender's advantage.

Remember that Rule 32(d)(3) requires, in essence, that any objection to a defect that can be cured at the deposition must be timely made during the deposition or the objection is deemed waived. All of the foregoing versions of the stipulation relieve the defender of the burden of interposing a timely objection to certain aspects of the deposition. The defender can then contemplate what objections to make during the months or even years between the date of the deposition and the attempt to use the deposition at trial, in a summary judgment motion, or for some other purpose.

The degree to which the defender is relieved of the duty to object to curable errors depends on the version of the stipulation. Obviously, reserving "all" objections provides the defender with the greatest advantage; reserving all objections to form provides less but still considerable advantage; and reserving objections except to form and foundation confers the least benefit on the defender. But all the versions extend the defender's strategic position beyond what Rule 32(d) provides. While reserving "all" objections might not seem much more than reserving objections to "form and foundation," and reserving objections except to form and foundation may not seem that significant, Rule 32(d)(3)(B) includes objections to matters other than form and foundation such as problems in the manner of taking the deposition and in the "answer, the oath or affirmation, a party's conduct, or other matters."

Does the deposition taker gain anything from the stipulation? Theoretically, with objections being reserved, it is less likely the witness's attorney will make them, so there will be less interruption of the flow of the questions and answers and less coaching of the witness. In theory. As a practical matter, the stipulation does not preclude the defending attorney from objecting (unless you get the defending attorney to stipulate to that too), so the deposing attorney ends up gaining little. And while the stipulation would allow the deposing attorney to reserve objections to the defender's behavior or the witness's answer (for example, to nonresponsive answers), this would rarely tip the scales in favor of agreeing to the stipulation.

In fact, for the deposing attorney, the consequences of the stipulation can be outright nightmarish. Imagine, for example, an antitrust action where plaintiff's counsel is deposing an assistant employed by the defendant. The assistant had been assigned to take notes at a key meeting of several of the defendant's employees. At the beginning of the deposition, counsel stipulated to reserve all objections. During the deposition, the assistant testified to several highly damaging statements by the employees about having met with competitors to set prices in an effort to drive the plaintiff out of business. In short, the deposition was an unqualified success for the plaintiff.

The plaintiff's attorney, patting herself on the back for the brilliance of her questions at the deposition, has prepared a devastating cross-examination of the assistant at the upcoming trial based on the damaging statements given during the deposition. Unfortunately, unbeknownst to the plaintiff's attorney, during the time between the deposition and trial the assistant has disappeared and, even if found, would likely be beyond the subpoena powers of the court. Our attorney is undaunted, however, because she recalls that she can use the assistant's deposition testimony if the assistant becomes unavailable for trial. At the appropriate point in the trial, the plaintiff's attorney produces the deposition and announces to the court that she now wishes to read key questions and answers to the jurors.

This is where the fun starts. In response, the defendant's attorney stands up and says to the court, "Your Honor, before counsel reads the deposition portions in question, I have several objections I wish to raise. We stipulated at the time of the deposition to reserve all objections. Here are my objections. On page 42, line 13 the question was . . ." Much to the plaintiff attorney's dismay, the court sustains all of the defendant's objections and rules that none of the offered deposition testimony is admissible. In retrospect, the plaintiff's attorney realizes that all of the objections could have been easily cured at the deposition with some additional questions, if she had only been aware of them, but of course she was not aware of them because of the stipulation to reserve all objections.

The moral of this story? As the deposing attorney, do not stipulate to reserving objections.

As the defending attorney, on the other hand, strongly consider proposing such a stipulation in light of all that we have said. The only potential disadvantage is that the stipulation to reserve objections removes much of the good-faith basis for objecting, and the absence of good faith objections means the witness will not hear counsel's concerns about a question. In fact, since the stipulation removes the need to make an objection to preserve it, any objection that is made will appear to be to coach the witness, and objecting solely to coach the witness is forbidden.[5] If the deposing attorney files a motion to compel further answers or for sanctions for interfering with legitimate discovery, the defendant's motives in objecting become readily apparent to the judge.

6.2.3   *Waiving Reading and Signing*

Another common stipulation, which is also a frequent candidate for inclusion in the "usual stipulations," is to waive the reading and signing of the deposition. In other words, the parties agree that the witness does not have to read the deposition transcript and sign it. This stipulation is made only in jurisdictions that make reading and signing the deposition the default position.

---

5. *See* section 18.8.

Under Rule 30(e), a party or the witness must affirmatively demand, before the conclusion of the deposition, the opportunity to review and change or correct the transcript or recording. Otherwise, the right is waived. In federal cases, therefore, a further stipulation to waive the reading of the transcript does not add much, since waiver will occur automatically by simply not requesting the reading. And because a deposition does not need to be signed unless corrections are made (Rule 30(e)(1)), a stipulation waiving the signing does not add much either.

Other jurisdictions, including those that follow the pre-1993 version of the Federal Rules of Civil Procedure, may require the witness to read and sign the deposition. In those jurisdictions, it is common for the parties (and the witness, if a nonparty) to stipulate to waiving the obligation. Sometimes, the stipulation will be deferred to the end of the deposition, giving the lawyers an opportunity to evaluate the witness's performance before deciding whether to waive the right to read (and make corrections) and sign.

There is just one small problem with waiving the reading, correction, and signing of the deposition: it's a bad idea.

As the defending attorney, never waive the witness's right to read (and correct) the deposition transcript or recording (and, in federal court, always demand the right to read and correct it). Witnesses may misspeak or make other mistakes; lawyers may lose focus and start daydreaming, causing mistakes to go unnoticed until the transcript or recording is later reviewed in the more relaxed atmosphere of the office after the deposition is concluded; court reporters may mishear an answer or transcribe a question or answer incorrectly. All of these errors dictate the need for the witness (and defending attorney) to review the deposition transcript or recording and for the witness to make changes and corrections when necessary. If no changes to the transcript are needed after reading it, the witness could sign the transcript and return it (signing is not necessary in federal court if no corrections are made), or the witness could simply do nothing. The defending attorney only invites trouble by waiving the right to read and correct the transcript.[6]

As the deposing attorney, never waive the reading, correction, or signing requirements. If there are statements in the transcript that the witness thinks are incorrect for some reason, the time to hear about their corrections and their explanation is before they take the stand at trial. If the witness has had the opportunity to make corrections before trial, they cannot avoid an impeachment with the deposition transcript at trial by saying, "Well, I think that this transcript is wrong," because the impeaching attorney can respond with the following questions: "You had the

---

6. There is no disadvantage in the defending attorney waiving the witness's right to sign the deposition transcript, as opposed to the right to read and correct it. The witness's signature on the transcript only helps those who might use the deposition to later impeach the witness. Therefore, it is the deposing attorney who should not waive the requirement that the witness sign the transcript after receiving it.

right to sit down with your attorney and review every word of this transcript, didn't you?" "You never changed this answer, right?" "And [if applicable] this is your signature right here, below where it says, 'I have read the above transcript, and it is true and correct to the best of my knowledge and belief.'"

6.2.4 *Waiving Notice of Receipt or Filing*

In federal cases, depositions are ordinarily not filed with the court (Rule 5(d)). The court reporter transmits the transcript or recording to the deposing attorney for safekeeping, sends a copy to other counsel, and retains a copy (Rule 30(f)), leaving it to the attorney to file the transcript or recording with the court only if it is to be used in the proceeding (Rule 5(d)). Rule 30(f)(4) requires a party who files the deposition to promptly notify all other parties of the filing. It is better not to waive this requirement, because notice of filing will alert the nonfiling party that the filing party is planning to use the deposition.

Some state jurisdictions require the court reporter to serve notice of the preparation of the deposition transcript or notice of its delivery. In those jurisdictions, the parties routinely stipulate to the waiver of this requirement, because both sides usually receive copies of the deposition soon after it is transcribed.

6.2.5 *Other Potential Stipulations*

Several additional stipulations require less discussion, so we note them only briefly here.

- **A direction by the attorney not to answer a question will be considered a refusal by the witness to answer.** For some judges, a mere direction to a witness not to answer a question is not a sufficient basis for granting a motion to compel—the deponent must also refuse to answer the question. This stipulation eliminates the requirement that the witness refuse to answer the question, thereby speeding up the deposition and ensuring that an inadvertent oversight by the questioner does not foreclose consideration of a motion to compel. On the other hand, absent such a stipulation, the questioner can ask the witness directly whether they will answer the question—and explain the ramifications that may occur if they do not—and that may be enough to push the deponent to answer.

- **Copies of exhibits may be substituted for the originals.** This is already provided for by Rule 30(f)(2)(A)(i). There is no need for this stipulation, but it is sometimes made, perhaps because the attorneys do not remember the rule, or it is needed in state practice.

- **Where multiple parties are attending a deposition, an objection by one party will be considered an objection by all.** This stipulation reduces the time consumed by multiple objections in multiparty depositions and the resulting chaos of more than one lawyer making objections. However, where one of the parties has interests divergent from the other parties, that party may choose for tactical reasons not to be bound by the objections of the other parties, either by rejecting the blanket stipulation or by entering an objection to a specific question.

- **The deposition has been properly noticed and the time and place are proper under the rules.** Because an objection to an error or irregularity in a deposition notice is waived unless promptly served in writing under Rule 32(d)(1), there is no need for this stipulation, but it is sometimes made.

- **The deposition officer is duly qualified.** Rule 32(d)(2) requires that objections to the officer's qualifications be made before the deposition begins or promptly after the basis for disqualification becomes known or, with reasonable diligence, could have been known. There is some utility to this stipulation because it is possible that an objection to the officer's qualifications could arise during the deposition. This possibility is forestalled by the stipulation. The witness, however, could be affected by a defect in the officer's qualifications, if, for example, the witness is charged with perjury and a lack of qualifications to administer the oath would be a defense. A represented witness could be counseled by their attorney to agree to the stipulation. An unrepresented witness might not recognize the benefit of not being under oath. If the witness does not join the stipulation, it may be enforceable against the parties, but it is almost surely not enforceable against the witness.

- **In the context of a remote deposition,** there may be stipulations regarding protocols if an internet connection is lost, the availability of breakout rooms, breaks, electronic devices in the possession of the witness, the court reporter's authority to administer the oath to a witness not in their presence, and, possibly, that objections made after the witness answers the question are deemed to have been made before the answer. (*See* section 24.7.)

- **Where an expert is also a percipient witness (e.g., a treating physician), the deposition on eyewitness information will be separate from the deposition regarding expert opinions.** This stipulation can be made at the outset of the percipient witness deposition taken first, without compromising the right to take the expert deposition later; the stipulation should state that no expert opinions shall be elicited during the first deposition.

6.2.6   A Final Note on Stipulations

Once again, if you are in doubt about a stipulation, just say no. The federal rules strike a fair balance between the interests of the taker and defender, and things usually go quite smoothly when the deposition follows those rules. There is nothing inappropriate about responding to a request for a stipulation with the simple statement that, "We'll proceed under the [state] [Federal] Rules of Civil Procedure." By making this statement, you have prevented any later debates about what a stipulation meant.

On the other hand, if you and the opposing attorneys do decide to enter into a stipulation—the "usual stipulations" or otherwise—be sure the stipulation is clear on the record, preferably at the beginning of the deposition. There is nothing wrong with discussing potential stipulations off the record as long as any final agreement is clear and read into the record or reduced to a writing that is signed and affixed to the deposition. Take the time to make sure the agreement spells out exactly and clearly what is contemplated. Too many cases end up in motions or on appeal because the parties later disagree about the terms of a stipulation and what was accomplished by poorly chosen words.

Lastly, sometimes attorneys outsmart themselves. There is at least one case where the court has said in dicta that failing to object to the opposing party's statement that there is a stipulation amounts to agreeing that there is such a stipulation.[7] So if one side incorrectly states there is a stipulation when there is none, and the other side stands mute, a stipulation on that point may in fact be recognized. If you do not want to be bound by a proposed stipulation, clearly state your refusal to stipulate.

6.3 Witness Commitments

After going "on the record" at the start of the deposition, and after the court reporter or videographer have made the necessary opening remarks and counsel have stated their appearances and any stipulations, greet the deponent and identify yourself. Next, make a clear record that the witness understands and commits to the rules of the deposition process and their rights and obligations. This is a vital part of the deposition, serving several purposes:

- Reciting the ground rules establishes that you are the one in charge.

- The ground rules help to facilitate the orderly acquisition of complete and honest testimony.

- You develop a level of rapport with the witness, in a nonchallenging, non-substantive part of the examination.

- Most importantly, when worded correctly, the witness's commitments will undermine any later attempt by the witness to refute or explain their deposition testimony with cries of foul play or confusion, which is critical to your use of the testimony in summary judgment motions or trial.

---

7. *See* Garcia v. Co-Con, Inc., 629 P.2d 1237, 1240 (N.M. App. 1981) ("Silence amounts to assent when one lawyer says 'it is stipulated and agreed' and the opposing lawyer remains silent.").

Here, then, is a sample introduction for an in-person deposition:

Q: Mr. Bergis, my name is Joanne Backus. I represent XYZ Corporation, and I will be taking your deposition. Are you represented by Mr. Shine as your attorney today?

A: Yes, I am.

Q: Alright. And have you ever been to a deposition before?

A: No.

Q: Have you ever testified under oath in any type of proceeding?

A: No, I haven't.[8]

Q: Let's go over the ground rules for this deposition, so we all have the same understanding. Alright?

A: Yes.

Q: In this deposition, I will be asking you questions and you will be answering them truthfully under oath. Do you understand that?

A: Yes.

Q: My questions and your answers will be recorded by Mr. Emanuel, the court reporter at the end of the table. For him to do that, you need to speak up and answer with words so he can hear you, rather than giving a nod or a shake of your head. Do you understand that?

A: Yes, I understand.

Q: And will you do your best to give audible, oral answers?

A: Yes.

Q: Mr. Emanuel also might have trouble if we talk over each other. I'll try not to cut you off while you're answering a question, and I ask you wait until I finish my question before you begin to answer, even if you think you know what the rest of the question will be. Will you try to wait for me to finish my question before answering?

A: Sure.

---

8. If the witness has attended a deposition, ask if they gave testimony. If the witness has testified previously, in deposition or otherwise, find out about the prior testimony. Some attorneys elicit the information about the prior testimony right away—striking while the iron is hot, so to speak—but the importance of the commitments generally suggests finishing them first. Even if the witness has testified in deposition before, obtain the commitments set forth in this introduction.

Q: You have just taken an oath that requires you to tell the truth, the whole truth, and nothing but the truth. Do you understand that?

A: Yes.

Q: And that is the same oath you would take if you were to testify in court, do you understand?

A: Yes.

Q: We're interested in finding out everything you know about the events and facts that underlie this lawsuit. We are looking for full, complete, and accurate answers to my questions—the "whole truth" that you just took an oath to give. Will you tell me the whole truth today?

A: Yes.

Q: If you don't understand any of my questions, please let me know.

A: Okay.

Q: If you do answer, I'm going to assume that you do understand the question, alright?

A: Yes.

Q: I intend to take one break in the morning, a break for lunch, and one break in the afternoon. If you need a break at another time, please let me know. I will finish my line of questioning, but then we'll break at the next appropriate time. Sound good?

A: Yes, thank you. That sounds fine.

Q: And you see that we have water and coffee here for you. Feel free to get up and get whatever you need during the break, okay?

A: Yes, thank you.

Q: I know I asked you before we started, but do you need any water or coffee now?

A: No, I'm good, thanks.

Q: If you need to talk to your attorney at some point, let me know. But if I've asked you a question, you have to finish your answer before speaking to him, unless you need to talk to him about whether your answer would be privileged.[9] Okay?

---

9. Reword this to reflect the rules of the jurisdiction regarding conferences between the deponent and their lawyer.

A: Okay.

Q: If your attorney objects to one of my questions, you still have to answer the question unless he specifically directs you not to answer. Do you understand that?

A: Yes, I do.

Q: Sometimes it happens that you'll give an answer as completely or as accurately as you can, but then later on you'll remember some additional information or a clarification to give to the earlier question. If that happens, will you tell us that you'd like to add to your answer?

A: Yes.

Q: Now, because I'm entitled to your full, complete, and accurate answers, I have to ask you this. Are you taking any medication or drugs of any kind that make it difficult for you to understand and answer my questions today?

A: No.

Q: Have you taken any cough syrup or anything containing alcohol that might make it difficult for you to understand and answer my questions?

A: No.

Q: Are you at all sick today?

A: No.

Q: Is there any reason why you cannot give full, complete, and accurate testimony today?

A: Nothing comes to mind.

Q: And you'll let me know if it does, won't you?

A: Okay, sure.

This introduction makes a record of the fairness of the deposition process and provides for an orderly deposition.[10] Moreover, as discussed in the next section, it makes it more difficult for the witness to avoid the effect of the deposition answers later at trial, and as addressed in a later section, it can be used to establish the

---

10. If the witness is not represented by counsel, such as a nonparty witness, it is all the more important for the record to show that the treatment of the witness and the questioning techniques were fair. In addition, when the deponent is unrepresented, questions concerning representation with counsel should be amended to note that the witness chose not to retain counsel for the deposition.

National Institute for Trial Advocacy

deposing counsel's authority and to develop a rapport with the witness. You may ultimately elect not to include all the commitments mentioned in this sample introduction, but consider each one with its strategic aim and rationale.

6.3.1 A Closer Look at the Commitments

Let's go through the foregoing questions and commitments one by one, analyzing exactly what is going on.[11]

> *"Have you ever been to a deposition before?"*
>
> *Or "Have you ever been deposed before?"*
>
> *Or "Have you ever testified under oath?"*

This question sounds innocent enough, but there is a good reason for it: if the witness has been deposed, that fact can be used to undermine any claim by the witness in front of the jury that they were confused or uncertain about the deposition procedure. For example, in closing argument:

> Members of the jury, you heard Mr. Bergis admit in his deposition that he attended the pricing meeting in Chicago. Then you heard him try to deny it here on the stand in front of you. He claims now he was "confused" about the deposition procedures and oh so very nervous. But you also heard him testify that he had been in a deposition three previous times. Three. He was a deposition veteran! He was not nervous. He was not confused. He was telling the truth at the deposition—he *was* at the meeting in Chicago—and his attempts to deny it now here in front of you show he is not very credible.

There is another good reason for the question. If the witness has been deposed previously, you can inquire about the nature of that testimony and potentially gain evidence relevant to the current litigation. Do not make the mistake, however, of forgoing the rest of the introductory instructions and commitments just to find

---

11. Some attorneys ask the witness, "Have you ever been deposed before" or "Have you ever had your deposition taken before." Those questions are generally fine, but a small but surprising number of witnesses do not understand the intended meaning of being "deposed" or having their deposition "taken," so the broader question of whether the witness has attended a deposition may be more helpful as a starting point. If the witness answers "yes," it is simple enough to follow up by asking whether they were the witness at the prior deposition. Other attorneys ask the even broader question of, "Have you ever testified before," particularly in practice areas where the deponent may well have testified under oath in an administrative proceeding. Similarly, persons who were deposed on Zoom may not recall they were deposed, but they do recall they answered questions after taking an oath to tell the truth.

out about the prior deposition. The better approach is to stick with obtaining all the commitments first, and then ask about the prior deposition: Was the witness a party or a nonparty in that case? What kind of case was it? What court? Where? When? What was the name of the case? Why were you a witness? What did you testify about? There may be a protective order barring the witness's testimony, but you may pursue the matter until counsel instructs the witness not to answer and the witness refuses to do so.

If the witness has not been deposed, it is all the more reasonable for you to proceed by telling the witness the rules of the deposition and obtaining the witness's commitment to abide by them. Deposing counsel can easily segue to something like, "Okay, well, let's talk about the ground rules for this deposition then."

> *"You need to speak up, rather than nodding or shaking your head."*

Alerting the witness to the need to answer audibly helps the court reporter take down what is said, and it results in a clearer record that is easier to use at trial or summary judgment. The commitment to "speak up" is particularly important in a remote deposition, where the microphone and audio quality may not be the best.

The commitment also helps the attorney taking the deposition, because it keeps the witness from letting their voice trail off toward the end of an embarrassing answer and reminds the witness that the testimony is being recorded. You might add on to this commitment by asking, "So you'll forgive me if you give a nod instead of an audible answer and I say, 'Is that a "yes"?'"

Some attorneys believe, however, that the deposing attorney should do as little as possible to remind the witness that the answers are being recorded, in the hope that the witness will be more spontaneous and less guarded. If you take that approach, watch for nods or headshakes and confirm their meaning to keep the record clear, like this: "You are shaking your head from side to side. Is your answer 'no'?"

> *"Wait until I finish my question before you begin answering."*

This commitment sets an expectation of order and respect in the question-and-answer format. It also makes court reporters happy—I have seen them nod their head in agreement as they're recording the commitment. Some attorneys add, "That said, there may be times when I have to cut you off for sake of time, just to help you understand my question." This, of all the commitments, may be the most basic, the most easily accepted, and the most important. If the deposition transcript is ever going to be used for summary judgment, trial, or a similar opportunity, the fact that the witness understood they had undertaken to tell the truth is the biggest support for the veracity of the information they gave in the deposition.

> *"You have just taken an oath to tell the truth."*

Some attorneys add an interesting twist to this commitment (and, in fact, to a number of the commitments). After the witness acknowledges that they have taken an oath to tell the truth, the attorney asks, "What does that mean to you?" The witness typically responds with something like, "Tell the truth and not lie." The record demonstrates from the witness's own mouth their understanding of the oath, and their statement presumably invests them in living up to it.

> *"I'm interested in finding out everything you know."*
>
> *Or "I'm looking for full and complete answers."*

Your goal is to obtain a reliable transcript of the witness's full recollection of the facts of the case, so for that reason alone it is worth having the witness commit to providing full and complete answers.

Moreover, this commitment undermines a witness's most frequent attempt to avoid unfavorable deposition testimony when confronted with it at trial or summary judgment: the witness, without directly contradicting the deposition testimony, will try to add facts or nuance to their description of the events to make their position more plausible. It is unclear whether the phenomenon is better explained by the witness testifying to a new falsehood, the witness innocently filling in and reconstructing the events in question, or the witness adopting their attorney's suggestions, but in any case, it must be countered.

If the witness tries to add facts at trial, you can impeach the witness under the theory of inconsistency by omission. A good start to the impeachment is to remind the witness that, during the deposition, the witness was under oath, agreed to tell the "whole truth," and was asked to give "full and complete" testimony. When the witness must acknowledge that the idea was to disclose everything at the deposition, the attempt to add to the facts at trial seems suspicious and damages the witness's credibility. The cross-examination at trial might proceed like this:

Q: You just told us on direct examination that you had a good view of the accident?

A: Yes.

Q: In that regard, you said that even though it was dark and rainy that night, there was a streetlight directly behind you that illuminated the intersection?

A: That's right.

Q: In fact, Mr. Jones, there was no streetlight at the intersection, was there?

A: No, I remember the light.

Q: Well, let's see what you said about this earlier when under oath. You had your deposition taken in this case, correct?

A: Yes.

Q: And at this deposition, I asked you questions and you gave answers?

A: Yes.

Q: Your attorney was there?

A: Yes.

Q: You took an oath at that deposition to tell the truth?

A: I did.

Q: The whole truth?

A: That's right.

Q: I told you at the deposition that we were interested in finding out everything you knew about the accident, right?

A: Yeah.

Q: And you agreed to give full and complete testimony, didn't you?

A: I did.

Q: You weren't trying to hide anything while under oath, were you?

A: No.

Q: You were also told that if you realized you'd given an incomplete answer you could make the answer complete at any time during the deposition, correct?

A: Yeah.

Q: And in fact, after every break I asked you if you wanted to complete or change a previous answer, didn't I?

A: I guess so.

Q: My questions and your answers were transcribed by a court reporter into a booklet-like form?

A: Yeah.

Q: You never changed or corrected any of your answers at the deposition, did you?

A: No, I didn't.

Q: Let me show you what has been marked as Exhibit 77. [Or, "Let me draw the court's and counsel's attention to the witness's deposition transcript, which has been lodged with the court."] Exhibit 77 is your signed deposition, isn't it?

A: It is.

Q: Directing your attention to page 34, line 1 of your deposition, please read along with me, silently, as I read it aloud.

"Question: Did you have a good view of the accident?

Answer: Yeah, pretty much.

Question: What was the lighting like?

Answer: Well, it was night and raining, so it was dark out.

Question: How is it that you still think you could see what happened?

Answer: Well, I was about forty feet away. When I heard a squeal of brakes, I turned and there was nothing between the accident and where I was standing.

Question: Was there anything else that helped you see what happened?

Answer: Just that. I was close and looking right at it with nothing in the way.

Question: Were then any other reasons why you believe you had a good view of the accident?

Answer: No."

Q: I read the transcript correctly, didn't I?

A: Yes.

Q: In this deposition transcript, you made no mention of this streetlight you today claim was there, did you?

A: Well, no.

> *"If you don't understand any of my questions, please let me know."*

When trapped between the testimony given at trial or in a declaration, and answers given at a prior deposition, the embarrassed or desperate witness often tries to explain away the deposition testimony by claiming, "I didn't understand the deposition question; I was confused." If the jurors can see that the deposition question was in fact understandable, the witness's credibility takes a hit. And if the jurors also learn that the witness agreed to tell you if a question was unclear or not understood, the jurors should infer from the witness's answering the question that the witness did understand it. Admittedly, failing to understand a question posed during the deposition and recognizing a failure to understand the question can be two different things, but obtaining the commitment is better than nothing.

Attorneys are divided on whether to also tell the witness, "If you answer my question, I will assume you understood the question." Those who balk at the idea express concern that the witness's attorney might object: "Counsel, you can assume anything you want. The witness is here to answer questions. Let's get on with it." While that objection may come, the deposing counsel is not doing anything wrong. It is inappropriate for a deposing lawyer to "threaten" the witness with assumptions, but the point here is merely to emphasize to the witness the need to alert counsel if the witness does not understand a question.

Note that the sample introduction obtained only the witness's commitment to "let me know" if the witness does not understand a question. Some attorneys also volunteer that they will "rephrase the question" if the witness does not understand it. It is better not to make this promise, however, to avoid suggesting that the witness can play the game of not understanding a question and forcing you to come up with a different one—this gets old and time-consuming very quickly. If the witness claims a lack of understanding for a particular question, you might end up rephrasing it, but you might alternatively inquire what the witness doesn't understand about the question or define the terms used in the question; there is no reason for deposing attorneys to lock themselves into rephrasing their questions.

> *"If you need a break at any time . . . ."*
>
> *"We have water and coffee here."*

This commitment may put the witness a bit more at ease and reduce the likelihood that they disrupt your questioning by asking for a break, since the witness knows that a break is not too far away. On the other hand, it may increase the likelihood that the witness requests a break because it confirms for the witness—as the witness's attorney no doubt advised already—that it is okay to request one. Whichever effect the commitment might have—and it likely depends on the witness—the purpose of the commitment is twofold.

First, to the extent the deposition testimony will ever be used in a motion or at trial, the offer of breaks and refreshments conveys to the judge or jurors that the deposition was not a "third-degree" interrogation in which the witness was questioned until the point of exhaustion and discomfort. Similarly, if the witness has committed to request a break when needed, it is more difficult for the witness to say at trial, when impeached by the deposition: "Yes, I did give that answer about stealing from the church coffer, but I was very tired at that point of the deposition, and you just kept pressing me and pressing me without giving me a chance to breathe."

Second, the commitment can minimize the disruption that occurs during the deposition when witnesses do proclaim they need a break. The general idea is that, if a witness needs a break, the witness is going to take one (especially if represented by counsel) whether the deposing attorney explicitly says they can or not. But by giving the admonition that a break will be taken "at the next appropriate time" after finishing the line of questioning, the witness knows that the deposing attorney's pending question must be answered and the break may not be taken right away.

> **"If you need to talk to your attorney . . ."**

It may be counter-intuitive for deposing counsel to tell the witness it is alright to confer with the witness's attorney during the deposition.[12] After all, you would prefer that the witness testify without attorney input. But the fact is, when the questioning gets intense and the witness becomes anxious, the witness may want to check with their attorney before answering a tough question. By acknowledging that the witness can talk with the attorney, but telling the witness the conference cannot occur while a question is pending, the commitment gives the deposing attorney a bit of leverage later:

> Now, Mr. Smally, when we started, you agreed that you would answer my question before you talked with your attorney. Please give me your answer, and then we can take some time for you to talk with your attorney.

---

12. Before including this commitment in your repertoire, check the jurisdiction's rules and possible court orders on attorney conferences during a deposition. Omit the commitment if the jurisdiction does not allow such conferences.

Although this commitment is not guaranteed to prevent attorney-witness discussions between your questions and the witness's answers, experience shows that it can help.

Note that the commitment tells the witness there is an exception allowing the witness to talk to their attorney about matters of privilege even before giving an answer. In the absence of case law peculiar to the jurisdiction or a court order to the contrary, that is the law. If this exception is not included in the statement to the witness, opposing counsel may well interject: "Of course, you may talk with me while a question is pending if you need to ask about a matter of privilege." Avoid such an interjection, because it may undo any rapport you have achieved with the witness and interrupts the flow of the questioning.

The commitment also helps if the deposition is later used at trial because it suggests a fair procedure: the witness had a chance to talk with their lawyer. It may even enhance the reliability of incriminating statements that the witness made notwithstanding the opportunity to consult with counsel.

> **"If your attorney objects to one of my questions . . ."**

This commitment derives from Rule 30(c)(2), which states that "an objection must be noted on the record, but the examination still proceeds; the testimony is subject to any objection." Most represented witnesses know this, but the reinforcement does not hurt.

> **"If you remember some additional information or clarification . . ."**

This commitment helps you obtain more accurate and complete information, because witnesses may not otherwise know they are allowed to supplement their answers at the deposition. In addition, the witness's commitment to clarify or add to their answers, coupled with your request for the "whole truth" and "full and complete" answers, enhances the likelihood that you get the witness's full story or, at least, bolsters the impeachment of a witness who expands or changes their deposition testimony later at trial, as demonstrated above.

For best effect, supplement the commitment by giving the witness an opportunity after every break to make corrections or additions to previous answers. For example:

Q: Alright, Mr. Smally, we are back on the record after our lunch-time break. I remind you that you are under oath. Before we go

National Institute for Trial Advocacy

ahead, would you like to correct or expand on any of your previous answers to my questions?

A: No, I'm good.

Be forewarned that some defending lawyers feel the need to say something to the effect of: "Counsel, we will supplement the record as required by the rules." The propriety of that approach is questionable because the rules allow for correcting the transcript, not supplementing a witness's answer with new information after eschewing your invitation to supplement it during the deposition. To the extent the defending attorney is concerned that the witness may volunteer information unknown to the attorney, the better approach is to request another brief break to discuss the matter with the witness.

What should you do if the witness does want to add to their answer? Find out what answer the witness wants to supplement, obtain the facts the witness wants to add, inquire why the witness wants to add them, and take it from there. You might also ask how the witness happened to remember the new information and whether anything was shown to the witness that jogged their memory, which can entitle the deposing attorney to see it under Fed. R. Evid. 612 (*see* section 7.2.2).

Doesn't this allow the witness to parrot what the witness's attorney "reminded" the witness to say during the break? Yes, it does. But a witness who has been reminded of what to say will likely find a way to say it after the break anyway. And again, we usually want the deposition to be where we learn *all* the information that the opponent might say later in summary judgment, arbitration, or trial so we can prepare for it. Of course, if you obtained some amazing admission before the break that you do not want the witness to clarify, you have discretion not to invite the witness to add anything.

> *"Are you taking any medications or drugs? Have you consumed any alcohol?"*

These questions, and a related question about feeling ill (or, for example, being under a doctor's care) are intended to cut off excuses that a witness might give at trial to avoid an unfavorable deposition answer. Because some witnesses find such questions intrusive, include the explanatory preamble about the need for full, complete, and accurate answers.

If the witness appears and behaves normally, some attorneys forgo these questions. We recommend, however, that in any personal injury or product liability case involving injuries, you ask the plaintiff about painkillers and other medications and any effect they might be having on the plaintiff's comprehension and memory.

Although not common, sometimes a witness testifies that they are, in fact, feeling ill or taking pain medication that affects memory or brings fatigue. When this happens, find out the extent of the issue and decide whether to postpone the deposition. If you decide to proceed with the deposition, get the witness to confirm that they will let you know if, later in the deposition, their ability to provide full, complete, and accurate answers becomes affected. The inquiry might look like this:

> Q: Are you taking any medications or drugs of any kind that might make it difficult for you to understand or answer my questions today?
>
> A: Well, I had my wisdom teeth pulled two days ago, and I am taking something for the pain.
>
> Q: What medication you are taking?
>
> A: I have the bottle here. Let's see. The label says it is Hydrocodone. I think 500 mg.
>
> Q: When did you last take one of those Hydrocodone tablets?
>
> A: At eight this morning.
>
> Q: How many did you take?
>
> A: Just one.
>
> Q: Have you taken any Hydrocodone before?
>
> A: About five or six since I had the operation.
>
> Q: What effect do they have on you?
>
> A: They make my mouth quit hurting, and I get a little sleepy.
>
> Q: Are you sleepy now?
>
> A: No.
>
> Q: Have you noticed any problem remembering things since you started taking the medication?
>
> A: No.
>
> Q: You haven't noticed any problem understanding or answering questions since you started taking the medication?
>
> A: No.
>
> Q: Has anyone told you, since you started taking medication, that you have trouble understanding or remembering things?
>
> A: No.

Q: How about having your wisdom teeth pulled? Is that causing you any pain or difficulty now?

A: Not since I took the pill.

Q: You mean the Hydrocodone?

A: Yes.

Q: Are you feeling okay now?

A: Yes.

Q: Will you be sure to tell me if you feel that your teeth or the medication is causing you any problem in understanding or answering my questions?

A: Sure.

If, after questioning, it appears the witness's situation will cause difficulties with the deposition—for example, the witness seems sleepy to the point of having trouble staying awake—your best response is to reschedule the deposition, telling opposing counsel on the record what you intend to do and why. But there is, of course, a tension: do you postpone the deposition and give up the chance to depose the witness that day, at the risk of difficulty rescheduling it; or do you continue with the deposition and risk a later objection or an attempt to explain away testimony due to the effect of their medication, illness, or injury? This calculus will depend much on the situation and the witness, but think hard before going forward with a deposition that could turn out to be an unusable waste of time and expense.[13]

> *"Is there any reason you cannot give full, complete, and accurate testimony?"*

This is an indispensable question, because it gets to the heart of the matter: are we going to get the witness's full story? If you choose not to ask the intrusive questions about medications, drug use, alcohol consumption, medical conditions, and a doctor's care, this generic inquiry must be included. If the witness says there is a reason they might not be able to give full, complete, and accurate testimony, ask why and probe further as needed.

---

13. One other note. If you decide to ask about alcohol, particularly if the witness appears to be under the influence, ask again following the lunch break, to find out whether the witness had a couple of drinks over lunch to relieve their anxiety from the morning. Yes, it happens.

In addition, ask the question even if you have inquired about medications and the like, because there are other reasons a witness might not be able to give full, complete, and accurate testimony. For example, just before the deposition or during a break, a witness might learn about trouble in their business or a family illness that will compromise the witness's testimony.

6.3.2 *Additional Commitments for Remote Depositions*

In addition to the commitments and questions set forth above, there are commitments and questions to ask the witness at the beginning of the deposition if the deposition is held remotely via an online videoconference. These commitments and questions are designed to make sure that 1) the deposition is private; 2) the witness's testimony is not aided by any outside source—which could range from documents, information on computer websites, scripted answers opened on their laptop, or even texts from the witness's boss or attorney; and 3) there is an agreed protocol if the witness or other participants in the deposition lose their internet connection. It can go something like this:

Q: Since we're holding this deposition remotely, let's cover a few extra items. First, let me ask you: is there anyone else in the room with you right now?

A: No.

Q: Will you tell me if anyone else comes in the room?

A: Sure. I told them I'm in a deposition, but yeah, sure.

Q: Now I'm entitled to your unaided testimony, so let's talk about that for a moment.

A: Okay.

Q: Do you agree to answer my questions from your own recollection, without referring to any document, device, or anything else unless I specifically ask you to?

A: Sure.

Q: That means you can't communicate with any person in answering the questions either, other than your attorney as we've already discussed.

A: That's fine.

Q: And if you want to talk with your attorney, tell me that you would like to do so, rather than just doing it, okay?

A: Okay.

Q: Other than the computer that you're using to connect to this deposition, do you have any other computers, laptops, cellphones, or other electronic devices visible to you right now?

A: Yeah, my phone.

Q: Please turn it off and place it face down on the desk. [Or, Please turn it to silent mode and place it face down on the desk where I can see it.]

A: Fine. There.

Q: And please keep it turned off unless we're on a break, okay?

A: Okay.[14]

Q: Are there any other electronic devices visible to you now?

A: No.

Q: Are there any hard-copy documents, photos, diagrams, or anything else concerning the case within your reach or visible to you?

A: No.

Q: Are there any documents, apps, programs, or anything else open on your computer other than the Zoom connection for this deposition?

A: Just Facebook.

Q: Please close Facebook and anything that's open other than the Zoom connection.

A: Okay, done.

Q: And do you agree not to have any document, app, or program open on your computer during the deposition, other than Zoom, unless I ask you to open it?

A: Yeah, okay.

Q: If you lose your internet connection or your connection to this deposition, will you to try to reconnect right away?

A: Yes.

---

14. Commitments to turn off, put away, and not refer to a phone during questioning are a good idea in all depositions. Witnesses check texts and emails even when the deposition is conducted in person.

Q: If you have trouble reconnecting, let your attorney or the court reporter know, okay?

A: Okay.

Q: Do you have their number or email address?

A: Yeah, my attorney's.

For further discussion of remote depositions, see Chapter Twenty-Four.

> **Extra Commitments for Remote Depositions**
>
> - *the deposition is private,*
> - *the witness's testimony is not aided by any outside source, and*
> - *there is an agreed protocol if the witness or other participants in the deposition lose their internet connection.*

6.3.3 Commit to Commitments

In going through this introductory portion of the deposition, too many deposing attorneys just present the witness with a list of do's and don'ts. The mere fact that you have told the witness your expectations for the deposition is not enough. Do not simply describe the rule; ask whether the witness understands the rule and will follow it—thereby making a commitment—so it has the desired effect both during the deposition and after. Examples have been included in the sample introductory section set forth above.

6.3.4 Admonitions or Commitments Usually to Avoid

Speculating or Guessing

Some attorneys like to advise the deponent not to speculate or guess when answering a question. They argue that by putting this advisement on the record, it is harder for the witness to later avoid an unfavorable answer by claiming it was a guess or speculation. The commitment questions go something like this:

Q: Now, Ms. Huang, I'm entitled to learn what you know, and that includes your giving me your best estimate in response to my questions, but I don't want you to guess or speculate, okay?

A: Okay.

Q: Let me explain the difference between an estimate and a guess. If I asked you the width of this table, you might not know precisely, but you could still give me an estimate. On the other hand, if I asked you the width of the table in my dining room, you would just be guessing or speculating, because you've never seen the table in my dining room. Do you understand the distinction?

A: Uh, I think so.

We recommend against this instruction, however, because it is unnecessary and counterproductive. Most jurisdictions have no rule against guessing at a deposition. Moreover, a witness's speculation may be more valuable than their limited personal knowledge. Although speculation might not itself be admissible, it may well lead to another witness or to a document that can be used as admissible evidence. For example, consider these questions to the executive assistant about his boss's activities ("DC" refers to defending counsel):

Q: Mr. Smally, how much time did your boss spend on the Century account in May?

A: Well, I'm not exactly sure. You know, I don't keep track of her every minute.

Q: Yes, I understand that. Give me your estimate of how much of her time she spent.

A: Well, it would be more of a guess, I suppose.

Q: All right, give me your guess.

DC: Objection. Calls for speculation. No personal knowledge. No foundation. He already told you he's not sure.

Q: Mr. Smally, tell us what you know of your boss's time on the Century matter in May.

A: I don't know for sure how much time she spent.

Q: Fine. Now, give me your best speculation or guess.

DC: Same objections. We've been through this.

Q: Answer the question, please, Mr. Smally. Give us your best estimate, even if it is a guess, how much time she spent on the account in May.

A: I guess it was about half of her time.

Q: What do you base that on?

A: Well, we only had one other big account in the office then, and she seemed to be working on Century almost all the time. Actually, it could have been more than half.

Q: If you had to find out the answer, what would you do to find it out?

A: I don't know. Ask the boss. Or check the time logs on her computer.

While this testimony might not be entirely admissible at trial, it is clearly useful to know what the witness believes because he presumably observed "the boss" on a daily basis. Speculation such as this can lead to admissible evidence through further discovery, by suggesting document requests for diaries and time logs or questions you can ask at the depositions of other witnesses, thereby bringing the request for a "guess" within the permissible scope of discovery under Rule 26.

"You might not know or remember the answer."

Sometimes deposing attorneys include commitments like these:

Q: I may ask you a question to which you don't know the answer. Will you be sure to tell me you do not know the answer and not guess at what you think the right answer is unless I tell you to do so?

A: Sure.

Q: Similarly, I may ask you a question that at one time you knew the answer, but can now no longer remember the answer. Again, will you be sure to tell me you do not know the answer and not guess at what you think might be the correct answer unless I tell you to do so?

A: Yes.

These commitments have the same rationale and downside as the one that told the witness to give an estimate rather than a guess. The upside is that, if the witness later says, "I answered but I didn't really know (or remember)," the deposing attorney can point to the commitment and say the witness was allowed to say if they did not know or recall. The most important task at the deposition, however, is to get information from the witness. That goal is impeded by suggesting to the witness that they can get out of answering a question by saying they do not know or do not remember.

"If you think of some documents that might help . . ."

Some attorneys instruct the witness to this effect:

Q: When you are answering, you may think of some documents that might help you remember the answer or might help you give a more accurate answer. If you do, tell us. We may have those documents right here, or we may be able to get them to help you answer completely and accurately. Is that okay?

A: Yes.

The idea of this commitment is to encourage the witness to mention documents that come to mind. The purpose is threefold. First, the fact that the witness knew they could refer to a document precludes the witness from later saying, "Well, if I had the documents in front of me then, I might have remembered this other bank account." Second, if there is a document that helps the witness remember, using the document will make the examination more efficient. Third, the invitation to mention relevant documents can result in the witness disclosing documents not yet produced or even known to the defending attorney.[15]

The theory against including this commitment, however, is that the deposing attorney should first obtain the witness's recollection of any event, conversation, meeting, or other matter without aid from any documents, so giving the witness permission to ignore those questions and demand a document is counterproductive. The better approach is not to offer this commitment at the beginning of the deposition, but to instead insist on the witness providing any unaided recollection of the event and then asking if there is any document that would assist their recollection. Or, if you choose to give the commitment, add to it that you will ask the witness "to give your unaided recollection before you look at the document."

Trouble words

Finally, there are a couple of words deposing attorneys use in the setup and commitment questions that generate a contentious response from opposing counsel, at least in those areas of the country where contentiousness is a hallmark of deposition practice. Those words are "promise" and "agree." The colloquy goes something like this. The deposing attorney asks the witness, "Will you promise to tell me if you do not understand a question so I can rephrase it?" or "Will you agree to let me know if you later remember some additional information that should have been included in your original answer?" Defending counsel then roars into action, exclaiming: "Counsel, the witness isn't here to make promises or agreements. They are here to answer questions. Now, if you have a question, ask it. Otherwise, I suggest we all go home." After such an outburst—as inappropriate as it is—your efforts at building rapport with the witness may be for naught.

The solution: avoid using the words "promise" and "agree" when asking the commitment questions. Of course, you do want the witness to agree to follow

---

15. If the witness mentions a document that falls within the scope of a request for production but has not been produced, demand that the document be produced before the deposition ends. If it is not produced during the deposition, state that the deposition may be reconvened after the production of the document. If the document is not produced after an agreed or reasonable time, bring a motion to compel and request additional deposition time. If, on the other hand, the document was not the subject of an earlier request for production, ask to see the document and submit a formal document request for it immediately. An informal request on the record that the document be produced is likely insufficient. The typical response by defending counsel is "we'll take that under advisement." Such a response is code for, "If you don't send a formal request for production, you will probably never see that document."

the ground rules—again, that is why we call them "commitments"—but you do not need to use that word. The previous questions are just as effective if phrased like this: "Will you tell me if you do not understand a question?" or "Will you let me know if you later remember?" This alternative phrasing seems to avoid giving defending counsel an excuse to act in an obstructionist manner. If you get pushback even to that phrasing, ask, "Please let me know if you do not understand a question, okay?" and make sure the witness responds with "okay" or its equivalent.

6.3.5   *Demeanor, Rapport, and Control in Obtaining Commitments*

Remember at the outset of this subchapter we stated that obtaining the witness's commitments to the deposition ground rules not only helps the deposition run smoothly and minimizes the witness's later effort to explain away their testimony, and also helps to establish a rapport with the witness. The nature of explaining ground rules and obtaining the witness's commitments puts you in a position of authority—you are running the show. Because the commitments give the impression of a fair and reasonable proceeding, they may suggest that you are not the monster or trickster that the witness's counsel described; the more the witness is comfortable in the deposition and used to agreeing with your propositions, the more the witness will be forthcoming in their substantive testimony and abide by their undertaking to provide full, complete and accurate testimony. And, if performed smoothly, the commitments section of the deposition offers an easy way for deposing counsel to display professionalism, competence, and credibility.

> *Commitments protect against the witness later reneging on testimony, establish who's running the show, give place to develop rapport, and facilitate the orderly acquisition of information.*

With all of this in mind, be familiar enough with the commitment questions stated above that you can deliver them in a manner that not only conveys confidence but also suggests you are a normal person. Do not read them off a script. Do not state them as if you were ticking off items on a list. Be conversational. You might even smile occasionally. And look at the witness—not only to develop rapport, but to size up how the witness might be feeling or approaching the deposition.

To view a video demonstration of Beginning the Deposition (Commitments), scan the QR code (print version) or click here.

CHECKLIST
BEGINNING THE DEPOSITION

✔ Set up the deposition room.

✔ Consider possible stipulations to request, accept, or decline.

✔ Place any stipulations on the record once the deposition begins.

✔ Decline to enter into the "usual stipulations" or others without confirming what they are.

✔ Address the witness in a confident, conversational manner to set the tone and build rapport.

✔ Learn if the witness testified previously, particularly in a deposition, and learn about those proceedings.

✔ Obtain the witness's commitments; e.g., ensure that the witness:

- ✓ will give audible, verbal answers;
- ✓ will let the question end before answering;
- ✓ understands they are under oath to tell the truth;
- ✓ will provide the whole truth—full, complete, and accurate answers;
- ✓ will tell the deposing attorney if a question is not understood;
- ✓ can ask for a break at the next appropriate time;
- ✓ will answer the question before conferring with counsel (unless a privilege is involved);
- ✓ can supplement an earlier answer with additional information or clarification;
- ✓ has no reason not to be able to testify fully, accurately, and completely;
- ✓ will tell the deposing attorney if the ability to do so changes;
- ✓ accepts additional commitments as needed for remote depositions.

CHAPTER SEVEN

PRELIMINARY INQUIRIES

You have to know the past to understand the present.

—Carl Sagan

A deposition will be more effective if you cover preliminary matters—including the witness's background and preparation for the deposition—to the extent required by the needs of the case.

Once you have started the deposition confidently and conversationally to obtain the witness's commitments to the deposition ground rules (Chapter Six), consider how much information to elicit from the witness about their background, preparation for the deposition, and other preliminary matters before delving into substantive issues. Sometimes this background information is critical to the case or useful for setting the witness up for later testimony; sometimes, however, attorneys waste far too much time on questions that have no possibility of contributing to the deposition goals.

> **In This Chapter:**
>
> - *Three potential areas of preliminary inquiry*
>
> - *Deciding when and to what extent the inquiries should be made*
>
> - *Segueing to substantive topics*

In this chapter, we examine three potential areas of inquiry and how to decide when and to what extent the inquiries should be made. We conclude with a segue to eliciting testimony on the more substantive topics of the deposition.

7.1 Background of the Witness

Inquiries into the witness's background may include all or some of the following:

- **Basic personal and identifying information:** address or city of residence; age; marital status; children.

- **Education:** how far the witness progressed in school; college major and degrees earned; specific courses if related to the issues.

- **Training:** informal education, including apprenticeship and training relevant to the case.

- **Employment:** jobs held; for each job, dates of employment, location, duties, supervisor, and reason for leaving; further detail on the employment most germane to the case; if employed by a party, pertinent aspects of the company they work for; licenses and accreditation.

7.1.1 Purposes of the Inquiry

Asking questions about the witness's background serves several purposes. First, the background inquiry accustoms the witness to the deposition process and can encourage the witness to give full narrative answers to your later questions on substantive issues. Asking relatively nonthreatening, nonchallenging questions early on, which inquire about the witness rather than the events underlying the lawsuit, may put the witness more at ease. The witness learns to answer questions with something more than a monosyllabic answer. By responding to the witness's answers in an interested, conversational way, you may dispel the witness's preconceived idea that you are the evil enemy and build some degree of rapport. The time spent in this mode will be repaid severalfold later when the witness is more forthcoming on substantive issues and the inquiries take less time.

A second purpose for background questioning is to assess the witness's personality, intelligence, savvy, and articulateness. This in turn will help you judge how to handle the witness in substantive areas. The way the witness answers background questions, for example, can tell you how confident or adversarial the witness is and whether you need to be more precise or less formal in your questioning.

A third purpose for background questioning is to find out facts directly relevant to the substantive issues in a low-key manner. A witness's competence and experience, for example, may be directly relevant to the issues that decide the case. Moreover, a witness's answers to background questions can set them up to give the answers you want later on substantive questions. For example, due to their job duties, a witness should know about certain procedures at the plant; due to their lack of training, the witness may concede they had no ability to take the steps that would have avoided the mishap in the case. Conversely, the witness's background in a field may suggest they could have handled the events differently. These facts can be obtained more easily if asked in the context of background inquiries rather than interrogation on the substantive events.

Finally, a fourth purpose for background questioning is to uncover an unexpected gold nugget of information—prior firings, other litigation, criminal convictions, and the like—that compromises the witness's credibility or the persuasiveness of the opponent's position. (A bit of finesse is required if you ask about these matters directly, however. Because your goal in asking background questions includes putting the witness at ease and developing rapport, save these more invasive inquiries for a strategic point later in the deposition.)

7.1.2   How Much Background Information Is Needed

Despite the many purposes for learning the witness's background, the amount of time to devote to the background inquiry depends on the witness and the circumstances, including the direct relevance of the witness's background to the substantive issues in the case and the number of other topics that must be covered during the allotted deposition time. Before the deposition begins, decide what background questioning will be appropriate, considering the following:

> • What role does the witness play in the story of the case?
>
> • How important is the witness's background to the issues in the case?
>
> • What is the likelihood that a background inquiry will lead the witness to divulge information later on?
>
> • How much time is needed for other, substantive inquiries?

What role does the witness play in the story of the case? If the witness merely had the misfortune of standing on the corner when the plaintiff's and defendant's cars collided, it is unlikely you will need to do a great deal of background questioning—the only ostensible reason for a background inquiry in this situation would be to help the witness feel more comfortable in answering questions. On the other hand, if the allegation is, for example, that the witness is the principal inventor of a type of business software, you will need more background information to evaluate the witness and the testimony.

How important is the witness's background to the issues in the case? When the witness's background helps prove some issue in the case, the background questioning takes on greater significance because it has substantive importance. For instance, in a securities fraud case where the broker is accused of taking advantage of a customer's naiveté, the customer's educational history is more than just background—it directly addresses the issue of the customer's sophistication in relation to the broker's representations.

What is the likelihood that a background inquiry will lead the witness to divulge information later on? This is a tough call until you start deposing the witness, so you may have to make this assessment after questioning begins. Generally, if the witness is not a party to the case and may be intimidated by the proceedings, putting the witness at ease during background inquiries may indeed make the witness more forthcoming during the rest of the deposition. On the other hand, if the witness is a party, a senior executive, or an expert witness, it is unlikely a background inquiry will lull the witness into being more talkative. With these witnesses, any gains you might make in building rapport will evaporate by the time the witness and counsel return from a break. If there is no other reason to believe exploring the witness's background will yield significant positive results, ask about the background only as needed for substantive purposes. Alternatively, relegate background inquiries to the *end* of the deposition, so you get through the substantive topics first. This option is especially appropriate where the witness's needed background information is easy to find through internet research (or, in the case of an expert, a curriculum vitae and expert witness disclosures).

How much time is needed for other, substantive inquiries? The seven-hour, one-day time limit on depositions in Rule 30(d)(1) is another factor. Unless the length of the deposition has been extended by stipulation or court order, decide what topics to cover and what topics to jettison if the deposition begins to bump up against the time limit. Minimize questioning on the witness's background— except to the extent it directly bears on the merits—if more important topics are likely to take the full seven hours. Even if there is no likelihood of taking the time allotted or there is no time limit at all, developing the witness's background has a cost in dollars for the client, both in attorney time and the expense of the transcript preparation.

To sum up these factors, do not ask background questions merely because you or others have asked them of other deponents in the past; have a specific purpose for asking them. If the witness's background has no relevance to the substantive issues, a few questions about where the witness lives and what the witness currently does for work will often suffice. To the extent delving into the witness's background is worthwhile, ask the questions in a friendly, accepting, and interested manner to facilitate warming the witness up for later testimony.

7.1.3   *How to Elicit Background Information*

To the extent you decide to inquire about the witness's background, it is typically best to begin with basic personal information about the witness and then proceed chronologically through the witness's educational background and employment history. By proceeding chronologically, you are less likely to miss a period or event that the witness may not want to talk about—like the eight months they spent in jail. To this end, ask the witness to supply specific dates to make sure no period of time has been omitted, as might happen if the witness is allowed to say, for example, "Well, three years ago I left my job at American, and then I started work at Century." While it might be true that the witness left the American job three years ago and his next job was at Century, checking the dates of each employment will reveal any unaccounted time between the two jobs.

How you obtain the details of employment and education depends on the witness. For witnesses with little education or employment history, the details of which are not germane to the case, you might combine their education and employment history by starting with whether they finished high school and then proceeding with what they did after that, and after that, and after that. For witnesses who have a lot of education or employment that directly bears on the case, take education first, starting with a relevant point (e.g., college) and proceeding chronologically; then address employment, starting with a relevant point (e.g., first job after college) and proceeding chronologically to the present. For each job the witness lists, ask where the witness worked, what they did, who they worked for, and why they left. The extent you elicit the details of each job and the witness's education will also depend, of course, on what you need for the case.

7.2 Witness's Preparation for the Deposition

In this section of the deposition, which can come before or after the inquiry into the witness's background, ask what the witness did to prepare for the deposition. The inquiry typically includes:

- Who the witness talked to about the deposition.

- The contents of those conversations, to the extent not privileged (make certain nonparty witnesses understand that they do not have a privileged relationship with the party's attorney).

- If the conversation was with an attorney, nonprivileged information about the witness's consultation with the attorney to see if the attorney-client privilege attached and whether it was subsequently waived.

- Documents, photos, videos, or other material the witness reviewed to prepare for the deposition.

- If any of this material helped the witness remember the events.

7.2.1   *Purposes of the Inquiry*

There are several reasons to ask about the witness's preparation for the deposition. First, who the witness talked to about their upcoming deposition can lead to the discovery of additional potential witnesses. Find out the name of each person to whom the witness spoke, why the witness discussed the deposition with that person, how many times they communicated, what was said, and what the witness did as a result of the communication. Although the witness may be hesitant to provide it, ask how to get in contact with the person(s) they spoke with.

Second, although discussions the witness had with the witness's attorney would ordinarily be undiscoverable due to the attorney-client privilege, you may ask questions that probe whether the privilege attached to the particular communication, whether the privilege was waived, or whether circumstances support an exception to the privilege rules. For example, ask: "Without telling me the content of your conversation with your attorney, when did you meet with your attorney?" "For how long?" "Where?" "Who else besides your attorney was there?" "Did you tell anyone about the conversation?" (If a third party was present, or if the communication was disclosed to others, the attorney-client privilege may have been waived, allowing further inquiry into the conversation.) "Besides legal advice, what else was discussed?"

In addition, inquiring about the documents, videos, photographs, and recordings the witness reviewed may lead to material you have not seen—as when a witness volunteers, "Oh yeah, last night I looked through the box of files in my garage and that video that's still on my phone"—and opposing counsel gets a queasy look on their face. If the witness discloses the existence of material that has not been produced, ask the witness where the material is, what it contains, where the witness got it, and whether and when the witness provided it to counsel. If the material falls within the scope of a document production request, demand that the witness's attorney produce the material; if it does not fall within the scope of a production request, send a new request for production.

Finally, and relatedly, asking what material the witness reviewed, and whether the material refreshed the witness's recollection of the events, may lead to the recovery of otherwise-privileged documents that could be helpful in litigating the case. Let's look at that more closely in the next section.

7.2.2   *Inquiring About Documents Used to Refresh the Witness's Memory*

Deposing attorneys commonly ask the witness a question to the effect of: "Did you review documents while preparing for your deposition?" So phrased, this yes or no question is not objectionable. If the witness answers "no," there is no issue. But if the witness answers "yes," there may be.

If the witness answers "yes," the follow-up question would logically be: "What documents did you review while preparing for your deposition?" If the witness reviewed documents of their own choosing, the witness must divulge the documents reviewed. But if—as is likely—the witness reviewed documents selected by the witness's attorney, the witness's attorney typically objects on the ground that the attorney's selection of those documents reflects the attorney's work product; on that basis, the attorney instructs the witness not to answer (or at least not to identify any documents the attorney asked the witness to review).

> *Watch out for party attorneys who mistakenly believe that when they prepare a nonparty witness it creates an attorney-client privilege with that witness. It does not; in fact, evidence shared with that witness loses its privileged status. This can be an excellent source for solid information.*

The work product objection and instruction may well be valid. At least in cases involving a large number of documents, an attorney's selection of a subset of documents for the witness to review during deposition preparation likely reflects the lawyer's thinking about the case. Therefore, even if the documents themselves are not privileged, and the fact that the witness reviewed documents is not privileged, "the selection process itself represents . . . counsel's mental impressions and legal opinions of how the evidence in the documents relates to the issues and defenses in the litigation."[1]

The analysis changes, however, if the witness's review of the documents shown by counsel refreshed the witness's memory about the events in the case. In that instance, many courts have held that, in fairness, those documents must be identified by the witness and produced to the deposing attorney pursuant to Fed. R. Evid. 612, even if the selection process constituted attorney work product.

Under Fed. R. Evid. 612, "when a witness uses a writing to refresh memory . . . before testifying, . . . an adverse party is entitled to have the writing produced at the [deposition], to inspect it, to cross-examine the witness about it, and to introduce in evidence any portion that relates to the witness's testimony," if the court decides that justice so requires.[2] Rule 612 thus creates a tension between the need

---

1. Sporck v. Peil, 759 F.2d 312, 315 (3d Cir. 1985); *see* James Julian, Inc. v. Raytheon Co., 93 F.R.D. 138, 144 (D.C. Del. 1982). Not every court reaches this exact conclusion, however. Depending on the jurisdiction, a judge may decide that the witness must divulge the documents that were reviewed; it is just that the witness cannot say which ones were chosen by counsel. If counsel volunteered that they selected all the documents, that is counsel's fault, and counsel cannot insulate from discovery the identity of the documents reviewed by volunteering that the attorney selected them. Pradaxa Products Litigation, 2013 WL 1776433 (S.D. Ill. 2013).
2. Fed. R. Evid. 612 is applicable to depositions pursuant to Fed. R. Civ. P. 30(c). *See* U.S. ex rel. Bagley v. TRW, Inc., 212 F.R.D. 554, 565 (C.D. Cal. 2003).

for the deposing attorney to be able
to question the witness on how the
deposition testimony was affected
by the refreshing of the witness's
memory, and the need to protect the
work-product status of the defending
attorney's decision to use the documents in preparation. As stated by
one court two decades ago, "A review

> **Witness Preparation Inquiries:**
> - *Who the witness talked to.*
> - *What the witness looked at.*
> - *Anything else the witness did to prepare.*

of the cases in general . . . indicates that courts have been grappling with the scope
of Rule 612 with varying degrees of clarity."[3] The observation remains somewhat
true today.

When faced with this situation, some judges issue a blanket order that all documents reviewed in preparation for testimony must be produced. These judges
reason that it is impossible to determine reliably whether a document that was reviewed actually "refreshed memory" or not, so in fairness, if the deponent reviewed
it, the document is certainly relevant to the deponent's testimony and it must be
produced. In jurisdictions following this rule, if the deposing attorney asks, "What
documents did you review in preparation for your deposition," the witness must
identify those documents and, subject to an issue addressed below, the documents
must be produced.

Another position holds that, if the witness testifies that they reviewed a document that helped them recall the events surrounding the lawsuit, the document
must be produced to the extent that it refreshed memory. That is, if a ten-page document was reviewed and only the middle two paragraphs on page six refreshed the
witness's memory, then all that need be produced is some identifying information
regarding the document (e.g., Memorandum of August 10, 2009, from J. Smith
to D. Jones) and the two paragraphs from the document on page six. These courts
appear to hold that, if a document is used to refresh the recollection of a witness,
the privilege is waived and the document must be produced to the other side without further consideration of, for example, a balancing of the relevant interests.[4] In
these jurisdictions, if the deposing attorney asks, "In preparing for your deposition,
did you review any documents that helped you remember the events alleged in this
case?" the witness must answer and those documents must be produced.

As a third alternative—and the most cited rule today—courts hold that a document need not be produced pursuant to Rule 612 unless it is shown not only that
the document refreshed the memory of the witness about the events underlying

---

3. Suss v. MSX Int'l Eng'g. Servs., Inc., 212 F.R.D. 159, 163 (S.D.N.Y. 2002).
4. *E.g.*, Marshall v. U.S. Postal Serv., 88 F.R.D. 348, 350 (D.C. 1980); *see* Adidas Am., Inc. v. TRB
Acquisitions LLC, 324 F.R.D. 389 (D. Or. 2017) (describing alternative approaches to the Rule 612
issue).

the lawsuit, but that the document refreshed the memory of the witness about testimony actually given at the deposition and production would be in the interest of justice.[5] These courts reason that, unless there was actual testimony about the topic that was refreshed, there is no reason for the document to be produced under the rubric of Rule 612. In these jurisdictions, ask, "In preparing for your deposition, did you review any documents that helped you remember the matters you testified about today?" (In these jurisdictions, this question would come toward the end of the deposition, not the beginning.)

> *You may learn new sources of information, and extensive preparation suggests they should remember the facts during the deposition.*

To sum up, know your jurisdiction. If in doubt, ask, "In preparing for your deposition, did you review any documents that refreshed your recollection of [or jogged your memory about, etc.] the matters you testified to today?" The defending attorney should allow the witness to answer "yes" or "no." If the witness answers "no," then the witness need not identify the documents reviewed. If the witness answers "yes," any work product protection is likely gone. Next, ask, "What documents did you review that refreshed your recollection of the matters you testified to today?" At that point, the defending attorney should allow the witness to identify the documents. Whether those documents need to be produced will depend on whether the parties can work out an agreement or, ultimately, if the court finds it necessary in the interest of justice to compel production.[6]

---

5. *E.g.*, Sporck v. Peil, 759 F.2d 312, 317 (3d Cir. 1985) (before ordering production of documents counsel selected for the witness to review, court must determine that the witness used the writing to refresh memory, used the writing for the purpose of testifying, and production is necessary in the interest of justice); Nutramax Labs., Inc. v. Twin Labs., Inc., 183 F.R.D. 458, 468–70 (D. Md. 1998) (if the document refreshed memory and was used for testifying, it should be ordered produced notwithstanding the attorney work product doctrine upon application of a balancing test to balance the need for disclosure and the need for work product protection, setting forth nine factors to consider); Berkey Photo, Inc. v. Eastman Kodak Co., 74 F.R.D. 613, 615 (S.D.N.Y. 1977) (production not required unless the documents had sufficient "impact" on the expert's testimony); Bank Hapoalim, B.M. v. American Home Assurance Co. 1994 U.S. Dist. LEXIS 4091 (S.D.N.Y. April 6, 1994) ("[b]efore ordering production of privileged documents, courts require that the documents 'can be said to have had "impact" on the [witness's] testimony to trigger the application of Rule 612'. . . . If this threshold is met, courts then engage in a balancing test considering such factors as whether production is necessary for fair cross-examination or whether the examining party is simply engaged in a 'fishing expedition.'"); Abu Dhabi Com. Bank v. Morgan Stanley & Co., 2011 U.S. Dist. LEXIS 122325 (S.D.N.Y. Oct. 14, 2011) (following *Bank Hapoalim*); Campbell v. Pa. School Bds. Ass'n, No. 18-892, 2018 U.S. Dist. LEXIS 120257 (E.D. Pa. July 17, 2018) (denying request for documents due to lack of showing that they influenced testimony); Adidas Am., Inc. v. TRB Acquisitions LLC, 324 F.R.D. 389 (D. Or. 2017) (adopting modified approach as to Rule 30(b)(6) witnesses).
6. Derderian v. Polaroid Corp., 121 F.R.D. 13 (D. Mass. 1988) (disclosure of notes used to refresh recollection was not ordered where it was not shown to be in the interest of justice).

But that brings us to a second issue. Let's say the witness identifies the documents they reviewed—whether or not those documents were shown to them by counsel—and mentions a document that is itself an attorney-client communication or reflects the mental impressions of counsel: "Well, let's see. I reviewed the letters from the government about the contamination spill site, internal memoranda concerning the clean-up efforts, diagrams and maps of the area, and, oh yeah, my attorney's letter about the deposition subjects." If the unprivileged documents (e.g., the letters from the government) have not been produced and fall within the scope of the Rule 26 mandatory disclosures, a Rule 34 document request, or a Rule 45 subpoena (and were in the possession, custody, or control of the recipient of the document demand), the documents must be produced. If any of the documents are privileged or protected by the work product doctrine (i.e., the attorney's letter about the deposition subjects), you are nonetheless entitled to immediate production of the document under Rule 612 if it refreshed the witness's recollection about the events testified to and justice so requires.[7]

Thus, Rule 612 rears its head in two respects: 1) you may learn what documents the defending attorney told the witness to review and obtain a copy of them to the extent they refreshed the witness's recollection, and 2) privileged or work-product documents the witness reviewed, even on their own, are subject to production if they refreshed the witness's recollection about the events on which the witness testified. This can be a goldmine. It's rare, but occasionally the defending counsel is sloppy; that is why these lines of questions are pursued.

Your takeaway: ask witnesses if they reviewed any document that refreshed their recollection of the events to which they testified. The takeaway for the defending attorney: in preparing a witness for deposition, never provide to the witness a privileged or work-product document, and provide only those documents that have either been produced already or present no tactical disadvantage if they have to be produced later to opposing counsel.[8]

7.3   Confirming the Sufficiency of the Witness's Document Production

Another preliminary topic is whether the deponent produced all the documents you requested in discovery. Normally, you send document requests

---

7. *E.g.*, Ehrlich v. Howe, 848 F. Supp. 482, 493 (S.D.N.Y. 1994) ("when confronted with the conflict between the command of Rule 612 to disclose materials used to refresh recollection and the protection provided by the attorney-client privilege . . . the weight of authority holds that the privilege . . . is waived").

8. If the deposition witness uses a privileged or work product document during the deposition to refresh the witness's recollection for purposes of testifying, the other side is automatically entitled to it at the deposition under Rule 612. *E.g.*, Sperling v. City of Kennesaw Police Dep't, 202 F.R.D. 325, 329 (N.D. Ga. 2001). By the terms of Rule 612, in that circumstance the court does not need to engage in any balancing test to determine whether disclosure is necessitated by the interest of justice.

pursuant to Rule 34 or subpoenas pursuant to Rule 45 to obtain responsive documents before the deposition of key witnesses, so you have plenty of time to receive and review them. If time is tight or if there are only a few documents involved, however, the deposition and document production can be scheduled for the same time. In that instance, the witness comes to the deposition with the documents, and you have an additional preliminary matter to cover during the deposition: the sufficiency of the witness's production. Even if the documents were produced before the deposition, ask the witness about the sufficiency of the production if the witness has knowledge of how the documents were collected and produced.

> *After every break in the deposition, ask the witness what they did during the break: Who did you speak to? Why? What was said (unless privileged)? What did you look at related to this case?*

You can easily determine whether a subpoena or request for production has been complied with if the subpoena or request called for specific documents (e.g., "the insurance policy," "the lease") by comparing the documents specifically asked for with the documents turned over. But where the subpoena or production request refers to categories of documents rather than specific documents (e.g., "all documents relating to . . ."), you cannot tell if all the responsive documents were produced, so examine the witness about the efforts taken to locate and produce them.

Let's take a situation where a nonparty witness received a document subpoena and is not represented by counsel:

Q: Mr. Vidas, I am handing you what has been marked as Exhibit 1, the subpoena duces tecum that was served on you. Do you recognize it?

A: It looks like the subpoena I got.

Q: Have you read the subpoena?

A: I did.

Q: Do you understand that the subpoena required you to search for all documents in your possession, custody, or control that the subpoena was asking for?

A: Yes.

Q: Did you bring documents with you in response to this subpoena?

A: Yes. Do you want them now?

Q: Yes, thank you. [Receives documents.] Just for the record, I note that the documents bear Bates numbers AG 1 to AG 237. Did anyone help you with the search for responsive documents?

A: No, I did it by myself.

Q: Did you talk with anyone about it?

A: No.

Q: Have you collected and provided all the documents in your possession, custody, or control that were called for by the subpoena?

A: I did my best.

Q: What does that mean?

A: I searched everywhere I could think of.

Q: Were there any documents that you found that were requested by the subpoena, but that you withheld for any reason?

A: No.

Q: Were there any locations you decided not to search because you thought that location might have responsive documents?

A: No.

Q: Do you know of any documents that were covered by the subpoena, but that you couldn't find?

A: No.

Q: When did you undertake the search?

A: Just last week.

Q: How long did the search take?

A: About an hour.

Q: Tell me everything you did to collect the documents called for by the subpoena.

A: Well . . . .

After the witness has fully described the search made, including the locations searched, why, and what was found, be sure to suggest other possible locations of covered documents.

Explore whether the witness used to have responsive documents that were destroyed (and when and why they were destroyed) and, if so, whether anyone might have copies of the destroyed documents. In the context of this last question, ask about document retention and destruction policies.

> **Possible locations for covered documents**
>
> - *email archives;*
> - *computer files, including those on personal computers and servers, in backup files, and in archives;*
> - *documents in the possession of other individuals and entities;*
> - *notes and diaries;*
> - *microfilms, PowerPoint displays, spreadsheets, and other electronic files;*
> - *scanned documents; and*
> - *other devices with a memory such as iPads, smartphones, etc.*

If the witness is represented by counsel, it is still worth asking the witness how the search was conducted to ensure that all reasonable steps were taken to recover and provide responsive documents. If a privilege log has been provided, inquire about the entries on that log, including whether copies of the documents were sent to third parties and other facts that might undermine the privilege.

7.4 Moving on to Substantive Topics

While you should cover the foregoing preliminary matters to the extent appropriate, the bulk of the deposition must be devoted to the substantive issues in the case: the events underlying the claims and defenses in the litigation, as germane to the witness at hand. Keep an eye on your time, and move at an appropriate pace. Conduct the inquiry by applying to your specific circumstances the advice and techniques addressed more fully in other chapters, including the following:

> - **Use your outline as your guide:** you built a strong framework for the examination by researching the witness, deciding what facts you need to learn or confirm in light of your case theories, strategizing the order and priority of the topics, and choosing documents and other material to use as exhibits (Chapter Five).
>
> - **Be flexible:** deviate from the outline if the testimony calls for it (section 5.4).

- **Keep your eye on the goal:** focus on what you want from this witness (obtaining information, gaining admissions, preserving testimony, etc.) and why (summary judgment, trial) so you get what you need (Chapter One; section 5.4).

- **Use the right questioning techniques:** ask concise and clear questions that are phrased to gather information or obtain admissions most efficiently (Chapters Eight and Nine).

- **Use documents** as needed (Chapters Ten and Eleven).

CHECKLIST
PRELIMINARY MATTERS

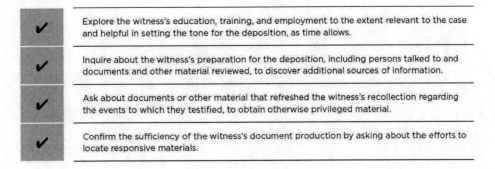

✔ Explore the witness's education, training, and employment to the extent relevant to the case and helpful in setting the tone for the deposition, as time allows.

✔ Inquire about the witness's preparation for the deposition, including persons talked to and documents and other material reviewed, to discover additional sources of information.

✔ Ask about documents or other material that refreshed the witness's recollection regarding the events to which they testified, to obtain otherwise privileged material.

✔ Confirm the sufficiency of the witness's document production by asking about the efforts to locate responsive materials.

CHAPTER EIGHT

QUESTIONING TECHNIQUES: GATHERING INFORMATION

If you do not know how to ask the right questions, you discover nothing.

—W. Edwards Deming

If one tells the truth, one is sure, sooner or later, to be found out.

—Oscar Wilde

A deposition will be more effective if you use the questioning techniques most suitable to your goal. While all questions should be concise and clear to maximize the chance the witness gives the desired information and to minimize opposing counsel's objections, your purpose for the questioning dictates how you phrase each question and what combination of questions you ask.

If the goal is to gather all the information the witness has on a subject, ask open-ended questions with exhaustive follow-up. If the goal is to get the witness to admit specific facts that can be used against the opposing party in a summary judgment motion or at trial, precise leading questions are in order. While it is possible to obtain new information with leading questions and elicit admissions through open-ended questions, it is far more efficient and beneficial to use open-ended questions to gather information and leading questions to obtain targeted admissions. In short,

In This Chapter:

- *How different purposes for depositions lead to different questioning methods*

- *Four essential techniques for learning what a witness knows*

- *The "funnel method"*

- *Different approaches to one universal subject of inquiry—conversations* match your questioning approach to the purpose of the inquiry and the type of response you want to get.

Let's look more closely at deposition purposes and how to gather all the witness's information.[1]

8.1 Revisiting Deposition Purposes and Their Relation to Question Form

In Chapter Two, we discussed four primary purposes of depositions: 1) gathering (and confirming) information, by which we obtain all the witness's knowledge on the issues in the litigation so we can best prepare our case; 2) obtaining admissions, so we get the specific facts we need to use against the opponent in a motion or at trial; 3) preserving testimony, particularly of persons who might not be available at the time of the motion or trial; and 4) facilitating settlement, by exposing the weakness of the other side's case, presenting the strength of our client's case, and gauging the effectiveness of the witness and opposing counsel.

In the chapters that followed, we saw how the purpose(s) of a deposition affect the choice of topics to be pursued. Now we address how the purpose of the deposition—and the purpose of each line of inquiry during the deposition—dictates the question form and techniques to accomplish that purpose most efficiently.

For any topic we tackle in a deposition, there will be one or more purposes for our questions. One purpose may be to find out the full extent of what the witness knows—for example, all of what a nonparty witness observed of the traffic accident, what the plaintiff claims their supervisor did that constitutes sexual harassment, or what the defendant says regarding her company's development of an allegedly infringing product. Even if we

> **Four Primary Purposes of Depositions**
>
> 1) *gathering (and confirming) information*
>
> 2) *obtaining admissions*
>
> 3) *preserving testimony*
>
> 4) *facilitating settlement*

already have an idea about some of the details based on our client's story, the allegations in the pleadings, our informal investigation, and the opponent's responses to our formal discovery requests, we want to confirm these facts with the witness to support our factual theory and case chronology (*see* Chapter Four). Usually, we can accomplish all of this through information-gathering questioning techniques, with open-ended questions and thorough follow-up designed to get the witness talking.

---

1. In Chapter Nine, we will address how to adapt cross-examination techniques to obtain usable admissions.

On these same subjects, we may have additional purposes that require us to incorporate other questioning techniques. We may want the witness to confess to very specific facts pertaining directly to an element of a claim for relief or a defense—in other words, facts that establish the legal theory suggested by our proof chart (*see* Chapter Four). This purpose—obtaining admissions—calls for asking leading questions in a calculated order.

And suppose we know that for health or other reasons the witness will not be available to sign an affidavit later or to testify at trial. In this deposition in lieu of an affidavit or live testimony, our purpose is to preserve testimony favorable to our case, without preserving harmful information as well. If the witness is favorable to our client and we can work with the witness before the deposition, we can ask open-ended questions as if conducting a direct examination at trial. But if we are deposing an adverse witness who might give unfavorable testimony, we will use the questioning techniques for gaining admissions.

Lastly, we may want the deposition to facilitate settlement. We can demonstrate the strength of our case by combining techniques for information-gathering and obtaining admissions, gaining settlement leverage and encouraging the other side to come to the negotiation table. We can also test our broader case theories by seeking admissions—challenging the witness with our characterization of the facts to which the witness has testified (such as, "it was your poor job performance that led to your dismissal," "the information was not treated confidentially as a trade secret") to gain a whopping concession. If the witness rejects our characterization, we turn to information-gathering follow-up questions to explore the reasons why.

The questioning techniques to accomplish our deposition purposes therefore fall into one of two broad categories: 1) techniques to gather information, and 2) techniques to obtain admissions. There is a difference between these two, as we've already hinted at. When gathering information, ask open-ended questions to encourage the witness to talk at length (e.g., "How did you discover the new protein-pump inhibitor?" "When?" "Where?" "Why?") and then follow up, exhausting the witness's knowledge. When seeking admissions, ask leading questions to encourage the witness to answer concisely—preferably "yes" or "no"—to one fact at a time, resulting in the clear admissions needed in summary judgment motions and trial.

Keeping these questioning goals and techniques straight is important. Do I want to get everything out of the witness's brain? That's information-gathering. Do I want to put words in the witness's mouth? That's gaining admissions.

In most situations, depose witnesses using information-gathering techniques to find out all the witness knows on material points, whether their testimony is good or bad for your client's position. The reason to obtain the good facts is obvious: it helps win the motion or trial or favorably settle the case. The reason to obtain the bad facts is equally important: it reveals what the other side will argue and attempt to prove, so we can attack their position, find contrary evidence, and refine our own position while we still have time to do so before summary judgment or trial.

Only rarely—very rarely—should you forsake information-gathering altogether. It is possible, as mentioned above, that you know an adverse witness will become unavailable to sign a declaration or to testify at trial. Because you do not want any negative information preserved in the transcript, choose only to obtain admissions favorable to your case. You may also elect to bypass information-gathering for a witness whose versions of events are circumscribed by documentary evidence and testimony from other deponents. There is still a serious risk in not finding out all of what the witness might say in a declaration or at trial, but that may be your strategic decision.

What happens much more often, however, is that deposing attorneys default to attempting to obtain admissions in a quasi-cross-examination that, due to poor design and execution, yields neither the witness's information nor usable admissions. This happens time and again. That is why the National Institute for Trial Advocacy has focused its deposition training programs on information-gathering skills, as well as skills in obtaining admissions, resulting in better deposition-takers across the country for the last half a century.

To be sure, gathering information and obtaining admissions are not mutually exclusive, and they can (and should, as necessary to obtain your deposition purposes) coexist and complement each other in a deposition. For example, while gathering information through exhaustive open-ended questioning, the answers may contain information that helps prove your case; or, while using open-ended questions to find out what the witness has to say, you may briefly turn to leading questions to grab admissions you need on that subject, and then return to open-ended questions. As an alternative, after gathering all the witness's information on a topic (conversation, meeting, etc.), you can switch to questioning techniques to gain admissions, asking leading questions to highlight the key facts and create a stand-alone segment in the transcript or video recording that can be used readily for summary judgment or powerfully at trial. As yet another example, in your attempt to obtain admissions with leading questions, it may be that the witness denies your efforts, and you bring into play your information-gathering skills to obtain all the facts and reasons the witness can muster for the denial, allowing you to plan how to rebut it later.

> **Information-gathering:**
>
> *I want to get everything out of the witness's brain.*
>
> **Gaining admissions:**
>
> *I want to put words in the witness's mouth.*

Nonetheless, you must first be able to distinguish in your own mind the difference between questioning to gather information and questioning to obtain admissions. Now let's look at the techniques for gathering all the witness's information.

8.2 Essential Questioning Techniques for Gathering Information

When engaged in information-gathering, you want to know everything the witness has to say on a topic, both good and bad. To gather this information thoroughly and efficiently, apply three essential techniques: open-ended questions, as discussed above; follow up to obtain the witness's full answer to the question; and clarification of the witness's answer and elicitation of further detail. Incorporate a fourth technique—closing off—to make sure that the witness is locked into the deposition testimony and cannot vary from it in a summary judgment motion or at trial.

8.2.1 Open-Ended Questions

Fundamentally, obtaining information efficiently involves the use of open-ended questions—such as "who," "what," "when," "where," "why," or "how"—which encourage the witness to disclose all their responsive information, as opposed to leading questions that invite the witness to say just "yes" or "no" to one specific fact. To contrast the use of leading questions and the use of open-ended questions in the search for information, here is a silly example that will make the point. The use of narrow, leading, suggestive questions would look like this:

Q: Once you got to the store, did you buy meat?

A: No.

Q: Didn't you buy ham?

A: No.

Q: Did you buy any kind of meat?

A: No.

Q: Did you buy vegetables?

A: Yes.

Q: You bought green vegetables, correct?

A: No.

Q: You didn't buy green vegetables?

A: No.

Q: You bought potatoes?

A: Are potatoes a vegetable?

Q: Well, I don't know. But did you buy potatoes?

A: No.

> Q: You bought squash?
>
> A: No.

As opposed to this approach, with a single open-ended question:

> Q: Once you got to the store, what did you buy?
>
> A: Tomatoes.

This scenario is simplistic, but the first example's floundering adherence to leading questions, or "did you" questions, reflects the poor attempts at gaining information that we see all too often in actual depositions. Open-ended questions are a much more efficient means of getting information out of a witness, particularly because of the way witnesses are prepared for their deposition. A standard directive in witness preparation is, "Listen to the question, answer only the question asked, do not volunteer." That advice results in the witness giving "yes" or "no" responses to leading questions that inquire into one specific fact, but it does not have much effect on the witness's response to open-ended questions, which force the witness to answer with substantive information.

8.2.2 Pursuing the Witness's Entire Answer

The witness's initial answer may disclose only part of the information the witness has in response to a question. Sometimes witnesses are not forthcoming with the entirety of their information because they are hiding something; sometimes it is because they just forgot about it, or they might not think all the information is necessary. Whatever the witness's motivation, follow up on the answer to make sure the witness has disclosed everything. A typical follow-up is as simple as "What else?" or "Anything else?" Here's an example, returning to our hypothetical:

> Q: Once you got to the store, what did you buy?
>
> A: Tomatoes.
>
> Q: What else did you buy?
>
> A: Uh, onions.
>
> Q: What else?
>
> A: That's it.
>
> Q: So you bought tomatoes and onions, and nothing else?
>
> A: Yes, that's it.

8.2.3 Clarifying and Obtaining Further Details

Once you obtain the witness's full response to a question, it's time to flesh out the witness's response to obtain greater clarity and detail. This is accomplished with open-ended questions, supplemented by narrower, more suggestive questions as needed to prompt the witness to add details you believe exist—or hope exist. Here is an example:

Q: Let's talk about the tomatoes you bought. What kind of tomatoes did you buy?

A: Heirloom. Always heirloom.

Q: Why always heirloom?

A: Oh my gosh, they taste so much better.

Q: Why do they taste better?

A: They're more . . . tomato-ish.

Q: Interesting. What do you mean by tomato-ish?

A: I can't explain it, really.

Q: Do you mean less bland?

A: Yes, right. Stronger. More tomato-ish.

Q: Besides their taste, why else do you choose heirlooms for your tomatoes?

A: That's it.

Q: Is it because of their color?

A: No.

Q: Is it because of their shape?

A: No. Well, yes. They have more interesting shapes.

Q: How so?

A: They're not always round and smooth; they have more creases.

Q: Are there any other reasons you always choose heirloom tomatoes?

A: No.

Q: Were there any other reasons you chose heirloom tomatoes in June?

A: No.

> **The Four Essential Techniques for Obtaining Information:**
>
> - Use open-ended questions;
> - follow up to ensure a full answer;
> - clarify and explore the details; and
> - close off the witness from giving a different or additional answer after the deposition is over.

Of course, you would continue eliciting details relevant to the case—perhaps the number of tomatoes, their size, why tomatoes were purchased, etc.—but you get the idea.

8.2.4   *Locking the Witness In*

After using primarily open-ended questions to elicit the witness's information and following up with some probing questions, we need the witness to say they have no further information about the topic so it will be more difficult for the witness to later say—in a declaration opposing a summary judgment motion or on cross-examination at trial—that they had more to relate on the topic but were never specifically asked at the deposition. As we'll discuss a bit later in the chapter, the technique may recap what the witness has said and include a more leading question to the effect of, "Have you now told me everything about [the meeting / the conversation / your duties / your process]?" Returning to our hypothetical, here is an example:

> Q: So just to confirm, you bought two tomatoes and one onion at the store for roughly $7, and nothing else, because you were making guacamole and had the other ingredients at home. Correct?
>
> A: Yeah, that's right.
>
> Q: Have you now told me all that you bought at the store?
>
> A: Yes.
>
> Q: Have you now told me all the reasons you bought what you bought?
>
> A: Yes.

To sum up, the four essential techniques for obtaining information from the witness are: use open-ended questions, follow up to make sure the witness has given a full answer, clarify and explore the details of the witness's answer, and ultimately close off the witness from later giving a different or additional answer after the deposition is over.

While these are the fundamental techniques, to apply them well we need to have a framework for using them. And the best framework for implementing these techniques in an orderly trek through a topic is the "funnel method," to which we turn next.

8.3   The Funnel Method

The funnel method is the most foolproof mechanism for gathering information in a deposition. Its name derives from the shape of a funnel—broad and open at the top, increasingly narrow toward the bottom—and resulting in a focused output of material ready for use. The funnel method of deposition questioning starts at the top of a topic with broad and open-ended questions, proceeds with increasingly narrow questions as you exhaust the witness's knowledge and hone in on the details, and results in fixed testimony ready for use in case planning, motions, and trial.

To help conceptualize the funnel method and its essential techniques of gathering information, check out this diagram:

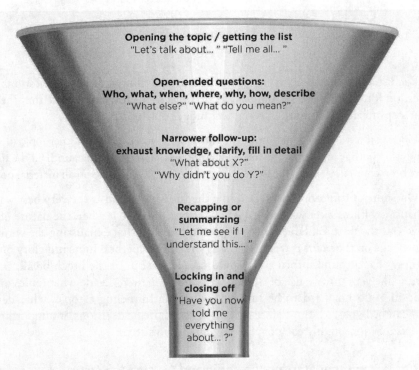

Opening the topic / getting the list
"Let's talk about... " "Tell me all... "

Open-ended questions:
Who, what, when, where, why, how, describe
"What else?" "What do you mean?"

Narrower follow-up:
exhaust knowledge, clarify, fill in detail
"What about X?"
"Why didn't you do Y?"

Recapping or
summarizing
"Let me see if I
understand this... "

Locking in and
closing off
"Have you now
told me
everything
about... ?"

There are five fundamental steps of the funnel method:[2]

1) Start the topic and get a "list";

2) explore each item on the list initially through open-ended questions;

---

2. The funnel method has endured numerous iterations over the years. It has been said to have five levels, six levels, and as many as thirteen levels. The description in this edition synthesizes what the author has found easiest for attorneys to digest and apply. The essential point, no matter how many levels or stages or steps it might be described as having, is that the questioner starts the topic broadly with open-ended questions, follows up to exhaust the witness's knowledge and clarify the witness's answer, and locks in the witness to their testimony, through progressively narrower and more leading questions. (Yet another concept of the funnel, embodying all aspects of witness examination, is described in section 9.7.)

> 3) follow up with narrower questions to clarify the witness's answer and obtain additional details to exhaust the witness's knowledge;
>
> 4) recap or summarize the witness's testimony to confirm completeness and understanding; and
>
> 5) close off the witness's testimony.

Each step has a different function with correspondingly different questions and question form, proceeding from broad questions to narrow ones. Note that the last four steps relate to the four essential techniques outlined previously.

Once you have applied the funnel method to one topic, go to another topic in your deposition outline and apply the funnel method to that second topic, until all the topics have been covered, yielding the fullness of the witness's knowledge on all material points.

One note of caution, however. While the funnel method is the very best way to exhaust a witness's knowledge, it takes a lot of time. Use it when the nature of the topic and the time available for the deposition suggest that exhausting the witness's knowledge on the point is worth it. Using the funnel method in its full glory on the witness's background information could take at least until the lunch break, which is very likely an unwise use of time. As a strategic matter, decide what topics of the deposition do not need to be funneled, or while funneling a topic, what details that can be bypassed. But before making those strategic decisions, it's important to understand thoroughly each of the funnel method's steps.

8.3.1 Step One: Starting the Topic and Getting the List

Begin the topic of inquiry by asking a broad question or questions that elicit the general scope of the witness's relevant knowledge. There are several goals here: get the witness talking; get an idea of the breadth of the witness's knowledge on the topic at the outset—before delving into any of the details—so you don't get lost in the minutia of one aspect of the witness's testimony and never get to the rest of what the witness has to say; and get the witness to offer a list of facts or subtopics that give you a structure for asking follow-up questions and obtaining all the witness's information.

Depending on the nature of the topic, here are a few specific ways to start out: the overview, the structured overview, or generating a list.

The Overview

When addressing a new topic, some attorneys begin with an overview question to get an idea of what the witness will be offering as the questioning proceeds.

The overview question prompts the witness to reveal the facts they consider important—or, at least, the facts they are willing to tell you initially. Generally, the more open the question, the more you will learn from the witness.

In a contract case, for example, the overview question might be: "Tell me how this transaction came about." In a personal injury case, it could be: "Tell me about this accident." The witness would answer with a barrage of facts, each one of which you would then explore, asking follow-up questions. Such broadly-worded overview questions, however, may be *too* broad, leaving a witness bewildered and prompting opposing counsel to object that the question calls for a narrative.

The Structured Overview

Another way to start the topic is to ask the broad but more structured questions of "who," "what," "when," "where," "why," and "how." So, in our personal injury scenario, the opening of the topic may include questions like this:

> Q: I'd like to talk to you about the accident you witnessed in this case. When did the accident take place?
>
> Q: Where was it?
>
> Q: Where were you?
>
> Q: What did you see?

Each of these questions—when, where, and what—elicits answers requiring follow-up questions. In particular, the "what did you see" question will elicit an answer referring to more than one fact: a person typically sees more than one thing when observing any event or transaction. Regarding a motor vehicle accident, for example, the witness will have seen the cars approach each other, the cars colliding, people scattering, the victims displaying injuries, etc. In the ensuing phases of the funnel method, you will elicit the details of each thing the witness observed.

Generating a List

A similar way of starting a topic is to think of it as asking questions that will prompt the witness to answer with a list of facts, on each of which you can follow up. The key to this approach is to get the *whole* list—all the witness's answers to your initial broad question—using the follow-up questions "what else" and "what about." Only after getting the whole list in response to the initial question should you seek out the details of each item on the list.

This approach works well where the topic has to do with job duties, components, processes, and procedures. Let's look at some examples.

Example: Job duties. Assume that the shipping manager at a parts supplier is being deposed about the topic of their job responsibilities. Getting "the list" of responsibilities might look like this:

Q: What are your responsibilities as shipping manager?

A: I am in charge of all shipments going out of the company.

Q: What other responsibilities do you have as shipping manager?

A: If insurance is required on a shipment, I also arrange that.

Q: What else?

A: I have to arrange the type of shipping used.

Q: Do you have any other responsibilities as shipping manager?

A: I have to make sure that the amount of the shipping charges is passed on to billing.

Q: What else?

A: That's everything.

Q: What about ordering shipping supplies?

A: No.

Q: So you're in charge of outgoing shipments, arrange insurance and type of shipping, and make sure the shipping charges are passed on to billing. Have you now told me all of your responsibilities as shipping manager?

A: Yes, that's it.

Notice what the deposing attorney did in this example to get the *full list* of job responsibilities.

- **First, the deposing attorney asked about possible additional items that might belong on the list,** asking "What else?" and probing with the more suggestive question, "What about ordering shipping supplies?" Witnesses sometimes answer initially with only the information they want you to have or feel comfortable sharing, hoping you will move on to another question. Probing with "what else" and suggestive questions makes sure that we get the whole list of items responsive to the question.

- **Second, the deposing attorney had the witness confirm it was a complete list,** using the question, "have you now told me all of your responsibilities as shipping manager?" This type of question gets the witness to commit, as much as possible, that the witness has answered fully, so it is less likely or less credible for the witness to come up with additional information after the deposition in a summary judgment declaration or at trial.

- **Third, the deposing attorney got the list of responsibilities first,** before trying to explore or go into detail about any part of the witness's answer. This avoids distracting the witness from recalling information (or distracting ourselves from seeking all this information) by interrupting with questions about details. The idea is to get an overview of the witness's knowledge—the entirety of the list—with the details to follow later. The list, the whole list, and nothing but the list.

Example: Procedures. If the topic is a witness's or company's processes or procedures—anything that has different steps in it—it is easy to generate a list for further inquiry. Here is an example:

Q: I'd like to talk about the procedure you have for investigating a sexual harassment complaint, as you've defined it. Basically, I want to start by having you identify all the different steps in your procedure from beginning to end. So, after a sexual harassment complaint has been received by your office, what is the first step in your response?

A: Either I or another HR person reads it.

Q: Does the procedure after that differ depending on whether you read it or another HR person reads it?

A: No.

Q: Okay. So, after you read the complaint, what do you do?

A: Check the files for any other complaints by the complainant or against the alleged wrongdoer.

Q: What comes next?

A: We interview the complainant.

Q: And then what?

. . .

Q: What's next?

A: That's it.

Q: We'll go over each of these steps in more detail, but have you now told me each step in your response to a sexual harassment complaint?

A: Yes.

Notice that, in this example, the attorney started the questioning by explaining to the witness exactly what the attorney wanted the witness to provide in the examination: "identify all the different steps in your procedure from beginning to end." Not only does this help the witness understand what they are being asked to do, it encourages the witness to give complete information. It also gives the deposing attorney something to point to later if the witness tries to testify in a motion or at trial that there is another step in the procedure. The attempt will not seem credible if it is clear from the deposition transcript that the witness had been asked for all the steps at the deposition.

Example: Chronology. Obtaining a chronology of an event can accomplish the purposes of "getting a list." For example, getting a chronological list from the plaintiff in a personal injury case might go something like this:

Q: I want you to take me through what happened that day from the moment you left the house until the accident occurred. When did you leave the house?

A: About 8:15 in the morning.

Q: What's the first thing you did after you left the house?

A: I got in the car, started it, pulled out of the driveway, and drove down 15th Street.

Q: What next?

A: As I approached the intersection with Yale Street, I saw a car stopped at the stop sign on Yale.

Q: What happened next?

A: I was going through the intersection, and the car at the stop sign suddenly shot forward and hit my car.

Q: What next?

A: I heard a big crash, and I was thrown against the door.

Q: What happened next?

A: I was in a lot of pain, and someone must have called an ambulance because I was then taken to the hospital.

Once you have obtained the full "list" of what occurred, it will be time to proceed to step two in the funnel method and explore one or more of the items on that list.

8.3.2 Step Two: Top of the Funnel—Open-Ended Questions

Having gotten the full list, decide which items on the list are worth exploring and which items can be ignored or postponed for later inquiry if time permits. For example, having learned the full list of the witness's duties, you can examine the witness on each of those duties in turn or simply choose one or two. Generally, the more important the topic, the more you will want to explore each item—e.g., each job duty, each step in the investigation procedure, each thing the witness observed of the accident, or each conversation the defendant had with the plaintiff. If you are worried about how much time this will take, pursue the important items first. If multiple items are important, tackle them chronologically or in order of importance to the case. But be methodical, addressing each of these items one at a time.

To explore ("funnel") an item on the list, start at the top of the funnel with open-ended questions. Again, the classic "reporter's questions"—who, what, when, where, why, and how—supplemented by "describe," "explain," and "tell me about"—invite narrative answers and encourage witnesses to reveal what they know. Open-ended questions make it much more difficult for the witness to hide information or evade the question.[3]

Using one of our prior scenarios, the deposing attorney could learn more about one of the witness's job duties by asking the witness to "explain" it or to "describe" how the witness does it. A more thorough examination results, however, if the deposing attorney includes the "who," "what," "when," "where," "why," and "how" questions. Here is an example:

Q: Let's look at one of the job duties you mentioned—arranging insurance if required. What do you mean by, "if required."

A: If the customer asked for it on the order form.

Q: What other ways would it be "required?"

A: Well, none. That's it.

Q: When do you arrange for insurance?

A: As soon as I've confirmed inventory, but before I've forwarded the order to the shipping department.

Q: How do you arrange for the insurance?

A: I figure out the value and refer to the shipper's price for insurance.

Q: How do you figure out the value?

A: It's declared by the customer on the order form.

---

3. Many lawyers never get the full benefit of a deposition because they ask only narrow questions calling for "yes" or "no" answers. We are not sure why there is this aversion to open-ended questions—perhaps a need to maintain control, a view of the case that goes no further than what is already in their head, or a fear of a "bad" answer—but they should keep the open-ended questioning techniques of the funnel method in mind as a way to organize the inquiry and maximize the chance to learn all the witness's relevant information.

Q: Is there any other way to figure out the value?

A: No, just their declaration.

Q: How do you get the shipper's price?

A: It's listed on their website. Sometimes I call if I have to.

Q: When do you have to call?

A: If it's not on the website.

Q: What other times do you have to call?

A: None that I can think of. Well, wait. I call to check if there's a difference depending on the ship method and date and maybe a discount is available. That doesn't happen very often, but yeah.

Of course, the exact "who," "what," "when," "where," "why," "how" questions you ask will depend on the information you need in the case, but again, you get the idea.

8.3.3 *Step Three: Middle Funnel—Narrower Suggestive Questions for Detail and Clarity*

Although broad, open-ended questions are important to start with because they elicit the witness's information most efficiently, they are usually not enough to obtain the witness's full knowledge. To unearth the relevant details that the witness is less likely or less willing to disclose, ask more focused follow-up questions that exhaust the witness's knowledge and fill in the gaps left in their testimony. To put it another way, move the inquiry down to a narrower part of the funnel: make your questioning narrower and more suggestive as you progress from hearing what the witness has volunteered to clarifying and adding to what the witness has said.[4]

Some of these follow-up questions will still be open-ended but will be more narrowly tailored to the specific facts the deposing attorney is seeking. For example:

Q: Where was the accident?

A: In San Francisco.

Q: Where in San Francisco?

A: The Mission District.

Q: Where in the Mission District?

---

4. This can also be a good juncture to introduce documents, photographs, and other exhibits to jog the witness's memory. Alternatively, present the exhibits to the witness further down the line. Either way, the funnel method seeks the witness's unaided recollection before turning to documents that might shape the witness's testimony. We discuss the use of documents in detail in Chapter Ten.

National Institute for Trial Advocacy

A: The intersection of Van Ness and 16th Street.

Q: In what part of the intersection did the cars collide?

A: Just entering the intersection from the left turn lane on 16th.

Q: How many feet from the crosswalk did your car strike the plaintiff's car?

A: About 10 feet.

Other follow-up questions will be less open-ended and more suggestive, starting with "was it," "did you," "were you," "what about," "did you consider," and the like. For example:

Q: What color was the car?

A: Red.

Q: What shade of red?

A: Oh my gosh, I don't know. It was red.

Q: Was it closer to dark red like blood, or closer to bright red like a fire engine?

A: It was closer to a fire engine.

Returning to a previous scenario, here is yet another example of suggesting additional facts to see if they trigger the witness's further recall. (Asking about these additional facts is also a good way of confirming favorable facts you've learned from the client or from other discovery.)

Q: What do you do when arranging shipping?

A: I choose a shipper and fill out the shipping documents online, which generates a shipping date. Then I have the shipment ready at that time, and the shipper comes and takes the shipment away.

Q: What else?

A: That's it.

Q: Do you also arrange for insurance on the shipment?

A: Oh, that's right. I do arrange for insurance by filling out an insurance form.

Q: Do you email the customer to confirm the shipment date?

A: Yes, I do that, too.[5]

---

5. When suggesting new facts to find out more information, the deposing attorney should usually only suggest facts that are neutral or helpful to the client's case. It is possible, however, to ask

Last but not least, here is an example of using an exhibit to prompt the disclosure of additional information.

Q: What do you do when arranging shipping?

A: I choose a shipper and fill out the shipping documents online, which generates a shipping date. Then I have the shipment ready at that time, and the shipper comes and takes the shipment away.

Q: What else?

A: That's it.

Q: Do you also arrange for insurance on the shipment?

A: Uh, well, I don't arrange for insurance, no.

Q: Let me show you what's been premarked as Exhibit 32. That's a letter to you from Tompkins Insurance dated June 16, 2019, correct?

A: Yeah.

Q: Does it appear to you to be a true and accurate copy?

A: Yeah . . . Oh, yeah, I see. Yeah, I did arrange for them to handle the insurance.

8.3.4 Step Four: Middle/Bottom of the Funnel—Recapping and Summarizing

The process of asking open-ended questions (top of the funnel) and following up with narrower and more suggestive questions (mid-funnel) elicits a lot of information, some of which may be difficult to follow. Therefore, towards the bottom of the funnel, recapitulate or summarize the testimony and ask if the witness agrees with the synopsis. If you have not summarized the testimony correctly, or if the witness realizes that they omitted responsive information, the witness may provide further clarification or details. If the witness agrees that you summarized the testimony correctly, proceed to the next step in the funnel.

Summary questions have a bonus effect of distilling dozens of pages of testimony to a smaller passage of text that can be more easily used in cross-examination or motions practice.

---

questions about potential bad facts to try to get the witness to deny them. "Q: You aren't responsible for packing the shipment, are you? A: No, they are packed by the production division." Notice how the question form changed to a leading question to prompt the witness to answer a certain way. This is where the information-gathering function of the funnel method meshes with (or momentarily gives way to) the questioning techniques for gaining admissions, discussed in the next chapter.

Here's an example. Assume that the deposition focuses on obtaining a list of a purchasing agent's job responsibilities. After a series of long and rambling answers, you become concerned whether you understand the testimony correctly. One method of bringing clarity is to recapitulate the answers:

> Q: Let me see if I understand you. One of your duties as purchasing agent is to determine what items need to be purchased for a production job?
>
> A: Correct.
>
> Q: You are also responsible for determining from which vendor the parts should be purchased?
>
> A: Right.
>
> Q: You also have to decide on the shipping method?
>
> A: Yes.

Continue in this vein until you have fully summarized the witness's testimony about duties. Another approach is to accomplish the task with just one question:

> Q: Let me see if I understand. Your duties are to determine what needs to be purchased, determine what vendor to use, and decide on a shipping method. Is that right?
>
> A: Yes.

Sometimes the recapitulation or summarization prompts the witness to provide clarifying information:

> Q: Let me see if I understand. Your duties are to determine what needs to be purchased, determine what vendor to use, and decide on a shipping method. Is that right?
>
> A: Well, technically, I recommend the shipping method to the boss and he decides it.
>
> Q: Okay, so you determine what needs to be purchased, determine what vendor to use, and recommend the shipping method to your boss.
>
> A: That's right.

Before we leave our discussion of Step Four, there are two more things to note about summarizing the witness's testimony. First, when you provide the summary and ask if it was accurate, opposing counsel will inevitably object that the question "misstates the witness's testimony." The witness is still supposed to answer. If the witness takes up counsel's refrain and claims that the summary is incorrect, have the witness explain exactly why it is inaccurate.

Second, use summarizing with caution if the witness blurted out some very helpful information: upon hearing the prior answer summarized, the witness may not like what they said and try to qualify or retract it. Therefore, be wary of repeating what you think is a favorable answer if you believe the witness may take the answer back. This is a judgment call; weigh the need to make sure you understand the witness's testimony, the possibility of locking the witness into a favorable disclosure, and the risk of the witness recanting.

8.3.5 Step Five: Bottom of the Funnel—Locking In and Closing Off

An important goal at a deposition is to prevent the witness from later

Keys to Using the Funnel:

- Use open-ended questions as much as possible before probing with narrower, suggestive questions and closing off.

- Keep questions clear and concise.

- Listen to the witness and watch for nonverbal clues.

- Funnel within the funnel.

- Return to another part of the funnel as needed.

- Use the funnel to obtain exhaustive discovery on important topics.

surprising you at trial or in a motion for summary judgment with new information that the witness did not disclose during their deposition.[6] After finding out what the witness knows (or doesn't know) about a topic through open-ended questions, narrower follow-up questions, and perhaps a summary or recapitulation, lock the witness into their answers so there will be no surprises later.

One method of locking in the witness and closing the witness off from changing the testimony is to ask: "Have you now told me everything that was [said, done, etc.] about [this topic]?" For example, if examining a human resources manager at a defendant company about everything they had done in response to receiving an employee's complaint about an incident of sexual harassment, close off the

---

6. Most jurisdictions limit the extent to which a deponent can contradict deposition testimony in a later affidavit supporting or opposing a summary judgment motion, especially if the affidavit is being used to create a triable issue of material fact to avoid summary judgment. *E.g.*, Perma Rsch. & Dev. Co. v. Singer Co., 410 F.2d 572, 577–78 (2d Cir. 1969) (conversation described in affidavit was disregarded where it was not mentioned in response to repeated inquiry about the basis for an alleged fraud); Yeager v. Bowlin, 693 F.3d 1076, 1080–81 (9th Cir. 2012) (facts asserted in affidavit were disregarded where they would have been responsive to deposition questions answered "I don't recall"). In addition, a deponent who testifies at trial inconsistent with their deposition testimony can be impeached with the prior inconsistent statements in the deposition (Rule 32(a)(2)). In both situations, it will be important for the deposition transcript to show that the testimony in the deposition was the witness's complete answer to the questions posed.

examination on that topic by asking: "Have you now told me everything you did in response to the plaintiff's complaint to your office about sexual harassment?"

This technique flows naturally from the recapping and summarizing step. Here's how it would be done using the example given in the preceding subchapter:

Q: Okay, so you determine what needs to be purchased, determine what vendor to use, and recommend to your boss the shipping method.

A: That's right.

Q: Have you now told me all the steps in performing your duty of ordering parts?

A: Yes.

Witnesses and defending counsel may resist your efforts to lock in and close off the witness. Sometimes witnesses are trying to hide information; sometimes they are just concerned they might have forgotten something and do not want to be precluded from testifying about it later. Whatever the motivation, witnesses may resort to evasive or qualified answers that could give them an out from their deposition testimony, such as "that's all I recall at this time," "generally that's it," or "that's about all." We deal with these situations in section 12.4, but for now suffice to say: challenge these answers with queries such as "what might help you recall more information," "where is that material," "who would you talk with to get more information," "you said 'generally that's it,' but is there anything you've not mentioned," or "you said 'that's about all,' so what else is there?" Such questions, along with some follow-up, limit the chances the witness can legitimately come up with additional information later, thereby locking in their testimony as much as possible.

8.3.6   Going to the Next Item on the List

After locking in and closing off the witness, you have finished funneling the first item on the list (e.g., the first duty on the witness's list of job duties). Proceed to the next item on the list that is worthy of inquiry (e.g., another job duty), funneling that item to the extent it is useful and time allows. After covering all the items on the "list" that you want to cover (e.g., all the job duties), you would proceed to your next topic in the deposition outline (e.g., what occurred on the day the plant exploded).

> *To view a video demonstration of Questioning Techniques: Gathering Information (Using the Funnel Method), scan the QR code (print version) or click here.*

8.4 Tips on Using the Funnel Method

As a practical matter, keep the following in mind when using the funnel method to find out the witness's information, follow up on the witness's answers, and exhaust the witness's knowledge of the subject.

8.4.1 *Stick with Open-Ended Questions as Much as Possible*

There is a natural tendency to ask an open-ended "who," "what," "where," "when," "why," or "how" question and then quickly resort to "did you" or leading questions to get the answer you want or expect. Resist that temptation. Remember that open-ended questions are the most efficient way to get information out of the witness and will prompt the witness to say far more than any other question form. If the purpose of the deposition is to gather information, you want to get everything that the witness might say, not just what you hope or expect. Only when you cannot think of any more open-ended questions (both broad and narrow) should you resort to the "did you" or leading questions.

8.4.2 *Keep Questions Concise and Clear*

Omit filler words that add nothing but length to your question. For example, instead of "Can you tell me what you said at the meeting," which technically calls for "yes" or "no," just ask, "What did you say at the meeting?" Extra words cost a lot of time over the course of the deposition.

Avoid words that undermine your efforts to get the witness's full information. For example, omit language that suggests the witness might not recall: "Do you remember what you said at the meeting" often results in the witness not remembering. "Tell me a little about that" or "What were some of the things discussed" gets you only part of the story. By contrast, broad questions encourage a broad response: "What did you look at" elicits more than "What documents did you review."

When you resort to a "did you" or "were you" question, incorporate a temporal element for clarity (and to minimize a vagueness objection): "Did you tell Ms. Katsumura at the July meeting?" or "Did you ever tell Ms. Katsumura?"

8.4.3   *Listen, Observe, and Take Notes*

To obtain the witness's complete information, carefully listen to what the witness is saying (and not saying) and observe how the witness is saying it. There may be an aspect of a question that the witness is ignoring, something the witness is leaving out of an answer, or a nonverbal gesture or expression that provides clues to the witness's response. All of this is important for asking follow-up questions.

Listen to make sure you really comprehend the witness's answers. This is more difficult than it seems because we tend to hear what we want to hear based on our own mindset or our pre-existing understanding of the facts. Make sure that you understand how the witness is using a word; do not assume that it is being used as you might use it. Similarly, make sure the witness's depiction of an event or conversation is so clear and complete that a disinterested third party who knows nothing about the case could picture what occurred. If the witness's testimony does not create a clear and complete picture, ask more follow-up questions to fill in the gaps. Follow-up questions as simple as, "What do you mean," and "Why" are indispensable to the funnel method. Only then will you exhaust the witness's knowledge and discover how the witness might testify in trial or in a declaration.

Listen for non-responsive, evasive, or hedged answers. An inattentive deposing attorney can miss things like the following:

Q: Did you talk with the defendant about what had happened?

A: Not on that day.

Q: Did you let your employer know what had happened? [switching to a different topic]

The witness's answer begged for a follow-up question. The lawyer should have detected the nuance in "Not on *that* day" and asked:

Q: If you didn't talk with the defendant that day about what happened, when did you talk with him? [or]

Q: What day did you talk with the defendant about what happened? [or]

Q: Was there any day you talked with the defendant about what happened?

Witnesses hedge in other ways, inserting into their answers "as far as I remember now," "generally," "usually," and the like. We address this in section 12.4.4 at length, but the upshot is to follow up with the witness to obtain the entirety of their information (for example, "You said 'generally'; what are the exceptions?").

Take a few notes but observe the witness. Getting the witness's complete information also requires some level of notetaking on your part, because the funnel method involves eliciting a list (e.g., all the duties of the defendant at their current job position) and then following up on each item on that list one at a time. Without jotting down the list, it will be harder to make sure the items on the list get covered.

At the same time, keep your notes simple and jot them quickly. Do not be so focused on taking notes that you look at the laptop screen or the yellow pad more than the witness. Looking at the witness is important, not only to put the witness on the spot, but also to observe nonverbal clues the witness may display. If you are busy looking at notes, you will miss the witness's fidgeting and tells of deception, the witness looking at defending counsel as if begging for help in answering the question, and the witness's look of distress when the questioning ventures into an area the witness wants to avoid because of what they might have to disclose.

8.4.4 *Funnel within a Funnel*

Sometimes while you funnel a topic by asking open-ended and then increasingly narrow questions to exhaust the witness's knowledge, the witness's answer will indicate that you need to find out more information about part of the answer before proceeding. Here is an example:

Q: So, let's talk about your observations after the cars collided. Where were you?

A: Still on the sidewalk.

Q: In the same exact location?

A: Yeah, I was still standing there on the corner. I mean, I think I took a step closer to get a better look but yeah, I was there on the corner still.

Q: What did you see?

A: Some guy ran up to the red car with a baseball bat and started pounding on the blue car and denting it like in the hood and stuff and then smashed the window and I thought he was going to, like, kill that guy. Like, seriously.

Q: Ok, let's focus on the guy for a moment. What did he look like?

A: Heavy-set, like muscular, light skinned.

Q: What color was his hair?

A: Red.

Q: How long was his hair?

A: Uh, I don't know. Like, regular. Not like a buzz cut, not shoulder length. Just regular.

Q: What was he wearing?

A: Jeans and some kind of white shirt.

Q: What kind of shirt?

A: T-shirt, you know. Not like undershirt, but some T-shirt with a logo on it.

Q: What logo was it?

A: I have no idea.

Q: What else was he wearing?

A: Uh, sunglasses, I think.

Q: How tall was he?

A: About 6 feet, give or take an inch or two.

Q: Was there anything else about the guy who hit the blue car with the baseball bat?

A: No.

Q: Did he have any facial hair?

A: Oh yeah, I think so. Yeah, like a goatee. That's right.

Q: Anything else you can tell me about him?

A: Nah.

Q: Did you get a picture of him?

A: No.

Q: Hear anyone call out his name?

A: No.

Q: Have you ever seen him before that time or since that time?

A: Never.

Q: Ok, let's go back to what you saw him do. . . .

8.4.5 *Return to the Top of the Funnel If Needed*

Toward the bottom of the funnel, while recapping the witness's testimony and asking more pointed questions, the witness may respond with new information that must be explored; to do so, return to the top of the funnel, so to speak. Ask open-ended questions and follow up to obtain all the details about the new information the witness has revealed.

For example, assume the deposition is of a key witness to an automobile collision, and the witness has earlier testified about seeing the accident occur. The questioning has proceeded to the bottom of the funnel:

Q: So, you said you were working in the service bay of the BP station around 3:30, looked up when you heard the screech of brakes, and saw the red car hit the blue car?

A: Well, yeah. When she screamed.

Q: Wait, who screamed?

A: Some lady.

Q: What was she screaming?

A: "Look out!"

Q: How many times did she scream "look out"?

A: Just once that I heard.

Q: Did you see this lady?

A: No.

Q: When did she scream in relation to the screech of the brakes?

A: Right before.

Q: So, was the sequence that you heard the scream, then you heard the brakes, and then you looked?

A: Yeah, that was it.

Q: Okay. So, you were working in the service bay of the BP station around 3:30, heard a lady scream "look out," then heard brakes screech, and then you looked and saw the red car hit the blue car?

A: Exactly.

8.4.6   *Exhausting Does Not Have to Be Exhausting*

The time limit on depositions means you must judge how far to exhaust the witness's information about a topic. Your decision will turn on factors including the time available in the deposition, the importance of the topic in relationship to the other topics to be covered, and the constraints of the litigation budget in the case. Generally, less-experienced attorneys do not follow up enough. But it is also quite common, particularly in high-stakes litigation, to encounter lawyers who spend what seems to be endless hours exhausting the witness's knowledge about marginally relevant topics in what are known as "scorched earth depositions." Such an approach is expensive to the client and loses sight of the true issues in the litigation.

Your goal is finding out everything reasonably important to understanding, analyzing, and presenting the case—but not to waste time exhausting the witness's knowledge about details that will never play a role in adjudicating the dispute.

8.5 Obtaining Information About Conversations

One of the most common topics of inquiry in a deposition is a conversation the party or parties had in the events underlying the litigation. The conversation may have been held in person, by phone, by online chat, by videoconference, or even electronically in the form of emails and texts. No matter what form the conversation took, you must know how to obtain the witness's full information about the conversation in an efficient manner.

The standard funnel method works well. For each conversation, ask "who (was there)," "when (was the conversation)," "how long (did it last), "where (did it occur)," "why (was the conversation held)," and "how (were people connected)," and then explore the "what"—that is, what was said during the conversation—following up with further open-ended questions and increasingly more focused and suggestive questions to obtain the witness's full information.

Some more specialized templates have been developed for examinations about conversations. These are essentially applications of the funnel method, worth considering for conversations critical to the case. We'll begin by looking at the necessary components of an examination about a conversation, and then turn to the amount of detail to elicit, a standard litany for an examination on a conversation, and the "Four Cs" approach to conversations.

8.5.1 Necessary Components

In examining the witness about conversations, explore these key points:

- **The mode of conversation**—whether conducted in person, by telephone, by text, by Zoom or FaceTime, by some other method, or some combination;

- **The witness's basis for knowing about the conversation**—preferably the witness will say that they participated in the conversation or overheard it, giving the witness personal knowledge; if the witness heard about the conversation secondhand, then their account is less likely admissible at an evidentiary hearing or trial—but you may still inquire about it in deposition for discovery purposes;[7]

---

7. For the testimony to be admissible at trial, the proponent may need to ask additional foundational questions for telephone conversations and conversations where the witness identifies the speaker by familiarity with their voice. *See* Chapter Eleven.

- **When the conversation occurred**—this is important for placing the conversation in context and later identifying it; also learn how long the conversation lasted, which serves as a check on the witness's description of the content of the conversation—it is not credible for a witness to say that "not much" was discussed in a forty-five-minute conversation;

- **Who participated in the conversation**—who might provide more information about the conversation and who might have additional responsibility or knowledge about the subject matter; and

- **What each person said**—obtain the actual words each participant used when you can, both for admissibility purposes and for persuasive purposes, but realize few witnesses recall conversations so vividly after months or years have passed; if they do recall the exact words, ask how they can still remember; and if they don't recall the exact words, get the witness to be as specific as they can about who said what.

Additional questions about the circumstances of the conversation may elicit details that help you understand the significance of the conversation, lead to additional evidence, and increase the weight a judge or jurors give the testimony. Questions such as:

- the location of each participant in the conversation;

- what the witness was doing at the time of the conversation;

- what other participants were doing;

- the participants' tone of voice, gestures, and demeanor;

- any notes or recording of the conversation;

- documents referring to the conversation; and

- actions taken as a result of the conversation.

8.5.2 How Much Detail to Elicit

A key consideration is how much detail to elicit about the conversation. Is it sufficient to find out just the general topic of the conversation? Is it enough to confirm that the conversation did not touch upon any relevant topic? Or is it necessary to know every subject that was discussed, and for each of those subjects, what the first person said about it, what the next person said about it, how the first person responded, and so forth? Or, to put it another way, to what extent do we need to "funnel" the conversation? That is a strategic matter based on the needs of the case.

Consider, for example, this segment of deposition testimony concerning a conversation after an accident, as reported by a witness:

Q: Mr. Richie, did anyone say anything at the scene of the accident?

A: Well, when the owner got there, he was really upset. You know, it sounded like the driver was trying to explain what happened, but the boss just wouldn't listen. I thought he was going to fire him. He—the boss, I mean—kept yelling and screaming about the brakes, and he was getting madder and madder. The driver finally sat down on the bumper of the truck, and he didn't say anything.

Compare that testimony with the additional testimony elicited when the attorney follows up to obtain the actual words used by the parties to the conversation:

Q: Okay, let's just go through this one piece at a time. Tell me the exact words the driver first said to the boss.

A: Okay. As best I can recall, the driver said, "The brakes went soft; they just didn't grab."

Q: How did the boss respond to that?

A: He got really mad and started yelling at the driver.

Q: What words did he yell at the driver?

A: I can't remember everything he said, but I remember him saying, "Don't say that to anybody; don't say anything about the brakes. Just tell them it happened too fast." I don't know, I was kind of embarrassed about hearing this, you know. I mean, obviously, they didn't know I could hear them.

Q: Did the driver say anything back to the owner?

A: No. He just sat down on the bumper of the truck and didn't say anything else.

Q: Where were you when you heard this conversation?

A: I was standing at the back of the truck, about fifteen feet from them.

Q: Was there anyone else who might have heard this conversation?

A: I'm not sure. Maybe the woman who was driving the Cadillac, because she was standing next to me. Both of us were waiting for the police to come.

Q: Do you think anyone besides the Cadillac driver could have overheard this conversation between the boss and the driver?

A: I don't think so.

Q: Is that all that you heard of the conversation between them?

A: Yes, then the police came, and I was talking to them.

Q: Do you remember anything else about that conversation between the boss and the driver?

A: No, that's it.

Q: Did you make any notes about that conversation?

A: Well, no, I didn't make any notes, but I told the police officer about what I had heard, and he was writing while I was telling him.

Q: And that was Officer Davis, who you mentioned before?

A: Yes.

On the other hand, sometimes all you want to know about a conversation is the summary and, particularly, that the conversation has no bearing on the case. If the summary suggests that nothing important to the case was discussed, move on to another topic. For example, assume a case where the issue is whether the defendant had notice that ordered goods were required by a particular date:

Q: Did you talk with the defendant the next day?

A: I gave him a call.

Q: What did you talk about?

A: It was just a social call. I asked him if he was going to be playing in the golf tournament at the club that weekend.

Q: Was there anything said about when the goods were needed?

A: No, that didn't come up.

Q: Let's talk about the next time you spoke with the defendant. When was that?

8.5.3 *The Standard Litany*

While we focused in the above example on the extent of the inquiry into the content of the conversation, there are other aspects of the conversation to elicit, both to get a full understanding of the conversation and its significance and to lay a foundation for the admissibility of the testimony: the mode of conversation, how the witness knows about the conversation, when it occurred, and who was involved. To that end, we will provide two approaches: the "standard litany" and the "Four Cs."

In the standard litany, the first step is to lay the foundation for the conversation. Let's take a wrongful death action where the plaintiff is attempting to show that the defendant, after drinking at a bar, was intoxicated at the time of the accident:

Q: Ms. Huang, were you at the Top Hat Tavern on March 4th of this year?

A: Yes.

Q: Was the defendant, Hudson Woodbridge, there that night as well?

A: Yes.

Q: Did you hear Mr. Woodbridge say anything that evening?

A: I heard him talk with the bartender.

Q: Were you able to hear what was said by Mr. Woodbridge and the bartender?

A: Yes, I was standing right next to them at the time.

Q: Was anyone else there at the conversation?

A: No one else was close.

After the foundation has been laid, the standard litany requires that the witness be asked what was said, followed by a series of "What else?" questions until the witness says, in effect, "that's everything." Here is what it might look like in the same wrongful death action:

Q: Who said what to start the conversation between Mr. Woodbridge and the bartender?

A: The bartender told Woodbridge he was looking three sheets to the wind and maybe he should let someone else drive him home.

Q: What else was said during the conversation?

A: Well, Woodbridge replied, "Nah, I'm fine."

Q: What else was said?

A: The bartender said, "It's your life."

Q: What else?

A: That's it. Woodbridge walked out of the bar.

In this example, the attorney took the witness through the entire conversation without asking specifically whether those were the participant's exact words. If you follow this approach, ask for the exact words used and other details (tone of voice, gestures, etc.) after the witness has testified that nothing more was said in the conversation, but do not interrupt the witness's initial recounting of the conversation because it could derail the witness from remembering the conversation's flow. (There is a contrary view that since you are proceeding through the conversation virtually line by line anyway, you might as well get the exact words and details attendant to each line as you go.)

8.5.4 The "Four Cs" Approach

Some conversations are so important to the issues in the case that you will want to go beyond the basic foundational requirements. Using the Four Cs technique developed by Henry Hecht, a leading teacher and scholar on depositions, will ensure

The Four Cs

- Context
- Conversation
- Close Off
- Confirm

that you will find out everything the witness knows about the conversation.[8] Our approach is slightly modified from the approach suggested by Mr. Hecht.

Context

The first "C," context, is designed to do two things: 1) lay the necessary foundation for the conversation to be admissible at trial or on a motion for summary judgment, and 2) take the witness back to the time of the conversation to prod their memory about what was said (a concept sometimes called "memory flooding").

Q: Did you ever talk with the defendant about risk of loss insurance?

A: Yes.

Q: How many times?

A: Just once.

Q: When did this conversation take place?

A: It was back in March of last year. I don't remember the exact date, but it was early in the month.

Q: Where did this conversation take place?

A: I talked with him on the phone.

Q: Where were you at the time?

A: I was in my office.

Q: Who placed the call?

A: I did.

---

8. *See* HENRY HECHT, EFFECTIVE DEPOSITIONS, 761, Appendix 6.

Q: At what number did you call the defendant?

A: I called him at his office.

Q: Where did you get the number?

A: From his email signature block.

Q: What time of day did you call him?

A: As I recall, it was in the morning.

Q: What were you doing at the time?

A: I was working on ordering the parts we needed.

Q: Was there anyone else with you when you placed the call?

A: No.

Q: Did the defendant say whether anyone was with him?

A: No.

Q: Could you hear anyone else in the room with the defendant?

A: No.

Q: Who answered the phone when you called?

A: The defendant.

Conversation

The second "C" is the conversation itself. Go through the conversation at least twice to make sure the witness has recounted as fully as possible what was said. The first run-through is phrased broadly:

Q: What was said in that conversation?

A: I told him we wanted the shipment to be insured, and he said that would not be a problem.

Q: What else? [repeating this until the witness says everything has been covered]

A: I think we discussed the date when we should expect the shipment to arrive.

On the second time through, counsel should seek a verbatim rendition of what was said by each participant in the conversation:

Q: Let's go back. Who spoke first?

A: I guess I did.

Q: What did you say?

A: I think I started out by saying "hello."

Q: What did he say?

A: He said "hello" back.

Q: What did you say to that? [repeating this litany until the entire conversation has been elicited]

A: I told him I needed to know when the shipment will be arriving so we could prepare for our production run.

Q: Were those your exact words?

A: As best as I can recall.

After the witness has recounted everything that was said, ask for any further details about the conversation and favorable facts the witness has failed to mention.

Close Off

The third "C," closing off, makes sure the witness has testified to everything they can remember so they cannot later add to their testimony.

Q: Have you now told me everything you can remember about what was said in that conversation?

A: Yes.

Q: Is there anything that would help you remember more of what was said in that conversation?

A: Not that I can think of.

Confirm

The final "C," confirming, is directed at checking the accuracy of what the witness has said by looking for corroborating evidence.

Q: Did you make any notes of that conversation either during or after the conversation?

A: I jotted down a few notes while we were talking, but I threw them away.

Q: Are there any documents that refer to the conversation?

A: I sent an email to the CEO recounting what was said.

Q: Is that Exhibit No. 3?

A: Yes.

Q: What other documents refer to that conversation.

A: None that I know of.

Q: Have you ever heard of any?

A: Nope.

Q: Who did you tell about the conversation?

A: No one.

Q: Are you positive you didn't discuss the conversation with anyone?

A: Positive.

Q: What happened as a result of that conversation?

A: Nothing really, other than I kept waiting for the parts to arrive.

As you can see, following the "Four Cs" approach can be very tedious and time consuming. Reserve it for those conversations where knowing everything about the conversation is important.

CHECKLIST

GATHERING INFORMATION

✔	Decide not only what topics to cover, but also your purposes for the deposition and for each topic of inquiry (gathering information, obtaining admissions, preserving testimony, facilitating settlement).
✔	For information-gathering purposes, use the funnel method.
✔	Start a topic by getting an overview and a list.
✔	Explore the topic with broad open-ended questions ("who," "what," "when," "where," "why," "how," "describe").
✔	Get the full answer to each question ("Who else?" "What else?").
✔	Follow up, clarify the answer, obtain more details, and exhaust the witness's knowledge of the topic by probing the witness's testimony with more focused open-ended questions and more suggestive questions ("What do you mean?" "Tell me more," "What about X?" "Did you consider Y?").
✔	Follow up on nonresponsive, evasive, and hedged answers, as well as lack of recollection or lack of knowledge.
✔	Ask clear, concise questions that encourage full answers, avoiding "can you tell me," "do you recall," and "tell me some of."
✔	Recap and summarize the witness's testimony to confirm completeness and proper understanding ("Let's see if I understand this correctly").
✔	Lock the witness into the answers and close off the witness from later changing the testimony ("Have you now told me everything you know about X?").
✔	Have a method for jotting down notes on an outline without sacrificing eye contact and attentiveness to the witness's verbal and nonverbal responses.

CHAPTER NINE

QUESTIONING TECHNIQUES: OBTAINING ADMISSIONS

*In a lawsuit the first to speak seems
right, until someone comes forward and
cross-examines.*

—Proverbs 18:17

*Only those who will risk going too far can
possibly find out how far one can go.*

—T.S. Eliot

A deposition will be more effective if you obtain targeted factual admissions to help your case. The questioning techniques in Chapter Eight, as valuable as they are for gathering information, will not suffice. This chapter explains how leading questions and other techniques provide the greatest chance of getting the witness to admit specific facts—and make whopping concessions—that can be used against the opposing party.

Seek these admissions from the witness even in depositions that are primarily focused on information gathering. In a grocery store slip-and-fall case, for example, question the store manager to learn everything she knows about the spilled mayonnaise on which the plaintiff slipped, and then use leading questions to get the store manager to admit that, despite learning about the spilled mayonnaise, she had not gotten around to calling for a "clean-up in Aisle 4." In a wrongful death case alleging that suicidal thoughts were caused by a pharmaceutical company's antidepressant, question the witness for all their knowledge of the nature and testing of the drug, then seek a specific admission that the company had never tested the drug on teenagers diagnosed with depression.

> **In This Chapter:**
>
> - The importance of admissions
>
> - Planning for admissions
>
> - Techniques for obtaining admissions
>
> - Theory testing
>
> - Turning facts into soundbites

These admissions of fact are gold nuggets. You will use them to support or oppose motions for summary judgment and other evidentiary motions, support or oppose challenges to expert witnesses, gain leverage in negotiations or mediation, and encourage favorable settlements. They can also be used at trial as affirmative evidence or as impeachment on cross-examination.

The techniques highlighted in Chapter Eight for gathering the witness's full knowledge can elicit admissions along the way, but that laborious process is not the most efficient means of eliciting them, for multiple reasons. First, for some topics, you only need the witness to confirm a couple of facts that will dispositively resolve the issue. In that (rare) case, forgo the exhaustive information-gathering techniques for that topic and use the techniques in this chapter that target admissions.

Second, information-gathering techniques may yield all the facts needed for your motions or trial, but those facts will be scattered over many different pages of the transcript. The facts will be much more powerful if presented to the factfinder in one concise passage from the deposition; for that purpose, apply the techniques explicitly suited for gaining admissions to create a section of the transcript or video recording for use in motions and trial. Indeed, if following the funnel method to gather all possible information from the witness (*see* Chapter Eight), the bottom of the funnel—at which the questions have become much more suggestive and leading anyway—is a great place to switch to these techniques to get specific admissions before returning to open-ended questioning on the next topic.

Third, these techniques for obtaining admissions can result in more than just dry, factual admissions. They can be adapted to test case theories and gain characterizations and soundbites from the witness that are much more powerful than what can be obtained using the information-gathering approach.

This most efficient way to obtain admissions from the deposition witness involves:

1) planning what admissions to get;

2) distinguishing techniques for obtaining admissions in deposition from conducting cross-examination at trial;

3) applying the techniques of leading questions, loaded questions, boxing in the witness, and controlling the witness, which increase the odds of the witness admitting the facts you need;

4) pushing the witness to admit more than bare objective facts (e.g., theory testing);

5) knowing what to do if things go awry; and

6) coordinating information-gathering with obtaining admissions.

After addressing these topics, we close the chapter by revisiting the funnel method and emphasizing the overarching takeaway for the reader: align question purpose with question form.

9.1   Planning for Admissions

Obtaining admissions is an intentional process that requires you to know before the deposition exactly what admissions to seek. Determine the needed admissions regarding facts that establish the elements of the client's claims for relief (or defenses); facts that tend to negate the elements that the opposing party must prove; and facts germane to witness credibility. Once you identify these facts, consider which ones this deponent may admit and incorporate those inquiries in the deposition outline.

Alternatively, decide what events this witness knows about; for each of those events, consider what facts you want the witness to admit that will help the client's case; and jot down those facts in your deposition outline as admissions to get.

During the deposition, if your examination of the witness's full story using the funnel method has not elicited the admissions you need (or in the rare case when you choose not to elicit the full story for strategic reasons), gain the admissions through the techniques described below. Of course, witnesses are usually not keen on admitting facts that will hurt their case, so obtaining admissions requires both strategic thought before the deposition and application of these techniques during the deposition. Before we get to the specific techniques, however, let's dispel a misperception: that getting admissions in a deposition is the same as cross-examining at trial.

9.2   Distinguishing Trial Cross-Examination

The process of obtaining admissions in a deposition is similar—but not identical—to cross-examination in the courtroom. The similarity is largely in the use of short, one-fact, leading questions and specific strategies to encourage witnesses to answer as you like. However, there are several significant differences.

Dramatic skills count for little in a deposition. Good cross-examiners in jury trials use their voices and gestures to keep the jurors' attention and impress on them the significance of the questions and answers. These techniques have little effect in a stenographically-recorded deposition because the transcript reflects only the words spoken. A video deposition picks up voice inflection and volume, but because the camera is usually solely on the witness, much of the examiner's dramatic efforts are lost to the viewer. Worse, the aggressiveness that can accompany courtroom cross-examination will tell the deposition witness that the question is meant to elicit a harmful response. Therefore, a firm but conversational questioning style is normally the most effective way to conduct a deposition, with perhaps a bit of vocal emphasis at important points in a video deposition.

Deposition admissions can be obtained in any order. In a trial, the cross-examiner will usually group together all the questions on a topic to increase clarity and to maximize the impact on the jurors. In depositions recorded stenographically, it theoretically makes no difference whether the questions are grouped together or interspersed throughout the deposition, because you can rearrange the questions and answers later when bringing or opposing motions, planning cross-examination for trial, or preparing to read portions of the deposition to a jury.[1] This means that in a deposition, you can obtain admissions by spreading out or ordering your questions in a way that makes the significance of the questions less obvious. As a practical matter, however, grouping the relevant admissions together even in a deposition has a benefit, because it makes the testimony easier to cite in a motion or to read as a continuing passage. Moreover, grouping the admissions together makes for a better video recording to play at trial; having to rearrange and piece together video deposition questions and answers results in a choppy video presentation.

It is generally a good idea in a deposition to ask "one question too many." One of Irving Younger's "Ten Commandments" of cross-examination at trial is never to ask "one question too many." If you've led the defendant's witness on cross-examination to state the essential facts (e.g., that the defendant threw the first punch in the fight with the plaintiff), do not ask a follow-up conclusory question, "And so, it was the defendant who started the fight?" The answer may come back, "No. Before the defendant got in a punch, the plaintiff had pushed the plaintiff to the ground and was kicking him in the head!" At trial, once you get the facts you need to draw an inference for the jurors, the better course is not to give the witness an opportunity to explain it away.

This rule generally does not apply in depositions, where asking the conclusory question can be beneficial. Even if the witness can explain away the significance of the factual admissions, you will want to hear that explanation at the deposition rather than for the first time at trial or in opposition to a summary judgment motion. Refraining from asking "one question too many" does not make the explanatory answer go away—it just means you don't learn about it until it is too late. And if the witness does concede the conclusion you ask, the more favorable the deposition testimony. Therefore, while there are situations where you may not want to ask one question too many even in a deposition (where, for example, the deposition transcript will be used at trial in lieu of the witness's testimony), the general rule is to do so.

In a deposition, it is generally good to ask questions to which you don't know the answer. Another of Irving Younger's commandments for cross-examining a witness at trial is, "Never ask a question to which you don't know the

---

1. This practice is subject to the caveat, however, that presenting a question and answer out of context, in a way that changes the meaning, may entitle the opposing party to present other parts of the deposition testimony for the sake of fairness. Fed. R. Civ. P. 32(a)(6); Fed. R. Evid. 106.

answer." Generally, the opposite of that rule applies in deposition, where you do not know the answer to most of the questions being asked. One of the purposes of most depositions is to find out those answers so you will know what to expect in motion practice and trial.

> *Seeking admissions in depositions employs concise, leading questions and other cross-examination techniques, but is typically more subtle and more daring than cross-examination at trial.*

9.3 Essential Questioning Techniques for Obtaining Admissions

Notwithstanding the differences between cross-examination at trial and obtaining admissions at a deposition, the two pursuits share several techniques: leading questions, short and one-fact questions, controlling the witness through eye contact and inflection, loading the question, and boxing in the witness.

9.3.1 Leading Questions

When seeking admissions, ask leading questions that call for a "yes" or "no" answer. The degree of suggestiveness can range from marginally suggestive ("was the car red?" or "did you go to the store next?") to trial-type questions that make a declarative statement and invite the witness only to agree ("the car was red, wasn't it;" "then you went to the store, right?").

Use leading questions for two reasons. First, by encouraging the witness to answer only "yes" or "no," they reduce the witness's role to merely agreeing with the fact contained in the question rather than giving a narrative response. With leading questions, you can put words into the witness's mouth. Second, by reducing the witness's answer to "yes" or "no," it is easy for jurors to understand the admission, without having to sort through superfluous information in narrative responses.

Here is an example of leading questions at a deposition in a case claiming that a work site was not properly supervised:

> Q: You work for the Lone Star Trucking Company?
>
> A: Yes.
>
> Q: You have worked there for ten years?
>
> A: Yes.
>
> Q: Your job there is to direct the loading of the moving trucks?
>
> A: Yes.

Q: If you are not there the other workers cannot begin loading the trucks?

A: That's right.

Q: If the workers are not loading trucks they are usually just sitting around?

A: Yes.

Q: You often leave the work site when there is no loading of the trucks going on?

A: I often do.

Q: That's because there is nothing for you to do on the work site when the trucks are not being loaded?

A: That's true.

Q: But you do have paperwork to do in your office?

A: Yes, there is always lots of paperwork.

Q: You often go to your office to work on paperwork when there are no trucks being loaded?

A: Sometimes.

Q: When you are in your office, there is no one at the work site supervising the men?

A: They really do not need supervision if they are not loading the trucks.

Q: My question is, there is no one at the work site supervising the men when you are in your office doing paperwork, true?

A: True.

Through these leading questions, the deposing attorney has established that the workers were unsupervised at the job site. If the accident could have been avoided by proper supervision, this admission takes the plaintiff's case a long way toward success.

As mentioned previously, leading questions sometimes alert the witness and opposing lawyer that you are trying to get the witness to give a particular answer, prompting both to be on guard. The increased use of leading questions can result in more objections and obstructive behavior by opposing counsel. If this is a concern, you can "soften the lead."

One way to soften the lead is to speak in a matter-of-fact tone that is not as accusatory as we associate with cross-examination at trial. Another way is to start out with open-ended questions such as "What did you discuss with her in that conversation," "How long did you talk," and "Who else was there," and then nonchalantly follow up with a leading question such as, "The chances of her promotion didn't come up at that time?" A third way is to be less leading but still directive: instead of using the most leading cross-examination form ("You didn't discuss her chances of promotion, did you?"), you might use a less intimidating question ("You can't recall discussing her chances of promotion?"). For some witnesses, the less intimidating form can increase the odds they will agree; for other witnesses, it will decrease those odds, so always consider the type of witness you are deposing.

9.3.2 Short and One-Fact Questions

Keep questions short. Ask about only a single fact to maintain the pace of the examination. Keep questions clear, omitting vague language and unnecessary qualifiers the witness can quibble with. Short, one-fact, clear questions are harder for the witness to evade. They give the witness less time to craft an answer. They draw fewer objections because counsel cannot think fast enough to object. And they are easier to understand when the question is quoted in a summary judgment motion or read to jurors.

For example, an attempt to gain admissions that a defendant was speeding to avoid being late to work might proceed like this.

Q: The collision happened at the intersection of Westheimer and Kirby Streets?

A: Yes.

Q: That intersection is about three miles from your work?

A: Right.

Q: There are traffic lights between that intersection and your work?

A: Yes.

Q: The accident happened at 8:50 a.m.?

A: Yes, ten of nine.

Q: You start work at 9:00 a.m.?

A: I do.

Q: The collision occurred ten minutes before your start time?

A: Yeah.

Q: To get to work on time, you had to travel two miles in ten minutes?

A: Yeah.

Q: To get to work on time, you had to go through six traffic lights in ten minutes?

A: Yes.

Note that the advice here is to ask one-fact questions. If the goal is to encourage the witness to respond "yes" or "no," the likelihood of accomplishing this goal is increased if questions seek the admission of facts rather than characterizations. In the example above, the attorney asked whether the collision occurred "ten minutes before your start time"—an objective fact—rather than "shortly before your start time"—a subjective conclusion. We may choose later on to ask more subjective and characterization questions (*see* section 9.4.2) to get a more significant admission, but it is almost always better to start with the objective facts that the witness is more likely to concede; if we can at least get those concessions, the deposing counsel has clean factual admissions to cite to and argue inferences from.

9.3.3   Other Means of Controlling the Witness

What we say about style and demeanor in section 12.1 bears mentioning here. In particular, to increase the odds of the witness admitting what you want, consider the manner in which you are asking the questions, including your eye contact, inflection, and pace.

Maintain good eye contact while asking the questions; most witnesses struggle to lie or be evasive when you are looking at them. Eye contact facilitates the questioning throughout the deposition (with some cultural exceptions), but it is particularly important when seeking admissions.

A downward inflection at the end of the question subtly encourages a witness to agree with the question's premise, which is what you want when seeking admissions. By comparison, an upward inflection invites the witness to give an explanation or narrative response, which you do not want if you're desiring a nice, clean admission usable at trial. Therefore, just as you switch your question form from open-ended to leading when moving from information-gathering to obtaining admissions, switch your inflection from upward to downward.

Finally, rapidly follow the witness's answer with the next question; give the witness no time to think about the implications of the last question and answer or to consider how to avoid giving the answer you want. Of course, rapid-fire questioning also gives you less time to think of the next question, so know your line of inquiry. Beware that defending counsel sometimes make (spurious) objections to slow things down, so be prepared to ignore the objections, keep looking at the witness, and immediately tell the witness to "go ahead and answer." (*See* section 13.3.1.)

9.3.4   Loading the Question

Loading the question is a technique that encourages admissions by including the witness's prior answers in the question. Essentially, once the witness admits a fact in your question, "load" that fact into the next question, so the second question incorporates the fact the witness just admitted; once the witness admits a new fact in the second question, load that new fact into a third question; and so forth. Because the questions embrace a fact the witness has already admitted, the witness feels more constrained to agree. The technique works particularly well if the information you load into the question makes anything other than an affirmative answer seem foolish. Here is an example of the technique in the deposition of a pharmaceutical company executive in a products liability case:

> Q: In September, you were told that the drug was dangerous if taken by people with a heart condition?
>
> A: Yes.
>
> Q: The drug was dangerous because it can cause heart attacks, strokes, and death in users?
>
> A: Yes.
>
> Q: After finding out the drug can cause heart attacks, strokes, and death in users, you were concerned?
>
> A: Yes.
>
> Q: You were concerned about possible death, heart attacks, and strokes in users, so you wanted the company to take some action regarding the drug?
>
> A: Yes.

9.3.5   "Boxing in" the Witness

Obtaining admissions would be easier if every witness was completely honest and forthcoming. Not all witnesses, however, are fully committed to the truth. Furthermore, the recollection of even a truthful and well-intentioned witness may be distorted by the passage of time, their preparation sessions, and pressures to perform. Consequently, build up to important question areas by first establishing subsidiary facts that make the witness's admissions more likely.

Boxing in the witness—also known as "setting up" or "priming" the witness— uses a progression of questions and answers that make it increasingly difficult for the witness to deny the important facts you ultimately want the witness to admit. Begin by obtaining the witness's agreement on relatively benign points the witness must concede. These concessions compel the witness to admit more critical facts or conclusions because denying them would contradict logic and the witness's earlier answers; the witness is forced to choose between truth on the one hand and foolish inconsistency on the other. The technique requires both planning before the deposition and execution during the deposition.

Before the deposition, decide what facts you will use to box in the witness. To do this, work backwards from your goal. Let's say your goal is to get the witness to admit that they read a contract before signing it, but you anticipate the witness will balk if asked up front, "You read the contract before you signed it, didn't you?" Think of facts that would make it more likely the witness will eventually agree that they read the contract—the witness was given the contract two days ahead of time; the witness was asked to read it; the contract contained the terms of the deal; those terms included what the witness would have to pay, when to pay it, how the payments might change, when a breach could be declared, and what would happen if there was a breach; the terms of the contract were not unimportant; the witness would be responsible for fulfilling the terms; the other side had the chance to read the contract and learn the terms; being in breach of the contract could result in losing money; signing the contract would bind the witness to the contract terms; it would be better to know the terms than not know them; the witness did not want to be surprised to find out after signing the contract that it contained unfavorable terms, etc. Once you have identified those prefatory facts, you know to ask the witness those questions before getting close to asking the witness the ultimate question of, "You read the contract, didn't you?"

Note that the "box" is more easily set up if the prefatory facts have to be admitted by the witness. A fact must be admitted if the witness has previously written it, said it, or was photographed doing it, or because the fact is indisputably true. Other facts will likely have to be admitted if the witness knows they are contained in a document or can be easily corroborated. Still other facts should be admitted if to deny them would make the witness look illogical, foolish, ignorant or a liar.

At the deposition, first question the witness about facts the witness must admit and then ask about facts you would like the witness to admit. Start by asking the prefatory type of facts that we just discussed, which will make it more likely the witness will give you your goal admission. After the witness admits all or most of these facts, continue to box the witness in with logical statements the witness can no longer readily deny—in our example, the questions might be "it wouldn't have been a bad idea to look at the contract before signing it" or "it would have made sense to read the contract before signing it." Then inch toward the ultimate admission: "You looked at the contract before signing it." "You signed it after you'd read it."

Conceal your objective for as long as possible. A witness who figures out where the questioning is headed and the ultimate admission you are seeking is more likely to resist conceding the facts that lead to that objective. Start with prefatory facts that the witness would look foolish to deny. The longer you can conceal the objective, the better. Keep your questioning nonchalant and matter-of-fact. Maintain a poker face when you hear a favorable answer.

Anticipate escape routes and close them off early. Before the deposition, think of the excuses the witness might use to deny or avoid the admission you want the witness to make. Include prefatory fact questions to take away those excuses before the witness realizes where the examination is going.

Here is an example. Assume the admission being sought is that a stockbroker, employed by a major brokerage house, heard a statement at an analyst meeting that a company in which the broker had been advising clients to invest was projecting a loss for the year. The plaintiff contends that after hearing the statement, the broker failed to inform clients of this information and continued to place their orders to buy the company's shares. What escape routes might the stockbroker take to avoid this admission? He might say he was not at the meeting, that he didn't hear the statement, that he did not recall that his clients were investing in the company, that he did not have time to inform his clients of the news. The questioning to close off those escape routes could go like this:

Q: It is part of your job to attend meetings with the investment house's analysts?

A: Yes.

Q: Attending these meetings helps you to know how to advise your clients regarding their investments?

A: Yes.

Q: You were at your office on May 13 of last year when there was one of these analyst meetings?

A: That's what my calendar says.

Q: Yes, that is what your calendar says. So, you were at your office on May 13 of last year when there was an analyst meeting?

A: Yes.

Q: You attended that meeting?

A: Yes.

> **Boxing in the Witness to Get Admissions**
>
> - Before the deposition, decide what facts you will use to box in the witness.
>
> - At the deposition, first question the witness about facts the witness must admit.
>
> - Then ask about facts you would like the witness to admit.
>
> - Conceal your objective for as long as possible.
>
> - Anticipate escape routes and close them off early.

Q: There was a written agenda containing the names of the stocks that would be discussed that day?

A: Yes.

Q: You look at these agendas to see if any of the companies listed are companies in which your clients are investing?

A: I usually do.

Q: Well, you didn't decide to ignore the agenda for this meeting, did you?

A: No.

Q: Handing you what has been marked as Exhibit 1, you saw that NCP was on the agenda for the May 13 meeting?

A: Yes.

Q: You knew that five of your clients had investments in NCP?

A: Yes.

Q: The total investment of these five clients was over $1,000,000?

A: Something like that.

Q: A million dollars in investment is not a trivial amount?

A: I've seen larger.

Q: I didn't ask you that. A million dollars in investment is not trivial?

A: It's not trivial.

Q: The analyst meeting was held in the twelfth-floor conference room?

A: Yes.

Q: It only holds a dozen people or so?

A: That sounds right.

Q: You can easily hear the analyst when she is making her presentation?

A: Yes.

Q: You were paying attention because she would be discussing a stock in which your clients had invested?

A: Yes.

Q: May 13 was a week before the purchase of NCP stock on May 20?

A: Yes.

Q: At the May 13 analyst meeting, the analyst stated that NCP would be showing a loss for the year.

A: Yeah.

The deposing lawyer closed off possible escape routes—that the witness did not attend the meeting, was not paying attention, etc.—before asking the witness whether he heard the analyst say NCP would be showing a loss.

> *To view a video demonstration of Questioning Techniques: Obtaining Admissions, scan the QR code (print version) or click here.*

9.4 Techniques for More Powerful Admissions and Theory Testing

Depositions—unlike cross-examination at trial—give deposing counsel a relatively safe opportunity to obtain not just admissions of facts, but admissions of characterizations, inferences, theories, and sound bites that make the case more powerful and persuasive. Here are some ways to do that.

9.4.1 Asking More Than What You Know

In this example, we have a personal injury case involving a collision with a pedestrian. The deposing counsel knows some facts that the defendant witness must admit; now she goes further and attempts to obtain admission of a fact counsel is unsure of—that the defendant was not looking out for pedestrians.

Q: As you approached the intersection, you were looking straight ahead at the cars in front of you?

A: Yes.

Q: You were keeping your eye on the traffic light?

A: Yes.

Q: You wanted to get through the intersection before the light changed?

A: Yes.

Q: You weren't looking to the sides of the road?

A: Not as much as I was looking at the light.

Q: The light was over the middle of the road, not over the sidewalk?

A: True.

Q: Since you were looking at the light, you weren't looking for pedestrians?

A: I wasn't.

Counsel has obtained a nice admission. But what if it happened this way?

Q: As you approached the intersection, you were looking straight ahead at the cars in front of you?

A: Yes.

Q: You were keeping your eye on the traffic light?

A: Yes.

Q: You wanted to get through the intersection before the light changed?

A: Yes.

Q: You weren't looking to the sides of the road?

A: Not as much as I was looking at the light.

Q: The light was over the middle of the road, not over the sidewalk?

A: True.

Q: Since you were looking at the light, you weren't looking for pedestrians?

A: That's not true. Even when I was looking at the light, I could see the people on the sidewalk out of the corner of my eye. I was definitely looking out for pedestrians.

The attorney did not get a favorable admission, but she still benefitted from the questioning. Now aware of the witness's answers, the attorney planning her cross-examination for trial will know to ask whether the defendant was looking straight ahead, was concentrating on the traffic light, wanted to get through the intersection before the light changed, and was not looking to the sides of the road as much as he was looking at the traffic light. If the defendant denies these facts at the trial, the deposition testimony can be used for impeachment. The attorney will also know not to ask at trial whether the defendant was looking out for pedestrians, because the deposition revealed how the defendant will answer that question. Simply put, by asking the question about looking out for pedestrians, the deposing attorney learned the limits of the future trial cross-examination. Although the deposition does preserve on the record that the defendant claims to have been "looking out for pedestrians," this assertion would have been made anyway at trial or in connection with a summary judgment motion.

9.4.2 Getting the Witness to Agree to Subjective Words and Phrases

Good cross-examination questions at trial do not include subjective words and phrases, such as adjectives, adverbs, conclusions, or characterizations. Subjective language provides the witness with more room to disagree with the proposition contained in the question. For example, a witness at trial should normally not be asked on cross-examination to agree that one of the parties was driving "very fast" at the time of the accident. Without an agreed definition of "very fast," the witness can interpret the words however they choose. Therefore, the cross-examiner's questions should suggest the party was driving very fast by eliciting facts that lead to that conclusion, but the attorney would not raise the conclusion itself until closing argument.

An exception, however, to the rule against using subjective words and phrases in cross-examination at trial is when the witness has already agreed to that very language during the deposition. The witness's use of those subjective words and phrases then stands as a provable, conceded fact. For example, if the witness answers during the deposition that the party was going "very fast" and later refuses on cross-examination at trial to say the same thing, you can use the deposition to introduce the statement "very fast" through impeachment.

Therefore, at the deposition, after obtaining admissions on the objective facts (e.g., miles per hour, pounds, dates, times), push the witness to agree to favorable subjective words and phrases as well.

There are two methods for getting the witness to agree to subjective words and phrases. One way is to ask the witness to provide them. If this method is not as successful as you hoped, then suggest the subjective words and phrases to the witness. To illustrate these methods, let's turn to part of a deposition in a personal injury case:

Q: How fast were you going?

A: About 75 miles per hour.

Q: The speed limit in that stretch is 55 miles per hour?

A: Yes.

Q: You were going 20 miles over the speed limit?

A: I guess that's about right.

Q: How would you describe your speed?

A: Uh, I was going . . . fast, I guess.

Q: About 20 miles over the speed limit is fast?

A: Yeah.

Q: Wouldn't you say that 20 miles faster than the speed limit is very fast?

A: Maybe.

Q: In fact, 20 miles faster than the speed limit can potentially be dangerous?

A: It could be.

Q: You were going at a dangerous rate of speed, weren't you?

A: No, no, that's not true.

Note that the attorney first obtained the facts (75 miles per hour in a 55 mile-per-hour zone), which would allow the attorney to argue any characterization they wanted from those facts at trial or in a motion. Then they obtained the witness's characterization ("fast") and, pushing further, obtained some agreement on the attorney's characterization (maybe "very fast," and it could potentially be dangerous). From this deposition testimony, the deposing attorney can argue in a motion or at trial that the defendant admitted to driving fast and at a speed that "could be" potentially dangerous. Furthermore, at trial, the witness would have to admit these characterizations in cross-examination or be impeached by the deposition testimony. The defendant's refusal to admit to driving at a "dangerous" rate of speed does not hurt the deposing attorney, because the deposing attorney can still argue to the judge or jury that, in fact, the defendant was driving dangerously.

9.4.3   *Testing Theories*

Getting the witness to agree to subjective characterizations is fundamental to another technique—theory testing. In preparing for the deposition, you will form a theory that explains what happened in the case favorable to the client (e.g., the plaintiff theorizes that the defendant was not paying attention, the defendant theorizes that the plaintiffs brought the trouble on themselves by not following the rules). Test that theory with the witness to see if the witness will agree to that proposition or something close to it, and if not, why not. This will end either with a colossal admission that cripples the other side's case, or an explanation of the other side's defense to the theory. Either way, you are that much more prepared for summary judgment and trial.

> *To test a case theory:*
>
> - *think of facts supporting the theory;*
> - *ask a leading question for each fact;*
> - *suggest benign characterizations of those facts, building toward the conclusion (your theory);*
> - *ask the ultimate conclusion;*
> - *if the witness pushes back, ask why.*

To test a theory with the deposition witness, think of the ultimate theory (e.g., the defendant was not paying attention), the facts supporting the theory (e.g., the defendant had been thinking about an argument with a colleague, was tired, and was texting), and some relatively benign characterizations of those facts that would support the theory (the defendant was not laser-focused the entire time, had other things on their mind). Then in the deposition, ask leading questions progressing from the facts to the benign characterizations to the ultimate theory. If the witness admits the theory, great. If the witness balks at a question somewhere along the way, you learn the limits of potential testimony at trial and can ask the witness why they do not agree, gleaning further information about the witness's perspective and the opponent's case.[2]

To view a video demonstration of Theory-Testing, scan the QR code (print version) or click here.

---

2. If the purpose of the deposition is to preserve only favorable testimony of a witness who will not be available for trial, and you are unsure how the witness will respond to the questions, be wary of testing theories. You may spur the witness to testify unfavorably and the testimony could be used at trial.

9.4.4 *Turning from Facts to Soundbites*

It is one thing to get the witness to admit a fact, which you can cite and use to create an argument. It is quite another when you phrase your deposition questioning to get a soundbite—a damaging admission that *sounds* damaging. You can incorporate these soundbites into a summary judgment motion or read or show them to the jurors for dramatic effect.

A soundbite's impact is greatest when captured in a video deposition. A video soundbite allows the jurors to watch and listen as the damaging words come out of the witness's mouth. Video also shows the witness's nonverbal reactions to the question—their demeanor, gestures, expressions, perspiration, twitches, jitters, smirks, and other visual indicators that can strongly influence the jury's assessment of the answer.

Let's look at this example from a products liability case:

Q: The data that would be used to estimate the dangerousness of the drug was maintained by the company as confidential information?

A: Correct.

Q: A family physician out in West Texas could not find out how dangerous the drug is from the package insert that comes with the drug?

A: It wasn't on there.

Q: That family physician out in West Texas could not find out how dangerous the drug is from any of the literature and advertising the company sent to doctors all over the United States?

A: No.

Q: Knowing the dangers of taking a particular drug is something a physician would want to know before prescribing the drug to one of the doctor's patients?

A: Well, yes.

Q: Without knowing about the dangers of a drug, doctors don't have the information they need to make an intelligent decision whether the drug's benefits outweigh its risks?

A: I guess not.

Q: Of course, if doctors don't have information about the drug's dangers, they can't inform their patients about the risks that come with that drug such as heart attacks and strokes?

A: . . . Correct.

Any of these questions and answers can be used later as a freestanding soundbite, or a number of them can be presented together for cumulative impact.

9.5 Techniques If the Witness Refuses to Admit the Facts

Despite your best efforts to work logically toward the admission you want, the witness may refuse to comply. You have some options: revert to open-ended, information-gathering skills to find out the reasons for the witness's denial, wrestle with the witness over the logic of the witness's denial, or both. And if you anticipate that the witness is going to resist every line of questioning, consider "leading in the opposite direction," as described below.

9.5.1 Returning to Information-Gathering

The first option simply strives to find out the basis for the witness's refusal to provide the admission. Consider the following:

Q: The failure to tighten bolts in the construction of a building might cause the building to be structurally unsound, correct?

A: No.

Q: The building would be structurally sound even if the bolts are not tightened completely?

A: That's right.

Q: Why?

In this instance, the deposing attorney has switched to the open-ended, information-gathering approach with a "why" question and will make sure that the witness states all reasons by continuing to ask "why else."

9.5.2 Wrestling with the Witness

The second option is the wrestling approach.

Q: The failure to tighten bolts in the construction of a building might cause the building to be structurally unsound, correct?

A: No.

Q: The building would be structurally sound even if the bolts are not tightened completely?

A: That's right.

Q: Well, let's see. The bolts are designed to hold the struts together?

A: Yes.

Q: The struts are necessary for the building's structural soundness?

A: That may or may not be true.

Q: If the struts were not installed, the building would likely collapse?

A: That's true.

Q: So the struts are necessary to the building's structural soundness?

A: Put that way, yes.

Q: The struts only work if they are connected to one another and to the upright beams?

A: True.

Q: If the struts are not connected, they cannot work to hold the building together?

A: Correct.

Q: The bolts hold the struts together?

A: Yes.

Q: The plans for constructing the building indicate the bolts should be tightened to at least ninety foot-pounds of torque, right?

A: Yes.

Q: The construction details specify that the bolts should be tightened to at least ninety foot-pounds of torque for a solid connection between the pairs of struts?

A: Yes, that's true.

Q: Is it your testimony that tightening the bolts to less than ninety foot-pounds still achieves a solid connection?

A: It probably would not be as safe.

Q: And it wouldn't be as safe because there would be a possibility of the building being structurally unsound?

A: Yes.

Q: The bolts in this case were tightened to only sixty-seven foot-pounds?

A: That is my understanding.

Q: Torque of sixty-seven foot-pounds would not be as safe as ninety foot-pounds?

A: That's true.

Q: And that is because there is a possibility of the building being structurally unsound?

A: That would be true.

As you can see, the "wrestling" approach requires a high-level understanding of the subject matter on your part, and in practice it can devolve into more of an argument than an inquiry. When successful, however, it does result ultimately in an on-the-record concession of your point.

Sometimes it is helpful to combine the approaches, first finding out "why" the witness will not give the admission initially and then, armed with the facts and reasons the witness has offered, engage in some wrestling.

9.5.3   *Leading in the Opposite Direction*

Some witnesses are such contrarians that they will resist giving you the slightest concession on any topic. These witnesses refuse to admit whatever proposition your question contains, no matter how harmless an admission might be. You can try to capitalize on this by appearing to lead the witness in a direction opposite to where you really want the witness to go.

For example, assume that you want the witness to admit that they are supposed to read, and did read, the terms and conditions in a price list. Expecting the witness to fight you on any question you ask, you might choose not to ask, "you read the entirely of the price list, didn't you," but instead approach it like this:

Q: Your job must be very busy with a lot of responsibilities?

A: It isn't always busy.

Q: Well, as the plaintiff's purchasing agent, you must receive hundreds of catalogs and price lists and other sorts of advertising literature?

A: There's not that many that come in.

Q: Certainly too many for you to read all of them?

A: That's not true. I read them all.

Q: You can probably glance at them, but surely it's beyond you to read all the fine print and terms and conditions in them?

A: That's my job. I am required to stay on top of that sort of information.

Q: But when the defendant's price list came in, you just glanced at it?

A: No, I read everything on it, front and back.

Use the technique of leading in the opposite direction only after you determine that the witness, out of sheer contrariness, is likely to resist the line of examination.

9.6 Correlation of Obtaining Admissions and Gathering Information

Chapter Eight focused on techniques for gathering information. This chapter focuses on techniques for obtaining admissions. In both chapters, we note that most depositions will include both techniques.

A common approach is to start a given topic with information-gathering questions (using the funnel method described in Chapter Eight) and then switch to leading questions to obtain specific admissions as necessary, based on the witness's prior answers and any other information at hand. After you obtain the admissions and exhaust the topic, you move to a new topic and repeat the process. There are, however, a couple of variations on this theme.

9.6.1 Obtaining Admissions to Isolate the Information Gathered

Sometimes the witness admits the fact you wanted the witness to admit, but the admission is buried in the middle of a long answer that also contains unfavorable information or has been interrupted by attorney objections and colloquy. Reading the entire answer to the jurors, quoting it in a summary judgment motion, or attempting to impeach with it runs the risk of the judge or jury not understanding the significance of the admission. You need to isolate the favorable admission from the rest of the answer to make it useful.

Here is an example in which the deposing attorney wants the witness to say there was snow on the ground. The attorney starts with an open-ended question to find out what the witness will say about the road surface.

Q: What was the road surface like where the collision occurred?

A: Well, it had been sunny earlier that day, and the roads had been dry and clear ever since I passed the intersection with I-45, but then it started snowing, and there was a fair amount of snow on the ground, although I don't think the snow was the cause of the accident since I had snow tires on, so I really do not know what caused us to collide.

The deposing attorney, who wants to isolate the witness's admission that there was snow on the ground, could simply switch to a leading question form and ask, "It started snowing and there was a fair amount of snow on the ground, right?" If the witness answers "yes," counsel has obtained a clean admission of the important facts. But counsel may be concerned that asking the witness to repeat only this favorable part of the answer will signal that counsel deems it important and cause the witness to back off the admission. An alternative approach would be for the deposing attorney to go through the entire answer and have the witness agree to each part of it, yielding a clean admission without alerting the witness. It might go like this:

Q: Let me see if I understand this. You said it had been sunny earlier that day?

A: Yes.

Q: The roads had been dry and clear after the intersection with I-45?

A: That's right.

Q: Then it started snowing?

A: Yes.

Q: There was a fair amount of snow on the ground?

A: Right.

Many lawyers, while switching from gathering information to obtaining admissions, change their tone and demeanor when they ask about the key admission. Avoid this—it tips off the witness to the importance of the answer.

9.6.2 *Starting with Obtaining Admissions*

Sometimes it makes sense to start the deposition by immediately asking leading questions designed to obtain admissions. The witness is unlikely to expect such aggressive questioning so early in the proceeding, especially if their lawyer told them that the questioning will start with the witness's background and not touch upon the merits until later. Starting with questions seeking admissions may find the witness surprised and unprepared, which may, in turn, result in the witness giving the desired answers. In fact, if you obtain enough favorable admissions early on, and you believe you have enough information to file a persuasive motion for summary judgment, you may be able to shorten the deposition substantially.

A drawback of the "hit 'em early" approach, however, is that seeking admissions usually requires you to push the witness to get the desired answer. As you ask leading questions and attack any unfavorable answers with more leading questions, your tone may become sharp, confirming for most witnesses that you are the adversary out to do them harm. If you then shift to information-gathering mode, where the witness's cooperation is important, the witness will probably be in no mood to be helpful. In short, it is much easier to go from gathering information to obtaining admissions than the other way around.

9.7 The Funnel Method—Revisited and Reimagined

The correlation between gathering information and obtaining admissions, and the real-world interplay between the two, leads to a different use of a funnel to describe how to inquire of a witness. Instead of limiting the funnel to explain just the phases of gathering information for discovery purposes (Chapter Eight), you can use the funnel to explain the entire examination of a witness on any given topic, including everything you want from the witness on that topic—all the information-gathering phases plus, at the bottom of the funnel, phases dedicated to obtaining admissions and testing theories. In that conceptualization, the different levels of our master funnel of any topic would be:

1) Broad introductory question to start the topic

    "List all the job duties you had as provost of the university."

    "What else?"

2) Broad, open-ended questions to elicit as much information as possible

    "Who," "what," "when," "where," "why," "how," "describe"

    "What do you mean by 'periodic faculty retention and remuneration capacities?'"

3) Narrower suggestive questions and use of exhibits for detail, clarity, and exhausting knowledge

    "What role did you play in tenure decisions?"

    "Weren't you copied on some of the correspondence regarding Professor Barrett's tenure decision?

    "Let me show you what's been premarked as Exhibit 2, a letter to you dated July 4, 2022."

4) Narrower questions that recap and summarize the witness's testimony to make sure you understand, elicit more information, and condense drawn-out information into a succinct excerpt

    "Let's see if I have this right . . . "

    "So you . . . "

5)   Questions to lock in and close off the testimony so the witness cannot add more later

> "Have you now told me all your involvement as provost in regard to the tenure decisions?"

6)   Leading, cross-examination questions to obtain admissions of specific facts, gain soundbites, and put words in the witness's mouth

> "You didn't call for an investigation of the plagiarism charges against Professor Barrett, did you?"

> "You never found an example of plagiarism by Professor Barrett?"

7)   Leading, characterization questions to test your case theories and swing for the fences

> "You found it unnecessary to evaluate the plagiarism claim in light of the other allegations."

> "In the scheme of things, the plagiarism allegation wasn't important."

> "You kind of knew what your decision was going to be before the investigation began."

> "Professor Barrett really never had a chance, did she?"

With this conceptualization of the funnel, your examination on a topic does not have to start at the top and proceed lockstep to the bottom. Start in the funnel wherever you want according to the purposes for the deposition and, more importantly, according to your purposes for inquiring about the topic. Do you want to find out everything the witness knows and might say about a particular topic? Start at the top of the funnel with the broad, open questions and work your way down the funnel as you see fit. Are you looking for admissions only, to keep the record clean for purposes of seeking summary judgment, or to avoid preserving unfavorable facts that can be used at trial if the witness becomes unavailable? Start the topic lower in the funnel with the leading questions targeting the admissions you want. Remember that each choice has a risk (exploring every detail with exhaustive open-ended follow-up takes a lot of time; forgoing information-gathering will deprive you of knowing what the witness might say later), but it is a strategy and judgment call for you to make.

Moreover, depending on the answers you get during the examination, jump from level to level, anywhere on the funnel. Got an unexpected answer to your leading questions or a big "no" in response to your theory testing? Jump back up to the top of the funnel and explore the witness's answer. Did you start with broad information-gathering questions but now need to cut to the chase due to time? Jump down to leading questions.

Whatever conceptualization is more helpful for you—a funnel for information-gathering and a separate pursuit for obtaining admissions, or one funnel that includes it all—embrace it. Because the point, of course, is not what is properly contained in the rubric of a "funnel." The point is that there are many ways to ask questions, but they will be most effective only if we remember that different purposes cry out for different question forms, and different question forms yield different types of testimony. Know your purpose, know what you want, and ask the right type of question.

CHECKLIST
OBTAINING ADMISSIONS

✔	Before the deposition, decide what admissions to obtain from the witness.
✔	Ask leading questions.
✔	Keep questions short, inquiring about one fact at a time.
✔	Increase witness control with eye contact and a slight downward inflection.
✔	Distinguish trial cross-examination and soften the lead where necessary.
✔	Load the question by incorporating facts the witness has already admitted.
✔	Box in the witness by obtaining concessions on relatively neutral subsidiary facts that make it more difficult for the witness to deny the critical facts.
✔	Press the witness for facts beyond what you already knew.
✔	After obtaining admissions of the objective facts, get the witness to provide or agree to subjective words and phrases characterizing those facts.
✔	Test your case theories.
✔	Turn facts into soundbites through the phrasing of your questions.
✔	If the witness refuses to give an admission, ask why and return to information-gathering techniques to find out more.
✔	Wrestle with the witness as needed.
✔	Lead contrarians in the opposite direction.
✔	Move between gathering information and gaining admissions, while keeping the question form distinct.

CHAPTER TEN

DOCUMENTS AND ESI

The historian, essentially, wants more documents than he can really use . . . .

—Henry James

Documents create a paper reality we call proof.

—Mason Cooley

A deposition will be more effective if you use documents and electronically stored information (ESI) in an efficient, strategic manner. Documents can include receipts, letters, notes, contracts, reports, and memoranda, as well as photographs, diagrams and more. ESI can include emails, voicemail, texts, tweets, video, audio, social media pages, and webpages. Each has its place, and each should be kept in place.

Documents and ESI must be used in questioning the deposition witness. They are especially persuasive items of evidence, and they are critical to most civil litigation. Not only do they provide substantive information, you can use them to lead or challenge the witness and refresh the witness's memory.

On the other hand, do not let documents and ESI control the deposition. While some lawyers do not use documents enough, many lawyers obtain every available document and

> **In This Chapter:**
>
> - *Reasons for using documents and ESI in a deposition.*
>
> - *Preparing to use them.*
>
> - *Marking them as exhibits.*
>
> - *Questioning about them during the deposition.*

shred of ESI, even if only marginally relevant, and then devote much of the deposition to marking and discussing each item, even if the witness's oral testimony would replace dozens or hundreds of them. Take the full opportunity to find out what is in the witness's mind, not merely what is on the face of a document you already have.

In this chapter, we consider the many uses for documents and ESI in a deposition, preparing to use them, marking them as exhibits, questioning the witness about them, and related matters.

10.1 Uses for Documents and ESI in Depositions

First, let's define our terms. The word "document" is sometimes equated with the term "writing" as defined in Rule 1001(a) of the Federal Rules of Evidence, namely anything that "consists of letters, words, numbers, or their equivalent set down in any form," as opposed to a "recording" or a "photograph." FRCP 34(a)(1)(A) distinguishes between "documents" and ESI, allowing inspection requests for "any designated documents *or* electronically stored information—including writings, drawings, graphs, charts, photographs, sound recordings, images, and other data or data compilations—stored in any medium from which information can be obtained either directly or, if necessary, after translation by the responding party into a reasonably usable form." (Italics added.) Sometimes, then, the term "document" is relegated to what appears in hard copy form. In this chapter, unless stated otherwise, for brevity we will use the word "document" to include hard-copy writings, photographs, recordings, and all ESI.

Defined in this broad way, documents are used in connection with depositions for numerous purposes. In fact, part of carefully planning for a deposition is deciding in advance exactly what documents to use, why you want to use them, and how best to use them. Let's start by identifying some common uses.

10.1.1 To Generate Questions for the Deposition

One of the more important uses of documents—occurring before the deposition—is developing questions to ask at the deposition. Some documents have an obvious impact on the facts in the case: the contract at issue in the litigation, the receipt for rent, the prospectus in a securities case, the accident report, the architectural drawings, the patent, the environmental impact report, the employee's performance review, and letters, emails, texts, voicemails, and other communications pertinent to the case, as well as disclosures on social media, photographs or diagrams of the scene, representations on websites, and so forth. Always consider these documents while developing your factual theory and a chronology of the case, a legal theory and "proof chart," and the deposition outline (*see* Chapters Four and Five).

Review the salient documents line by line before the deposition to elicit questions about the document itself (what the author meant, what the recipient understood, the meaning of terms and figures in the document, what actions were taken as a result, etc.), as well as about the events depicted or referenced in the document.

10.1.2 To Establish an Evidentiary Foundation for the Document

Sometimes a document is used in a deposition to have the witness authenticate it and, to the extent needed, to lay any additional evidentiary foundation for its use at trial or in a summary judgment motion. For example, you can depose the person in charge of managing records at the local hospital solely to certify and authenticate a party's medical records if the records have not already been certified by affidavit. More frequently, documents are authenticated, and their evidentiary foundation is established, as part of a broader examination of the witness about the issues in a case. (We discuss foundations further in Chapter Eleven.)

> *Plan for your deposition by deciding in advance:*
>
> - *what documents you will use,*
>
> - *why you want to use them, and*
>
> - *how best to use them.*

10.1.3 To Discover Other Facts, Witnesses, and Documents

Examining a witness about a document will often reveal the existence of additional facts, witnesses, and documents, opening the way to further discovery. For example, the witness's responses about an email announcing a company meeting can divulge follow-up emails, the identities of persons mentioned in the email, the names of everyone who attended the meeting, what each person said, and any notes or minutes taken.

10.1.4 To Refresh the Witness's Memory

Just as at trial, documents can be used to refresh a witness's memory at a deposition. At trial, the goal in refreshing recollection with a document is usually to bring a particular fact to the witness's mind; in deposition, the goal is more often to remind the witness of the entire array of facts related to a referenced event, such as a meeting or decision.

10.1.5 To Impeach the Witness and Encourage Candor

When a deposition witness testifies to facts inconsistent with what the witness said previously in a document, one option is to impeach the witness with the document at the deposition. An alternative tactic is to save the impeachment for trial, where it would have greater impact on the factfinder; since most cases are now resolved before trial, however, impeaching the witness at the deposition is better because it can influence settlement negotiations or the judge's view of the deposition testimony when ruling on a summary judgment motion.

Impeaching with a document at the deposition also lets the witness know you have a firm grasp on the facts in the case and there are consequences to lying. Particularly when the impeachment occurs early in the deposition, the witness may become more truthful—if for no other reason than to avoid the embarrassment of being impeached again. If the impeachment stings enough, the witness might even go along with an answer unfavorable to their party because it was suggested by the "all-knowing" deposing attorney—you.

10.1.6 To Force Admissions

Documents can help you extract an admission from a witness. The printed (or digitized) word has a force that evanescent oral information may not. A witness who will eagerly disagree with the testimony of another witness is usually more hesitant to contradict facts contained in, for example, a letter written by that other witness.

Take advantage of this dynamic when seeking an admission by first showing the witness a document that contains the answer you want the witness to adopt. Although it is usually preferable to elicit the witness's recollection of the events before presenting the document, this can be a strategic exception.

10.2 Preparing to Use the Documents: Review, Selection, Premarking, Copying

The initial step toward using documents in the deposition is planning their use before the deposition. Determine the universe of potentially relevant documents to prepare for the examination generally, cull those documents down to a manageable number of deposition exhibits, and prepare that subset of documents for use by premarking, copying, or uploading them as the case may be. Let's look at these steps more closely.

10.2.1 Gather All Potential Documents for Review

First, collect all the documents possibly relevant to the examination. In smaller cases, conduct a "search and arrange" mission, in which all documents having any relationship to the case or the witness are pulled together and organized in some way—often chronologically or chronologically within subject matter. Because the case is small, with few documents, the process is quite straightforward.

In the larger, document-intensive case, use document management software to gather the documents that the deponent wrote, that the deponent received, or in which the deponent is mentioned. Do not rely, however, on a name-only search; perform supplemental searches to gather relevant documents in which the witness's name may not appear (e.g., blueprints or plan drawings in a construction case). Make—and keep a record of—a list of keywords relevant to the witness with which to enact your searches. (With a record of your searches, when a potentially vital term comes to light you can easily determine whether you have already searched for that term or if you need to perform a new document search.)

The assembled material may have originated in hard-copy (paper) or digital (electronic) form. Some attorneys prefer to work with hard copies, while others prefer to work with digital copies. Electronic material, such as emails, texts, and voicemails, may be put into hard-copy form by printing them out.[1] Or, to work entirely in electronic form, scan hard-copy documents and convert them into a digital format such as a PDF or, for photographs, JPG. Preserve the original of the document—even a digital document, which would include the metadata associated with that digital information.

In reviewing the relevant documents and preparing for the deposition, many attorneys arrange the documents they anticipate using in chronological order. This can be useful to confirm the factual theory of the case. In a more complex lawsuit with many topics and many documents, however, it is better to arrange the material first topically and then, within each topic, chronologically. This approach helps you generate questions topic by topic and lends itself to probing the witness's knowledge in each area, yet still helps identify what the witness knew and when the witness learned it. Of course, if all the material has been digitized, it can easily be ordered and re-sorted to fit your tasks. By placing the documents for each topic in a tabbed

> *This research and document management work is ideal for a paralegal. A well-trained paralegal is a terrific asset and will help you contain client costs. Many attorneys squander this asset, though, by treating this professional as a glorified secretary. Do not make this mistake! Instead of just saying, "look for all documents referring to the meeting on October 17," explain the case and the overall picture of the proof you are seeking. Looking at the documents with an understanding of the case and a fresh set of eyes, your paralegal is likely to "strike gold"— and make you look good in front of the client.*

---

1. If you are an attorney who wants all electronic documents printed out for review, it's time to reconsider that habit. Not only is it a waste of paper and ink, it wastes time—time printing and collating the documents, time locating and transferring any notes you make on the paper copy back to the electronic document, and time (and materials) when you lose the first paper copy. It also creates the hazard of lost notes when multiple members of the litigation team are looking at multiple paper copies.

Applications like Google Documents, Microsoft Office 365, and DropBox—to name just a few—have the tools your litigation team needs to share ideas and concerns as you consider each piece of evidence. If this all seems overwhelming, start small. Decide to review emails electronically, for example. With a little effort, you can become proficient at electronic review and save yourself all that time and expense.

notebook, labeled file folder, or digital folder of electronic documents, they will be readily accessible when needed.

10.2.2 Generate Questions for the Deposition Topics

Once you have pulled and organized the relevant documents, review what the witness wrote or received to understand the witness's role in the case. The documents may show an involvement that the witness would otherwise deny.

Also review the documents to evaluate how their content relates to the issues and to see what questions arise. Keep in mind the deposition outline topics, as well as the facts that need to be learned or confirmed given the factual theory, chronology, legal theory (elements of the claims for relief and defenses), proof chart, and the persuasive theory (*see* Chapter Four). How does this document apply to the case? Why was the information in this document recorded and why were these statements made? What was their source? What was meant? How was it understood?

Consider also what questions arise about the events the documents depict. For example, in a design defect case, a simple email message from a company's president requiring the company's safety officer to attend a meeting about the design of the company's product can generate a variety of questions for the deposition: Was the meeting held? Where was the meeting held? How long did the meeting last? What was the purpose of the meeting? Why was the meeting held? Who decided to hold the meeting? Who attended the meeting? Why was each person invited to attend the meeting? What was discussed at the meeting? Were any notes made at or following the meeting? Were there any later discussions concerning the meeting? Are there any documents that refer to the meeting? What actions were taken as a result of the meeting? Why were those actions taken? Why was the safety office invited? What did the safety officer contribute to the discussions? What other meetings were there about the safety of this product?

Examine the documents chronologically (overall or within a particular topic), paying attention to what happened first, and what happened next. Look for temporal relationships between statements in documents. For example, if one document mentions "customer acceptance problems in Texas" and a document dated a few days later mentions the need for a trip to Texas without specifying a purpose, use both documents with the witness to find out if the trip was to solve the problems or find their source. If the witness says that the first document had nothing to do with their responsibilities, the second document putting them in Texas may prod their memory or honesty.

10.2.3 Select Documents to Use as Exhibits

Although you may pull and review a huge number of documents to familiarize yourself with the deponent and to prepare deposition questions, not all those documents must be—or should be—used as exhibits at the deposition. Thoroughly examine on a few key documents rather than superficially examining on many that have marginal relevance to the witness or to the issues. In selecting documents for use as exhibits, here are some considerations:

- Based on your case theories and the opponent's case theories, how important is the content, timing, or other circumstances of the document to the issues in the case?

- Is this witness the only person, or most important person, who can testify about the document (e.g., the author or addressee, or the only available person to identify it or explain its creation)?

- Is this the only witness, or the best witness, to provide an evidentiary foundation for the document?

- Will the document aid the witness's explanation or your understanding of their testimony (e.g., diagrams, maps, photographs)?

- Does the document contain predicate facts (e.g., a report of sales figures or other data the witness would likely not remember precisely) necessary to elicit this witness's testimony on a topic?

- Do you need this witness to explain the content of the document (e.g., meaning of terms, figures, data; identity of people referenced in the document)?

- Do other documents or oral testimony evince the same fact, so the document is less essential to the case?

- Will this document help "box in" the witness to get a favorable admission at the deposition (*see* section 9.3.5) or impeach the witness's story?

Applying these criteria, you will eliminate unneeded documents, pinpoint "must use" documents for the key topics in your deposition outline, identify "just in case" documents for refreshing recollection, and "bullpen" documents pertaining to less important topics you might not get to.

The bottom line is this: if a document does not help your case or the other person's case, there is probably no reason to question about the document; if it does make a difference in the case, you must know your purposes for using the document and scour it to develop the questions you need to ask of the upcoming deponent.

10.2.4 Double-Check for Privilege and Confidentiality

Once you select your likely exhibits, double-check to see if any of them are privileged and appear on a privilege log or are confidential and subject to a protective order. As the deposing attorney, do not waive privilege or breach confidentiality by using the document in the deposition. If a confidential document must be used, make sure that a protective order is in place and the court reporter is apprised so that the exhibit and the corresponding portion of the deposition transcript will be sealed as confidential.

10.2.5 Decide Where the Selected Documents Fit in the Deposition Outline

Indicate in your deposition outline (*see* Chapter Five) what documents you want to use as exhibits and when. This lets you introduce each document in its most effective place. To do this, first consider the topic(s) to which the document corresponds, and then decide when to present the document during your questioning on those topic(s).

The documents themselves will reveal the topic(s) to which they correspond. The documents will also reveal the questions to ask, including substantive questions about their content as just discussed. In addition, plan to ask basic foundational questions such as authentication (*see* sections 10.3.3, 10.3.11) and essential questions about any important document (e.g., confirming important information on the document, why it was written, existence of drafts, meaning or understanding of words and phrases, action taken as a result). Note the specific aspects of the document you want to inquire about in your deposition outline or, more conveniently, on a copy of the document that you will retain during the questioning.

When in your questioning should you present the document? It is generally better to probe the witness's unaided recollection of a conversation, meeting, or other event before showing the witness a document that describes it. If their account is favorable, then turn to the documents to confirm it; if their account is unfavorable, use the documents to attack it. Also use the documents to prompt the witness to add facts or explain them. By contrast, if you present the witness with the document before getting the witness's unaided account of the event, they are more likely to conform their recollection to what is in the document in front of them, and less likely to reveal new information. The preferred sequence might look something like the following:

Q: Tell me how the agreement between you and the defendant came about?

A: I wrote him a letter back in June of this year asking if he was interested in selling me his business.

Q: Why did you write him?

A: Well, two reasons. We needed the cash flow, and it was important to stay ahead of our competitors by diversifying, and his business offered us both.

Q: What terms did you have in mind at the time?

A: We offered him $1.2 million.

Q: How did you come up with that amount?

A: It seemed reasonable based on the preliminary figures he showed us—that Exhibit 26 we've talked about.

Q: I am handing you what has been marked as Exhibit 31. Is that the letter you wrote to the defendant?

A: Yes.

Q: That letter is dated June 4 of last year?

A: Yes.

Q: Looking at the first page of the letter, in the second sentence, you stated, "We are pleased to offer you the sum of $1.2 million to purchase the business on terms heretofore discussed." What did you mean by "terms heretofore discussed"?

The questioning on the document would continue. In a further example of the "story, then document" approach, you might elicit more facts about the underlying event, withholding any documents until the witness's memory of events is exhausted—particularly where the document describes a fact-rich meeting or series of occurrences.

Asking about documents after, but in connection with, the witness providing an account of the depicted events elicits a better understanding of the events than examining about the documents in a separate part of the deposition. The approach both draws from the witness information you had not known and serves as a check on the witness's narrative. If, after hearing the witness's story, there are documents containing additional information about the event, turn to the documents to fill in the gaps in the witness's story; with a more complete understanding of the events, you will be in a better position to attack the unfavorable aspects of that story.

There is an exception to trying to get the witness's story first, alluded to above: if the document is favorable for your case, and the witness has no story to tell about the event, you can more readily obtain an admission of the facts depicted in a document by simply showing the witness the document.

Though planning out your use of the document is important, during the deposition you might decide to spring the exhibit on the witness earlier to surprise them, to refresh their memory, or to cut through the witness's inaccurate recollection and speed up the coverage of a topic. Alternatively, you might opt to withhold the exhibit until later for some other strategic reason. It is nonetheless best to have an idea of what you are going to ask about the document, and when you are going to ask it, before the deposition begins.

10.2.6 *Decide Whether to Use Hard-Copy or Digital Exhibits*

You have the choice of presenting the document to the witness in hard-copy (paper) form, which requires making a sufficient number of copies and distributing them by hand at the deposition, or in digital (electronic) form—such as a PDF or JPG—uploaded to a server before the deposition, accessed on your laptop at the deposition, and distributed to the other participants' laptops electronically when you use the exhibit. Hard-copy exhibits are traditional and are certainly fine if the litigation involves relatively few exhibits, few depositions, and few attorneys; digital exhibits save the time, paper, and client expense otherwise required to make multiple hard copies, organize them, and lug them to the deposition in multiparty litigation. Digital exhibits also make sense if much of the documentation is comprised of ESI such as emails, texts, voicemail, social media, and the like. Although ESI material could be printed out as a hard copy and used in that format, a digital image in a PDF, JPG, or MP3 format (or a more native format for more complicated manipulation of the data) is considered best. For those wary of technology, preparing digital exhibits and using them at a deposition is not much more complicated than dragging and dropping a file from one folder to another, as we discuss below. As we shall see, your choice between hard copies and electronic copies will vary the tasks of preparing and presenting the exhibit.

10.2.7 *Confirm the System for Marking Exhibits*

Before using a hard-copy or digital document as an exhibit at a deposition, it must be "marked" by affixing an exhibit number to it. Just as at trial, documents used at a deposition need unique names—exhibit numbers—so the documents can be clearly identified in the record. Not only do the people at the deposition need to know what piece of paper is being referred to at any particular time, people using the deposition later (at a summary judgment motion, at another deposition, or at trial) need to know whether the piece of paper they are looking at is the same piece of paper the deposition witness was testifying about.

There are two decisions to make about marking deposition exhibits. First, at least if you intend to use hard-copy (paper) exhibits, decide whether to premark the exhibits before the deposition, as opposed to having them marked at the deposition by the court reporter as you introduce them during the questioning. Second, decide what method you will use to assign an exhibit number to the exhibit. These decisions go hand in hand.[2]

Premarking takes a modicum of effort and forethought but ultimately saves time. Specifically, premarking the exhibits saves the time the court reporter

---

2. Communicate these decisions to the court reporter in advance, so everything runs smoothly on deposition day. When entering a litigation in midstream, ascertain whether conventions have already been established by other counsel or the court.

must take during the deposition to mark them, which can be significant if you are using many exhibits. Premarking is also the way to go if, as discussed next, the parties have decided in advance what exhibit number each document will receive.

There are two customary methods for assigning a number to an exhibit: 1) at each deposition, give the documents numbers as they are introduced, so they are labeled Barnes Depo. Ex. 1, Barnes Depo. Ex. 2, etc.; or 2) in advance of the depositions, identify all (or most) key documents and give each a universal number that they will have for *every* deposition, so a document will always bear the mark of "Ex. 1," for example. The latter approach involves more upfront work and coordination between counsel, but it avoids much confusion and work later if there are many documents and deponents. Furthermore, most courts today require, by pretrial order or otherwise, that documents for trial be premarked, and using the same exhibit number for the documents at every deposition and at trial makes a lot of sense. Indeed, gathering information for any use—a motion in limine, summary judgment motion, trial, and so forth—is much easier and more efficient if each document bears the same exhibit number throughout the lawsuit. This is especially so when the deposition transcripts are delivered in digital form and are readily searchable: if a question arises whether a certain document should be admitted over a hearsay objection, for example, or it becomes necessary to know what was said about the document by numerous witnesses, the lawyers need only search the deposition transcripts for the assigned universal exhibit number to access all the relevant testimony.

To make the universal numbering system work, reach an agreement with opposing counsel. You might agree on a list of primary documents that will bear the same exhibit number for every deposition and other use in the litigation. Alternatively, you could agree to be responsible for assigning numbers within a certain range to documents of your choosing, with other counsel responsible for assigning numbers within a different range to their documents. Or a number could be assigned to a document when it is used the first time, with the document retaining that number for all subsequent uses. The numbering and marking protocol is often a matter of attorney stipulation set forth in a scheduling or discovery order.

Numbering exhibits separately for each deposition may seem like a time-saver up front, but if you choose to give documents a new number for each deposition, you take on more work to keep things straight. Unless you use the same documents in the same order for each deposition, the same document—a contract, for example—might have been identified as Johnson Depo. Ex. 2, Barnes Depo. Ex. 7, and Wong Depo. Ex. 32. Attorneys on both sides must keep a meticulous "table of concordance" (which, before computers, often provided a paralegal with many wearisome hours of work).

SUGIS / JONAS
DEPOSITION EXHIBITS

Sugis 1	=	Jonas 17
Sugis 2	=	Jonas 4
Sugis 3	=	Jonas 39
Sugis 4	=	Jonas 1

JONAS / SUGIS
DEPOSITION EXHIBITS

Jonas 1	=	Sugis 4
Jonas 2	=	Sugis 9
Jonas 3	=	Sugis 42
Jonas 4	=	Sugis 2

If there are only two deponents, only two lists have to be prepared, with two columns. If there are three deponents, three lists are necessary with three columns, and so forth. A database program can take care of this recordkeeping rather easily, although the burden of putting the information into the database still exists.[3]

The final pretrial product, after all depositions are complete and all trial numbers have been assigned, can look like this:

If you want to refer to a witness's deposition testimony when you use it at trial, take an additional foundational step to relate the deposition document to the trial document:

Q: Ms. Vardas, you then wrote a letter to the president of the Shadis Company, didn't you?

A: I'm not sure what you are referring to. I don't think I ever wrote to him.

---

3. The additional risk of this system is that if everyone is bringing their own version of a contract, can you be certain that the version of the contract the opposition is presenting is identical to the version you used in your deposition? An agreed upon set of documents prevents varied versions of an exhibit—whether by error or malice—from muddying the waters when it comes time for settlement, motions practice, or trial.

FINAL CONCORDANCE

Exhibit Number	Sugis No. / Depo Tr. Pg. #	Jonas No. / Depo Tr. Pg. #
DX-1	73 / 153–157	14 / 43–44
DX-2	74 / 168, 179	3 / 10
DX-3	5 / 23	72 / 198–199
DX-4	15 / 68	31 / 97, 201
DX-5	46 / 109	62 / 153

Q: In the same deposition we have talked about, Ms. Vardas, I asked you this question, didn't I? Page 73, counsel: "Isn't Vardas Deposition Exhibit 15 a letter from you to the president of the Shadis Company?" And you answered, "Yes, I wrote that to him." Wasn't that your answer?

A: Yes, I said that.

Q: Ms. Vardas, let me show you what has been marked as Defendant's Exhibit 142. That's the Deposition Exhibit 15 we've been talking about, isn't it?

A: Yes, it looks like the same letter.

Obviously, the trial examination will be much cleaner if only one set of numbers is involved—yet another reason to assign numbers before the depositions of significant witnesses.

10.2.8 Prepare and Copy Hard-Copy Documents for Use at an In-Person Deposition

If you plan to use hard-copy exhibits at an in-person deposition, there are three preparatory tasks once every document is in hard-copy form (including ESI printed out or transcribed): premarking (optional), making sufficient copies, and getting the copies to the deposition.

Premarking

As discussed, you must mark documents before they can be used as an exhibit at a deposition. Premarking hard-copy exhibits before the deposition saves time during the deposition and keeps the examination flowing. (Another option is to ask the court reporter to mark the exhibits at some point before the witness is sworn.)

Premarking is simply affixing an exhibit number to the document. In the absence of a court rule or order dictating how exhibits should be premarked, the best approach is to emulate the practice of the court reporter. In some jurisdictions, exhibits at trial or in the deposition are marked using exhibit stickers with different colors for plaintiff and defendant; in other jurisdictions, the labels are white because they are more readable on copies of the exhibit. Whatever the practice in your jurisdiction, conform to that custom so the premarked exhibits will resemble any exhibits that are not premarked (e.g., marked for the first time at trial).

If there is a system for giving certain documents the same exhibit number, follow that system. If there is no system, you can number them in any order you wish—usually, the order in which you anticipate using them at the deposition.

If an exhibit consists of several pages and each page has already been Bates-stamped, each page of the document has been sufficiently identified so it can be referenced during the deposition and the record will remain clear. If the pages of the document have not been Bates-stamped, however, assign an exhibit identifier to each page: assign a number to the exhibit, put that number on the first page of the exhibit, and use a letter suffix for each page thereafter (e.g., Exhibit 4-A, Exhibit 4-B).

Using numbers for exhibits works better than letters. Some courts require that one side use numbers and the other side use letters, but if the choice is up to you, choose numbers. A sequence of numbers can extend infinitely, but after 26 letters the sequence must start over, usually with a doubling of the letters, e.g., AA, BB, CC or AA, AB, AC, and so forth. If a case involves hundreds, or even thousands of documents, a letter system becomes cumbersome.

Copies

Prepare and bring at least enough copies to provide:

- One for the witness;
- One for each party's attorney, including the attorney for the witness;
- One for the court reporter; and

- A working copy for yourself, which can be marked up with notes about what questions to ask concerning the exhibit.[4]

Some deposing attorneys resist providing a copy to the witness's counsel, thinking there is no reason to make the deposition easier for them. But handing the witness's lawyer a copy makes the deposition easier for you too. Otherwise, a time-consuming ritual occurs where the witness's lawyer either demands a copy—forcing you to make a trip to the copier—or takes the exhibit from the court reporter (or witness) and proceeds to read it from the first word to the last and then hands it to the witness with the instruction to do the same. This slows the deposition, breaks the flow of questioning, and turns a bit of control over to your opponent. Shorten this process by providing a copy to the lawyer, as well as to the witness, so they can look over their copies simultaneously. Furthermore, giving the witness's lawyer their own copy avoids the lawyer and witness huddling together over the same piece of paper during review and questioning, in a position where the lawyer can more easily point to a part of the document that would assist the witness.

Transport

A good way to transport the hard-copy documents you plan to use as exhibits is in a banker's box containing a file folder for each exhibit; in the file folder, place all the copies for that exhibit, with your annotated copy on top in each file folder so you don't inadvertently turn that one over to the other side. When the deposition outline or the testimony prompts you to use one of the documents, pull the file folder from the box, distribute the copies, and proceed as we describe later in this chapter.

10.2.9   *Prepare Digital Documents for Use at an In-Person Deposition*

Preparing digital exhibits for the deposition is relatively simple. Scan any remaining hard-copy documents you want to use at the deposition (or have on hand to use). Once all needed documents are digitized, upload them to a secure cloud server managed by a third-party software vendor or court reporting service. Label and organize the documents in any manner you like for easy recognition and retrieval during the deposition. The software may allow you to annotate the documents with your questions and comments.

At the deposition, all participants sign into a web portal. When you want to use the exhibit, select it from your laptop or tablet, use the software to mark it as an

---

4. Some attorneys write questions on the face of their working copies of the documents as a substitute for preparing a deposition outline. However, exploring and confirming the information on a document is only one deposition objective; obtaining new information is usually a more important goal, and a topic outline that helps direct the examination, with reference to the documents as needed, assures that the documents support the deposition but do not control it.

exhibit, and place the exhibit into a shared folder or otherwise distribute it electronically to the other participants, who can review the exhibit on their own laptop or device. (Any annotations you added to the document are not visible to the others.) As easy as that, marking is accomplished and there is no need to make physical copies or transport them to the deposition.

10.2.10   Prepare Documents for Use at a Remote Deposition

If the deposition is conducted remotely, consider how to get the documents in front of the witness during the deposition and, in turn, if you need to take any steps before the deposition to facilitate that task. As discussed further in section 24.7.7, documents can be presented to the deponent in a remote deposition either by referring the deponent to a document that was sent to the witness and their counsel ahead of time, by screensharing the document during the deposition, or—similar to the use of digital exhibits we just discussed—using special software that enables you to drag and drop the document into a shared folder that the witness and counsel can see during the deposition.

10.2.11   Provide Exhibits in Advance If There Is a Strategic Advantage

The Advisory Committee Notes to Rule 30 of the Federal Rules of Civil Procedure suggest that the impact of the seven-hour time limit on depositions in federal cases can be lessened if you send copies of the deposition exhibits to the witness (via counsel, if represented) in advance of the deposition. The witness can review the documents before the deposition and avoid the time consumed by reading each document during the deposition.

There are obvious problems with giving the witness copies of the exhibits in advance. First, any element of surprise is lost. While a well-prepared witness is unlikely to be shocked by any document introduced during the deposition, not all witnesses are well-prepared, and any amount of uncertainty, even with prepared witnesses, gives you a psychological edge. Second, providing the documents in advance gives the witness's attorney a roadmap to your case theory and strategy.

Nonetheless, advance delivery of the exhibits may be called for in the right case. In some lawsuits, everybody knows (and possesses) the documents that are going to be used with a given witness, as well as the legal theories and likely lines of questioning. In that instance, giving the witness and counsel the exhibits ahead of time might expedite the proceedings. Furthermore, as just mentioned, providing exhibits in advance is one way of bridging the physical gap between you and the witness in a remote deposition.

When you deliver exhibits in advance, remember that their contents may be confidential. If providing a digital copy of the documents by email or a filesharing service (e.g., GoogleDrive, OneDrive, Dropbox), send the file password-protected for reasons of both security and strategy. You may choose not to disclose the password to the witness or opposing counsel until right before or during the deposition, to maintain the secrecy of the exhibits for as long as possible. If providing a hard copy of the documents by mail or delivery, take precautions to protect any sensitive or proprietary information.

10.3 Using the Documents at the Deposition

Handling exhibits at a deposition is governed by a series of rote steps that you can quickly master, but which you should follow faithfully to avoid problems later. As a general rule, you want to elicit the witness's recollection of a conversation or other event before presenting the exhibit, but whenever you decide to present the exhibit, here are the essential steps.

10.3.1 Ask the Court Reporter to Mark the Document (If Not Premarked)

If you premarked your documents, skip this step. If you choose instead to have the court reporter mark the documents during the deposition, hand the document to the reporter when you first want to use it and say, "Please mark this document as Exhibit 1" (or "Please mark this January 17, 2022, email from Ms. Thurgood to Mr. Garces as Exhibit 2"). If you use so many exhibits that you forget which number is next, ask, "Please mark this document as Exhibit next in order," and the court reporter will know which number to give it. The court reporter affixes an exhibit sticker to the exhibit (or stamps it), indicating the exhibit number and the date. When asking the court reporter to mark a document, *stop talking* so the court reporter can stop taking things down stenographically and affix the exhibit sticker to the document.

10.3.2 Present the Exhibit to the Witness, Identifying It for the Record

In an in-person deposition with hard-copy exhibits, if the exhibit has been premarked, simply hand the premarked document to the witness and a copy to the court reporter and the witness's attorney, stating to the effect of, "Handing witness, counsel, and the court reporter what has been premarked as Exhibit 13." If other parties are represented at the deposition, also give them copies while noting it on the record.

If the court reporter is marking hard-copy exhibits during an in-person deposition, the reporter usually hands the exhibit to the witness once the exhibit is marked. As the reporter is doing so, say, "Ms. Witness, the reporter has just handed you a document that has been marked Exhibit 13." Hand a copy of the exhibit to opposing counsel, saying, "Mr. Mouth, here is a copy of Exhibit 13 for you." If other parties are represented at the deposition, also give copies to them at this point.

While the exhibit is handed to the witness and the witness's attorney, give a short, non-argumentative description of the exhibit (if you haven't already). That way, if there is any later confusion about what exhibit number was assigned to a particular exhibit—when the same exhibit number is inadvertently assigned to two separate exhibits, for example—the description can clear up the confusion. This description can merely be something like: "The exhibit that you have been handed, Exhibit 13, appears to be a letter from Mr. Vardas to Ms. Jones at the Shadis Company, dated January 13, 2022."

Next, give the witness some amount of time to look at the exhibit. On the record, state, "Please take a look at Exhibit 13 and let me know when you're finished." Patience is required at this point as opposing counsel and the witness will usually take their time carefully reading the exhibit from beginning to end. Once the witness has looked up from reading the exhibit, begin your questioning. If the exhibit has many pages, you might save some time by representing that you will only be asking about a certain portion, e.g., the first page (if that's true).

In an in-person deposition with electronic exhibits, select the document you want to use from a folder on your laptop or tablet, use the software to affix an exhibit sticker, and place the exhibit into a shared folder or send it electronically to the other participants, who can then review the exhibit on their own laptop or device. For the record, state what you are doing—something like, "Let's look at what I've marked and displayed as Exhibit 17, which appears to be a letter from Ms. Jones to Mr. Vardas dated August 1, 2022. Does everyone see that?" After the participants confirm they see the exhibit, ask the witness to "take a look at Exhibit 17 and let me know when you're finished." The witness and the other participants can review the exhibit independently and can scroll from page to page on their own; in some applications, you can adjust the display to see where in the document the witness is looking, and highlight any part of the exhibit you want the witness to focus on.

In remote depositions, we recommend using software that allows the witness and counsel to see and review the document on their screen as soon as you place it into a shared folder, very similar to what occurs with electronic exhibits at an in-person deposition. Alternatively, screenshare a premarked document, or direct the deponent and counsel to an exhibit you provided before the deposition. If you provided the document electronically in a password-protected file, give the participants the password so they can open the file on their computer. No matter what method you choose, the concern is essentially the same: making sure all participants can view the exhibit.

10.3.3 Lay Any Necessary Foundation for the Exhibit

You do not need to lay any evidentiary foundation for an exhibit just to ask the witness questions about it at the deposition. However, if your goal is to use the exhibit at trial or in a summary judgment motion or other evidentiary proceeding, take the time during the deposition to establish the evidentiary foundation for such later use.

The subject of evidentiary foundations is so broad and nuanced that we devote Chapter Eleven to it. For now, the takeaway is that in most situations, the primary task is to get the witness to authenticate the exhibit by saying what it is and how they know. There are several ways to establish this authentication—essentially, that the exhibit is the document it purports to be—such as by the witness remembering writing it, recognizing a signature, recognizing a logo, and the like. *See* Fed. R. Evid. 901.

Authentication can be obtained using nonleading questions or leading questions. One way to do it, therefore, would be like this:

Q: What is Exhibit 27?

A: It's a letter I wrote to Vardas.

Q: How do you know?

A: I remember writing it, and it has my signature.

Q: It bears a date of January 20, 2022. Do you have any reason to believe that date is incorrect?

A: Nope.

Or you could simply do it this way:

Q: Exhibit 27 is a letter you wrote to Vardas dated January 20, 2022, right?

A: Yeah.

Things seem a bit more complicated when authenticating emails, voicemail, texts, and other ESI, but the same evidentiary rules apply. Generally, an email can be authenticated by a person who wrote or received it, a voicemail by someone who recognizes the voice or observed the caller leave the message, a text by the sender or by the recipient who recognizes the phone number or something unique about its content, and so forth. Authentication can also be established by circumstantial evidence, such as information in the email, voicemail, or text that suggests it is a communication from the purported sender to the recipient. For a more detailed discussion of authentication—as well as laying a further foundation for a business record exception to the hearsay rule or a foundation that the document reflects a statement by a party-opponent—*see* Chapter Eleven.

If the witness might be wary of authenticating a document that is harmful to the opponent's case, ask instead for the witness to authenticate a nonthreatening— but representative—document of a similar type. For example, present the witness with a document that is benign or may even support the opponent's case to gain an admission that a signature is genuine, a logo or trademark belongs to the company, or the author was speaking for the company. Doing so may be enough to authenticate all other documents with the same signature, logo, or author, or at least make it more likely that the witness will feel compelled to authenticate the damaging document.[5]

10.3.4 Ask If Anything Is Missing from the Document

Always ask the witness if the document is missing anything that was present when the witness saw it previously. There are a few reasons to do so. First, the question is germane to the evidentiary foundation for the document, to the extent the witness is not disputing that the document is a true and correct copy of the original. *See* Fed. R. Evid. 901, 1002. Second, you want to know if you have not received all the pages of the document in a document production. Third, you want to know if the witness or opposing party is going to claim something else was attached.

The inquiry can be part of laying the foundation for the document, with a question such as the following: "Is Exhibit 5 in the same condition it was in when you first received it?" "Is there anything missing from Exhibit 5 that was there when you saw it at any time before the deposition?" "Does Exhibit 5 appear to be a true and correct copy of the email?" "Do you have any reason to believe Exhibit 5 is not a true and correct copy of the original?"

10.3.5 Refer to the Document by Its Exhibit Number

Once an exhibit has been marked and given to the witness, include the exhibit number in every, or nearly every, question about the exhibit, to ensure that the record is clear.

> Q: Ms. Vardas, let me hand you what has been marked as Vardas Deposition Exhibit 13, which appears to be a letter from you to Ms. Jones at the Shadis Company dated January 13, 2020. Counsel, here's another copy you may use. Would you look at Exhibit 13 please, Ms. Vardas?
>
> A: Yes, this is the letter we were talking about.

---

5. If a document is bad for your case, and there is no likelihood you would want to use it in a motion or at trial, do not authenticate it or otherwise lay the evidentiary foundation. Nor is it good practice, even for helpful documents, to mindlessly authenticate them without making a further inquiry. Some lawyers start the deposition by working through a stack of documents by taking each one, handing it to the witness, and asking a series of questions like this: "Q: Handing you Exhibit 1, do you recognize it? A: I do. Q: Is Exhibit 1 that letter you sent the defendant in June 2020? A: It is. Q: Handing you Exhibit 2; do you recognize it? A: I do. Q: Is Exhibit 2 a letter you received from the defendant in July 2020 in response to Exhibit 1? Q: I think so. Q: Handing you Exhibit 3; . . . ." And so on until the pile has been exhausted. The deposing attorney has obtained authentication of the documents but not learned about the witness's understanding of them.

Q: And is Exhibit 13 the same letter that you say you wrote after rejecting the Shadis Company offer?

A: No, there's another letter that I was thinking of.

Q: Let me show you another letter. Mr. Emmanuel, please mark this document as Vardas Deposition Exhibit 14, which appears to be a letter from Ms. Vardas to Ms. Jones at the Shadis Company dated January 26, 2022. Now, Ms. Vardas, take a look at Exhibit 14. Counsel, here's an extra copy for you. Is Exhibit 14 the letter you wrote after receiving the Shadis offer?

A: Yes, that's the one.

Q: Exhibit 14 is dated January 26, 2022, isn't it?

A: Yes.

Q: Now, please tell us how this letter, Exhibit 14, relates to your rejection of the Shadis offer . . .

Any lawyer who has worked on a summary judgment brief or attempted to use deposition testimony at trial will understand the importance of using the exhibit number in as many questions as possible. It is cumbersome to cite to a question that reads, "After you received this letter, what was the next thing you did?" and then go back several questions or even pages to identify what letter was being referenced. Using the exhibit's "proper name"—its number—allows all counsel and the court to know exactly what document you and the witness were talking about.[6] A clear record makes everyone happier, including judges and senior partners.

10.3.6 *Refer the Witness to the Relevant Portion of the Exhibit*

When questioning the witness about something that appears on the document, direct the witness to the part of the exhibit you want to ask about. Not only does this ensure that you, the witness, and the witness's attorney are all on the same page (literally), it makes the transcript clear for future readers. The preferred method is to refer the witness to the page and line of interest and read at least part of it into the record:

Q: Ms. Vardas, would you please look at the fifth page of Vardas Deposition Exhibit 57. That's the page that begins with the language "and to tour the plant with Jonas and his employees." Do you have that page in front of you?

A: Yes, I have it.

---

6. Electronic transcripts provide another benefit to referring to exhibits by their numbers. When searching the transcript database for references to the document, you will pick up more occurrences if the number has been used instead of "this document," "that letter," or "the first memo."

> Q: Now, please look at the first full paragraph on that page, the second line, which starts with, "It is most important that you . . ." Do you see that?
>
> A: Uh . . . yes, yes, got it.
>
> Q: I'll read this sentence into the record just to be clear. "It is most important that you do not let any rank-and-filers know about this." Ms. Vardas, why did you write that sentence?

Many lawyers use a less preferred method of asking the witness to read a sentence or paragraph in the document. If you ask the witness to read it silently, there is no way to know if the witness is reading the correct portion of the exhibit. And if you ask the witness to read it aloud, they may read the wrong part or (relevant to a video deposition) the wrong way or unintelligibly. You may also get the objection, "Counsel, this is not a reading test. If you have a question, ask it." Absent some clear strategic purpose to the contrary, it makes more sense for you to read the relevant sentence.

10.3.7 Question on the Exhibit

The questions you ask about a document will be determined, of course, by the document itself. Given the universe of cases, theories, documents, and witnesses, it is impossible to list the exact questions here for any given case or exhibit. Certainly, your deposition preparation session will generate questions to ask, and additional questions will become apparent as the deposition proceeds. Key, of course, is keeping in mind your deposition outline and your factual and legal theories of the case.

Nonetheless, here are some basic types of substantive questions typical for any document that is worth addressing with the witness. If the witness wrote the document:

- Was it written on the date indicated?
- Why was it written?
- Were there drafts, how did they differ, and where are they now?
- Who helped create the document, and what was their input?
- Meaning of phrases
- Intent behind phrases
- Who received copies?
- Discussions about the document and responses

If the witness received the document:

- When and by whom was it received?
- Who reviewed it and when?
- Understanding of phrases
- Action taken as a result
- Conversations about the document

10.3.8   Ignore "The Document Speaks for Itself" Objections

If you attempt to characterize a document or ask about its content, you will frequently draw an objection that "the document speaks for itself." This is silly. I have never heard a document "speak," and there is no such evidentiary objection. Does counsel mean that the question calls for hearsay? That asking about the content of the document violates the best evidence (or original document) rule? That it is harassment to ask a witness what is written on the document? As with all other objections, ignore the objecting attorney and tell the witness to answer.

10.3.9   Keep Track of the Exhibits

Once an exhibit is marked and used with the witness during the deposition, leave a hard copy on the conference table for the court reporter or make sure the court reporter has an electronic copy. After the deposition is completed, the court reporter will add the exhibits to the deposition transcript.

Keep track of your copy of the exhibits. For electronic documents, this means avoid inadvertently transmitting your annotated exhibits to the other party—easy to do unless you clearly name files with a designation such as "DO NOT SHARE."

Hard-copy exhibits offer a variety of handling styles. Some deposing attorneys place a pile of hard-copy documents they intend to use as exhibits on the conference table, and as they ask about them during the deposition, shift them from a "to be asked about" pile to an "already asked about" pile. This two-pile arrangement can lead to the documents controlling the course and content of the deposition, since it suggests that once a document reaches the "already asked about" pile, you are finished with the document once and for all. It may also signal to the defending attorney and the witness how much of the deposition is left, since they can watch the "to be asked about" pile dwindle. (An attorney with a sense of humor, like one of the originating authors, might add pieces of paper to the bottom of the "to be asked about" pile during breaks, so that it actually grows during the deposition.) A solution is to keep the documents you intend to use as exhibits in a file box below table level, so only you know how many documents remain for inquiry. As you use the exhibits, make a note in your deposition outline and place your copy face-down on the table, accessible for later reference if needed.

> *To view a video demonstration of Using Documents at the Deposition, scan the QR code (print version) or click here.*

10.4 Witness Creation and Annotation of Exhibits

As a general matter, you can give a witness a piece of paper and ask the witness to draw a diagram or perform a calculation on it, and then mark the paper as an exhibit. It may prompt an objection from the witness's attorney, but the more the process is described as merely illustrative and not to scale, the greater the possibilities. Alternatively, ask a witness to mark on an existing hard-copy document or on an electronic exhibit (using annotation features of the exhibit presentation software), to indicate, for example, the location of a car at an intersection or to highlight language in a document.

If you do ask a witness to mark on an exhibit, make sure the record is clear regarding exactly what marking is being made. For example, assume you are asking a witness the location of a structural defect in a support beam. The following line of questions would not be clear:

Q: Would you please take this red pen and mark where the beam was cracked?

A: Yes, sure. It was right about there.

Q: Could it have been up here a bit further? [Indicating.]

A: It may have. It could have been up to here.

Q: Here? Or are you saying as far as there?

A: No, here.

Q: Thank you.

Readers of the transcript cannot follow this discussion, even with the document in front of them. Instead, approach it more like this:

Q: Would you please take this red pen and mark with your initials where the beam was cracked?

A: Yes, sure. It was right about there.

Q: You have put your initials near where the beam cracked. Could the break have been further up the beam, nearer to where I am placing this X in blue?

A: Perhaps. It might even have been up to there.

Q: Would you please place a Y where you have just indicated as "up to there"?

A: Yes.

Q: Do you mean it was where you have placed the Y on Exhibit 13, or could it have been as low as this spot, where I am placing a Z?

A: It was not as low as your Z. I think it was where I placed my initials.

10.5 Refreshing the Witness's Recollection

To be certain that a witness's knowledge has been exhausted at the deposition, you may need to use a document to refresh the recollection of a witness who claims no memory, or an incomplete memory, about a given event. Here is a simple example.

Q: Mr. Johnson, who was at the meeting?

A: I don't remember.

Q: You were there?

A: Yes.

Q: Who else?

A: Elsa.

Q: Who else?

A: I really don't remember.

Q: Would it help to see the minutes of the meeting?

A: Yeah, sure.

Q: I'm showing you what was premarked as Exhibit 17, appearing to be the meeting minutes. Does that help you remember?

A: Oh, yes.

Q: I'll take Exhibit 17 back from you for a moment. Who else was at the meeting?

A: Mr. Schniffel and Ms. Port.

When attempting to refresh recollection with a document, however, do so with care. Showing the witness the document may indeed refresh the witness's memory, but it will likely have a limiting effect as well. For example, if the witness testifies that they remember three subjects discussed at a meeting, and then you show them a memorandum that lists four subjects, the witness will adopt those four as the complete meeting agenda, regardless of how many more subjects were really discussed. To avoid this premature closure, keep the document in reserve for as long as possible, until other attempts at jogging recollection have failed.

10.6 Other Document and ESI Issues

So far in this chapter, we have been talking about using documents and ESI during a deposition. Other questions arise, however, concerning whether the deposing counsel has obtained all the documents and ESI that would allow counsel to conduct the deposition. In section 7.3, for example, we explained how to question a witness to make sure all documents and ESI have been produced responsive to a production request or subpoena. Let's turn now to two related matters: 1) conducting a separate deposition to determine compliance with document and ESI requests; and 2) addressing a witness's reference to documents that have not yet been received in discovery.

10.6.1 Depositions to Determine Compliance with Document and ESI Requests

If the request for production or subpoena was directed to an entity—a corporation, partnership, or other organization—you may need to depose the entity's custodian of records or Rule 30(b)(6) designee regarding the entity's document creation, maintenance, and destruction policies, as well as the scope of the search conducted to comply with the request or subpoena at hand. For example:

Q: Ms. Arrowsmith, as office manager of the corporation and custodian of its records, what responsibilities do you have regarding the corporation's records?

A: I supervise all the recordkeeping procedures in the company. All the important records are maintained under my ultimate supervision.

Q: What do you mean by important records?

A: Well, the records that the company needs to operate, like sales orders, invoices in and out, bills of lading, inventory records, disbursements, receipts, everything that goes into compiling balance sheets.

Q: Where are those records maintained?

A: It's all in files up to 2017. We digitized starting January 1, 2017, and all of those records are on our servers.

Q: Where is your server?

A: At the office.

Q: Do you mean that you converted existing hard-copy documents to digital form beginning in January 2017, or beginning in January 2017 and from then on, all documents were created and stored digitally.

A: No, no, no. Documents created before January 2017 are still in hard copy. Documents created beginning in January 2017 are electronic.

Q: Okay. You've talked about financial records. What are the procedures for collecting and maintaining nonfinancial records, like correspondence and memoranda?

A: Well, those are not quite so rigorous. Files are kept up in each office according to client, and those contain the correspondence and memoranda. Everyone has a computer and company laptop. All of those documents are automatically uploaded to our server, saved every twelve minutes. So, there could be some on our server, there could be some in office files.

Q: What is the company's retention policy?

A: Each office has to keep the files of correspondence and memoranda for one year at least, then we move the files to an inactive file area, unless there has been activity within the past year. After three years in the inactive file storage, those types of documents are destroyed. Our financial records, of course, we keep much longer; some of them we keep forever.

Q: What about for the items on your server?

A: Well, we actually don't have a policy yet for that. We keep everything. Storage is cheap.

The deposing attorney would continue to ask follow-up questions, but you get the idea. Regarding the adequacy of the search for responsive documents, the custodian of records may not know how the search was conducted; in that case, you could depose whoever conducted the search or a Rule 30(b)(6) designee.

Where the entity relies extensively on electronic communications and records and maintains a large amount of ESI, a more intense inquiry would be made regarding the creation, storage, retrieval, and retention policy concerning that material, as well as the methods of retrieving and producing ESI responsive to a particular discovery request or subpoena. Remember also that a company's ESI will be found not just on company servers and its employees' devices, but in the hands of third parties such as telecommunications companies, internet service providers, and social media organizations, all subject to subpoenas for ESI production and deposition.

Navigating a company's ESI and the adequacy of its discovery responses goes far beyond receiving documents at a deposition and asking a few questions of the records custodian who brought them. The following are three primary sources of information, one or more of which may be pursued at the beginning of discovery (to help word discovery requests) and during discovery (to ascertain the sufficiency of the responses to those requests). Note also that, in federal court, there are typically disclosures, meet and confer sessions, and orders early in the case to address ESI specifically (*see, e.g.,* Rule 26).

IT Officer

Depose the person responsible for designing and/or maintaining the company's electronic document systems to learn the nature of the systems the company uses to store electronic documents (personal computers, cell phones, tablets, servers, outside vendors, etc.), the methods by which ESI is created, the type of electronic documents maintained, and the retention system that can track the electronic document from accessible data retention systems (e.g., hard drives) to back-up systems, archives, and final repositories.

Rule 30(b)(6) Designees

A deposition of a party or nonparty corporation, partnership, or other organization can be noticed under Rule 30(b)(6), obligating the organization to designate one or more individuals to testify on the organization's behalf on topics set forth in the notice (*see* Chapter Twenty-One). In this context, the topics of inquiry would pertain to the location of relevant ESI and the efforts to preserve and produce it. Specific topics might include the following:

- organization of the company and its departments
- the records maintained and the means of communication among employees
- categories of ESI created or maintained by the company

- manner in which ESI is created and maintained (to establish business record exception in the absence of suitable certification for document production)

- location of ESI (hard drives, servers, individual laptops, cellphones, etc.)

- native format of the ESI

- ESI retention policy

- if a party—whether and when it instigated a litigation hold and whether ESI was destroyed, deleted, or altered thereafter

- identity of the custodians of ESI records, IT personnel, and the workers involved in the party's ESI retrieval and production

- method employed to retrieve ESI responsive to the production request or subpoena

- method used to decide whether attorney-client privilege or other privilege should be asserted

- former employees, third parties, and others not under the company's control, who may possess the company's ESI

Electronic Document Custodians

These individuals, who may or may not be the IT professionals or Rule 30(b)(6) designees discussed above, can authenticate the ESI produced in discovery and provide a foundation for its admissibility in summary judgment proceedings or at trial.

Other sources of information include a consulting expert witness, who can explain the company's systems and the value of the company's ESI, and forensic computer experts familiar with recovering deleted files. Also ask employees deposed for substantive reasons how they record information at the company and communicate on a daily basis. Former employees may be deposed to learn about the day-to-day creation, storage, and retrieval of ESI and its whereabouts (they may have even retained the party's ESI on cellphones and flash drives after their departure).

10.6.2 Addressing a Witness's Reference to Documents That Have Not Been Produced

Let's turn next to another document-related topic that can arise during a deposition: the witness refers to documents that have not been produced in discovery but appear to be relevant to the case.

When a witness mentions documents that have not yet been obtained by the deposing attorney, the deposing attorney typically turns to the witness's attorney to engage in the following type of colloquy:

Deposing Counsel:	Vito, will you provide us with these documents we've been talking about?
Defending Counsel:	Well, I don't think they were on any of your requests to produce, Ann, and they certainly weren't among the documents subject to mandatory disclosure under Rule 26(a)(1)(B).
Deposing Counsel:	I'm not saying they were. I'm just asking whether you will agree to provide us with the file of letters and the other materials, the memoranda, that Mr. Shadis has referred to in the last hour or so.
Defending Counsel:	We don't have them here.
Deposing Counsel:	When can you produce them?
Defending Counsel:	I don't know. I'll have to get back to you.
Deposing Counsel:	Well, it's going to have to be soon, because you can see that we're probably going to have to have some more time with Mr. Shadis after we get the documents.
Defending Counsel:	I'm not going to agree to that. You could have asked for the documents before you scheduled this deposition. We're not going to just hold it open and let you keep coming back again and again.
Deposing Counsel:	Well, we scheduled the deposition to fit your witness's schedule, and you know that. If you've held back some documents we have to ask him about, then we'll get an order for him to return.
Defending Counsel:	Ann, we'll look at the transcript when we get it and do the best we can, consistent with our need to represent our client's best interests and to avoid subjecting him to harassment through repetitive depositions.
Deposing Counsel:	You're being unreasonable and I'm seeking sanctions.

Defending Counsel: Oh, get off it. Do you have a question for this witness or are we done?

This type of unproductive dialogue occurs so frequently that we ought to give it a number, and whenever the situation arises, we could simply announce, "Document production argument number three" and it would be understood that all the above worthless verbiage was intended.

Why was it worthless verbiage? Because the defending counsel agreed to nothing more than to look at the transcript and make a decision. If, after two months, counsel finally decides not to produce the documents, he has not violated any agreement or order and no motion to compel discovery is teed up. If counsel does agree to produce the requested documents, often the record is not clear on what documents must be provided or when. If a few pages have been produced a month later, the record does not clearly support an order compelling further production. Even if the deposing counsel is unable to get more out of the defending attorney at the deposition, counsel must pursue the matter afterwards.

How should you handle this situation?

If the document to which the witness referred falls within the scope of a request for production of documents (or document subpoena) that has already been served, state on the record: "Counsel, I don't believe that the document has been produced to us, and it's clearly within the scope of our discovery request. I ask that you produce it to me now, so I have a chance to ask questions of the witness."

If defending counsel knows the document and is comfortable releasing it without further review (for privilege or otherwise), they can and should promptly agree to produce it, since the scope of their obligation is clear. Specify the document(s) to be produced on the record. If the document is readily available, defending counsel should produce it during the deposition to avoid a later squabble over whether the deposition must be reconvened so you can ask the witness about it. If necessary, defending counsel should have the document couriered to the deposition (or, of course, delivered electronically). You are in a much stronger position to demand that the deposition be continued or resumed at some future time, and even recover your costs for doing so, if counsel failed to comply with a valid request to produce. If defending counsel refuses to produce the document at the deposition, attempt to get an on-the-record agreement that the document will be produced by a specified date. Follow up with a letter immediately after the deposition, requesting a reconvening of the deposition (if reasonable) and reserving the right to pursue all appropriate remedies for the failure to provide timely discovery.

Some defending counsel may respond, "Write me a letter to tell me exactly which document you want, and we'll review it," or something to the effect of, "I will take your request under advisement." Do not engage in a battle over this on the record, upending your deposition; you might discuss the matter with defending counsel during a break, and you should certainly follow up with a letter after the deposition—and a motion to compel and for sanctions if appropriate—but defending counsel may well have a good faith reason for wanting to review the document before agreeing to turn it over. (Surprisingly, we estimate that no follow-up letter is ever sent in over half the times defending counsel makes this kind of response.)

If the document to which the witness referred is not the subject of a prior document request, state something like this on the record: "Counsel, I don't believe that the document has been produced to us, and it's clearly relevant. Will you provide it now without another formal request for discovery so I can ask the witness questions about it?"

If defending counsel agrees, great. More likely, particularly if defending counsel is not sure what document the witness has in mind, they may choose to take the matter under advisement pending their review of the document. In that case, try to obtain an on-the-record agreement that the document will be provided by a certain date without a formal discovery request, or at least defending counsel will provide a response by that time; if no such agreement is reached by the close of the deposition, however, immediately serve a formal request for the document, because time is a-ticking.

Some defending attorneys do insist on a formal production request instead of a mere letter or oral request, but the advantage is not clear. Giving counsel the benefit of the doubt, it is possible that they find it easier to get their clients' attention if they can tell them, "These documents are subject to a request for production," than if they have to say, "Well, they wrote me a letter asking for them." Check your jurisdiction's civility rules.

The takeaway? Stuff happens in depositions, including revelations that the other side has not provided all the documents and other material it should have. State your position, take a reasonable but firm approach, and neither forget about the situation nor let it distract you from the remainder of the deposition.

CHECKLIST
DOCUMENTS AND ESI

✔	Select documents and ESI to use as exhibits.
✔	Incorporate the exhibits into the deposition outline.
✔	Decide whether the exhibits will be presented in hard copy or digital form.
✔	Confirm the system for marking exhibits, including whether to premark and any required or agreed numbering system.
✔	Prepare the documents and ESI as exhibits, depending on whether they are hard copies or digital copies, and whether the deposition is in person or remote.
✔	Think through the steps for using the documents at the deposition, including: ✓ marking (if not premarked); ✓ presenting the exhibit to the witness; ✓ laying an evidentiary foundation; ✓ referring to the document by exhibit number; ✓ pointing the witness to the portion of the exhibit; ✓ asking the essential document questions.
✔	Decide whether and how to ask the witness to create or annotate exhibits.
✔	Conduct other depositions to confirm compliance with document and ESI requests, as needed.
✔	Determine how to address a witness's reference to documents that have not been produced.

CHAPTER ELEVEN

EVIDENTIARY FOUNDATIONS

He who has not first laid his foundations
may be able with great ability to lay
them afterwards, but they will be laid
with trouble to the architect and danger
to the building.

—Niccolo Machiavelli

A deposition will be more effective if you take the opportunity to lay the necessary evidentiary foundation for the later use of favorable deposition testimony and exhibits. Although no foundation is required to question the witness about the evidence at the deposition, the deposition is not your end goal. Elicit facts about the evidence from the witness to ensure its later admissibility in evidentiary proceedings such as a summary judgment motion or trial.

In this chapter, we discuss evidentiary foundations generally and, more specifically, the foundational facts to establish through the deposition witness in common situations. We also consider tips to make the process go smoother and the possibility of negating an evidentiary foundation for unfavorable evidence.

> **In This Chapter:**
> - *Evidentiary foundations*
> - *Foundational facts to establish through the deposition witness*
> - *Tips to make the process go smoother*
> - *Techniques to negate the foundation for unfavorable evidence*

11.1 What Is an Evidentiary Foundation?

Every trial lawyer knows the importance of "laying a foundation"; few agree what that phrase means. Some commentators and judges limit the concept to establishing that an item of evidence is authentic—that it is what its proponent claims it to be.[1] The concept of "foundation" may also reflect the principle that a lay witness can testify only from their personal knowledge. In other instances, however, the term is used more broadly to mean the proof of any fact that is a prerequisite to admissibility.[2]

- is **relevant**, in that it has a "tendency to make a fact more or less probable than it would be without the evidence" and "the fact is of consequence in determining the action" (Fed. R. Evid. 401, 402; *see* 403, 404)

- is **authentic**, in that it "is what the proponent claims it is" (Fed. R. Evid. 901, 902)

- is not **hearsay**, or it falls within an exception to the hearsay rule (Fed. R. Evid. 801–804)

- is an **original (or duplicate)** of a writing, recording, or photograph if offered to prove its content (Fed. R. Evid. 1001–1003) or constitutes permissible secondary evidence under Fed. R. Evid. 1004

Used in this broader sense, to lay the foundation for the admission of evidence, the attorney must establish that the item of evidence:

Furthermore, this foundation must be established by someone who is competent to testify and has personal knowledge of the facts supporting the requirements (Fed. R. Evid. 601, 602).

It is beyond the scope of this book, of course, to list the foundational facts for all the different types of evidence. For depositions, the question is essentially this: in light of the requirements for the admissibility at trial of a writing, recording, or photograph (which you are also using as an exhibit at the deposition) or the deposition testimony itself, what can you do during the deposition to make the later admission of that document or testimony into evidence more likely? Let's look at writings, recordings, and photographs first.[3]

---

1. Fed. R. Evid. 901(a): "To satisfy the requirement of authenticating or identifying an item of evidence, the proponent must produce evidence sufficient to support a finding that the item is what the proponent claims it is."
2. Black's Law Dictionary (8th ed.) defines "Laying a Foundation" as "Introducing evidence of certain facts needed to render later evidence relevant, material, or competent."
3. For the evidentiary requirements related to the admission of expert witness testimony, see Chapter Twenty-Two. Those seeking a more detailed discussion of evidentiary foundations should refer to any of the major trial advocacy treatises for their discussions of relevance, authenticity, hearsay, the best evidence (or "original document") rule, and the competence of witnesses. An excellent trial advocacy treatise containing a chapter devoted to foundations and exhibits is STEVEN LUBET AND

11.2 Writings, Recordings, and Photographs

As mentioned, the admission into evidence of a writing, recording or photograph requires the proponent to make a threshold showing that the item is relevant, authentic, not hearsay, and, if applicable, either the "original" or "duplicate" of the item. We will take these in a slightly different order.

11.2.1 Relevance

Relevance depends on the writing, recording, or photograph at hand and the issues in the case. Because the questions establishing relevance are so case-dependent, we will simply remind you to ask the witness questions showing that the item has a "tendency to make a fact more or less probable than it would be without the evidence" and "the fact is of consequence in determining the action" (Fed. R. Evid. 401), which your good deposition questions will be showing anyway.

11.2.2 Original Document/Best Evidence

The "original document" or "best evidence" rule rarely poses an obstacle to the admissibility of a document. To the extent the rule requires the original document to prove the document's contents, the term "original" is broad: for photographs, it includes the negative or a print from the negative; for ESI, it includes "any print-out—or other output readable by sight—if it accurately reflects the information." Fed. R. Evid. 1101(d). Moreover, the rules provide that a "duplicate," defined essentially as an accurate reproduction (such as a photocopy), is "admissible to the same extent as the original unless a genuine question is raised about the original's authenticity or the circumstances make it unfair to admit the duplicate." Fed. R. Evid. 1101(e), 1103.

In deposition, therefore, there is not much to do to lay the groundwork for meeting the "original document" or "best evidence" rule, except perhaps to forestall a claim that the exhibit is not an accurate copy. To that end, ask the witness, "Is this an accurate photocopy of the original?" or "You have no reason to think this is an inaccurate copy, do you?"[4]

---

j.c. Lore, Modern Trial Advocacy: Analysis and Practice, 6th ed. (NITA 2020). There also exists an "encyclopedia" of evidentiary foundations by Edward J. Imwinkelried with the catchy title of *Evidentiary Foundations*.

4. The original document rule can come into play when a party tries to prove the content of a document by oral testimony rather than by the original or duplicate of the document. The issue in that instance is not one of laying a foundation for the document, but one of phrasing questions when asking about its content: seek what the witness recalls or understands about the document as opposed to what is written in the document. Consult the evidence rules of your jurisdiction.

That leaves authentication and hearsay, which we discuss in turn, with some example lines of questioning.[5]

11.2.3 *Authentication*

As a practical matter, authenticating writings, particularly paper documents, is usually resolved by the time of trial. The standard for authentication is low—merely that there is some evidence from which a trier of fact could conclude that the document is authentic. Few documents are truly subject to a claim that the proponent has fabricated or adulterated them. As long as there is someone with knowledge of the preparation or receipt of the document (or even documents like it), authentication is routinely satisfied. In fact, some types of documents are self-authenticating, and many courts rule that the party who produced a document from its files in response to a discovery request cannot later raise an authentication objection.[6]

There are exceptions, of course. Photographs can be photoshopped, and social media can be manipulated. Video and audio recordings can be edited, and ESI can be adulterated. If there is a key document the other side desperately wants to keep out of evidence, they might argue that there is no person with sufficient personal knowledge to authenticate it. But these instances are relatively few. As a result, the authenticity of most documents is stipulated by the parties, either shortly before trial or in response to requests for admission. Even without a stipulation, the document may be admitted because no objection is asserted when offered at the trial.

Regardless, familiarize yourself with the way writings, recordings, and photographs can be authenticated—including in a deposition. After all, your efforts to authenticate documents at the deposition may reduce the debate over authentication at the time of trial. As suggested in Chapter Ten, try to get the witness to authenticate every exhibit used in the deposition (with the possible exception of documents that are so bad you would never want them to be in evidence—as to those, see the "negative foundation" discussion at the end of this chapter).

There are two key concepts to satisfying the authentication requirement. First, the facts you need to elicit for authentication depend on the purpose for which you are offering the writing, recording, or photograph. If a letter is being offered to prove

---

5. Of course, an item of evidence might raise all sorts of other evidentiary issues such as undue prejudice, cumulative evidence, character evidence, and the like, but here we are focusing on common issues that can be addressed in deposition. If you want to ensure the admission of a particularly great piece of evidence at a future evidentiary proceeding, think through in advance the entirety of the foundation that will have to be laid, as well as all other potential evidentiary issues, and then consider if there is anything you can do about it during pretrial, including in a deposition.
6. *See* Nola Fine Art, Inc. v. Ducks Unlimited, Inc., 88 F. Supp. 3d 602, 607–08 (E.D. La., 2015) (party who produced an email in discovery "cannot seriously dispute the email's authenticity"); John Paul Mitchell Sys. v. Quality King Distribution, Inc., 106 F. Supp. 2d 462, 467 (S.D.N.Y. 2000) ("the act of production implicitly authenticated the documents").

that the witness wrote it, then the examination must establish by direct evidence ("I wrote that") or circumstantial evidence ("That's the stationery he uses") that the witness authored the letter. On the other hand, if you are offering the exhibit to establish that the addressee received it, you must establish that the addressee or some other witness recognizes the exhibit as the letter she received, or find circumstantial evidence to that effect. As another example, if a photo appearing on a social media site is being offered just to show what the defendant was doing in the photograph, the authentication is much less extensive than if you are offering it as a photograph that was posted by the defendant.

Second, authentication—that the contract, voicemail, email, text, etc. is what the proponent says it is—can be established in various ways, including direct evidence ("I saw them write it") and circumstantial evidence ("they must have written it because . . ."). An item can be authenticated as set forth in Fed. R. Evid. 901(b) (and state laws generally follow suit) as follows:

- **testimony by a witness with knowledge** that the item is what it is claimed to be ("that is the letter I wrote");

- **testimony by a lay witness that identifies the handwriting** as genuine, based on a familiarity with the handwriting that was not acquired for the litigation ("that's the letter he wrote, I recognize this handwriting from working with him for thirty years"); or

- **the appearance, contents, substance, or other distinctive characteristics** of an item ("that's the letter he wrote, no one else would have known to say those things and look, there's his company logo at the top").

There are other methods of authentication mentioned in the federal rule as well. For example, you may establish authentication by evidence describing a process or system and showing that it produces an accurate result, such as an x-ray. And, as discussed later in this chapter, audio recordings such as voicemail can be authenticated by a person identifying the voice, having heard it previously in circumstances confirming it was in fact that person's voice.

Federal Rule of Evidence 902 provides that some types of documents are "self-authenticating." Included are certain public documents, foreign documents, certified copies of public records, official publications issued by a public authority, newspapers and periodicals; trade inscriptions, signs, tags or labels affixed in the course of business and indicating origin, origin or control; commercial paper; certified records of a regularly conducted activity; certified records generated by an electronic process or system; and certified data copied from an electronic device, storage medium, or file. Because these items are self-authenticating, they do not require anything at trial (or in deposition) to authenticate them—just obtain any necessary certification and fulfill any other requirement mentioned in the rule.

What does all of this mean when you show the witness a document during a deposition? Unless the documents are self-authenticating, ask the witness "What is Exhibit [#]?" and "How do you know?" or elicit that information by leading questions. That alone will go a long way toward establishing authentication. For a deeper understanding of the issues and possible additional requirements, let's look at some examples.

Authenticating a Contract through Witness with Knowledge

Under Fed. R. Evid. 901(b)(1), a witness can authenticate evidence by testifying that the document is what it purports to be based on the witness's recognition of the item.

Q: Mr. Woodbridge, I am handing you what has been marked as Exhibit 14, which appears to be a contract between you and Mr. Morganfield for the sale of your mobile home. Do you recognize it?

A: Yes.

Q: What is Exhibit 14?

A: It is in fact the contract Morganfield and I signed for him to buy my mobile home.

Q: How do you recognize Exhibit 14 as the contract for the sale of your mobile home?

A: Well, I got the form out of a book of business forms a friend had. That's my signature right above the "Seller" line, and I saw Morganfield sign it right above the line marked "Buyer."[7]

Authenticating a Letter through Witness Who Recognizes Handwriting

Federal Rule of Evidence 901(b)(2) states that a writing or document can be authenticated by "[a] nonexpert's opinion that the handwriting is genuine, based on familiarity with it that was not acquired for the current litigation." Note the requirement that the familiarity cannot have been acquired for purposes of the litigation. If the witness became familiar with the signer's handwriting or signature before the lawsuit, testimony such as the following should suffice:

---

7. Some insist that you should also ask, "Is Exhibit [#] in substantially the same condition as you observed it at the time of the [relevant meeting, etc.]." In practice, this is more important in criminal cases where a chain of custody must be established. In civil cases, the deposing attorney should check the requirements and custom of the applicable jurisdiction; in any event, counsel may add that question to their inquiry about a document if they like.

National Institute for Trial Advocacy

Q: When did you receive the letter in question?

A: Christmas week of last year.

Q: Are you familiar with Mr. Sajid's handwriting?

A: Yes.

Q: How are you familiar with his handwriting?

A: I worked with him for ten years. I saw many notes and letters he wrote over that time. I saw his handwriting at least several hundred times.

Q: Are you also familiar with his signature?

A: Yes.

Q: How are you familiar with his signature?

A: Same way. Over those ten years I must have seen him sign more than a thousand letters and documents.

Q: I am handing you what has been marked as Exhibit 4 and ask if you recognize it?

A: Yes, this is the letter I received.

Q: Do you recognize the writing on that letter, Exhibit 4?

A: I do.

Q: Whose handwriting is it on Exhibit 4?

A: Mr. Sajid.

Q: Do you also recognize the signature on Exhibit 4?

A: Yes.

Q: Whose signature is it on Exhibit 4?

A: Mr. Sajid.

Authentication of Letter by Circumstantial Evidence

Under Federal Rule of Evidence 901(b)(4), a writing can be authenticated through circumstantial evidence. For example, in the prosecution of Alger Hiss in the 1940s, an FBI agent testified that transcriptions of certain government documents were typed on a typewriter owned by Hiss. This testimony was based on the unique characteristics of the letters produced by the Hiss typewriter. Similarly, if a note contained misspellings unique to the alleged author, there would be circumstantial evidence that the note was written by that person. Or, as another example, if a letter referred to facts that only the alleged author would likely know, there is circumstantial evidence of authorship.

Here is an example of authenticating a letter through circumstantial evidence:

Q: Did you ever have a discussion with a Mr. Chester Burnett about purchasing baseball bats from him?

A: Yes.

Q: Where was that discussion?

A: We were both attending a preseason game between the Cubs and the White Sox.

Q: When was that discussion?

A: I don't remember the exact date, but it was in the spring of this year.

Q: What was said in that discussion?

A: Burnett offered to sell me 1,500 of his top-of-the-line bats for $27.00 each. I told him I would get back with him.

Q: Did you ever hear from Mr. Burnett again?

A: Yes, I received a letter from him at the end of March offering again to sell me the bats.

Q: I am handing you what has been marked as Exhibit 2. Do you recognize it?

A: I do. This is the letter that Burnett sent me.

Q: Is the letter, Exhibit 2, on letterhead?

A: Yes, it is on the letterhead of Big Bat, Inc., Mr. Burnett's company.

Q: How do you know that's his letterhead?

A: I have conducted business with his company before, and he used that letterhead.

Q: Does Exhibit 2 refer to the meeting between you and Mr. Burnett that was held at the Cubs-White Sox preseason game?

A: Yes. It says right here that he enjoyed meeting me at the game and that he is renewing his offer to sell me 1,500 bats for $27.00 each.

Here, there were two bases for authentication: the letter was on the letterhead of Big Bat, Inc., and it contained information that would likely be known only by the purported sender. The more evidence supporting authentication, the better.

The Reply Letter Doctrine, adopted in some states, is a variant on the use of circumstantial evidence to establish authenticity. Under this doctrine, if the witness sent a letter to Ms. X and then received in the mail a letter purportedly signed by Ms. X and referring to or in purported reply to the first letter, there is sufficient circumstantial evidence of the authenticity of the second letter—that it came from Ms. X.

Q: Did you ever notify the defendant of your concerns?

A: Yes, I wrote her detailing my complaints.

Q: How did you do that?

A: I wrote a letter, put it in an envelope, stamped it, and mailed it.

Q: What address did you use on the letter?

A: The one in the ad she sent me.

Q: When did you send this letter?

A: That day, August 3, 2022.

Q: What happened after that?

A: I got a letter back in the mail.

Q: When did you receive that reply?

A: About two weeks later.

Q: Did that second letter have a signature?

A: Yes, above the defendant's name.

Q: Did the letter you received refer in any way to the letter you sent?

A: Yes, it responded to the concerns I raised in my letter to the defendant.

Q: I am handing you what has been marked as Exhibit 8. Do you recognize it?

A: Yes.

Q: What is Exhibit 8?

A: This is the letter I received from the defendant.

Of course, nowadays communications are much more often by email or text than by letter. That makes authentication even easier, because you can see that the other party's correspondence was sent in reply.

Authenticating Audio Recordings

Assume here that we do not have a paper document but an audio recording used as an exhibit at the deposition. To establish authentication for purposes of admission at a later evidentiary proceeding, ask the following:

Q: Do you hear the recording of Exhibit 101, which we just played?

A: Yeah.

Q: Whose voices are on the recording?

A: Dennis and Nami.

Q: How do you know?

A: I recognize them from work. Nami sits next to me, Dennis is always hanging around.

That may be enough to establish authentication of the voices on the recording. There may still be an issue of whether it is a fair and accurate recording of the conversation. If the witness has knowledge of the conversation, ask this question as well:

Q: Since you were there too, is Exhibit 101 a fair and accurate recording of the conversation?

A: Yeah, sounds like it.

It may also be necessary, for relevance purposes, to establish the date and time of the conversation. Again, to the extent possible with the witness, elicit those facts too. Alternatively, obtain the necessary testimony by deposing the participants in the conversation (Dennis or Nami), a custodian of the recording, or an expert witness.

Authenticating Voicemail

Authenticate a voicemail the way you authenticate other audio recordings— identify the speaker and, in some scenarios, confirm that it appears to be a fair and accurate recording of the message. For example, authenticate the voicemail recording by testimony that the witness recognizes the voice on the message or observed the message being sent.

Authenticating ESI—Generally

Authenticating ESI essentially follows the same rules as authenticating hard-copy documents. Often the authentication is established through the deposition testimony of the source's custodian of electronic records, a certificate of records or data from that custodian (Fed. R. Evid. 902(b)(13)–(14)), or your own expert witness.[8] But as with other evidence, a lay witness may authenticate the item based on that person's knowledge of the item's creation or receipt, or by circumstantial evidence such as the item's contents and the production of the item in discovery by the purported authoring party.[9]

Authenticating Emails and Texts

The sender or recipient of an email or text can authenticate the item as one they personally sent or received. Someone else can authenticate the item through circumstantial evidence. For example, to authenticate an email as one sent by "Mr. Sledge," the witness can testify that the sender's address stated on the email belonged to Mr. Sledge, the content of the email reflected information told to Mr. Sledge, and the witness had received emails from Mr. Sledge in the past. For texts, testimony that the deponent recognizes the sender's phone number, or content of the message, may provide the necessary authentication.[10]

Of course, the opposing party can argue at trial that someone other than Mr. Sledge used his email account (or used his phone to send the text), but in the absence of evidence to that effect, the low threshold for authentication will likely be met. In fact, even if there were evidence of someone else posing as Mr. Sledge—thus creating a factual issue for the jury—there is a good chance the court would allow the evidence, concluding the dispute goes to the weight of the evidence, not its admissibility.[11]

> *Authenticate ESI as you would anything else: direct or circumstantial evidence that it is what it purports to be.*

---

8. Federal Rule of Evidence 902(b)(13)–(14) is particularly helpful in this regard. Rule 902(b)(13) deems the following to be self-authenticating: "A record generated by an electronic process or system that produces an accurate result, as shown by a certification of a qualified person that complies with the certification requirements of Rule 902(11) or (12). The proponent must also meet the notice requirements of Rule 902(11)." Rule 902(b)(14) applies to "Data copied from an electronic device, storage medium, or file, if authenticated by a process of digital identification, as shown by a certification of a qualified person that complies with the certification requirements of Rule 902(11) or (12). The proponent must meet the notice requirements of Rule 902(11)."

9. American Federation of Musicians of the United States v. Paramount Pictures Corp., 903 F.3d 968, 976 (9th Cir. 2018) (despite failure to authenticate email in deposition, document was admissible because it was produced by the opposing party and bore an electronic signature and address).

10. *E.g.*, United States v. Teran, 496 F. App'x 287, 292 (4th Cir. 2012).

11. There are other ways of authenticating emails, such as by expert witness testimony or identifying hash marks. Lorraine v. Markel Am. Ins. Co., 241 F.R.D. 534, 538–39, 546–47 (D. Md. 2007). An email may also be deemed authentic if produced in discovery. Nola Fine Art, Inc. v. Ducks Unlimited, Inc., 88 F. Supp. 3d 602, 607–08 (E.D. La., 2015) (party who produced the email in discovery "cannot seriously dispute the email's authenticity"); John Paul Mitchell Sys. v. Quality King Distribution, Inc., 106 F. Supp. 2d 462, 467 (S.D.N.Y. 2000) ("the act of production implicitly authenticated the documents").

Authenticating a Witness's Social Media Post

Let's now address the world of social media posts. If it is a post of the witness, the witness has personal knowledge and can easily authenticate it.

Q: Is Exhibit 14 a fair and accurate printout of a post you made on the PostOnMe webpage?

A: Yes.

Q: It has a date of "05/07/21." What do you understand that to be?

A: May 7, 2021.

Q: Do you have reason to believe the date is inaccurate?

A: Huh?

Q: Does May 7, 2021, sound about right as the day you posted?

A: Yeah.

Authenticating Another Person's Social Media Post

It is more difficult to authenticate a post supposedly made by someone other than the witness. The key, once again, is to elicit circumstantial evidence from which a trier of fact could reasonably conclude it was posted by that other person. Evidence of the name on the page and the page's content (such as photos of the individual and their family, and other matters related to the individual) is circumstantial evidence that the account belongs to that person and, assuming an account has a password and access is needed to post, that the posts were made by that person.[12] So, in deposition, it might be profitable to ask the witness to state those facts.

Q: Is Exhibit 15 a printout of one of the plaintiff's posts on the PostOnMe webpage?

A: Yes, it is.

Q: How do you know?

A: It has her name and photo on the page.

Q: Is there anything else that makes you think it is her page?

A: Oh look, there's a picture of her cat. Aww. And her pet monkey.

Q: Is there anything about the language used by the poster that makes you think it was the plaintiff?

---

12. *E.g.*, Taylor v. Sullivan, 2019 U.S. Dist. LEXIS 7308 (E.D. Cal. 2019); People v. Valdez, 201 Cal. App. 4th 1429, 1434–35 (2011).

A: Yeah, sounds like the way she talks.

Q: What do you mean?

A: Those words "indisputably obnoxious" are something she says all the time. Like, all the time.

Q: Are you familiar with PostOnMe?

A: Yes, I have an account.

Q: Do PostOnMe accounts have passwords?

A: Duh.

Q: Is that a "yes"?

A: Yes.

Q: Can anyone post on your PostOnMe page without entering your password to get into the account?

A: No. Not that I know of. I mean, people get hacked.

Q: I understand, but as a general rule, if someone does not have the password to your account, they cannot post on your page, right?

A: Right.

Q: Did you ever hear that plaintiff's PostOnMe account had been hacked?

A: No.[13]

You need a much less extensive foundation if you just want to authenticate a photo that appears on the page—not caring who posted it or whose account it appears on, but only what it depicts.

Q: Is Exhibit 33 a photo of Barrata kissing her assistant?

A: Yes.

Q: Does it fairly and accurately depict Barrata kissing her assistant in June 2020, before her divorce?

A: Yes.

---

13. Again, there are various ways of authenticating a post, including through the poster's testimony that they created and posted it, evidence gained from the hard drive of the alleged poster, or information from the hosting site that connects the post to the poster. Griffin v. State, 19 A.3d 415, 427–28 (Md. 2011); United States v. Browne, 834 F.3d 403, 410–14 (3d Cir. 2016), cert. denied, 137 S. Ct. 695 (2017); United States v. Encarnacion-La Fontaine, 639 F. App'x 710, 713 (2d Cir. 2016).

Q: How do you know?

A: I was there.[14]

Authenticating Video Recordings

Video is ubiquitous these days: cellphone video, GoPro and other brands of personal video recorders, Ring doorbells and other brands of video doorbells, home security footage, commercial security cameras, government security cameras, traffic cameras, private investigator or law enforcement surveillance, police bodycams, drone cameras, and more. Furthermore, videos are often uploaded to the web and broadly shared through social media sites and across cyberspace.

If a video was created by or in the possession of an organization, it might be authenticated via a certificate from the organization's electronic records custodian. The opposing party may still object to its admission at trial, contending for example that the video was altered; it recorded the scene from a misleading angle, in poor lighting, with a lens that distorted the scene; or it captured only part of the event and therefore is more misleading and prejudicial than probative. The challenges may be such that an expert witness or electronic records custodian will have to testify. The video may even violate an individual's constitutional or statutory right to privacy, their reasonable expectation of privacy, or their rights under two-party consent laws.

Nonetheless, there are some basic questions that you can ask in a deposition that contribute to a finding of authentication, whether or not you have the custodian's certificate or testimony. For example, if the video is played as an exhibit at the deposition, and the witness shot the footage or has personal knowledge of the scene, you might ask questions like these:

Q: Is Exhibit 3 a fair and accurate depiction of Mr. Bannister leaving the office?

A: Yeah, that's him alright. That's our office. He's going out and down the steps.

Q: I note that the first frame is time-stamped July 25, 2022, 04:32:11. Do you have any reason to believe that this information is incorrect?

A: No, I don't. He usually left around 4:30 in the morning, so, yeah.

---

14. If the witness can identify Barrata and her assistant but does not know when the photo was taken, other evidence would have to be obtained showing when the kiss occurred to satisfy the relevance requirement.

Q: Do you have any reason to believe that this video has been edited or altered in any way?

OC: Objection, no foundation. No personal knowledge. Not an expert.

Q: You may answer.

A: No, the video didn't skip or anything.

Q: What is Mr. Bannister carrying in his right hand?

OC: Objection, speculation.

A: Looks like a company laptop, given the shape and the logo and all.

Authenticating Public Records

Under Federal Rule of Evidence 901(b)(7), a document may be authenticated as a public record with evidence that it was recorded or filed with a public office. Laying the foundation through deposition testimony is possible, but rarely necessary.

Federal Rule of Evidence 902(4) provides the most convenient way of authenticating a public record: authentication by certification. The document is certified as correct either by a custodian or by a certificate that complies with Federal Rule of Evidence 902(1)–(3). The specifics of certification under Rule 902(1)–(3) depend on whether the record is that of a foreign government or a U.S. governmental unit and whether the document bears a seal of that governmental entity. As an example, a document is self-authenticating if it bears a seal of the United States and a signature of attestation. Fed. R. Evid. 902(1).

If a public record is self-authenticating and falls within the hearsay exception for public records (Fed. R. Evid. 803(8)), it is unnecessary to question a witness to lay a foundation.

Authenticating Demonstrative Exhibits—Photos, Maps, and Diagrams

The foundations for photographs, maps, and diagrams as illustrative or demonstrative exhibits—in other words, as an aid to understanding a scene—all have similar requirements. First, the witness must identify the photograph, map, or diagram as portraying the relevant scene (of the crime, of the accident, of the layout of the building, etc.) based on their knowledge of the scene. Second, the witness must testify that the photograph, map, or diagram "fairly and accurately" depicts or represents the scene at the relevant time (of the crime, accident, or other event).

A map or diagram need not be drawn to scale, although you may want to elicit that information for clarity (and to help rebut an objection that the map or diagram distorts the scene). Nor does the witness need to be the one who drew the map or diagram or took the photograph of the scene; familiarity with the scene itself is sufficient, so the witness has a basis for comparing the image to reality. So, for a photograph:

Q: Is Exhibit 32 a photograph of the intersection of Lakeshore and Grand?

A: Yes.

Q: Does it fairly and accurately depict that intersection at the time of the accident?

A: Yes.

Q: How do you know?

A: I've been there a thousand times, including that day.

For a diagram:

Q: Is Exhibit 33 a diagram of the intersection of Lakeshore and Grand?

A: Yes.

Q: Does it fairly and accurately represent that intersection at the time of the accident?

A: Yes.

Q: How do you know?

A: I've been there a thousand times, including that day.

And here is another version:

Q: Are you familiar with the intersection of Kirby and Richmond?

A: I am.

Q: How did you become familiar with that intersection?

A: I drive through that intersection nearly every day.

Q: Are you familiar with the way it looked in December of last year?

A: Yes. It hasn't changed much since then.

Q: Are you familiar with the way it looked when you are facing north?

A: Sure, that's the way I drive through it going to work in the mornings.

Q: I am handing you what has been marked as Exhibit 12 and ask if you recognize what is shown in the photograph?

A: I do. That's the intersection of Kirby and Richmond.

Q: Does Exhibit 12 fairly and accurately show the intersection of Kirby and Richmond as it appeared during the month of December last year?

A: Yes.

Q: Does it fairly and accurately show the intersection as it appeared when facing north?

A: Yes.[15]

11.2.4 Hearsay

Any out-of-court oral or written statement, if offered to prove the truth of the matter asserted in the statement, is hearsay under the Federal Rules of Evidence unless it is

- **a prior inconsistent statement** (Fed. R. Evid. 801(d)(1)) (or, in some circumstances, a prior consistent statement): inconsistent with the declarant's testimony at trial and was given under penalty of perjury, such as at a deposition; or

- **a statement of a party-opponent** (Fed. R. Evid. 801(d)(2)): offered against an opposing party and made "by the party in an individual or representative capacity," adopted by the party, by a person authorized by the party to speak on the subject, "by the party's agent or employee on a matter within the scope of that relationship and while it existed," or by the party's coconspirator during and in furtherance of the conspiracy.

When you ask a deposition witness about a document in the case, the document is obviously an out-of-court statement. Whether the document is offered to prove that its content is true will depend on how the document is used at trial (or summary judgment), so there is nothing we can do about that in the deposition. Nor can we determine until trial whether the document is inconsistent with the witness's trial testimony.

We can, however, ascertain during the deposition whether the document is a statement made by the opposing party, and thus not subject to the hearsay rules. While that is an easy thing to figure out if the document is written or created by an individual who is the opposing party, it is sometimes less clear when the document

---

15. At trial, the proponent of the evidence should also ask the witness if the demonstrative or illustrative exhibit would assist in giving testimony.

was written or created by an individual who is an agent or employee of the opposing party. The question, essentially, is whether the individual was authorized by the party to speak on the subject, was acting within the scope of their employment, or wrote something that the party later adopted. In deposition, therefore, when asking the witness who created the document, also ask a question that addresses these issues.

> Q: Who wrote this letter?
>
> A: I did.
>
> Q: You wrote this as part of your job duties?
>
> A: Yes.

Or here is another example:

> Q: Do you see that the email is from Ms. Taylor's work email account?
>
> A: Yes.
>
> Q: The email address is jtaylor@wembler.com so that was a company email account?
>
> A: Uh, yeah. True.
>
> Q: At the time this was written, Ms. Taylor was an employee of Wembler Company?
>
> A: She was.
>
> Q: You authorized her to write letters like this to customers as part of her job duties?
>
> A: Yeah, that was part of her job.

You do not have to do this for every document, and you may not have to do it at all if there is no way the opponent can quibble about whether the document was created by the witness within the scope of their employment. If there is a potential issue, however, the deposition is a great place to head it off at the pass.

Let's continue now with our hearsay analysis. If the statement is hearsay according to the foregoing rules, it is generally inadmissible unless it:

- **falls within an exception to the hearsay rule under Federal Rule of Evidence 803,** regardless of whether the declarant is available for trial, such as exceptions for a present sense impression, an excited utterance, a statement of then-existing mental, emotional, or physical condition, statements made for medical diagnosis or treatment, recorded recollection, records of a "regularly conducted activity," and seventeen other exceptions; or

National Institute for Trial Advocacy

- **falls within an exception to the hearsay rule under Federal Rules of Evidence 804** because the declarant is not available for trial and the statement constitutes the witness's former testimony, was made while under the belief of imminent death (a "dying declaration"), was against their proprietary or pecuniary interest or exposed them to civil or criminal liability, or otherwise satisfies Fed. R. Evid. 804(b).

Of all these exceptions, the ones you can most likely set up during a deposition are those dealing with excited utterances, statements made for medical diagnosis or treatment, recorded recollection, and—most of all—records of a regularly conducted activity, otherwise known as the "business records exception."

Hearsay—Excited Utterance

An excited utterance is a "statement relating to a startling event or condition, made while the declarant was under the stress of excitement that it caused." (Fed. R. Evid. 803(2).) A deponent, asked about a diary entry, journal, blog, or social media post, might be asked the following questions to lay a foundation for the excited utterance exception:

Q: When you wrote this in your diary, were you still stressed or excited about that event?

Hearsay—Statement for Medical Treatment

A statement is not made inadmissible by the hearsay rules if it was made for (and reasonably pertinent to) medical diagnosis or treatment and it describes medical history, symptoms, their inception, or general cause. (Fed. R. Evid. 803(4).) When a deponent is recounting statements made to medical personnel, if the reason is not otherwise obvious, the deponent may be asked in the deposition:

Q: Did you tell them these things so they could diagnose or treat you?

Hearsay—Recorded Recollection

Recorded recollection is a record that "is on a matter the witness once knew about but now cannot recall well enough to testify fully and accurately," "was made or adopted by the witness when the matter was fresh in the witness's memory," and "accurately reflects the witness's knowledge." (Fed. R. Evid. 803(5).)

To lay a foundation for a document under the exception for recorded recollection, ask the witness something like the following:

Q: Is it fair to say you can't recall [the topics discussed at the meeting] fully and accurately now?

Q: But you did know what topics were discussed when you were at the meeting?

Q: Let me show you what's been premarked as Exhibit 99. Counsel, here's a copy. Is Exhibit 99 a memo you made about the topics that were discussed at the meeting?

Q: Did you make this memo during or shortly after the meeting?

Q: When you made this memo, were the topics fresh in your mind?

Q: And the memo was accurate when you made it?

Hearsay—Business Records

Rule 803(6) of the Federal Rules of Evidence states that a "record of an act, event, condition, opinion, or diagnosis" is not made inadmissible by the hearsay rule if "the record was made at or near the time by—or from information transmitted by—someone with knowledge," "the record was kept in the course of a regularly conducted activity of a business, organization, occupation, or calling, whether or not for profit," "making the record was a regular practice of that activity," and "all these conditions are shown by the testimony of the custodian or another qualified witness, or by a certification that complies with Rule 902(11) or (12) . . ."

The foundation for the business record exception can be established either by testimony or by a certification that complies with Federal Rule of Evidence 902(11) or (12) and accompanies, for example, the company's production of documents. If you already have a certificate that fully establishes the elements of the business record exception, you do not need to lay the foundation through the deponent.

If you need to establish the business records exception through a deponent, ask the following questions:

Q: Does Exhibit 19 record an [act, event, condition, opinion, diagnosis]?

A: Yes.

Q: Was Exhibit 19 made at or near the time of the [act, event, condition, opinion, diagnosis]?

A: Yes.

Q: Was Exhibit 19 made by someone with knowledge of the event?

A: Yes, me.

Q: Was Exhibit 19 kept in the course of a regularly conducted activity of your business [organization, occupation, calling]?

A: Yes.

Q: Was making Exhibit 19 a regular practice of that activity?

A: Yes.

To lay the foundation for the business record exception, the witness has to know about the creation of the document—or, at least, must know how such documents are created in the regular course of the business. In other words, it will be sufficient if the witness understands how the type of document is created by the party, even if the witness lacks personal knowledge about the creation of the specific exhibit. So, for example, the custodian of records can be asked as follows:

Q: Are you the custodian of records for Nita Memorial Hospital?

A: Yes.

Q: Are you familiar with the making and keeping of the medical records at the hospital?

A: Yes.

Q: Are those records made and kept as part of the regularly conducted business activities of the hospital?

A: Yes.

Q: Are those records made at or near the time of the events recorded in them?

A: Yes.

Q: Are those records made by, or from information transmitted by, persons with firsthand knowledge of the events recorded in them?

A: Yes.

Q: Does the person reporting the information have a business duty to do so?

A: Yes.

Q: When you came to court today, did you bring with you the medical records for the plaintiff?

A: Yes.

Q: I hand you what has now been marked as Exhibit 14 and ask if you recognize it?

A: I do.

Q: Is Exhibit 14 the hospital's medical record for the plaintiff?

A: Yes.

Q: Is Exhibit 14 one of the records whose making and keeping you have just described?

A: Yes.

In establishing the business records exception through the testimony of a witness, you can ask the formal "litany" of questions set forth in the preceding examples, which tracks the words of the rule and is therefore most easily recognized by judges and attorneys; you could also ask a "prose" version, which uses less legalese and is therefore more jury-friendly and informative. This prose version can be added to (or supplant) the litany version when establishing the business record exception at trial. In deposition, however, it makes sense to use the litany version, unless the witness is unable to understand the questions.

Here, for your comparison, is an example of the prose version of the business record exception.

Q: What is your position at the Nita Memorial Hospital?

A: I am the custodian of medical records.

Q: What does the custodian of medical records at Nita Memorial Hospital do?

A: I am responsible for making sure that all the hospital's medical records are properly prepared and stored at the hospital.

Q: How are the records prepared?

A: The nurses and doctors make entries on a patient's medical chart of all information concerning the patient's treatment. For instance, when a doctor prescribes a medication, this is put on the chart; or when the patient's temperature is taken, that information is also put on the chart.

Q: Who makes these entries on the chart?

A: The nurses and doctors treating the patient.

Q: When are these entries made?

A: When the treatment is given. For example, when the patient's temperature is taken, the nurse will write the temperature on the chart right after taking it.

Q: How are these records kept?

A: When the patient is discharged, all of the patient's records are sent to the Medical Records Department, where we keep them for a specified period.

11.3 Deposition Testimony

Introducing deposition testimony at trial (or in connection with an evidentiary motion) is discussed at length in section 15.3. Essentially, FRCP 32(a) allows depositions to be used in court proceedings against parties to the extent permissible under the rules of evidence, against witnesses for impeachment as allowed under the rules of evidence, and, if the witness is "unavailable," for any purpose. In this chapter on evidentiary foundations, we again focus on the constraints imposed by the rules of relevance, authentication, and the original document and hearsay rules.

Relevance, as mentioned, depends on the facts and law of the case. Authentication and the original document rule should be satisfied by the court reporter's certificate on the deposition transcript or other recording.[16] So that leaves hearsay.

The witness's statements in the deposition are out-of-court statements and, offered for the truth,[17] would constitute inadmissible hearsay unless:

- **the statement is of a party opponent** and therefore not hearsay (Fed. R. Evid. 801(d)(2)); this would apply if the deposition was taken of an individual who is the opposing party; it may also apply if the deposition was of someone who was the party's officer, director, managing agent, or Rule 30(b)(6) designee, but usually not if the deponent was a lower-level employee (FRCP 32(a)(3));

- **the statement is a prior inconsistent statement** or consistent statement and therefore not hearsay (Fed. R. Evid. 801(d)(1)(A); *see* FRCP 32(a)(2)); or

- **the witness is unavailable** and the statement constitutes the witness's former testimony, offered against a party who had an opportunity and similar motive to develop it by examination at the deposition (Fed. R. Evid. 804(b)(1); *see* FRCP 32(a)(4))[18]

---

16. *See, e.g.*, Orr v. Bank of Am., 285 F.3d 764, 774 (9th Cir. 2002) ("A deposition or an extract therefrom is authenticated in a motion for summary judgment when it identifies the names of the deponent and the action and includes the reporter's certification that the deposition is a true record of the testimony of the deposition."); Contreras v. Am. Family Mut. Ins. Co., 135 F. Supp. 3d 1208, 1217 (D. Nev. 2015) ("Plaintiffs have failed to authenticate the deposition because it is not signed by the court reporter.").

17. Deposition testimony, taken under oath, is admissible both for impeachment of the declarant and for its truth (FRCP 32 (a)(2)). Deposition testimony not offered for its truth would not be hearsay. If the deposition testimony is used at trial merely to refresh the witness's recollection, the transcript and statements would not come into evidence and would not be read aloud (*see* Fed. R. Evid. 612, FRCP 32(a)(2)).

18. Rule 32(a)(4) of the Federal Rules of Civil Procedure, which governs when deposition testimony of an unavailable witness may be used at trial, provides that a witness is unavailable if the witness is deceased; the witness is more than 100 miles away; their attendance could not be secured by subpoena; they cannot testify due to age, illness, infirmity, or imprisonment; or other exceptional circumstances. Under Rule 804 of the Federal Rules of Evidence, which allows hearsay statements if the declarant is unavailable as a witness, provides that a witness is unavailable if the declarant is

There is, however, a caveat. Even if the witness's testimony at the deposition is made admissible under the foregoing rules, the testimony may be inadmissible to the extent the witness spoke of what someone else said or what was contained in a document. For example, there is a difference between a deposition witness giving a narrative description of what occurred at a party, and a deposition witness who also testifies, "Oh yeah, and then Michael said that a big shipment is coming in tonight and I said, 'money, money, money!'" To authenticate this testimony, you would have to show that it was, in fact, Michael who made the statement now attributed to him. Furthermore, the purported out-of-court statement of Michael and the purported out-of-court reply of the witness ("money, money, money") must be evaluated under the hearsay rule. To put it another way, the witness's deposition testimony might be admissible at trial generally because the witness has become unavailable, but Michael's purported statement and the witness's reply may still be ruled inadmissible unless some additional foundation has been laid at the deposition.

Let's take hearsay first. We again employ the usual analysis: is Michael's statement (or the witness's reply) offered for its truth; is it the statement of a party opponent or a prior inconsistent statement and therefore not hearsay under the federal rules; does the statement fall within an exception for a present sense impression, an excited utterance, a statement of then-existing mental, emotional, or physical condition, a statement made for medical diagnosis or treatment, or another exception under Fed. R. Evid. 803; or, if the declarant Michael is unavailable, was his statement made, for example, while under the belief of imminent death or against his proprietary or pecuniary interest (Fed. R. Evid. 804)?

Next, let's take the issue of authentication. While the witness obviously knew that they were the one who said, "money, money, money," you would have to establish what basis the witness had for concluding it was indeed Michael who said that a big shipment was coming in. Explore that foundation during the deposition. It might turn out to be obvious from context or it might take just one question—"how did you know it was Michael who said that"—but let's look at the broader issue in a variety of contexts.

11.3.1   Authenticating a Speaker's Voice

Authenticating a conversation—specifically, identifying who was speaking in that conversation—can be accomplished by a witness who heard the statement and knows the other person's voice, and/or by their knowledge of the time, place, and

---

exempted from testifying due to a privilege, refuses to testify despite court order, testifies to not remembering, or cannot be present due to death, infirmity, or physical or mental illness, or the proponent has not been able to secure their attendance as set forth in the rule. These rules provide alternative grounds for admissibility; you only need to satisfy one of them. *See* Ureland v. United States, 291 F.3d 993, 996 (7th Cir. 2002).

circumstances of the statement, from which it can be inferred it was that other person who spoke.

Here is the easiest situation: a witness who authenticates a conversation by stating they know the other person and were in attendance.

Q: Do you know Mr. Shrackle, the defendant?

A: I do.

Q: Were you present during the month of May 2022 at a conversation in which Mr. Shrackle participated?

A: I was.

Q: Where was that conversation held?

A: It was at my house.

Q: When was that conversation?

A: On May 10 at about 3:00 p.m.

Q: Who else was present?

A: It was just me and Mr. Shrackle.

Q: What did Mr. Shrackle say?

A: He said that he was ashamed of how he behaved the previous night.

Authenticating by Voice Identification

Sometimes the witness was not in the physical presence of the speaker when the speaker made the statement, as during a telephone conversation. One way to identify the speaker and authenticate the statement is to show the witness's familiarity with the speaker's voice (Fed. R. Evid. 901(b)(5)).[19]

Q: Are you familiar with Ms. Holton's voice?

A: Yes.

Q: How did you become familiar with her voice?

A: I dated her for a number of years.

Q: Did you receive a telephone call on June 8, 2018?

---

19. Note that the familiarity with the speaker's voice can be acquired after the statement was made and can even be acquired for purposes of litigation, unlike familiarity with handwriting. *See* Fed. R. Evid. 901(b)(2).

A: I did.

Q: Who called?

A: Ms. Holton.

Q: What did Ms. Holton say?

A: She said she was going out of town.

Circumstantial Evidence of Speaker's Identity

As with documents, circumstantial evidence can be used to establish the identity of a speaker. For example, if the speaker talks about information only the claimed speaker would know, there is circumstantial evidence of the speaker's identity. The elements and example of this type of foundation are the same as for circumstantial evidence of the author of a document.

Authentication of Call Where Voice Not Recognized

Under Federal Rule of Evidence 901(b)(6), an outgoing telephone call—one made by the witness—can be authenticated as a call made to the purported recipient by showing that it was made to the number assigned by the telephone company to that person or company; and, if made to a person, circumstances such as self-authentication showing that was the person who answered; if made to a company, that the call concerned business reasonably transacted over the phone.

Q: Did you ever place an order with the company by phone?

A: I did.

Q: When did you do that?

A: On Thursday of that week, sometime in the morning.

Q: Where did you get the number?

A: I looked it up on their website.

Q: When you called, how was the phone answered?

A: It was a man, and he said "Cut-Rate Order Department. May I help you?"

Q: What did you do?

A: I placed my order.

11.3.2 What This Means for Your Depositions

The takeaway for depositions is simply this: if the witness is testifying in deposition about a conversation in which the witness could not see one of the speakers, ask how the witness knows who the speaker was:

Q: You just testified that Mr. Shrackle said you had a screw loose. How did you know it was Shrackle?

A: After working for him for a year, his voice is etched into my mind forever. I recognized his voice.

This requirement also applies if the witness is testifying about a voicemail that the witness listened to. Again, authentication can be established in a number of ways; here are some options:

Q: You testified that you retrieved a message on your cell phone from Mr. Genghis. How did you know it was him?

A: I recognized his voice.

A: He said, "Hey, Genghis here, I got your new tires."

A: My cellphone showed his number next to the voicemail.

A: My old-fashioned message machine announced his phone number when it played back the message.

11.4 Laying Foundations Efficiently

Laying the foundation for the future admission of evidence takes time and can be frustrated by an uncooperative deposition witness. The following techniques will help.

11.4.1 Use Leading Questions When Permissible

It is more efficient to use leading questions when establishing an evidentiary foundation, especially with an adverse party, an agent or employee of an adverse party, or a hostile witness. Using leading questions in the deposition should suffice when the matter is later presented to the court at trial or on summary judgment for a decision: They are permitted at trial when questioning "a hostile party, an adverse party, or a witness identified with an adverse party," and even on direct examination "as necessary to develop the witness's testimony," as in the case of undisputed preliminary matters. Fed. R. Evid. 611(c). Moreover, Federal Rule of Evidence 104(a) states that a court is not even bound by the evidentiary rules when determining the admissibility of evidence. Nonetheless, it remains possible that a judge will not tolerate leading questions even for purposes of laying an evidentiary foundation, so it may be safest to avoid leading questions when establishing foundation in circumstances where it would be improper to lead the witness in questioning on the merits.

Where leading questions are permitted—with an adverse party or a witness aligned with that party, for example—leading is the way to go:

Q: I am handing you what has been marked as Exhibit 13, which appears to be a letter the witness sent to the plaintiff. This is a letter you wrote, correct?

A: Yes.

Q: You wrote that letter, Exhibit 13, on June 30 of last year?

A: Yes.

Q: And you mailed Exhibit 13 on that same day?

A: Yes.

11.4.2   Lay Foundations for Groups of Exhibits

You can frequently save time discussing categories of documents rather than laying the foundation for each exhibit separately:

Q: Mr. Shadis, Exhibit 76 is one of your company's invoices, correct?

A: Yes, it is.

Q: Was Exhibit 76 your company's standard form for invoices at the time of the sale we've been talking about?

A: Yes.

Q: I notice Exhibit 76 has "Shadis Co." in the upper right-hand corner and "Invoice No." and a blank line in the left corner, and then spaces for entering items and amounts. That was on your standard form of invoice in June 2022 for bulk purchases of Shadis construction materials?

A: Yes, that's the form we used then and we use now.

Q: All of your company invoices would be in the same form?

A: Yes, they would.

Q; You don't know of any other company that uses invoices with this form, with Shadis Co. in the upper-right corner?

A: No, I don't.

11.4.3   Ask for the Basis of a Foundation Objection

Sometimes opposing counsel will object using just the word, "foundation," and you will not know what counsel believes is wrong. As we have urged throughout this book, do not squabble with opposing counsel, but simply ask the witness to go ahead and answer the question. After the witness has answered, however, if you still do not know what opposing counsel was talking about, ask. There is no sense in floundering around, attempting to figure out what question you may have omitted. If the opponent refuses to reveal the basis for the objection, it will be harder later, under Rule 32(D)(3)(B), for them to argue that the objection was preserved; it is virtually impossible to cure a lack of foundation if the objector refuses to identify what is lacking. On the other hand, if opposing counsel clarifies the objection and you believe a judge might agree, you can cure the infirmity during the deposition.

11.4.4 Do Not Offer the Exhibit

There is no judge at the deposition and no need to offer an exhibit into evidence after laying a foundation. If you seek to use the exhibit and corresponding deposition testimony later, at that time the judge will rule on any objection that was properly asserted. Offering the exhibit into evidence at the deposition will produce either confusion or bemusement on the part of opposing counsel and the court reporter.

11.5 Negative Foundations: Precluding Admission of Bad Evidence

Up until now we have been talking about questions you should ask to facilitate the later use of favorable testimony at trial or another proceeding. Now let's look at what to ask in deposition that will lead to the exclusion of unfavorable evidence— that is, how we can establish a "negative" foundation for an exhibit or testimony that is bad for our case.

In our first example, the witness has made a damaging statement, so the deposing attorney seeks to show that there is no foundation for it.

Q: What is your basis for saying the customer list was the subject of reasonable efforts to keep it confidential?

A: Well, I mean, I never saw it on the internet or nothing.

Q: You were not an employee until May of 2021.

A: Yeah.

Q: You do not know firsthand what the company did to keep the customer list confidential before you started working in May 2021.

A: Well, no, not firsthand.

Q: Your conclusion is based on what you heard others say.

A: Well yeah, I wasn't there.

Q: Exactly. You did not personally see any nondisclosure agreements.

A: No, I didn't.

Q: You didn't see if copies of the customer list were stamped confidential.

A: Well, no.

This line of questioning suggests that the witness had no personal knowledge for their damaging assertion, which would likely render it inadmissible even if they become unavailable at trial or, if they are available for trial, provide a basis for a motion in limine to preclude such testimony.

As another example, consider a situation where a company has been sued for gender discrimination. As a precursor to bringing the action, a complaint was filed with the Equal Employment Opportunity Commission, which in turn requested a reply from the now-defendant company. In response to the request, the defendant company's human relations department investigated and prepared a report disclaiming any discrimination on the company's part and asserting that the now-plaintiff was discharged for poor work performance. The following, in pursuit of a "negative foundation," occurs at the deposition of the human relations officer, Ms. Wilson, by plaintiff's counsel:

Q: Ms. Wilson, were you the person who investigated my client's claim of gender discrimination at the Acme Paper Company?

A: Yes, I was.

Q: Did you prepare a report of your investigation for Acme's vice president for personnel?

A: I did.

Q: Let me show you a six-page document that we have marked as Exhibit 23, which appears to be a memorandum prepared by you on January 28, 2023, and sent to Joyce O'Toole, vice president for personnel at Acme Paper Company. Do you recognize Exhibit 23?

A: Yes, that's the memorandum I just told you about that contains my report on your client's complaint.

Q: Why was Exhibit 23 prepared?

A: As I understand it, your client had made a complaint of gender discrimination against Acme, and we had been asked by the EEOC to respond to that complaint.

Q: So when you conducted your investigation you knew that a complaint had been made by my client to the EEOC?

A: Yes, this has happened a few times in my ten years at Acme—someone complains to the EEOC, they ask for a response, and we respond.

Q: In the past when this has happened, has there ever been a lawsuit filed against Acme by the person who complained to the EEOC?

A: Yes, that has happened several times.

Q: Were you aware of that when you prepared Exhibit 23?

A: Yes.

Q: In addition to sending Exhibit 23 to Ms. O'Toole, does Exhibit 23 show that any copies were sent to anyone else, and I refer you to the last page, page six of Exhibit 23?

A: Yes, a copy was sent to Bob Burns, Acme's general counsel.

Q: Why was that?

A: Because there is always a possibility of litigation when an EEOC complaint is made.

Q: Am I correct then, that Exhibit 23 was prepared for two purposes—one, to respond to the EEOC, and two, in anticipation of possible litigation?

A: That's right.

With this "negative foundation," Exhibit 23 will likely be excluded as hearsay if offered at trial or summary judgment by the defendant company, because it was prepared in anticipation of litigation, which would disqualify it as a record of a regularly conducted activity (business record). (The plaintiff, however, could still offer Exhibit 23 into evidence as an opposing party statement if so desired.)

CHECKLIST

EVIDENTIARY FOUNDATIONS

✔	Review all intended exhibits and consider any evidentiary obstacles to their admission at trial or summary judgment.
✔	Consider to what extent those evidentiary issues might be resolved by inquiries of the witness at the deposition.
✔	For each deposition exhibit, ask the witness questions to authenticate it (what the item is and how the witness knows), especially if the exhibit is not self-authenticating (unless the exhibit is entirely bad).
✔	Consider different methods of authentication: knowledge of the item's creation or receipt; familiarity with handwriting or voice; appearance (e.g., logo); content.
✔	Ask if photos, maps, and diagrams "fairly and accurately depict" the scene at the relevant time.
✔	Ask if the exhibit appears to be a true and accurate copy.
✔	If the witness testifies in deposition to a voicemail or what somebody else said in a conversation outside their view, ask how they knew who was speaking.

✔	As to favorable hearsay, including out of court statements referenced in the witness's deposition testimony, elicit facts showing admissibility on the ground the statement was
	
	   ✓ Made by (or adopted by) a party opponent or representative;
	   ✓ An excited utterance;
	   ✓ A statement for medical treatment;
	   ✓ A recorded recollection;
	   ✓ Regarding regularly conducted business activity (business record).

✔	When laying a foundation, use leading questions when permissible.
✔	Preclude the admission of bad evidence by laying a negative foundation.

CHAPTER TWELVE

DEALING WITH WITNESSES

A hot-tempered person stirs up conflict,
but the one who is patient calms a quarrel.

—Proverbs 15:18

A deposition will be more effective if you adopt an approach geared specifically to the individual who is being deposed and their behavior during the deposition.

In this chapter, we discuss: 1) encouraging witnesses to talk by adopting an appropriate style, incorporating active listening and critical listening skills to gauge how to follow up with the witness, and exploiting the power of silence and other nonverbal techniques; 2) approaching special situations where the witness requires an interpreter or the witness is not represented by counsel; 3) handling common witness prototypes and witness behaviors, such as the witness who claims they cannot remember, knows nothing, evades the question, provides a vague or conditional answer, lies, or is combative; 4) dealing with a witness's harmful testimony; and 5) adjusting and reorganizing your planned inquiry in light of the witness's testimony and behavior.

> **In This Chapter:**
> - *Methods to encourage witnesses to talk*
> - *Approaching special situations such as the witness who needs an interpreter*
> - *Handling common witness prototypes and witness behaviors*
> - *Dealing with a witness's harmful testimony*
> - *Adjusting and reorganizing your deposition plan when the testimony is not going as planned*

12.1 Choosing an Appropriate Style

Each of us differs in personality, temperament, and demeanor. Each of has our own style. We must be ourselves, of course, and not try to imitate anyone else's personality even in a deposition. Nonetheless, in a deposition we may have to summon from deep within the various facets of who we are: hospitable, fair, patient, friendly, empathetic, and down-to-earth; formal, business-like, no-nonsense, assertive, and demanding; intelligent, precise, persistent, thorough, suspicious, and shrewd; yet flexible, unflappable, and undaunted. From deposition to deposition, witness to witness, case to case—and from time to time in the same deposition—we may need to summon any of these characteristics, while remaining professional in every situation.

The best style or demeanor to use with any given witness will largely depend on who the witness is and what the witness does during the deposition. But it will also depend on the context: how opposing counsel is behaving, what has happened previously in the deposition, how much material there is left to cover, and your perception of what the witness is trying to accomplish. As a result, despite your best preparation, you may not be able to predict the most profitable demeanor ahead of the deposition. Nevertheless, here are some essential observations.

12.1.1   *Generally, You Catch More Flies with Honey*

Your style and tone of voice when asking questions make a difference in the way a witness responds. Typically, a witness who sees you as being respectful, interested, and friendly is much more likely to provide full answers—and even volunteer information—than is a witness who believes you are conniving and judgmental.

Here are two possible responses to the identical question:

Q: What was your relationship like with Mr. Salas?

A: Fine.

versus

Q: What was your relationship like with Mr. Salas?

A: We got along well most of the time. You know, we chatted a lot about things, like what he had done that weekend and what I had done. Real friendly like. But then some days he would come in and be kind of nasty. Nothing he actually said, but just his tone of voice. Really hurtful, if you know what I mean. He made me cry once. But whatever.

The first answer reflects a witness providing as little information as possible. This could be for a variety of reasons, but experience tells us that one potential reason is that the witness distrusts or dislikes the questioning lawyer. By contrast, the second answer is more typical of a witness who is holding a conversation with the questioning lawyer and is willing to "help" the questioner by providing information readily.

The extent to which style and tone get the witness to spill the beans (or the tea) depends on other factors as well, including the personality of the witness and how invested the witness is in the outcome of the case. Nonetheless, maintaining a pleasant demeanor matters, if for no other reason than you do not want to give witnesses any greater motivation to withhold information than they already have.

So what precisely causes a witness to perceive you as someone worthy of help rather than an enemy inquisitor to evade and rebuff? Well, ask yourself how you would respond if you met the following two people for the first time at a business reception:

Person A

- approaches you confidently and with a smile;
- leans forward in a friendly way while talking with you;
- has a pleasant tone of voice;
- has relaxed posture;
- is courteous;
- asks open questions (about your interests) in an informal and pleasant way;
- responds with affirmation and positive feedback to your answers.

Person B

- talks to you without smiling;
- stands or sits rigidly erect;
- uses a stern, formal tone of voice;
- has an edge to his voice;
- is abrupt, bordering on rudeness;
- asks questions using formal or legalistic language and in an aggressive fashion;
- gives no response or frowns in response to your answers to their questions; and
- interrupts.

Most of us would respond favorably to Person A and react in kind. If we met Person B, most of us would immediately wonder how to end the conversation.

The same goes during a deposition. Leaning forward, speaking in a pleasant tone of voice, using straightforward language, and offering an occasional smile or nod conveying interest encourages the witness to do what they do every day—have a conversation. Yet many lawyers act like Person B, engaging in what could pass as a police interrogation of a suspected criminal, with formal, complicated, and perhaps aggressive and intimidating questions and style. These lawyers come across as dislikeable creatures and receive responses reflecting their demeanor. Think of the number of times you have seen a deposition begin with the taking lawyer asking in a stern, formal voice: "State your name and address for the record" followed by "State your occupation" and other equally terse, legalistic questions.

The adage "you catch more flies with honey than with vinegar" applies as much to depositions as it does to life. Coupled with other tactics—such as warming up the witness with background questions (section 7.1) and using open-ended questions (section 8.2)—a confident yet pleasant approach tends to get witnesses talking. And getting the witness talking is the key to any deposition conducted to gather information.

12.1.2   A No-Nonsense Approach Is Better for Some Witnesses and Situations

For some witnesses, the "nice guy" approach fails. They perceive cordiality and amiability as weakness and a lack of resolve. These witnesses, often executives and others with positions of power, see this style as an invitation to play games with the questioning attorney. For other witnesses who believe the deposition to be a major inconvenience in their lives, a pleasant style can confirm that their time is being wasted. The best style with these witnesses may be a no-nonsense approach, with little time invested in pleasantries.

In addition, there are witnesses who melt under aggressive questioning. These witnesses become meek and malleable, willing to agree to almost anything suggested by the deposing lawyer. Sometimes you can shock the witness into this defeated attitude with difficult or embarrassing questions at the beginning of the deposition; other times by pressing the witness who is unsure of the facts into repeatedly admitting, "I don't remember" or "I don't know." Sometimes, through persistent questioning, you can anger the witness until they lash out with intemperate responses that can be quite revealing.

Finally, a witness who is the opposing party, or who closely associates with the opposing party, is obviously less likely moved by your efforts to be pleasant. These witnesses come to the deposition believing firmly that you are an evil person whose goal is to ruin them or someone close to them—and sometimes losing the lawsuit would mean just that. Their cooperation is rarely forthcoming. If the friendly approach is not working, switching to a no-nonsense approach may make sense.

With any witness, you may also need to take on a different demeanor depending on what happens in the deposition. If a witness becomes evasive, it is time to make sure they answer your questions. When it is time to obtain admissions, your demeanor may be slightly more authoritative. The witness may change too as the deposition proceeds; their cooperation level may wane when your questions shift from inquiring about the witness's background and noncontroversial subjects to inquiring about issues directly related to the merits of the case, or when you change from open-ended questions to cross-examination style questions; their resistance may decrease after 4:00 p.m., when the weariness of a long day settles in. It is therefore wise to bring a variety of styles to the deposition, equipped for every occasion.

So which style do you start with? Despite your preparation for the deposition, you might not know at the outset if it will be more effective to treat the witness in a friendly, disarming manner or a more business-like, no-nonsense way. If so, it is wisest to start with the pleasant style and shift to other styles if needed. Doing the opposite—starting aggressively and then trying to shift to a more pleasant style— leaves the witness doubting your sincerity and remaining cautious when answering your questions.

12.1.3 Active Listening and Critical Listening

To be effective in deposition, pay attention to both the witness's answers and the witness's nonverbal cues. That's the first hurdle—observing both what the witness is saying and how the witness is saying it, rather than thinking of the next question or hearing merely what you expected the witness to say. Moreover, conducting a deposition involves more than just listening in the sense of hearing—it involves the attributes of active listening and critical listening.

Active listening expresses attention and interest in what the other person is saying to build trust, to encourage the other person to talk, and to understand what the other person is saying and feeling. It fits in very well with the "get more with honey" deposition style but can be used with the "vinegar" or "no-nonsense" style too. Typical active listening skills include:

- **Nods of encouragement:** nodding in apparent acceptance or understanding of what the witness is saying tends to keep the witness talking (if using this skill in a no-nonsense manner, nod only when the witness provides information helpful to your case); words of empathy may also encourage the witness to say more ("Yeah, I understand that"; "I can see how you feel that way").

- **Eye contact:** in the United States, maintaining eye contact with the witness is generally a sign of respect and of interest in what the witness is saying (note, however, that some people find eye contact intimidating; in some Asian and Middle Eastern cultures, eye contact may be considered rude).

- **Noting nonverbal cues:** to understand the situation from the witness's perspective, consider not just the words the person is saying, but also their tone of voice and body language, which discloses how the witness feels about what they are describing. Consider, for example, the inflection in the witness's voice, the expression on their face, and whether the person is fidgeting (nervous about the topic) or covering their mouth with their hand (a classic sign of deceit). Are their eyes no longer directed at you but instead looking away in embarrassment or regret? Are their arms folded defensively, or are they looking at their attorney as if unsure how to answer a tough question?

- **Paraphrasing:** stating back what you heard the witness say indicates your interest and understanding and encourages the witness to elaborate.

While deploying active listening skills, simultaneously listen with a critical ear. Critical listening evaluates and judges what the other person is saying, discerning whether the witness's testimony is true and whether facts are being withheld, thereby equipping the listener to respond with another question. As the witness answers, therefore, ask yourself: Does that answer really make sense? Would a reasonable person have acted the way the witness is describing? Would I have reacted that way? Is the witness's answer consistent with other evidence in the case? Is something missing in this story? This internal mental process fuels good follow-up questions.

Although critical listening is viewed as the antithesis of active listening in most fields, the two must coexist in depositions when the goal is to obtain everything the witness knows about a subject. The key is to outwardly demonstrate active listening skills—nodding, encouraging, maintaining eye contact, noting nonverbal cues, and paraphrasing—while inwardly using critical listening skills, assessing what more needs to be asked.

12.1.4   *The Power of Inflection, Silence, and Eyebrows*

We all know from daily conversations that other techniques encourage people to talk. These techniques work in depositions, too.

- **Inflection.** If the pitch of our voice rises at the end of a sentence, it makes a statement seem like a question and makes a question seem like more of a question. This upward inflection prompts the other person to say more in response. By contrast, if the pitch of our voice goes down at the end of a sentence—sometimes called "landing"—it makes a statement more authoritative and a question seem to invite a "yes" or "no" answer rather than a narrative. An upward inflection is good when you want the witness to elaborate—that is, when we are gathering their information. A downward inflection is good when you want the witness to agree with you—as when obtaining an admission.

- **Silence.** Many people feel uncomfortable with silence, especially in a situation where they think they should be talking. They want to fill the silence with words, and that makes them tend to elaborate on an answer. After a witness has given an answer and you think it is not all they know in response to the question, try just looking at them in silence for a moment.

- **Eyebrows.** While you are waiting in silence for the witness to continue their answer, raising your eyebrows, as if to say "go ahead" or "keep going," can further spur the witness to talk.

12.1.5 Avoiding Unnecessary Offense

In addition to encouraging witnesses to talk, we want to avoid doing anything unnecessary that would give the witness a reason not to talk. On this point, we need to distinguish between two things.

On the one hand, while a witness might take offense to deposition questions that delve into private matters or insinuate wrongdoing or bad character, much of that is an inevitable part of the litigation process. After all, we cannot shrink away from asking difficult questions and inquiring persistently about matters germane to the case out of fear the witness's feelings may be hurt. If, for example, a plaintiff has placed their medical condition or mental health at issue, those topics are fair game for discovery. While it would be inappropriate to exploit the situation to harass or deprecate the witness unnecessarily, pointed questions will be needed and may even demonstrate to the witness and counsel that their allegations fall apart once exposed to the light. If the witness is offended by a professional inquiry into sensitive subjects at issue, so be it.

On the other hand, be aware of other ways we might offend a witness, which are not only unnecessary but counterproductive. The truth is, we can easily sabotage our efforts to achieve an effective deposition with offhand language, actions, or suppositions. Words that insult a deponent (or a court reporter or opposing counsel) may derail the deposition, reflect poorly on the attorney and the attorney's law firm, and make a deponent less willing to provide information. Sensitivity to the perspectives and experiences of other cultures is not just important, it is expected. Moreover, we all have unconscious biases (assumptions we carry about people without realizing it), which, if left unchecked, may lead us to presume what a witness did and why they did it or anticipate answers to unasked questions so that we fail to ask questions that would elicit vital information. In short, every litigator, regardless of their personal views, must avoid suppositions based on an individual's education, career, work ethic, race, sexuality, religious beliefs, or politics.

12.1.6 Professionalism and Civility

In the same vein, local court rules and bar association opinions increasingly deal with issues of attorney professionalism in the treatment of opposing counsel, witnesses, and court personnel. For example, the "Guidelines for Civility in

> *Some key ingredients: honey, vinegar, active listening, critical listening, inflection, silence, facial expressions, professionalism.*

Litigation" in the Los Angeles Superior Court Local Rules, as well as the "Guidelines for Professional Conduct" of the U.S. District Court for the Northern District of California, provide that attorneys should "refrain from repetitive or argumentative questions or those asked solely for purposes of harassment." They also "limit objections to those that are well founded and necessary for protection of a client's interest" and warn not to "coach the deponent or suggest answers" while a question is pending. Many states have now incorporated in their rules of professional conduct the idea that civility is necessary, appropriate, and consistent with zealous advocacy.[1]

12.2 Examining Witnesses Through Interpreters

Having talked about our style and demeanor, let's shift gears and discuss witnesses. We'll start with the witness who requires an interpreter.

If the deponent requires a foreign language or sign language interpreter, arrange for the services of a professional interpreter certified or licensed in the jurisdiction and include in the deposition notice that an interpreter will be used and what language will be interpreted. There are two main methods of interpretation: simultaneous interpretation (real-time, such that the witness is hearing a translation of your question just about the same time you are asking it) and consecutive interpretation (where the deponent or deposing attorney finishes a sentence, and then the interpreter translates it). Usually consecutive interpretation is employed, which more than doubles the time it takes for the deposition.

At the deposition, speak slowly, use short sentences, and avoid idioms and double negatives. This makes it much easier on the interpreter, which in turn results in a better translation. When asking questions and listening to the

---

1. States such as Alaska, Arizona, Colorado, Delaware, District of Columbia, Hawaii, Illinois, Massachusetts, Minnesota, New Mexico, New York, South Carolina, Utah, and Wyoming provide that counsel's duty of reasonable diligence does not require the use of offensive tactics. Additional rules target behavior that is demeaning or obstreperous. The California Civility Task Force, comprised of judges and practitioners, issued an initial report in September 2021 that proposed, among other things, civility-focused continuing education requirements and revisions to the California Rules of Professional Conduct that would deem repeated incivility as professional misconduct and clarify that civility is not inconsistent with zealous advocacy. Local bar associations in California have expressed support for these efforts.

answers—including the translation provided by the interpreter—look at the witness rather than the interpreter. More breaks will be needed, particularly for the interpreter, and if the deposition is going to last more than three or four hours, more than one interpreter may be required to avoid interpreter fatigue. Professional interpreters are typically a better choice than friends of the witness or family members, because they are disinterested in the outcome, maintain confidentiality, and have an aura of credibility as licensed professionals. Some courts and practice areas have developed full protocols for the use of interpreters in depositions, so check to see if that applies in your case.[2]

12.3 Examining Unrepresented Witnesses

If the witness is not represented by an attorney, the deposition proceeds as it normally would, but there are a few things to keep in mind. At the very beginning of the deposition, confirm on the record that the witness is not represented by an attorney and has chosen to appear at the deposition without a lawyer. Identify on the record the party that you represent. Also ask if the witness has consulted with an attorney in preparation for the deposition.

The witness commitments to the deposition ground rules (section 6.3) are particularly important when the witness is not represented by an attorney. Emphasize the duty to tell the truth and to give full and accurate testimony. Without providing legal advice, explain to the witness the opportunity to review the transcript of the deposition and make corrections (and, under federal law, the need to make such a request of the court reporter before the end of the deposition). During the deposition, appropriately remind the witness of the ground rules if the witness goes astray.

> *After a break, ask the witness:*
> - *Do you understand you're still under oath?*
> - *What did you do during the break?*
> - *Who did you talk to? Why? What was said?*
> - *What did you look at related to the case?*
> - *Do you want to change your testimony?*

After any break in the deposition, remind the witness—as you would with any witness—that they are under oath, and ask what the witness did during the break,

---

2. *See, e.g.*, In re Lithium Ion Batteries Antitrust Litigation, No. 13-md-2420-YGR (N.D. Cal., Oct. 19, 2015); In re Chrysler-Dodge-Jeep "Ecodiesel" Marketing, Sales Practices, and Products Liability Litigation, MDL No. 17-MD-2777-EMC (N.D. Cal., Nov. 3, 2017).

who if anyone they spoke to, why, what was said, what they read or watched, and if they want to change any of their testimony.

12.4 Dealing with Prototype Witnesses

Every witness is a unique individual, and you must deal with them based on what the witness is saying in the testimony, the witness's background, and the witness's personality. There are, however, some common witness types and behaviors that can be addressed in tried and true ways.

12.4.1 The Forgetful Witness

The forgetful witness is the one who repeatedly says, "I don't remember." Some legitimately do not remember because the events occurred long ago or the detail they are asked about was never important to them. Others use "I don't remember" as a way of avoiding a substantive answer that would embarrass them or hurt their case. Some use "I don't remember" because it is easier than answering the question substantively and their attorney said during preparation that it was okay not to remember (or, worse still, their attorney interjected "if you remember" during the deposition). Still others use "I don't remember" or "I can't recall at this time" to protect themselves in case they remember later.

The initial thing for you as the deposing attorney to do—even before the deposition—is to decide whether you want the witness to remember. Usually you do, so you can get information. But if you prefer instead to make it so the witness cannot later testify credibly to what occurred, getting the witness to admit at the deposition both that they do not remember and that there is nothing that would refresh their memory goes a long way to making any testimony they come up with later look suspicious and unbelievable.

If You Want the Witness to Remember

Assuming you do want the witness to remember the event (conversation, meeting, etc.), set the witness up to make it more likely the witness will recall it. Ask about time periods immediately before and after the event you care about. Ask about the event generally and inquire about some details that are innocuous or even favorable for the witness. The more details you elicit, the more likely an honest witness will be flooded with memories of what occurred. And if the witness recalls those benign aspects of the event, the more likely even a recalcitrant witness will feel obliged to recall the more significant and damaging aspects of the event; the witness will not appear credible if the only details that escape the witness's memory are those that hurt their case.

In addition, your questions about the event should presuppose that the witness remembers. In other words, do not start the questions with "If you recall" or "Do you remember." For example, instead of, "Do you recall if Art was there," ask "Who was there?" and then, "Was Art there?" or "Art was there, right?"

If the Witness Nonetheless Claims Not to Remember

If the witness claims a lack of recollection, make sure the record is clear what the witness means by that, attempt to jog the witness's memory, and decrease the odds the witness can credibly refresh their recollection after the deposition. Here are some examples.

First, if it is unclear from the context what the witness meant by "I don't recall," have the witness clarify.

> Q: Was Art there?
>
> A: I don't recall that.
>
> Q: Do you mean, as far as you can recall, Art wasn't there; or do you mean you can't recall one way or the other whether Art was there?
>
> A: I can't remember if he was there or not.

Then see if you can help the witness remember. "Wasn't it part of Art's job to attend?" Or, in another context where the witness does not recall the subjects covered in a conversation: "Is it possible you discussed Ms. Horvitz's health?" "Did you talk about the complaints from customers?"

Next, try to get the witness to agree that, because they cannot remember whether something happened or not, the witness cannot state definitively that it did not happen (or that it did happen).

> Q: Since you can't remember if Art was there or not, you cannot state that he was there.
>
> A: No, I don't remember.
>
> Q: Since you don't remember one way or the other, you're not denying that he was there?
>
> A: No, I just don't remember.

Finally—and this is most important—if the witness claims a lack of recollection, make it more difficult for the witness to justify at trial or summary judgment that they had an epiphany after the deposition was over:

> Q: What would help you remember if Art was there or not?
>
> A: Uh, I don't know.
>
> Q: Is there a document or notes that would help you recall?

A: No.

Q: Who would you talk to remember if Art was there?

A: No one.

Q: If later today you remember as we go through the rest of my questions, will you let me know?

A: Yeah, sure.

If You Do Not Want the Witness to Remember

If you do not want the witness to recall an event, suggest through your questions that the witness does not remember.

Q: When was the meeting?

A: About four years ago.

Q: I know that was a long time ago, so I guess you don't remember if Art was there.

A: Nah, I don't.

Q: And at this point there's probably nothing to make you remember if Art was there.

A: Can't think of anything.

Q: If asking you these questions about what happened brings that back to mind, you'll tell me before the deposition is over, right?

A: Sure.

12.4.2 *The Know-Nothing Witness*

The know-nothing witness is the one who repeatedly answers, "I don't know." Similar to the situation with the "I don't remember" witness, decide before the deposition if it is more desirable for the witness to know the requested information so you get a substantive answer at the deposition, or whether it is better if the witness claims not to know, so the witness is less able to testify credibly to the facts in a declaration or at trial.

For forgetful and know-nothing witnesses:

- *Set them up;*
- *clarify their claimed lack of memory or knowledge;*
- *suggest the answer;*
- *if they disagree, ask why;*
- *close off their ability to recall later.*

If You Want the Witness to Know

If you want the witness to provide a substantive answer to your question, set the witness up by first establishing facts that would make it more likely that the witness would know the information. For example, if the witness had any supervisory duties, establish that the witness was responsible for keeping abreast of what the employees were doing, saw the employees every day, checked in on them once a week, used that information to train the employees, had a duty to report the information to headquarters, and took all those responsibilities seriously. Once the witness gives this testimony, it will be harder for the witness to claim ignorance about the employee's conduct that is at the crux of the case.

If the witness nonetheless answers, "I don't know," there are some things to clarify. First, clarify whether the witness means that they never knew the information or that they once knew it but since forgot. If it turns out the witness just has a lack of memory, handle the situation as with an "I don't remember" witness. If the witness concedes that they never knew the information, explore what the witness means by "knew." (Some witnesses normally use the word "know," "knew," or "knowledge" very narrowly, allowing them to later say, "Well, I meant not for sure, but had a suspicion based on these facts.") Inquire, therefore, if the witness means they never had any information at all about the issue, or whether they really mean they did not have personal knowledge and therefore do not know the answer for sure. Finally, accepting that the witness does not have any knowledge in response to the question, explore with the witness how to get the information, which can lead you to other sources of discovery. The questioning may go something like this:

Q: Was Art there?

A: I don't know.

Q: Do you mean you never knew if Art was there, or you knew at some point but just can't remember now?

A: I don't think I ever knew.

Q: Okay, and by you don't know, do you mean you never had any clue, or just that you don't know for sure?

A: Never had a clue.

Q: So you never heard that he was there?

A: Nope.

Q: You never read that he was there?

A: Nope.

Q: And you didn't see him there?

A: No.

Q: So you don't have any reason to believe Art was there, correct?

A: Yeah, I just don't know.

Q: You can't say whether he was there or wasn't?

A: Right.

Q: If you had to find out now if Art was there, how would you do it?

A: Ask Julio, I guess.

(At this point, if you do not know who Julio is, explore with the witness who Julio is and how to reach him.)

Get a Range or Best Estimate

Another approach to the "I don't know" witness is to help the witness provide a range or a set of possibilities. An example might go like this:

Q: How many of last year's twelve meetings did Art attend?

A: I don't know.

Q: Did he attend any meetings?

A: Yeah.

Q: More than one?

A: Yes.

Q: More than six?

A: Yeah, probably.

Q: More than nine?

A: Um, yeah, about that.

Q: Could it have been ten?

A: Maybe.

Q: Did he attend all of them?

A: No.

Q: So he attended approximately nine or ten meetings last year.

A: Yeah, that sounds right.

. . .

Q: How long was the meeting of April 27, 2021?

A: I don't know.

Q: What is your best estimate?

A: About an hour.

Q: What's the longest you think it lasted?

A: Maybe an hour and a half.

Q: What's the shortest it could have been?

A: I would say an hour. Between an hour and an hour and a half.

Similarly, as with the forgetful witness, suggest what the answer to your question might be: if they disagree, ask why; if they agree despite a speculation objection, ask the basis of the witness's answer.

If You Don't Want the Witness to Know

If you are content if the witness professes their lack of knowledge, making it difficult for that witness to testify to the facts later in a declaration or at trial, confirm for the record that the witness has no information in response to the question.

12.4.3 *The Evasive Witness*

The evasive witness is the one who does not answer the call of your question. There can be two reasons for this—the witness does not want to answer the question, or the witness just did not understand the question. Either way, persist in getting a responsive answer.

Q: Did you report the harassment to anyone?

A: What was I supposed to do? They were all against me.

Q: I understand, but that wasn't my question. My question is, did you report the harassment to anyone?

A: No, I didn't.

Once you get an answer responsive to your question, you may choose to explore the nonresponsive answer the witness gave originally. In the foregoing example, a follow-up question might be "Who was against you?" "What do you mean by 'against you'?" "How were they against you?" Whether to follow up on the witness's original nonresponsive answer is, of course, a judgment call. Was there something in the witness's answer worth exploring, or is it a red herring that distracts you from getting the relevant information you need?

Sometimes it is more difficult to get the witness back on track, but if you really need the answer to your question, you must persevere:

Q: What time did you get home that day?

A: I hadn't eaten and I was like, starving. I had one of those, what do you call it, they're these pastry-like things that you put in the toaster—Pop-Tarts, that's it. I love the cinnamon sugar ones. So, yeah.

Q: I appreciate that, but I was asking something specific. What time did you get home that day?

A: Well, before I ate the Pop-Tarts, obviously.

Q: What time did you eat the Pop-Tarts?

A: I finished before Taylor got home from school.

Q: What time did Taylor get home from school?

A: He gets home about 3:30.

Q: So you must have gotten home that day before 3:30 then?

A: Yeah.

Q: And earlier than that because you made and ate your Pop-Tarts before he got home?

A: Yeah.

Q: So if you made your Pop-Tarts and ate them before 3:30, what time did you get home?

A: Well, uh, around . . . 3:00.

When a witness is not giving a responsive answer to the question, you may object to the answer as—you guessed it—nonresponsive. Again, contemplate whether this will be productive with the particular witness, but the colloquy might go like this:

Q: Was it raining at the time?

A: Dude, it was at night.

Q: [To the court reporter:] I object to the witness's answer as non-responsive. [To the witness:] You didn't answer my question. I'll ask it again. Was it raining at the time?

"I Don't Understand"

Another form of evasive witness is the one who claims not to understand your questions, particularly after their attorney has objected that the question is vague or ambiguous. We will revisit this phenomenon when we talk about dealing with defending attorneys' improper conduct in Chapter Thirteen, but we discuss it here because it also pertains to dealing with witness behavior.

Here is an example of the problematic exchange ("OC" refers to opposing counsel):

Q: Ms. Lemontas, how large is the sales department at the Crab-tree Company?

OC: Objection, vague.

Q: Ms. Lemontas, do you understand the question?

A: No, I don't understand it.

There are ways to avoid this situation. First, when counsel objects on the ground of vagueness, do not respond by asking the witness if they understand the question (as counsel did in the example), because the witness will inevitably say "no" in deference or obedience to their attorney. Instead, just ask the witness to answer the question. If the witness has not conspired with their attorney to say they do not understand any question to which counsel objected, the witness will likely answer the question.

Next, if the witness does respond by saying, "I don't understand the question," you have essentially two options: either rephrase the question or ask, "What is it about the question you don't understand?" If you have an easy rephrasing in mind (e.g., "How many people are currently employed in the sales department at the Crabtree Company?"), it might be simplest to rephrase it. But if you suspect the witness is playing a game, asking the witness to articulate what the witness does not understand may make the witness grow weary of the charade.

Sometimes witnesses insist they do not understand questions without any objection from counsel. Here is an example:

Q: What procedure does the purchasing department follow in plac-ing orders for computer parts?

A: What do you mean by "procedure"?

Q: Well, I mean what does the purchasing department routinely do when it buys computer parts?

A: What do you mean by "routinely"?

Q: I mean regularly. Do you have a regular practice for ordering parts?

A: I am not sure what you mean by "regular" practice.

It could be that the witness is genuinely confused by the question. In the forego-ing example, however, it is more likely that this is a sharp witness who is attempting to lure deposing counsel into playing the game of "dictionary," in which the witness tries to divert attention from a question the witness would prefer not to answer. One response is to have a dictionary on hand and look up the word, choose a definition, and read it into the record. But the less burdensome approach is to turn it back on the witness.

Q: Mr. Vitar, what precaution did you take when you learned that the boiler was overheating?

A: What do you mean by precaution?

Q: Are you familiar with the word "precaution"?

A: Yes.

Q: What does that word mean to you?

A: Well, I guess it means what you do to prevent problems.

Q: Okay, using that definition, what precautions did you take when you learned that the boiler was overheating?

If the definition used by the witness differs from yours, first get the information using the witness's definition. Then insert your own definition and ask the question again.

12.4.4 *The Vague Witness*

The vague witness uses phrases such as "generally," "not specifically," "sort of," "basically," "mainly," "primarily," and "that's all I can remember at this time" to avoid being pinned down. The witness may be earnestly concerned that they cannot recall all the details in the heat of the deposition. Alternatively, the witness may just be evasive. Regardless, unless the witness's answer is unimportant, clarify their answer.

"Generally."

If the witness qualifies an answer with a word like "generally," follow up and ask what they mean.

Q: Do you inform new hires of the company's procedures for reporting accusations of sexual harassment?

A: Generally, no.

Q: You said "generally, no." Are there any times you tell them?

A: I can't think of any instances, but I suppose it must come up sometime when we interview new hires.

Q: Why do you suppose that?

A: I'm just speculating.

"Not Specifically."

If the witness qualifies an answer with "not specifically," the witness is probably trying to limit your question or withhold information. Again, follow up.

Q: Did you discuss the amount of time it would take to complete the job?

A: Not specifically.

Q: What do you mean, "not specifically"?

A: We didn't talk specifically about the amount of time, but some things that kind of relate.

Q: What did you discuss that "kind of" related to the amount of time to complete the job?

A: Well, there's a big backlog in getting supplies, so it takes a couple of months just to get the parts.

"That's All I Can Remember at This Time."

Often the witness, with or without counsel's advice, will try to carve out some wiggle room in their deposition answer in case the witness needs to embellish the answer in later proceedings. While there is no perfect response to this ploy, try to limit its usefulness by making it difficult for the witness to claim later that they remember additional facts. The approach is similar to the one to try if the witness claims not to remember at all, discussed above.

Q: Have you now told me the names of everyone who was at that meeting?

A: That is all I can remember at this time.

Q: Is there anything you can think of that would help you remember more names?

A: No.

Q: Did you make any notes about the meeting that could help you remember?

A: No.

Q: Do you know if anyone else made such notes?

A: Nobody that I know about.

Q: Have you talked with anyone about the meeting?

A: No.

Q: Is there anything you could check—letters, emails, whatever— about who was at the meeting?

A: Nothing I can think of.

Q: There's nothing that might help you remember who was at the meeting?

A: No, I don't think so.

Q: Is there anyone you could talk to who might help you remember?

A: No, I don't think anyone knows it better than me.

If the witness tries to testify later to more than the information given at the deposition, refer to this line of questioning and argue that the witness had not recalled new information legitimately.

Another type of vague witness offers characterizations without facts or explanation, claiming someone or something was "inferior," "better," "normal," "standard," "reasonable," etc. Ask them to clarify.

> *For evasive and vague witnesses: persevere to get a responsive answer and ask what they mean.*

12.4.5 The Lying Witness

The lying witness is the one who decides not to tell the truth. Prevarication typically derives from fear—the witness's fear that telling the truth will cause the witness to lose face, lose the case, harm the witness's friend or employer, or reveal an earlier lie. The first task is to detect that the statement is, in fact, a lie; the second task is to deal with it.

Detecting the Lie

Most obviously, a witness may be lying if the witness has a motive to lie and either the witness's account is inconsistent with the rest of the evidence, or the witness is claiming to have acted or reacted on the subject occasion in a way they had never acted or reacted in similar situations before or since.

An unusual degree of detail in the witness's answer may reflect a lie. The witness who is lying about what happened at an event will either not want to talk about it and under-elaborate (offering only a hazy picture of what occurred), or overelaborate and volunteer far more details in response to an initial question than a person ordinarily would.

Someone who is lying may try not to answer the question. Instead of responding to the query directly, the lying witness may repeat the question, protest the question, announce they are offended by the question, challenge your motives in asking it, or respond to the question with a question directed to you.

Duplicitous witnesses also tend to distance themselves from the situation. For example, if asked if they did something, instead of saying "no," the lying witness might say, "I would never do that." They might respond to a question without referring to themselves as "I" ("That's not something a person would do" or "No one in their right mind would resort to violence"). In their denial, they might not refer to another person by name (e.g., saying "I never had sexual relations with that woman" rather than "no, I did not have sexual relations with Monica Lewinsky").[3]

There are also nonverbal clues that the witness is lying. The witness may not be telling the truth if their words say one thing (they were happy) but their facial expression (a frown) says another. Several "tells" have traditionally been heralded as indications of prevarication, such as facial "micro-expressions": staring too intensely at the questioner or refusing to look the questioner in the eye; shifting the body from side to side; putting a hand over the mouth; speaking louder or in a higher pitch; or fidgeting. Scientific research has questioned how well these behaviors detect lies, however, and the tells are difficult to notice in a fast-paced deposition, where you do not know the witness and therefore have less ability to discern whether the witness is acting differently than normal.

Dealing with the Lie

When you suspect that a witness is lying (or, before the deposition, anticipate that the witness will lie), there are various ways to handle the situation.

- **Focus on the details.** After asking open-ended questions to get the witness's general version of what occurred, switch to granular questions that get down to the nitty-gritty details. (This is one reason for using the funnel method to gather information at a deposition, discussed in Chapter Eight.) This approach is helpful for two reasons. First, while those details would typically be remembered by someone telling the truth, the lying witness may not have thought through all the details of their fabricated story. Second, requiring the liar to recount details puts pressure on them and requires a lot of mental energy. Going over the event in a different order (not chronologically) makes it particularly taxing for the liar to keep the made-up details straight.

- **Confront the witness with evidence that contradicts the witness's story**. This is an obvious one, but it helps. A witness confronted at the deposition

---

3. A variation occurs when someone responds to an accusation by debating whether it can be proven rather than whether they did it: "Q: You killed the busboy, didn't you? A: You got no proof, detective." This is more of a confession than a lie.

with contradictory evidence may be persuaded to back away from the lie and testify truthfully in accord with the evidence. Alternatively, the witness caught in their lie may become flustered or combative, and if the deposition is being recorded by video, the witness's demeanor may speak volumes. Some attorneys prefer not to confront the witness at the deposition, in the hope of saving the contradictory evidence for a blockbuster cross-examination at trial; with the miniscule number of civil cases that go to trial these days, that strategy may lose you any chance at confrontation. We cannot recommend it.

- **Express to the witness the reasons you do not believe their testimony and give them an easy way out.** If you suspect the witness is not telling the truth, you might point out what leads you to that inference and confront the witness with lines something like this: "Ms. Crowley, I noticed you were looking at the table when you gave me that answer rather than looking at me, and what you said is different than what Ms. Tippleberry said in her deposition. There's maybe the slightest possibility that your answer is a bit inaccurate, isn't there." "Reasonable minds might differ on what happened, right?"

- **Up the fear ante.** Assuming witnesses lie because they fear the negative consequences of telling the truth, they can become motivated to tell the truth if they realize that the consequences will be even worse if they lie. For example, emphasize that at the beginning of the deposition, the witness took an oath to tell the truth and there are penalties for perjury.

12.4.6 *The Combative Witness*

The combative witness argues with you, refuses to answer questions, calls you names, or worse. YouTube contains numerous examples of combative witnesses, including excerpts from the video depositions of Lil Wayne and Justin Bieber. There is also a milder form of combative witness—the questioning witness—who demands that you clarify far too many questions. Consider the infamous deposition of Bill Gates, who questioned the meaning of words such as "ask," "compete," "support," and "concerned." While this can be a sign of a very precise person, it can also be a combative form of evasion. Consider, too, the snarky witness who more subtly expresses contempt for the questions and questioner through sarcasm, tone of voice, and facial expressions.

There can be several reasons for the witness's combativeness. It may be that the witness comes to the deposition with disdain for your client and your client's case—and therefore for you—and resents the imposition on their time. Other witnesses, unused to anyone trying to pin them down through interrogation, become hostile because the questioning is intrusive or makes them defensive. Still other witnesses become aggressive because of a perceived slight or offense from a line of questioning. Others may be combative just because they think it is fun or they want to mess with you.

Whatever the source of the witness's hostility, the main thing to remember is to remain calm, stay the course, and persevere with respectful questioning. If the witness's combativeness is an act, the witness will tire of the ruse as it becomes clear you are moving forward with the questioning undaunted. And if the combativeness continues notwithstanding your professionalism, it is the witness who will end up looking bad to the court and to the trier of fact; in turn, this can

> **Key Responses for Prototype Witnesses**
> - **Forgetful** —"What would help you remember?"
> - **Know-nothing** —"How would you find out?"
> - **Evasive**—"I'll ask my question again."
> - **Vague**—"What did you mean by that?"
> - **Lying**—"What about this [evidence]?"

give your client leverage in settlement negotiations and, if it goes that far, at trial.

Depending on what you perceive to be the cause of the witness's aggression, there may be additional tactics to consider. If you believe that the witness, who has otherwise cooperated in the deposition, has become hostile because you offended them by your questions, get things back on track by telling the witness it was not your intent to offend and you are just trying to do your job. If you believe the witness's behavior is based on the witness's sincere sense of injustice regarding what happened to them, or genuine frustration with the system and the deposition process, let the witness know that you hear and understand what they are saying. If the witness's hostility leads them to resist answering questions, explain that the deposition is the opportunity for the witness to tell their story by answering your questions. But be careful. The idea is not to give in to the witness or to let the witness run the deposition; it is merely another way of attempting to accomplish your deposition goals.

Also consider asking the defending attorney to speak with the witness about the impropriety of refusing to answer questions and any other antics. Point out that the witness's behavior will result in further deposition time and, if necessary, a motion to compel answers and the imposition of sanctions. Note that the failure of defending counsel to make a genuine effort to curb their witness's improper behavior is a basis for sanctions against the attorney.[4]

Finally, if you suspect before the deposition that the witness may be hostile, keep two things in mind. First, plan to demonstrate your credibility and professionalism

---

4. Luangisa v. Interface Operations, No. 2:11-cv-00951-RCJ-CWH, 2011 U.S. Dist. LEXIS 139700, at *33 (D. Nev. Dec. 5, 2011); GMAC Bank v. HTFC Corp., 248 F.R.D. 182, 186, 195–99 (E.D. Pa. 2008); *see* State ex rel. Secretary of the DOT v. Mumford, 731 A.2d 831, 833–34, 836 (Del. Super. 1999) (pro hac vice admission revoked).

from the very beginning of the deposition by knowing the facts, the case, and your questions—including the nomenclature of the industry in which the witness is involved—so as not to increase the witness's disdain for you or provide a reason for the witness to debate and quibble. Second, as discussed next, make sure the deposition will be recorded by audiovisual means to curb or document the witness's combativeness.

12.4.7   *Video Is Your Friend*

All the witness behaviors we have discussed—failing to remember what they should be able to remember, claiming not to know what they should know, evading the question, offering only vague and qualified answers, lying, and combativeness—tend to diminish when the deposition is videorecorded. There is something about a camera staring the witness in the face that puts the witness—at least most witnesses—on their best behavior. It tends to keep defending counsel in line as well. And for those witnesses who are not daunted by the camera, their antics are recorded for the court and jurors to see. If you believe the witness may not cooperate, strongly consider including in the deposition notice that the deposition will be recorded by audiovisual as well as stenographic means and arrange for a videographer.

12.5   Dealing with Bad Testimony

Inevitably, the deposition witness will testify to facts that hurt your client and help the opposing party. As a general matter, this is not a terrible thing in depositions conducted for the purpose of obtaining information, because you learn the opponent's strongest evidence while there is still time to deal with it. Moreover, you can take the following steps to get the witness to back off their harmful testimony.

12.5.1   *Explore Fully the Witness's Basis for Their View*

This tip overlaps with the earlier chapters on questioning technique, but it is important to mention here. When you get an answer from the witness that is not helpful to your case, explore all the witness's reasons and bases for it. By learning the witness's supporting facts, you can determine if those facts are accurate and how best to attack them, and you can evaluate how the witness's version will stack up against your client's version. Note that, while you cannot ask a witness to state all facts supporting a legal claim or defense (on the ground it calls for a legal analysis and conclusion),[5] you can certainly ask for all the facts that the witness believes support the witness's view of the events underlying the case.

---

5. Lance, Inc. v. Ginsburg, 32 F.R.D. 51, 53 (E.D. Pa. 1962); Rifkind v. Superior Court, 22 Cal. App. 4th 1255, 1259–63 (Cal. Ct. App. 1994).

National Institute for Trial Advocacy

12.5.2   Question the Witness's Personal Knowledge and Recollection

Try to get the witness to retreat from their unfavorable testimony by pointing out that they did not observe what happened firsthand, they are speculating, or they merely have an opinion that other observers do not share.

Q: What happened next?

A: He hit her in the face with his briefcase.

Q: How do you know?

A: I heard the scream and then she ran out the door holding her face.

Q: You didn't see her being hit in the face?

A: No, I didn't see it.

Q: You weren't in their office at the time?

A: No.

Q: You are just assuming that he hit her.

A: Well, yeah.

As another example, through leading questions and a "gee, I certainly understand it would be hard to remember things from way back then" attitude, you may get the witness to acknowledge that their version of what occurred may be faulty.

12.5.3   Confront the Witness with Contrary Evidence

Confronting the witness with the testimony of other witnesses or documents can sometimes shake the witness's confidence in their testimony. To increase the likelihood of success in this regard, ask the witness early on what their view is of the person or other source of the information that contradicts their story. If the witness speaks highly of that source, the witness will more likely accept the source's account of what occurred and reconsider their own view. If the witness holds firm to their testimony notwithstanding the contrary evidence, consider asking if the witness believes that the person providing the contrary evidence was lying.[6] Certainly ask the witness if, in light of the evidence contrary to the witness's view, the witness might have made a mistake. At the least, ask the witness to acknowledge that different people can have different views of what occurred at an event.

---

6. Asking a witness at trial if someone else was lying will draw an objection; the witness has no personal knowledge of the reason the other person said what they did, and whether the other witness lied is a matter for the jury. In deposition, however, explore what, in the witness's view, caused the difference between the witness's version of the event and another witness's version.

12.6 Asking Witnesses to Do a Demonstration

There is no rule precluding you from asking the witness to demonstrate or reenact how an event occurred. This can be very useful for understanding what the witness means by their testimony, and if the deposition is recorded by video, provides a means of evaluating the witness's claim later and limiting what the witness can say at trial. Several reported cases have granted motions allowing a demonstration in personal injury cases.[7]

12.7 Encouraging Answers Through (Re)Organization of the Inquiry

In Chapter Five on preparing for the deposition, we explained why it is better to move through the substantive portions of the deposition in a logical progression, chronologically or topically, rather than employing a "leapfrog" approach that randomly jumps from topic to topic. We also discussed that there may be a strategic reason to diverge from a chronological order to make it more likely you will elicit the information and admissions you want.

We revisit that concept here as it applies to dealing with witnesses. While the deposition outline is critical for mapping out what you want to cover with the witness and estimating the best approach to the deposition, the deponent's answers (or resistance to answering) may suggest an on-the-fly modification. In listening to the witness's responses, you will likely hear unexpected information that you need to follow up on, forcing you to decide between pursuing the matter right away—striking while the iron is hot—or noting the subject in your outline, saving it for later, and continuing with your planned approach so as not to be sidetracked. (As a general rule, if the witness's volunteered information seems fresh and emotional, it is worth pursuing immediately; if it is tangential objective information, it may be something to consider pursuing later.) The witness could also resist your attempts to obtain admissions at one point in the deposition despite your use of the techniques

---

7. Carson v. Burlington N., Inc. 52 F.R.D. 492 (D. Neb. 1971) (granting motion to record deposition of plaintiff by stenographic and photographic means to show how the plaintiff approached and operated the machine that resulted in his injuries, although plaintiff would not have to touch or operate the machine but use a pointer); Roberts v. Homelite Div. of Textron, Inc., 109 F.R.D. 664 (D. Ind. 1986) (granting motion to conduct deposition at place of accident and record by videotape a reenactment of plaintiff attempting to start a lawn mower that had injured his hand, without jeopardizing parties' safety); Gillen v. Nissan Motor Corp. in United States, 156 F.R.D. 120 (E.D. Pa. 1994) (granting motion to compel plaintiff to submit to a videotaped demonstration of the alleged defect of her car's seatbelts). Bassily v. Louisville Ladder, 2:20-cv-01120-BHH, 2021 U.S. Dist. LEXIS 224563 (D. S.C. March 30, 2021) (granting motion to allow plaintiff's deposition to include video reenactment of the plaintiff's position and actions when he fell off a ladder at the scene where the accident occurred, without jeopardizing plaintiff's safety). The earlier cases pertain more to the court's discretion in ordering videotaped depositions under then-existing law, but they generally confirm an openness to demonstrations during depositions.

described above, and your return to the topic later in the day, when the witness's weariness or desire to end the deposition have set in, will elicit a favorable response.

In sum, dealing with witnesses requires you to have a plan to *listen* to the witness's responses and to react accordingly, always keeping in mind the primary goals of discovering the witness's knowledge and obtaining the admissions you need to win the case.

CHECKLIST

DEALING WITH WITNESSES

✔	Decide what style ("catch more with honey" or "no-nonsense") to use with the witness.
✔	Listen actively: nods of encouragement, eye contact, and noting and responding to nonverbal cues.
✔	Listen critically: evaluate the witness's answer to know what follow-up questions are needed.
✔	Encourage the witness to talk with upward inflection and silence.
✔	Avoid unnecessary offense and uncivil conduct that might lead a witness to shut down.
✔	If an interpreter will be used, prepare for the extra time necessitated by consecutive translation, speak slowly, and avoid idioms and double negatives.
✔	For the forgetful witness, decide if you want the witness to remember and attempt to refresh recollection, or clarify a claim of no recollection and close off the possibility of later recollection.
✔	For the know-nothing witness, decide if you want the witness to know, find out who would know, and attempt to obtain estimates or ranges, or clarify a claim of no knowledge and close off the possibility of later recollection.
✔	For the evasive witness, persist in getting an answer.
✔	For the vague witness, follow up to clarify answers containing qualifying words such as "generally," "not specifically," or "that's all I remember at this time."
✔	For the lying witness, focus on minute details, consider confronting with contradictory evidence or other "tells" of prevarication, and up the fear ante.
✔	For the combative witness, remain calm, stay the course, persevere.
✔	To minimize all difficult witness behaviors, video record the deposition.
✔	In dealing with harmful testimony, explore and question the basis for the witness's testimony.
✔	Consider asking the witness to do a demonstration, particularly in a video deposition.
✔	Encourage the desired answers by ordering the topics strategically.

National Institute for Trial Advocacy

CHAPTER THIRTEEN

DEALING WITH THE OBJECTING, OBNOXIOUS, OR OBSTRUCTIONIST OPPOSING COUNSEL

*A gentle answer turns away wrath, but a
harsh word stirs up anger.*

—Proverbs 15:1

*[The enemy] must be hounded and annihilated
at every step and all their measures frustrated.*

—Joseph Stalin

A deposition will be more effective if you deal with the objections, instructions, and other conduct of the witness's attorney in a way that contributes to the primary goals of the deposition: to obtain information and admissions from the witness.

In this chapter, we focus on three categories of behavior displayed by witnesses' attorneys:

- **Objecting counsel:** attorneys objecting and instructing a witness in good faith and in line with the rules applicable to the jurisdiction.

- **Obnoxious counsel:** attorneys acting in an unpleasant, offensive, or obstreperous manner that can derail the deposition, such as making meritless objections, "speaking" objections, and offhand comments; throat clearing, coughing, and other intentional interruptions; and impatience with or disdain for the questions and deposing counsel.

- **Obstructionist counsel:** attorneys deliberately delaying or preventing the deposing attorney from obtaining the information to which the deposing attorney is

> **In This Chapter:**
>
> - Dealing with the three categories of problem attorneys
> - Making the record
> - When to go to the judge

entitled, through coaching the witness and baseless instructions not to answer.

"Objecting" counsel is merely doing their job of protecting the record and the interests of the witness and the client; do not respond to these interruptions in a way that undermines the acquisition of information from the witness. Do not engage "obnoxious counsel" for the same reason, unless the behavior gets to the point where the witness is not answering questions or is giving answers that reflect counsel's improper interjections. "Obstructionist counsel" cannot be tolerated; the behavior must be addressed firmly in a manner that allows for later (or occasionally immediate) judicial intervention and sanction.

13.1 The Nature of the Beast

By its nature, a deposition places the participants in conflict. The deposing attorney wants the witness to provide information that supports the attorney's case and reveals or undermines the other side's case. The witness may not have the information, remember the information, or want to disclose the information. The witness's attorney wants to limit the extent to which the deposition hurts their client, harms the witness, or benefits the deposing attorney. Furthermore, reasonable people may disagree on how rules apply and whether questions, objections, or instructions are appropriate. Often, the stakes of the litigation are tremendous—at least to the witness and the clients—and elements of ignorance, fear, insecurity, suspicion, pride, and frustration too often catapult the conflict inherent in depositions to a boiling point that does no one any good.

While it is the right and responsibility of defending counsel to interpose objections where appropriate, too many attorneys have the wrong idea, thinking their job in defending a deposition is to prevent the discovery of information at virtually any cost. There may be several reasons for this. The attorney may be unprepared to defend the deposition and therefore desperate to avoid inquiry into the substance of the case. The attorney may be inexperienced in defending depositions and afraid to allow the facts to come out. The attorney may be ignorant of the Federal Rules of Civil Procedure or other applicable law. The attorney may be following the lead of unprofessional role models, mentors, and TV attorneys, presuming that's just the way it's done. Or the attorney may reject the premise that pretrial discovery of the opponent's information is favored[1] and trial by ambush, obfuscation, and surprise is disfavored, and intentionally violate the rules to try to win the case. Or the attorney may be unequipped to litigate the case properly.[2]

---

1. The goal of the discovery rules is to promote "free and open" exchange of information between the parties and to prevent surprise and delay. *See, e.g.,* Davis v. Romney, 55 F.R.D. 337 (D. Pa. 1972); United States v. I.B.M., 68 F.R.D. 315 (S.D.N.Y. 1975); Wiener King, Inc. v. Wiener King Corp., 615 F.2d 512 (C.C.P.A. 1980).
2. "The Federal Rules of Civil Procedure . . . are designed to prevent trial by ambush." Yohannon v. Keene Corp., 924 F.2d 1255, 1259 n.4 (3d Cir. 1991).

Many obnoxious, obstreperous, offensive, and obstructionist lawyers prey on young or inexperienced deposing attorneys; female attorneys and attorneys of color are also disproportionately targeted. Other lawyers attempt these tactics on any deposing attorney and in any deposition, from the small tort case to multidistrict commercial litigation.

Because obnoxious, obstreperous, offensive, and obstructionist behavior interferes with the legitimate goals of discovery, it has been the topic of criticism and numerous proposals by the organized bar, trial judges, rule makers, and others. And because spurious objections and instructions not to answer have been the primary form of obstructive behavior, the Federal Rules of Civil Procedure dictate how and under what conditions objections and instructions not to answer may be asserted. Rule 30(c)(2) provides:

> An objection must be stated concisely in a nonargumentative and nonsuggestive manner. A person may instruct a deponent not to answer only when necessary to preserve a privilege, to enforce a limitation directed by the court, or to present a motion under Rule 30(d)(3) [seeking limitation or termination of the deposition due to, e.g, harassment].[3]

Strict adherence to Rule 30(c)(2) would eliminate an overwhelming majority of the obstructive behaviors that occur at depositions, and judges—especially those in the federal courts—are more and more often insisting on just that. Some federal districts and state courts have gone further, enacting local rules that more severely limit the form of objections that can be made. For example, local rules in several districts limit objections to stating the word "objection" or to a limited range of permissible phrases such as, "Objection, form." In those jurisdictions, the defending attorney can say nothing more about the objection during the deposition unless questioning counsel requests the basis for the objection so it can be cured.

Individual courts and judges have also fashioned discovery orders that severely limit defending counsel in other ways, including communications with the deponent during the deposition. These orders are designed to prevent defending counsel from coaching the witness, and they usually allow—and properly so—appropriate consultation with the client to discuss a potential claim of privilege or a defending attorney's concern that the deponent may have given false testimony.

Published cases now reflect a judicial willingness to sanction attorneys for a wide range of obstructionist behavior at depositions, including improper coaching and

---

3. Fed. R. Civ. P. 30(c)(2). Objections and instructions not to answer questions are discussed in Chapter Eighteen from the perspective of the defending attorney.

improper instructions not to answer.[4] The increasing prevalence of video depositions has tempered misconduct as well. Even though the camera usually catches only the image of the deponent, the recording picks up the tone and volume of attorney antics, and in severe cases, a camera may be trained on insolent counsel.

Recently, local courts and bar associations have more seriously embraced the notion that attorneys should be civil with each other, as well as with witnesses, court reporters, and court personnel. For example, the "Guidelines for Civility in Litigation" in the Los Angeles Superior Court Local Rules, as well as the "Guidelines for Professional Conduct" of the U.S. District Court for the Northern District of California, target improper deposition behavior by advising that attorneys should "refrain from repetitive or argumentative questions or those asked solely for purposes of harassment," "limit objections to those that are well founded and necessary for protection of a client's interest," and not "coach the deponent or suggest answers" while a question is pending. In addition, the rules of professional conduct in several jurisdictions now communicate the idea that civility can and should coexist with zealous advocacy.[5]

---

4. Cases approving sanctions or censure in response to improper behavior by defending attorneys are far too numerous to list, but here is a sampling. Craig v. St. Anthony's Med. Ctr., 384 F. App'x 531, 532–33 (8th Cir. 2010) (upholding sanctions imposed against attorney who made argumentative objections and suggestive objections, conferred with the witness, answered questions in place of the witness, and directed the witness not to answer); Redwood v. Dobson, 476 F.3d 462, 468–70 (7th Cir. 2007) (censure imposed against deposing attorney who asked irrelevant and harassing questions, against defending lawyer who engaged in speaking objections and improperly instructed the witness not to answer (rather than suspending deposition to obtain a protective order), and against the witness, also a lawyer, who pretended not to understand or remember); Deville v. Givuadan Fragrances Corp., 419 F. App'x 201, 207 (3rd Cir. 2011) (upholding sanctions against attorney for behaving in an "abusive, unprofessional and obstructionist manner during the deposition"); Luangisa v. Interface Operations, No. 2:11-cv-00951-RCJ-CWH, 2011 U.S. Dist. LEXIS 139700, 2011 WL 6029880, at *11 (D. Nev. Dec. 5, 2011) (inappropriate to demand that deposing attorney state the relevance of his questions); Specht v. Google, Inc., 268 F.R.D. 596, 598–99, 603 (N.D. Ill. 2010) ("objections that are argumentative or that suggest an answer to a witness are called 'speaking objections' and are improper under Rule 30(c)(2)"; sanctions imposed); Van Pilsum v. Iowa State Univ. of Science & Technology, 152 F.R.D. 179, 181 (S.D. Iowa 1993) (sanctions imposed where defending attorney lacked justification for monopolizing 20 percent of the deposition, where objections were mostly "groundless, and were only disputatious grandstanding"); Hall v. Clifton Precision, 150 F.R.D. 525, 528–30 (E.D. Pa. 1993) (prohibiting conferences between attorney and witness except for assertion of privilege); *see also* Corsini v. U-Haul Int'l, Inc., 212 A.D.2d 288 (N.Y. App. Div. 1995) (attorney representing himself violated ethics rules by evading or refusing to answer questions, giving improper responses, and making personal attacks against defense counsel; complaint dismissed as a sanction).

5. As recognized explicitly in at least Alaska, Arizona, Colorado, Delaware, District of Columbia, Hawaii, Illinois, Massachusetts, Minnesota, New Mexico, New York, South Carolina, Utah, and Wyoming, counsel's duty of reasonable diligence does not require the use of offensive tactics. Conduct that is demeaning or obstreperous is beginning to be specifically addressed as well. The California Civility Task Force, comprised of judges and practitioners, issued an initial report in September 2021 that proposed measures such as a continuing education requirement on civility and revisions to the California Rules of Professional Conduct, which would characterize repeated incivility as professional misconduct and affirm that civility is not inconsistent with zealous advocacy.

But obnoxious, offensive, obstreperous, and obstructionist attorneys are still out there. While the worst of the worst obstructionists are a vanishing breed, you need to know how to deal with them when they show up across the table at a deposition. Fortunately, a few techniques will help you attain your deposition goals despite the defending attorney's behaviors, whether the defending conduct is within the rules or not.

13.2 General Principles

13.2.1 Size Up the Behavior

The first step in dealing with defending counsel is to decide whether their behavior is merely irritating, thereby making the deposition more difficult, or is in fact obstructing the acquisition of information from the deponent. An attorney who interposes objections even in good faith can be an irritant because, although the conduct is permissible (and wise from the witness's perspective), it interrupts the flow of the deposition at some level. A greater irritant is the opposing counsel who constantly makes objections, makes long speaking objections, makes improper objections, or asks for unnecessary clarifications of questions. An obstructionist opposing counsel is more blatant in their antics and directly impedes the witness's testimony, whispering in the witness's ear while a question is pending or impermissibly instructing the witness to refuse to answer due to, for example, relevance or question form. The effects on the deposition of these three types of behavior— objecting, obnoxious and obstructing—are different, and the response to the three should reflect that difference, as we discuss further below.

13.2.2 Assume Good Faith Unless Proven Otherwise

Although some attorneys behave like jerks, it may be that the defending counsel is simply trying to do their job in good faith. Not every instance of opposing counsel asking for a question to be clarified or conferring with the witness while a question is pending is an obstructionist tactic. Some lawyers ask for clarification because they genuinely find your question confusing and believe the witness may be similarly confused or the witness's answer will lead to a misleading transcript on an important matter. Some lawyers confer with the witness while a question is pending because a legitimate issue of privilege must be cleared up before the witness can answer. Some objections are made because they are valid and legitimate, and the lawyer is trying to address the problem. Even obnoxious, offensive, and obstreperous attorneys may think they are doing something permissible or, at least, traditional.

Unless there were prior bad experiences with the opposing counsel, or the lawyer has a reputation as an obstructionist, assume until shown otherwise that opposing counsel is acting in good faith. That does not mean you fail to follow the steps suggested in this chapter to ensure you attain your deposition goals. But responding with a nuclear outburst to a polite request for clarification of a question is guaranteed to turn the deposition into an unpleasant experience for all involved. More importantly, it may interfere with your ability to obtain the maximum amount of information from the witness.

Treating opposing counsel as the enemy every time they object can also lead you to miss a valid objection and the need to rephrase an inquiry or clarify the record. Consider counsel's objection, while ignoring counsel's tone and volume, to determine if the question or the record can be improved so the sought-after information is admissible and understandable. If you later offer the deposition testimony at trial or use it as support for a summary judgment motion, you will have favorable evidence available because you adjusted the inquiry in response to the shouted or nastily-made objection.

13.2.3   It's Not Personal (Usually)

Along the same lines, assume that the other lawyer's conduct is not targeting you personally—the attorney would pull the same stunts no matter who was taking the deposition. Making objections and appropriate instructions not to answer is far from a personal attack. Even obnoxious, obstreperous, and obstructionist behavior is usually not a personal attack, even if it is intended to keep information from you. And even if the behavior is designed to irritate or offend you personally, don't think of it that way. The less you think of it as a personal attack, the less your emotions will take over; and the less your emotions take over, the better you will handle the situation strategically and the better your response will appear in the record when a judge reviews it.

13.2.4   Ask Good Questions

One of the most effective ways of nullifying an objecting, obnoxious, offensive, or obstreperous attorney, waiting to pounce on every minor flaw in your questioning, is simply to ask good questions. While not every question can or should be planned in advance, spend time before the deposition thinking through the form of your questions and the proper handling of exhibits (*see* Chapters Eight through Ten). For example, if you follow the advice to ask simple, clear, open-ended questions beginning with "who, what, where, why, when, how, tell us, describe, and explain" (section 8.2.1), you provide defending counsel little opportunity for proper objection. You also send the message that you are a competent and professional attorney.

If, on the other hand, you give opposing counsel a legitimate reason to object to your questions—as compound, for example—debating or justifying those questions merely wastes time. Instead, correct the problem with the form of the question (in this example, by asking two questions instead of one). Of course, counsel's success in calling you on your faulty question and forcing you to ask better ones will no doubt encourage counsel to do it some more. But there is nothing obstructionist about making legitimate objections. And, if you ask for intervention from the court, it does not help your position when opposing counsel proves to have made a meritorious objection. Bottom line? If you are getting a lot of irritating objections because you are asking long, unclear, run-on, compound questions, well my friend, that's on you.

13.2.5 Keep the Deposition Goals in Mind

In all discovery depositions, the primary goal is to obtain information, helpful or harmful, to better prepare for the rest of the case. To accomplish this goal within the given time constraints, operate efficiently. An opposing attorney's objections and obnoxious, offensive, obstreperous, or obstructionist behavior invites you to behave inefficiently by arguing with opposing counsel. If you are addressing opposing counsel instead of questioning the witness, you have abandoned the primary goal of obtaining information. Do so only where the flow of information from the witness is already being improperly denied by opposing counsel's behavior.

13.2.6 Make Sure It's All on the Record

For the most part, the court reporter will take down all the objections, instructions, and obnoxious, offensive, obstreperous, and obstructionist statements of opposing counsel, and there is no need to make special note of it or characterize it on the record. There are exceptions, where counsel's behavior needs to be called out, as we mention later in this chapter. But we must always be mindful of what the record may not be reflecting—the volume or tone of counsel's voice in a stenographically-recorded deposition, or the finger pointing and other gestures that may accompany counsel's statements. All of this you need to describe on the record, so the record recites anything that can be used as ammunition if recourse to the court is needed.

With the foregoing principles in mind, let's turn to our three categories of behavior of defending attorneys: objecting, being obnoxious, and being obstructionist. The line between these three prototypes may not be clear in the heat of a deposition, and defending counsel's behavior may reflect a spectrum or combination of these attributes at different points in the deposition, but the categories will frame our discussion.

13.3 Dealing with the Objecting Counsel

We begin with the defending attorney who interposes objections and instructs the witness not to answer on a good faith basis and in a manner consistent with the applicable rules. That is, we may not agree with the objections or the instructions, and the number of objections may be irritating, but the objections have a colorable basis and are stated simply and to the point.

13.3.1   Objections: Outwardly Ignore, Inwardly Consider

In dealing with opposing counsel's objections, do two ostensibly opposite things simultaneously: ignore and listen. More specifically, outwardly ignore the objection in the sense of not engaging with opposing counsel. At the same time, inwardly listen to the objection, considering whether it has some merit.

Outwardly Ignore

When the defending attorney objects, do not debate or even acknowledge the defending attorney's objection. Trying to persuade the defender that they are incorrect, misunderstand the rules of evidence or depositions, or are unduly interfering with the deposition is rarely successful; the witness's attorney was motivated to make the objection and is unlikely to back down in front of the witness, who may be their client. Moreover, engaging with opposing counsel takes up time and distracts you from questioning the witness. The colloquy between counsel gives the witness a break to further consider the line of questioning and where it is headed, and the exchange often escalates to prolonged diatribes in which counsel go back and forth on the record to elaborate their positions with increasing emphasis and frustration. Resist the temptation. Do not even look at opposing counsel in response to the objection. Instead, continue looking at the witness and ask the witness to answer the question—which the witness must do unless the witness's attorney has not only objected but also instructed them not to answer (*see* Rule 30(c)(2)).

Inwardly Consider

Listen to the objection nevertheless, so you can judge whether it is valid. If you think the objection has no merit, your question can stand as-is. If you believe the objection might have merit, rephrase the question (after trying to get the witness to answer your first one) to ensure there is no evidentiary impediment to your later use of the testimony at trial or on summary judgment.

Here is how it may play out if you outwardly ignore the objection but listen to it and conclude internally that the objection was valid ("OC" refers to opposing counsel):

> Q: Mr. Vito, just a moment ago you said that as you approached the intersection, you started to brake. How far away from the intersection were you when you started to brake and how fast were you going when you started to brake?
>
> OC: Objection, compound question.

Q: Please go ahead and answer, Mr. Vito.

A: About 150 feet, and I was going thirty-five miles per hour.

Q: Okay, let me break that apart. You were about 150 feet away from the intersection when you started braking?

A: That's right.

Q: And you were going thirty-five miles per hour when you first started braking?

A: Yes.

Notice that the deposing attorney ignored the objection by not engaging with counsel, but listened to the objection and decided, correctly, that it was valid. Rather than correcting the question immediately, the deposing attorney insisted on an answer to the objectionable question, sending the message that objections were not going to throw the deposition off track. Then, after the witness answered the question, the deposing attorney rephrased the question to make it nonobjectionable, ensuring that the answer will be usable for summary judgment or trial.

Here is how it may play out if you outwardly ignore the objection but listen to it and conclude internally that the objection was not valid:

Q: Sir, before you sent Mr. Tiltson Exhibit 1 canceling the contract, you did not telephone him to discuss the problem?

OC: You're leading the witness, counsel. I object.

Q: Sir, go ahead and answer.

A: That's right, I didn't.

The deposing attorney did not argue with opposing counsel about the objection or try to convince opposing counsel that the objection was invalid. The deposing attorney simply insisted on an answer and, confident that a "leading" objection makes no sense when the inquiry is of an adverse witness, left it at that.

It may not always play out so cleanly. There may be times that you ignore the objection outwardly, conclude internally that the objection is valid, and insist that the witness answer it, but the question is so poorly phrased that it cannot be answered:

Q: Mr. Vito, how long did it take you to go from here to there?

OC: Objection, vague. Counsel, we have been talking about so many "heres" and "theres" that I don't know which ones you are referring to in your question.

Q: Please answer the question.

A: I'm sorry, I don't know what you're talking about either.

Or, the objection may not have been valid, and the question may indeed be perfectly answerable, but the witness goes along with the characterization offered by the witness's attorney anyway.

Q: Mr. Vito, what is the name of your cat?

OC: Objection, vague, ambiguous, unintelligible, uncertain.

Q: Do you understand the question, Mr. Vito?

A: Nope.

In this example, the deposing attorney made the mistake of asking the witness if he understood the question, which makes it too easy for the witness to say "no," in line with the opposing attorney's objection. Instead, simply say to the witness, "Please answer the question." (You already told the witness, at the beginning of the deposition, that if he did not understand the question, he should let you know. *See* section 6.3.)

As shown in the two foregoing examples, there may be times when the witness claims an inability to provide an answer due to the phrasing of the question. At that juncture, as explained in Chapter Twelve, you have a choice. One option is to give in and rephrase the question to make it clearer. This can solve the problem, although it forces you to do more work, may not get to the witness's actual concern, and could suggest to the witness or opposing counsel that they can easily stall your questioning by continually claiming not to understand the questions. Another option is to ask the witness, "What about the question don't you understand?" This forces the witness to identify what in the question is problematic and gives you a head start on clarifying or rephrasing. It may also discourage the witness from saying they do not understand the question unless they truly do not understand it. As a follow up, ask the witness what they understand the word that is confusing them to mean, and then adopt that meaning in your question. After the witness answers the question using a word that they have defined, you can follow up by asking the question and defining the word as you would define it. It might go like this:

Q: Mr. Vito, what is the name of your cat?

OC: Objection, vague, ambiguous, unintelligible, uncertain.

Q: You may answer, Mr. Vito.

A: I don't understand the question.

Q: What do you not understand about it?

A: Uh, I don't understand what you mean by "name."

Q: Do you have an understanding of what the word "name" means.

A: Well, yeah. What you call someone.

Q: Let's use that meaning, then. What is the name of your cat?

A: I call him Hoppity Blue. Or HB for short.

Q: By what name did you identify your cat to the vet?

A: HB.

As mentioned in Chapter Twelve on witness behaviors, sometimes the witness and the defending counsel have worked out a scheme by which the attorney makes an objection, particularly on the ground that a question is "vague," and the witness automatically proclaims that they do not understand the question (whether the witness understands it or not). Such a scheme constitutes improper coaching on the part of counsel and improper conduct by the witness. Persevere to the extent you can, but if it occurs frequently you may need to respond more aggressively with the approaches we will suggest for obnoxious and obstructionist behavior later in this chapter.

In dealing with defending counsel's objections, remember that the only person who can rule on them is the judge or magistrate, and that ruling comes only if you or your opponent attempts to use the deposition for some purpose such as introducing the answers at trial or in a summary judgment proceeding. This leads to two observations. First, most questions, objections, and answers do not end up amounting to much, so do not let an objection to a question distract you from your overall deposition goals.

But second, if there *is* a chance you will want to use the witness's answer as evidence, take steps so the objection to your question is not later sustained by the court, which would throw out the question and the witness's answer. Assume, for example, that you deposed a key witness and obtained many helpful admissions, but the witness is deceased by the time of trial; you must introduce their deposition testimony. If the trial judge sustains opposing counsel's objections made at the deposition, you are left not only without a witness, but without the witness's deposition testimony too. The rule, therefore, is this: when in doubt, cure the objection. The perils of ignoring a possibly valid objection are too great to do otherwise.

13.3.2 Instructions Not to Answer: Get the Details

Three fundamental rules about instructions should inform your response if a defending attorney instructs a witness not to answer a question.

First, as mentioned, the defending attorney may instruct a witness not to answer under Rule 30(d)(1) only to 1) preserve a privilege, 2) enforce a court order limiting discovery, or 3) make a motion to the court under Rule 30(d)(3) to limit or terminate the deposition due to harassment, etc.

Second, if the defending attorney bases the instruction not to answer on a claim of privilege, Rule 26(b)(5) requires the defending counsel to claim the privilege expressly and to describe the withheld communication or material in such a way that, without revealing the claimed privileged information, the other parties will be able to determine whether the claim of privilege is valid.

Third, if you conclude that the privilege claim or other basis for the instruction is without merit, you may pursue a motion for sanctions and an extension of the time for the deposition (Rule 30(d)(1)) and to compel the witness to answer the question (Rule 37(a)). To prevail on that motion, it must be clear that the witness refused to answer pursuant to counsel's instruction (a requirement in some jurisdictions), and counsel's instruction was erroneous.

In light of these three rules, whenever the defending attorney instructs a witness not to answer a question, make sure of the following:

- the witness's attorney is, in fact, instructing the witness not to answer;

- the basis for counsel's instruction—that is, which of the grounds stated in Rule 30(c)(2);

- the witness is going to follow the attorney's instruction not to answer;

- the witness has information responsive to the question;

- the information, including underlying facts, is responsive and not privileged or subject to a prior discovery order;

- the scope of the subject matter to which instructions will be asserted; and

- if a privilege is claimed, the applicability of the privilege to the question being asked.

Let's look at these ideas more closely with some examples.

Confirm the Instruction, Ground, and Refusal to Answer

Confirm that the defending attorney is indeed instructing the witness not to answer, as opposed to merely objecting. In a future motion to compel, you will need to show that the attorney precluded the witness from answering. Also establish the ground on which defending counsel is basing the instruction, to ascertain whether it falls within the permissible grounds set forth in Rule 30(d)(1). Some jurisdictions require you to show that the witness opted to follow the attorney's instruction (especially where the instruction is on the ground of privilege, and the witness, as the client, is the one who decides whether to waive it).

> Q: Mr. Valencia, what information did you hear about the plaintiff before you decided to terminate him?

OC: Objection. You don't have to answer that.

Q: Are you instructing the witness not to answer?

OC: Yes.

Q: Counsel, please state the reason you are instructing the witness not to answer.

OC: It calls for information protected by the attorney-client privilege.

Q: Counsel, are you claiming the attorney-client privilege for communications between you and the witness concerning the plaintiff?

OC: Yes.

Q: Mr. Valencia, are you going to follow your attorney's instruction not answer on grounds of the attorney-client privilege?

A: Yes.

In this example, the defending attorney asserted the attorney-client privilege, which is one of the permissible grounds for instruction under Rule 30(c)(2). If it were on a ground not recognized by Rule 30(c)(2), such as relevance, the instruction would be impermissible as a matter of law, entitling the deposing attorney to file a motion for sanctions and to compel an answer. We address this more fully later in this chapter in our discussion of obstructionist counsel.

In response to a facially valid assertion of the privilege (or to forestall one), ask a question that avoids the privilege—one that asks for facts and information, rather than a communication (e.g., "What information did you have about the plaintiff before you decided to terminate him?"). Rephrasing the question can be the simplest way to deal with defending counsel's instruction; if that is not possible or successful, proceed with the following additional steps.

Confirm the Witness Has Responsive Information and Explore the Underlying Facts

As a practical matter, make sure that the witness did, in fact, have a substantive answer to give if they had been allowed to answer the question at the deposition—otherwise you could go to the expense of obtaining an order reconvening the deposition, only to have the witness say they have no responsive information. This is important regardless of the ground that defending counsel asserts as the basis for the instruction.

If the basis for the instruction was privilege, probe the witness for the facts known to the witness from any means, as opposed to asking the witness to specify the words spoken to the attorney or by the attorney.[6]

> Q: Ms. Desmond, what did you learn about the checks you received from Enterprise Systems?

> OC: Objection, attorney-client privilege. I instruct you not to answer.

> Q: Are you going to follow your attorney's instruction not to answer?

> A: Yes.

> Q: Without telling me the words your attorney spoke to you, yes or no, did you ever learn any facts about the checks you received from Enterprise Systems?

[The defending attorney might object and instruct at this point, but the question is proper because it does not seek the communication, only whether the witness knows of any facts. If an instruction is given, confirm the ground and that the witness is refusing to answer.]

> A: Yes, I did.

> Q: What facts did you learn about the checks received from Enterprise System?

[Again, opposing counsel may object and instruct the witness not to answer, but the inquiry is proper.]

> A: The checks were fake.

Seek Non-Privileged Responsive Information

Similarly, even though counsel has instructed the witness not to answer the question on the ground of privilege, it is possible that the witness has responsive information that was obtained independent of any attorney-client communication. Ask for that information.

> Q: Mr. Valencia, did you learn any information about the plaintiff outside of any communications from your attorney?

> A: Yes.

> Q: Tell me what you learned.

---

6. *E.g.*, Specht v. Google, Inc., 268 F.R.D. 596, 601 (N.D. Ill. 2010) ("The privilege protects communications, not facts."); Thurmond v. Compaq Comput. Corp, 198 F.R.D. 475, 479 (E.D. Tex. 2000).

Ascertain the Scope of the Subject Matter to Which the Instruction Will Be Asserted

Explore the scope of the subject matter to which the privilege (or, e.g., prior protective order) is being asserted. This can be important for a future motion to compel, to avoid the defending attorney's argument that they instructed only about one question and would have allowed the witness to answer questions in related areas, but you never asked them.

Q: Ms. Desmond, what did you learn about the checks you received from Enterprise Systems?

OC: Objection, attorney-client privilege. I instruct you not to answer.

Q: Are you going to follow your attorney's instruction not to answer?

A: Yes.

Q: Counsel, I have a number of related questions I could go through one by one. Do you want to just stipulate that you are instructing the witness not to answer, and the witness will not answer, all questions regarding her conversations with her attorneys in the three different cases, on the ground of attorney-client privilege?

OC: Sure.

The defending attorney may or may not enter into this type of stipulation. If not, then ask all the questions you intended to ask, forcing the defending attorney to instruct on each one and the witness to confirm they will not answer each one.

Probe Any Assertion of Privilege

When the defending attorney bases the instruction not to answer on the ground of privilege, ask questions that will enable you to determine whether the claim of privilege is proper. The defending attorney should allow the witness to answer. Rule 25(b)(5)(A). The witness's answers will help the judge rule on your motion to compel further answers or the defending attorney's motion to obtain a protective order.

In particular, probe an assertion of privilege to determine 1) whether there was a privileged relationship when the communication was made; 2) if the privilege applies to the communication (whether the communication was confidential and intended to be confidential and for the purpose of, e.g., obtaining or providing legal advice); 3) if the privilege was waived (as by disclosure to third parties); and 4) if there is an exception that allows for disclosure (such as, depending on the applicable law, communications for the purpose of perpetrating a crime or fraud). To this end, inquiries might include:

- the name of the client;

- the name of the person spoken to (to make sure it was a person with whom a privilege exists, such as a licensed lawyer or their agent);

- the date of the communication and the period of the privileged relationship (to make sure the communication was made while the privileged relationship existed);

- the place of the communication (to determine if it was made in a place where there was a reasonable expectation of confidentiality, such as a lawyer's office as opposed to a crowded restaurant);

- the people present during the communication (to ascertain the attendance of people whose presence might negate the privilege);

- any person with whom the communication was shared orally or in writing (to ascertain waiver);

- the general nature and purpose of the communication (such as an oral or written communication for the purpose of obtaining legal advice, as opposed to business advice or perpetrating a crime or fraud);

- whether the communication was recorded and, if so, to whom the record was disclosed and where it currently is kept (to show lack of an intention of confidentiality or a waiver).

Armed with the information about the circumstances of the communication, you can seek a motion to extend the time for the deposition (Rule 30(d)(1)) and a motion to compel disclosure of the substance of the communication (Rule 37(a)) or seek the court's in camera inspection of a written communication (or a recording of an oral communication) to determine whether the privilege is properly claimed, if there has been waiver, or if an exception to the privilege exists.[7]

13.4 Dealing with the Obnoxious Counsel

Unlike the objecting attorney, the obnoxious, offensive, or obstreperous opposing counsel is irritating and acting beyond the rules; but unlike the obstructionist attorney we will discuss in a bit, they do not appear to be successful in blocking the flow

---

7. If the objection and instruction is asserted on the ground of attorney work product or material prepared in anticipation of litigation or trial pursuant to Rule 26(b)(3), the question is whether the information was the type that can be protected from discovery and whether the protection for the material was waived. For some types of material under the federal rules, you may try to convince the court that disclosure should be ordered due to your substantial need for it and the inability, without undue hardship, to obtain its substantial equivalent by some other means (as where one party has obtained a statement from a witness who has unique information and the witness has become unavailable). Some state laws (e.g., California) afford broader protection for the work product of attorneys, regardless of whether the material was prepared in anticipation of litigation.

of information from the witness and are not directly impeding the proceedings. Typical behaviors are these:

- periodic "speaking" objections, in the sense that they exceed the limitations of the rules but do not directly coach the witness how to answer (which would be obstructionist) (such as, "Objection, vague as to time; it is not clear whether you mean today, 2020, 1820, or any other time");

- an excessive number of objections, although properly stated;

Essential points for the objecting attorney:
• Objections
○ ignore outwardly;
○ consider inwardly.
• Instructions
○ ask the basis;
○ confirm the witness's refusal to answer;
○ explore any assertion of privilege;
○ seek nonprivileged information.

- meritless objections that would be appropriate only at trial (relevance, hearsay, etc.);

- throat-clearing and coughing that distract and might be signaling the witness (but do not appear to be having an effect);

- offhand, gratuitous comments that serve as a distraction;

- expressions of disdain for the deposing attorney and their questions;[8]

- checking emails and texts and then insisting that a question or answer be read back.

The defending attorney's conduct in these instances is inappropriate. For example, speaking objections—stating anything beyond "Objection" and the ground (e.g., "compound question")—are impermissible under the rules and case law.[9] Rule 30(c)(2), as we discussed, requires that an objection "be stated concisely in a nonargumentative and nonsuggestive manner." Long-winded objections and other obnoxious, offensive, or obstreperous behavior may be an intentional attempt to fluster you or derail the deposition, or it may be just a demonstration of the defending counsel's ignorance or unprofessionalism. Regardless, it is inconsistent with the rules.

---

8. *See, e.g.,* Mullaney v. Aude, 126 Md. 639, 730 A.2d 759, 767 (Md. Ct. Spec. App. 1999) (calling female opposing counsel "babe"); Principe v. Assay Partners, 154 Misc. 2d 702, 704; 586 N.Y.S.2d 182, 186 (N.Y. Sup. Ct. 1992) (telling female opposing counsel, "Be quiet, little girl," and the like).
9. Fed. R. Civ. P. 30(c)(2); *E.g.,* Specht v. Google, Inc., 268 F.R.D. 596, 598–99, 603 (N.D. Ill. 2010) ("objections that are argumentative or that suggest an answer to a witness are called 'speaking objections' and are improper under Rule 30(c)(2)").

Nevertheless, assuming the conduct is not getting to the point where the witness declines to answer a question or answers in a way that reflects counsel's coaching, it is generally best to ignore these antics, focus on the witness, and persevere. There is, of course, a thin line between a few speaking objections or throat-clearings here and there and outright coaching the witness—which is an obstructionist tactic that calls for a strong response—but for as long as possible, stay the course.

13.4.1 Do Not React or Play Opposing Counsel's Game

The acts of an obnoxious defending attorney threaten to slow the flow of information from the witness; the behavior, therefore, is inconsistent with your goals for the deposition. Assuming the antics are not actually working, however, engaging with the defending attorney takes yet more time away from asking the witness questions. The defending counsel wants to derail you, to fluster you, and to make you focus more on the objections than on pursuing answers from the witness. Just as it is important not to engage with the defending attorney who is making legitimate objections, so too is it important not to engage when the objections are improper and counsel's behavior is more "in your face." It just takes more self-control.

Do not play the defending attorney's game. Do not look at the defending attorney; ignore the behavior. Focus on the witness. Show that the attorney's conduct is futile and beneath you. You must be disciplined and patient, and the witness may be confused about what is happening as the defending attorney screams (figuratively or literally) to be recognized ("Won't you even give me the courtesy of looking at me and answering my question about why this is relevant?"). But overall, demonstrating the futility of obnoxious behavior at the outset results in a much better remainder of the deposition: you stay in control of the deposition, not by shouting down the defending lawyer, but by refusing to be distracted from your goals.[10] The defending lawyer, seeing you will not take the bait, may eventually settle down.

Ignoring the obnoxious defending attorney is not easy. The temptation is to debate the objection. You may unconsciously adopt a different tone with the witness, become formalistic, switch from open-ended questions to cross-examination style questions, or move to another topic. Your blood pressure may rise as the attorney launches into a harangue about your purported inability to ask proper questions.

---

10. Some attorneys insist that deposing counsel must immediately crack down on a defending attorney's first speaking objection to nip the practice in the bud. That may work for some, but I join the original authors in concluding it is not the best tactic. Of course, in any given case, and depending on the defending attorney and the witness, the deposing attorney will have to make a judgment call whether it is more powerful—and more effective in fulfilling the goals of the deposition—to ignore the defending attorney, focus on the witness, and ask for an answer, or to say sharply to the defending attorney, "speaking objections are not permitted, stop it," or "enough!" and then turn amicably back to the witness and resume your questioning.

It is often not long before you explode in anger at defending counsel's behavior, threatening to call the magistrate judge.

But remember, these responses have nothing to do with your goal of obtaining answers to questions about facts in the case while you have the witness in front of you. If the defending counsel goads you into these responses, they win the round: you are at least temporarily prevented from getting the information you need, and the witness gets a breather while the attorneys squabble. Arguing with or berating the defending counsel accomplishes nothing anyway, since there is virtually no chance of convincing another lawyer of their wrongheadedness during a deposition. The colloquy more likely results in a record that suggests to the judge that neither attorney knows how to act correctly.

Therefore, treat the defending attorney's antics as white noise. Do not even wince at them. Make it clear to the defending attorney and to the witness that the defending attorney is doing nothing more than babbling—"a tale told by an idiot, full of sound and fury, signifying nothing." Let the witness see the calm resolve in your eyes as you doggedly pursue the information you have a right to obtain. In that way, you win.

Let's look at an example of the tactic of ignoring an obnoxious opposing counsel:

Q: Ms. Adobayo, what makes you believe that your broker was not handling your stock account properly?

OC: Well, wait; let's just get our time periods straightened out here before we all get confused. What are you talking about? When she first believed that he was churning, or what?

Q: Ms. Adobayo, please answer the question.

OC: Counsel, now, you haven't answered my question. I don't know when we are talking about here, and I'm sure that the witness doesn't either. That's just not the way to take an intelligent deposition, and I'm surprised your senior partners didn't tell you that, because maybe you just don't know. But you've got to have a time period for all these things.

Q: You can answer, Ms. Adobayo.

OC: Counsel, you are just trying to confuse the witness now, by not telling her when you are asking about her knowledge. Clearly, she knows a lot of things today that she didn't know back when this guy was handling her account, and it's not fair for you to just ask about what she knows or what she knew without saying "when." So, why don't you ask a better question?[11]

---

11. "Why don't you ask a better question?" or "Why don't you ask the witness . . . ?" are among the sharpest needles a defending attorney can jab into a deposing attorney. There are reported instances

Q: [Nods at witness to proceed with her answer.]

A: Yes. I think that I was first, you know, a little suspicious when I saw some interest charges on my monthly statements, and he wasn't very direct when I asked him about them.

The deposing attorney in this example never responded to the defending attorney's challenge and continued to press the witness for an answer. If we were watching this little drama, we would have seen that the deposing attorney's eyes were always on the witness, never looking at the defending counsel. By watching the witness throughout the defending counsel's comments and then immediately telling the witness, "please answer the question," counsel communicated that such interruptions will not succeed in hiding information and the witness should not gain any courage from them. The implicit message to the witness from deposing counsel is: "I will stay here until next Tuesday if it's necessary because of the loudmouth sitting next to you; so you decide—do we do this the easy way, or do we do this the hard way? Because we are going to do it."

In fact, subtly relating to the witness can further dampen both the impact of defending counsel's interjections and defending counsel's stamina. Adding a reassuring nod to your encouragement of the witness to "please answer the question," as if to say, "yeah, your attorney's barking a lot, but you and I know we need to get through this deposition," seems to work with many witnesses. Even when the witness is the chief executive officer of the opposing company, you may have enough of a rapport (sparked at the beginning of the deposition, *see* section 6.3.5) that you and the time-pressed witness can stay on track with questions and answers while opposing counsel indulges in obnoxious behavior.

Having said this, we should add two points. First, sometimes a quick acknowledgment of opposing counsel's objection will allow the deposition to move forward. If opposing counsel feels it necessary, for reasons of ego or otherwise, to receive some sort of recognition of their comments and statements, the disruptive behavior may continue until that recognition is given. If opposing counsel does not soften their disruptive stance after being ignored for fifteen minutes, consider a simple response, without looking at the defending attorney. "Objection noted. Ms. Adobayo, please answer my question." The objective still is to get answers to questions, not to fight with opposing counsel.

---

of attorneys getting into physical wrestling matches in the deposition room, spilling out into the hallway, over who has the right to suggest questions at a deposition, and there is one instance, recorded in what we understand became a famous page of transcript in Washington, D.C., where the attorneys end a series of bitter exchanges about "suggested" questions with the taking attorney shouting at the defending attorney, "%&#$ you, I'll ask whatever questions I want to!" This is not the most efficient way to obtain information from the witness.

National Institute for Trial Advocacy

Second, note that the witness in the preceding example ultimately provided information to the deposing attorney. If, on the other hand, the defending attorney's antics start working and the witness begins to not answer questions or to answer them as counsel clearly signaled her to, then we have a problem. Or, if the conduct continues with nearly every question posed, we again have a problem. At some point, the defending attorney's antics cross the line from merely obnoxious to obstructionist; address them as we discuss next.[12]

13.5 Dealing with the Obstructionist Counsel

While the approach for dealing with the obnoxious, offensive, or obstreperous opposing counsel is (almost always) to ignore the behavior, this tactic is inadequate in responding to the obstructionist who is precluding you from obtaining necessary information. Ignoring defending counsel who coaches the witness's answers or improperly instructs the witness not to answer rewards clearly improper behavior that deprives you and your client of the evidence to which you are entitled. Obstructionist behavior can take many forms:

- Frequent speaking objections that inform the witness of how the question should be handled ("Objection, vague, ambiguous, uncertain, unintelligible—no one could possibly answer that question it's so poorly worded and incapable of comprehension."), resulting in the witness not answering questions or answering in a way that reflects the attorney's coaching;

- Whispering in the witness's ear or taking the witness out of the deposition room, while the question is pending, to discuss how to respond substantively to a question;

- Signaling the witness by nudging, kicking, nodding, gesturing, or mouthing words;

- Pointing out portions of a document to help the witness answer a question;

---

12. We can imagine three other contexts in which something more than ignoring the defending attorney's behavior might be in order, even though the behavior has not yet succeeded in blocking the flow of information. First, you may invoke a zero-tolerance policy on defending counsel's comments that are personally offensive, especially if the witness may also find them offensive ("Look here, sweetie") ("Here in America, buddy, we do things this way") ("You people are all alike"). Second, if the defending attorney's overzealousness (in speaking objections, for example) appears to be more a matter of ignorance or misguided exuberance than design, it may be worth talking to the attorney in a break, outside the presence of the witness, and matter-of-factly saying that speaking objections are sanctionable and the defending attorney needs to cut it out. Third, while a defending attorney's obnoxious behavior is usually verbal and therefore automatically included in the transcript or other record of the deposition, if the behavior is nonverbal or would otherwise not be discernable from the record, strongly consider describing it aloud, succinctly, so the record will reflect it. Videorecording the deposition works wonders, too.

- Writing notes to the witness or, during a remote deposition, sending text messages to the witness;

- Making "helpful" suggestions to the deposing lawyer on how to ask a question, which actually coaches the witness (e.g., "Why don't you ask the witness whether she ever, even once in her life, had anything at all to do with even the slightest instance of driving under the influence?");

- Interjecting "answer only if you know," which prompts the witness to blandly claim, "I don't know";

- Improper instructions not to answer a question.

While these are some of the more common examples of obstructionist conduct, it is not a complete catalog; the creativity and ingenuity of opposing counsel in continuing to find ways of behaving inappropriately precludes a definitive list. Coaching a witness, such as by conferring with a witness while a question is pending, is clearly improper under the federal rules.[13] So is instructing the witness not to answer on the ground of relevance or any other ground not specified in Rule 30(c)(2).[14] Here are some ways to deal with it.

13.5.1 Continue Relating to the Witness

As mentioned in the context of dealing with obnoxious behavior, it is often helpful to ignore the defending attorney's objections and instead relate to the witness, as by asking the witness in a reassuring manner to answer the question. Even if this does not work initially, and the witness has followed the attorney's promptings on earlier questions, the approach may end up working as the deposition wears on, bringing the witness back to answering the question. When a simple question is asked and opposing counsel claims that it is actually as complicated as the Theory of Relativity, the witness may be too honest, too embarrassed, or too expedient to continue going along with it.

One might think that a witness who is a corporate executive or professional would dutifully follow the defending attorney's lead, but that is not always so, for several

---

13. Conferring with the client while a question is pending, or pulling the witness out of the deposition room while a question is pending, is improper except to discuss assertion of a privilege. *E.g.,* In re Stratosphere Corp. Sec. Litig., 182 F.R.D. 614, 621 (D.C. Nev. 1998). Some courts, and some judges by standing order, prohibit any conference between the witness and the attorney—even during recess in the deposition—except to ascertain whether a privilege should be asserted. *E.g.,* Hall v. Clifton Precision, 150 F.R.D. 525, 528–30 (E.D. Pa. 1993) (conferences between the witness and counsel during the deposition and recesses are prohibited, even if requested by the witness, except to confer regarding assertion of privilege). Know the rule applicable in your jurisdiction.
14. *E.g.,* Resolution Trust Corp. v. Dabney, 73 F.3d 262, 266 (10th Cir. 1995) ("It is inappropriate to instruct a witness not to answer a question on the basis of relevance."); Specht v. Google, Inc., 268 F.R.D. 596, 599 (N.D. Ill. 2010) ("[Defending counsel] egregiously violated Rule 30(c)(2) by instructing [the witness] not to answer a question because his answer would be a 'guess.'").

reasons. First, the witness may feel offended by their own lawyer suggesting that the witness does not understand something, especially when that something seems perfectly clear and understandable. Second, while witnesses may be willing to sit quietly while the lawyer makes a speech about simple things being complicated, it is quite another thing for witnesses to say they lack the ability to comprehend a simple question. Third, as the witness may have learned in the deposition already, the net effect of these squabbles is that the deposing attorney eventually obtains the information, but it just takes longer. It wastes the witness's time and the company's money. This consideration is especially persuasive with executives and professionals, who have a healthy appreciation for the value of their own time. In fact, it is the strong-willed and independent executive or professional who is more likely to shun the defending attorney's advice. Reality can be brought home to the witness like this:

> Q: Doctor, I am sure your time is worth more than mine, but it appears that at the pace we are moving it will not be possible to finish up your deposition this morning. At this rate it will take much longer, and now it looks like we'll be here until the end of the day. We would prefer to avoid having to go to the judge to ask for an extension of the deposition at your expense, but we'll see. So let me again ask the question I just asked and to which your counsel objected.

We also addressed the idea earlier that defending counsel and the witness sometimes make a pact that whenever the defending attorney objects on the ground that a question is vague, the witness will say that they do not understand the question. If, at the deposition, the witness repeatedly claims to lack an understanding of clear questions after the attorney objects on vagueness grounds—such that the pattern is affecting your ability to obtain discoverable information—it may be time to be more confrontational. This approach can work:

> Q: Now, I've noticed that when your attorney objects that something is vague, you always say you can't understand the question. Is that because you really can't comprehend the question or because you're just following whatever your attorney is saying?

At this point, the defending attorney may explode in protest, and the witness may insist they were unable to understand the questions. But ignore the explosion and go on with your questions. You may very well see a subtle and welcome change in the witness for the rest of the deposition.

13.5.2 Make a Specific Record of Counsel's Behavior

If you need to ask the court for more time to conduct the deposition or for sanctions due to defending counsel's behavior, you will need proof of that behavior. Therefore, if any of the defending attorney's obstructionist conduct is nonverbal and thus unlikely to appear on the record—whispering in the witness's ear, nudging or signaling the witness, etc.—make sure that you refer to it orally so the transcript or recording of the deposition mentions it (e.g., "Let the record reflect that counsel is conferring with the witness while the question is pending").

Even when statements by opposing counsel are on the record, it may be helpful to call out the behavior to show opposing counsel that you are tracking it for potential presentation to the court. While making such a record runs the risk of defending counsel protesting and giving their side of the story (to which you need not respond, to avoid a lengthy colloquy that distracts from your questioning), it accomplishes two things: it may dissuade the defending attorney from continuing to obstruct the deposition, and, at the least, it shows the court that you pointed the issue out to counsel (For example, "This is about the twentieth time you've resorted to speaking objections and coached the witness. Stop it.")

13.5.3 Escalate Your Response as Needed

If a low-intensity "note for the record" approach does not discourage counsel's interruptions, up your response as appropriate. Here are some possibilities.

- **Invoke the rules.** While it may not always be evident, some defending lawyers cool their jets when confronted by a clear statement that their conduct is prohibited. Bringing to the offending lawyer's attention the prohibitions of the rules may sound something like this: "That last objection was suggestive and clearly designed to coach the witness. That's improper. Rule 30(c)(2) requires an objection to be concise, nonargumentative, and nonsuggestive. Back to my question."

- **Ask the court reporter to mark the record where the offending conduct is occurring.** Most court reporting machines allow the court reporter to mark the point in the transcript where something occurs, so the reporter can locate it later. It is also code for, "I want this part of the deposition easily found because I'm going to use it in a motion to compel further testimony and to obtain sanctions." For that purpose, say, for example, "This is the third time in a row that defending counsel has conferred with the witness while a question is pending. I ask that the court reporter mark the deposition."

- **Note on the record the time consumed by the obstructionist counsel in taking breaks, conferring while a question is pending, and engaging in other disruptive conduct.** The Advisory Committee Note to Rule 30(d)(1)—the rule limiting depositions to seven hours on one day—states that the court must grant additional time if the witness or counsel engages in inappropriate, time-consuming conduct. Transcription equipment has evolved such that the amount of time in the deposition devoted to obstructionist conduct can be calculated; it can also be estimated from real-time transcript feeds. Use this to make statements on the record such as, "Counsel and the witness took a break while a question was pending and were gone for seventeen minutes."

- **Take a break and talk with opposing counsel away from the witness.** Although defending counsel cannot afford to back down in front of the client or even a witness, a reasonable request made in the hallway during a break, apart from the client, has better prospects for success. For example: "Bill, this is getting out of hand. I don't want to break this off and call Judge Acosta—you're busy and so am I, and the judge won't like it—but you're putting me in a corner. You've got to stop the conferring and interruptions. You know it's improper." The defending counsel will bicker with you, but the tactic may still work.

13.5.4   Deal with Improper Instructions Not to Answer

Previously in this chapter, we addressed how to handle a defending counsel's instruction not to answer a question when the instruction appears colorable—that is, when there may be a legitimate ground for the witness not to answer. Here, we address how to handle an instruction that is plainly improper—one that is not based on a ground recognized by Rule 30(c)(2), which allows instructions only to 1) preserve a privilege, 2) enforce a limitation ordered by the court, or 3) present a motion under Rule 30(d)(3) to terminate or limit the deposition due to harassment. When defending counsel instructs or otherwise prevents a witness from answering for any other reason, the conduct is improper. Period.

Dealing with an improper instruction is not too different from dealing with a colorable one. In both situations, ascertain from the defending counsel the basis and scope of the instruction, ask the witness questions to see if the instruction is well taken, and see what other information on the topic you can get. There are, however, a couple of additional things to keep in mind: 1) beware an obstructionist attorney's "phantom" instruction; and 2) revisit the subject matter later in the deposition. And of course, where the basis of the instruction is clearly not supported by the rules, you have better odds when turning to the court for a ruling and sanctions (addressed in the next section).

Beware of Phantom Instructions

Obstructionist counsel often try to discourage the witness from answering a question without using the word "instruct," perhaps hoping that the deposing attorney will move on to another topic and the issue will go away. To deal with this situation, confirm that counsel is, in fact, instructing the witness not to answer (and the witness is not going to answer and has responsive information), ask counsel to identify the specific basis for the instruction, and take it from there.

Q: Mr. Goldstein, when did you first learn about the problems with the computer design?

OC: Hold on. I have no idea of what you mean by first learning about the problems. You make it sound like all of a sudden he learned this. He could have gradually learned about it.

Q: Please answer the question.

OC: No way. I am not going to let him answer that question the way you are asking it.

Q: Again, please answer the question.

OC: Are you deaf? That is improper and the witness does not have to answer.

Q: (To counsel.) Are you instructing the witness not to answer?

OC: You bet I am. (To witness): Don't answer that.

Q: Mr. Goldstein, are you going to follow your lawyer's instruction and refuse to answer?

A: Yes.

Q: Counsel, what is the reason for your instruction not to answer?

OC: Your question stinks.

Q: Under Rule 30(c)(2), you can't instruct a witness not to answer except to preserve a privilege, prevent a violation of a protective order which we don't have in this case, or to adjourn the deposition and seek an order limiting or terminating the deposition based on harassment, annoyance, or embarrassment of the deponent. Which one of these are you relying on?

OC: I don't have to tell you that. Figure it out, bright boy.

Q: Are you refusing to give the basis for your instruction?

OC: Yes, I am.

Q: If it's on grounds of privilege, Rule 26(b)(5) requires you to claim the privilege specifically and allow me to explore the applicability of the privilege. And Rule 37(a)(1) requires that we confer to see if I can obtain the information called for by my question without seeking court action. Are you going to comply?[15]

---

15. It would be a good idea for lawyers to include these statements in a deposition outline or some other place for easy retrieval during the deposition.

OC: You guys who sit there and spout off rules make me sick. There's nothing to talk about. I instructed him not to answer. Okay? Okay? If you don't have any more questions, I suggest we end this deposition right now.

At this juncture, the deposing attorney may feel frustrated or defeated, but a record has been created that will allow the court to provide relief and—quite likely—impose sanctions.

Try Again Later

Many defending attorneys are in a feisty mood at the beginning of the deposition but become subdued as the day drags on. Lawyers who are quick to make objections and instruct not to answer become increasingly interested in just getting the deposition over with. They also might reconsider their position, or at least be in a better frame of mind to do the right thing. This means that, around four in the afternoon, it is worth repeating the question that earlier in the day had drawn an instruction not to answer. Phrase the second attempt differently than the first. The question might now be answered without interference by opposing counsel because they do not recognize the question as being the same, because they do not care anymore, or because they realize they have no basis for stopping the witness from answering and do not want to be sanctioned.

> **Essential points for the obnoxious or obstructionist attorney:**
>
> - *Do not engage:*
>   - *keep your cool and persevere when counsel is obnoxious, but*
>   - *if counsel blocks information by coaching or instructing improperly, be prepared to take action.*
> - *If you anticipate counsel will be obnoxious or obstructionist, consider videorecording the deposition.*

13.5.5 Seek Judicial Intervention During the Deposition as a Last Resort

In severe situations, where coaching or instructions are occurring unabated, you may have to enlist or threaten to enlist judicial intervention. This is a last resort. Think through (preferably before the deposition) the point at which you might pursue this option, how you will do it, and what record you will need to be successful.

Warn of Your Intent to Seek the Assistance of the Court

A warning may be something like this: "Let the record reflect again that counsel is conferring with the witness while a question is pending. Counsel, if you keep doing this, I'll have no choice but to ask the court to intervene, and I'll be asking that your client be ordered to pay the costs and expenses for having to do so." Or this: "An instruction on that ground is not allowed under Rule 30(c)(2). If the witness does not answer, I'm going to the court to compel the answer and extend the time to finish the deposition." The threat of judicial intervention—and all the time and money it takes—can persuade the defending counsel to abide by the rules.

Do not, however, threaten to go to the court unless you are willing and able to do it. If the defending attorney calls your bluff and you do not go to the magistrate or judge, you lose your credibility for the rest of the deposition, if not the entire case.

Seek the Assistance of the Court During the Deposition

After there is a sufficient record of obstruction, suspend the deposition to contact the court and obtain an order from the magistrate judge or other applicable judicial officer. Ask the reporter to mark the sections of the transcript where defending counsel acted inappropriately (if that has not already been done) and be prepared to read those sections if the phone call, video conference, or in-person meeting with the magistrate can be arranged. Have the rules and case law citations ready to support your argument (assemble these in advance and have them on hand for every deposition). Call the magistrate and ask for a short hearing. Keep your presentation short, specific, and to the point. Do not whine—you are not asking the magistrate to help you, but simply to ensure that the deposition proceeds according to the applicable rules of the jurisdiction. Seek an order that allows questioning on specific areas of inquiry and directs opposing counsel to obey the relevant rule—to refrain from making improper objections, conferring with the witness before an answer unless privilege is involved, or instructing on impermissible grounds.

Before you make this call or threaten to make the call, however, remember this: while most courts offer telephonic judicial intervention as an option,[16] not all do. For many jurists, telephone conferences are a quick and efficient method of resolving disputes without burdening the court's docket, and they are preferred over formal in-court hearings with written motions and supporting briefs. Telephonic conferences also resolve the dispute more quickly and allow the deposition to reconvene without waiting weeks or months for a written motion to be drafted, placed on

---

16. Paramount Commc'ns v. QVC Network, 637 A.2d 34, 55 (Del. Super. Ct. 1994) ("Although busy and overburdened, Delaware trial courts are 'but a phone call away' and would be responsive to the plight of a party and its counsel bearing the brunt of such misconduct [inappropriate conduct by defending counsel].."); Brinko v. Rio Props., 278 F.R.D. 576, 584 (D. Nev. 2011) ("The magistrate judges in this district routinely make themselves available for emergency dispute resolution conferences.").

the motion calendar, heard, and decided. However, some judicial officers will not hear discovery disputes over the telephone. So before the deposition—and certainly before breaking off the deposition to call the judge—check to see if the assigned judge or magistrate is willing to take such calls.

Moreover, even where federal magistrates and judges (and their state counterparts) are willing to make themselves available for emergency discovery conferences, they are not sitting around waiting for your call. You may not reach one during the deposition, or at least not right away. When you do pry them away from their other responsibilities, settling attorney squabbles in a deposition is not likely their favorite pastime. Be sure that it will be clear to a neutral observer that the opposing counsel has committed a serious infraction that violates the rules and neither conversation among counsel nor even a later motion to compel will suffice.

With that said, let's see how an example dispute might arise during a deposition and review the process for obtaining a hearing over the telephone:

> Q: Mr. Stefanos, let me ask you a few questions about the early days of your corporation. Who were the original shareholders?
>
> OC: Objection. That was ten years ago. It has nothing at all to do with this case. Let's try to stick to relevant questions here, Adrienne.
>
> Q: Mr. Stefanos, will you answer the question, please? Who were the original shareholders?
>
> OC: Adrienne, I just objected to that question. Now, you're not going to try to play hardball here, are you? Why don't you move on?
>
> Q: Are you going to answer the question, Mr. Stefanos?
>
> OC: I'm sorry, you are being so unreasonable, Adrienne. I'm going to instruct the witness not to answer.
>
> Q: Mr. Stefanos, will you answer the question, please?
>
> A: No, I am going to follow the instructions of my lawyer.
>
> Q: Counsel, what is the basis of your instruction? Under Rule 30(c)(2), it can only be to preserve a privilege, enforce an existing order, or seek a new protective order.
>
> OC: I'm claiming these questions have nothing to do with the claims or defenses in the case, or with discovering admissible evidence in the case, so the witness does not have to answer them.

Q: Well, let me ask this, then. Were the shares originally held by more than ten people?

OC: Again, this just has nothing to do with the issues here, and I instruct Mr. Stefanos that he need not answer this question.

Q: Mr. Stefanos, how many people held the shares originally?

A: I'm not going to answer the question, on the advice of my attorney.

Q: Counsel, what's the basis for your instruction?

OC: I told you. It's outside the scope of discovery. Please move on.

Q: You're seriously instructing the witness based on relevance?

OC: You heard me, Adrienne. Move on.

Q: Mr. Stefanos, let me see if I can get at the information in another way. There is some question whether the owners on the certificate of incorporation were all of the original owners. Let me show you that certificate, which is Stefanos Deposition Exhibit 13. Are those all of the original owners?

OC: Same objection, Adrienne. You are way out of line here. Just ask relevant questions, and we will have no problems, but you're just not going to snoop around on some fishing expedition.

Q: Mr. Stefanos, will you answer my last question about the certificate?

A: No, I'm going to follow my lawyer's advice.

Q: Counsel, this is important to me, so before I call the magistrate, let me confer with you, as required by the rules, to see if there's a way to work this out.

OC: I think I have made my position very clear. I am not budging.

Q: Well, since this is probably the last area I need to question the witness about, I might as well see if we can get the magistrate on the phone right now rather than waiting until the deposition is concluded.

Since the deposing attorney has now asked about the same subject matter in three different ways, a solid record has been made that discovery in the area is being precluded by directions to the witness not to answer. The defending attorney has not claimed privilege or other ground permitted under Rule 30(c)(2), relying instead on a relevance argument. Although defending counsel could claim that a question exceeding the proper scope of discovery is designed to oppress, embarrass, or harass, the deposing attorney sees no basis for that conclusion. Let's return to the deposition room.

Counsel: Ms. Reporter, please mark those last few pages, where I am asking about the original owners of the corporation and the certificate of incorporation. Then, let's just go off the record until I can get the magistrate on the telephone.

Reporter: Does counsel agree to go off the record?

OC: This is ridiculous, but fine.

[After the magistrate is on the phone, preferably on speaker:]

Counsel: Your Honor, we have a problem here in the Smith case, Docket Number C-931443. I'm representing the plaintiff, taking the deposition of Mr. Julius Stefanos, the vice president of the defendant corporation. I've asked him in different ways who the original shareholders were and how many there were. The defendant's attorney has instructed the witness not to answer those questions on the ground that the information being sought is not relevant, which as you know is not a proper ground for instruction. I attempted in good faith to confer with opposing counsel to avoid having to call you, but that was unsuccessful. We have the reporter here, prepared to read the questions and objections, if you would like.

Magistrate: No, counsel, not at this point. Let me talk to defendant's counsel.

OC: Your Honor, what plaintiff's counsel has been doing here is egregious. These questions about original ownership have nothing to do with the issues in this case, and she knows it. She's just trying to fish around to see if she can bring other people into this controversy, people who have nothing to do with the problems that her client has experienced, so that she can inconvenience and embarrass them. Besides that, I know she's working with other counsel in a different case against my client, and she may very well be intending to share the answers in this deposition with that other lawyer to give her an advantage in that other lawsuit. That's why I had no choice but to direct the witness not to answer these improper questions.

Magistrate: OK, let me hear the questions from the reporter.

[The questions are read by the reporter.]

Magistrate: Counsel, I understand we're on speakerphone, so here's my ruling for everyone to hear. The witness is directed to answer these questions, and other questions reasonably related to them. There is nothing privileged here, and, as I understand it, defense counsel is not arguing privilege. These questions may not be on matters directly part of the claims or defenses in the case, but they are relevant to the claims and defenses in this case and are proportionate to the needs of the case. If counsel in some other lawsuit can take advantage of these answers, that has nothing to do with whether the answers should be given in this case. Their use in the other case depends on a determination of the judge in that matter on the relevance of the information to that other case.[17] Of course, if you think it justified, you can always seek a protective order in the other case. I find that these questions present a legitimate area for discovery, and, counsel for the defendant, you will not interfere by directing this witness, or other witnesses who may be asked about these topics, not to answer.

After the telephone conference with the magistrate, resume questioning. Start, of course, with the questions that were the subject of the application to the magistrate and which the witness refused to answer, and follow up as appropriate.

13.6 Filing a Motion with the Court

As an alternative to calling for judicial intervention during the deposition, finish as much of the questioning as possible, suspend the deposition pending a ruling by the court, and file a written motion to extend the deposition time and compel additional witness responses. Note that this option is available not only when the defending counsel has been obstructionist through coaching or making clearly improper instructions, but also when the defending counsel may have had a good-faith basis for the instruction yet you conclude the instruction has no merit.

---

17. However, the magistrate or judge ruling on this application has the discretionary power to order deposing counsel not to release the information obtained during the deposition to anyone, including counsel in another case. *See* Scott v. Monsanto Co., 868 F.2d 786, 792 (5th Cir. 1989).

13.6.1   *Rule 30(d)(1) Motion to Extend the Deposition and for Sanctions*

Rule 30(d)(1) permits the district court to issue an order extending the time for a deposition beyond the ordinary limit of one seven-hour day[18] "if needed to fairly examine the deponent or if the deponent, another person, or any other circumstance impedes or delays the examination." The motion is made to the court in which the action is pending and, if the court finds that a person has impeded, delayed, or frustrated the fair examination of the deponent, the court may impose sanctions, including the reasonable expenses and attorney's fees incurred by the moving party, against that person.

It is for purposes of motions like these that modern court-reporting systems can track the time spent examining the witness (by recording the starting and ending times of questioning sessions) and the time expended for breaks, arguing objections, conferences with the deponent by defending counsel, or any other interruption. Submit this information, along with relevant excerpts from the deposition transcript, in support of the motion.

13.6.2   *Rule 37(a) Motion to Compel Answers*

If a witness refuses to answer a question at a deposition—whether on the witness's own initiative or following counsel's instruction—you may move for an order compelling an answer under Rule 37(a)(3)(B). Rule 37(a)(4) treats an evasive or incomplete answer as a failure to answer. Under Rule 37(a)(2), a motion seeking an order against a party is made to the court in which the action is pending, while a motion seeking an order against a nonparty is made to the court in the district where the deposition is being taken (because that is where the witness is subject to the court's power). You have the option of completing the examination, or adjourning the examination, before filing the motion. Pursuant to Rule 37(a)(5), the court may order payment of the other side's expenses, including reasonable attorney's fees, for unsuccessfully bringing or opposing the motion without substantial justification.

If the court issues an order under Rule 37(a) compelling a witness to answer a question at the deposition, and the witness refuses to obey the order, the court may impose a variety of sanctions under Rule 37(b). For example, the court in the district where the deposition is being taken may hold a witness in contempt for refusing to obey an order to answer (or refusing to be sworn). A party who refuses to answer a question after being ordered to do so is subject to the further sanctions listed in Rule 37(b)(2), including issue or evidence sanctions and even dismissal or default. A party failing to abide by the court's order, the attorney advising the

---

18. Most courts and the Advisory Committee view the seven-hour time limit as the time during which the actual questioning of the deponent by the examining lawyer is occurring.

party, or both can be required to pay the reasonable expenses, including attorney fees, caused by the failure.

As a prerequisite to filing a Rule 37 motion, the moving party must include a certificate that it conferred in good faith with the other party, or attempted to confer, to resolve the problem without court intervention (Rule 37(a)(1)). Always check the local rules of the court in which the motion is being filed to determine how to comply with meet and confer requirements. Most state courts have a similar requirement for discovery-related motions, and even in the absence of this obligation, it makes good sense to discuss the possibility of resolving the problem with opposing counsel before appearing before the court. Not only might the parties reach agreement, the attorneys gain an advantage if the court believes they can behave professionally.

Consult the applicable rules to determine what must be filed along with the written motion. Typically, the materials would include a memorandum of law, a declaration or affidavit, relevant excerpts from the deposition transcript, and a proposed order.

13.7 Videorecording the Deposition

The most effective method for controlling inappropriate attorney behavior is to discourage it from happening in the first place, by opting under Rule 30(b)(3) for the deposition to be recorded by audiovisual means. If, before the deposition, you know that opposing counsel has a reputation for obnoxious or obstructionist behavior, or your previous experience with the lawyer suggests it is likely that improper behavior will occur, use the notice of deposition to announce that it will be a videorecorded deposition.

For whatever reason, lawyers who engage in the most outrageous conduct when only a court reporter is present tend to be on their best behavior when the deposition is being recorded by video. Perhaps their knowledge that the video can be shown to the judge or magistrate accounts for this, but regardless of the reason, it

> *Lawyers who engage in the most outrageous conduct when only a court reporter is present tend to be on their best behavior when the deposition is being recorded by video.*

works. For those opponents who obstruct not merely by objections and instructions not to answer, but also by coughing, sighing, making faces and gestures, and other activity not shown on the transcript or on the head-and-shoulders shot of the deponent used in most videotaped depositions, a second camera, operated by a second videographer, can be brought to the deposition and aimed at the defending lawyer, or at the taking attorney, defending lawyer, and the witness. This can be expensive, but if the witness is important and the defending attorney's conduct is severe, enduring this expense may well be worth it. If it does not discourage improper behavior altogether, there will at least be indisputable videographic support for a claim that opposing counsel has obstructed the deposition.

Even if the deposition was not originally noticed as a video deposition, a deposing attorney subjected to improper behavior can announce, perhaps just before the lunch break, that the remainder of the deposition will be recorded on video. Opposing counsel can object, but continue the video recording subject to later resolution of the objection (*see* Rule 30(c)(2); *accord* Rule 30(b)(3)(B)).[19]

To view a video demonstration of Dealing with Opposing Counsel (Objections and Instructions), scan the QR code (print version) or click here.

---

19. As a final note, although not geared to seeking judicial assistance or obtaining answers from the deponent, consider whether the defending attorney's conduct is so egregious that it must be reported to the ethics or disciplinary unit of the relevant state bar. The defending attorney's conduct may violate the jurisdiction's rules of professional conduct, particularly with the advent of civility rules, and some jurisdictions require an attorney to report the unethical conduct of another attorney. *See* ABA Model Rules 3.4, 8.3, 8.4. To date in California, reporting another attorney's ethical violation is not mandatory; in fact, threatening to report an attorney to the California State Bar is itself an ethical violation, if it is done to obtain an advantage in a civil dispute. Cal. R. Prof. Conduct 3.10(a). California is currently considering an ethical rule that would require reporting an attorney in some circumstances.

CHECKLIST

DEALING WITH OBJECTING,
OBNOXIOUS, OR OBSTRUCTIONIST OPPOSING COUNSEL

When confronted with the defending attorney's objections, instructions, and other conduct:

✓ Size up the defending attorney's behavior;

✓ Ask good questions of the witness;

✓ Keep the deposition goals in mind;

✓ Get everything on the record.

When an objection is made:

✓ Outwardly ignore the objection and the defending attorney;

✓ Inwardly consider whether the record should be clarified, or a different question must be asked for evidentiary purposes.

When the defending attorney instructs the witness not to answer:

✓ Confirm that the witness's attorney is, in fact, instructing the witness not to answer;

✓ Ask the witness's attorney for the basis of the instruction (see Rule 30(c)(2));

✓ Ask the witness if they are going to follow the attorney's instruction not to answer;

✓ Ask the witness if they have information responsive to the question;

✓ Ask for any information, including underlying facts, that is responsive and not privileged or subject to a prior discovery order;

✓ Ask counsel the scope of the subject matter to which instructions would be asserted.

If the instruction not to answer is based on a claim of privilege, ask the witness questions to probe whether:

✓ There was a privileged relationship when the communication was made;

✓ The communication was confidential and for the purpose of a confidential relationship;

✓ The privilege was waived by disclosure to third parties;

✓ The crime-fraud or other exception allows for disclosure;

✓ A written communication would refresh the witness's recollection of the subject of the testimony.

Ignore the obnoxious counsel's efforts to goad you into debates and distract you.

If the defending attorney obstructs the deposition by coaching or by improperly instructing the witness not to answer:

✓ Continue relating to the witness;

✓ Invoke the rules, make the record clear, and mark the record;

✓ Consider judicial intervention during the deposition, if available, as a last resort;

✓ File a motion to compel further answers, to extend the deposition time, and to impose sanctions.

CHAPTER FOURTEEN

CONCLUDING THE DEPOSITION

It ain't over 'til it's over.

—Yogi Berra

A deposition will be more effective if you finish all lines of inquiry before the deposition is deemed completed. Normally there is only one opportunity to depose the witness, and once the deposition is concluded, there is little chance to persuade the opponent or the court to call the witness back for more questioning. In this chapter, we discuss how to ensure all important subject areas have been covered, to follow up on any examination conducted by other attorneys, and to adjourn the deposition without waiving any rights.

14.1 Ensuring Completeness

Before concluding the deposition, call a recess to consider whether the goals of the deposition have been accomplished as much as possible given the available time and the number of issues. Review the deposition outline to see what has been addressed and if anything remains. If a client, co-counsel, paralegal, or consulting expert is present, check with them as well to see if more questioning is needed in any area. Consider the ul-

> **In This Chapter:**
>
> - *Ensuring complete coverage of all important subject areas*
> - *Following up on other attorneys' examinations*
> - *Adjourning the deposition without waiving rights*

timate question: do I now have everything I need from this witness for my summary judgment motion, evidence at trial, or whatever other purpose I had for the deposition?

Once assured that there is nothing more to cover with the witness, attorneys often ask the witness questions like these:

Q: Now Mr. Tilts, are there any answers to my questions that you wish to change before we close this deposition?

A: Not that I can think of.

Q: Do you have any information in response to any of my earlier questions, which you didn't recall when I asked you the question, but that you remember now?

A: No.

Q: Do you have anything to add that would allow me to present your side of this dispute to my client more fully?

A: No, I don't think so.

A witness rarely claims to remember anything new or changes an earlier answer. But the value of these questions becomes apparent if you need to later impeach the witness with their deposition testimony at trial, because the witness's answers make the deposition testimony seem all the more reliable and make any conflicting testimony at trial seem all the more suspect.

14.2 Arrests and Convictions

Consider asking the witness if they have any prior convictions and arrests. Under appropriate circumstances, a witness can be impeached at trial with a criminal conviction under Federal Rule of Evidence 609 or with prior bad acts under Federal Rule of Evidence 404. The court also has discretion during the cross-examination of a character witness to allow inquiry about arrests and other bad acts to show that the character witness does not really know the person well or has a faulty notion of what it means to have good character.

Witnesses may resent being asked if they have been arrested or convicted and cease cooperating once you ask. Reserve such questions until the end of the deposition, when cooperation no longer matters. But these questions should be asked, because in this day of numerous regulatory crimes, the possibility of a criminal conviction is more likely than one might think. Even if the information is not worth bringing out at trial, the mere possibility that testifying may reveal a prior undisclosed conviction can induce the opposing party to settle the case.

14.3 Ending Without Ending

When you finish questioning the witness (or the time for the deposition has expired), state for the record, "I have no further questions," "I have no further questions at this time," or words to that effect. The defending attorney and counsel for any other parties may then ask their own questions of the witness.

14.3.1 Dealing with Questions from Other Lawyers

You may not be happy with the questions from other counsel or the witness's answers to their queries. The witness's counsel may elicit facts from the witness that explain away admissions that you obtained. The witness may come up with factual assertions that muddy the possibility of obtaining summary judgment or cloud testimony that could otherwise be used for impeachment at trial. Attorneys representing other parties may elicit evidence shifting blame from their client to yours or otherwise confound your client's interests. But here is the deal. All that information would have come out anyway sometime in the future—in mediation, in arbitration, in summary judgment proceedings, or at trial. The examinations of other counsel give insight into their case theories. They give you an opportunity to hear the good, the bad, and the ugly and to prepare for it. And you can conduct a follow-up examination of the witness to test the testimony that other counsel elicited. Therefore, listen to the examinations conducted by the other lawyers and be prepared to ask further questions.

14.3.2 Final Words Without Waiver

When all counsel have finished their questioning (if any) of the witness, the deposing attorney typically closes out the deposition. If something arose during the deposition that leads you to believe the questioning should be reconvened later pursuant to a court order—such as the defending attorney's impermissible instructions not to answer or a revelation that documents have been withheld improperly from production (*see* section 13.5), preserve the right to seek such relief. Say the deposition is "adjourned at this time," is "suspended until a time to be identified in the future," is "adjourned until such time as the court rules on motions to be brought," is "terminated pending further discussions between the parties on the production of documents," is "in recess until the production of the documents referred to," is "suspended to permit a motion for an order to compel discovery," or is "concluded subject to the right to recall the witness for further questioning should that be required," as the case may be.

What is the legal effect of these phrases? Usually nothing, although they do preclude a later argument that you abandoned any such right by closing the deposition. Which one is the best alternative? Usually, it doesn't matter. Unless there is an agreement among the parties or a court order to continue the deposition, Rule 30(b)(5)(C) requires the deposition officer to state on the record that the deposition is complete and to set out any stipulations made by the lawyers. If you have not offered any further questions, the deponent can go home and not come back unless a court says otherwise.

In the final analysis, any right to have a witness return to answer more questions is governed not by whether you chose the proper phrase at the end of the session, but by whether there is sufficient justification for calling the witness back.

In other words, if the court is later persuaded to deny the witness's privilege claims and orders the deposition to resume, the witness will have to return regardless of the language used at the end of the last deposition day. Conversely, if you cannot demonstrate a sufficient reason for resuming the deposition, the witness does not have to come back, no matter how careful the attorney was to say at the deposition, "Adjourned, subject to my right to recall."

CHECKLIST
CONCLUDING THE DEPOSITION

✔	Check the deposition outline, and confer with a co-counsel, client, or consulting expert to the extent available, to confirm that all intended topics were covered.
✔	Give the witness another opportunity to add to their testimony, at the risk they will undo a favorable admission.
✔	Inquire about arrests and convictions or other matters that might alienate the wtiness, if raised earlier in the deposition.
✔	Follow up as needed after other attorneys examine the witness.
✔	Adjourn the deposition without waiving any right to reopen the deposition.

CHAPTER FIFTEEN

USING DEPOSITIONS IN MOTIONS AND TRIAL

That which is used—develops. That which
is not used wastes away.

—Hippocrates

A deposition will be more effective if you know how to use the deposition transcript or recording beneficially in the lawsuit. Usually, the deposing attorney selects excerpts from the transcript or recording to use as evidence in motions or at trial, although the defending attorney and other parties can offer excerpts as well. All counsel can use the deposition testimony to better prepare the case.

In this chapter, we consider the primary uses of deposition testimony in summary judgment motions and trial preparation, as well as seven uses of the deposition at trial.

15.1 Motions for Summary Judgment

Deposition testimony is commonly used to support or oppose motions for summary judgment.[1] Typically, portions of the transcript are attached as exhibits to a declaration from an attorney, authenticating the deposition excerpts based on counsel's presence at the deposition or the reporter's signed certification page. The deposition excerpts are cited as support for an assertion that a material fact is undisputed or disputed, as the case may

> **In This Chapter:**
>
> - *The primary uses of deposition testimony in summary judgment motions*
>
> - *The primary uses of deposition testimony in trial preparation*
>
> - *Seven uses of the deposition at trial*

---

1. *See, e.g.,* Rule 56(c) (party may cite to materials in the record, including depositions); Cal. Code Civ. P. § 437c (same). A jurisdiction's local rules may dictate how the material should be presented to the court. A party can use their own deposition testimony in summary judgment proceedings, but usually not at trial (except, e.g., to refresh recollection) unless the party becomes unavailable.

be. The opposing party may object to the consideration of the deposition excerpts on procedural or evidentiary grounds, and the court should rule on those objections in conjunction with its ruling on the summary judgment motion.

Because deposition testimony is so often used in summary judgment proceedings, attorneys taking a deposition may be concerned about the way they ask their questions. In particular, attorneys intending to seek summary judgment may be wary of asking open-ended questions of an opposing party's witness, because it leaves the witness free to state information creating a triable factual issue that the opponent can use to defeat the motion. As a practical matter, however, opposing counsel could manufacture triable issues of fact even if the evidence was not elicited at the deposition by the deposing counsel by merely asking their own questions at the deposition or having the witness later sign an affidavit opposing the summary judgment motion (with some limitations for "sham affidavits").[2] For that reason, it is generally advisable to ask the open-ended questions and find out all the witness has to say, close off any future elaboration, and then follow up with leading questions that will specifically support summary judgment (*see* Chapter Eight).

Nonetheless, some attorneys prefer to enter the deposition with the exclusive goal of gaining certain admissions that will remove any possibility of a genuine issue of material fact, without attempting to find out what the witness knows more globally about the issues in the case. That can work if the deposing attorney is masterful enough to obtain admissions that the witness cannot undo by a subsequent affidavit. If summary judgment is not granted, however, the attorney will be stuck without knowing the full scope of what the witness will say at trial. Both approaches have their place in appropriate circumstances, and counsel must weigh the costs and benefits of each approach.

15.2 Preparing for Trial

Depositions play an important role in trial preparation, particularly as you craft your direct examinations and cross-examinations of the trial witnesses. To that end, you must have a way of organizing and recalling the deposition testimony, using the testimony to draft the examination outlines, and readying the outlines and deposition materials so that excerpts from the testimony can be presented promptly when needed at the trial.

---

2. The "sham affidavit" doctrine holds that an affidavit submitted in a summary judgment proceeding may be stricken or ignored to the extent it contradicts prior deposition testimony. *E.g.*, Perma Rsch. & Dev. Co. v. Singer Co., 410 F.2d 572, 577–78 (2d Cir. 1969); Yeager v. Bowlin, 693 F.3d 1076, 1080–81 (9th Cir. 2012). However, the rule may not apply if the inconsistency is not extreme enough to suggest a sham or if the affidavit presents an adequate reason for the disparity. *E.g.*, Button v. Dakota, Minn. & E. R.R. Corp., 963 F.3d 824, 830–31 (8th Cir. 2020) (court did not err in relying on affidavit that expanded on deposition testimony rather than contradicting it and affidavit did not present sham facts).

15.2.1 *Summaries, Abstracts, and Digests of the Deposition Testimony*

To help prepare for trial (and for motions as well), deposition transcripts are frequently summarized to help counsel understand the gist of each witness's testimony and quickly locate specific testimony on any given topic. These summaries, sometimes called abstracts or digests, can be created by paralegals or more junior attorneys. Alternatively, senior attorneys on the case may choose to create the summaries to become more familiar with the testimony. Outsourcing the work is also an option. Not only do the summaries assist counsel, they lead to greater client participation in the trial preparation, because clients are better able to consume summaries than entire transcripts.

There are numerous ways to summarize a deposition, but they all come down to two basic methods. The full summary method condenses all the deposition testimony from beginning to end; the subject method summarizes the testimony regarding predefined topics or issues.

A summary abstract is more complete. It might take the following form, providing a short description by page and line:

14:6   Founded own construction co. after graduation from college.

14:12 Had only 5 to 10 employees for 1st 10 years.

14:16 Now has 50 employees.

14:20 Does all engineering work and bidding on contracts.

It can also appear in narrative form, like this:

> Founded own company after college (14:6) where he does all the engineering and bidding work on the contracts (14:20). The company has grown from 5 employees to 50 in 10 years (14:12, 14:16). He has plans to grow it to 100 (43:25) and then to sell it to his younger sister and brother-in-law (45:13).

A summary abstract tends to include more information than is needed, because it deals with all the testimony at the deposition from start to finish.

A subject abstract is more practical. It organizes the deposition testimony by topic, summarizing the testimony pertinent to each topic under a topic heading. The abstract can also be presented in a sortable electronic table or database, with columns for 1) the page and line range of testimony, 2) a summary of the testimony, and 3) the topic to which it pertains. Counsel can then search for testimony according to where it occurred in the deposition ("I know the witness said something about that right before lunch"), can sort the testimony by topic, or can search for particular words of interest.

A variety of software applications also handle the task efficiently. Typically, counsel uploads the electronic transcript (and synched video recording, if applicable) to the cloud and, using the software, can read the transcript, perform searches, annotate testimony, highlight testimony, color-code testimony by topic or priority, and generate reports that contain, for example, all the testimony on a particular topic by multiple deponents. The software can also create deposition summaries from the highlighted and color-coded testimony. Instead of using summaries or abstracts, attorneys may rely on electronic searches of a digital copy of the deposition transcript for specific words and phrases.

15.2.2 Crafting Direct and Cross-Examinations

The witness's deposition testimony shows what facts the witness must admit at the trial or face impeachment with the deposition testimony. It also shows what questions to avoid on cross-examination (because the witness will respond unfavorably). Many trial lawyers therefore construct their cross-examinations based on the answers given at the witness's deposition.

Reorganize the deposition questions as necessary to make the intended points on cross-examination most effectively. For example, a critical point for trial may not have been covered until the end of the deposition, but nothing prevents beginning the cross-examination with this point. Not only may the order of points and questions be changed, but questions that elicited unimportant or harmful information at the deposition may be omitted, and unartfully worded questions can be rephrased.

> *Reorganizing Deposition Testimony to Prepare for Cross-Examination:*
> - *Reorder topics and questions to focus attention on critical points.*
> - *Omit questions that elicited unimportant or harmful information.*
> - *Rephrase unartfully worded questions.*

That said, having critical cross-examination questions mirror the questions asked at the deposition will facilitate using the deposition transcript as an impeachment tool. The key to impeachment is showing a definite inconsistency between the trial testimony and the deposition testimony. When the question at trial is the same as the question at the deposition, the difference in the trial answer and the deposition answer will be clear. When the question at trial is slightly different than the question at the deposition, a clever witness can avoid the sting of impeachment and make the cross-examiner look foolish. Consider the following example:

Q: Isn't it true, sir, that you never even bothered to read the contract?

A: No, that's not true.

Q: Are you telling these jurors that you did read the contract?

A: Yes.

Q: Well sir, do you remember having your deposition taken?

A: Yes.

Q: Showing you that deposition, do you see on page 14, line 6 that you were asked, "Did you read the contract before you signed it?" and your answer was "No"?

A: Yes, but that's different than what you just asked me. You asked whether I had ever read the contract, and I did read it about two weeks after the signing.

Q: Oh. Well, let's move on.

15.2.3 Other Trial Planning

Use deposition testimony in planning the rest of the trial as well. Consider if there is any admissible deposition testimony—for example, statements of the opposing party or testimony of witnesses unavailable for trial—that would be effective to use in opening statement (with the court's permission), in the presentation of evidence, or in closing argument. Conversely, in preparing direct examination of the witnesses you intend to call, review how the witness testified in the deposition to avoid subjecting the witness to impeachment with prior inconsistent statements. Indeed, consider the witness's deposition testimony carefully when readying the witness for trial.

15.2.4 Preparing to Use the Deposition Testimony at Trial

When preparing direct examination outlines and cross-examination outlines for the various witnesses who will be testifying at trial, annotate the outlines with the page and line of the deposition that supports the desired answer. That will ready you to refresh a witness's recollection on direct examination or impeach a witness on cross-examination with a prior inconsistent statement. Cross-examination outlines should also reference, by page and line number, any excerpts from an opposing party's deposition testimony that you plan to introduce as a statement of a party opponent. In addition, identify any deposition excerpts that should be introduced as evidence in lieu of an unavailable witness's live testimony.

Taking this preparation one step further, the trial examination outlines can include bar codes or QR codes and electronic versions of the deposition transcripts can be bookmarked to facilitate display of admissible deposition testimony on monitors in the courtroom (for example, admissions of the opposing party). Similarly, if the deposition is recorded using digital video, and the video has been synchronized with the transcript, knowing the page and line of the desired testimony will allow you or an associate to quickly access the relevant video excerpt and display it to the jurors, so the witness can be seen and heard delivering the testimony.

15.3 At Trial

Rule 32(a)(1) provides that all or part of a deposition may be used at a trial or hearing against a party who was present or represented at the deposition or had reasonable notice of it to the extent it would be admissible under the Federal Rules of Evidence if the deponent were present and testifying, if the use is permitted by Rule 32(a)(2) through (8). In essence, deposition testimony can be used against a party for any purpose set forth in Rule 32(a)(2)–(8).

Rule 32(a)(2)–(8) authorizes a broad variety of uses. Rule 32(a)(2), for example, allows use of a deposition for impeachment and "for any other purpose allowed by the Federal Rules of Evidence." Rule 32(a)(3) provides that an adverse party may use the deposition testimony of a party or the party's officer, director, managing agent or Rule 30(b)(6) designee. Rule 32(a)(4) allows the use of a deposition of any witness who is unavailable for trial in that the witness is dead, is outside geographical limits, cannot attend due to age, illness, infirmity, or imprisonment, or meets other criteria (*see also* Fed. R. Evid. 804).[3]

Pertinent as well is Rule 32(a)(6), which reflects the rule of completeness. Rule 32(a)(6) reads: "If a party offers in evidence only part of a deposition, an adverse party may require the offeror to introduce other parts that in fairness should be considered with the part introduced, and any party may itself introduce any other parts." Federal Rule of Evidence 106 similarly provides: "If a party introduces all or part of a writing or recorded statement, an adverse party may require the introduction, at that time, of any other part—or any other writing or recorded statement—that in fairness ought to be considered at the same time."[4]

Given the broad scope of Rule 32(a), there are at least seven ways a deposition transcript may be used at trial. We address them in detail next.

---

3. Limitations on the use of depositions are set forth in Rule 32(a)(5), which refers to depositions taken on short notice while a motion for a protective order was pending and the use of a deposition against an unavailable party who shows they could not obtain counsel for the deposition. Rule 32(a)(7) provides that substituting a party under Rule 25 does not affect the right to use a deposition. Rule 32(a)(8) generally allows use of a deposition taken in an earlier action between the same parties (or their representatives or successors in interest) involving the same subject matter.
4. A proposed amendment to Rule 106 would allow the completing statement even if hearsay and would apply the rule to unrecorded oral statements.

15.3.1 Seven Ways to Use a Deposition at Trial

Under the federal rules—and state laws as well—the most common uses for a deposition at trial are:

- as the testimony of an unavailable witness;
- as a source of opposing party statements;
- as a basis for a proffer;
- as a means of refreshing recollection;
- as the testimony of a witness who is unable to testify because of lapse of memory;
- as a means of impeaching a witness; and
- as a means of accomplishing a "phantom" impeachment.

These uses have different foundations, deriving from the underlying evidentiary rules. Because depositions are out-of-court statements, for example, the rules regarding hearsay often come into play. Furthermore, for many of these uses, you must decide how best to present the material to the jurors. Here then is a closer look at each of these uses of deposition testimony at trial.

15.3.2 Testimony of an Unavailable Witness

By the time of trial, a witness may have become "unavailable" within the meaning of Rule 32(a)(4) or Federal Rule of Evidence 804(a) (*see* section 11.3). Common examples of unavailability are that the witness has died, is too ill to attend, or is outside the geographical reach of subpoena power. Whether or not you anticipated the witness's availability at the time of the deposition, the deposition transcript or recording may be used in lieu of the missing witness's live testimony (Rule 32(a)(4)). Such use is not precluded by the hearsay rule if the deposition testimony is offered against a party who had an opportunity and similar motive to examine the witness at the deposition (Fed. R. Evid. 804(b)(1)).[5]

There are two prerequisites to presenting the deposition testimony of an unavailable witness: selecting and designating the deposition excerpts you want to use and obtaining rulings on any objections to their use. Counsel must then decide how to display the testimony to the jurors.

---

5. Federal Rule of Evidence 804(b) does not apply if the witness's unavailability was procured by the proponent of the testimony. Fed. R. Evid. 804(a).

Designating Deposition Excerpts

The first task is to determine and disclose the portions of the depositions you want to use. Usually this is done by reference to the page and line numbers of the transcript, the time codes in a videorecording, or both.

Edit the excerpt of the deposition transcript or recording in a manner that will convey the testimony to the jurors appropriately. Purge the excerpt of any false starts, irrelevancies, arguments between counsel, and objections asserted by the defending attorney. To avoid disputes over this editing and any objections, follow the designation and counter-designation protocols that provide all parties the opportunity to respond to deposition testimony that is anticipated for use at trial.

Most courts will order the parties to designate before trial the depositions or portions of depositions each intends to offer. In federal district courts, Rule 26(a)(3)(A) requires the parties to file and serve, at least thirty days before trial, the evidence it may present at trial other than solely for impeachment. Not only does this include a list of witnesses and the exhibits the party intends to use, it also includes the designation of "those witnesses whose testimony the party expects to present by deposition and, if not taken stenographically, a transcript of the pertinent parts of the deposition."

Local rules and the court's standing orders may contain further requirements. For example, the parties may have to designate their deposition excerpts simultaneously. Under this procedure, each side identifies the portions of depositions it intends to offer, either by making a list of witnesses, pages, and lines (the usual procedure under the current federal rules) or by marking on a copy of the transcripts. The parties then exchange the lists or transcript volumes and make counter-designations under Rule 32(a)(6) (i.e., if the opposing party gets to introduce their excerpts, then we get to introduce these additional excerpts). Be sure to read the court's rules carefully to understand the manner and timing of the designations, counter-designations, and objections.

Many lawyers make the mistake of designating long portions of the deposition because they want to give context or convey completeness, even if not all of the excerpt contributes to

> **The Most Common Uses for a Deposition at Trial:**
> - As the testimony of an unavailable witness
> - As a source of opposing party statements
> - As a basis for a proffer
> - To refresh recollection
> - As the testimony of a witness who is unable to testify because of lapse of memory
> - To impeach a witness
> - To accomplish a "phantom" impeachment

the point they are trying to make. Do not do this. Designate only those questions and answers that will help the jurors' understanding and persuade them.

If the deposition was recorded by audiovisual means, make sure the video clip conveys the right point and creates the desired impression of the witness. If the court reporting service delivered the deposition testimony in a written transcript that can be synchronized with the video recording, review the testimony in the transcript and the corresponding video clip to evaluate whether to designate that portion of testimony (and how ultimately to present it at trial, knowing that opposing counsel has the right to require the presentation by video, as discussed below).

Objections and Rulings

Once the parties have made their designations and counter-designations, they submit objections to the other parties' designations and counter-designations. Under the federal rules, each party has fourteen days after the opposing party's designation (unless the court sets a different time) to file and serve any objections to the use under Rule 32(a) of a deposition designated by the other party. Any objection (except for relevancy and lack of probative value under Fed. R. Evid. 402 and 403) is waived if it is not made within those fourteen days, unless the court allows a tardy objection for good cause.

The objections may include those asserted at the deposition and thus already contained in the deposition transcript or recording, as well as new objections that by rule or stipulation were preserved (e.g., objections to the deponent's competence or to the competence, relevance, or materiality of the testimony, unless the ground for the objection might have been corrected at the deposition—*see* section 18.8.1).

The court will rule on the objections, sometimes holding a hearing first. Some judges prefer not to rule until a lawyer tries to use the deposition excerpt at the trial, but that leaves the attorneys uncertain whether the excerpt will be admitted. On the other hand, ruling before the trial can cause the court to spend a lot of time evaluating objections to deposition excerpts that may never be used. The best procedure may be to ask the court to review the designations a few days before their intended use at trial, after the jury has left for the day. That will be close enough to the presentation for you to have a relatively firm idea of what you want to use at trial, and for the court to have more of a context for their use, yet still far enough in advance for you to formulate a plan based on the judge's rulings.

After the parties have made their designations, registered their objections, and obtained rulings, the court will usually not consider other designations or objections. The court should allow additional deposition material only on a showing that the need to use it could not reasonably have been anticipated. (Uses of deposition testimony for other reasons, such as impeachment, proffers, and refreshing recollection, would still be available.)

Presentation at the Trial

Under Rule 32(c), the proponent of a deposition excerpt must offer a written transcript of the excerpt, has the option of also showing a video of the testimony if it was recorded by audiovisual means, and might have to show the video upon another party's request (unless offered for impeachment purposes).[6] As relevant to the deposition testimony of an unavailable witness, counsel must decide whether to present the material by reading it or by displaying the video.

The exact manner of presenting deposition testimony to the trier of fact is very much a matter of local custom and procedure. In bench trials, judges may simply read or view the designated testimony at a convenient time in chambers. In jury trials, the testimony is almost always read or shown (if video) to the jury in the courtroom, although the transcript or recording itself may not be given to the jury during its deliberations. The testimony is typically presented to the jury during the proponent's case-in-chief. With the court's permission, video can be displayed in opening statement and, if admitted into evidence, may be shown in closing argument.

There are three main ways of reading or showing the deposition testimony to a jury: the attorney offering the testimony reads it aloud; the attorney and an associate or paralegal (or even an actor) assume the roles of the deposing attorney and the witness and read the testimony aloud; or the video recording of the deposition testimony is played. In addition, some courts have the bailiff read the designated portions to the jury.

Presentation by Reading. The option of having just the attorney read the questions and answers is best only for very short excerpts, where the attorney can hold the jury's attention. Using an associate or paralegal to play the role of the witness and read the deposition answers from the witness stand is suitable for lengthier excerpts and is preferred by many attorneys (and, no doubt, most jurors). The give-and-take in questioning a live person, albeit in a reenactment, offers greater realism, believability, and a dramatic element that is not present in a straight reading.

There are, however, some things to keep in mind when presenting the material by reading it. First, deposition readings are a tedious experience for the jurors. One study of jury comprehension noted that "[t]he jurors' response to reading of depositions into evidence was uniformly negative. They found it boring, difficult to follow, and uninformative."[7] The more mercifully brief the experience, the more

---

6. Rule 32(c) provides: "Unless the court orders otherwise, a party must provide a transcript of any deposition testimony the party offers, but may provide the court with the testimony in a nontranscript form as well. On any party's request, deposition testimony offered in a jury trial for any purpose other than impeachment must be presented in nontranscript form, if available, unless the court for good cause orders otherwise."

7. Special Committee of the ABA Section of Litigation, Jury Comprehension in Complex Cases, 37 (1990).

likely the jurors will understand, remember, and be persuaded by what they hear. If lawyers will be reading the testimony, they should animate their voices and, within reason, emphasize those questions and answers they particularly wish the jurors to focus upon. While the reading of depositions is boring, reading in a monotone turns it into torture.

Second, be careful in selecting the person to play the role of the witness, because the jury may color the deposition testimony in light of the appearance and personality of the witness-reader. If the unavailable witness gave helpful deposition testimony, select a witness-reader who presents an appropriate yet favorable demeanor in terms of age, attire, and bearing. If your absent witness is a middle-aged executive, for example, select a middle-aged reader dressed in a suit and tie; if the witness is a male assembly line worker, select a reader who looks as though he could make a living with his hands, and perhaps have him wear a sports coat and open-collared shirt; if the witness is a woman who owns a small business, select a reader who presents the appropriate appearance of experience, competence, and success.

On the flip side, the court will look dimly on a reader who creates a false impression of the deposition witness or inserts emotion into the deposition through exaggerated intonation or pauses. If the actual deponent is a twenty-five-year-old high school dropout who happened to be present when his boss discussed contract terms, it is misleading to present to the jurors a reader who looks and speaks as though he has a graduate degree in business administration. If your opponent engages in such abuse, object, under Rule 403, that use of that reader will mislead and confuse the jurors by inviting them to associate greater credibility with the testimony than would have occurred if the actual witness had been available. The court may have difficulty appreciating this objection because it will not have seen the actual deponent, so point out the witness's educational background, for example, as elicited in the deposition. Because you may have no advance notice of the identity of the reader selected by the other side, have ready a generic brief reminding the court of its power to control the mode of the presentation of the deposition testimony and the need to avoid confusing or misleading the jurors.[8]

If you have no objection to the reader your opponent selected to portray the unavailable witness—or any such objection has been overruled—be prepared to present any additional testimony of the unavailable witness that should be read in fairness under Rule 32(a)(6). Here is what the presentation of deposition testimony might sound like if the excerpts were read aloud from a written transcript by counsel and

---

8. Sometimes during discovery you may suspect the opponent is taking a deposition because the witness is going to be unavailable for trial and chose to record it stenographically because the witness would be less persuasive on video. Counter the opponent's strategy by arranging, under Rule 30(b)(3), for the deposition to be recorded by audiovisual means. At trial, when the opponent presents the deposition to a jury, insist under Rule 32(c) that the jurors view the video rather than the opponent's associate or actor reading the stenographic version.

a paralegal, and opposing counsel called for additional portions of the deposition to be read. ("PC" refers to plaintiff's counsel; "DC" for defendant's counsel.)

PC: Your Honor, Mr. Adrian Jamal was scheduled to be our next witness, but he has been called out of the state due to an illness in his family. Counsel for the defendant has been kind enough to stipulate to Mr. Jamal's unavailability and to the fact that this transcript sets forth his deposition testimony.[9] In place of Mr. Jamal's live testimony, we would like to now read certain limited portions of his deposition testimony for the jury. In total, there are about fifteen pages, Your Honor.

Court: That's fine, Mr. Moreland. I presume that these portions have been redacted pursuant to the pretrial rulings?

PC: Yes, Your Honor, and defendant's counsel also has had an opportunity to review the portions we intend to read as redacted. With the court's permission, we would like to have Mr. Richie, a paralegal who works with us, read Mr. Jamal's answers from the witness stand as I read the questions.

Court: All right. There being no objection, you may proceed.

PC: Mr. Richie, if you will go up to the witness stand, we can start with page 27, at line 17.

Q: (By defendant's counsel) Mr. Jamal, what was your position with Vitas Industries in 1992 and 1993?

A: I was the vice president for purchasing for the company.

Q: What were your responsibilities in that position?

A: I oversaw the purchasing of all materials that we required to manufacture all of our products. That included everything from the copper wire that we wound around the cores to make the armatures for the generators, to the decals that we put on the transformer boxes telling about the high voltage.

Q: During that time, from whom did Vitas Industries purchase refined copper?

---

9. Reciting the stipulation lays the foundation for using the deposition under Fed. R. Evid. 804: the witness is unavailable, not through the fault of the proponent of the evidence, and this is in fact their deposition. If opposing counsel refuses to stipulate, you may have to offer competent evidence establishing the witness's unavailability.

A: We had several suppliers, but the main ones for those two years were Chilean Copper Conglomerate, Incorporated, and Python Industrial Metals.

PC: Now, Mr. Richie, will you please turn to page 43 in the deposition of Mr. Jamal? We'll begin with line 4.

Q: Mr. Jamal, why do you think that Chilean Copper and Python Industries were engaged in some kind of agreement to fix copper prices to your company, as is alleged in the complaint in this case?

A: Well, during that time, I often tried to get one or the other of them to give me a better price, you know, to bid against a price I had from the other. But they'd never break the line. Right in lockstep, all the time. On my other metal purchases, I could make deals by going from one supplier to the next, but on copper, those two never gave even a penny off.

DC: Your Honor, at this point, we ask that the next two questions and answers be read, pursuant to Rule 32(a)(6), because they contain material which, in fairness, the jury ought to be allowed to consider along with this last answer.

Court: Well, let me just look at that material for a moment. [Reviewing.] . . . Yes, we'll have that read at this point, please, Mr. Moreland.

PC: Yes, Your Honor.

Q: Mr. Jamal, isn't it true that there was a terrific demand for copper during that period and a shortage of supply due to unrest in the government of Chile?

A: Well, there were some political problems down there that made the supply of copper a little less predictable. But we were getting all that we needed.

Q: And isn't it also true, Mr. Jamal, based on your experience in the purchase of metals, that no one discounts their prices on metals during periods of shortage, because they can clear their inventories without price reductions?

A: Yes, I suppose that is true in general, but I still think that Chilean Copper and Python were fixing prices.

Some courts believe that Rule 32(a)(6) material can just as well be presented during cross-examination, rather than immediately after the testimony is given during the direct examination. If the condition of Rule 32(a)(6) has been met— that is, the proffered material is so closely related to what has already been read, the jurors ought in fairness to consider the two selections together—then the two selections should be presented together, not separated by the remainder of the direct examination. The fact that the additional material could be presented on cross-examination does not make it the best way to promote juror understanding.

Presentation by Video. If the deposition of the unavailable witness was recorded by video, strongly consider showing the relevant video clip rather than reading the testimony. The video will usually be more powerful and less tedious than a reading. It allows the jurors to hear and see the testimony rather than hearing it only, which increases their comprehension and recall of the witness's statements. Moreover, observing how the witness made the statements in the deposition often speaks volumes about what the witness meant and the witness's character. Many courtrooms are set up so counsel can connect their laptop to the courtroom audio-visual equipment and display on courtroom monitors the relevant testimony from electronic transcripts and synchronized video stored on the laptop or the cloud. For further discussion of the presentation of video testimony, see Chapter Twenty-Three on video depositions.

15.3.3 Source of Opposing Party Statements

One of the most powerful uses of deposition testimony at trial is reading or showing the testimony of an opposing party. Under Rule 32(a)(3), opposing party testimony can be presented at trial even if the opposing party is available for trial and, indeed, sitting in the courtroom. Rule 32(a)(3) specifically authorizes using the deposition of a party, officer, director or managing agent of a party, or a person designated to testify under Rule 30(b)(6). The testimony is nonhearsay under Fed. R. Evid. 801(d)(2).

Designation of Deposition Excerpts and Rulings on Objections

Using deposition testimony of an opposing party may or may not be subject to a court's requirements for designating deposition excerpts ahead of the trial. If you do not intend to use the opponent's deposition testimony unless the need arises at trial, it may not be necessary to designate it. But if, for example, a plaintiff anticipates using the defendant's deposition transcript to help establish the plaintiff's prima facie case without calling the defendant as an adverse witness, the plaintiff will likely need to designate it in advance. Any objections asserted at the deposition, or asserted after the excerpt has been designated, will be ruled on by the court.

Presentation at the Trial

Like deposition testimony of unavailable witnesses, deposition testimony of opposing parties may be presented by reading the transcript or, if the deposition was recorded by audiovisual means, by playing the video (Rule 32(c)). If the excerpt is short, it may suffice for you to read the questions and answers aloud. If it is of greater length, it may be presented akin to the way testimony of unavailable witnesses is presented: with readers or by video display. Again, keep in mind that showing the video will usually be less boring and more impactful, allowing the jurors to watch the opposing party utter incriminating admissions from their own mouths and, perhaps, squirm when nailed on a difficult point. The excerpt can be presented during the proponent's case in chief, during the cross-examination of the witness, or any other time amenable to the court, as well as opening statement and (if admitted into evidence) closing argument.

Here is an example where the excerpt is short and the testimony is read by counsel. It occurs during the examination of another witness.

Q: What, if anything, was the person carrying when he came out of the building and threatened you?

A: It looked like he had a knife.

Q: What kind of knife?

A: It was like a big-blade hunting knife, you know. And he was like twirling it and I could see it had, like, a blue like feather like.

Q: I'm sorry, what did the knife have on it?

A: A blue feather was attached to the handle.

Q: Your Honor, at this time we would like to read a section of one page of the defendant Sugis's deposition, which is an opposing party's statement under Federal Rule of Evidence 801(d)(2). The deposition has been stipulated as authentic.

Court: You may proceed, but let's keep it short, since you have this witness on the stand.

Q: Yes, Your Honor. The portion appears on page 17 of the deposition, beginning at line 11. Quote:

Q: Mr. Sugis, did you own any hunting knives in October 2017?

A: Maybe, yeah.

> Q: One of those knives had a blue feather attached to
>   the handle?
>
> A: Yeah.

Counsel would then return to the examination of the trial witness.

15.3.4   *Basis for a Proffer*

Sometimes at trial, you must persuade the court that certain examination questions seek relevant information or a line of questioning has a good-faith basis. Deposition testimony may provide this foundation, even if the deposition testimony is not itself admitted into evidence. Consider the following example from a cross-examination by defense counsel:

> Q: Mr. Taras, isn't it true that you never saw the plaintiff
>   before he went into the hospital?
>
> A: No, that's not true at all. I saw him several times. We were
>   good friends, and we visited a lot.
>
> Q: Mr. Taras, you were good friends a year before the plain-
>   tiff's car accident, weren't you?
>
> A: Yes, yes, of course.
>
> Q: And you are good friends now, aren't you?
>
> A: Yes, that's true, of course.
>
> Q: But at the time of the accident, you and the plaintiff were
>   not even on speaking terms, were you?
>
> A: I don't understand what you're saying. He's my friend, and
>   I see him all the time.
>
> Q: Mr. Taras, you used to play poker with the plaintiff once
>   a week, didn't you?
>
> PC: I object, Your Honor. This is irrelevant and prejudicial.
>
> DC: Your Honor, since this has to do with relevance, may we
>   approach the bench?
>
> Court: Yes, step up, counsel. [At bench:] Now, where are you go-
>   ing with this, Mr. Kaunas?
>
> DC: Your Honor, based on this witness's deposition testimony,
>   which I can show you here at pages 34 and 35 of the tran-
>   script, I believe he will testify that he and the plaintiff
>   used to play poker once a week, but that two weeks before

the accident they had an argument over a poker hand and that they didn't speak to one another for several months. That testimony impeaches his testimony on direct that he visited with the plaintiff in the weeks after the accident and could see the pain and limited movement that the plaintiff now claims he had.

Court: Let me see the deposition. [Reading.] All right. Based on this deposition testimony, I am going to overrule the objections and permit the questioning. You may proceed, Mr. Kaunas.

DC: Mr. Taras, the question is, didn't you and the plaintiff play poker once a week before the accident?

A: Yes, but he was never very good.

Q: But just a week or so before the accident, you stopped playing poker, right?

A: Yeah.

Q: You had an argument about a poker hand, didn't you?

A: Yes. He never had a pair of aces. He had one ace, and he took the other from his pocket.

Q: And because of that argument, you and the plaintiff didn't talk to each other for almost a year?

A: Yeah, I guess. It was silly. I've had aces in my pocket, too.

Q: And you didn't spend time with him and visit with him right after the accident, did you?

A: Well, no. He just told me last week he had been in a lot of pain then.

15.3.5 *Means of Refreshing Recollection*

Witnesses at trial can have a lapse of memory. Their recollection may be refreshed with anything from a simple leading question to a photograph, a snippet of a song, or a letter from mom. The question is not, "What was used to refresh recollection?" but rather, "Is the witness actually testifying from refreshed recollection?"

Depositions are useful tools for refreshing recollection because they are usually taken months or years closer to the relevant events. The foundation at trial for this use of depositions is essentially the same as that for any attempt to refresh recollection: establishing that the witness does not recall the answer to a question but that their recollection may be refreshed; showing the material to the witness; taking the material away from the witness; and asking the question again so the witness can testify based on their refreshed recollection. It would sound something like this:

Q: Now, Ms. Vardas, what was the next step in trying to persuade United Lumber and Hardware to finance the expansion of your business?

A: Well, I think that I met with Mr. Shadis at the bank. No, that wasn't it. Maybe . . . . I'm sorry, I'm just not sure what was next. There were a number of meetings. I don't remember.

Q: Might taking a look at your deposition help you remember?

A: Oh, yes, I think we covered this at my deposition.

Q: Okay, let me hand you your deposition and ask if you would turn there to page 73.[10] Read lines 8–10 silently to yourself, please, and look up at me when you've finished.

A: All right. Yes, I've read it.

Q: Now, just let me have the transcript back, please. Thank you. Is your memory refreshed?

A: Yes, it is, it is.

Q: Let me ask you again, what was the next step in trying to persuade United Lumber and Hardware to finance your business expansion?

A: I met with their accountant, and I brought my accountant and architect with me. It was at that meeting and United told me to go ahead with obtaining the permits and negotiating with your general contractor.

Note that neither the deposition transcript nor the deposition testimony is admitted into evidence or presented to the jurors. Using the deposition transcript to refresh recollection therefore does not give rise to any hearsay issue, and it is permitted under the Federal Rules of Evidence just like any other type of refreshing recollection.

---

10. Courts express different views on whether material used to refresh recollection must be marked as an exhibit and shown to opposing counsel before showing it to the witness. On the one hand, the document is not going to be admitted into evidence, so it is not necessary to have it marked. On the other hand, marking the document as an exhibit keeps a clear record of what the witness was shown. In the example given, it is unlikely a deposition would be marked as an ordinary exhibit in any event, since typically the original deposition transcript would be lodged with the court, with counsel in possession of a copy.

        National Institute for Trial Advocacy

15.3.6 *Former Testimony of a Witness Who Cannot Remember*

A deposition can be used in another way when the trial witness has a lapse of memory. If the witness cannot remember a fact at trial but had testified to the fact in a deposition, the statement from the deposition can be offered into evidence at the trial under Rule 32(a)(1)(B) and Rule 32(a)(2).

Rules 32(a)(1)(B) and 32(a)(2) indicate that a deposition may be used by any party for any purpose permitted by the Federal Rules of Evidence. Federal Rule of Evidence 804(a)(3) provides that "not remembering the subject matter" renders the witness unavailable, and Federal Rule of Evidence 804(b)(1) states that the former deposition testimony of an unavailable witness is not excluded by the hearsay rule when offered against a party who had an opportunity and similar motive to examine the witness.

In other words, instead of refreshing the witness's memory with the transcript so that the witness testifies from their refreshed recollection, we admit the relevant portion of the testimony. And we admit that testimony under the same rules that allow for the admission of the deposition testimony of an unavailable witness generally (discussed above), although in this case the witness is only "unavailable" for one question area and, because the lapse of memory at trial could not have been reasonably anticipated, the relevant excerpt did not have to be designated before the trial. (Another option, if the forgetful witness was the opposing party, would be to admit the deposition excerpt under Rule 32(a)(3).)

The foundation under Federal Rule of Evidence 804(a)(3) (unavailability due to lapse of memory) and Federal Rule of Evidence 804(b)(1) (former testimony) is quite simple. You merely need to show that the witness has testified that they cannot remember the subject matter of the deposition excerpt being offered and that the other party had notice of the deposition (which, except in extremely rare situations, establishes opportunity and similar motive to examine).

Depending on the length of the deposition excerpt, it could be presented to the jurors by reading or by video. Reading normally suffices. Here is an example during a cross-examination, although the same thing could be accomplished on direct examination using nonleading questions.

> Q: Didn't you tell Mr. Shadis that you thought it was a fair contract and he shouldn't breach it?
>
> A: I don't recall.
>
> Q: Mr. Jamal, let's go back to your deposition we discussed earlier this morning. When you answered questions during that deposition, you were under oath?
>
> A: Yes.

Q: Your attorney was there?

A: Yep.

Q: Counsel, I'll be referring to page 46 of the deposition transcript. In the deposition, Mr. Jamal, you were asked this question and you gave this answer: "Question: What did you discuss about the McLean contract? Answer: Well, I told Shadis that he seemed to be getting his money's worth, and that it looked to me like Vardas was doing a good job. I mean, he asked if I thought it was a fair deal, and I said, 'Yeah, it looks fair to me'."

So is it better to refresh recollection, or to read the transcript as former testimony under Rule 32(a)(1)(B) or as a statement of an opposing party under Rule 32(a)(3)? On the one hand, refreshing recollection leaves the witness with more credibility, because the witness testifies from their refreshed recollection. It also sidesteps the rule of completeness under Rule 32(a)(6) and Federal Rule of Evidence 106—since the transcript is not offered into evidence when refreshing recollection, there is no basis under those rules for the other side to demand that additional portions of the transcript be read "in fairness." On the other hand, refreshing recollection requires the witness to be amenable to having their memory refreshed. Traditionally, refreshing recollection is best for friendly witnesses, and introduction of the transcript is best for unfriendly witnesses.

15.3.7 Means of Impeachment

Sometimes the problem with trial witnesses is not that they have a lapse of memory, but that they have a change of heart. Having testified one way in deposition, they now testify at trial to something different.

Under Rule 32(a)(2), a witness's deposition testimony can be used to "contradict or impeach" the witness's trial testimony. Similarly, under Federal Rule of Evidence 801(d)(1)(A), deposition testimony that is "inconsistent" with trial testimony is classified as nonhearsay and may be considered by the trier of fact both as substantive evidence and as a reflection on the witness's credibility.[11] In short, a deposition

---

11. A prior inconsistent statement made under oath, as in a deposition, is admissible under the federal rules both to impeach the witness's credibility (the witness has been inconsistent in, e.g., describing the color of the traffic light) and as substantive proof (the traffic light was red as stated in the deposition, not green as the witness now claims). By contrast, prior inconsistent statements not made under oath can be used under the federal rules only for impeachment. State laws may treat prior inconsistent statements differently. In California, for example, a prior inconsistent statement constitutes a hearsay exception, such that the statement may be considered both for impeachment and for its truth as substantive proof, regardless of whether made under oath. Cal. Code Civ. P. § 1235.

excerpt can be used to impeach a witness with a statement that is inconsistent with their trial testimony.[12]

Presentation at the Trial

The following is an example of the impeachment of a nonparty witness during cross-examination at trial, the first time an impeachment of the witness has been necessary. Note that the attorney initially confirms with the witness that they are sticking with their current (errant) testimony, then credits the earlier (true) deposition testimony by showing it was made when the witness was likely telling the truth, and finally confronts the witness by reading the earlier testimony.

Q: Mr. Lapitis, on direct examination did you really say the traffic signal for the defendant's Cadillac was green?

A: Yep. It was green.[13]

Q: Well, let's see what you testified to previously under oath. Mr. Lapitis, you remember going to my office a few months ago, don't you?

A: Uh yes, I remember that.

Q: And you were there to have your deposition taken, right?

A: Yes. Well, I got a subpoena, so I showed up like I was supposed to.

Q: And in this deposition, I asked you questions and you gave answers under oath?

A: Yeah.

Q: And the defendant's attorney was there, wasn't she?

---

12. Note that, if the witness is a party-opponent, the deposition testimony would be admissible under Rule 32(a)(3) and constitute nonhearsay under Federal Rule of Evidence 801(d)(2)(A). In those situations, one might wonder which is better—to introduce the deposition excerpt as a prior inconsistent statement under Rule 32(a)(2) and Federal Rule of Evidence 801(d)(1), or as the statement of an opposing party under Rule 32(a)(3) and Federal Rule of Evidence 801(d)(2)? On the one hand, Rule 32(a)(2) applies to any witness, while Rule 32(a)(3) applies only to a party and to certain of its personnel. On the other hand, admitting the testimony under Rule 32(a)(3) avoids a squabble over whether the prior testimony is sufficiently "inconsistent" for purposes of Federal Rule of Evidence 801(d)(1). Depending on the circumstances, both grounds can be asserted as justification for admitting the excerpt. And no matter which ground is pursued, it should be elicited from the witness that the deposition entailed answering questions under oath in the presence of counsel and a court reporter, to demonstrate that the witness had incentive to be truthful.
13. Of course, if the witness disclaims the trial testimony ("What, green? No, I meant red!"), then no impeachment is necessary. The witness simply made a mistake. At most, you would ask, "If on direct examination you said the light was green for the Cadillac, you misspoke and really meant it was red for the Cadillac?"

Q: Yes.

Q: She sat right next to you during the deposition, didn't she?

A: Yes, she was very nice.

Q: There was a court reporter there, who gave you an oath to tell the truth?

A: Yes.

Q: And you promised then to tell the truth?

A: Yes.

Q: Because you swore to tell the truth, you testified at the deposition accurately and truthfully?

A: Well, yes, I'd hope so.

Q: The court reporter took down what was said at the deposition?

A: Yes, he had this little machine he was typing on.

Q: After the deposition was over, you received a booklet from the court reporter that contained my questions and your answers?

A: Yes, the transcript, I think.

Q: That's right. And you signed the transcript without making any corrections?

A: Yes.

Q: Let me show you that deposition transcript, Mr. Lapitis, and I'd like you to look at page 76. That's your signature there at the bottom, isn't it?

A: Yes.

Q: Your Honor and counsel, I will be referring to page 16, lines 32 through 34. Mr. Lapitis, in your deposition, let's turn to page 16. Beginning on page 16, line 32, I asked you a question and you gave an answer. Please read along silently while I read it aloud. "Question: What color was the traffic light for the westbound car, the defendant's Cadillac? Answer: For the Caddy, let me see … for the Caddy *it was red*." I read that correctly, didn't I.

A: Well, uh, yes you did.

In addition to the structure of **confirming** the current statement, then **crediting** the deposition statement, and lastly **confronting** with the deposition statement, several aspects of the attorney's examination are worth noting.

- The deposition testimony ("green light") was clearly inconsistent with the trial testimony ("red light") and was on an important point in the case—impeaching with a prior statement takes time, and it must be worth the effort.

- In crediting the prior deposition testimony, the attorney asked the witness about what occurred at the deposition, so jurors would know what a "deposition" is—and not all will; subsequent impeachments do not need to go into as much detail.

- In crediting the deposition testimony, the attorney emphasized that the witness was sworn to tell the truth.

- When confronting the witness with the deposition testimony, the attorney identified for the court and counsel the portion that the attorney was about to read—thus heading off an interruption.

- The attorney read the deposition testimony aloud himself, thereby maintaining control over the delivery and emphasizing the important words—in this case "it was red."

- After confronting the witness with the deposition testimony, the attorney only asked if they had read the words of the transcript correctly—the attorney did not invite the witness to explain the inconsistency, or demand to know if the witness was "lying then" or "lying now;" the point is that the prior inconsistent statement was made, and the attorney can argue in closing which version is more likely true.

As the facts warrant, make the favorable deposition statement appear more truthful than the later trial testimony by suggesting a reason for the witness's change in testimony. One obvious reason is that the deposition occurred closer to the time of the events. A more unsettling reason can be pursued as follows:

Q: Mr. Lapitis, between the time of the deposition, when you said the light was red, and your testimony today, when you changed and said the light was green, you met with the defendant's attorney, didn't you?

A: Yes.

Q: You testified today the light was green, after talking with the defendant's attorney.

A: Well, yes, but I just remembered it better.

Q: I didn't ask you if you remembered the accident better today than you did way back when you had your deposition taken. I asked you this question, yes or no: You testified today the light was green, after having talked with the defendant's attorney, right?

A: Yes.

Dealing with the Wriggling Witness

Expect opposing counsel to elicit information from the witness on redirect examination to explain the discrepancy between the deposition and trial testimony and support the veracity of the current version. (Better opposing counsel would have brought out such information on direct examination!) Quite often, whether in response to such inquiries on direct or redirect, or on their own volition when confronted with their prior testimony on cross-examination, the witness tries to wriggle out of their deposition testimony by claiming they did not understand the question, they were fatigued, or they had not understood the importance of providing all the information comprising their answer at the deposition. If the witness tries to make such a claim, refer the witness to the commitments obtained early in the deposition to counter the witness's assertion. (*See* section 6.3.)

Using Video

If the deposition was videorecorded, consider in advance whether to impeach witnesses by reading the prior inconsistent statement from the written transcript or by showing the relevant video excerpt. This decision turns largely on the content of the video, the courtroom's facility for displaying video, whether the transcript and video have been synced and loaded onto your laptop or other device, and your comfort level with the technology. Technology allows counsel to display video clips as quickly as reading the written transcript, by going to the page and lines in a deposition that has been loaded onto a laptop, selecting the corresponding video clip, and displaying it on the courtroom monitors or other viewing device for the jury to see.

If the video shows that the witness was confident and earnest in giving the prior inconsistent statement during the deposition, jurors tend to credit the prior inconsistent statement and dismiss assertions by the witness at trial that they did not understand the question or were too fatigued at the time. On the other hand, depending on how clear or convincing the witness's testimony appears in the video, it may be more advantageous for counsel to read the prior inconsistent testimony from the written transcript, with appropriate inflection and emphasis.

15.3.8 Means of "Phantom" Impeachment

The "phantom" or "ghost" impeachment is so called because, although no true impeachment occurs, the witness answers truthfully because they think impeachment is possible. The success of this tactic depends on convincing the witness at trial that the cross-examiner has mastered the facts in the deposition and can call them up virtually instantaneously.

Some attorneys put the witness's deposition transcript in a booklet with bright covers, with the witness's name two inches high across the front so that, perhaps during the direct examination, but certainly during the cross-examination, the witness recognizes that the cross-examiner has the deposition transcript readily available. When impeaching the witness's testimony during the cross-examination, the attorney makes conspicuous use of the brightly bound volume, moving from the cross-examination outline directly to the right page and line of the deposition without fumbling or delay.

After a number of such impeachments, the witness will become "disciplined"—that is, will be much more inclined to tell the truth and accept the propositions in counsel's leading cross-examination questions, wanting to avoid further embarrassing impeachment with the deposition.

Video excerpts of transcripts, animated simulations, and PowerPoint presentations can all enhance your trial proficiency.

But they can also distract you from listening to testimony and throw off your timing. Your delivery will suffer if you must continually pause to find and load media materials.

Solve this by having someone assist you. Whether an associate, a paralegal, or an administrative assistant, someone who can search out and upload transcripts and other materials to the courtroom monitors will keep your questioning smooth and avoid awkward delays.

If the case is high-stakes enough to warrant it, consider hiring a courtroom technology company. Their trial teams will bring an extra level of professionalism to your video presentations.

CHECKLIST

USING DEPOSITIONS IN MOTIONS AND TRIALS

✔ Identify deposition excerpts for use in supporting or opposing motions for summary judgment.

✔ Summarize the deposition transcripts and digitize them for searches and sorting.

✔ Use deposition testimony to craft direct and cross-examinations for trial by evaluating how the witness answered questions.

✔ Consider deposition testimony in preparing witnesses for trial testimony.

✔ Identify deposition excerpts to be introduced as testimony of an unavailable witness.

✔ Identify deposition excerpts to be introduced into evidence as opposing party statements.

✔ Consider video deposition excerpts to be used in opening statement.

✔ Annotate witness examination outlines with page and line references for refreshing recollection and/or impeachment.

✔ Determine whether deposition excerpts will be presented by reading, by reading with a partner, or by video.

✔ Think through how the deposition excerpts will be located and displayed in the courtroom.

✔ Consider other uses of the deposition, including proffer and former testimony.

✔ Prepare to deal with the witness who, upon being impeached, tries to wriggle out of the deposition testimony by claiming they were fatigued, misunderstood the deposition question, or did not know the need to provide a full and complete answer to the question.

PART THREE

DEFENDING DEPOSITIONS

CHAPTER SIXTEEN

INITIAL ANALYSIS AND MOTIONS FOR PROTECTIVE ORDERS

They say that the first inclination an animal has is to protect itself.

—Diogenes Laertius

Chapters Four through Fifteen focused on you, as the deposing attorney, asking the questions and running the show. But your deposition notices and subpoenas will be met with notices and subpoenas from the opposing party, and your client's witnesses will be on the receiving end of tough questions, too. Defending a deposition witness will be more effective if you discern in advance what information the deposing party wants, determine what the witness knows, and seek protection for your witness and client before the deposi-

> **In This Chapter:**
>
> - *Protecting your client's interests*
> - *When to object to a deposition notice*
> - *Protective orders*
> - *Preparing yourself for defending the deposition*
> - *Addressing whether the witness is a client*

tion. While ultimately you must prepare the witness for the deposition (Chapter Seventeen) and protect the client's interests through permissible objections and instructions (Chapter Eighteen), this chapter covers how the defense begins long before that.

16.1 Review of the Deposition Notice or Subpoena

The first task after receiving a notice of the deposition of a party you represent, or a subpoena ordering the deposition of a nonparty you represent, is to review the deposition notice or subpoena and decide what, if any, immediate action to take. This review includes checking for compliance with the applicable rules, court orders, and any prior stipulations with counsel; considering whether the witness will need an interpreter or assistive device or accommodation; and deciding whether to request that the deposition be videorecorded.

16.1.1 Requirements for Deposition Notice or Subpoena

As discussed in Chapter One, the deposition notice served under Rule 30(b) must state the time and place of the deposition, whether it will be conducted remotely, the deponent's name and address (if known), and the method for recording the testimony (stenographic, audio, or audiovisual). If the named deponent is a public or private corporation, partnership, association, governmental agency, or other entity under Rule 30(b)(6), the deposition notice must "describe with reasonable particularity the matters for examination" so the entity can designate persons to testify on the entity's behalf (*see* section 21.3).

For a deponent who is not a party to the litigation, a deposition notice must be served on the parties but will not suffice to compel the witness's attendance; instead, a subpoena must be issued and served pursuant to Rule 45. The requirements for the subpoena are similar to those for the Rule 30 deposition notice: the subpoena must state the court from which it is issued, the title of the action, what the recipient is supposed to do (including attending the deposition and testifying), and when and where the recipient is supposed to do it. The subpoena must also identify the method of recording the deposition and comply with the requirements for Rule 30(b)(6) if applicable. In addition, it must be accompanied by a witness fee as required by Rule 45(b)(1).

Determine whether the subpoena was issued by the proper court (the court in which the litigation is pending) pursuant to Rule 45(a); whether the subpoena was properly served under Rule 45(b); and whether the subpoena requests compliance within the geographic range set forth in Rule 45(c).

16.1.2 Attend to Time, Place, Manner, Issues, and Any Document Request

The attorneys should have already agreed to the time and place for the deposition. Upon receiving the notice (or subpoena), confirm that the time and place are set forth correctly.

If no agreement was reached, determine whether, in fact, the time and place set forth in the notice or subpoena are appropriate. Under the federal rules, a deposition notice or subpoena need only provide a reasonable amount of notice—estimated by some to be between seven and ten (or fourteen) days. The location of an in-person deposition is typically the deposing attorney's office or at times the court reporter's office; those locations would suffice unless circumstances suggest otherwise.

A deposition notice may be accompanied by a request under Rule 34 that the party produce documents, electronically stored information, or tangible things

(Rule 30(b)(2)); confirm the date requested for any such production and make sure a written response is served. A nonparty may be requested to produce documents, etc., in addition to attending and testifying (Rule 30(b)(2), Rule 45); in that case, the subpoena must set forth the documents or other material requested (and the format of ESI), and the notice served on the parties must also list or attach a list of the requested materials. The subpoenaed party has fourteen days after service to object to the production (Rule 45(d)(2)(B)). Rule 45(e) sets forth the duties in responding to the subpoena.

Inform the client and the witness of the receipt of the deposition notice or subpoena. Make sure that the witness (and counsel) are available for the deposition on the scheduled date and that there is time, pre-deposition, to prepare the witness. Also inform the client of any request for production and arrange for coordinating a response. If there are problems with any of these issues, negotiate with opposing counsel and, if necessary, object to the deposition notice or subpoena and bring an appropriate motion (*see* below).

16.1.3   *Determine If an Interpreter or Other Assistance Is Needed*

To the extent not previously explored, determine if the witness requires an interpreter. If the deposing attorney was aware of the need for an interpreter, the deposition notice should specify, as a matter of good practice, that an interpreter will be used and the language that will be interpreted. If the deposing attorney was unaware of the need, raise the matter.

Although there is no absolute right to an interpreter in federal civil cases, protocols for using interpreters in depositions have been developed.[1] Even if the deposing attorney has already arranged for an interpreter consider hiring a "check" interpreter to ensure that the questions and answers are translated satisfactorily (the downside being that disputes over the translation can arise during the deposition, which may lead a court to forbid the practice).[2]

If the proposed deponent requires an assistive listening device, is deaf (requiring an ASL interpreter), has a visual impairment, or has another disability, address those issues. Remember to arrange accommodations for the deposition preparation session as well.

---

1. In re Lithium Ion Batteries Antitrust Litigation, No. 13-MD-2420-YGR (N.D. Cal. Oct. 19, 2015); In re Chrysler-Dodge-Jeep "Ecodiesel" Marketing, Sales Practices, and Products Liability Litigation, MDL No. 17-MD-2777-EMC (N.D. Cal. Nov. 3, 2017).
2. Malpico v. Newman Machine Co., Inc., 107 F. Supp. 2d 712, 714 (W.D. Va. 2000).

16.1.4 Serve Notice of Additional Method of Recording

The identification in the notice or subpoena of the method by which the deposition will be recorded—by stenographic, audio, or audiovisual means—will affect how you prepare the witness for the deposition (*see* Chapter Seventeen).

Moreover, if the deposition notice advises that the deposition will be recorded by stenographic means only, consider whether to send your own notice to record the deposition by nonstenographic means such as video, as allowed by Rule 30(b)(3)(B). For example, you might want the deposition videotaped if the deposing attorney tends to be abusive when questioning witnesses or if having a videotaped recording for trial would put the client in a more favorable light. If you request that the deposition be recorded by video, your client must pay the cost for it (Rule 30(b)(3)(B)).

16.1.5 Serve Objections to the Deposition Notice

Rule 32(d)(1) states that errors and irregularities in the deposition notice are waived unless a written objection is promptly served on the party giving the notice. If the irregularities are not corrected and you believe they will substantially affect the deposition, seek a protective order, discussed below.

Rule 32(d)(2) states that, unless an objection is made before the deposition begins, or as soon thereafter as the disqualification becomes known or could be discovered with reasonable diligence, any objection to the qualifications of the officer before whom the deposition is being taken is waived. Occasionally, for example, the reporter assigned by the reporting service is not a notary in the jurisdiction in which the deposition is being held. This can be cured, however, by having a notary come to the deposition for the purpose of swearing in the witness; the "officer" notary would then have to remain in the deposition room, because the deposition is to be recorded "in the officer's presence" pursuant to Rule 30(c), although the parties could waive the requirement by stipulation. Sometimes a similar problem arises in the context of remote depositions, which we discuss in section 24.7.3.

16.1.6 File a Motion to Quash in Response to a Subpoena

Rule 45(d)(3) provides that, upon timely motion, the court for the district where compliance is required must quash or modify a subpoena that fails to allow a reasonable time to comply with the subpoena, requires a person to comply outside the geographical limits, requires disclosure of privileged or other protected matter, or subjects a person to undue burden. The court may quash or modify a subpoena if it requires disclosing a trade secret or other confidential research, development, or commercial information, or if it requires disclosing certain opinions or information of an unretained expert.

16.2 Protective Orders

Defending attorneys can often anticipate the problems that will occur at the deposition or conclude that no deposition should be taken at all. Although it would have been best if the issues were addressed earlier—in the Rule 26 conference and Rule 16 scheduling order, at some point before the deposition was noticed (or subpoena served), or at the very least in a dialogue between counsel after the notice or subpoena was served—motion practice can address the issues.

Under Rule 26(c), a party or person from whom discovery is sought may move for a protective order in the court where the action is pending or in the court for the district where the deposition will be taken. The movant must submit a certification that the movant undertook a good-faith effort with the deposing attorney to resolve the dispute without court action.

Rule 26(c) gives the court discretion, upon a showing of good cause, to "issue an order to protect a party or person from annoyance, embarrassment, oppression, or undue burden or expense." Potential relief, as applicable to depositions, includes one or more of the following:

* forbidding the deposition;

* specifying the terms of the deposition, including the time, place, and allocation of expense;

* prescribing a discovery method other than a deposition;

* forbidding or limiting inquiry into certain matters;

* designating the persons who may be present during the deposition;

* requiring that a deposition be sealed and opened only on court order;

* requiring that a trade secret or other confidential research, development, or commercial information not be revealed or be revealed only in a specified way.

In the context of depositions, there are a few circumstances, often apparent from the deposition notice or subpoena itself, that give rise to the need for a protective order under Rule 26(c) if the parties cannot reach an agreement. (Of course, an issue may arise during the deposition that indicates the need to protect the witness—improper harassment and the like—which can be addressed by a motion under Rule 37, as discussed in section 18.10.) Here are some potential grounds for a protective order.

Apex Witnesses

If the proposed deponent is a high-ranking individual in a government agency or corporation—the so-called "apex" witness—the person may not be the proper subject of a deposition at all. The question is whether the witness has "unique, first-hand, non-repetitive knowledge of the facts at issue in the case" and "whether the party seeking the deposition has exhausted other less intrusive discovery methods."[3] In resisting the deposition of the apex witness on this ground, the party has a heavy burden, but courts "generally do not permit depositions of high-ranking officials to occur before the depositions of lower ranking employees with more direct knowledge of the case have been taken," and the protection may apply even if the high-ranking official or employee has left the employment.[4]

The motion for a protective order should demonstrate that the witness lacks relevant knowledge and other sources of relevant information are available. If the court is unconvinced that the deposition should be canceled altogether, it might be

> *If applying for a protective order, support your arguments with specific facts attested to in sworn affidavits or declarations*

convinced that the witness should not be deposed at least until interrogatories have been served and answered, lower-ranking employees have been deposed, and perhaps a Rule 30(b)(6) deposition has been held.

Attorney Witnesses

At times the deposing attorney wants to take the deposition of opposing counsel—particularly, the in-house counsel of the opposing party. The deposition of an attorney raises obvious concerns in terms of attorney work product, the attorney-client privilege, and disclosure of client confidences. While objections and instructions could be interposed at the deposition, the mere fact of the deposition increases litigation costs for witness preparation and representation, threatens the attorney-client relationship, and potentially disrupts the adversarial system.

---

3. Apple Inc. v. Samsung Elec. Co., Ltd., 282 F.R.D. 259, 263 (N.D. Cal. 2012). *See* Salter v. Upjohn Co., 593 F.2d 649, 651 (5th Cir. 1979); Mulvey v. Chrysler Corp., 106 F.R.D. 364, 366 (D.R.I. 1985). *See also* Contractors' State License Bd. v. Superior Court, 23 Cal. App. 5th 125, 131 (Cal. Ct. App. 2018) (government official); Liberty Mut. Ins. Co. v. Superior Court, 10 Cal. App. 4th 1282, 1289 (Cal. Ct. App. 1979) (corporate executive). In California, the burden appears to be on the deposing party to show that the high-ranking individual has direct factual information pertinent to the material issues and the information to be gained from the deposition is not available through any other source. Contractors' State License Bd., *supra* at 132; Liberty Mut. Ins. Co., *supra* at 1289. Note that not all state courts extend the doctrine to corporate as well as government employees.
4. Rembrandt Diagnostics, LP v. Innovacom, Inc., No. 16-cv-0698 CAB (NLS), 2018 U.S. Dist. LEXIS 17766, at *16 (S.D. Cal. Feb. 2, 2018).

Depositions of opposing attorneys are therefore disfavored, although not improper per se. As a general rule, a court presented with a motion for a protective order will consider the importance of the information sought, the extent to which the attorney witness may have nonprivileged information, and the extent to which there is no other source for the deposing party to obtain it.[5]

Deposing Side Exceeded Deposition Limit or Witness Deposed Previously

Depositions may not be taken without leave of court in certain circumstances under Rule 30(a)(2), such as where the deposition would result in more than ten depositions for the deposing side or the proposed witness has already been deposed. A witness who has testified on behalf of an organization under Rule 30(b)(6) is not deemed to have been deposed before, since it is the organization that was the "deponent." The Rule 30(b)(6) deposition maybe a factor, however, in the court's determination of whether to issue a protective order to limit or preclude the individual's deposition.[6]

Time and Place

If for some reason—and there is rarely a good one—the parties cannot reach an agreement on where or when the deposition will take place, file a motion for a protective order that would designate the time and location. In the motion, provide specific, documented, fact-based reasons to support the request.

Confidential or Privileged Information

A frequent ground for seeking a protective order is that the deposition will inevitably disclose confidential, proprietary, or trade secret information, or it will disclose information protected by the attorney-client privilege or attorney work product doctrine.

Where there is a risk that trade secrets or other proprietary information will be disclosed, the typical solution is to craft an order that protects the information so the deposition can move forward. This can include limiting who attends the

---

5. *See, e.g.*, Shelton v. Am. Motors Corp., 805 F.2d 1323, 1327 (8th Cir. 1986) (party seeking deposition must establish that there is no other means to obtain the information, the information is relevant and nonprivileged, and the information is crucial to the preparation of the case); Nationwide Mut. Ins. Co. v. Home Ins. Co., 278 F.3d 621, 628 (6th Cir. 2002) (following *Shelton*); Johnston Dev. Group, Inc. v. Carpenters Local Union No. 1578, 130 F.R.D. 348, 353 (D.N.J. 1990) (party seeking to preclude deposition of its attorney must show good cause in light of the quality of the information held by the attorney, the ability to obtain the information from other, less burdensome sources, and the harm to the party's representational rights). *See also* Carehouse Convalescent Hosp. v. Superior Court, 143 Cal. App. 4th 1558, 1562 (Cal. Ct. App. 2006).
6. Rule 30(b)(6) and Notes of Advisory Committee on Rules—1970 Amendment.

deposition, sealing the deposition transcript or a relevant portion, limiting dissemination of the information to attorney's eyes only, and the like. Again, try to reach an agreement on these issues at the outset of the litigation (in federal cases, during the Rule 26 conference) or through a meet-and-confer process before the deposition.

When a party claims that the anticipated questioning will infringe on a claim of privilege or work product, the court will assess whether the privilege or work product protection applies. If the argument is that certain documents should not be inquired into, the court often conducts an in camera review of the material.

Remote Depositions

It may be that the deposition was noticed to take place in person, but you or the witness cannot travel to the destination due to health, expense, or some other reason. Rather than postponing the deposition or seeking to preclude it altogether, consider offering to participate in the deposition remotely by videoconference. Conversely, the deposing attorney may have sent notice of a remote deposition, but you may have a good-faith basis for wanting the deposition to proceed only in person. Discuss these matters with opposing counsel; if no resolution is reached, seek a protective order. A caveat, however: a hesitance to embrace remote depositions was not a strong argument even when such depositions were novel, and it is very unlikely that a lack of technological savvy will let you postpone a deposition until in-person testimony is available.

Deposing Attorney's Prior Impermissible Conduct

If, in the past, the deposing attorney has engaged in impermissible behavior such as harassing or insulting the deposition witness, seek a protective order barring such conduct. Provide the court with relevant transcript excerpts and video clips, if available, from the prior depositions.

The risk of bringing a motion for a protective order on any of the foregoing grounds is that, if the motion is unsuccessful, the court may order you or your client to pay the opposing party's reasonable expenses, including attorney fees, in opposing the motion. Conversely, if the motion is granted, the opposing party may be required to pay your reasonable expenses, including attorney fees, for bringing the motion. Again, try to resolve the dispute without judicial intervention. But if you cannot, it is usually worth the risk to bring the motion. It is less costly and more convenient to solve anticipated problems before they arise than to attempt to resolve them after they crop up at the deposition.

16.3 Advance Preparation for the Deposition

Before preparing the witness for the deposition, prepare yourself. Become intimately familiar with the substantive law and the facts, the witness, the rules of the jurisdiction, and the opposing attorney. This might be quick and easy if you are representing a party in a locale where you usually practice, you have been working on the case for a while, and you are familiar with the witness. It will be more time-consuming if you are new to the litigation.

16.3.1 Know the Law and the Facts

Just as the deposing attorney must know and research the legal issues in the case, so must you. The pleadings disclose the claims for relief and defenses, and legal research will identify the legal elements that have to be proven, which in turn show the factual issues likely to be explored at the deposition. As the defending attorney, equip yourself to prepare the witness to testify by thoroughly knowing the facts developed by informal investigation and other discovery, your case theories, and your opponent's likely case theories (*see* Chapter Four). Ultimately, you must be able to answer, "What does the deposing attorney want from this witness?"

This task is harder if you are a defending attorney representing a nonparty that was subpoenaed to testify. In that instance, allow plenty of time to get up to speed on the case. Obtain the pleadings from the court. Discuss with the client what they know about the litigation. If appropriate, contact counsel for whomever might be an ally in the litigation to gather intelligence about the litigation and the deposing party and counsel.

16.3.2 Know Your Witness

Of course, you may already know the individual who is scheduled to be deposed. Nonetheless, it is prudent to research the witness just as the deposing lawyer should do (*see* section 5.1). Consult the client, conduct social media and internet searches, review the allegations of the pleadings, review documents in the case (particularly those bearing the witness's name as author or recipient), and consider any possible testimony the witness may have given in other litigation (including criminal proceedings). This information will help you prepare the witness for the deposition.

16.3.3 Know Your Jurisdiction

While there is universal agreement on some aspects of depositions, there is still quite a lot of variation among jurisdictions, and courts within jurisdictions, and judges within those courts, as to some of the details. Learn the applicable law, including the local rules and orders in the case, that govern the taking and defending of the deposition at hand. In particular, consider:

- the applicable law of attorney-client privilege (*see* section 16.4.2, below);
- the permissible form for stating objections (*see* section 18.8);

- the extent to which you can confer with a witness during the deposition (*see* section 18.5);

- whether the judge or magistrate assigned to the case applies the procedural rules strictly or gives attorneys broader latitude (e.g., are speaking objections tolerated or are sanctions promptly imposed);

- whether the judge or magistrate will entertain emergency hearings by telephone or Zoom to resolve matters that arise during the deposition, and what procedures are required (*see* section 18.10).

16.3.4 *Know Your Opposing Attorney*

In deciding how to prepare the witness for the deposition, and to prepare yourself for the deposition, find out the ability, demeanor, and predilections of the opposing attorney. Is the attorney abusive to witnesses and defending attorneys? Are they easily distracted? How does the attorney respond when objections are made? What is the order in which topics are addressed? What tricks does the attorney like to pull?

> *Based on the case and your witness, what will opposing counsel try to get in the deposition? What are the jurisdiction's rules on privilege, work product, breaks, conferences, and availability of the court? What are opposing counsel's tendencies?*

16.4 Determine Whether the Witness Is the Client

How you prepare the witness for the deposition and defend the witness at the deposition depends on whether the witness is your client, a current employee of your client, or a former employee not represented by counsel. The answer to this question has ramifications in several areas: 1) to whom counsel owes a duty of loyalty and other ethical obligations; 2) whether the attorney-client privilege attaches to the predeposition preparation session and to conferences with the witness during the deposition; and 3) the extent to which you can object or instruct the witness not to answer. These are knotty questions, and it is imperative that you nail down the rules applicable to the pertinent jurisdiction. The following is a general overview.[7]

---

7. Another possibility, addressed in Chapter Twenty-Two, is that the deponent is an expert witness. Communications between the attorney and a testifying expert usually do not fall within the scope of the attorney-client privilege. Some communications may be protected from disclosure under Rule 26(b)(4)(C), but not all states follow suit.

16.4.1 Who Is Your Client for Ethical Duties?

For our purposes, the issue arises when defending counsel was retained by a corporation or other entity, and employees of that corporation (who may or may not be named parties) are scheduled for deposition. The key point here is that the client is the entity, not any of the individual employees. Therefore, the corporation holds the attorney-client privilege and decides whether to waive it, the corporation makes certain case-related decisions (e.g., settlement), and the corporation commands your duties of loyalty, confidentiality, and communication.

16.4.2 Are Conversations During Preparation and the Deposition Privileged?

The attorney-client privilege attaches to confidential communications between the attorney and the client for the purpose of seeking or providing legal advice. When the witness is your client, your communications during the preparation session and during breaks in the deposition are privileged (unless waived by disclosure). Other situations, however, require more analysis.

Witness Is Current Employee of Client

When the witness is a current employee of your client, whether the corporation's attorney-client privilege extends to the employee depends on whether the case is in a "control group" jurisdiction or an "*Upjohn*" jurisdiction. Some jurisdictions follow a variation on the two approaches.

In a control group jurisdiction—constituting a dwindling number of states (including Illinois)—the attorney-client privilege extends only to those individuals in the corporation or collective entity who can make legal decisions on behalf of the organization or have the authority to bind the organization. Many of these jurisdictions limit the "control group" to persons such as the directors or officers of the organization.

By contrast, *Upjohn* jurisdictions[8] extend the attorney-client privilege to communications between counsel and any employee of the corporation or collective entity, as long as the communications are to obtain information or provide legal advice, which in turn is necessary to provide legal representation for the organization.

When the witness is covered by the client's attorney-client privilege, any communications between you and the witness, for the purpose of preparing the witness to testify at the witness's deposition, are privileged and not subject to discovery by the other side. Similarly, the witness can consult privately with you during the deposition, and those discussions are privileged too. Conversely, in a control group

---

8. Named after Upjohn Co. v. United States, 449 U.S. 383 (1981).

jurisdiction, communications between counsel and employees outside the control group are subject to discovery, so be cautious in what you say to the employee.

Even in an *Upjohn* jurisdiction, the privilege belongs to the organization and may be waived only by the organization, and, because the organization operates through individuals, through those persons within the organization with the power to make legal decisions on behalf of the organization. Make certain the employee witness understands that the privilege belongs to the client organization, the client organization determines whether to waive the privilege and potentially disclose the communication, and the employee must not disclose any of the communications to a third party.[9]

As defending counsel, how do you know whether you are in a control group jurisdiction or an *Upjohn* jurisdiction? It depends on the court in which the action is pending. If the action is pending in a federal court, Federal Rule of Evidence 501 controls issues of privilege. Privileges in federal question cases (and federal criminal proceedings) are governed by federal common law, which follows *Upjohn*. Privileges in diversity actions are controlled by the laws of the state providing the rules of decision. In most state court cases, the law of the forum state will dictate application of the attorney-client privilege (and other privileges and privacy rights). *Upjohn* jurisdictions are in the clear majority, but check to be sure.

Witness Is Unrepresented Former Employee of Client

If the witness is a former employee of the client and is not represented by another attorney, there may be some protections afforded to discussions between you and the witness, but research the law applicable to the jurisdiction. Some courts have applied *Upjohn* to former employees, some have not, and some take the approach that whether a communication between the attorney and former employee is privileged depends on what was communicated and when. Several but not all courts hold that for former employees unrepresented at the deposition, communications with the employer's attorney that occurred during employment and communications whose nature and purpose were for the corporation's counsel to learn facts related to a legal action that the former employee was aware of due to their employment (regardless of when the communication occurred) are privileged. Communications between the corporation's counsel and the former employee about how to testify (e.g., guidance during breaks) are not privileged.[10]

---

9. Employees covered by the organization's attorney-client privilege may also be covered by an independent privilege arising from their own attorney-client relationship with separate counsel. For example, the CEO of a corporation may be represented by the CEO's own attorney. Generally, communications between the CEO and the CEO's attorney will be protected by the CEO's attorney-client privilege, which communications between the CEO and the corporation's attorneys will be protected by the corporation's attorney-client privilege.

10. *E.g.*, Peralta v. Cendant Corp., 190 F.R.D. 38 (D. Conn. 1999).

National Institute for Trial Advocacy

Witness Is Unrepresented Nonemployee Third Party

Sometimes you will want to contact a third-party witness, who is neither a client's employee nor within the scope of the attorney-client privilege, to see how the witness may testify at an upcoming deposition.

If the witness is not represented by other counsel (and not an employee or constituent of the opposing party), you may speak to the witness and discuss their likely deposition testimony. You may, in fact, prepare that person for their deposition in the sense of letting them know what to expect and walking through their testimony on substantive matters. Subject to any ethical rules in the jurisdiction limiting communications with unrepresented persons (*see* ABA Model Rule 4.3), you may discuss the witness's recollection of the events, how the law applies to the case, documents from the case, and possible lines of inquiry by the deposing attorney.

As a general matter, however, the communications during the preparation session and during breaks at the deposition will not be privileged and may not be protected by the attorney work-product doctrine. Everything you say or show to the witness can be discovered; everything they tell you, they can disclose; everything that happens, they can talk in the deposition, to opposing counsel before the deposition, and to the press, as well as posting it on social media and the internet absent some form of protective order.[11]

Third-party witnesses are often lay people unfamiliar with the law who think they can rely on you for protection and guidance. You must make clear to the witness that you do not represent them. Rather than considering this a true deposition preparation session, engage in an informal "what do you know" session, where you ask open-ended questions that do not disclose your analysis of the case. You are not there to provide legal advice; your only statement about the upcoming deposition would be, "Just tell the truth."

> Be especially cautious about preparing third-party, unrepresented witnesses with your client present—the client might unthinkingly volunteer information known only to you and the client.
>
> Deposing counsel will have a field day, drilling the witness for privileged information that was inadvertently waived.

---

11. On the other hand, there can be instances where an attorney who represents a party to the litigation is also hired to represent the nonparty witness for the sole purpose of the deposition. This may be permissible as a limited-scope representation to the extent allowed by the jurisdiction's ethical rules, including rules on conflict of interest.

Witness Is Represented by Another Attorney

If you know the witness is represented by another attorney, you cannot contact the witness without obtaining permission from their attorney.[12] Moreover, there is no attorney-client relationship between you and the witness, so there is no protection for communications. So even if you obtained permission from a co-defendant's attorney to speak directly with their client in preparation for a deposition, it is not a good idea for either the codefendant's attorney or for you. If you really want to know how the witness is likely to testify, ask the codefendant's attorney instead— although they cannot disclose attorney-client information, they might be able to disclose facts that help you understand the codefendant's position.

16.4.3   Can You Object and Instruct?

You can object to questions and instruct the witness not to answer, where appropriate, when the witness is your client. If the witness is not your client, you may object to the opposing attorney's questions on behalf of your client, but the witness is not obligated to follow any instruction you attempt to assert to stop the witness from answering. Because things can get dicey when the witness is about to spill the client's privileged information in the middle of a deposition, if you foresee that possibility, research the law in the applicable jurisdiction and consider filing a motion for a protective order that would preclude inquiry into those subjects.

Because preparing a witness represented by another attorney and preparing an unrepresented witness are relatively uncommon, our upcoming discussion in Chapters Seventeen and Eighteen focuses on preparing and representing a witness who is a client or who is within the scope of *Upjohn* or the control group, as applicable to the jurisdiction, such that the attorney-client privilege applies.

---

12. ABA Model Rule 4.2 provides that an attorney shall not "communicate about the subject of the representation with a person the lawyer knows to be represented by another lawyer in the matter, unless the lawyer has the consent of the other lawyer or is authorized to do so by law or a court order." If the person is a current or former employee of an organization that is represented by counsel, the attorney must take heed of ABA Model Rule 4.2, Comment [7]. State ethics rules are similar.

CHECKLIST
INITIAL ANALYSIS AND MOTIONS
FOR PROTECTIVE ORDERS

✔ Review the deposition notice or subpoena for
  - ✓ compliance with any prior agreement on time, place, and manner of the deposition;
  - ✓ a request to produce documents, ESI, or things.

✔ Confirm the witness's availability and schedule preparation sessions.

✔ Determine if an interpreter, accommodation, or assistive device is needed.

✔ Decide whether to serve notice of audiovisual recording if not designated in the notice.

✔ Serve any written objections to the notice within the time allowed.

✔ File, after meeting and conferring, a motion to quash the subpoena if necessary.

✔ File, after meeting and conferring, a motion for a protective order to
  - ✓ preclude the deposition of apex witnesses or other improper witnesses;
  - ✓ preclude the deposition because the limits are exceeded or the witness was previously deposed;
  - ✓ change the time and place or whether the deposition is conducted remotely;
  - ✓ protect confidential or privileged information;
  - ✓ protect the witness against harassment.

✔ Prepare for witness preparation by knowing
  - ✓ the applicable law and facts;
  - ✓ the opposing attorney;
  - ✓ the laws in the jurisdiction regarding attorney-client privilege, attorney-client conferences and breaks during the deposition, required form of objections, and the availability of judges for emergency rulings during depositions.

✔ Determine whether the witness is a client, a current employee covered by the attorney-client privilege, or a non-employee to whom no privilege applies.

CHAPTER SEVENTEEN

PREPARING THE WITNESS TO BE DEPOSED

An ounce of prevention is worth a pound of cure.

—Benjamin Franklin

Oh the nerves, the nerves; the mysteries of this machine called Man!
Oh the little that unhinges it; poor creature that we are!

—Charles Dickens

Defending a deposition witness will be more effective if, during a preparation session, the witness told you everything they know about the case, became familiar with the deposition process and how to answer questions, worked on answering questions about the events underlying the litigation, and now feels protected and confident heading into the deposition.

Witness preparation requires more than just discussing the facts of the case and the questions to expect. No matter how many facts the witness knows, they will not give clear and persuasive testimony unless calm enough to understand the questions and respond appropriately. In addition, the witness's demeanor—especially in video depositions—must reflect credibility and confidence. Because witnesses are frequently unfamiliar with the deposition process and may be nervous, wary, angry, or overzealous about testifying, the preparation session must address these issues.

In This Chapter:

- *Anticipating witness anxiety*
- *Emphasizing your need to know everything*
- *Familiarizing the witness with deposition procedures*
- *Giving clear rules for answering questions*
- *Preparing the witness substantively*
- *Practicing the testimony*

Too many attorneys exacerbate the witness's feelings about the deposition by burying the witness with dozens of documents to review or by reciting a long list of dos and don'ts the witness must recall and apply. That is not the best way to prepare the witness on the substance of their testimony or on the deposition procedures. Moreover, it fails to strengthen the witness's confidence in their ability to perform in the deposition environment. Instead, use the preparation session to take unnecessary burdens off the witness's shoulders, equip the witness, and rehearse with the witness what the deposition will be like so they are prepared mentally and psychologically, as well as substantively, to think straight during the deposition and answer honestly, accurately, and believably.

As such, there are four important phases of witness preparation:

> 1) opening check-in: ascertaining and responding to the witness's mindset and setting expectations;
>
> 2) procedural preparation: explaining what a deposition is, the role of each participant, and the importance of telling the truth and following a limited number of rules in responding to questions;
>
> 3) substantive preparation: finding out the witness's account of events, working with the witness to articulate their account honestly and favorably, and rehearsing the deposition in a mock examination that is more difficult than the real deposition will be;
>
> 4) final instructions: explaining where to meet, what to wear, and what (not) to bring.

This chapter addresses each of these phases. But first, let's consider some general preparation concepts.

17.1 General Preparation Concepts

Before the witness preparation session, complete the background work described in Chapter Sixteen: review the deposition notice or subpoena; determine or modify the method of recording the deposition; seek a protective order as needed; know the pleadings, the facts, the law, case theories, the role of the witness in the case, and the relevant industry; and confirm the jurisdiction's rules about privilege, objections, instructions, conferences, and breaks, and whether the attorney-client privilege applies to the preparation session. All of this will come in handy in setting up the preparation sessions and adapting them to the witness and the case.

17.1.1 *Timing and Duration*

Hold the preparation session one to two days before the deposition. That way, it will be close enough to the deposition for the witness to remember the preparation, but still leave at least a night to think things over before the deposition begins. If the preparation is going to take more than one day, hold the second session the day prior to the deposition.

Schedule as many hours as needed to prepare the witness fully. This means a lot of time for witnesses who were intimately involved with the events in the case. As a rule of thumb, some attorneys allot three hours of preparation for each hour of anticipated testimony—or at least for each hour of anticipated testimony on the facts in the case (as opposed to the witness's background). Most witnesses can be prepared in a day, but consider multiple days of preparation for critical witnesses in a big-ticket case—perhaps one day for substantive preparation on the facts, and a second day on the deposition process and mock examination. While preparation is a time-consuming and onerous process for the witness, it will greatly ease the ultimate load on the witness during the deposition.

To the extent possible, finish one phase of the preparation session (e.g., the check-in) before turning to another phase (e.g., procedural preparation). Of course, there will be some overlap among these phases; if the preparation session extends over multiple days, you will want to have a check-in on each day; during the phase where the witness is being prepared on the deposition procedure and the rules of answering questions, the witness may ask how the rules apply when talking about a particular aspect of the events; and during the substantive preparation phase, you will remind the witness of the rules you discussed while preparing how to answer questions. But to the extent it remains logical and efficient to do so, keep the phases separate so each can sink in.

Attorneys differ on the order of the preparation phases. Some suggest that, after the check-in, substantive preparation should come before procedural preparation, because the witness is more naturally familiar with the facts. That may be best when the preparation is going to take more than a day, leaving the procedural preparation for a time immediately preceding the deposition. If the preparation is going to last only one day, however, tackle the procedural preparation before the substantive preparation (as we do in this chapter).

Regardless of the order, if the preparation session lasts multiple days, start the second day by asking whether new or different facts or concerns have come to light since the last session. The witness might have remembered more information, discovered or looked at a new document, or talked with another person who has knowledge of the events.

17.1.2   Tailoring the Preparation Session to the Case and the Witness

The best preparation session reflects what is really going to happen in the deposition. Include a mock examination conducted by you or another member of your litigation team, so the witness can experience the interrogation format and practice responding to the tough cross-examination tactics the deposing counsel will likely use (*see* section 17.4.7).

To further create a deposition-like environment, hold the preparation session at a place, time, and mode similar to what the witness will experience during the deposition. If the deposition will be held in the morning in a conference room in person, prepare in the morning in a conference room, in person. If the deposition will be held remotely, hold at least one preparation session remotely, not only so the witness can get used to the format but also so you can learn of any problems the witness may have connecting to the platform, maintaining sufficient lighting, and accessing documents. If the deposition will be videorecorded, video the mock examination so you can see how the deposition recording will look.

Witness preparation is extremely dependent on the personality of the witness, the witness's role in the case, and the type of case. Because each witness and each case is different, there is no cookie-cutter witness preparation. Some witnesses need uplifting, others need focus, still others need restraint. The extent to which the witness is vulnerable to suggestion will impact how much the witness might cave in to deposing counsel; it also indicates how vulnerable the witness might be to your substantive comments on their proposed testimony, which affects the care you must take in preparing the witness without running afoul of the ethical rules.

Nevertheless, with some adaptation to account for these witness-dependent and case-specific factors, the guidelines and considerations discussed in the rest of this chapter can be applied to any case at hand.[1]

17.2   The Check-In Phase

Witnesses arrive at a deposition preparation session with emotional baggage. The witness may feel guilt (for their part in the underlying events), denial (refusing to accept that certain things happened), fear of the outcome (losing the case, getting fired), anger (at being sued or at the underlying injustice of what the other side did), impatience (at the pace of the lawsuit or having to do the preparation session), or

---

1. Most preparation techniques apply no matter how the deposition will be conducted or whether it will be held in person or remotely. There are, however, some differences that we talk about in this chapter and in the respective chapters on video depositions (Chapter Twenty-Three) and remote depositions (Chapter Twenty-Four). Among other things, a video deposition obviously requires additional attention to how the witness appears on camera, and a remote deposition requires greater concern about connectivity and attorney-client conferences.

a host of other emotions caused by the lawsuit or anything else in the witness's life. Sometimes witnesses have been deposed before or they are not the worrying type, but if there is any turmoil going on inside, the witness needs to get it out—vent, so to speak—enough to get in the right frame of mind for the preparation session.

> **Check-in phase:**
>
> - *Explain confidentiality.*
> - *Allow the witness to vent.*
> - *Set expectations, including*
>   - *length of the session, and*
>   - *the need to provide all information.*

Help the witness vent and focus in your own way, as befits your personality, the witness, and the setting. At the risk of being too elementary, however, let's walk through one approach to the task, beginning with the witness's arrival at your office for the preparation session.

17.2.1 Welcome

Make the witness feel welcome and as comfortable as possible. Maybe you've met, maybe you haven't. If you're good at small talk and the witness is up for it, a couple of minutes of that may help break the ice. Offer water, coffee, or a snack. Make it obvious, however, that you are well-prepared for the session and know exactly how it will proceed, communicating that you are not wasting the witness's time. At every juncture, inspire the witness's confidence. After all, you need the witness to trust you enough to open up to you about themselves and about the case.

17.2.2 Confidentiality of the Session and Privilege

We discussed in Chapter Sixteen the importance of knowing whether the witness is the client, an employee of a client, or a third party. To the client, you owe ethical duties of loyalty, communication, and confidentiality, and confidential communications between the lawyer and the client for purposes of legal advice are privileged from discovery. Depending on the law of the jurisdiction, confidential communications with employees of the client may be privileged too. Because communications between the attorney and persons not covered by the privilege are subject to discovery by the opposing side, remain mindful of the extent to which the privilege applies during the preparation session.

Inform the witness if the preparation session is privileged and confidential. A sense of confidentiality will encourage the witness to be forthright. At the same time, make certain a nonclient witness understands that their employer is the actual client even though the attorney is defending the witness at the deposition.

Privilege and Confidentiality

If the sessions with the witness are covered by the attorney-client privilege, tell the witness that the communications between you and the witness (but not the underlying facts) are confidential from the other side, that the witness should maintain that confidentiality, and that the witness should feel free to disclose everything to you due to that confidentiality. The explanation might go something like this:

> Everything we say to each other while preparing for your deposition is privileged and confidential. That means the other side can't force you to disclose what we say to each other. The attorney at the deposition can ask you about the facts that you know about the underlying events, even if we talk about them today; but the attorney can't ask you about the words I say to you today or the words you say to me.

> Here's an example. What if you told me, "the traffic light was green." If you're asked in the deposition, "what did you tell the attorney about the color of the light," the statement you made to me is privileged and you do not disclose it. But if you're simply asked what color the light was, you knew that before our meeting, so you'd have to answer what color the light was. Do you understand the distinction there? [witness affirms]

> The only way the other side might find out our confidential statements to each other is if you tell someone [besides the client]. So, keep everything we say here today confidential. Don't talk to anyone about what we said, don't take any notes during the session, and don't make any notes in preparing for the deposition on your own. Okay? [witness affirms]

> Now, here's the reason I'm telling you all this. Because the other side is not entitled to learn about what we say here, I want you to feel comfortable in telling me everything you know during our preparation. The good, the bad, and the ugly. Whether you think it's important or trivial, I'll need to know everything you know. If I don't know about it, I can't help with it. So, today, tell me everything that comes to mind, and we'll talk about it. Is that a deal? [witness affirms]

Upjohn Warning

If the witness is an employee of the client, clarify that you represent the interests of the client. Specifically, give employees what is known as an *"Upjohn* warning:" you represent the company and not the witness; the attorney-client privilege belongs to the company rather than the witness; and the company has the right to waive the privilege and disclose what is said at the interview (*see also* ABA Model R. 1.13(f), (g)).

> Now, just to be clear, I'll be with you at the deposition, but my actual client is Acme Corporation rather than you. Also, the attorney-client privilege we talked about belongs to Acme Corporation rather than you, so Acme Corporation has the right to waive the privilege and disclose what is said during our preparation session. I may share what you tell me with Acme. Again, you must not disclose our communications to anyone else.

No Privilege

If the sessions with the witness are not covered by a privilege, explain the following:

> I want you to understand that whatever we say here can be asked about during the deposition, and you will have to tell the other side's lawyer what you remember about our conversation. What this means is that we must not talk about anything or say anything to each other we would not want the other side to hear. And understand this: at no time today am I telling you what facts to say or what story to tell. The two things we are talking about here are the procedures of the deposition and whatever you can tell me about how this dispute developed. My overall direction is for you to be accurate and tell the truth.

In this situation, do not reveal client or attorney confidences to the nonclient witness.[2]

---

2. If the witness is an unrepresented third party, the attorney will not likely be "defending" the witness and the session will not be covered by the attorney-client privilege. The attorney should make clear who the client is and that the witness is not the attorney's client. It varies from jurisdiction to jurisdiction the extent to which an attorney who represents a nonparty at a deposition may object to questions and examine the witness. For this chapter and the following chapter, we assume that the preparation session falls within the scope of the attorney-client privilege.

17.2.3 Venting

Check in with the witness by asking something to the effect of, "How are you feeling today?" or "How are you feeling about the deposition?" Note the witness's response, including body language. A witness may say they are doing great—but the look on their face says otherwise. Or a witness may say, "I'm feeling okay, I guess, just a little nervous," and try to play it off. Explore what they mean: "That's understandable. What in particular are you nervous about?" And then, so often, will come the witness's gush. It starts out with, "Well . . . " and out pours whatever is on the witness's mind.

Then address the witness's concerns. Show that you heard the witness; respond to them in a realistic but positive way. Further assure the witness that you will address their concerns during the preparation session and, by the time you finish, they will be thoroughly equipped for their deposition. How can we communicate all this to the witness? Well, let's look at a "wrong" way and a much better way.

The Wrong Way

Here is an example of how **not** to deal with a witness's expression of concerns.

Q: So, John, how about this deposition coming up? You're not nervous about it, are you?

A: Well, I guess I am, a little. I'm not sure exactly what to expect, you know. I don't want to make any mistakes.

Q: Well, that's right, it's important that you don't make any mistakes, so we'll go over your testimony, what you know about the facts in this case. All right?

A: Sure, that seems like a good idea. But, you know, I was just wondering—are they going to try to make me look stupid or forgetful or anything? I'm just not sure what to do if I get confused about what they're asking.

Q: Well, it's very important that you be sure about what they are asking. Don't answer any question that's unclear to you or that is ambiguous. They may try to make you look forgetful, so watch out for that.

A: Well, you'll be there, right?

Q: Yes, of course, I'll be there. There are some rules about how much I can do, but I'll object if they try to take advantage of you. And make sure that you pause, okay, maybe take a deep breath before every answer, so that I have time to object if I think it's necessary. Then pay attention to what I say in my objection, because there may be something in the question that's unfair or improper, and you should be aware of that when you answer.

A: Wait, is their attorney allowed to ask unfair or improper questions?

Q: Oh, lawyers do it all the time. They'll try to trick you. They ask questions that have a double meaning, or they try to get you to admit things you don't really mean, or they only put in part of the story—those kinds of things. Et cetera, et cetera. So you really have to watch it, right? And that reminds me, another thing for you to remember is not to volunteer information. Don't answer with more than you were asked for. If the opposing attorney asks you, "Where do you work?" your answer should be, "Strongis Ironworks," not, "I've worked as a foreman at Strongis for the past seventeen years." You see, he didn't ask, "What is your position?" or "How long have you worked there?" So just answer what is asked; answers that go beyond that just cause trouble, believe me.

So, did the attorney help the witness? Unlikely. At the start, the attorney asked whether the witness was nervous in a way that suggested it was wrong to be nervous—and it's not. When the witness explained that he was nervous because he did not want to make any mistakes, the attorney emphasized the importance of not making mistakes, no doubt raising the witness's anxiety. Next, the witness expressed concern that the other side would try to make him look stupid or forgetful and he did not know what to do if he got confused during the questioning. Instead of providing reassurance and guidance, the attorney said, "Watch out for that;" he might as well have said, "You're right, they may confuse you, and if that happens, it's your job to avoid it."

Next, the witness in the example asked, "You'll be there, right?" This clearly signaled the witness's lack of comfort with the proceedings. By responding that he would be there to object "if they try to take advantage of you," the attorney made things worse: the ominous phrase, "take advantage of you," raises the specter of greater problems than the witness had imagined. The attorney then burdened the witness by instructing him to "maybe take a deep breath" before every answer. Now, besides worrying about the content of his answers and being taken advantage of, the witness must worry about his breathing and the timing of his words. Then the attorney told the witness to interpret any objections before giving his answer, without providing a suitable explanation, adding yet another ill-defined burden.

Finally, the attorney in the example reminded the witness that lawyers ask unfair and improper questions all the time but, again, failed to give the witness any tools for dealing with those questions, telling him only to "watch it." By next instructing the witness not to volunteer information, and failing to provide any rationale, the attorney suggested to the witness that there are hidden rules with hidden purposes that must be followed to avoid "trouble." None of this puts the witness at ease.

The Better Way

The witness would be more comforted and in a better space if the attorney gave the following responses to the concerns that so many witnesses share. Of course, there will be a later time and place to explain to the witness about listening carefully to the question, not volunteering information, and the like, but for now, we want to provide some realistic assurances so the witness can focus on the preparation.

"I don't want to make any mistakes"

This is a rational witness concern, and one that calls out for some encouragement. Maybe something like this:

> I know you don't want to make any mistakes, and I appreciate that. I have a feeling that after we get through our preparation session you won't be worrying too much about that anymore. We'll go over what I think will be the substance of the other lawyer's questions. We'll even do some practice deposition questions and answers, where one of my partners will come in and ask questions as though she is the opposing counsel, so you'll have some practice time before the real thing. At the deposition I'll be right there, and if I think that anything is important enough to correct, I'll make a note of it and can ask you questions after the other attorney is finished. And after the deposition, you'll have a chance to read over your testimony once it is typed up, and I'll read it with you. If we see any mistakes, we can deal with them. You don't need to feel you have to be perfect— no one's ever given a mistake-free deposition. Prepare today, and you'll do fine.

"I don't want to look stupid or forgetful"

Here is another valid witness concern. No one wants to look stupid or forgetful. Let the witness know they will be prepared by the time of the deposition, and that during the deposition it is alright to say they do not know an answer if they do not know, or that they do not remember an answer if they cannot remember. The assurance to the witness could be like this:

> Yeah, I get that. With our preparation session today, though, you'll be ready. We're going to go over what happened and some of the documents in the case. And here's the deal. If you're asked a question at the deposition and you don't understand it, you can just say you don't understand it. If you're asked a question and you can't remember the answer, or you don't know the answer, you can say you don't remember or you don't know. There's no shame in that. You have the right to do it.

"Am I going to be asked trick questions?"

In response to this concern, you want to send two messages to the witness: 1) the witness does have to be careful about what the opposing attorney is asking, but 2) you are going to be working with them on it during the preparation session and will be at the deposition to object if there are unfair questions.

> You know, you might get some difficult questions, and today we'll discuss how to handle them. That's really why we're spending this preparation session together. I think you'll find that they won't be able to trick you because you'll be paying close attention to the question. And also remember that I'm going to be there with you at the deposition, so if they try to pull anything that's truly unfair, I'll object and we'll take it from there. Okay?

Additional Witness Concerns

Here are some other concerns that can pop up during the preparation session, along with possible attorney responses.

"Who else is going to be there?"

This question can be motivated by anything from idle curiosity to an overriding fear that an abuser is going to attend the deposition and intimidate the witness. Some exploration of the underlying concern may be in order.

> I'm going to be there, the opposing attorney will be there, they may bring a colleague, and there will

be a court reporter who takes down what is being said. I don't expect anyone else to be there [adjust as needed—such as the opposing party]. Is there someone in particular you're concerned about being there?

"Will I get fired?"

This one's a bit tricky. On the one hand, you cannot tell the employee that they are not going to get fired, because you don't know and you don't want to make a representation one way or the other. And yet, it is unhelpful to tell the witness that yes, they might get fired, because that just increases their anxiety. The best you can do is to say (if honest) something to the effect of this:

> I don't know anything about that, but what I do know is this: you want to do well in your deposition, and that's what we're here for right now. So that's what we need to focus on. Can I get your agreement on that, to focus on this preparation?

"This is stupid."

This comment reflects a different type of witness who believes the litigation, the deposition, and perhaps the deposition preparation session is not worth their time. Ultimately, the witness must be told that the litigation, the deposition, and the preparation session are serious matters.

> I understand. We can agree that the case shouldn't have been filed and it's a pain for you to have this hanging over your head and taking up your time. I get that. But here's the deal. We don't want anything happening in the deposition that is going to make it look like they have a good case or even convince some judge or jury that they should win. So we need to set aside this time to prepare, knuckle down, and treat this seriously. I need your commitment on that.

"I'm going to jam these idiots up."

This statement indicates the mindset of yet another type of witness, who is bent on going into the deposition, telling the deposing attorney what-for, and attempting to win the case singlehandedly. Although the witness's exclamation might be false bravado, it reflects a loose-cannon witness you must bring under control. In the preparation session, see if the witness is merely exuberant or is actually going to try to outsmart and outtalk the deposing attorney. At some point, you may need to communicate something like this:

> You know, the way to win this case is not for you to go into the deposition all Rambo-style, but to leave this deposition unscathed and attack them later when the time is right. I understand what you're saying completely—I'd probably want to argue my case too if I were in your shoes. But we just can't approach it that way. Too many times I've seen it boomerang on the witness and they end up looking bad—you can watch clips on YouTube of all sorts of feisty witnesses that don't look good to a neutral observer. You don't have to win the case at this deposition. Today we'll work on how you're going to answer questions and maybe we can include some zingers in there, but you have to start with the mindset that you're just going to answer what they ask, truthfully, and that's it. Are we good?

A final caveat on dealing with your witness's venting and concerns: false or insincere reassurances do not work. Comments such as, "Don't worry, everything will be fine," do little to comfort the witness when the witness fears that the wrong answer may cost them their job, their house, their esteem, and everything else they hold dear. It is far better to be honest yet upbeat and constructive.

17.2.4 Setting Expectations for the Preparation Session

After you have welcomed the witness and explored any initial concerns the witness might have, you will want to lay the foundation for the rest of the preparation session.

The Road Map

Explain how the preparation session will proceed:

> Okay, so we've set aside the next four hours for this session. We'll talk about what a deposition is, who will be there, what each person's role is, what your role is, what my role is, and some rules to follow in answering questions at a deposition. When you're comfortable with that, we'll talk about the substance of the case—what the issues are, what they're likely going to ask you about. We'll go over the documents

they might ask you about. We'll practice answering questions at a deposition. And you can ask me any questions that you have.

Witness Commitment

Although you should have already obtained a commitment from the witness to stay at the preparation session for the planned number of hours, confirm this commitment with the witness at the start of the session. Work out the extent to which the witness can turn off or put away their phone and give their 100 percent attention, so the session does not have to last longer than necessary. Witnesses can be concerned about work matters, attending to childcare, responding to the office, or their parking meter running out or the parking garage closing, so plan for a break or two that allows the witness to deal with those things so they can be focused during the preparation.

Tell Me Everything

The phrase "tell me everything" bears repeating, both in this chapter and in the preparation session: it is critical for the witness to tell you everything they know about the facts, even if they think it might not be material, and even if they think it is going to be bad for the case. Similarly, the witness must be forthright about anything that the other side might use to make the witness look bad. Reiterate the sage admonition, "If I know about it, I can help you with it; If I don't know about it, I can't."

17.3 Procedural Phase: Preparing the Witness for the Deposition Process

In this phase of the preparation session, explain what a deposition is and what the witness can expect, the "one concept and three rules" of answering questions, ways to deal with the tactics of deposing attorneys, the need to stay calm, how breaks and conferences work, objections and instructions, and tips on handling documents during the deposition.

17.3.1 Explaining the Deposition Environment

Many witnesses have not had their deposition taken before and have no real idea what it entails. It helps the witness to be able to picture the environment and the process. Start out by asking if the witness has been in a deposition before. If so, have the witness explain their impressions of the process and how they felt about it, and then follow up as needed. If the witness has not been deposed before, no worries; you will provide an overview. Here is an example you can adjust to the situation.

What Is a Deposition?

A deposition is an official proceeding where the other side's lawyer asks you questions and you respond to those questions under oath. The opposing attorney may show you some documents and ask you questions about them. A court reporter takes everything down and puts it into written form called a transcript. [If applicable:] There will also be a videographer there who records the deposition by video.

Preparing the Witness on Process:

- *what a deposition is and what the witness can expect*
- *the "one concept and three rules" of answering questions*
- *ways to deal with the tactics of deposing attorneys*
- *the need to stay calm*
- *how breaks and conferences work*
- *objections and instructions*
- *tips on handling documents during the deposition*

Who Sits Where?

Here's how the deposition will be set up physically.

[In-person stenographic deposition.] The deposition will be held at the opposing attorney's law firm, in a conference room like this one. You and I will sit on one side of the table, and the opposing attorney will sit on the other side of the table. At the head of the table will be the court reporter who takes everything down.

[In-person video deposition.] The deposition is going to be held at the opposing attorney's law firm, in a conference room like this one. You'll likely be at the head of the table. The court reporter will be near you, and I'll be near you on the side of the table. Across from me will be the opposing attorney. The videographer will set up a camera behind the opposing attorney (or across from you) and monitor the equipment. The camera will record you looking at the opposing attorney.

[Remote deposition, lawyer and witness in same room.] The deposition is going to be held remotely, over Zoom. It's very similar to the Zoom meetings we have. We'll connect using a link, and we'll be sitting in the same room. You'll be able to see the court reporter and the opposing attorney on the screen. We'll need to keep your camera and mic on unless we go on a break. During the break, we'll turn off our mics and cameras and go into another room to confer.

[Remote deposition, different locations.] The deposition is going to be held remotely, over Zoom. It's very similar to the Zoom meetings we have. You'll connect using a link, and you'll be able to see me, the court reporter, and the opposing attorney. You'll need to keep your camera and mic on unless we go on a break. During the break, we'll turn off our mics and cameras and I'll call you on your cell.

I'll Be There

No matter how the deposition is set up physically, I will be there the whole time for you. As we'll cover at length today, essentially you have to answer the questions at the deposition without my help, but we will be able to talk during breaks and you'll be ready for it.

Use of the Deposition

The deposition transcript can be used in motions and at trial as evidence. The other side might try to use what you say to get the case dismissed, although we'll work hard today to make sure that doesn't work.

Opposing Counsel

I'll mention for now a little something about the opposing attorney who is going to be doing the questioning. She tends to be [a straightshooter/polite/aggressive/nasty/devious]. No matter how she acts, though, no matter how nice she is to you, the opposing counsel is not your friend. She will try to get you to say things to use against [you/the company]. That's no reason for you to be afraid or to be dishonest, but the point is that a deposition is not the place for a conversational chat with the other side's attorney. There's a reason we're preparing here today, and I will be right there with you at the deposition.

17.3.2 Making Witness Preparation Stick

Before we get to other specifics about witness preparation, a word about the style of preparation is appropriate. Too often, the lawyer gives the witness an uninterrupted lecture for nearly an hour, spouting a laundry list of a dozen so-called rules for the witness to follow during the deposition. At the end of this lecture, the attorney asks the witness if they have any questions and sends them on their way, leaving the witness in a bewildering sea of unfamiliar commandments without context or practice—just more for the witness to worry about. Then at the deposition, the attorney is disappointed to see the witness deviate from everything the attorney told them to do.

To make witness preparation stick, we have to make it as clear as possible. Give the witness only a minimum number of "rules" to recall and, for each one:

- Tell the witness the rule you want them to remember, simple and to the point.

- Give an example.

- Give a reason for the rule.

- Tell them the rule again.

- Have them tell you the rule.

- Give the witness a chance to practice the rule, and provide feedback. (For example, during the mock examination exercise, point out if the witness answered more than the question asked, etc.)

With this in mind, let's continue with our witness preparation.

17.3.3 The One Concept and Three Rules of Answering Questions

Distill how to answer questions to a very few precepts the witness can easily remember. Overall, the witness must be honest and, in most cases, provide the shortest responsive answer. Here's a way to explain it without overwhelming the witness.

Give the witness one overriding concept—tell the truth. The concept of telling the truth can then be expressed in just three principles the witness needs to remember about answering questions: 1) make sure you understand the question; 2) answer the question honestly; and 3) that's it!—don't say anything else. Of course, as all attorneys know, there are many other "rules" and guidelines that relate to those three principles. But the more we use the framework of just three rules, all within the umbrella of one main concept of truth-telling, the better the witness will retain what we teach, the less anxious the witness will feel about complying, and the better the witness's performance at the deposition.

Describe it something like this:

> There's just one main concept for you to keep in mind when you're answering a question. Tell the truth. You'll be under oath to tell the truth, and what you say is under penalty of perjury, so of course you have to tell the truth. I know you will, because you're an honest person, but even if you weren't, I'd implore you to tell the truth because not only is it the law, it turns out very badly when people are caught lying, and it can be utterly disastrous for the case. Sometimes the truth

is hard to tell, and people can be afraid that the truth is going to be harmful, but I can deal with that as long as I know about it in advance. Telling the truth is the overall concept.

So what's the overall concept? [*Witness responds.*]

Now, telling the truth in a deposition comes down to just three rules that all have to do with telling the truth. Since we're going to answer a question truthfully, we have to

1) make sure we understand what the question is asking

2) answer honestly in response to the question, and

3) that's it. Stop. You're done.

So, in total we have just three rules: understand the question, answer honestly, and that's it. We're going to work on each one, but again, it's just three rules: make sure you understand the question, answer the question honestly, and that's it.

Next, explain each of the three rules to the witness, giving a description and examples to the extent they would assist the witness. Take your time. This is a conversation with the witness, not a speech. It's not condescending, but it is instructional. You'll do it in your own style with your own words, but the following provides a sample discussion for each rule.

1) Make sure you understand the question

For our first rule, make sure you understand the question before you start to answer it. Sometimes in daily life we start to answer someone's question before they finish asking it, thinking we know what the person wants even if we're not sure. But a deposition is not daily life. If a witness in a deposition starts to answer without waiting for the attorney to finish the question, the witness typically says the wrong thing or says more than what was asked, and that can be dangerous because it gives the other side more information to work with.

So, listen to the question all the way through, and make sure you understand it before answering. If the opposing attorney is using words you don't understand, it's perfectly fine to say, "I don't understand the question." If the opposing attorney's question is just too long and confusing, it is perfectly fine to say, "I don't understand the question." It's the opposing attorney's job to ask understandable questions, and we don't want you to guess at what they meant. If you do understand the question, then you can answer it.

W: Okay, simple enough.[3]

Here's an example. What if the attorney said, "What did you say after you did that thing?"

W: Did what thing?

Okay. Did you understand the question?

W: No.

So how might you respond?

W: I don't understand the question.

Perfect.

2)   Answer the question honestly.

So let's go on to rule number two. Answer the question honestly. Like I said, you're under oath, so you have to tell the truth and give an honest answer in response to the question. We've already discussed one honest answer, "I don't understand the question," when you don't understand the question. But assuming you do understand the question, an honest answer could be, "I don't know the answer to your question." Another honest answer could be, "I don't remember." Or, depending on the question, an honest answer could be "two o'clock" or "yes," or "yes but" or "no because."

Those are all examples of honest answers, which you have to give because you took an oath to tell the truth. So let's look at these examples.

"I don't know." It's hard for us to admit that we don't know something, because we might think that we need to know all the answers because of our position or whatever. But if you don't know the answer to the attorney's question, the honest answer is "I don't know," and our case does not depend on you having all the answers. You don't want to guess. Why? Because a guess makes it sound like you know

---

3. Some attorneys tell the witness to take a moment, or pause, before answering each question, to make sure they understand it. I join the original authors of this book in disagreeing with that idea, because it gives the witness just one more thing to do and tends to heighten rather than reduce the witness's anxiety. Furthermore, repeated pauses can look odd on the recording of a video deposition. The better idea is for the witness to wait for the attorney to finish the question and make sure they understand it before answering, even if they have to pause. The emphasis should be on understanding, not pausing. The witness should have permission to pause, not an obligation to do so. That said, when preparing for a remote deposition, the "brief pause" idea might be appropriate if you will not be in the room with the witness and expect a lag in the connection; it will give you more time to interpose an objection.

something for sure when you don't. What you do know, tell them; if you don't know, say you don't know.

So how about this example. Here's the question: What was I thinking about before I came to work today?

W: Well, probably this deposition.

Well, do you *know* what I was thinking?

W: Oh, no, I guess I was guessing.

Right. What would be a better response if I asked you what I was thinking before I came to work?

W: I'd say, "I don't know."[4]

[Note to the Reader: Practically, there will be some situations where the witness should be limited to answering what they know in the sense of what they saw, heard, touched, tasted, or smelled, and other situations where the witness should answer what they know in the broader sense of what they figured out based on what they saw, heard, etc. Rather than confusing the witness at this juncture when the witness has no context for the distinction, it is easier to deal with these nuances in the substantive preparation. For now, keep it simple.]

"I don't remember." It's also hard to admit that our memories aren't perfect, but if you don't remember what the attorney is asking about, the honest answer is "I don't remember." There's no shame in that. Again, you don't want to guess and make it sound like you remember something for certain. If you remember later in the deposition, then let me know and we'll deal with it. So what would be an honest answer if the attorney asked you, "What did you have for breakfast on August 19, 2017?"

W: I don't remember.

Giving the information. Okay, now, we've talked about saying "I don't understand the question," "I don't know," and "I don't remember," which can all be acceptable and honest answers. But of course we're not going to play games here. If you do know the answer, answer

---

4. Some attorneys tell the witness, "Don't speculate." However, the deposing attorney can properly ask for the witness's speculation if it is reasonably calculated to lead to the production of admissible information. For example, suppose the question is: "Who was the last person to adjust the temperature settings on the boiler?" The witness answers, "Well, I'd really have to guess, based on who was there." The next question could properly be, "Okay, what's your guess?" There is no basis for directing the witness not to answer, because there is no issue of privilege, protective order, or harassment (Rule 30(c)(2)). Therefore, instead of telling the witness during preparation that they should not speculate, the better approach is to tell the witness not to volunteer a guess, and any speculation should be explicitly characterized as such.

whatever the question has asked for. Don't withhold information that's been asked for, because if you don't say it at the deposition, you might not be able to testify to it later. If the question calls for the information, go ahead and say it. Okay?

W: Fine.

"Yes" or "No." Sometimes the attorney will ask questions that let you answer "yes" or "no"—questions like "is it raining?" or "do you know Dan Porter?" It's either raining or it's not. "Yes" or "no" is the honest answer. So when the opposing attorney asks a yes-or-no question, go ahead and answer "yes" or "no." If the opposing attorney wants more information, it's their job to ask for it.

Now later today we may discuss some particular situations where you'll say "yes, but" or "no, and" and provide an explanation, but we'll cover that later. For now, just remember the basic rule—there's nothing rude about just saying "yes" or "no." So, for example, if you're asked at the deposition, "Do you know Dan Porter?" your answer would be, "No," rather than "No, but I know a David Porter." Or your answer could be, "Yes" rather than "Yes, and I've always suspected him of being shady." The "yes" or the "no" answers the question. Do you understand what I mean?

W: Yes.

[Note to the Reader: We used to instruct witnesses to answer yes-or-no questions with "yes" or "no," period. So, we would tell the witness in a preparation session, if the question is "Do you know what time it is," the correct answer would be "yes," not "12:15 p.m." For several reasons, however, this is no longer adequate advice. First, as trials have become rarer and deposition responses become the only opportunity for opposing counsel to get the information to evaluate the case, defending attorneys may want their witnesses to be more forthcoming. If, in fair response to a question, an opportunity is provided to inform opposing counsel—and put in the record—facts that are helpful to the deponent's (client's) position in the matter, a witness might be prepared to take that opportunity with a "yes but" or "no, however" type of response. Second, especially if the deposition is recorded by video, the short "yes" or "no" answers that do not volunteer any information can appear to be evasive if people in the real world (like jurors) would respond with an explanation. Third, a more complete answer will make its use at trial by the opposing party more difficult. When looking for admissions, as described in an earlier chapter, deposing counsel is seeking short, specific answers that can be read or shown to the jurors. The more expansive answer is harder to dissect and use as an admission. For all these reasons, it will often be prudent for defending counsel to prepare competent witnesses to answer fully, with appropriate explanatory material, to the most important questions in the lawsuit. But that should be a strategic departure from the general rule that we teach the witness at the outset.]

3) That's It!

The third rule is "That's It!"—which means to answer only what the question really asked for and then stop. Kind of like the "yes" or "no" situation, but more so.

This is new for most deposition witnesses because it's not like our normal conversations. In ordinary life, if you're asked, "What color is your car," you might respond, "Red. I love that car. I got such a great deal on it and it's getting great mileage."

But a deposition is not a conversation. Let me repeat that. A deposition is not a conversation. If the question is "What color is your car?" then the answer is, "Red." That's it. Stop. You gave the honest answer. You don't need to embellish, argue the case, or fill in the silence. The same thing with "When did you come home in the afternoon?" or "Where do you keep your canceled checks?" The answers would be "3 p.m." or "in a file at home." You don't have to help the opposing counsel by continuing on and saying what you think they might also want to know about. If they want more information, they can ask for it. You've done your job by answering honestly what was asked, and it's not your part to volunteer.

To put it another way, for each question you will give the shortest honest answer that responds to that question.

Let me tell you why this is important. Answering only what you were asked gives the shortest honest answer. Anything more than the shortest honest answer gives the opposing attorney a gift. The opposing attorney will take the extra things you've said and chase them all down to see if they lead to anything. We don't have any desire to prolong this deposition unnecessarily, so it helps to just answer what the question asked for. Do you understand what I mean by that?

Finally, wrap up this part of the preparation, although you will refer back to it when you do the mock examination. The wrap-up could go something like this:

So let's sum up. The overall concept is to tell the truth. And to tell the truth in response to a question, there are three things to do. And what are those three things?

W: Understand the question. Answer honestly. That's it.

Excellent. Let's take a break.

National Institute for Trial Advocacy

17.3.4   Equipping the Witness to Meet Common Tactics of the Deposing Attorney

We all know there are lots of ways deposing counsel can try to get the witness to reveal information and admit propositions—some are fair and legitimate, while others are not. Prepare the witness for these tactics, or at least the ones you believe the deposing counsel will employ.

Avoid giving the witness a list that will overwhelm them. Depending on how much preparation time you have, you might mention just two or three of the ones that are discussed below during the procedural preparation phase (e.g., the deposing attorney's tactics of silence, having the witness adopt other's testimony, and rephrasing the witness's testimony). Give an example of each and make sure the witness understands them. Then later incorporate them, and the rest that might apply, into your mock examination during the substantive phase of the preparation, so the witness has practice dealing with them.

Also avoid characterizing these matters as more "rules" for the witness to remember. Instead, offer them as examples of how the opposing counsel will try to distract the witness from following the three rules already mentioned—understand the question, answer it honestly, and that's it. To put it another way, the antidote for the opposing attorney's tricks and tactics is to steadfastly follow the three rules the witness has already learned. You could start the discussion as follows:

> Remember I said that the opposing lawyer is not your friend and is not truly there to have a nice conversation but to get you to say things that help your opponent's case? There are certain tactics or tricks they pull to get you to stray from our three rules—understanding the question, answering honestly what was asked, and then stopping. It's nothing to be afraid of, but you must be aware. Here they are [choose the most likely ones]:
>
> - **Silence.** Silence makes people feel uncomfortable, and the natural inclination is to fill the silence with words. After you give an answer, the opposing counsel may look at you in silence, hoping that you will start talking about something in addition to your answer. But if you have understood the question and answered honestly, that's it. Do not say anything to ease the silence. The attorney can ask another question.
>
> - **Efforts to lull you into sloppiness.** Opposing counsel may say things like, "I'm just having a hard time figuring this out, will you help me" or "I'm only here to chat a bit to find out what you know." Do not let your guard down. Opposing counsel is not your friend and is not an innocent questioner; they have an agenda to get you

to say things that will not be good for you (or for our client). No matter how nice they try to be, make sure you understand the question, answer it honestly, and that's it.

- **Rephrasing your testimony.** Opposing counsel will often try to sum up your testimony, saying things like, "So let me see if I got this right" or "In other words . . . " It may be an accurate summary that you can agree with, but usually it is not. It's either unintentionally inaccurate or intentionally trying to put words in your mouth. If the attorney tries to rephrase or paraphrase your testimony, listen carefully. If it is not accurate, then say so.

- **Saying "it's fair to say . . . "** Questions that begin with "is it fair to say" or "it's fair to say, then," make it sound like the opposing counsel is being "fair" in drawing a conclusion—but chances are, it is not fair to draw that conclusion at all. Again, make sure you understand the question and know what the opposing counsel is trying to get you to agree to.

- **"It's okay if you don't know."** This is a correct statement, but it is usually said by opposing counsel to get you to give in and just say you don't know something when in fact you do. The problem is that, if you say you don't know, it will be in the transcript, and it might prohibit you from telling the court what you know later. Whether you "know" something is up to you to decide based on our preparation today.

- **Asking you to agree to a leading question.** The lawyer may ask you an open-ended question like "what" or "where" that leaves you free to answer. But sometimes the lawyer will ask you a leading question that's really more like a statement they want you to agree with. Like, "You went to the store, didn't you?" Those questions try to put words in your mouth. The question, "you went to the store, didn't you" is trying to get you to agree that you went to the store. The natural inclination is to go along with the attorney's suggestion—you think to yourself, well, I might have gone to the store or, yeah, at some point I went to the store, so you say yes to the question. But that might not be accurate. So we want to give honest answers. Maybe the answer is, "I don't know." Maybe the answer is, "no." Maybe the answer is, "I don't remember."

- **Limiting your choices.** Questions may suggest that your answer has to be one of two alternatives embedded in the question. For example, "Did you learn that from Nicole or from Matty?" Don't be boxed in by the question. Maybe you learned it from someone else. The shortest honest answer may be "yes" or "no."

- **The third degree.** Sometimes the opposing attorney will not only ask you leading questions, but ask them in an intimidating manner at a brisk pace, mirroring the interrogations of police detectives we see on TV. To some extent, the attorney is allowed to do this. I'll be there and will put a stop to it if it gets out of hand, and you can take a break if you need one. But remember, make sure you understand the question, answer honestly, and that's it.

- **Reminders that you have taken an oath to tell the truth.** While it is true that you have taken an oath, sometimes opposing counsel uses this to get you to confess to what they are proposing. You must give honest answers in response to the opposing attorney's questions, but that doesn't mean you admit to something you do not believe is true.

- **Adopting other people's statements.** Opposing counsel may attempt this in two ways. One way is to say that another person has testified to a certain statement, to try to get you to agree with that proposition. Another way is to get you to agree to a proposition that is contained in a document that you didn't write. In both of those instances, resist the urge to automatically go along with what opposing counsel is saying. What is the question really asking? Do you know the answer? Is your knowledge the same as the knowledge of the other person?

- **Right after lunch and after 4:00.** Opposing attorneys often ask the hardest questions, or try to get you to admit things, right after lunch when the lunch fatigue sets in, or after 4:00 p.m. when you become weary. If you have trouble focusing on the question and need a break, say so.

17.3.5   Breaks and Conferences

During the preparation session, explain to the witness how breaks will be taken during the deposition, how to ask for a break, and expectations for conferences between the witness and counsel. As discussed in sections 18.5 and 18.6, this will depend on the jurisdiction. Generally, the witness can take a break to discuss issues of privilege with the defending lawyer even if a question is pending. A break may be taken for other reasons, at least if requested by the witness, but only if there is no question pending.[5] Depending on the rules of the jurisdiction, the explanation to the witness may be something like this:

---

5. *See, e.g.*, Hall v. Clifton Precision, 150 F.R.D. 525, 528–30 (E.D. Pa. 1993); In re Stratosphere Corp. Sec. Litig., 182 F.R.D. 614, 621 (D.C. Nev. 1998).

The other side's attorney will probably call a short break in the deposition once in the morning and one or two times in the afternoon, along with a break for lunch. In addition to that, there may be times when you feel you need to take a break. You may need to use the restroom or call to check on your kids, or you may feel you're getting angry or just need a chance to stretch and collect your thoughts. Let me or the opposing attorney know you need to take a break. If the opposing attorney already asked a question, you may have to answer it first, but then we can take a break. Does that make sense? [*witness affirms*]

Also, if there's ever a time when you think your answer might be privileged, because it's something said between you and an attorney, then tell me or the opposing attorney and don't answer the question. We'll stop so you and I can discuss it before you have to answer. It's better to take a break and talk about it—to either figure out how to make you comfortable with going forward or to decide whether the question is objectionable—than it is to go forward and perhaps give the other side private information that it's not entitled to.

So, bottom line, if you want a break for what seems to you to be a good reason, just say, "I'd like to take a break," and we'll take it from there.

17.3.6   What to Do When Objections Are Made

There are two things the witness needs to know about objections during a deposition: 1) the witness still has to answer the question to the best of their ability; and 2) the objection may remind the witness about some of the rules they should be following when giving truthful responsive answers.

"Unless you are told otherwise, you must still answer the question."

In a preparation session, witnesses often ask what to do if the deposing attorney asks a personally invasive question, irrelevant questions, or the same question repeatedly. The attorney's typical response is: "Well, if they do that, I'll object." Unfortunately, the attorney usually does not tell the witness that the witness will still have to answer the question. Explain to the witness that, even though you object to those types of questions—and to other questions as well—the witness must still answer the question (if they understand it) unless, in a rare instance, you specifically instruct them not to.

Sometimes the opposing attorney will ask you a question that isn't phrased well or there is something wrong with it in terms of the law.

> I will interrupt and say "objection" and why I'm objecting, and the court reporter takes it down. But since there is no judge in the room, you must go ahead and answer. Then later, if the other side tries to use your answer, the judge decides whether my objection is correct and the testimony shouldn't be used. But the main thing to know is that you still have to answer as best you can. That's just the way depositions work.

"The objection may remind you of some of the rules."

You cannot tell a witness that if you object to a question as "vague," they should conclude that they do not understand it and should parrot your statement. Objections are not made to coach the witness. But a good-faith objection that a question is "vague" may remind the witness to do what they should be doing anyway for every question—making sure they understand what the question is asking, including the timeframe. Similarly, an objection that a question "misstates prior testimony" may remind the witness to make sure the deposing attorney's summary of what the witness said is accurate.

> When I object, my objection may remind you of some of the rules we discussed in answering questions honestly. If I object that a question is vague, do what you would do anyway in making sure you understand the question before answering. If I object that a question misstates prior testimony, do what you would do anyway—be sure that the question is summarizing your earlier testimony correctly—before you answer.

17.3.7 *What to Do If I Instruct You Not to Answer*

The witness must understand that there is one exception to the rule that a witness must try to answer every question: when you instruct the witness not to answer, in protection of a privilege or some other extreme situation. In that instance, the witness must not answer the question. Remind the witness what you discussed regarding privilege at the outset of the preparation session, and provide clear direction on the point.

> There may be times when I not only object, but I also say to you, "I instruct you not to answer." That means that a question is so bad that under the rules I can tell you not to answer. It's usually because the question would get you to disclose something that is privileged. Remember what we talked about earlier, that what you say to me or I say to you for purposes of legal advice is privileged and should not be told to the other side. So, if the opposing attorney asks for information that is privileged, I'll say, "Objection, attorney-client

privilege, I instruct you not to answer." Don't answer that question. If opposing counsel asks you if you are going to follow my instruction, your answer should be yes.[6]

Similarly, if applicable, be sure the witness knows that, if a question calls for information covered by a protective order already in existence, you may have to instruct the witness not to answer, and the witness should not answer the question.

17.3.8   How to Handle Documents

While this topic logically falls within the scope of procedural preparation for the deposition, it might instead be addressed in the phase that deals with substantive preparation. Either way, teach the witness to do the following if the deposing attorney presents an exhibit to the witness:

- Make sure it is the true and complete document. Check to see that it is not missing any pages or attachments and is not actually two documents mistakenly stapled together.

- Take the time to refresh your memory of the document; for lengthy documents, look through the table of contents or skim through it; consider whether you have ever seen it before.

- If you have not reviewed the document recently, read it in its entirety.

- Determine whether you authored or received the document.

- If you did not write it, do not adopt what is in the document as if it is a fact or accurate—only that it is contained in the document.

- If the questioner directs your attention to one portion of the document, look at related portions to guard against something being taken out of context.

- Listen carefully to opposing counsel's characterization of the document before you agree to it.

Again, when communicating all this to the witness, try not to make it just a recitation of rules for the witness to have to remember. Show the witness a potential exhibit and model the steps the witness should take if presented with it at the deposition. Also use documents in the mock examination so the witness gets used to handling them.

---

6. Technically, the client has a choice to waive the privilege or not, but the client must have a chance to discuss the matter with counsel before exercising that choice; it is rarely in the client's best interest to waive the privilege.

17.3.9   Keep Cool, Look Calm, Be Serious

Tell the witness to keep their emotions in check during the deposition. When a witness becomes emotional, their words deviate from what they planned to say, usually not for the best. Expressions of anger typically do not play well with the trier of fact. If the witness feels they are becoming upset, they can and should ask for a break.

Similarly, body language is important. If the witness appears confident and credible, it suggests to the deposing attorney that the witness will do well at trial, which increases the settlement value of the case. Body language is even more important in video depositions, of course, since use of the deposition at trial results in the trier of fact seeing the witness's demeanor when answering the questions. Have the witness practice sitting up, with hands on their lap or folded, without rocking or swiveling their chair (practice this in a chair that does rock and swivel, since you cannot be sure what kind of chair they will have at the deposition). This helps the witness avoid nervous mannerisms—drumming fingers, rocking or swiveling, twirling their hair or moustache, clicking a pen, or putting their hand over their mouth.

Remind the witness to be businesslike during the deposition. The witness should not joke around: a deposition is not a joking matter, and a witness who jokes with the deposing attorney tends to let their guard down and fall into a free-flowing conversation, which is just what the deposing attorney wants. In addition, admonish the witness not to be sarcastic: sarcasm can be perceived as disrespectful, and it can be manipulated to suggest the witness was being serious.

17.3.10   Where to Look

For an in-person deposition, have the witness practice maintaining an appropriate amount of eye contact with the questioner to portray sincerity and confidence. If the deposition is recorded by video, this means the witness will not be looking at the camera (or at the judge or jurors who will eventually view the witness from the camera's perspective). Nevertheless, the generally accepted advice—in most parts of the country—is that the witness should look at the questioner even in a video deposition, with a result similar to a videotaped interview that might be seen on television.

In remote depositions, however, it is ideal for the witness to look into the camera on their computer or electronic device, so it appears to deposing counsel—and all the other participants as well as the trier of fact—that the witness is making eye contact with them; the result is akin to an anchorman presenting information during a television newscast. This takes a lot of practice, because the natural tendency is to look at the questioner on the screen rather than at the device's camera.

17.4   Substantive Phase: Preparing the Witness on the Facts

In this phase of the preparation, remind the witness of your need to know everything the witness knows about the facts and anything that could be used to attack their credibility; explain the issues in the case and the witness's role; prepare the witness for the inquiries the deposing attorney will likely make; and have the witness practice answering questions while familiarizing the witness with the aggressive examination they may face. But first, let's talk about ethics.

17.4.1 The Ethics of Witness Preparation

A key issue in witness preparation is the extent to which the defending attorney may ethically aid the witness in preparing the testimony. Essentially, counsel must not knowingly assist a witness to testify falsely, but counsel may work with the witness to reach an honest and accurate rendition of the facts that is worded as favorably as possible for the client.

No False Testimony

Rule 3.4(b) of the American Bar Association Model Rules of Professional Conduct ("ABA Rules"), adopted in some form and extent in all jurisdictions, states that an attorney shall not "counsel or assist a witness to testify falsely." Similarly, ABA Rule 3.3(a)(3) states that an attorney shall not knowingly "offer evidence that the lawyer knows to be false."

If a defending attorney has actual knowledge that evidence is false, the attorney cannot prepare the witness to testify to it. Rather, the attorney should attempt to persuade the witness not to so testify, such as by explaining the perjury laws, the potential ramifications for the case, and the attorney's ethical obligations.[7]

If the lawyer does not have actual knowledge that the evidence is false, the lawyer may prepare the witness to give the testimony that the witness wants to give, even if the lawyer suspects it is untrue.[8]

Strategically, even if you are not ethically barred from offering evidence suspected to be false, it may be unwise to prepare the witness to present that evidence. After all, defending counsel's suspicion came from somewhere—perhaps the testimony of other witnesses, documentary evidence, or the witness's demeanor in talking about it—and opposing counsel may have access to the same information. The witness's false statement can be exposed at trial or at the deposition, damage the witness's credibility, and potentially ruin the client's case.

Honest, Accurate, and Favorable Testimony

As we have just discussed, you cannot prompt the witness to testify to something you know is false or something the witness believes is false. Nor can you

---

7. *See* ABA Rule 1.2(d); ABA Rule 3.3 (a)(3), (b), and Comment [6]; Nix v. Whiteside, 475 U.S. 157, 169 (1986).
8. *But see* ABA Rule 3.3, Comment [8]; ABA Rule 8.4(c).

instruct the witness what to say.[9] But that does not mean you must accept whatever comes out of the witness's mouth in the preparation session.

You may—and likely must, to fulfill duties to the client—attempt to persuade the witness that their recollection of the facts is incomplete or inaccurate, in light of other documents, testimony, or reason. You must have a factual basis for believing the witness's version is errant, and make sure the witness is not so susceptible to your suggestions that they would be influenced to testify falsely.[10]

To this end, talk to the witness about the issues in the case and the applicable law, so the witness knows what facts might be relevant and the reasons certain questions may be asked. Do this with care, making sure it does not assist or lead the witness to make up facts or otherwise testify falsely to provide an answer they believe you want.[11] Avoid instructing the witness with something like, "Unless you testify this way, you are going to lose." But it may be appropriate to say, "What we have to prove is a breach of the contract, which means that we have to show that the defendant did not do what it was supposed to do."

> **Preparing the Witness on Facts:**
>
> - *Remind the witness that you need to know everything they know about the facts of the case (and anything that could be used to attack their credibility)*
>
> - *explain the issues in the case*
>
> - *explain the witness's role*
>
> - *prepare the witness for the inquiries the deposing attorney will likely make*
>
> - *practice with the witness answering questions*
>
> - *familiarize the witness with aggressive examination tactics*

Rehearse testimony with the witness and suggest word choice and language—again, as long you are not helping the witness to testify falsely.[12] If, for instance, a witness uses a word that has a negative connotation, inform the witness of the connotation, explore whether it reflects what the witness was intending to convey, and work with the witness to find an accurate and truthful word that better reflects the witness's understanding.

Often, a fine line exists between appropriate suggestions of word choice, confrontation with the evidence, and discussion of what is important legally in the

---

9. *See* In re Eldridge, 82 N.Y. 161, 171 (N.Y. 1880).
10. *See* RTC v. Bright, 6 F.3d 336, 341 (5th Cir. 1993); Restatement (Third) of Law Governing Lawyers § 116 (Am. Law Inst. 2000).
11. Restatement (Third) of Law Governing Lawyers § 116.
12. Restatement (Third) of Law Governing Lawyers § 116; D.C. Bar Ethics Opinion No. 79 (1979).

case, and inappropriate encouragement to make up facts and parrot the attorney's proposed answer. Conscientiously assess how susceptible the witness might be to suggestions and do not take advantage of it. Ensure at every step that any revision to the witness's proposed testimony does, in fact, reflect what the witness believes to be true. Ask the witness if the revised testimony can be given honestly and be sure that the witness's demeanor does not suggest otherwise.

17.4.2   Air the Dirty Laundry in the Preparation

A continuing task in witness preparation is getting the witness to disclose everything they know about the case and anything the deposing attorney might discover that could bear on the witness's credibility. A witness might not volunteer this information in the preparation session due to embarrassment or a belief that the information is unimportant or will not surface at the deposition. But you must explore these matters before the deposition so you and the witness can prepare how to handle them if they do arise.

Explain to the witness the need to discuss this type of information and ask the witness directly if there is anything they should tell you. Examples include: criminal history; other lawsuits; social media posts and negative communications concerning the case, the other parties to the litigation, a party's injuries, or unflattering information even if not related to the case; the witness's medical history (if at issue) and psychological history; substance abuse issues; improper workplace activity or accusations, such as taking documents, supplies, or confidential material from the office, or obtaining unauthorized access to computer networks; employer disciplinary actions; failure to turn over all documents responsive to discovery requests; and anything else the opposing party might know about or the opposing counsel's investigators might find.

17.4.3   Explain the Issues in the Case and Role of the Witness

At the beginning of the substantive preparation, explain the nature of the case and each side's position on the issues. This is not a long legal explanation or attempt to bring the witness up to your level of understanding. Instead, the goal is to instill in the witness a basic grasp of the issues so they have an overall framework and context for the substantive preparation and appreciate the significance of pertinent factual disputes. If the witness is also the client, they should already have a good idea of these matters; in corporate and similar cases, however, lower-level employees and others not directly interested in the outcome may have only vague notions of what the lawsuit is about.

After providing a general overview, explain the case issue by issue, succinctly stating the parties' positions on each one or what the parties are trying to prove.[13] If the

---

13. Again, we are assuming in this chapter that the preparation session is protected by the attorney-client privilege and work product doctrine.

witness's participation in the underlying events was limited, the discussion can focus on the issues in which the witness was involved. Like every other aspect of witness preparation, tailor the explanations to the witness's needs and comprehension, without making it more complex than the witness can understand and remember.

Here is an example of a defending attorney explaining the issues to a nonparty witness:

> **Lawyer:** Let's now talk about what this lawsuit concerns and how you fit into it. As you know, this is an antitrust action. Dr. Rimard is claiming Hospital Pathology, Inc., unfairly took all of the pathology business for itself and prevented Dr. Rimard from getting any of the business. Have you heard about that?
>
> **Witness:** Yes, there has been a lot of talk in the doctors' lounge about the case.
>
> **Lawyer:** Opposing counsel is taking your deposition next week to find out whether Hospital Pathology uses general practitioners such as yourself to steer pathology patients to themselves and away from Dr. Rimard. Dr. Rimard claims that when a patient requires pathology work, the hospital automatically refers the patient to Hospital Pathology without letting the patient or the patient's primary care physician know about alternative sources of pathology services. Hospital Pathology, on the other hand, claims it and the hospital always give the patient and the primary care physician a choice about what pathology services to use.
>
> **Witness:** Okay.
>
> **Lawyer:** Your deposition is being taken because you are a primary care doctor, and Hospital Pathology wants to find out what your experience has been with the referral of patients for pathology services. Does this all make sense?
>
> **Witness:** Yes.

Tell the witness what their role is in the deposition. (Even if discussed in the procedural preparation, it bears repeating.) That role, usually, is not to win the lawsuit, but to answer honestly the questions put to the witness and then to leave. There are times when you need the witness to put forth certain information either to protect the record, plan for a summary judgment motion, educate the opponent, or fulfill some other strategic purpose, and if you think the witness can do that and hold up under cross-examination, then prepare the witness to do it. But as a general matter, remind the witness to answer only the question put to them and not to argue or volunteer information to prove the case.

17.4.4 Cover Questions on Background and Preparation

Inform the witness what types of questions typically occur at the beginning of the deposition—including the commitments (ground rules), the witness's background, and the witness's preparation for the deposition (*see* Chapters Six and Seven). Usually this will not take up much of the preparation session; include it, nonetheless.

Briefly discussing the commitments lets the witness know what to expect at the start of the deposition and affords you an opportunity to reinforce what you discussed in the procedural preparation, such as the importance of understanding the question and the opportunity for breaks. You will also learn how the witness might answer questions about medications and prior deposition experience.

As to questions about the witness's background, explain that the opposing attorney will likely ask questions about the witness's educational and employment history. If the witness's background is important for the case—for example, the witness's training and knowledge of protocols—explore how the witness would answer those queries, similar to preparing the witness on substantive issues.

In addition, explain how to handle questions about the witness's preparation for the deposition. Remind the witness that inquiries into what was said in the preparation session are objectionable because they call for privileged communications, you will instruct the witness not to answer, and the witness should not answer questions that ask for those communications. (If you are preparing a witness for whom the attorney-client privilege does not apply, the witness will likely have to answer queries about the preparation session.)

Finally, ready the witness to answer questions about their review of documents in preparing for the deposition. Instruct the witness to respond truthfully, e.g., "Yes, I have reviewed documents with my attorney in preparation for this deposition."[14] Depending on the jurisdiction, you may object to any follow-up questions that ask which documents were reviewed with counsel and direct the witness not to identify those documents (on the ground of attorney work product) unless the questioning attorney can establish that a document refreshed the witness's memory on a relevant point (*see* section 7.2.2). If the deposing attorney asks the witness if the documents refreshed the witness's recollection on the subject matter of the witness's testimony, the witness must answer honestly; this puts the onus on you not to jeopardize privileged or work product material by showing it to the witness during the preparation session, as discussed next.

---

14. At this juncture, it is also helpful to tell the witness not to review any material on their own without checking with you first.

17.4.5 Use Documents in Preparation—Carefully

Documents are critical to witness preparation for two reasons: 1) the witness may be asked about them during the deposition; and 2) they help the witness recall what happened in the case. Do not overwhelm the witness with a barrage of documents during the preparation session and do not to show the witness any document that is privileged, work product, or otherwise not subject to discovery.

Manageable Number of Documents

In the relatively small case involving ten to thirty crucial documents, carefully review each one with the witness before the deposition. Witnesses are sometimes unnerved if confronted in the deposition with documents they have not seen in months or years. The pre-deposition review prevents this and assures the witness that their testimony will be consistent with the documentary evidence—or at least the witness will be prepared to explain any inconsistencies if need be. Similarly, the pre-deposition review provides a check on reconstructed memories that build up over time, often with inaccuracies that seem perfectly real to the witness until contemporaneous documents reveal otherwise.

Larger cases, involving hundreds or thousands of documents obtained from the client and in discovery, require a different approach. Even if the witness had the time and energy to read through—or even just scan—each page, they could not retain all the information. No matter how well organized the documents are—by topic, by recipient, by author, or by date—the number of documents shown to the witness must be limited. In a complex case, therefore, cull the documents to those that are most important to the witness's testimony and most likely to be used at the deposition. Some attorneys recommend the "fourteen document rule," showing the witness no more than fourteen documents—or perhaps fourteen documents per topic—because the witness cannot be expected to remember 100, 1,000, or 10,000 documents accurately.

Because merely handing documents to a witness for review does not ensure that the witness will review them—or notice everything in the documents that the witness needs to see—take time during the preparation session to review the documents with the witness, incorporating them in the discussion of the issues or events in the case. For each issue or event, organize a manageable number of documents chronologically to see if the witness agrees that those are the key documents or if anything is missing. By arranging the documents chronologically, the witness will be better able to recount what occurred and realize cause and effect: "Oh, I see. I called him on the tenth because he sent me this email on the eighth asking if we could fill his order. I wondered why I called." If the documents seem at odds with the witness's independent recollection, work with the witness to reconcile the discrepancy.

No Privilege or Work Product

As explained in section 7.2.2, take care in deciding what documents to show the witness during a preparation session. If the witness is not a person to whom the client's attorney-client privilege applies, showing that person a privileged document may waive the privilege. Even if the witness is the client or otherwise within the scope of the attorney-client privilege, showing the witness a privileged document (or allowing the witness to review it on their own) may lead to the production of that document to the opposing party if the document refreshed the witness's recollection of the events in the case. Bottom line: Never show any witness any document that is privileged or otherwise protected from discovery (e.g., attorney work product and trial preparation materials).[15]

17.4.6 *Proceed Through the Substantive Topics and Events*

The manner of preparing the witness to answer questions that probe the events in the case depends on the witness. If the witness was involved in a limited way—the eyewitness to an accident or an employee who participated in only a couple of meetings—it will suffice to ask the witness what happened, follow up to explore the details they recall, and supplement the discussion with any documents the witness might be shown at the deposition. If the witness was involved extensively in the matters underlying a complicated case, you will have to be more methodical in proceeding chronologically through the relevant events, spending more time on the important ones.

The general approach in preparing the witness is nonetheless the same: obtain the witness's recollection of the event, probe and clarify what the witness is saying, and supplement the questioning by confronting the witness with documents the witness might be shown at the deposition. Once you understand the witness's information and the witness seems to have an adequate recollection of what occurred, pose questions the deposing attorney might ask and see how the witness would answer.

Ignorant or Informed?

Unless the witness has been designated to testify on behalf of an organization under Rule 30(b)(6) with the information reasonably available to the organization, the deposition of a nonexpert targets the witness's personal knowledge. An inevitable tension arises between allowing a witness to remain hazy on the facts, so the witness gives a lot of "I don't know" and "I don't remember" answers at the deposition, and refreshing the witness's recollection so the witness provides substantive answers at the deposition.

---

15. Some lawyers provide witnesses with summaries of what other witnesses have said in their depositions. This practice has some risk, because if the witness's recollection of the events is refreshed by these lawyer-prepared summaries, a judge could order that they be turned over to opposing counsel pursuant to Federal Rule of Evidence 612.

It is almost always better to prepare witnesses by reminding them of what they once knew. Deposing counsel will know of the witness's participation in the underlying events, so prepare the witness to address likely deposition questions. While using a witness's lack of memory to avoid disclosing information may seem like a good tactic, it often backfires. The witness's "I don't know" and "I don't remember" answers in the deposition—although ethical and appropriate if offered honestly[16]—can preclude the witness from later testifying to facts that the client may need to win the case. As touched upon previously in Chapters Eight and Fifteen, the sham affidavit doctrine may lead the court to disregard a later summary judgment affidavit from the witness if it contradicts the witness's deposition testimony—including if it contradicts repeated claims of lack of recollection.[17] Furthermore, if the witness tries to testify to the facts at trial, the opposing counsel can impeach the witness with their claims of ignorance at the deposition (Rule 32(a)(2)).

17.4.7 Conduct a Mock Deposition

The heart of witness preparation is having the witness practice answering questions. Only through practice and feedback will the witness fully understand how to phrase their answers to get their meaning across accurately, how to respond to an aggressive cross-examination style, how to display an appropriate demeanor, how to apply the "one concept and three rules" of answering questions, and how to deal with many other nuanced situations that occur during deposition. While it is neither possible nor necessary to rehearse answers to every likely deposition question, have the witness practice answering questions in the key areas on which they are reasonably certain to be examined.

Begin the mock deposition session by explaining to the witness what is going to happen: your colleague will play the role of opposing counsel and ask the witness questions as in a real deposition, the witness will answer questions as if it were the real deposition, and you will act as the defending attorney. At some point, everyone

---

16. Of course, it would be unethical to instruct a witness to testify "I don't know" or "I don't remember" if that was not the truth.

17. *E.g.*, Perma Rsch. & Dev. Co. v. Singer Co., 410 F.2d 572, 577–78 (2d Cir. 1969) (affidavit did not raise genuine factual issue to preclude summary judgment, where the affiant had made no reference to the newly-raised conversation in the deposition, despite being asked repeatedly to specify the basis of an alleged fraud); Yeager v. Bowlin, 693 F.3d 1076, 1080–81 (9th Cir. 2012) (district court did not err in disregarding plaintiff's affidavit in opposition to summary judgment, where the affidavit asserted facts that would have been responsive to many unambiguous deposition questions to which the plaintiff had answered "I don't recall," the district court could have reasonably concluded that no juror would have believed the plaintiff's explanation for his newfound recollection, and his recollection could not have been credibly refreshed). On the other hand, the affidavit may not be excluded if it expands on testimony rather than contradicts it, includes a good reason for the change in testimony, or there is independent corroborating evidence. *E.g.*, Button v. Dakota, Minn. & E. R.R. Corp., 963 F.3d 824, 830–31 (8th Cir. 2020); Baer v. Chase, 392 F.3d 609, 625–26 (3d Cir. 2004).

will step out of their roles and you will provide the witness with feedback. If you do not have an available colleague to assist, play the role of the deposing attorney, too.

> *If you must do the mock examination without a colleague, wear a hat or suit jacket whenever you are in the role of the opposing lawyer, so it is clear to the witness what role you are playing at any given moment.*

Once the witness understands the task, the participants go into role and the mock examiner questions the witness on a chosen topic. Listen to the witness's answers for substance, gauging the accuracy of the proposed testimony and how the deposing attorney and the trier of fact might perceive the witness's wording of the answers. Observe, also, how the witness answers—gestures, facial expressions, and body language— especially if the deposition is going to be videorecorded.[18]

Provide feedback at regular intervals and whenever you have concerns about the substance of the witness's answers. Possibilities for feedback include exploring the witness's substantive responses for content and word choice, noting mannerisms or expressions of which the witness should be aware, and pointing out any way the witness deviated from the procedural "rules" for answering questions (*see* section 17.3.3). After explaining the feedback, have the witness practice answering the question(s) again, incorporating the feedback into the answer. (If you have more than one concern, address each one separately so the feedback does not become overwhelming or discouraging.) When satisfied, move on to the next series of questions.

Here is an example, where the defending attorney is also playing the role of the deposing attorney ("L" is for lawyer, "W" is for witness):

L: OK, let's imagine again I am the lawyer for Hospital Pathology, and let me ask you some questions about your efforts to generate pathology patients. Ready?

W: Sure.

L: Dr. Unitas, please tell me all the things you did to get pathology patients of your own.

W: Well, I contacted all the hospitals and told them I had left Hospital Pathology and was now accepting patients of my own. And I also sent a letter to all the primary care physicians telling them about the availability of my services.

---

18. Consider videorecording the mock examination. The witness can better understand your feedback if they see what the camera saw. Use this technique sparingly, however, so the witness does not become overly self-conscious about their appearance. *See* section 17.4.9.

L: Is that all?

W: Yeah, I think so.

L: Okay, let me become your lawyer again. What I heard from your answer was that you didn't do anything to get pathology patients except contact hospitals and PCPs. Didn't you tell me that when you went out on your own, you set up a website?

W: Oh yeah, that's true.

L: And as I recall, you also did some research on how to start your own practice and made some phone calls to doctors to let them know you were now taking patients?

W: That's true.

L: Did you ever tell other doctors at parties and medical association meetings that you were now out on your own and accepting patients?

W: Sure, it would come up, and I would let them know.

L: Okay, would it be truthful and accurate to include those facts in your answer?

W: Yes, it would.

L: How do you feel about including that in your response?

W: Yes, that's a better answer. It's true.

L: Okay, let's try it again. Imagine I am the lawyer for Hospital Pathology. Tell me everything you did to generate patients when you went out on your own.

Note what went on here. Based on what the witness had stated previously, the lawyer actively suggested what the full and true answer could be and even how it could be phrased. The lawyer was careful, however, to make sure the witness also believed the proposed answer was accurate and true, giving the witness space to disagree. The lawyer did not merely suggest a better way to answer, but had the witness practice giving the better answer. The substantive information came from the witness or documents in the case to avoid improper "coaching." The witness's response must reflect the witness's true understanding not only for ethical reasons, but also so the witness can confidently defend their answer if pressed further at the deposition.

In the above example, the lawyer first assumed the role of the deposing counsel (rather than having a colleague play that role) and from time to time stepped out of that role to help the witness complete and formulate answers as the preparing lawyer. This process can confuse the witness and, of course, takes the preparing lawyer out of the role they will ultimately play at the deposition—that of defending counsel. Assign another lawyer to the role of questioning counsel during the preparation session whenever possible. You can then stay in the role of defender and stop the questioning whenever the witness needs help in the manner or content of the answers.

17.4.8 Familiarize the Witness with Aggressive Questioning

The witness should not suffer the shock of an aggressive examination for the first time during the deposition. Instead, introduce the witness to this type of questioning during the preparation session, so they will less likely become angry or intimidated when deposing counsel tries the tactic at the deposition. Again, another lawyer should, ideally, play the role of the deposing attorney; whoever plays that role should act as much like deposing counsel as possible in style and demeanor. Consider the following example:

Lawyer 1: Sometimes aggressive questions can make a witness upset. The important thing is not to get angry or intimidated by what is happening. Just remain cool and answer the questions as best you can. Let me show you what I mean by this. Pretend we are at the deposition and Mary, my partner here, is opposing counsel. Go ahead, Mary.

Lawyer 2: Now Doctor, you never ran any advertisements in the *Nita Medical Association Journal* saying you were available to accept patients?

Witness: No, I didn't.

Lawyer 2: You know every doctor in the area receives a copy of the *Journal*, right?

Witness: Yes.

Lawyer 2: A three-by-five-inch ad would cost only $250?

Witness: I don't know what the advertising rates are.

Lawyer 2: You never bothered to check, did you?

Witness: Well, no.

Lawyer 2: But you'd agree the *Journal* is an inexpensive way of making sure the physicians in the area know about your services?

Witness:	Well, look, doctors don't read those ads or take them seriously. I've talked with lots of doctors through the years, and I never heard of any of them bothering to read those ads, and when I talked with other doctors who had started their own practices, none of them thought it was a good idea to run an ad like that.
Lawyer 2:	And you didn't bother checking on this inexpensive way of informing physicians in the area because you weren't relying on your own efforts to get patients.
Witness:	Well, I mean, it wasn't all up to me.
Lawyer 2:	That's right, because you were counting on the hospital to get you your participants.
Witness:	Well, yeah. I mean, no!

Lawyer 1: Okay. Let's take a break from the questioning for a moment and talk about what just happened. You did well remaining calm and answering the questions at the beginning. But as the questions continued, how did you feel?

Witness: Frustrated. Trapped.

Lawyer 1: Right. And you became defensive explaining why you didn't check into the *Journal* and that seemed to throw you off on the later questions. The question was simply whether you'd agree that the *Journal* was an inexpensive way of alerting physicians. If you agree, say "yes." If you don't agree, just say "no." If the attorney asks why, you can explain why.

Witness: Yes. I was starting to get angry.

Lawyer 1: Yes, and you know that anger won't help you. It won't help you focus. You may say more than you should, and more or less than you mean, when you speak from anger. Keep calm and listen to the question. If you understand it and know the answer, answer honestly and stop. That's how you defeat an aggressive questioner. So, let's try this again.

Note that the attorney was very specific about what the witness did well, what the witness could improve upon, and how the witness could improve.

Keep the examples of aggressive examination short. Even though the witness understands intellectually that your colleague is merely playing the role of opposing counsel, being treated in such a hostile fashion is still irritating. The idea is not to make the witness angry with their own lawyers, but to prepare the witness to deal with this type of questioning. Using one of your colleagues to conduct the cross will reduce the possibility of any damage to your relationship with the witness.

Also, use some of the tactics that you warned the witness about (*see* section 17.3.4), and see how the witness responds. If the witness responds well, point it out. If the witness does not do well, remind the witness in an encouraging way to follow your advice and try it again.

17.4.9   *Use Video to Prepare the Witness*

Some witnesses require intensive work to adjust speech habits or mannerisms that distract from their testimony. Often when you point out such things in your feedback, the witness does not believe they did what you claim they did, but it is difficult for them to argue with a video showing the problems. Stuffy corporate executives, pompous experts, and mumbling fact witnesses can all markedly step up their performances if they are shown video of the mock examination.

> *The most effective mock deposition simulates the actual deposition environment:*
>
> * *time of day;*
> * *whether in-person or remote;*
> * *video or not;*
> * *tough questions likely asked;*
> * *documents likely shown; and*
> * *tactics and personality of the deposing attorney.*

It can be helpful to record a fifteen-minute segment of the mock examination, review it with the witness, and then record another segment with further suggestions for improvement. For key witnesses in big-dollar cases, communications consultants can help identify and cure problems that interfere with the witness effectively presenting testimony.

That said, using video in preparation sessions for stenographic depositions is necessary only if the witness's problems are severe. Since the trier of fact will never see the witness's appearance at the deposition, the value of using video in the preparation is outweighed by the concern that too much focus on mannerisms and expressions will make the witness so worried about how they look that they blow an answer in the deposition. There is vastly greater reason to use video in the preparation sessions if the deposition is going to be recorded by video.[19]

17.5 Final Instructions

In this final portion of the preparation session, address any other concerns of the witness, make sure you have each other's best contact information, and take care of the remaining preparation details.

17.5.1 Where to Meet

Never meet the witness at the deposing attorney's office for the deposition. The chances are too great that the witness will have a conversation with a party, opposing counsel, or the opposing law firm personnel, which you do not want the witness to have. It is also very likely that the witness will have some last-minute questions or concerns to raise with you, which are best addressed outside of the opposing counsel's office. Meet the witness at a coffee shop or at your office for final preparations and go to the deposition site together. Allow plenty of time to get there.

17.5.2 What to Wear

The witness's attire affects their credibility. In general, a suit or business casual attire will be appropriate, so long as it is comfortable for the witness. If the deposition is to be recorded by video, other considerations apply: for a shirt or blouse, a light blue or other pastel color is more camera-friendly than white; avoid stripes, checkered patterns, distracting jewelry, or garish ties.

17.5.3 What to Bring

One of a defending attorney's less pleasant experiences at a deposition occurs when a witness suddenly reaches into his pocket and pulls out a set of notes that counsel has never seen. That unwelcome surprise gets worse when it becomes apparent that the witness has scribbled all sorts of damaging comments about the weakness of the case. If the witness uses the notes to refresh their memory, little can be done to keep them out of opposing counsel's hands.

The scene just described occurs if, after the preparation session, the witness goes home and starts worrying about what questions will be asked the next day. The witness

---

19. The question arises whether such video rehearsals are discoverable. The better rule is that these videos, like an attorney's notes taken during preparation sessions, constitute attorney work product and are protected from discovery. The order of questioning, the subjects prepared, the suggestions from the attorney or consultant all reflect the attorney's approach to and preparation of the case. The fact that video technology provides an especially effective way of preparing does not reduce the protection courts should accord the attorney's efforts.

thinks that a few notes will help keep events straight and keep counsel's comments in mind, and the witness can refer to the notes if they forget during the deposition.

To prevent this from happening, instruct witnesses not to make notes and to bring nothing to the deposition—no notes, documents, or anything else. When you meet on the morning of the deposition, ask whether the witness has any notes or other papers and, if so, take them away before the deposition begins. It is better to be safe than sorry.

CHECKLIST
PREPARING THE WITNESS TO BE DEPOSED

✔ Schedule ample time for the deposition preparation session(s).

✔ Tailor the session to the role, experience level, and personality of the witness.

✔ Organize the preparation session(s) into "check-in," "procedural," and "substantive" phases.

✔ In the check-in phase:
- ✓ Explain confidentiality and the attorney-client privilege, to the extent applicable;
- ✓ Allow the witness to vent concerns and respond with realistic assurances;
- ✓ Set expectations for the preparation session regarding length and content;
- ✓ Obtain the witness's commitment to the session and to telling you everything.

✔ In the procedural phase:
- ✓ Explain the deposition environment—how it looks, who is there, what happens;
- ✓ Explain and model the "One Concept and Three Rules" method of answering questions—tell the truth; understand the question, answer the question honestly, and that's it;
- ✓ Equip the witness to meet common tactics of deposing attorneys, including use of silence, misstating testimony, leading questions, "third degree" interrogation, exhortations to comply with the oath to tell the truth, and more;
- ✓ Inform the witness about the availability of breaks and conferences during the deposition, consistent with the law of the jurisdiction;
- ✓ Explain what to do with objections and instructions not to answer;
- ✓ Work with the witness on how to handle documents;
- ✓ Explain the need to keep cool and provide tools to do so.

✔ In the substantive phase:
- ✓ Exhort the witness to disclose all the dirty laundry of the case and the witness during the preparation session;
- ✓ Explain the issues in the case and the witness's role;
- ✓ Cover likely deposition questions on the witness's background and preparation for deposition, including how to answer questions on documents reviewed;
- ✓ Review the substantive events in an orderly manner, incorporating key non-privileged documents to assist recollection and documents likely to be used as exhibits at the deposition;
- ✓ Conduct a mock deposition, preferably using a colleague in the role of opposing counsel, and provide feedback to the witness on the substance and delivery of the witness's answers;
- ✓ Familiarize the witness with aggressive questioning;
- ✓ Use video to help prepare the witness.

✔ Instruct the witness on where to meet, what to wear, and what to bring.

CHAPTER EIGHTEEN

DEFENDING THE DEPOSITION

*The worst thing that can happen to a good
cause is not to be skillfully attacked, but to be
ineptly defended.*

—Frederic Bastiat

Defending a deposition witness will be more effective if you staunchly protect the witness in line with the client's interests and the applicable rules. The defense will ultimately be deemed successful if, as a result of these efforts, the witness leaves the deposition session with the client in at least as good a position as when the deposition started, and you leave with a better idea of the opponent's case. While much of the hard work of defending the witness is accomplished during the preparation session (*see* Chapter Seventeen), there is still plenty to do at the deposition.

To this end, this chapter addresses the following roles and responsibilities of the defending attorney during the deposition: supporting and protecting the witness; entering into only beneficial stipulations; clarifying the record when necessary and appropriate; discerning the deposing attorney's tactics and case theories; conferring with the witness and taking breaks to the extent the jurisdiction allows; curbing witness behavior; properly stating objections to preserve them for the court's later

> **In This Chapter:**
> - *Supporting and protecting the witness*
> - *Beneficial stipulations*
> - *Clarifying the record*
> - *Discerning tactics and case theories*
> - *Conferring with the witness and taking breaks*
> - *Curbing witness behavior*
> - *Properly stating objections*
> - *Instructing the witness not to answer*
> - *Seeking protective orders*
> - *Questioning the witness*
> - *Securing the right to correct the transcript*

ruling; instructing the witness not to answer to prevent disclosure of privileged and other confidential information; seeking protective orders and terminating the deposition as need be according to the rules; questioning the witness if prudent; and, in federal court, securing the witness's right to review and correct the deposition transcript.

18.1 Supporting and Protecting the Witness

Being deposed is not fun. It is stressful and usually unpleasant. It involves a foreign process in an unfamiliar location, with much at stake. Party witnesses worry whether they are answering correctly or in a way that might cause them to lose the case. Nonparty employees worry that their answers might lose them their jobs, that people whose opinion they value may think they did something wrong, or that they may get someone in trouble. Nonparty witnesses who have no connection to the case usually do not want to be there and have no need for the confrontation that typically arises in a deposition. The deposing attorney often challenges and argues with the witness, may ask personally embarrassing questions, and may even insinuate that the witness is a scoundrel and a liar. Being a witness at a deposition can be a horrible experience.

One of your most important tasks is providing the witness with emotional support and preventing the stress of the proceeding from interfering with the witness's efforts to give accurate and persuasive testimony. A witness who feels secure and protected will be more comfortable defending their actions, fending off the questioning attorney's efforts to shake their story, and avoiding unfortunate admissions.

There are limits, however, to what you can do to protect the witness at the deposition. Witnesses must answer the questions put to them except in very limited circumstances, even if those questions seek information that is embarrassing or harmful to the witness's position. You cannot object to questions without a good faith basis, tell the witness how to answer, or instruct them not to answer, except on very limited grounds. You cannot undermine the process or conceal evidence. Sanctions may be imposed if you do, and such conduct may violate civility rules and ethical canons.

So how do we help the witness feel secure during the deposition? We will talk about proper objections and instructions later in this chapter, but for now let's consider several other techniques.

18.1.1 Sit Close

In a stenographic, in-person deposition, some suggest that the defending attorney sit between the witness and the reporter, while others place the witness between the reporter and the attorney. Either way, sit close to the witness and sit forward (close to the table) to remain within the deponent's view, giving the witness a degree of comfort.

Sitting forward near the witness's elbow gives you, as the defending attorney, other advantages as well: you stay more involved in the deposition and have more of a presence; the witness will less likely fall into a conversation with deposing counsel that can lead to ill-advised volunteering; and when you make objections or instruct the witness not to answer, you can stop the witness from blurting out an answer by slightly raising a hand. At the witness's elbow, you are also positioned to exercise two of the more important—albeit, limited—rights available to the defending attorney: the opportunity to consult with the witness at the table and the ability to take a break for a brief period to confer with the witness outside the deposition room, to the extent permitted by the jurisdiction (*see* sections 18.5–18.6, below).

If the deposition is recorded by video, the deponent is usually filmed alone in the shot, so adjust your positioning so as not to appear in the frame. Nonetheless, sit as closely to the witness as possible. As the need arises, do what is necessary (and ethical) to support and protect the witness.

18.1.2   Always Be There

Protecting the witness starts before the deposition begins, continues after the deposition ends, and includes breaks. Again, never meet the witness at opposing counsel's office; arrange instead to meet the witness elsewhere and arrive at the deposition together. Once there, while everyone is filling up their coffee cups and getting comfortable, do not let the witness chat with opposing counsel before the deposition starts. Even if the witness does not disclose anything of substance, casual moments with opposing counsel can cause the witness to lower their guard. Never leave the witness alone in the deposition room: if you must leave the room for a telephone call or a restroom break, take the witness out of the room as well. During restroom breaks, instruct the witness not to speak with anyone—opposing counsel, paralegals, friends, strangers, or office staff. Even though it is inappropriate, deposing counsel frequently tries to engage the witness in conversation when defending counsel is absent or occupied. Although deposing counsel always defends those conversations as "merely trying to make the witness comfortable"—and usually that is true—avoid even those communications.

18.1.3   Beware After Lunch and 4:00

The two most hazardous times for a deposition witness are after lunch, roughly between 1:00 p.m. and 3:00 p.m., when our circadian rhythms hit a low point, and after 4:00 p.m., when the deposition participants become weary. These are deposing attorneys' favorite times to address complicated issues with the witness and lead the witness into admissions and traps. You will have warned the witness about this during the preparation session, but be especially vigilant at these times; carefully assess the witness's ability to discern the deposing attorney's questions and consider, as we discuss below, the need to take a quick break.

18.1.4 *Adapt to Remote Depositions*

Supporting and protecting the witness is more difficult when the deposition is held remotely and you are not in the same room as the witness. In that case, you cannot "sit close" and will not be at the witness's side physically, but your face will be on the screen for the witness to see. Keep your camera on during the deposition unless a court order requires otherwise. In remote depositions where you are in the witness's room, sit as close as possible. Before the deposition, hold an online deposition practice session to familiarize the witness with the remote configuration. Use the same platform and physical setup that will be used for the deposition.

18.2 Entering into Stipulations

We discussed the wisdom of agreeing (or not agreeing) to various stipulations in section 6.2. Essentially, do not enter into any stipulation, even the so-called "usual stipulations," without knowing what it means and specifying what it means on the record. As a default, decline any stipulation and insist on proceeding according to the federal rules (or the state rules if those apply). As the defending attorney, however, consider stipulating that all objections (except for privilege and other matters that would justify instructing the witness not to answer) are preserved—meaning that any objections that would otherwise have to be made at the deposition to avoid a waiver do not have to be made. This saves time; it also typically benefits you because it precludes any inadvertent waiver of an objection and gives you until trial (or a summary judgment motion) to digest the questions and answers and determine what objections you should assert. A downside of preserving objections is that without objections to make, you will appear less involved in the deposition.

18.3 Clarifying the Record

Depositions result in a transcript or video recording of the testimony that can be used for various purposes, including at trial (*see* Chapter Fifteen). The deposition transcript may be clear and understandable or a muddled jumble of words incomprehensible to both judge and jurors.

The question is: "Which is better—clear or muddled?" Is your client's best interest served by a clear record, or is the client better off if opposing counsel's transcript is a mass of confusion? The answer to this question depends on the topics under examination and whether the witness's answers are favorable or unfavorable to the client's position. It is best if helpful answers are clear and understandable; harmful answers are better left obtuse, incomprehensible, and less usable in the future.

To make this decision—clear or muddled—first be alert enough during the deposition to hear ambiguity in the witness's answers. Answers such as "It was from here to there," or "It was right here at this point on the map that I first saw the other car," are likely going to be useless if the deposition is later offered at trial. Even though everyone in the deposition room could see exactly where the witness was pointing when these answers were given, the judge or jurors will be left without a clue to the location of "here" and "there" or to the point on the map to which the witness was referring, especially if the deposition was not recorded by video.

If you prefer muddled because the answer is harmful to your client's claim or defense, sit quietly. You have no duty to clarify a record muddled by deposing counsel's carelessness. If the answer is helpful, on the other hand, state for the record what the witness is doing: "Let the record reflect that the witness is indicating from their chair to counsel's chair, a distance of approximately five feet," or "Counsel, perhaps you could have the witness mark with the letter 'A' where they are pointing on the map, which has been marked as Deposition Exhibit 12."[1]

18.4 Discerning the Deposing Attorney's Tactics and Case Theories

As you listen to the deposing counsel's questions, try to figure out what counsel is up to. Is counsel heading into an area that is more likely objectionable? Is counsel's approach one you had not anticipated or discussed with the witness? Is it clear from the questioning what factual theories and legal theories counsel is pursuing? These observations will help your discussions with the witness during breaks. It will also help you prepare other witnesses for their depositions, and it could spur legal research and prompt reassessment of case theories, the settlement value of the case, and prospects for trial.

18.5 Conferring with the Witness

As mentioned, one reason to sit next to the witness is to allow you and the witness to confer quickly and easily about a question or answer when appropriate. Assuming you do not abuse such conferences to obstruct the deposition, there is no limit on the number of times you and the witness can confer—unless, of course, such conferences are precluded by a discovery order, local rule, or the case law in the applicable jurisdiction.

More and more judges are issuing orders that do not allow conferences between the defending lawyer and the witness during the pendency of the deposition—even during breaks and recesses and even if requested by the witness—except when necessary to discuss whether to assert a privilege or when required as a matter of professional responsibility to ensure that the witness is not committing perjury.[2] It

---

1. All things considered, the default position should favor "clear" over "muddled." If the transcript is clear, at least you know what you've got and how it will later be interpreted.
2. *See, e.g.*, Hall v. Clifton Precision, 150 F.R.D. 525, 528–30 (E.D. Pa. 1993); Chapsky v. Baxter Healthcare, Mueller Div., 1995 WL 327348, 1995 U.S. Dist. LEXIS 2609 (N.D. Ill. 1994). Hall represents perhaps the extreme constraints on counsel at deposition, where the court opted to impose draconian restrictions due to counsel's behavior.

is therefore imperative that you know where the jurisdiction draws the line between permissible and impermissible conferences.

Assuming, however, that your jurisdiction permits attorney-client conferences for reasons other than exploring privilege, the following can occur.

If no question is pending, you can confer with the witness to advise about procedures as well as privilege. A witness may forget all that was discussed at the preparation session and start volunteering information that was not sought by the deposing attorney, advocate the merits of the case, or spout off intemperate statements. Your first reaction may be to simply remind the witness aloud, "just answer the question" after the witness has answered the question.[3]

Also, after the witness has answered, you can lean over and, *sotto voce*, remind the witness not to argue the case or volunteer information beyond what is called for by the question. This approach leaves the conference off the record because it is whispered and inaudible to the reporter and opposing counsel. The problem is that, for all the deposing counsel knows, you are telling the witness substantive information to include in the answers. If done too much, it will look bad to the deposing attorney—who will (and should) note the incident on the record—as well as to any judge who is called upon to review the videorecording of the deposition or a transcript containing the deposing attorney's protests.

In severe situations, after an answer is completed, some defending attorneys may invoke the "elbow rule," taking the client-witness by the elbow and stating, "We're taking a break here," and going into the hallway or a vacant office to straighten things out. Deposing counsel will probably try to prevent this interruption by saying something like, "You can't do that," or "You can take a break after I finish this line of questioning," or "Let's break after this next question," or "Get back here right now," but deposing counsel cannot prevent you and the witness from stepping outside for a moment. You can use the "elbow rule" if the witness is getting out of control and no break is imminent; it can take just a minute in the hallway to remind the witness of the rules discussed in witness preparation or to get the witness cooled down. But be careful here. Do not make this a normal practice. Know your jurisdiction's rules and do not unethically interfere with the deposing attorney legitimately obtaining testimony. You may have to defend what you did to the judge or

---

3. As a caveat, some view this to constitute coaching the witness. In most instances, however, if you are not cutting off the witness mid-answer but admonishing the witness after the witness has answered, this is merely reminding the witness not to respond with more information than the deposing attorney requested. The deposing attorney is not entitled to more than what they requested, so if your statement is not depriving the deposing attorney of anything to which they are entitled, it should not be deemed inappropriate. The oral reminder is also more upfront than whispering the reminder to the witness, out of the earshot of the deposing attorney and court reporter. Of course, whether the practice is appropriate depends heavily on the specifics of what was asked and what was volunteered, and the more the exhortation is repeated, the more suspicious and improper it seems.

magistrate, and your reason needs to be better than the witness was giving up too much discoverable information.

While a question is pending, you can confer with the witness about privilege. If a question is pending—that is, counsel asked a question but the witness has not yet answered—it is generally impermissible to confer with the witness. Doing so runs the risk of sanctions.[4] The exception is when privileged information might be disclosed in an answer or when the witness is unsure about how to answer without divulging confidential or personal information. In such a case, there is little choice but to confer with the witness before the witness answers, because once the witness answers, it may be too late.

> *Always know the jurisdiction rules on privilege, conferences, and breaks. Keep the rules and key case cites/summaries on your notepad or phone for ready access.*

This conference adds no meaningful interruption to the proceedings because without it, you would have to object, instruct the witness not to answer, and then typically confer with the witness anyway.

In remote depositions, of course, the defending attorney cannot whisper in the witness's ear. (Well, technologically it is possible to set up the witness with an earpiece receiving communications from counsel, but that would be inappropriate and deceptive because it would not be obvious to the deposing attorney.) You must, therefore, interrupt the deposing attorney, after the witness has finished the answer, and announce that it is necessary to take a break to confer with the witness (or, if it regards a privilege, even while the question is pending). You might announce it this way: "Counsel, I want to make sure you are getting the responsive answers you are entitled to," which sounds fair and is in fact true: the intent is to tell the witness to respond to the question but not to volunteer more than what the question is calling for. You and the witness would then mute your microphones, turn off your video, and consult via a virtual breakout room or, better yet, by phone or through some private channel separate from the deposition platform.

During a break, you can (usually) confer with the witness about nearly anything. You may confer with the witness during a recess, lunch, or other break (at least if requested by the witness) to make sure the witness understood the questions, to discuss the facts, and to remind the witness of good deposition procedures,

---

4. *See* Calzaturficio S.C.A.R.P.A. S.P.A. v. Fabiano Shoe Co., Inc., 201 F.R.D. 40 (D. Mass. 2001); McKinley Infuser, Inc. v. Zdeb, 200 F.R.D. 648, 650 (D. Colo. 2001); In re Stratosphere Sec. Litig., 182 F.R.D. 614, 621 (D. Nev. 1998); *see generally* United States v. Phillip Morris, 212 F.R.D. 418, 420 (D.D.C. 2002).

as well as to explore any privilege issues.[5] Again, however, make sure that the court or jurisdiction does not have a rule to the contrary.

18.6   Taking Breaks

Speaking of breaks, ensure that the witness gets enough of them. Answering questions at a deposition is exhausting, made more so by the witness's need to be constantly alert to the wording of the questions and to give complete and precise answers. Defending a deposition, if done correctly, takes a lot of concentration and is tiring as well. Both you and the witness will become increasingly fatigued as the deposition wears on; ask for breaks to relieve the weariness and the problems that come with it. Do not be misled by the witness's protests that they are doing fine and do not need a break. Resist the temptation to "power through" to finish the deposition.

Take breaks both periodically and as needed. In the morning portion of the deposition, the questioning should go no longer than an hour and a half without a break. In the afternoon, insist on a break every hour or so. Monitor the witness and their performance—yawning, rubbing eyes, looking haggard, and sloppy answers are signs the witness needs a break. In remote depositions, the same guidance applies. "Zoom fatigue" is real and even more breaks are needed.

There is no universal rule about the number of breaks to which a witness is entitled. Some jurisdictions require that the break be requested by the witness rather than the lawyer.[6] The more breaks you take, the more it looks like you are coaching the witness as opposed to merely getting a breather. But other than that, and as long as you take the break after the witness has answered the deposing attorney's question, insist on a break to ensure that a weary witness is giving accurate answers.

18.7   Curbing Witness Misbehavior

So far, we have discussed protecting the witness from the deposing attorney and the strain of testifying. But you also have an obligation to protect witnesses from themselves and to intervene in witness misbehavior that could derail the deposition.

Try to convince your witnesses to participate appropriately in the deposition; most notably, to answer the questions put to them. Failing to rein in a client's offensive or disruptive behavior during a deposition can lead to sanctions imposed on both the witness (client) and counsel.[7] If the witness's behavior is trending towards

---

5. *See* In re Stratosphere Corp. Sec. Litig., 182 F.R.D. 614, 621 (D.C. Nev. 1998) (with a question pending, counsel may not confer except to assert a claim of privilege; if the witness does not understand a question, the witness must ask the deposing attorney to clarify; during a recess, the attorney may make sure the client did not misunderstand the question, but only if the attorney was not the one who called the recess).

6. *E.g., id.*

7. Luangisa v. Interface Operations, No. 2:11-cv-00951-RCJ-CWH, 2011 U.S. Dist. LEXIS

incivility, request a recess, go off the record, pull the witness aside, and discuss the witness's behavior. Explain that such incivility is not in the witness's best interest and may harm the case and result in the levying of sanctions.

18.8 Stating Objections

Making and responding to deposition objections probably consumes more energy, causes more frustration, and wastes more time than any other aspect of discovery. Perhaps due to a lack of confidence in their knowledge of evidence, or because they are unsure what objections are waived and what objections are preserved, attorneys at depositions object and battle over objections inordinately. Most deposition disputes could be avoided if counsel paid more attention to the law—in federal cases, the requirements of the Federal Rules of Civil Procedure and the Federal Rules of Evidence.

Study the rules about objections. Rule 32(d)(3)(A) states: "An objection to a deponent's competence—or to the competence, relevance, or materiality of testimony—is not waived by a failure to make the objection before or during the deposition, unless the ground for it might have been corrected at that time." Rule 32(d)(3)(B) states: "An objection to an error or irregularity at an oral examination is waived if: (i) it relates to the manner of taking the deposition, the form of a question or answer, the oath or affirmation, a party's conduct, or other matters that might have been corrected at that time; and (ii) it is not timely made during the deposition."

In short, under the federal rules, you need not assert any objection that cannot be cured at the deposition (and can instead assert it later if someone tries to use that portion of the deposition in a summary judgment motion or at trial), but you must assert any objection that can be cured at the deposition—otherwise, the objection will be waived. So, what cannot be cured and what can be cured? The following answers that question and summarizes objections you should make at a deposition and how to make them.[8]

139700, at *33, (D. Nev. Dec. 5, 2011) (as an officer of the court, an attorney must "take some affirmative step to ensure the deponent complies with deposition rules"); GMAC Bank v. HTFC Corp., 248 F.R.D. 182, 186, 195–99 (E.D. Pa. 2008) (sanctions imposed against defending lawyer who sat "idly by" and did not meaningfully intervene in his witness's hostile, uncivil, and vulgar conduct, interference with a fair examination, failure to answer questions, and evasive answers); State ex rel. Secretary of the DOT v. Mumford, 731 A.2d 831, 833–34, 836 (Del. Super. Ct. 1999) (attorney's pro hac vice admission revoked because he "did not take any attempts to ameliorate the disruptive and offensive conduct" of his client, who was "crude, frequently used obscenities, and even threatened the deposing attorney with physical violence").

8. There are also objections that should be made before the deposition. Rule 32(d)(1) states that errors and irregularities in the deposition notice are waived unless a written objection is promptly served on the party giving the notice. Rule 32(d)(2) states that an objection based on disqualification of the officer before whom the deposition is to be taken is waived if not made before the deposition begins or promptly after the basis of disqualification becomes known or could have been known with reasonable diligence.

18.8.1   Objections That Do Not Have to Be Made at the Deposition

Rule 32(d)(3) tells us squarely that objections to the competence of the witness and the competence, relevance, and materiality of testimony are not waived unless the problem is curable at the deposition. While it is possible to imagine circumstances where additional questions might cure these objections, the reality is that most objections to competence, relevance, and materiality cannot be cured. So, here's our list of objections that do not have to be made:

- **Competence** (Fed. R. Evid. 601).

- **Relevance and materiality** (Fed. R. Evid. 401).

- **Undue prejudice, confusion of the issues, misleading the jury, etc.** (Fed. R. Evid. 403). This is akin to relevance in that it considers the probative value of the evidence compared to the ramifications of admitting it. Whether evidence is unduly prejudicial, etc., cannot be determined until trial or an evidentiary hearing.

- **Hearsay** (Fed. R. Evid. 801, et seq.). The conventional wisdom is that a hearsay objection is not curable and therefore the failure to make the objection at the deposition is not a waiver. That makes sense, because we cannot know until trial whether the statement is being offered for its truth. (Be aware, however, that an argument can be made that a hearsay problem can be "cured" to the extent it is possible to lay a foundation for a hearsay exception, such as the business record or excited utterance exceptions, and therefore the objection would have to be raised at the deposition.)

18.8.2   Form Objections—Waived Unless Made at the Deposition

Under Rule 32(d)(3)(B), failing to object to errors or irregularities that might have been corrected if an objection had been raised at the deposition waives those objections. This includes, but is not limited to, errors in the taking of the deposition (e.g., in remote depositions, the witness or other participant cannot hear, cannot be heard, or suffers connectivity or other issues), in the form of the questions or answers (addressed in this section), in the oath or affirmation, or in the conduct of the parties.

Most objections that fall into this category are objections to the form of the question. The following examples pertain to question form, target curable errors, and require a bit of explanation.[9]

---

9. Note that, except for leading questions, there is no Federal Rule of Evidence directly governing these objections. They are instead derived from the court's general authority to regulate the mode of witness questioning. Fed. R. Evid. 611(a). Also, our list includes objections on the grounds of "asked and answered" and "assumes facts not in evidence," even though some believe these are not proper form objections for a deposition; counsel should refer to the rules of their jurisdiction and any standing orders of the court. *See generally* Boyd v. Univ. of Maryland Med. Sys., 173 F.R.D.

Leading (Fed. R. Evid. 611(c))

A leading question suggests the desired answer (e.g., "wasn't the car red" or "the car was red, correct" rather than "what color was the car"). Rule 611(c) states that, at trial, the court should allow leading questions on cross-examination, as well as when a party calls a hostile witness, an adverse party, or a witness identified with an adverse party. At a deposition, therefore, those witnesses may be asked leading questions. If the witness is a nonparty and not associated with an adverse party, leading questions would likely be impermissible unless the witness is behaving in a hostile manner.

> **Objections that do not have to be made at the deposition:**
>
> - *Competence*
> - *Relevance and materiality*
> - *Undue prejudice, confusing of the issues, misleading the jury, etc.*
> - *Hearsay*

In short, you may object to leading questions put to a deponent who is not a party, not hostile to the deposing attorney, and not associated with a party adverse to the deposing attorney. Remember, however, that leading questions are not an efficient way for the deposing attorney to learn information, so objecting might help the deposing attorney, who rephrases the questions to a more open-ended form.

Ambiguous/Vague/Unintelligible/Complex/Confusing

All these terms, which mean different things but are often used interchangeably, describe questions that do not tell the witness in a clear and understandable manner what information is being sought—e.g., questions that ask if something occurred without disclosing the time period, or questions that contain words that have multiple meanings.

Making this objection protects against later efforts by deposing counsel to cite the witness's answer as evidence of something the witness had not intended. It also forces the deposing attorney to choose whether to take the risk of the objection later being sustained (such that the answer is inadmissible at trial or in motion practice), rephrase the question (which takes time and effort), or try to get the witness to agree they understand the question (which may not be successful).[10]

143, 147 n.8 (D. Md. 1997) (stating that the most frequent grounds for objecting to the form of a question are: 1) overbroad or narrative; 2) compound; 3) asked and answered; 4) calls for speculation; 5) ambiguous or vague; 6) argumentative; 7) assumes facts not in evidence; 8) misquotes earlier testimony; 9) opinion from unqualified witness; and 10) leading where improper under Fed. R. Evid. 611 (c)).

10. Because this type of objection is so often made by defending counsel, some courts have limited its use to situations where the question is so bad that a reasonable defending lawyer could not possibly discern the subject matter, or have put the onus of seeking clarification on the witness,

Argumentative

An argumentative question is one that is asked not for the purpose of obtaining information from the witness, but to argue with the witness about the answer or a fact in the case (e.g., "Are you seriously telling me that you thought that was appropriate conduct?"). Argumentative questions can intimidate a witness into agreeing with counsel's point. Object to any argumentative question.

Asked and Answered

Object to a question as "asked and answered" when the deposing attorney asks a question that the witness has already answered. The objection is often made to combat a deposing attorney's tactic of asking a previous question in a different way to test the witness's credibility and to see if a different answer can be obtained. A debate frequently arises whether the witness truly answered the prior question and whether the new question is really the same as the prior one.

Judges rarely sustain an asked-and-answered objection unless the repetition reaches the point of harassment. Some defending lawyers make the objection regardless of whether it will ultimately be sustained, hoping to throw off the deposing attorney, slow down the questioning, and alert the witness that the question was answered before and the answer this time should be the same. This is improper without a good-faith belief that the exact question has, in fact, been answered already.

Assumes Facts Not in Evidence

A question is objectionable if it assumes a fact for which there has not been evidence. For example, "When you went to the store, did you buy anything?" assumes that the witness went to the store, and the question is objectionable if there has not been evidence that the witness had gone to the store. The defect is curable, since the deposing attorney can ask the witness about the fact that the question assumed (i.e., "Did you go to the store?").

Some debate whether "assumes facts not in evidence" is an appropriate objection in a deposition. But the generally accepted view is that a defending attorney should object to questions that assume facts, at least where there is uncertainty about the truthfulness of the assumed fact. Some deposing attorneys will deliberately place

---

such that the witness works it out with the deposing attorney rather than the witness turning to the defending attorney or the defending attorney dueling with the deposing attorney. Hall v. Clifton Precision, 150 F.R.D. 525, 530 n.10 (E.D. Pa. 1993) ("If [a] witness needs clarification, the witness may ask the deposing lawyer for clarification. A lawyer's purported lack of understanding is not a proper reason to interrupt a deposition."); Phillips v. Mfrs. Hanover Trust Co., No. 92 Civ. 8257, 1994 U.S. Dist. LEXIS 3748 (S.D.N.Y. March 29, 1994) (it is "not counsel's place to interrupt if a question is perceived to be potentially unclear to the witness;" "the witness should make the determination as to whether a question is clear and answer to the best of [their] ability").

contested or unprovable facts in questions with the hope that the witness will not notice and proceed to answer the question, thus making it appear that the witness has adopted or admitted the assumed fact.

Compound Question

Compound questions are two questions combined into one, making it difficult to tell which question the witness is answering. For example, if the witness is asked "You were driving on the left side of the road and were driving at forty-five miles per hour?" and replies "yes," it is unclear whether the witness was driving on the left side of the road, driving at forty-five miles per hour, or both.

If the compound question is phrased to call for a yes-or-no answer, object, because the trier of fact may conclude that a "yes" answer applied to all the parts of the question. On the other hand, there is less need to object if the compound question calls for more than a yes-or-no answer, because witnesses tend to respond only to the last part of the question, and the deposing attorney will often not notice that some information was never provided. For example, a witness who is asked, "When was Mega Corporation formed and how is it organized?" may respond by describing the organization of Mega Corporation or, less frequently, the year the corporation was formed, but not both. Objecting to the question as compound would prompt the deposing attorney to ask two separate questions that result in more information being revealed.

Misleading Question

A misleading question is a deceitful question. For example, it would be misleading for the deposing attorney to misrepresent a fact to get the witness to agree to a proposition: "Mr. Kaunas, we have already deposed many witnesses who believe that your car was over the center line. Now, don't you agree that you were not in your lane?" If the deposing attorney has not, in fact, deposed many witnesses and obtained this information, the question deceives the witness and is inappropriate. Always object.

Misquoting the Witness/Misstates Prior Testimony

A question is objectionable when it includes a factual predicate that misstates the deponent's testimony. (For example, "Q: How far from the intersection did you start braking? A: About 500 feet away. Q: When you started braking 300 feet or so from the intersection, how fast were you going?") Always object.

Calls for a Narrative

A question calls for a narrative when it is unfocused and overbroad. (Such as, "Tell me everything you know about how the contract with Mammoth came about.") This places an unreasonable burden on the deponent and is dangerous because it could be used to argue that the witness knows nothing more than what the witness was able to include in the deposition response.

Calls for Speculation

Although some courts have ruled to the contrary, asking the witness to speculate in the deposition is generally proper because the speculation may lead to the discovery of admissible evidence. However, an objection to the question may properly be made because the testimony, if offered at trial or into evidence, would lack the requisite foundation of personal knowledge. An example of a question asking the witness to speculate is: "What did the defendant think when you told him that you could not deliver the parts as originally scheduled?" The question, as phrased, is asking the witness to read the defendant's mind.

Calls for a Legal Conclusion

Object if the question asks a witness about the legal significance of actions, words, or documents. For example, it is objectionable to ask a witness: "Was it negligence for the defendant to be driving at seventy-five miles per hour in a twenty-five-mile-per-hour zone?" It is also usually objectionable to ask the witness to opine on the law: "Tell me what 'mitigation of damages' means?" It is permissible, however, to ask what the witness believed to be the law or the legal significance of actions, words, or documents (if the witness's belief is relevant).

Calls for an Improper Lay Opinion

Fed. R. Evid. 701 permits a lay person to give an opinion only if it is rationally based on the witness's perception, helpful to understanding the witness's testimony or determining a fact in issue, and not based on scientific, technical, or other specialized knowledge within the scope of expert witness testimony. Object when the question asks the witness for an opinion beyond these limitations (e.g., "Do you have an opinion about whether the failure to administer blood thinners contributed to your stroke?"). Depending on the type of opinion being elicited, it may or may not be curable (by having, for example, the witness testify to the facts the witness perceived), but the objection should be made.

Calls for an Opinion Beyond an Expert's Qualifications

An expert witness may not opine on matters outside their specialized knowledge (*see* Fed. R. Evid. 702). So, for example, a physician qualified to give an opinion only in the field of hematology would not be qualified to express an opinion about the prognosis for the patient's fractured femur. At a deposition, the defect would be curable, because the deposing attorney could theoretically lay a foundation for the witness's qualification as an expert in the other field. To avoid waiving the objection, object.

Calls for Hearsay (Possibly)

As mentioned, a question calling for hearsay is traditionally treated as noncurable and thus an objection does not need to be made at the deposition. But if the hearsay statement can be placed within an exception under Federal Rules of Evidence 803, 804, or 807, the defect is arguably curable and, conceivably, the objection could be waived if not made at the deposition. A prudent defending lawyer may therefore object to questions calling for hearsay, both to potentially preclude admissibility of the answers and to avoid a later argument that the objection was waived.

Calls for Privileged Information or Work Product

Fed. R. Evid. 501 provides that, in civil cases, "state law governs privilege regarding a claim or defense for which state law supplies the rule of decision." The federal common law

> **Curable Form Objections:**
>
> - *Leading*
> - *Ambiguous/vague/ unintelligible/complex/ confusing*
> - *Argumentative*
> - *Asked and answered*
> - *Assumes facts not in evidence*
> - *Compound question*
> - *Misleading question*
> - *Misquoting the witness/misstates prior testimony*
> - *Calls for a narrative*
> - *Calls for speculation*
> - *Calls for a legal conclusion*
> - *Calls for an improper lay opinion*
> - *Calls for an opinion beyond an expert's qualifications*
> - *Calls for hearsay (possibly)*
> - *Calls for privileged information or work product*

generally governs a privilege claim otherwise. There are, of course, several different privileges that might apply in a given case, including those applicable to confidential communications between attorney and client, physician and patient, psychotherapist and patient, or clergy and penitent, as well as marital or spousal privileges. Similar protection may be afforded to trial preparation material and other attorney work product.

Object to a question that calls for privileged information or attorney work product. The defect in the question may be curable, in the sense that the inquiry might be rephrased so it seeks only non-privileged information, and therefore the objection must be made at the deposition to preserve it. Moreover, the objection must be made at the deposition and accompanied by an instruction not to answer, so the witness does not disclose the privileged information and thereby waive the protection regarding that answer and potentially other information that would otherwise be protected. Although the client holds the privilege and the client could theoretically choose to waive it, always assume at the deposition that the witness will want to invoke the privilege. Follow the same procedure to protect attorney work product and trial preparation materials[11] during the deposition. We discuss instructions later in this chapter.

18.8.3 Foundation Objections—Waived Unless Made at the Deposition

Like an objection to the form of a question, which can be cured by rephrasing it, an objection to a lack of foundation, which can be cured at the deposition by asking additional questions, must be made at the deposition or it will be deemed waived. The concept of evidentiary foundations is discussed in greater detail in Chapter Eleven, but we address it here in the context of objecting at the deposition.

No Authentication (Fed. R. Evid. 901–902)

Before a witness may testify at trial about what someone said, there must be evidence showing it really was that person who said it ("I recognized his voice from hearing it the last few months"). Before a writing, recording, or photograph can be admitted into evidence, there must be evidence that it really is the thing it is purported to be ("Exhibit 2 is the letter, I recognize it and there's my signature"). Rule 901 lists many ways of authenticating evidence and Rule 902 lists items that are self-authenticating. If the deposing attorney asks about a conversation or about a document and does not elicit evidence that the voice or document is what it purports to be, object to preserve the objection.[12]

Lack of Personal Knowledge (Fed. R. Evid. 602)

Rule 602 provides that "[a] witness may testify to a matter only if evidence is introduced sufficient to support a finding that the witness has personal knowledge of the matter." In other words, before lay witnesses (as opposed to expert witnesses) can testify about an event, it must be shown they have firsthand knowledge about

---

11. *See* Fed. R. Civ. P. 26(b)(3) (limiting discovery of documents and other tangible things prepared by or for a party in anticipation of trial); Fed. R. Civ. P. 26(b)(4)(D) (limiting discovery relating to consulting expert witnesses).

12. The defending attorney should usually object because, if no objection is made at the deposition, no objection can be made on that ground to the admission of the evidence for purposes of summary judgment or trial. Nonetheless, you might choose not to object at the deposition if the authentication can be easily established through the witness (i.e., objecting will not do any good) and if the deposing attorney proceeds to elicit the authentication, the evidence will seem that much more persuasive against the client (in other words, objecting will make things worse).

it. In deposition, if the deposing attorney fails to elicit the basis for the witness's knowledge, you must object or the objection will be waived. If waived, no objection under Rule 602 could be asserted later to prevent the deposition testimony from being admitted at trial or for purposes of summary judgment.

> ### *Curable Foundation Objections:*
> - *No authentication*
> - *Lack of personal knowledge*
> - *Argumentative*
> - *Not best evidence*
> - *No foundation*

Not the Best Evidence (Fed. R. Evid. 1001, et seq.)

Under the "best evidence rule," also known as the "original document rule," the contents of a writing, recording, or photograph can be proven only with the original (or "duplicate" original) of the writing, recording, or photograph, except for some circumstances set forth in the rules. If you object on this ground at the deposition, the deposing attorney can cure the problem by presenting the witness with the original or duplicate original or exploring a possible basis for an exception under the rules. Object at the deposition not only to avoid waiving the objection, but because the witness's testimony is more likely to be accurate if the witness is first given the opportunity to view the writing, photograph, or recording.[13]

No Foundation

In some jurisdictions, it may suffice to object to a question by stating "no foundation" as an omnibus objection to any shortcoming in the evidentiary foundation—authentication, personal knowledge, best evidence, and even relevance and hearsay. In other jurisdictions, the phrase "no foundation" may not be specific enough to preserve the objection.[14]

18.8.4 How to Object

The Federal Rules of Civil Procedure specify the way to object in a deposition. Rule 30(c)(2) decrees: "An objection must be stated concisely and in a non-argumentative and non-suggestive manner."

Rule 30(c)(2) contemplates that an objection will be made by stating the word "objection" and then briefly identifying the specific legal ground. For example,

---

13. An objection under the best evidence rule might be considered an objection to form in some circumstances. If, for example, the deposing attorney asks the witness, "What did the contract state about tariffs?", the defect could be cured by changing the form to, "What did you understand the contract required you to do in regard to tariffs?"

14. Chapter Twenty-Two lists other objections appropriate in expert witness depositions.

an objection to a compound question would be stated as "Objection, compound question." An objection to a confusing question would consist of "Objection, vague." In this way, the defending attorney says enough about the perceived shortcoming of the question so the deposing attorney can cure the problem, without saying so much that it would unduly interfere with the proceedings or coach the witness.

Courts are taking more seriously the problem of "speaking objections" that go beyond what Rule 30(c)(2) allows and tell the witness how to answer. Examples of speaking objections include "Objection, vague, ambiguous, uncertain, incomprehensible, I don't see how anyone can possibly understand what you just asked;" and "No personal knowledge, the witness did not see or hear what was said so there is no way the witness can really know what was said and can't tell you what was said." Speaking objections that coach the witness, and therefore interfere with the deposition, may well lead the court to sanction the defending attorney in state courts as well as in federal courts.[15]

Some federal district courts, as well as several state courts, have adopted rules that would prohibit even objections in the straightforward form of "Objection, compound question." These jurisdictions limit the defending attorney to something akin to "Objection: Form," to further reduce the possibility that a witness may be coached through counsel's objections. An example of such a rule is found in the local rules of the United States District Court for the Eastern District of Texas:

> Objections to questions during the oral deposition are limited to 'Objection, leading' and 'Objection, form.' Objections to testimony during the oral deposition are limited to 'Objection, nonresponsive.' These objections are waived if not stated as phrased during the oral deposition. All other objections need not be made or recorded during the oral deposition to be later raised with the court. The objecting party must give a clear and concise explanation of an objection if requested by the party taking the oral deposition, or the objection is waived.[16]

Discovery orders issued in the litigation may also restrict the form of objections, so check for those too.

---

15. *E.g.*, Craig v. St. Anthony's Med. Ctr., 384 F. App'x 531, 532–33 (8th Cir. 2010); Redwood v. Dobson, 476 F.3d 462, 468–70 (7th Cir. 2007); Specht v. Google, Inc., 268 F.R.D. 596, 598–99, 603 (N.D. Ill. 2010).
16. Tx. R. Civ. P. 199.5(e).

18.8.5 Whether to Object

Not every objectionable question deserves an objection. If time allowed, you would consider what potential objections could be asserted in response to the question, whether the objection pertains to form or foundation, or, more specifically, whether the problem is curable and thus must be asserted to avoid a waiver, or not curable and thus no potential for waiver exists, and whether the advantages of making the objection (e.g., avoiding waiver, forcing the deposing attorney to ask more questions, potentially precluding the later admission of the testimony) are outweighed by the disadvantages (e.g., prompting the deposing attorney to cure the problem and thereby not only secure the admissibility of the testimony but make it more persuasive). That assessment, however, must be made within the two or three seconds between the deposing attorney's question and the witness's answer, and it is therefore difficult to do.

As a default position, if the problem with the question goes to form or foundation, object so the objection is not waived; if the problem does not go to form or foundation, but to relevance, prejudice, or competence, do not object. As the deposition goes on, you may learn that the deposing attorney does not do a good job of curing the problems and your objections should continue; or the deposing attorney may use your objections to cure the problems and ask better questions and obtain better answers, leading you to rethink your strategy. Yet another consideration is the effect the objections have on the witness. Some witnesses thrive on the protection offered by objections, while others are distracted by them. If in doubt, object.

18.8.6 When to Object

To be timely, make the objection after the question and before the answer. If the witness answers before you have a chance to object, object as soon as possible, stating something like this for the record: "I'm objecting on the ground that the question called for speculation. The witness answered so quickly that I didn't have time to object before the answer."

Interjecting your objection before the witness answers is not always easy. In preparing the witness for the deposition, some defending attorneys tell the witness to pause after the question before answering, but that is just another unnatural thing for the witness to remember to do and can look odd when the deposition is videotaped. Here are some ways to increase your chances of objecting in a timely manner:

- Know cold the grounds for the objections you are going to assert—those to form, including privilege, and foundation. A list can be found in the appendix.

- As you prepare for the deposition, consider the topics deposing counsel may cover, and where counsel might ask vague or speculative questions or struggle laying a foundation.

- Sit close to the witness and in a position where you can place your hand in front of the witness after an objectionable question is asked, and say "Objection," which will signal the witness not to answer until you have a chance to object and give you a few more seconds to articulate the grounds (or withdraw the objection).

- If a deposing attorney's question starts with "if," chances are it calls for speculation.

- If a deposing attorney's question starts with "Is it fair to say" or "In other words," listen carefully because it may be misstating the witness's prior testimony.

- If a question starts with "did you," "were you," and the like, listen to make sure it is clear what time frame the deposing attorney is referencing; it may or may not be clear from the context of the question, but the deposing attorney may later take the answer out of context.

- If a question starts with "did you," "were you," or is otherwise leading, and the witness is a nonparty that is not associated with a party adverse to the deposing attorney, object that the question is leading.

18.8.7 Make a Correct and Specific Objection

Objecting on the wrong ground or failing to object with specificity can constitute a waiver of the objection. Therefore, object on all the grounds that come to mind and for which you have a good faith basis. For example, "Objection: Calls for speculation, lack of foundation, no personal knowledge."

How specific the objection must be depends on the jurisdiction. Unless required by local rule or court order, a generic statement of "Objection" or "Objection: Form" is usually insufficient. Make your objection specific enough for the taking lawyer to know the claimed defect in the question (e.g., "Objection, compound"). Otherwise, the opportunity to cure the defect—the presumed point of

Spotting Curable Objections	
Question starts with	Ground
• "If"	• Speculation
• "Is it fair to say" • "In other words"	• Misstating prior testimony
• "Did you" • "Were you"	• Vague (timeframe) • Leading

objections—would be meaningless. Similarly, the judge needs to know from the transcript what you were complaining about when the judge reviews the transcript at a later proceeding.

> *To view a video demonstration of Defending the Deposition (Objections), scan the QR code (print version) or click here.*

18.9   Instructing Not to Answer

As also discussed in Chapter Thirteen, Rule 30(c)(2) sharply curtails the situations in which an attorney may instruct a witness not to answer a question: "A person may instruct a deponent not to answer only when necessary to preserve a privilege, to enforce a limitation ordered by the court, or to present a motion under Rule 30(d)(3)." Rule 30(d)(3) refers to adjourning the deposition to seek an order terminating or limiting the deposition because it is being conducted in bad faith or in such a manner as unreasonably to annoy, embarrass, or oppress the deponent. Therefore, there are three—and only three—grounds for instructing the witness:

- **To preserve a privilege** such as protection for confidential communications between attorney and client, physician or psychiatrist and patient, or cleric and penitent; or a marital or spousal privilege; or attorney work product; *see* Fed. R. Evid. 501.

- **To enforce a limitation ordered by a court** such as a court order limiting inquiry into trade secret or confidential information.

- **To adjourn the deposition to seek an order ending or limiting the deposition** because it is conducted in bad faith or to unreasonably annoy, embarrass, or oppress the witness (such as impermissibly delving into irrelevant private information).

You cannot instruct a witness not to answer a question on the ground of relevance (unless it gets to the point of harassment and you intend to seek a protective order), or merely because you think the question is objectionable or too difficult to answer.

Attorneys who insist on doing so are at risk of being sanctioned.[17]

The decision to instruct a witness not to answer a question is a weighty one, because if you choose incorrectly, the consequences can be great. If you instruct the witness not to answer a question that the court later determines is proper, the court can require you or your client to pay the reasonable expenses, including attorney fees, of the questioning attorney

> **Instruct the witness *not to* answer:**
>
> - *To preserve a privilege.*
> - *To enforce a limitation ordered by a court.*
> - *To adjourn the deposition to seek an order ending or limiting the deposition.*

in obtaining the order compelling an answer. On the other hand, if you allow the witness to answer the question, you risk both losing the protections of the privilege, or the court protective order you had already obtained for that question, and waiving them for the future as well.

The full calculus of deciding whether to instruct the witness not to answer runs something like this. On the one hand, if I instruct the witness not to answer, how likely is it that opposing counsel will bring a motion to compel? If opposing counsel brings a motion to compel, how likely is it that the court will grant it and compel an answer? If the court grants the motion, how likely is it that I or my client will be required to pay the opponent's fees and expenses? On the other hand, what will be lost if I don't instruct? If the ground is privilege or an existing protective order, will I waive those protections? If the ground is harassment, will I be allowing the deposing attorney to engage in unacceptable conduct at the expense of the witness, who might respond or testify in all sorts of ways as a result? But how likely is it that the court will agree and grant a protective order?

If in doubt, and as a rule of thumb, so long as you have a good faith basis for the instruction, instruct. There is just too much to lose if you don't, and typically sanctions will not be imposed if you have a substantial justification for your position. And if you decide later in the deposition that your instruction was incorrect, you can allow the question to be asked while the deposition is still in session; if the deposition has ended, avoid expensive motion practice by offering to answer the question as an interrogatory. Failing that, work out some additional deposition time for the deposing attorney. And it is possible, of course, that the deposing attorney will not even pursue the matter.

---

17. *See, e.g.*, Resolution Trust Corp. v. Dabney, 73 F.3d 262, 266 (10th Cir. 1995) ("It is inappropriate to instruct a witness not to answer a question on the basis of relevance."); Specht v. Google, Inc., 268 F.R.D. 596, 599 (N.D. Ill. 2010) ("[Defending counsel] egregiously violated Rule 30(c)(2) by instructing [the witness] not to answer a question because his answer would be a 'guess.'")

If you decide to instruct the witness not to answer, make it clear to the witness that you do not want them to answer the question, and state for opposing counsel (and the record) one of the three bases under Rule 30(c)(2). If the instruction is on the ground of privilege, you must say so explicitly and, if not obvious from the context, "describe the nature of the documents, communications, or tangible things not . . . disclosed" in a manner that does not reveal the protected information but allows other parties to assess the privilege claim (Rule 26(b)(5)). In most instances, the instruction to the witness will therefore look like this ("DC" refers to defending counsel):

> Q: Now, Mr. Vargas, did you ever receive any advice from your attorney concerning whether it was proper to terminate the contract?

> DC: Objection. Calls for information protected by the attorney-client privilege. (Turning to witness.) I instruct the witness not to answer.

> Q: Mr. Vargas, are you going to follow your attorney's instruction?

> A: Yes.

Note that the defending attorney turned to the witness when stating that they were instructing the witness not to answer. Establish eye contact with the witness as if to say—or literally saying, if needed—"This is important: I am instructing you not to answer this question on the ground of attorney-client privilege." If the witness nevertheless starts to answer the question, interrupt and tell the witness not to answer. (One of the matters you must cover during deposition preparation is what to do when an instruction not to answer is given. As addressed in section 17.3.7, you must tell the witness not to answer the question: if asked by the deposing attorney whether an answer will be given, the witness should respond, "No"; if asked whether the witness is going to follow the attorney's instruction, the witness should respond, "Yes.")

If the instruction was on the ground of privilege, attorney work-product, or trial preparation materials, the defending counsel must allow the witness to provide sufficient information for the deposing attorney to determine whether the assertion of the privilege was proper, and for the judge to have sufficient information to rule on either a request for a protective order to enforce the claim of privilege or a motion to compel to overcome the claim of privilege. *See* Rule 26(b)(5)(A).

Therefore, be prepared to allow the deposing attorney to ask, and allow the witness to provide, the following information so the deposing attorney can explore the claimed basis for the privilege: name of the client; name of the person spoken to; date of the communication and date range of the privileged relationship; place of the communication; people present during the communication; anyone to whom the subject matter of the communication was given orally or in writing; the general nature and purpose of the communication; and whether the communication was recorded and, if so, to whom the recording was disclosed and where it is being kept. Deposing counsel can also ask follow-up questions about these factors to attempt to show that the communication does not fall within the privilege because no privilege attached, there was a waiver, or there is an exception that allows disclosure. Remain vigilant that privileged information is not being disclosed; you may want to raise a continuing objection on privilege grounds to make it clear that the substance of the communication is still being protected.

If the instruction was on the ground of a preexisting protective order, make sure you know the scope of the protective order; take a copy of the order with you to the deposition.

If the instruction was on the ground of harassment, with the intent of seeking a new protective order, other considerations apply. First, of course, you must have a sufficient and good-faith basis for the instruction. For example, the deposing attorney may be engaged in abusive behavior by yelling at the witness, the questions may be asking for trade secrets, the attorney may be asking about embarrassing matters that have absolutely nothing to do with the issues in the case ("beyond the scope of discovery under Rule 26"), the witness may be asked a misleading and derogatory question in the nature of "have you stopped beating your wife," and so forth.

Questions allowed during a privilege objection:

- *Who is the client?*
- *To whom did you speak?*
- *What was the date of the communication?*
- *During what dates was there a privileged relationship?*
- *Where did the communication take place?*
- *Who else was present during the communication?*
- *Was anyone else given information about the subject matter of the communication, either orally or in writing?*
- *What was the general nature and purpose of the communication?*
- *Was the communication was recorded?*
- *If so, to whom was the recording disclosed and where it is being kept?*

Second, federal cases caution defending attorneys against merely instructing the witness not to answer a question believed to be harassing, without also seeking a protective order by presenting the matter to the court under Rule 30(d)(3).[18] And while

---

18. *E.g.*, Brinko v. Rio Props., 278 F.R.D. 576, 584 (D. Nev. 2011) (defending attorney who believes questions are argumentative or harassing should suspend the deposition and seek a protective order, or contact the court for an emergency resolution, rather than just instructing the witness not to answer).

Rule 30(d)(3) suggests that the deposition will be adjourned immediately for the defending attorney to file a motion seeking a protective order, lawyers often agree to complete the deposition before filing a motion, unless the deposing attorney is abusing the witness (e.g., yelling) as opposed to venturing into improper subject matter.

The "beyond the scope of discovery under Rule 26" basis for the instruction results in much of the heat at depositions. In the eyes of the defender, the deposing attorney has gone so far beyond the scope of the pleadings that the information sought is not relevant to any party's claims and defenses, which is the outer bound for discovery under Rule 26(b)(1). The deposing attorney, however, believes the information is relevant and perceives the defender as obstructionist. Both sides require perspective: deposing attorneys should recognize they need not turn over every rock in the field to find the worms they need to go fishing; defending counsel should give the questioner a bit of latitude, as the court likely will. Indeed, if the inquiry is not harmful or harassing the witness by probing into private matters, why help opposing counsel get back on track? Just sit back and watch the allowed deposition time slip away.

> **Consider these issues while listening to the questions:**
>
> - *Can I object to that question in good faith?*
> - *Should I?*
> - *Do I need to instruct not to answer?*
> - *Does the witness need a break?*
> - *Is the record clear?*

Finally, be alert to the deposing attorney's tactic of returning to a line of questioning later in the deposition, often toward the end when everyone is tired, and inquiring into areas that had previously prompted an instruction not to answer. Unless you have decided that the previous instruction was a mistake, repeat your objection and instruction of the witness.

> *To view a video demonstration of Defending the Deposition (Instructions), scan the QR code (print version) or click here.*

18.10 Motions for a Protective Order or Termination of the Deposition

We discussed in Chapter Sixteen that the deposition notice might prompt the witness's attorney to seek a protective order under Rule 26(c) before the deposition, to limit inquiries of the witness and keep secure trade secret or other confidential information. An equivalent protection can be obtained under Rule 30(d)(3), after the deposition has begun, to address the deposing attorney's improper questions or conduct.

Rule 30(c)(2) allows a defending attorney to instruct a witness not to answer a question for the purpose of presenting a "motion under Rule 30(d)(3)." Rule 30(d)(3) authorizes the deponent (or a party) to move, at any time during a deposition, to terminate or limit the deposition "on the ground that it is being conducted in bad faith or in a manner that unreasonably annoys, embarrasses, or oppresses the deponent or party." The motion may be filed in the court where the action is pending or where the deposition is being taken.

Under Rule 30(d)(3)(B), the court may order that the deposition be terminated or may limit its scope and manner as provided in Rule 26(c), which includes forbidding the discovery entirely, limiting the scope of the inquiry, requiring that the deposition be sealed, and imposing limitations on the disclosure of trade secrets or other specified confidential information. If the deposition is terminated under Rule 30(d), it can be resumed only by order of the court where the action is pending. Expenses, including attorney fees, may be awarded to the prevailing party if the opposing party acted without substantial justification.

Under Rule 30(d)(3)(A), the objecting deponent or party can demand that the deposition be suspended for the period needed to obtain the order. This is a powerful tool to be wielded wisely. As a practical matter, attorneys may agree to finish the deposition regarding all other topics before suspending it, which potentially benefits both the deposing attorney, who gets the rest of the witness's information without having to reconvene later, and the defending attorney, because it is clear that if the deposition is reconvened it will only be about the disputed area. Also, attorneys may be in a better frame of mind to work out a solution after the other topics have been addressed. Of course, if the deposing attorney's wrongdoing is rude and harassing treatment of the witness, immediately suspending the deposition may be necessary.[19]

---

19. While Rule 30(d)(3) states that the motion must be "filed" in the court, relief under the rule may be available by way of a telephonic conference with the court during the deposition, which will be quicker.

18.11   Defending Counsel's Questioning of the Witness

After the deposing attorney has finished questioning the witness, you have a right to ask questions of the witness as well. Traditionally, defending counsel would not do so for an obvious reason: the witness whom counsel was defending would be the client or a friendly witness, and the best place to ask those people questions is in the privacy of the defending counsel's office. There, the details of future trial testimony could be worked out in light of all the other evidence, without the opposing lawyer overhearing. But all this assumed that the end game of the litigation was a trial, when information unknown to the other side could be used to surprise the opponent. Things have changed, and now there are some situations where you should consider asking questions of the witness at the deposition.[20]

18.11.1   Favorably Influencing Settlement

The end game for most litigation these days, if not resolved by a dispositive motion, is a mediated or negotiated settlement. Parties frequently use deposition testimony as leverage points in mediations and negotiations. Revealing favorable information in a deposition ahead of a mediation can have greater impact than waiting to spring it on the other side for the first time during the mediation. Therefore, consider priming your best witnesses to take selective opportunities during their depositions to reveal favorable information. If the opportunity to reveal the favorable information does not arise during the deposing attorney's examination, ask your own questions to elicit the information and convince the opposing party of the strength of your case.

18.11.2   Witness Unavailable for Trial

Consider questioning the deposition witness if you anticipate that the witness will be unavailable for trial and the deposition will be the vehicle for presenting that witness's information to the jury. Unavailability, you will recall, is a fairly broad concept under the federal rules, including situations where the witness (even your client's employee) is outside the reach of the court's subpoena power. If you expect the witness to be unavailable, prepare the witness not only to be deposed by the other side, but also to answer your questions as if at trial.

---

20. If you are not defending the witness, but attending the deposition solely as counsel for another party in the case, questioning the witness at the deposition may be your only opportunity to find out information from the witness. If the witness has refused to be interviewed informally or it would be unethical to interview them, question the witness at the deposition for the same reasons the deposing attorney has asked questions: to find out what the witness knows and, if possible, obtain favorable admissions. Even though another party has noticed the deposition, attorneys for the other parties may question the witness subject to any court orders.

Sometimes the deposing attorney will notice the deposition of their own client, or of a witness friendly to that side, in what is known as a preservation deposition—or a *de bene esse* ("of well being") deposition—which is taken for the sole purpose of preserving the witness's testimony for trial in lieu of live testimony (*see* Chapter Twenty). In fact, any time the deposing attorney is deposing a friendly witness, suspect that the deposition is being taken to preserve the witness's testimony and prepare accordingly. Although you will not be able to interview the witness before the deposition—and you will not be a "defending" attorney at all—prepare to question the witness in the same way you would prepare if you were noticing the deposition.

18.11.3   Clarifying Ambiguous Answers

Question a friendly witness whose deposition answers are unclear or capable of several interpretations, one of which would be inconsistent with the witness's expected trial testimony or declaration in support of or opposition to a summary judgment motion. This is important for two reasons. First, looking ahead to trial, asking clarifying questions during the deposition is wise because, as part of the deposition transcript, Rule 32(a)(6) provides that those clarifications can be read to the jurors if opposing counsel tries to impeach the witness.[21] Indeed, once the witness has clarified the supposed inconsistency at the deposition, opposing counsel will be less likely to attempt the possible impeachment at the trial. Second, for purposes of summary judgment, obtaining a clarification from the witness at the deposition will make it more likely the court will accept a subsequent affidavit from the witness consistent with that clarification, and not strike it as a sham affidavit (*see* section 17.4.6).

18.11.4   Modifying Incorrect or Incomplete Answers

Provide the witness an opportunity to correct an answer given in response to the deposing attorney's questioning. Before doing so, confirm with the witness during a break that the previous answer was a mistake; inquire how they would answer if asked again and if there was a reason for the earlier mistaken testimony. When the deposition resumes and it is your turn to question the witness, elicit the correction like this: "Earlier in the deposition you stated in a response to a question by Ms. Jones that you first began considering design modifications in 2019. Was 2019 the year you started considering a design modification, or was it earlier or later?"

---

21. Rule 32(a)(6) states: "If a party offers in evidence only part of a deposition, an adverse party may require the offeror to introduce other parts that in fairness should be considered with the part introduced, and any party may itself introduce any other parts."

18.11.5 Downside and Alternatives

A potential downside to asking your witness questions is that the deposing attorney, and counsel for any other party at the deposition, may then ask additional questions, too. This extends the deposition and continues to subject the witness to inquiries. Indeed, if the deposing attorney follows up with a "redirect" examination, it is not uncommon for the redirect to be followed by a "recross" and further redirects and recrosses until everyone reaches the point of exhaustion or the time limit runs out.[22]

An alternative method of correcting a previous answer is not to wait until the end of the deposition, but to have the witness announce a correction on the record following a break in the deposing attorney's questions (after you have confirmed the correct answer with the witness). Although this may still engender follow-up questions from the deposing attorney, it tends to attract less attention than if the correction arises during your time to question the witness.

Another alternative is to ask the witness—during the deposing attorney's questioning—to clarify. Do this sparingly because it is improper to highjack the deposing attorney's examination. It could be worded something like, "Excuse me, just to clarify the record, I think the witness said 2019. Is that the correct year?" If you direct the comment to the deposing attorney, it seems like you are not trying to take over the questioning but merely inviting the deposing attorney to elicit correct information and obtain a clear record. Again, however, do this infrequently and not in a manner that coaches the witness.

Yet another alternative, where available, is not to deal with the witness's error during the deposition, but to have the witness correct the answer in an errata sheet after reviewing the deposition transcript. Beware, however, that some jurisdictions limit this method of changing answers to clerical matters—the court reporter took down something incorrectly, for example—as opposed to changing the substance of the answer. The possibility of using an errata sheet takes us to our next subchapter and is addressed at greater length in section 19.1.

18.12 Demanding the Right to Review and Make Changes

Under Rule 30(e), the witness or a party must demand, before the conclusion of the deposition, the right to review the deposition transcript or recording and to make corrections. As discussed in section 6.2.3, it makes little sense to give up the right to correct mistakes the witness has made in answering or the court reporter has made in transcribing the testimony. Therefore, if not raised at the beginning of

---

22. Rule 30(c)(1) provides that "[t]he examination and cross-examination of a deponent [should] proceed as they would at trial under the provisions of the Federal Rules of Evidence."

the deposition in a federal case, always demand the witness's right to make corrections before the deposition concludes.

The demand is typically unnecessary in state cases because the right (or requirement) is preserved by statute. Check the law of the jurisdiction.

18.13   Concluding the Deposition

No particular words must be uttered by either counsel to formally end the deposition. The deposing attorney usually says something to the effect of, "I have no further questions." If you (and counsel for any other parties) have no questions, you might add, "The deposition is concluded." If the deposing attorney tries to hold open the deposition pending a court ruling or production of documents, express your disagreement, if any, on the record.

CHECKLIST
DEFENDING THE DEPOSITION

✔ Support and protect the witness by sitting close and maintaining a presence, whether in person or online.

✔ Enter into stipulations with opposing counsel only if clearly beneficial to the client (i.e., possibly, stipulating to preserving all objections) and place any such stipulation on the record.

✔ Clarify the record if necessary, without overreaching.

✔ Listen to the deposing attorney's questions to discern their tactics and case theories.

✔ Confer with the witness as allowed by the jurisdiction.

✔ Make sure the witness takes breaks in the deposition to discuss matters, especially any privilege issues, and to ensure that the witness is fresh and focused.

✔ Anticipate objectionable questions and lines of inquiry and prepare to make objections.

✔ Object to the deposing attorney's questions, particularly to form and foundation, as prudent and as required to avoid waiver

   ✓ **Form:** leading, vague, ambiguous, argumentative, asked and answered, assumes facts not in evidence, compound, misleading, misstating testimony, calls for narrative, calls for speculation, calls for legal conclusion, improper opinion, privilege, or work product.

   ✓ **Foundation:** no authentication, lack of personal knowledge, not the best evidence.

It is unnecessary to object on relevance grounds to preserve the objection unless the defect could be cured; you cannot instruct the witness not to answer merely because a question seeks irrelevant information.

✔ Phrase objections by identifying the ground, consistent with the rules of the jurisdiction (no speaking objections).

✔ Instruct the witness not to answer only on grounds consistent with applicable law—e.g., privilege, existing court order, or to get a protective order against harassment.

✔ File a motion for a protective order or termination of the deposition if needed.

✔ Ask questions of the witness if it will favorably influence settlement, the witness is expected to be unavailable for trial, or the witness's testimony requires clarification or correction and further questioning is the best way to accomplish it.

✔ (In federal court), demand the witness's right to review and make changes to the deposition transcript.

CHAPTER NINETEEN

REVIEWING, CORRECTING, AND SUPPLEMENTING THE TRANSCRIPT

You can't always get what you want. But if
you try sometimes, you just might find,
you get what you need.

—The Rolling Stones

An error doesn't become a mistake until
you refuse to correct it.

—Orlando Aloysius Battista, later attributed to John F. Kennedy

Defending a deposition witness will be more effective if you ensure that the witness reviews and corrects any errors in the deposition transcript or recording, consistent with the rules of the jurisdiction. In this chapter, we consider how, when, and to what effect a witness may make changes to the testimony after the deposition is concluded, and any circumstances in which the witness may need to supplement that testimony.

19.1 Reviewing and Correcting the Deposition

The witness's right to review and correct the deposition transcript depends on the jurisdiction governing the deposition. Under federal law, Rule 30(e) allows a party or the witness to request—before the completion of the deposition—the opportunity to review the transcript or recording and make changes. If

> **In This Chapter:**
>
> - How a witness may change the testimony after the deposition is concluded
>
> - When a witness may change the testimony after the deposition is concluded
>
> - The effect of a witness changing the testimony after the deposition is concluded

this request is not clearly and timely made, there is no right to correct the testimony.[1] If a request to review and correct the testimony is clear and timely, Rule 30(e)(1) gives the witness thirty days after the deposition officer provides notice of the availability of the transcript or recording to make any changes. Under state law, by contrast, the rule is typically that the witness has a statutory right to review and make corrections within a specified period, unless that right is explicitly waived.[2]

Ordinarily, both sides have a strong incentive for the witness to review and correct the transcript, as discussed more fully in section 6.2.3. A court reporter may err in transcribing the testimony, and the witness may misspeak, with potentially grave ramifications. There are, of course, some possible negative ramifications for the witness who corrects a transcript as well. Opposing counsel can comment on the changes at trial, a large number of changes may suggest the testimony is unreliable, any errors missed during the witness's review may be harder to explain away, and the witness's corrections may inform opposing counsel of problem testimony or case theories. Nonetheless, the advantages of having an accurate record typically override these concerns.

We therefore recommend that no one—witness, plaintiff's counsel, or defendant's counsel—waive the right to review and correct the transcript or recording. Accordingly, where federal rules apply, claim the right affirmatively and unequivocally, preferably at the outset of the deposition (so you will not forget) and at the very least before the deposition is concluded—just say, "We request review, correction, and signature." In state court, where the right to review and correct the transcript is established by statute, neither you nor the witness should do anything to suggest a waiver.

19.1.1   Making Corrections: The Errata Sheet

The law of the jurisdiction will also dictate how the witness records any changes the witness wants to make to the transcript. Rule 30(e)(1)(B) provides that "the changes and the reasons for making them" must be set forth in a signed statement. In practice, the process of crafting this statement begins once you receive the transcript from the reporter. Arrange for the witness to read the transcript at your office or a location convenient for the witness; if the witness reviews the transcript without you present, discuss proposed changes with the witness after their review. Conform to your ethical obligations not to suborn perjury or improperly influence the witness's testimony.

After the witness reviews the transcript, create an errata sheet—or use an errata sheet supplied by the reporter—identifying the page and line numbers of the deposition testimony, the corrections, and the reasons for making the changes. The

---

1. *See, e.g.*, EBC, Inc. v. Clark Bldg. Sys., 618 F.3d 253, 270–71 (3d Cir. 2010).
2. *E.g.*, Cal. Code Civ. P. § 2025.520; N.Y. C.P.L.R. 3116.

witness signs the errata sheet and, depending on the jurisdiction, may also need to have the signature notarized. Send the completed errata sheet to the deposition officer or reporter. Under Rule 30(e), the reporter attaches the sheet to the certificate prepared under Rule 30(f)(1) and indicates in the certificate that changes were made. The corrections are included in the final bound transcript of the deposition.

An errata sheet, including the changes to be made and the reasons for those changes, may look like the following:

Corrections to Vargas Deposition of May 17

Page 17, lines 2–5:

> "should have been considered a possible sort of supplier, but never really came to a close on supplying," should read, "should have been considered a possible source of supply, but never really came close to supplying." Reason for the change: the court reporter apparently misheard my actual answer.

43:1:

> "now that I see a difference" should read, "not that I see a difference." Reason for the change: the court reporter apparently misheard my actual answer.

114:10:

> "No" should read "Yes." Reason for the change: I did not understand that the question had been phrased in the negative.

Including the reason for the change is imperative in jurisdictions requiring a persuasive justification for the correction. If the errata sheet provided by the court reporter does not give enough room to explain the reason fully, use your own form. The reason for the change should make sense in light of the original answer and the new answer, the context of the transcript, and any video of the testimony.

19.1.2   *Kinds of Corrections*

Rule 30(e)(1)(B) provides that changes may be made "in form or substance." Courts are split whether the right to make "substance" changes extends to all substantive changes the witness wants to make, or only to mistakes made by the reporter or transcriber.[3]

---

3. *See, e.g.*, United States v. Lab. Corp. of Am. Holdings, 2021 U.S. Dist. LEXIS 105824 (D.S.C. June 7, 2021) (discussing the two views).

The traditional and majority view is that the witness may make any kind of change to the testimony, including one that alters the substance of the testimony (e.g., changing "no" to "yes" or "red" to "green"), even if the change is due not to a reporter's mistake but simply because the witness does not like how they originally answered.[4] Other courts restrict changes under Rule 30(e) to corrections of the reporter's transcription errors, and distinguish between corrective and contradictory changes, concluding that a witness should not be able to change the substance of an answer given at the deposition under oath. In other words, substance cannot be changed unless the change is due to an error of the court reporter.[5]

Of the courts that permit substantive changes, some allow the change even if unaccompanied by any explanation for it. Other courts require a persuasive explanation for making the change, or the change will be stricken from the errata sheet.[6]

A court may apply a more stringent standard where the changes are used to try to create a triable issue of material fact in opposition to a summary judgment motion. Akin to the "sham affidavit" doctrine, by which affidavits or declarations in opposition to a summary judgment motion may be stricken to the extent they contradict previous deposition testimony, a court may strike changes made to the substance of deposition testimony if they appear to sandbag deposing counsel or create sham factual disputes.[7]

Because case law remains split on the extent to which a witness can make substantive changes to a deposition transcript under Rule 30(e), and because of variations in state laws, always research the law of the applicable jurisdiction.

19.1.3 Effect of Corrections

If the witness's substantive changes are permissible but substantial, a court may treat the changes as if they resulted from examination by the witness's attorney

---

4. *E.g.*, Aetna v. Express Scripts, Inc., 261 F.R.D. 72, 75 (E.D. Pa. 2009) (majority rule allows changes that contradict the original answers, even if not supported by explanations, as long as the changes comply with the rule); Agrizap, Inc. v. Woodstream Corp., 232 F.R.D. 491, 493 & n.2 (E.D. Pa. 2006) (reciting cases).

5. Garcia v. Pueblo Country Club, 299 F.3d 1233, 1242 n.5 (10th Cir. 2002) ("We do not condone counsel's allowing for material changes to deposition testimony and certainly do not approve of the use of such altered testimony that is controverted by the original testimony."); Thorn v. Sundstrand Aerospace Corp., 207 F.3d 383, 389 (7th Cir. 2000); Greenway v. Int'l Paper Co., 144 F.R.D. 322, 324 (W.D. La. 1992) ("A deposition is not a take home examination.").

6. *See* Hambleton Bros. Lumber Co. v. Balkin Enters., Inc., 397 F.3d 1217, 1224 (9th Cir. 2005) (explaining the need to provide a reason for the change, but ultimately concluding that only corrective as opposed to contradictory change is allowed); Torres v. Bd. of Educ. of City of N.Y., 137 A.D.3d 1256 (N.Y. App. Div. 2016) (errata sheet should have been stricken where it contained substantive changes in conflict with earlier hearing testimony and the purported reason for the change—that the witness misspoke and was clarifying—was insufficient).

7. *See, e.g.*, EBC, Inc. v. Clark Bldg. Sys., 618 F.3d 253, 270–71 (3d Cir. 2010); Hambleton Bros. Lumber Co. v. Balkin Enters., Inc., 397 F.3d 1217, 1224–26 (9th Cir. 2005).

at the deposition and order a resumption of the deposition so the deposing attorney can explore the witness's changes and any justifications given.[8] The deponent may have to bear the costs and attorney fees associated with the re-examination.[9] Keep this in mind before your witness makes wholesale changes to the deposition transcript.

For similar reasons, if, as deposing counsel, you receive an errata sheet, determine if the corrections are timely and in compliance with the requirements of Rule 30(e) or applicable state law. Also assess the significance of the changes, the persuasiveness of the reasons given for making them, and the number and magnitude of the changes, and consider filing a motion (after conferring with opposing counsel) to strike the errata sheet or to obtain an order resuming the deposition.

Note, also, how corrected deposition answers are used at trial. Just because the witness made changes to the answers, the original answers do not vanish; instead, they are preserved in the transcript and may be used to impeach the witness. If the deposition was of a party-opponent, the original answers are party statements that can be offered at trial for the truth of the matter asserted as well as for impeachment, with the corrections or changes being available for arguable rehabilitation. Whether impeaching the witness or using the deposition as a party statement, the deposing attorney is entitled to read the original transcript (or show the video recording); the defending attorney can then request, under Rule 32(a)(4) and Fed. R. Evid. 106, that the corrected response be read immediately thereafter so the trier of fact can decide which answer to accept.

19.2 Supplementing the Deposition

Under the federal rules, a witness generally has no duty to supplement deposition testimony.[10] In other words, if the witness learns of information after the deposition that casts doubt on their testimony, or that improves upon their testimony, there is no obligation to inform the other parties.

There are, however, some things to keep in mind. First, an exception exists in the context of expert witness depositions. As set forth in the "Notes of Advisory Committee on Rules—1993 Amendment" to Rule 26(e), the exception applies to

---

8. *See* Colin v. Thompson, 16 F.R.D. 194 (W.D. Mo. 1954) (allowing further examination of plaintiff regarding matters covered by the changes); De Seversky v. Republic Aviation Corp., 2 F.R.D. 113, 115 (E.D.N.Y. 1941) (allowing further deposition to explore new answers); Sanford v. CBS, Inc., 594 F. Supp. 713, 715 (N.D. Ill. 1984) (allowing plaintiff further deposition of the witness about why the changes were made).
9. Sanford v. CBS, Inc., 594 F. Supp. 713, 715 (N.D. Ill. 1984).
10. This contrasts with the duty under Rule 26(e) to supplement Rule 26(a) disclosures and responses to interrogatories, production requests, and requests for admission if the party learns that the disclosure or response is materially incomplete or incorrect and the supplemental information has not been made known to the other parties during discovery or in writing.

"experts from whom a written report is required under [Rule 26](a)(2)(B)," in that "changes in the opinions expressed by the expert . . . in the report or at a subsequent deposition are subject to a duty of supplemental disclosure."

Second, as with nearly all discovery rules, the parties can stipulate to different obligations for supplementation under Rule 29. Therefore, when defending a deposition, recognize that an agreement with the deposing attorney to provide further information, to produce additional documents, or to check on the accuracy of an answer, imposes an enforceable obligation.

Third, remember that a witness who testifies at trial or submits testimony in the form of an affidavit during summary judgment proceedings may be limited by their deposition testimony. A statement at trial beyond what was said in the deposition is subject to impeachment with the deposition transcript (Rule 32(a)(2)). An affidavit attesting to matters beyond what was said in the deposition may be disregarded as a sham affidavit.[11] Therefore, weigh the importance of the witness's new information, consider the likelihood that the court will allow it if accompanied by a good explanation for not disclosing it earlier, and decide whether it would be prudent to supplement the testimony voluntarily—even if it leads to a limited reconvening of the deposition—to ensure that the new information can be presented to the trier of fact.

---

11. *E.g.*, Perma Rsch. & Dev. Co. v. Singer Co., 410 F.2d 572, 577–78 (2d. Cir. 1969); Yeager v. Bowlin, 693 F.3d 1076, 1080–81 (9th Cir. 2012); *but see* Button v. Dakota, Minn. & E. R.R. Corp., 963 F.3d 824, 830–31 (8th Cir. 2020); (Baer v. Chase, 392 F.3d 609, 625–26 (3d Cir. 2004). *See* section 17.4.6.

CHECKLIST

REVIEWING, CORRECTING,
AND SUPPLEMENTING THE TRANSCRIPT

✔	Demand the right of the witness to review and correct the transcript (federal court) and do not waive the right to do so (state courts).
✔	Review the deposition transcript with the witness and prepare an errata sheet.
✔	Correct clerical errors by the court reporter as well as substantive errors by the witness, to the extent permitted by the jurisdiction.
✔	State suitable reasons for each change.
✔	Consider the possibility that too many changes or too drastic a change may lead to the deposition being reopened.
✔	Consider the possibility that opposing counsel may comment on the changes, and too many substantive changes can make the witness appear unreliable.
✔	Consider the possibility of supplementing the deposition testimony upon the discovery of new material information not disclosed in the deposition transcript, to ensure the admissibility of the new information in later proceedings.

PART FOUR

SPECIALIZED DEPOSITIONS;
VIDEO AND REMOTE DEPOSITIONS

CHAPTER TWENTY

PRESERVATION DEPOSITIONS

Words are the only thing that last forever:
They are more durable than the eternal hills.

—William Hazlitt

A deposition will be more effective if it preserves the favorable testimony of a witness who will be unavailable for trial. The deposition testimony can then be used in lieu of direct examination. It can also be used in connection with other evidentiary proceedings such as summary judgment motions. In this chapter, we look at three aspects of the preservation deposition or "deposition *de bene esse*": preparing for the deposition, taking the deposition, and defending at the deposition.

20.1 The Nature of Preservation

As explained in section 15.3.2, any deposition can substitute at trial for the live testimony of a witness who thereafter becomes unavailable for trial within the meaning of Rule 32(a)(4) or Federal Rule of Evidence 804. This unavailability can be due to the witness's death, age, illness, infirmity, or imprisonment; the inability to procure the witness's attendance at trial by subpoena; or the witness being more than 100 miles from the place of trial or outside the United States (Rule 32(a)(4)). Unavailability also occurs upon the witness's refusal to testify despite a court order or if the witness suffers a lack of memory (Fed. R. Evid. 804(a), (b)(1)).

Because any party can introduce the deposition testimony of a witness who has become unavailable, contemplate the prospect of the witness becoming unavailable at every deposition. As the deposing attorney, make sure that favorable testimony is clear and without evidentiary issues, so there is no impediment to using it later if the witness is unavailable. Also consider the ramifications of eliciting unfavorable information. If the witness becomes unavailable, portions of the

> **In This Chapter:**
> - *Preparing for the* de bene esse *deposition*
> - *Taking the deposition*
> - *Defending at the deposition*

deposition that you took for discovery purposes—that is, to find out all the witness had to say about a topic, good or bad—may contain unfavorable information that opposing counsel can place into evidence. Even worse, if you opt not to confront the witness with impeachment evidence (hoping to save the attack for trial) and the witness becomes unavailable, you may not be able to present it. While the benefits of conducting a deposition that elicits all the witness's information almost always justifies the discovery-type deposition, consider how likely it is that the witness will become unavailable.

This chapter deals with a distinct situation where, during discovery, it already appears likely that a friendly witness will be unavailable for trial, typically due to declining health or being outside the court's subpoena power. In those circumstances, preserve the friendly witness's testimony in what is known as a "preservation deposition," "trial deposition," or "deposition *de bene esse*."

The key to this type of deposition is to craft it so the testimony can be presented at trial in lieu of the witness's live direct examination, often by video. There is typically no need to use the deposition to discover what the friendly witness knows, because a witness friendly to the client can disclose all they know to counsel informally. Essentially, the preservation deposition is a pretrial production of the direct examination debuting at trial.[1]

A preservation deposition may be taken of a witness who is likely to be unavailable for trial even if it is unclear whether the witness will provide favorable testimony. This can occur when, for example, the witness is thought to have important information that might be favorable, but neither side is quite sure and the witness refuses to be interviewed. When this "unknown" witness is expected to be unavailable for trial, counsel must make the hard decision whether to take the witness's deposition: it might preserve and render admissible favorable testimony, but it might preserve and render admissible unfavorable testimony.[2]

---

1. A similar type of deposition, permitted under Rule 27, pertains to depositions to perpetuate testimony before litigation begins. Under Rule 27, a person may file a petition in district court to obtain an order authorizing the petitioner to depose an individual to perpetuate their testimony, where the petitioner expects to be in litigation and can make a showing specified by the rule. The deposition can be used under Rule 32(a) in any subsequent district court action involving the same subject matter. Rule 27(a)(4).

2. In some states, attorneys try to control this risk by conducting a discovery deposition first, then proceeding with a "trial deposition" or *de bene esse* deposition if the evidence is favorable. There is no provision in the federal rules for taking two depositions of the same deponent; where two depositions are not permitted, the beginning portion of the preservation deposition could include discovery-type questions to ascertain what the witness knows. In any event, whether a *de bene esse* deposition is taken or not, whatever was said at the discovery deposition by a witness who becomes unavailable would be admissible under Rule 32, subject to any stipulation or court order to the contrary.

20.2   Preparing to Take the Preservation Deposition

Having decided to take a deposition to preserve a witness's testimony, keep a few things in mind. First, unless there is some strategic or logistical reason not to, schedule the deposition for as early in the discovery plan as possible, especially if the witness is in precarious health or is planning to leave the country. Wait too long, and you may miss the opportunity.

Next, remember that the deposition testimony will be presented in the courtroom, and that being read deposition transcripts can render jurors slightly comatose. Placing a colleague in the witness box to read the role of the witness will only marginally increase the jurors' interest level. Thus, if finances allow, and there is no reason you would not want the jury to see the witness's appearance or demeanor, videorecord the deposition, and disclose the recording method in the deposition notice or subpoena. The jurors' attention and retention are much greater when they see and hear the testimony on video rather than merely hearing it read from a written transcript.

Finally, assuming the witness is cooperative, prepare the witness for the deposition in the same way you would prepare them to testify at trial. In the preparation session, explain the deposition process and how you will use the deposition. Regarding the substantive issues, explore the witness's story and try to resolve any internal discrepancies or weaknesses. Know what facts to elicit through the witness and review with the witness the expected questions and the witness's answers. Consistent with the ethical rules, make suggestions for improving the presentation through better word choice, order, or emphasis (*see* section 17.4.1). Incorporate documents and graphics into the presentation, just as you would in a live direct examination in the courtroom. Also discuss cross-examination topics that opposing counsel may pursue at the deposition and give the witness a taste of what cross-examination will be like.

Remember, however, that the preparation session with the witness may not be privileged. Unless the witness is a client, or a person that falls within the client's control group or within the *Upjohn* parameters, assume that what is said at the preparation session is discoverable (*see* sections 16.4.2, 17.2.2).

20.3   Taking the Preservation Deposition

Examine the witness as if the witness were testifying at trial. If the deposition is not being videorecorded, the jurors or judge will not have an opportunity to observe the witness's demeanor, so you may need to develop a more complete accreditation of the witness in the deposition. This might include details of the witness's personal background that demonstrate the witness's reliability, as well as the witness's education and employment history. If the witness's substantive testimony relates to their work on the job, some details about the job and the witness's experience can bolster their credibility. If the witness has no ties to either side of the dispute and no interest in the outcome of the litigation, emphasize that fact as well.

Because the deposition substitutes for a direct examination in the courtroom, your questions must be clear and the witness's answers must be persuasive. Carefully thinking through the best method of explaining complex matters, and even writing out some questions, can help make the testimony understandable to the judge and jurors. An effective trial lawyer learns to "self-monitor," listening to their own questions and the witness's answers to ensure they are adequately communicating the witness's important information. Paying attention to the order in which facts are presented, and usually adhering to a chronological approach, will pay off by helping the judge and jurors follow the story.

If the deposition is not recorded by video, the witness's tone of voice, facial expressions, and gestures are not reflected in the record. Account for this. For example, describe the witness's expressions aloud ("I noticed your facial expression when you answer that question. What were you feeling then?"). If the witness must give distances or illustrate movements, obtain the information in a way that the jurors, hearing the testimony later, will understand what is going on: clarify all hand gestures and descriptions, such as "from here to there," with phrases such as "let the record show that the witness has pointed to an object ten feet from the witness chair."

Deal with objections differently in a preservation deposition. When an objection occurs at a deposition taken purely for discovery purposes, you will normally not respond to the objection except to ask the witness to answer the question; the interest is more in obtaining facts from the witness and maintaining control over the questioning than in ensuring that the question is unobjectionable. When the point of the deposition is eliciting and preserving admissible testimony, your incentive is to cure any defects in the question and avoid the court later sustaining the objection and precluding use of the answer (*see* section 13.3.1). At a *de bene esse* deposition, where the whole purpose of the deposition is to use the transcript at trial, this concern is paramount. Therefore, in a preservation deposition, request the witness to answer the original question, but follow up with another question that is rephrased to cure any purported defect.

In this regard, remember that the deposition will be presented at trial as a direct examination, and leading questions are permissible only in limited circumstances—preliminary matters; when examining an adverse party, a witness identified with an adverse party, or a witness who has demonstrated hostility; or when leading questions are necessary to develop the witness's testimony. In a preservation deposition, the witness will rarely be an adverse party, identified with an adverse party, or hostile. Therefore, avoid using leading questions. An added benefit is that open-ended questions—such as questions beginning with who, what, when, where, why and how—will more likely elicit the witness's answers in a way that makes the witness appear knowledgeable and credible.

If there are any favorable documents, electronically stored information, or tangible things that only the witness can authenticate, or the witness is the best person to establish other aspects of the evidentiary foundation or explanation for such material, be sure to incorporate questions to elicit this testimony in the examination.

20.4 Defending at the Preservation Deposition

Nothing in a notice of deposition states whether a deposition is a deposition *de bene esse* for use at trial. But anytime you receive a deposition notice from an opposing party for a witness you know to be friendly to that party, the deposition is probably being taken to preserve testimony. Otherwise, it would make little sense for your opponent to take the deposition of a witness who could be interviewed and sign a declaration without you being there to ask questions.

If you receive a deposition notice (or subpoena) of a witness friendly to the deposing party, prepare to cross-examine the witness at the deposition as if it were at trial. Be ready to object to the deposing attorney's questions. "Defending" at a preservation deposition of a witness friendly to the deposing party is about defending your client's interests rather than defending the witness.[3]

Witnesses friendly to the other side will probably not consent to being interviewed before the deposition (although it's worth a try if ethically permissible). Therefore, you may go into the *de bene esse* deposition without knowing what the witness's testimony will be. You may, however, get some idea from your client, internet searches, and other investigation. If the jurisdiction allows, consider noticing a discovery deposition to be held before a *de bene esse* deposition to find out what the witness knows.

As a practical matter, conduct your "defending" questioning at the *de bene esse* deposition in part as a discovery deposition—find out all the witness's information, beyond what was brought out by the deposing attorney. This might include facts favorable to your client or matters tending to discredit the witness. There is not much risk here, since it is unlikely the witness will say anything more unfavorable than what the witness has already said when questioned by the deposing attorney (unless the deposing attorney did a lousy job). After learning the totality of what the witness has to say, switch to trial-type cross-examination to emphasize the points you want. When the deposing counsel has the excerpts from the deposition transcript read or the video played at trial, you can present the trial-type cross-examination to the jurors.

---

3. In the preservation deposition of a friendly witness, the deposing attorney defends the witness during the other side's questioning, in the sense of making objections, guarding against overly aggressive behavior and attempts to obtain privileged information, and so forth.

CHECKLIST

PRESERVATION DEPOSITIONS

✔	Identify persons who may be unavailable for trial or summary judgment motions due to issues of health, distance, or other circumstance listed in Federal Rule of Civil Procedure 32(a)(4) or Federal Rule of Evidence 804 (or state law equivalent).
✔	Consider having the deposition videorecorded to best preserve and present the testimony.
✔	Prepare the witness, if cooperative, as if preparing them to testify on direct examination at trial and to withstand cross-examination, mindful that the preparation may not be protected by privilege or the work product doctrine.
✔	At the deposition, ask questions as if presenting direct examination at trial.
✔	At the deposition, have the witness lay the evidentiary foundation for favorable documents, ESI, or tangible things, at least to the extent that only the witness can provide the foundation.
✔	Maintain a clear record.
✔	If necessary, rephrase questions to which objections are made or could be made in the future, and clarify foundations for the witness's testimony to avoid evidentiary issues later.
✔	Defend the client's interests when other attorneys examine the witness.
✔	If not the deposing attorney, consider whether you can ethically communicate with the witness before the deposition, and, if so, discuss the witness's potential testimony to prepare for the deposition (remembering the discussion is likely not privileged).
✔	If not the deposing attorney, object at the deposition and examine the witness as appropriate, mindful that the testimony will be preserved for future evidentiary use.

National Institute for Trial Advocacy

CHAPTER TWENTY-ONE

RULE 30(b)(6) DEPOSITIONS

Knowledge is power.

—Sir Francis Bacon

A deposition to obtain the information of an organization will be more effective if pursued under Rule 30(b)(6) or its state-court equivalent. Pursuant to a notice that sets forth the topics of the deposition, the organization is required to select one or more individuals to testify on its behalf, prepare those witnesses with the information reasonably available to the organization, and present the witnesses for deposition. The witness's deposition answers are binding on the organization, even to the point where they may preclude the organization from introducing other evidence on the issue in summary judgment proceedings or at trial. For the deposing attorney, the Rule 30(b)(6) deposition is one of the most powerful and efficient discovery tools available; for the organization, it can be a daunting and perilous ordeal.

In this chapter, we consider the purposes and advantages of Rule 30(b)(6) depositions, the requirements of notice and specification of topics, the organization's task of selecting and preparing its designees, considerations for deposing attorneys when questioning those designees, and tips for defending counsel.

21.1 Purposes and Advantages of Rule 30(b)(6) Depositions

The Advisory Committee Notes to the federal rules cite multiple reasons for Rule 30(b)(6), but the main

> **In This Chapter:**
>
> - *The purposes and advantages of Rule 30(b)(6) depositions*
>
> - *The notice requirements and specification of topics*
>
> - *The organization's task of selecting and preparing its designees*
>
> - *Considerations for deposing attorneys when questioning those designees*
>
> - *Tips for defending counsel*

attraction for the deposing attorney is that it forces the organization to present a witness to testify to the organization's collective knowledge. This saves the time and expense of conducting multiple depositions to find the individual in the organization who has the needed information. As the Advisory Committee Notes state: "[The rule] will curb the 'bandying' by which officers or managing agents of a corporation are deposed in turn but each disclaims knowledge of facts that are clearly known to persons in the organization and thereby to it.' " On the other hand, the notes advise, Rule 30(b)(6) protects organizations from having "an unnecessarily large number of their officers and agents" subjected to individual depositions.

A Rule 30(b)(6) deposition may be taken at any stage of discovery. Depending on the needs of the case, it can make sense to take a Rule 30(b)(6) deposition at the beginning of discovery, near the end of discovery, or, in jurisdictions permitting more than one Rule 30(b)(6) deposition, both at the beginning and the end of discovery.[1]

At the start of discovery, consider using a Rule 30(b)(6) deposition to obtain the following information from the organization:

- the organizational structure, including lines of authority, identity of decision-makers, and other important players;

- the types of documents and ESI created by the organization, how that information is stored, maintained, and retrieved, and when such information is destroyed;

- other relevant policies and procedures;

- the relevant history of the organization; and

- collective organizational information and positions on every event in the case, the persons involved, and the relevant documents and ESI.

This early Rule 30(b)(6) deposition can take the place of other discovery efforts to obtain this information, such as interrogatories (the answers to which are heavily edited by counsel and do not allow for immediate follow-up questions) and deposing many individuals. By contrast, use a Rule 30(b)(6) deposition toward the end of discovery to clarify earlier testimony, obtain information that was not acquired from individual witnesses, and obtain party statements and admissions that will eliminate issues and shorten the trial.

---

1. Rule 30(a)(2) provides that, unless the parties stipulate, leave of court must be obtained to take the deposition of a "deponent" who was already deposed in the case. In State Farm Mut. Auto. Ins. Co. v. New Horizon, Inc., 254 F.R.D. 227, 234–35 (E.D. Pa. 2008), the court concluded that this limitation applied to Rule 30(b)(6) depositions. Other courts suggest that Rule 30(b)(6) depositions are unique and leave of court is not required to conduct a second Rule 30(b)(6) deposition, at least on different topics. *E.g.*, Quality Aero Tech., Inc. v. Telemetrie Elektronik GmbH, 212 F.R.D. 313, 319 (E.D.N.C. 2002).

A Rule 30(b)(6) deposition is treated as a single deposition no matter how many witnesses the organization designates to testify in response to the deposition notice. Therefore, not only is the deposing party spared the time and aggravation of conducting multiple depositions to find out information, the Rule 30(b)(6) deposition counts as only one deposition toward the ten per side Rule 30(a)(2) allows. Furthermore, you can spend up to seven hours for each designee without leave of court. So, for example, if the organization designates three witnesses to testify, the Rule 30(b)(6) deposition may last twenty-one hours and still count as only one deposition toward the ten-per-side limit.

Moreover, taking a Rule 30(b)(6) deposition of the organization does not necessarily preclude the deposing party from deposing individual officers or employees of the organization. This is true even if the individual was one of the organization's designees.[2] If an individual deposition is taken, however, the witness would be testifying only from their personal knowledge; it would be admissible to impeach the witness at trial or to use if the witness became unavailable for trial (Rule 32(a)), but it would probably not be admissible against the organization under Rule 32(a)(3) unless the individual was an officer, director, or managing agent of the organization.

21.2   The Rule 30(b)(6) Procedure

Rule 30(b)(6) reads as follows:

> In its notice or subpoena, a party may name as the deponent a public or private corporation, a partnership, an association, a governmental agency, or other entity and must describe with reasonable particularity the matters for examination. The named organization must designate one or more officers, directors, or managing agents, or designate other persons who consent to testify on its behalf; and it may set out the matters on which each person designated will testify. Before or promptly after the notice or subpoena is served, the serving party and the organization must confer in good faith about the matters for examination. A subpoena must advise a nonparty organization of its duty to confer with the serving party and to designate each person who will testify. The persons designated must testify about

---

2. The fact the deposing party availed itself of the Rule 30(b)(6) procedures might nevertheless factor into the court's decision whether to grant a protective order precluding an individual's deposition. *See* Notes of Advisory Committee on Rules—1970 Amendment (Rule 30(b)(6)).

> information known or reasonably available to the organization. This paragraph (6) does not preclude a deposition by any other procedure allowed by these rules.

The rule identifies three essential facets of the procedure. First, the party seeking discovery must notice the deposition of the organization and "describe with reasonable particularity the matters for examination." Second, the deponent organization must "designate one or more officers, directors, or managing agents, or designate other persons who consent to testify on its behalf."[3] Third, the organization's designees must then "testify about information known or reasonably available to the organization." While the latter obligation of learning and testifying to the organization's knowledge falls on the shoulders of the designee(s), it is the organization's burden to gather all that information and, though counsel, prepare the designee(s) to testify to it. Let's look more closely at these three aspects of Rule 30(b)(6) procedure.

21.3 Notice and Specification of the Matters for Examination

Depose a corporation, partnership, association, governmental agency, or other entity that is a party to the litigation by serving the organization (through counsel) with a deposition notice that meets the requirements for a regular deposition under Rule 30 (time and place of the deposition, manner of recording, etc.), except that it names the organization as the deponent and "describe[s] with reasonable particularity the matters for examination."[4] Also serve the organization with a request for production of documents, which tracks the matters for examination or requests all documents the organization used to prepare the designees for the deposition. Ideally, time the production request so the documents and ESI are provided before the deposition, allowing you to review them.

The matters for examination are critical. The organization will use them in deciding who to designate as witnesses and how to prepare them to testify. They also define the extent to which the designee's answers at the deposition will bind the organization. Although the deposing attorney may question a designee beyond the matters for examination, under Rule 30(b)(6) the designee's answer binds the organization only for matters specified in the deposition notice. Furthermore, because

---

3. The deposing party is not entitled to select the person to be produced as the organization's Rule 30(b)(6) designee—that is the prerogative of the organization. Therefore, a Rule 30(b)(6) notice that includes language like "the organization shall designate witnesses, including Robert W. Baldwin, vice president, to testify to the specified topics" has no effect on the selection of the designee.
4. If the party is using Rule 30(b)(6) to depose an organization that is not a party to the litigation, it must compel the organization's attendance by subpoena under Rule 45, name the organization as the deponent, describe the matters for examination with reasonable particularity, and inform the nonparty organization of its obligation to designate witnesses and to meet and confer about the matters for examination.

the matters for examination affect how many witnesses the organization might have to designate, they affect how long the deposition may last, since the deposing attorney is entitled to spend up to seven hours of deposition time per designee.

Difficulties frequently arise with the phrasing of the matters for examination. Often the deposing attorney does not know enough about the organization and its operations to craft examination topics that avoid ambiguity. The matters for examination may be broad, covering too long a period or inquiring into areas beyond the scope of discovery. For example, a fifteen-year period may be excessive if the central issue in the case is whether employment discrimination caused the firing of one worker, and the matters for examination may be too broad if they involve all branches of a multinational company when the issue is whether a single branch defectively manufactured a product. From the organization's perspective, the matters must be sufficiently specific so the organization knows how to prepare the witness, and too many matters for examination results in too great a burden to locate and prepare designees. On the other hand, a deposing attorney's attempt to be specific can result in an incomplete inquiry; efforts to be complete as well as specific necessitate a long list of matters for examination, and trying to limit the matters for examination can end up in broadly worded categories. These difficulties must be ironed out in a meet-and-confer process, discussed next.

21.4   Objections, Meet and Confer, and Protective Orders

The organization's attorney must carefully review the deposition notice and consider the matters identified for examination. If the organization or its counsel has any objection to the notice, counsel should promptly serve written objections on the deposing party.

Several types of objections may be levied regarding the matters for examination. The matters may be ambiguous or overbroad, as mentioned above. They may call for confidential or trade secret material. They may be irrelevant and thus outside the scope of discovery. In addition, the organization may claim that the matters for examination inquire about events that occurred long ago; no one presently employed by the organization has any knowledge of them, and there are no records at the organization that would get a designee up to speed without excessive burden and expense. Although the unavailability of current personnel with knowledge of the topics is not in itself a basis for an organization's failure to comply with Rule 30(b)(6), the infeasibility of the endeavor may eventually persuade a court to limit some of the matters for examination.

Whether or not the organization's attorney has objected to the notice, Rule 30(b)(6) provides—by virtue of an amendment effective December 2020—that "[b]efore or promptly after the notice or subpoena is served, the serving party and the organization must confer in good faith about the matters for examination." This meet-and-confer process is intended to address deficiencies the organization sees in the matters for examination; it also prevents otherwise unseen issues that can frequently arise at the deposition, when it becomes apparent that the matters for examination were intended by the deposing attorney to mean one thing but were interpreted differently by the organization and its attorney. Ideally, this conference should occur before the deposition notice is served.[5]

During the meet-and-confer, the organization's counsel, as a matter of strategy and good faith, may suggest a reasonable modification of the matters for examination, which would allow the deposing attorney to obtain the most relevant information that is feasible for the organization to assemble and impart to its designee(s).

Be wary, however, of efforts by the organization's attorney to dissuade you from taking the Rule 30(b)(6) deposition. The organization's attorney may claim that you have already deposed, as individual witnesses, the people the organization considers the most knowledgeable on the specified areas, so the Rule 30(b)(6) deposition of those same people as designees would just be duplicative. "Perhaps," counsel suggests, they might be willing to "just stipulate that their depositions will be treated as 30(b)(6) depositions and everyone can save some time and money." Sounds good, but it can be a bad idea. You do not have to settle for individuals who personally are the "most knowledgeable" from among the organization's individuals; you are entitled to all the reasonably available knowledge of the organization.[6] Relatedly, when the individuals were deposed previously, there was no obligation to inform them of the knowledge available to the organization; they were answering from personal knowledge, supplemented by whatever documents they were given or people to whom their attorney had them speak.

If the parties cannot agree on the matters for examination or other issues despite the meet-and-confer, the organization will file a motion for a protective order. Under Rule 26(c), the moving party must show that it has, in good faith, conferred or attempted to confer with the other party, and that there is good cause to protect it from the undue burden or expense involved in gathering the information and preparing the witness to testify. It is not necessary to show that the information is completely unavailable to the organization, but it is not enough to show that a large volume of documents will have to be reviewed; a proper showing would

---

5. If the witness is a nonparty served by subpoena, the subpoena must advise the nonparty organization of its duty to meet and confer regarding the matters for examination and to designate one or more witnesses to testify.

6. Some state rules permit "Person Most Knowledgeable" or "Person Most Qualified" depositions, which may be more limited than Rule 30(b)(6) depositions. *E.g.,* Cal. Code Civ. P. § 2025.230 (officers, directors, managing agents, employees, or agents who are most qualified to testify). Typically under these state rules, the organization still must provide designees (more than one, if necessary, despite the adjective "most") who can provide the specified information to the extent it can reasonably be found by the organization. Designees may be limited to employees or agents (like accountants) as opposed to outsiders. In other respects, entity depositions under the state rules are akin to those under the federal rules.

demonstrate that the burden in collecting and conveying it is too great given the relative probative value and need for the evidence. To make this showing, the organization must explain the effort that would be expended in gathering and conveying the specified information, supported by declarations or affidavits.

21.5 Selecting and Preparing the Designee

To whatever extent the matters for examination have been specified, modified by the parties, or ruled on by the court, the organization has a duty to designate one or more witnesses and to prepare them with the information reasonably available to the organization on each of those matters. This means the organization and its counsel must decide how many witnesses to designate, select those designees, and prepare them with the information; counsel then prepares the witnesses to testify at the deposition and represents them at the deposition.

21.5.1 Number of Designees

The number of witnesses to designate turns in part on the number and breadth of the matters for examination. In complex cases involving financial, securities, antitrust, or patent disputes, there could be scores of wide-ranging topics. In such cases, multiple designees are usually necessary because preparing a single designee on such a vast amount of information is extraordinarily difficult and time-consuming.

There are, however, other considerations to keep in mind. Having multiple designees extends the length of the deposition dramatically. As mentioned earlier, the deposing attorney is entitled to a seven-hour questioning session for each designee. The Rule 30(b)(6) deposition could easily become a thirty-five-hour deposition if five designees are chosen to testify.

Furthermore, each additional witness multiplies the possibility that the testimony of designees speaking for the organization will contain inconsistencies. Each witness requires time to review documents and prepare. And it may be hard to find enough suitable designees—a task we discuss next.

21.5.2 Selecting the Designees

Rule 30(b)(6) states that the designees can consist of "one or more officers, directors, or managing agents, or . . . other persons who consent to testify on its behalf." Note two things. First, the designee does not have to be the "person most knowledgeable" in the organization about any of the matters for examination; that is a phrase used in some states for similar entity depositions, but under the federal rules, what matters is that, by the time of the deposition, the designee is prepared with the reasonably available knowledge of the entire organization. Second, the organization is not limited in the type of person it can designate. The organization may choose a high-level executive, a lower-level employee, a mail clerk, a past employee, an independent contractor, a consultant, an expert, or even an actor. As far as the rules go, what matters is not who the person is, but whether the person consents to testify on the organization's behalf and is ultimately prepared with the information reasonably available to the organization on the matters for examination.

Because the object is to designate a person who is suitably prepared, the organization should look for someone who has the time and motivation to prepare. For each day of foreseeable deposition testimony, preparation might require as many as three days, depending on how much the person already knows about the subject matter. If a potential designee cannot spare that time, they are not the right choice; you will need to find someone else to do it alone or to share the load.

Although the preparation time may be reduced by selecting a designee who already knows about the subject matter, there is a risk to designating anyone who was involved in the events that gave rise to the lawsuit. The danger is that the witness will introduce their biases into the case, taking the deposition beyond the "organizational knowledge" into the designee's personal opinions and speculation—all of which could be deemed binding on the organization.[7]

From among the individuals who have the time and capacity to be satisfactorily prepared, the designee should be someone who can handle testifying at the deposition. Ideally, it would be someone used to (and proficient at) testifying in depositions or trials, or at least competent in expressing themselves in meetings and the like. Furthermore, Rule 30(b)(6) depositions are typically recorded by video as well as stenographically, so the Rule 30(b)(6) designee may become the face of the organization.

Sometimes it makes sense to enlist a former employee as the designee. For example, a good designee might be a recently retired senior executive who was not involved in the dispute leading to the lawsuit. They would have knowledge of the corporate structure and the lines of authority, so their preparation would be more efficient, and they would have an interest in doing a good job for their old company. In other instances, the matters for examination may address products or processes the organization no longer maintains, and turning to a former employee who worked in that area might be better than trying to bring a current employee up to speed.

> *In selecting the designee, consider persons who have the time and capacity to learn the organization's reasonably available information, testify persuasively, and represent the organization.*

---

7. If the witness was an officer, director, or managing agent of the organization, an adverse party could use the individual's testimony against the organization at trial anyway under Rule 32(a)(2), even if deposed as an individual.

There are some things to consider, however, before designating past employees or other third parties. First, be sure that the individual is sufficiently dedicated to the organization to do a good job. Second, deposing counsel may argue that, by designating a former employee or other third party, there is no attorney-client privilege or work product protection for the preparation session or for communications between the organization's counsel and the designee—check the law of the relevant jurisdiction. Third, the nonemployee may demand compensation for their time in preparing and testifying. If paying the designee is necessary, consider how the designee should address the compensation issue if asked at the deposition.

21.5.3 *Preparing the Designees with the Organization's Knowledge*

Rule 30(b)(6) requires the designee(s) to "testify about information known or reasonably available to the organization." The burden is on the organization to equip them to do so. Specifically, the organization must make a "conscientious, good-faith effort to designate knowledgeable persons for Rule 30(b)(6) depositions and to prepare them to fully and unevasively answer questions about the designated subject matter."[8]

To meet its obligation, the organization may have to locate multiple present and former employees; assemble and review its documents, records, and archives; and gather information that is "reasonably available" to the organization even if it is beyond the organization's possession, custody, or control. The organization (through counsel) must then instill the information in the designee—a task that may require several preparation sessions, interviews with other employees, and document reviews and study time by the designee. The designee may have to "review prior fact witness deposition testimony as well as documents and deposition exhibits."[9]

An insufficiently prepared designee can harm the organization in at least two ways. First, if the designee cannot answer the questions, the deposing attorney may obtain an order compelling the organization to prepare the designee, directing that the deposition reconvene regarding those matters, and imposing sanctions against the organization under Rule 37(d).[10] Second, if the designee has not been properly

---

8. Bd. of Trs. of the Leland Stanford Junior Univ. v. Tyco Int'l Ltd., 253 F.R.D. 524, 526 (C.D. Cal. 2008), *quoting* Sprint Commc'n Co., L.P. v. TheGlobe.com, Inc., 236 F.R.D. 524, 527 (D. Kan. 2006).

9. Calzaturficio S.C.A.R.P.A. S.P.A. v. Fabiano Shoe Co., 201 F.R.D. 33, 37 (D. Mass. 2001), *quoting* Prokosch v. Catalina Lighting, Inc., 193 F.R.D. 633, 639 (D. Minn. 2000).

10. *See* Starlight Int'l Inc. v. Herlihy, 186 F.R.D. 626, 639 (D. Kan. 1999) ("Defendants . . . have engaged in sanctionable misconduct by failing to adequately prepare their representative for deposition. The court also finds that Bruce, as a party to this action, engaged in sanctionable misconduct by not preparing himself adequately for the deposition. The court may find lack of preparation at a deposition to be a failure to appear.").

prepared but answers anyway, the designee may make a mistake or be more susceptible to the deposing attorney's leading questions, resulting in answers that bind the
organization to untrue facts or unfavorable positions.

21.5.4 *Preparing the Designee to Testify*

Preparing Rule 30(b)(6) designee(s) for the deposition is like preparing other
witnesses as discussed in Chapter Seventeen. There are, however, some important
differences.

Information of the Organization

Lay witnesses testify from their personal knowledge. Rule 30(b)(6) witnesses
testify from the knowledge reasonably available to the organization, which has been
downloaded into the witness. Stress to the designee that they are testifying as the
organization with the information reasonably available to the organization rather
than just upon the witness's own personal knowledge.

Also remind witnesses that their answers in a Rule 30(b)(6) deposition about
topics listed as matters for examination are binding on the organization. Generally,
the answers are not considered judicial admissions that the organization is unable
to controvert as a matter of law; instead, they are evidentiary admissions that are
admissible against the party but do not preclude the organization from introducing
evidence that is contrary to the admission (although such testimony may be subject
to impeachment with the Rule 30(b)(6) testimony).[11] All the witness needs to know
is that what they say will likely stick to the organization.

Matters for Examination

Unlike other depositions, the substantive topics for a Rule 30(b)(6) deposition
are set forth in the deposition notice or subpoena. You would think that would
make the task of preparing the witness straightforward. It does not. No matter how
well crafted the matters for examination are, there always seems to arise a question
whether some subject falls within their scope. That, plus the burden of answering questions on broad topics with all the information reasonably available to the
organization, makes the preparation task quite onerous. During the preparation
session, decide where the outer boundary of each matter for examination lies, so
you can object or note for the record when questions at the deposition fall outside
their scope.

---

11. U.S. v. Taylor, 166 F.R.D. 356, 362 n. 6 (M.D.N.C. 1996); W.R. Grace & Co. v. Viskase Corp.,
No. 09-C-5383, 1991 U.S. Dist. LEXIS 14651, 1991 WL 211647 (N.D. Ill. Oct. 15, 1991).

Questions Outside the Scope

To complicate things a bit more, in many jurisdictions the deposing attorney can question the witness about things outside the scope of the matters for examination specified in the deposition notice.[12] The rationale is that the specifications impose an obligation on the organization—to provide appropriately knowledgeable designees—but not a limitation on the questioner. The witness must answer these questions as best they can, but the answer need not be based on all the information of the organization and the answer will not be binding on the organization—at least so long as the witness is not an officer, director, or managing agent of the organization (Rule 32(a)(3)). As we shall discuss later in this chapter, the possibility of counsel asking about outlying subjects creates some issues for the deposing attorney and the defending attorney to deal with at the deposition, but the witness should know about it too. You may want to work with the witness on their testimony regarding subjects of which the witness has personal knowledge and could be asked at the deposition, just as you would work with any other witness.

Questions About the Witness's Preparation for the Deposition

Counsel preparing the designee to testify at a Rule 30(b)(6) deposition can be confident that the deposing attorney will ask the witness about their preparation for the deposition. The rules about inquiries into the Rule 30(b)(6) witness's preparation are fundamentally the same as the rules about inquiries into any other witness's preparation (*see* sections 7.2, 17.4). With a Rule 30(b)(6) witness, however, the preparation sessions may well constitute the time—or part of the time—when the designee obtained the substantive information about the matters for examination, participated in interviews of knowledgeable people with (or formerly with) the organization, and reviewed relevant documents.

As a general rule, the witness must tell the deposing attorney what material they reviewed in preparing for the deposition. Some jurisdictions might entertain an objection on attorney work product grounds if the question is unartfully phrased to the effect of, "who did counsel tell you to talk to" or "what documents did counsel show you," because those questions inquire about the attorney's mental processes. But the deposing attorney should be able to make a reasonable inquiry to ascertain whether, in fact, the designee was prepared with the information reasonably available to the organization.

---

12. *See, e.g.*, Chrimar Sys. v. Cisco Sys., 312 F.R.D. 560 (N.D. Cal. 2016); Am. Gen. Life Ins. Co. v. Billard, 2010 Dist. LEXIS 114961 (N.D. Iowa Oct. 28, 2010); Detoy v. City & County of San Francisco, 196 F.R.D. 362, 366 (N.D. Cal. 2000); King v. Pratt & Whitney, 161 F.R.D. 475, 476 (S.D. Fla. 1995); *but see* Paparelli v. Prudential Ins. Co. of Am., 108 F.R.D. 727, 730 (D. Mass. 1985).

Chapter Twenty-One

Answering Questions with "I Don't Know"

In section 17.3.3, we covered the "one concept, three rules" advice about listening to and answering questions. The overriding concept is for the witness to tell the truth. From that one concept derives three rules: make sure you understand the question; answer honestly; and that's it—don't embellish, explain, or volunteer. All of that applies to Rule 30(b)(6) witnesses generally, but with a slight twist.

Part of what we usually tell witnesses about understanding the question and answering honestly is to respond "I don't know" or "I don't remember" to a question if appropriate. We tell witnesses there is no shame in responding "I don't know" or "I don't remember," and indeed that is the correct response if it is the honest answer. In the Rule 30(b)(6) deposition, however, things work differently.

In the first place, the designee may not claim lack of their own personal knowledge in refusing to answer or in answering, "I don't know."[13] The reasonable search for information required by Rule 30(b)(6) extends beyond personal knowledge of the designees, as already explained.

In addition, the "I don't know" answer has consequences for the organization. If the organization's designee responds to a question within the scope of the matters for examination with, "I don't know," the response is binding on the organization and could be taken to mean that the organization has no information on the subject, no information was found, or the designee's preparation was inadequate. The organization might be precluded from introducing any evidence on that topic at the trial, because the designee was supposed to be prepared with all the information reasonably available to the organization. Otherwise, crafty lawyers could render the Rule 30(b)(6) procedure a sham by producing designees who have shirked their duties and are prepared to answer "I don't know" to all the questions.

On the other hand, if the Rule 30(b)(6) designee really does not know the answer, it makes no sense to have the designee hazard a guess on the organization's behalf. The takeaway is to prepare diligently with the knowledge of the organization concerning the substance of the matters for examination; if a topic comes up that the designee does not know or remember notwithstanding the preparation, so be it. Instruct the witness to answer honestly, and let you deal with it (as discussed below).

You May Not Be You

Rule 30(b)(6) depositions are depositions of the organization, seek the organization's information, and are binding on the organization. Inform the witness, therefore, that if a question uses the word "you," the question is probably asking about the organization, not the designee personally. Prepare the witness to respond with

---

13. Banco Del Atlantico, S.A. v. Woods Indus. Inc., 519 F.3d 350 (7th Cir. 2008).

the information known to the organization. For example, if asked, "What did you think of this person's work?" the designee should answer with the understanding that "you" in the question meant, "the organization."

But this can get complicated because, sometimes, the deposing attorney really is seeking the personal knowledge of the designee. Further, as discussed above, it is permissible for the deposing attorney to ask questions outside the scope of the matters for examination. Problems then arise. Is the question calling for information outside the scope of the deposition notice? If so, is the examiner asking for information of the organization? Asking for information from the witness's personal knowledge? In short, what does "you" really mean?

To address such doubts, prepare the witness to ask the deposing attorney, "Do you mean 'you' as in me or 'you' as in the organization?" Or simply, "What do you mean by 'you'?" Also be ready to object to any "you" questions.

21.6 Deposing Attorney's Inquiries of the Rule 30(b)(6) Designee(s)

Questioning a Rule 30(b)(6) witness is generally the same as questioning any other witness, in terms of starting the deposition with commitments to the ground rules (section 6.3), learning what the witness did to prepare for the deposition (section 7.2), using the funnel method to gather information (Chapter Eight), employing other questioning techniques to obtain admissions (Chapter Nine), incorporating documents and other exhibits (Chapter Ten), and all the rest. For substantive topics, the matters for examination listed in the deposition notice are natural headings for the deposition outline. There are, however, some additional considerations when deposing Rule 30(b)(6) designees.

21.6.1 Confirm Organizational Knowledge

Confirm at the start that the deposition is of the organization pursuant to Rule 30(b)(6), the witness is appearing on behalf of the organization as its designee, and the witness has been prepared to answer questions on the matters for examination with the information reasonably available to the organization. By now this seems redundant in this chapter, but you may be surprised at how many witnesses respond with a bewildered, "huh?" Mark the Rule 30(b)(6) notice as an exhibit. Ask if the witness has previously testified on behalf of the organization; an affirmative answer indicates they are familiar with the process—and may reveal other lawsuits involving the organization on the same issues.

Where the organization has designated multiple people to be witnesses, the organization may have disclosed (but need not disclose) the matters to which each designee will testify. Regardless, start each designee's deposition by asking to what specifications they are prepared to testify. You will then know how to allocate the deposition time with the designee. You do not want to be in a situation where there are multiple designees and, in the deposition of the last one, you ask about a topic only to have the organization's lawyer say, "Oh, that's a question you should have asked designee number one; he's the one who was prepared to speak to that."

At a Rule 30(b)(6) deposition of an opposing party, you do not have to worry much about laying a foundation for the answers—the organization has supplied that foundation by designating the witness as a company spokesperson, which turns answers relevant to the matters for examination into statements of a party-opponent.[14] It may nonetheless be helpful to ask the witness the source of their information to obtain clues for potential additional discovery and to prepare for the depositions of other individuals.

21.6.2   Ask About the Witness's Preparation for the Deposition

Pay special attention to how the designee prepared for the deposition. Obviously, this inquiry is important in a Rule 30(b)(6) deposition because it checks whether the organization did what it was supposed to do to equip the designee with all reasonably available information. Ask what material the witness reviewed, why the witness reviewed that material, what material the witness requested that was not provided, who the witness spoke to, the amount of time the witness spent in reviewing the materials and speaking with the others, and so forth.

21.6.3   Do Not Blur the Lines

Keep the record clear whether the witness is testifying based on the information known to the organization or the witness's personal knowledge. Avoid asking, "What were you trying to achieve by changing the blueprints for the brake pedal attachment?" Instead ask: "What was Aston-Martin trying to achieve . . . ." Although the witness is supposed to be testifying on behalf of the organization, an ambiguous query couched in terms of "you" may lead a judge to think that the answer might have been an expression of the designee's own opinions rather than a statement of the corporation's agent. Avoid this ambiguity to get the full benefit of the Rule 30(b)(6) process—party statements.

Another option is to say at the outset of the deposition, right after the witness confirms that they are testifying as the organization's designee for the information of the organization, that the questions will be asking for the organization's knowledge and, unless otherwise stated, the word "you" in a question means the organization. Whatever way you want to keep the record clear, keep it clear.

---

14. In the federal system under Fed. R. Evid. 801(d)(2), and in some states, opposing party statements are defined as "nonhearsay." In other states, such as California, opposing party statements are considered hearsay but fall within an exception to the hearsay rule.

Similarly, watch for answers like "My personal feeling is . . . ," or "Well, in my opinion . . . ," or "I think," so the court does not interpret those answers as expressing something other than the organization's knowledge uttered on the organization's behalf. If you like the information or opinion that the witness gave, and you want it attributed to the organization, subtly follow up with questions establishing that the opinion or feeling is based on the designee's review of organizational information and is expressed as the organization's designee.

If you do want to explore the witness's personal knowledge, as opposed to the organization's knowledge, the far better course is to depose the witness separately. For example, after serving the Rule 30(b)(6) notice, contact the organization's counsel, obtain the identity of the designee, and serve a deposition notice (or subpoena) for the individual deposition of the designee on the same day. Alternatively, include in the Rule 30(b)(6) deposition notice that, after the designee testifies on behalf of the organization pursuant to Rule 30(b)(6), additional questions will be asked of the witness based on the witness's personal knowledge under Rule 30(a).

Finally, have a good argument that each question you ask falls within the scope of the matters for examination. That way, the answer will be attributed to the organization's knowledge, the answer will be binding on the organization, and it will be difficult for the organization to present contrary evidence later.

21.7 Defending the 30(b)(6) Deposition

In addition to the techniques for defending witnesses described in Chapter Eighteen, the attorney defending at the Rule 30(b)(6) deposition must be vigilant of matters unique to those depositions.

21.7.1 Designee Does Not Know the Answer

Despite the best efforts to prepare the organization's designee, it can happen that the designee has no information in response to one or more of the deposing attorney's questions. The witness may blurt out, "I don't know." The significance of this answer depends on the circumstances, and the defending attorney should be prepared to handle it.

The first issue is whether the deposing attorney's question truly pertained to a matter for examination identified in the deposition notice. If not, the organization and designee had no obligation to provide information (at least not information beyond the personal knowledge of the witness). Object on that ground.

A second consideration is whether the organization has any information in response to the question. Although the organization is obligated to prepare the witness, its duty is only to provide information known or reasonably available to the organization. It may be that a reasonable effort was made to find information about the subject area, but none was found. In that case, the response is more to the effect of "we have (found) no information," rather than "I don't know." The witness should be ready, if asked, to testify to the efforts taken to locate the information. Assuming the efforts were reasonable, the organization should not be sanctioned for failing to prepare the designee, although it may be limited in presenting evidence on the issue later.

If the question is within the scope of the matters for examination and the designee was not prepared on the organization's information on the subject, acknowledge that the witness was inadvertently not prepared on the topic. Saying that is not enough, of course, because the organization would be subject to sanctions under Rule 37(d) for not adequately preparing the witness. Go on to say something like, "The organization has no answer at this time, but assuming the question seeks information within the scope of the matters for examination, the organization will not object to reconvening the deposition at a mutually convenient time with a designee equipped to answer the question." This avoids expensive motion practice and preserves the organization's opportunity to introduce evidence on the point.

21.7.2   Topics Outside the Matters for Examination

We have discussed that a Rule 30(b)(6) designee may be asked questions beyond the scope of the matters for examination, at least in some jurisdictions. If the deposing attorney does so, object to the question on that ground, state that the answer is not made on behalf of the corporation, and allow the witness to answer the question. Never instruct the witness not to answer unless there is some other basis for doing so.[15]

21.7.3   What Does "You" Mean

As mentioned, ambiguities arise when the deposing attorney asks the organization's designee a question containing the word "you," because it can be unclear whether the deposing attorney is referring to the organization or to the witness personally. If this crops up during the deposition, object, or ask a follow-up question to remove the ambiguity (e.g., "When you answered the question about 'how you liked Jackson's work,' did you understand that the 'you' meant 'the ABC Company,' your employer?"). If the ambiguity is missed during the deposition, the witness may be able to correct the transcript, if need be, when reviewing it after the deposition.

---

15. *Billard,* supra, observed that directions not to answer—on the grounds that the question goes beyond the Rule 30(b)(6) specifications— are improper primarily because the rules only authorize such directions when the questions involve privilege, a court order, or suspension of the deposition to file a motion for a protective order to limit or approve questioning. *See* Rule 30(c)(2), Rule 30(d)(3).

CHECKLIST
RULE 30(b)(6) DEPOSITIONS

✔ Study Rule 30(b)(6) procedure (or its state court equivalent).

✔ The deposing attorney serves a proper deposition notice (or subpoena) on the organization as the deponent and specifies the matters for examination.

✔ The parties, through counsel, meet and confer on the matters for examination.

✔ The organization selects one or more designees capable of adequate preparation and willing to serve as a designee.

✔ The organization and defending counsel prepare the designees substantively with the information reasonably available to the organization.

✔ The defending attorney prepares the designees for the deposition process, emphasizing:

- ✓ the obligation to testify with the organization's information on behalf of the organization;
- ✓ the onus of binding the organization;
- ✓ substantive responses to the matters for examination;
- ✓ the possibility of questions outside the scope of the matters for examination;
- ✓ questions about the witness's preparation for the deposition;
- ✓ issues that arise when answering questions with, "I don't know";
- ✓ the need for clarification of questions asking "you," or assuming it refers to the organization.

✔ The deposing attorney examines each Rule 30(b)(6) designee:

- ✓ confirming their role as designee and the matters for examination for which they are designated;
- ✓ inquiring about the witness's preparation with the organization's information and for the deposition;
- ✓ examining about the matters for examination;
- ✓ keeping the record clear that the questions seek the organization's information, unless explicitly stated otherwise.

✔ The defending attorney protects the witness and the rights of the organization by:

- ✓ addressing any inquiry outside the scope of the matters for examination;
- ✓ keeping the record clear regarding questions that could seek personal rather than organizational knowledge;
- ✓ dealing with instances in which the designee does not have information in response to the inquiry.

CHAPTER TWENTY-TWO

EXPERT WITNESS DEPOSITIONS

*He who would propagate an opinion must
begin by making sure of his ground and
holding it firmly.*

—Samuel Butler

*An expert is someone from out of town
who carries a briefcase.*

—Anonymous

An expert witness deposition will be more effective if you pin down the expert's opinions, methodology, and assumptions, laying the groundwork for attacking them at the deposition, by motion, or at trial.

Expert witness depositions are important, because expert witness testimony can be especially persuasive to the court on summary judgment or to the jurors at trial. In some cases, an expert's opinion is required for a party to establish an element of a claim or defense. The more you expose the flaws of the other party's expert at the deposition, the more likely the court will reject the expert as unqualified or unreliable, destroying the other side's case or drastically

> **In This Chapter:**
>
> - The law relative to expert witness testimony
>
> - The goals of deposing the opponent's expert witness
>
> - Preparing to take the deposition
>
> - The traditional topics to cover with the expert
>
> - Ordering the examination topics
>
> - As defending counsel, preparing and defending the expert witness

impacting the settlement value of the claims. Even if the matter proceeds to trial for each side's expert to battle it out, the deposition testimony provides ammunition to discredit the opponent's expert so that the factfinder finds your expert more persuasive.

The expert witness deposition is not easy. Experts have much more experience and knowledge in the subject matter because they are, well, experts. Some expert witnesses delight in confusing the deposing attorney and impeding the attorney's attempts to gain information and admissions, and most have the wherewithal to do so whether intentionally or not. On the other hand, using a few disciplined techniques and areas of inquiry can shift the balance of power to the deposing attorney.

In this chapter, we review the law relative to expert witness testimony, the goals of the attorney in taking the deposition of the opponent's expert witness, the preparation needed to take the deposition, the traditional topics to cover with the expert, and the best way to order those topics in the examination. For the defending attorney, we summarize some pointers in preparing and defending the expert witness.

22.1 The Law

The federal rules—and state laws as well—allow expert witness testimony to assist the trier of fact on matters outside a juror's common experience. In federal court, the rules suggest five considerations for the admission of expert opinion testimony in support of or opposition to a summary motion judgment or at trial. They embody three central requirements: 1) the expert must be qualified, 2) the expert's opinion must assist the jury, and 3) the expert's work must be reliable. Here are the five considerations derived from Federal Rules of Evidence 702 and 703:

- The expert must be qualified to give an opinion based on knowledge, skill, experience, training, or education (Fed. R. Evid. 702)

- The expert's specialized knowledge will help the trier of fact to understand the evidence or to determine a fact in issue (Fed. R. Evid. 702(a))

- The testimony must be based on sufficient facts or data and be the product of reliable principles and methods (Fed. R. Evid. 702(b), (c))

- The expert must have reliably applied the principles and methods to the facts of the case (Fed. R. Evid. 702(d))[1]

- The opinion must be based on the type of facts reasonably relied upon by experts in the field (Fed. R. Evid. 703)

---

1. A proposed amendment to Rule 702(d) would change the requirement from "the expert has reliably applied the principles and methods to the facts of the case" to "the expert's opinion reflects a reliable application of the principles and methods to the facts of the case."

Rule 702 reflects the holdings in two famous cases—*Daubert v. Merrell Dow Pharmaceuticals, Inc.*, 509 U.S. 579 (1993) and *Kumho Tire Co. v. Carmichael*, 526 U.S. 137 (1999), which charged trial courts to serve as gatekeepers and exclude unreliable expert testimony. This gatekeeping function is important due to the overpowering effect expert witness testimony can have on jurors and the difficulty jurors have in evaluating the reliability of expert witness testimony.

For expert witness opinions to be admissible under *Daubert, Kumho,* their progeny, and Rule 702, the proponent of the opinion must show, by a preponderance of the evidence, the reliability of the expert, their methodology, and their application of the methodology in reaching their opinion. Courts may consider, among other things: 1) whether the expert's methodology or theory can be tested objectively; 2) whether it has been subject to peer review and publication (the idea being that peers will understand the process and point out fallacies); 3) the methodology's rate of error; 4) whether there are standards and controls; and 5) whether the methodology or theory has been generally accepted in the scientific community. Not all these factors may apply in every case, particularly for nonscientific expert witness testimony. Other factors may apply, such as the extent to which the expert opinion derived from research independent of the litigation, whether the analysis reflects the same intellectual rigor as the expert would apply in their professional work outside the courtroom, and how well the opinion accounts for alternative methodologies, assumptions, and conclusions.[2]

If the court is not persuaded that the expert, the expert's methodology, and their application of the methodology are reliable, the expert's opinion will not be admissible and will not be considered in a motion for summary judgment or at trial. The deposition of the opposing expert witness therefore endeavors to unearth facts that will support a motion to strike or preclude the expert's testimony. And even if the court does not exclude or limit the testimony, the information casting doubt on the expert and the expert's qualifications, methodology, and assumptions can persuade a court or jury that their opinion is less convincing than the opinion of the client's expert.

---

2. Some state courts follow *Daubert.* Other state courts apply a similar standard based on Frye v. United States, 293 F. 1013 (D.C. Cir. 1923), which admits scientific expert opinions only if they are based on generally accepted scientific methods. In California, for example, courts apply *Frye* if the expert's testimony is based on a new scientific test or equipment. E.g., People v. Bui, 86 Cal. App. 4th 1187 (Cal. Ct. App. 2001). Case law later clarified that, for any expert witness opinion, the matter on which the expert has relied should be of a type an expert can rely on in rendering such an opinion. Lockheed Litig. Cases, 115 Cal. App. 4th 558 (Cal. Ct. App. 2004); *see* Sargon Enters., Inc. v. Univ. of S. Cal., 55 Cal. 4th 747, 770 (Cal. 2012); Cal. Evid. Code 801. Moreover, the trial court must serve as a gatekeeper by determining if the material on which the expert relied supports the expert's reasoning or if there is too great an "analytical gap" between the material and the opinion. *Sargon,* 55 Cal. 4th at 771; Cal. Evid. Code 802.

22.2 The Deposing Attorney's Goals

In light of the foregoing, consider the following goals in preparing for the deposition of the opposing party's expert witness and in deposing the expert:

Expert Deposition Goals

- Demonstrate that the expert lacks relevant qualification, to later argue that the witness should not be certified as an expert and the expert's testimony should be excluded.

- Show that the expert should not be trusted, is a professional witness ("hired gun"), an academic who lacks real-world experience, or a practitioner who lacks the latest research and training.

- Demonstrate that the expert's methodology is unreliable, in the sense of not being testable, trustworthy, or generally accepted in the scientific community, to preclude the expert's testimony.

- Discredit the expert witness's opinion by showing that the work was inadequate or incomplete or that the expert is biased.

- Discover and lock in the expert's opinions, methodology, and factual assumptions, so they can be attacked by your own expert.

- Ascertain the extent of the expert's understanding of the facts of the case, including any facts different than what discovery has shown.

- Discover the facts the expert relied upon in forming the opinion, to attack as not reasonably relied upon by an expert in the field.

- Gain admissions of any change in the opinion that would be prompted if the factual assumptions were changed.

- Gain admissions regarding the credibility and qualifications of your own expert and their methodology.

- Test theories to pin down the expert witness's response—setting before the opposing expert different portions of the client's explanations and your own expert's opinions, to learn the opposing expert's agreement or disagreement in advance of dispositive motions and trial.

- Evaluate the expert for a potential appearance as a witness at trial.

22.3 Preparing to Take the Expert Witness's Deposition

Keeping in mind the law regarding the admissibility of expert witness testimony and these goals, prepare for the deposition by learning as much as possible about the expert, the expert's opinions, and the subject matter. As discussed next, gather information from the client, other lawyers, and other experts; scrutinize the expert's written report, disclosures, and discovery; research the expert and their field and related law; consider expert witness tendencies and how to turn them into an advantage; and create workable timelines and an outline for the deposition.

22.3.1 Gather Information from the Client, Firm, and Experts

The attorney in a case involving expert witness testimony needs help. This help can come from the client and members of the law firm, from a paid consulting expert hired only to assist the attorney in preparation, and from the expert who has been retained to testify as the client's expert witness.

Client and Law Firm

Your client and colleagues are important sources of assistance during the preparation process. If the client is a technology company or engaged in scientific research, for example, their personnel will have expertise in the subject matter. Other attorneys in your firm may have handled similar cases with the same or similar expert witnesses. The client and the attorneys may know of the opposing party's expert and point you to prior deposition testimony and even transcripts or outlines of prior successful cross-examination of the opposing expert witness.

Using the client as a resource is less costly than hiring experts to consult with you. Furthermore, client confidences are not exposed and communications with the client for purposes of legal advice are protected by the attorney-client privilege and work product doctrine. How much time the client has to devote to your preparation, however, may be another question. Moreover,

> **Reliability factors courts may consider:**
>
> 1) whether the expert's methodology or theory can be tested objectively;
> 2) whether it has been subject to peer review and publication (the idea being that peers will understand the process and point out fallacies);
> 3) the methodology's rate of error;
> 4) whether there are standards and controls; and
> 5) whether the methodology or theory has been generally accepted in the scientific community.

the objectivity of an outside expert, untethered to the client, may be helpful. And it will be easier to inspire confidence in the client if, in addition to turning to the client for insight, you have accumulated familiarity with the technical or scientific subject matter on your own.

Consulting Expert

We briefly mentioned in section 5.2.1 the benefits of retaining consulting experts early in the litigation to guide you during the discovery process and to help you understand the relevant science, technology, industry practices, social science, or economics (including damage calculations) applicable to the case. These consulting experts are, of course, also invaluable when preparing to depose the opposing party's experts, helping you to understand the expert's report, opinions, methodologies, and assumptions and to craft the questions to ask the expert during the deposition. The consulting expert may even know the opposing party's expert—in fact, your expert may have testified against the opposing expert in other cases or worked side-by-side with them on projects or on boards.

The upside of working with one or more consulting experts—hired to help the attorney give legal advice to the client and not designated to testify—is that your communications with them generally fall within the scope of the attorney-client privilege and are protected from disclosure by the attorney work product doctrine. Under Rule 26(b)(4)(D), for example, a party generally may not discover facts known or opinions held by an expert who has been retained in anticipation of litigation or to prepare for trial and is not expected to be called to testify at trial.[3]

Testifying Expert

Whether or not a consulting expert has been hired, consider enlisting the assistance of any expert retained to testify at trial or in summary judgment proceedings. Beware, however, that unlike discussions with a consulting expert, discussions with a testifying expert have traditionally obtained little protection under the attorney-client privilege or attorney work product doctrine, especially under state law.[4]

---

3. A downside to using consulting experts is that it can add a lot of expense to the litigation. Due to the cost of consulting experts and potential problems with their availability, some attorneys find it helpful to hire graduate students in the field.

4. Communications between the attorney and a testifying expert usually do not fall within the scope of the attorney-client privilege, but they still may be protected from disclosure under the federal rules. Rule 26(b)(4)(C) protects communications between the attorney and the testifying expert (if the expert is required to provide a report under the rules), except to the extent the communications relate to the expert's compensation, identify facts or data that were provided by the attorney and considered by the expert in forming their opinion, or identify assumptions provided by the attorney and relied upon by the expert in forming the opinion. In addition, Rule 26(b)(4)(B) protects draft reports of the testifying expert. However, even these materials may be discovered upon a suitable showing of need (Rule 26(b)(3)(A)), except to the extent of the attorney's mental processes

22.3.2   *Review the Opposing Expert's Report and Discovery*

Rule 26(a)(2) requires each party to disclose the identity of any expert witness it may use at trial and provide (for most retained expert witnesses) a written report, prepared and signed by the witness, that includes "a complete statement of all opinions the witness will express and the basis and reasons for them," the "facts or data considered" in forming the opinions, exhibits that will be used to summarize or support the opinions, the "witness's qualifications, including a list of all publications authored in the previous 10 years," a list of all other cases in which the witness testified as an expert at trial or in deposition in the previous four years, and the witness's compensation (Rule 26(a)(2)(B)). Unless the court orders otherwise, the disclosure must be made at least 90 days before the trial date; for rebuttal experts, the deadline is 30 days after the other party's expert disclosures.[5]

As you review the opposing expert's report, look for the following—all of which will ultimately be part of your deposition inquiries.

Opinions, Bases, and Reasons

- What are the opinions?

- What is the stated basis and reasoning for each of those opinions?

- Is the methodology in reaching the opinion stated to be accepted in the field?

- What alternative methodologies exist and were tried?

Facts and Data Considered

- What facts and data did the expert consider?

- Where do those facts come from? Are they accurate?

(Rule 26(b)(3)(B)). Moreover, under state laws, no such protection may exist, rendering communications between counsel and a testifying expert discoverable. The deposing attorney, once again, must know the law of the applicable jurisdiction.

5. State courts vary in their procedures for expert witness disclosures. *E.g.*, Cal. Code Civ. P. §§ 2034.210, 2034.260 (simultaneous exchange of expert witness information; demand for discoverable reports; expert witness declaration prepared by attorney or party). Whatever reports and disclosures the jurisdiction requires, the deposing attorney should consider the issues raised in this chapter.

- What facts are omitted?

- What sources of information have not been consulted?

- Who participated in the data collection, testing, and analysis? Was it some-one trained (and licensed or certified, if required) to do this work?

- What interviews were conducted? What tests were performed? Did the ex-pert go to the scene (in an accident case, for example)? Has the expert used the subject equipment in their day-to-day work or at least examined it for the purpose of rendering an opinion in the case?

- What writings in the field or industry standards were reviewed?

- Was the research performed specifically for this case or was it already known to the expert?

Expert's Qualifications

The obligation to set forth the witness's qualifications, including publications authored in the last decade and expert testimony in the last four years, is sometimes fulfilled by delivering a list of the information or simply providing the expert's curriculum vitae (CV), list of credentials, or resumé. In whatever form you receive it, scrutinize the salient information and confirm it at least with online searches.

For instance, check out the information provided about the expert's employment and education. How relevant is the employment and education to the case? How long ago did the employment and education occur? Has the industry changed since then? Are there unexplained gaps between jobs? What does the employment and education reveal about the scope of the witness's true expertise? The witness may be credentialed in economics, for example, but their specialized knowledge may only be in a subset of the field that is not at issue and not germane to the subject of the witness's opinions.

If the expert claims membership in an organization, search for that organization to find out if it exists. Is it prestigious? Does it have rigorous membership standards or can anyone join for a fee? Does it reflect an affinity for a particular litigation side—i.e., the plaintiff or the defendant? Similarly, if the expert lists licenses or board certifications, contact the organization or visit its website to determine if the individual is in good standing.[6]

---

6. Although a longshot, a search of www.quackwatch.org can elicit whether a medical expert has been deemed a "quack" and whether certain tests and devices have been labeled dubious.

National Institute for Trial Advocacy

Prior writings and testimony are important too. For relevant publications, locate a copy to see if the expert has taken a position contrary to what the expert is taking in the case. For each case in which the expert has testified, search LexisNexis/Westlaw or the relevant court website to learn the nature of the case and the attorneys involved, who may have information on the expert's testimony.

Expert's Documents

Mandatory Rule 26 disclosures require identifying the exhibits that will be used to summarize or support the expert's opinions. There is no obligation to provide documents that do not support the expert's opinion. You want to get those too.

At least ten days before the deposition, serve a document request on the opposing party seeking production of all material (writings, recordings, photographs, objects, etc.) that was made available to the expert, that the expert may cite for the expert's opinions, that are inconsistent with the expert's opinions, that the expert reviewed (including witness statements, regardless of whether relied upon to support the opinion), or that refers or relates to the expert's reports or tests, as well as the expert's retention agreement in the case, resumes and CVs, time sheets, and billing statements.

Review thoroughly the documents received with the Rule 26 disclosures and in response to discovery requests. For those containing technical or scientific information—laboratory notes, chemical analysis, engineering diagrams, critical path flow charts, econometric calculations, medical charts, patents—your consulting expert can help you.

Have the consulting expert explain the documents to you—line by line, entry by entry, number by number if need be—describing sources for each entry and providing meaning to each entry. As the consultant guides you through the document, annotate your copy. Familiarize yourself to the point where you can explain the document to others, so you can ask about it at the deposition. Your goal at the deposition will not be to reveal your thorough knowledge of the documents; rather, your understanding of the document will allow you to recognize if the opposing expert has inadequate information, mistaken knowledge, or a mistaken conclusion, or tries to pull one over on you.

22.3.3 Research the Expert

Although the expert's CV or resume provides a glimpse into the expert's qualifications, publications, and testimony, do not stop there. That information is just what the expert or opposing party wanted you to see. There is much more available to help you assess whether the individual really is an expert relevant to the case.

An internet search of the expert's name will turn up the expert's website (if any), which typically touts experience, testimony, writings, and references. The search can also lead to websites that discuss the expert, organizations where the expert works or teaches, licensing information, and other testimony, writings, or lectures the expert did not disclose on their CV or exceeded the scope of the Rule 26 disclosures. You may even find YouTube videos.

LexisNexis is a particularly valuable resource. A case search uncovers references to the expert in briefs and court decisions. These decisions, from trial or appellate courts, may contain rulings or comments on the witness's qualifications or the reliability of the witness's methodology, as well as contact information for the attorneys involved. A search of LexisNexis's "Expert Research on Demand" database yields information about the cases in which the expert has testified, indications of a bias for plaintiffs or defendants, transcripts, *Daubert* challenges, disciplinary actions taken against the expert by a licensing board, newspaper articles mentioning the expert, and abstracts of articles and books the expert witness has written.

Other lawyers can provide helpful input too. Bar organizations such as the American Association for Justice (plaintiff-oriented) and Defense Research Institute (defense-oriented) maintain websites containing information on expert witnesses, including transcripts of prior testimony. Attorneys you know in the same practice area, even outside your firm, may know the expert and have copies of transcripts or recordings of the expert's prior testimony.

From all this information, you can often find material to use in the deposition—evidence that the expert exaggerated their credentials, conflicting expert opinions, literature from reliable authorities that contradicts the expert's approach, inconsistent views the expert has propounded in other cases, and other matters that raise questions about the expert and their work.

22.3.4 Research the Field of Expertise

Although you will never be as expert as the expert witness you are going to depose, become sufficiently familiar with the basics of the subject area on which the witness will opine.

For example, if the expert you are going to depose will opine on the value of a business, understand the different valuation approaches and the usefulness and weaknesses of each approach; if the witness is opining on the lost profits sustained by the plaintiff corporation or the lost wages suffered by the personal injury plaintiff, understand the different ways to calculate losses and essential concepts such as discount rates.

If you do not already know the basics of the field, start with a couple of reliable sources for novices, synthesize them, and get yourself to the point where you understand the material well enough to explain it to others.[7] Armed with some knowledge of the basics and the jargon and nomenclature, discuss the expert's report and the specified field with your client or with another expert or graduate student you have hired as a consultant.

During the deposition, as we discuss later in this chapter, you will adopt the persona of the ignorant but interested student, eager to be taught by the all-knowing expert witness. Ideally, however, that ignorance will be largely feigned, because you must detect and appreciate the nuances of the expert's methodologies and opinions, small changes in assumptions or facts that could result in major changes in conclusions, and word choice that is masking weaknesses or unfavorable alternatives.

22.3.5 Research Specifics of the Law

As with every deposition, keep in mind the substantive law of the claims and defenses alleged in the case and the legal theories of the client and the opponent. Beyond that, research matters specific to expert witness testimony. To what extent do the attorney-client privilege and the attorney work-product doctrine protect the communications between the opposing expert and the opposing attorney? Does the jurisdiction follow *Daubert* and *Kumho* in requiring the party offering the expert to show that the expert and methodology are reliable? If not, what standard must the opinion meet to be admissible? Is the requisite methodology dictated by statute or prior cases? Are there other requirements for admissibility peculiar to this type of expert? For example, in a medical malpractice case, must the opinion include knowledge of the local standard of care, or, in a legal malpractice case, must the opinion display knowledge of the level of practice within a particular legal specialty such as antitrust or products liability?

22.3.6 Consider How to Exploit Expert Witness Tendencies

Expert witnesses tend to share certain characteristics. Knowing them can help you prepare for the deposition. While some of these tendencies can make the deposition more difficult than deposing a lay witness, adjusting your deposition approach will allow you to exploit the tendencies and make them work for you.

An expert tends to teach, so become a student. Witnesses offered as experts have a lot of knowledge, experience, and information. Like us all, they do not mind

---

7. For example, the REFERENCE MANUAL ON SCIENTIFIC EVIDENCE, Third Edition (2011), is available from the Federal Judicial Center (www.fjc.gov). It describes "the basic tenets of key scientific fields from which legal evidence is typically derived" and provides "examples of cases in which that evidence has been used." The various chapters on scientific topics are "written for a non-technical audience" to provide judges with the "basic information in an area of science, to allow them to have an informed conversation with the experts and attorneys." It can be a great source for counsel looking for a general background and can be downloaded for free.

showing it. Academics are especially used to teaching students, and they carry that into the deposition room.

The expert's inclination to teach can give them an advantage at trial, because their comfort level in "teaching" the judge or jurors can help the trier of fact understand complicated material and make the expert seem persuasive. But if you can successfully encourage the expert to teach at the deposition with you in the role of student, the expert will ultimately give you more information than opposing counsel would like. Not only will this download of information help you understand the expert's work and opinion; it will help your own expert dissect and attack the opposing expert's position.

It is therefore very important, in deposing an expert witness, to assume the role of a student—someone who knows little to nothing about the expert's field but is interested in learning about it. You can step into this role in various ways. You can reflect it in your questions ("Why does . . ." "So do you mean that . . ." "Oh, I see, that's helpful," "I'm sorry, I just haven't quite gotten this yet . . ."). You can display sincere interest and respect. You can ask probing questions that appear derived from your intellectual curiosity (even if fueled by your own expert's advice to ask the question).

Giving the opposing expert some paper or a whiteboard to help explain the analysis may further encourage the expert to fall into a teaching role. The expert forgets that you are seeking material to undermine their credibility and opinions, and proceeds to sketch, diagram, instruct, repeat, simplify, and analogize in an effort to enlighten you about even the most esoteric aspects of the methodology and conclusions. Once the expert begins teaching at the deposition, the expert's advantage turns into your advantage.

As a corollary, take pains to understand what the expert witness is saying. If there are two questions to ask repeatedly when deposing an expert, they are "what do you mean?" and "why?" Too often, even with lay witnesses, deposing counsel will assume that they know what the witness meant by a specific word, phrase, or description, and that assumption may not be correct. The likelihood of this with expert witnesses is exponentially greater. Good advice on deposing the opposing expert is this: Do not assume you understand any answer the expert gives you.

An expert always could have done more, so elicit that admission. The time any expert has to devote to a case is finite, while the universe of information and inquiry is infinite. Therefore, experts must usually admit there is more they could have known and more they could have done in reaching their opinion. While they may claim it is only a remote possibility that their opinion would have changed if they had been told those unknown facts or performed those additional tasks, your eventual argument to the jurors is that the expert left the job unfinished and their opinion is unreliable.

An expert must make assumptions, so challenge them. To reach their opinions, experts rely on hypotheses and formulas that require the insertion of factual data they assume to be true—assumed facts of what occurred between the parties, what conditions and circumstances exist, or events in the future. Some of these factual assumptions can be challenged because they are contrary

> *Exploit an expert's tendencies, especially the tendency to teach; assume the role of interested student constantly asking "why," while being fully equipped to comprehend the answers and discern attempts to obfuscate or evade.*

to the evidence. For example, the expert may embrace facts alleged in the complaint, but discovery has demonstrated them to be untrue or the source of those facts has been shown to be a liar. Other factual assumptions can be challenged because they can never be confirmed. For instance, an expert in a wrongful death case attempting to calculate the present value of a future income stream involves future interest rates, future inflation rates, and future discount rates; while these can be estimated, they cannot be known with certainty.

Of course, your own expert (if there is one) must also rely on factual assumptions. The point is not that the opposing expert has made assumptions, but that the assumptions on which the opposing expert relies are less likely true than the assumptions made by your expert. The relative reliability of these assumptions affects the credibility of the expert, their opinion, and the opponent's entire case. (We address how to challenge the opposing expert's assumptions later in this chapter.)

An expert is concerned with professional standing, credibility, and livelihood, so hedge them in. Unlike most lay witnesses, experts bear the burden of belonging to a profession, and while they may wish to stand out as superior when compared to their colleagues, they have no desire to stand out because they are espousing a position so extreme that few if any of their peers would agree with them. In short, most experts are hesitant to become the outlier or to be perceived as a "radical" in their field. Moreover, they do not want to contradict their prior testimony, which would draw into question their credibility. Nor do they want to testify to opinions or methodology that might preclude them from future employment, which would affect their livelihood.

The tendency of the expert witness to remain consistent with mainstream beliefs and approaches can be leveraged in two respects. First, it can be used to get the expert witness to qualify or limit their opinion. Second, the expert will likely admit the authority of accepted treatises, theorems, or standards that can help your case or your own expert witness's testimony.

An expert loves jargon and complexities, so be prepared. Experts derive confidence from their belief that, if they encounter a question they do not want to answer, they can hide behind their expertise—plying jargon, insisting on hyper-technical definitions of terms, discussing the conditions they claim to see in questions—to the point where the deposing attorney has forgotten the question and lost all ability to determine whether it was answered. For example, when asked whether the assumed shape of the curve showing the receipt of profits for a project was more an ascending ramp than a descending ramp, an econometrician might answer:

> Well, counsel, that question presumes more informa-
> tion than is readily available from the few facts you
> seem to be implying, and without engaging in sub-
> stantial efforts at crafting a regression equation that
> produced a large enough R^2 to give us some comfort,
> an acceptable degree of confidence, perhaps at the 95
> percent level, we will be unsure whether we are deal-
> ing adequately with problems of heteroskedasticity or
> multicollinearity.

However, you can deal with an expert's use of jargon to avoid answering a question and turn it to your advantage. The expert, in using such jargon, is counting on your unwillingness to show your ignorance by asking for explanations. The expert presumes that your ego will keep you from admitting that you are unable to determine whether they have answered your question and you will therefore go blindly forward.

But because you are already playing the role of the interested but ignorant student, feel no shame in admitting your ignorance. When faced with jargon and other expert-speak, say: "I'm sorry. I don't understand that last answer. Can you help me? What do you mean by regression analysis? What do you mean by R^2? What do you mean by large enough R^2? What do you mean by heteroskedasticity? Why should we be concerned about that in your analysis?" Continue with your line of questioning until you have required the expert to define all their terms (even the ones you know) and have demonstrated the patience and resolve to cure your apparent ignorance with detailed questions.

Whether the expert has been intentionally trying to dissemble by hiding behind the jargon of their expertise or has merely forgotten that English is the language in which they are normally expected to converse, the lesson will eventually become clear: this is your arena, they will answer the questions eventually, and neither your ignorance nor your desire to get on to other topics will prevent you from slicing through the expert's attempts at obfuscation.

22.3.7 *Create Timelines and an Outline*

Many attorneys suggest creating multiple timelines to prepare for the deposition and then taking them along to the deposition. One such timeline is the chronology we discussed in section 4.1.1, which tracks everything that occurred during the events underlying the litigation. A second timeline shows the history of the opposing expert's involvement in the lawsuit, from first contact with opposing counsel through the completion of the work and the submission of the expert report. A possible third timeline would track the history of the science, scientific methods, and standards of care as germane to the issues in the case.

To quickly see the differences between the opposing expert's report and your expert's report, create a comparison table. Include rows for "qualifications," "opinion," "methodology," and "assumptions." Include a column for each expert and a column to record ideas for deposition inquiries.

As for an outline, list the topics and subtopics of the deposition, with annotations about documents and ESI to be used as exhibits. As in lay witness depositions, stick to using an outline form and bullet points rather than writing out specific questions—except for any questions that must be asked very precisely to make sense to the deponent or compel the answer you want. A consultant can help you word these questions as needed. An outline is also a good place to include a list of important terms that will come up in the deposition and a cheat sheet of definitions.

As for the items to include as topic headings in your outline, let's turn to what you will want to cover in your deposition of the expert.

22.4 Topics of the Deposition

The following topics provide good headings for your deposition outline and suitable areas of inquiry in the deposition: the expert's qualifications; the opponent's retention of the expert; work performed; work still to do; the expert's report; the expert's preparation for the deposition; the opinions, methodologies, and assumptions on which each opinion is based; changes to those assumptions and hypotheticals; questions about the certainty of the expert's opinion; critique of your own expert, and points of agreement with your expert. These topics are described below in what is ostensibly a logical order. At the deposition, however, there will likely be a strategic reason not to pursue these inquiries in this order, as we explain in section 22.5.

22.4.1 Qualifications and Experience as an Expert

The expert's qualifications include their education, training, certification, employment and real-world experience, teaching experience, experience as an expert witness, and relevant writings. The essential question is not whether the person has sufficient background to be an expert, but whether they have sufficient expertise to render specific opinions in this particular case.

In the deposition, the goal is not to spend hours poring over what is on the witness's curriculum vitae (CV) or resume. Simply mark the CV that you received from the opposing party as a deposition exhibit, show it to the witness, and have the witness confirm that it is current and accurate. If it is not current and accurate, ask what would need to be added, changed, or deleted. Ask what is not included on the CV that the expert had included on other versions. If there are gaps in the CV or an inconsistency between the CV and the expert's web page, ask about that too.

Other qualification questions to ask include narrow inquiries into the expert's background relevant to the specific area of the expert's opinions. So, for example, if the witness is giving an opinion on inspection and maintenance practices for a fitness center, ask what experience the witness has specific to inspection and maintenance practices in fitness centers, not anything else that might appear on the CV. The question can be as simple as, "What qualifies you to render your opinions in this case?"

The deponent's experience as an expert witness is another worthy topic. How many times has the witness testified as an expert witness? Has a court ever refused to certify the witness as an expert? On what topic? In what case? What percentage of time does the expert spend as an expert witness, as compared to teaching or working in the field or industry? What percentage of total net income does the expert derive as an expert witness? If the expert's time and revenue are largely tied to being an expert witness, the expert can be painted as a professional witness or hired gun. If most of the expert's time is spent in the laboratory or classroom, they may lack real-world experience; if most of the time is spent working in the field, the expert may lack the latest academic insights.

The witness's experience as an expert can show their biases. If the witness always testifies for the plaintiff's side, or always testifies for the defendant's side, the witness may have an apparent allegiance to that side. If the witness has testified frequently for a particular law firm, the witness might have a motive not to upset this source of income and an incentive to testify accordingly.

> **Deposition topics:**
> - *The expert's qualifications;*
> - *The opponent's retention of the expert;*
> - *Work performed;*
> - *Work still to do;*
> - *The expert's report;*
> - *The expert's deposition preparation;*
> - *The opinions, methodologies and assumptions on which each opinion is based;*
> - *Changes to those assumptions and hypotheticals;*
> - *The certainty of the expert's opinion;*
> - *Critique of your own expert; and*
> - *Points of agreement with your expert.*

Explore other possible biases at this juncture. The witness may have a result-oriented bias shown by their reaching the same conclusion in every case they handle—the driver in the accident is always intoxicated despite varying blood alcohol levels; every component part the expert witness examines is deemed safe; every invention they examine turns out to be novel, etc. Straight-up bias may exist if the expert has any monetary or financial interest in either of the parties or in their competitors.

The Rule 26(a) disclosures or discovery responses should identify the cases in which the expert witness has testified in the last few years. For each case in which the expert testified as a witness, you may inquire as follows, if you don't already know: What law firm retained them? For which party did the expert testify? Did the expert prepare a report? Was the expert's deposition taken? Was the expert a witness at trial? Did the court rule on the expert's qualifications to testify as an expert, and, if so, what was the ruling? What was the result of the lawsuit?

22.4.2   Retention of the Expert

Determine the circumstances in which the opposing party retained the expert. This inquiry may uncover an ongoing relationship to a client or to a law firm, exorbitant or result-oriented compensation, or the thinking of the party's counsel about the case. Specific questions may include: When was the witness first contacted by the opposing party or the opposing party's attorney? What was the witness told about the case? When was the witness retained? What rate of compensation was agreed to? Does that remain the rate of compensation? How much has been charged? Did the expert know the attorney, law firm, or party before being retained? How and in what way? What was the scope of the assignment given to the expert? How did the initial assignment change up to the time of the deposition? Some of this information will be covered by the retention agreement, timesheets, and billing statements provided in disclosures or discovery, too.

22.4.3   Work Done and to Do

Ask about the work the expert (or their associates) performed in response to their assignments from opposing counsel. This overlaps some with a later inquiry into the expert's methodology in reaching their opinions; the questions only need to be asked once. But asking about work performed overall will uncover any work of the expert that did not contribute to the expert's opinion and perhaps would have led to a different conclusion and can shed light on the opposing attorney's theory of the case.

Material Reviewed

In performing the assignment given by counsel, what material (equipment, hardcopies of writings, video, photographs, websites, etc.) did the expert or anyone else working on the project review? Where did this material come from? When was it received? What material did the expert ask for and why? What material did the expert request and not receive? What material was shown to the expert, whether in person, through screen-sharing, or otherwise? What material did the expert review but not rely upon in forming their opinions in the case?[8]

Communications with Others

Communications may be oral or written, formal or informal, and include interviews, correspondence, briefings, and texts. The communications may have been with the opposing party, with other experts or third parties, or with the opposing party's attorney. Communications with the opposing party, other experts, and third parties are fully discoverable. The discoverability of communications between the opposing expert and the opposing party's attorney may be much more limited, depending on the jurisdiction.

Under the federal rules, Rule 26(b)(4)(C) protects communications between the attorney and the testifying expert (if required to provide a report) as trial preparation material under Rule 26(b)(3)(A) and (B), "except to the extent that the communications . . . (i) relate to compensation for the expert's study or testimony; (ii) identify facts or data that the party's attorney provided and that the expert considered in forming the opinions to be expressed; or (iii) identify assumptions that the party's attorney provided and that the expert relied on in forming the opinions to be expressed." However, even these materials may be discovered upon a suitable showing of need (Rule 26(b)(3)(A)), except to the extent of the attorney's mental processes (Rule 26(b)(3)(B)). State laws, on the other hand, may or may not provide similar protections under attorney work product doctrines.

Subject to any applicable limitations in the jurisdiction, queries about the expert's communications might include the following: In working on the matter, with whom did the expert communicate about the case? When and why did these communications take place? When communicating with the opposing party or third parties, what was said? When communicating with the opposing party's attorney, what was said (or, in federal court, what was said about compensation, facts or data the expert considered, or assumptions the expert relied upon). Was any information about the facts conveyed in writing that you have not already disclosed? Was any information conveyed orally that you have not already disclosed? Were you instructed by the attorney to communicate orally, rather than in writing?

If unsure whether some of these communications may be protected under Rule 26(b)(4) or similar state law, go ahead and ask about them, provided you have a

---

8. Under the federal rules, this question may be subject to objection, to the extent it asks for a communication unrelated to facts or data the expert considered or assumptions the expert relied upon in forming their opinion. *See* Rule 26(b)(4).

good faith basis to do so. It is up to the defending counsel to decide whether to object.[9]

Research and Tasks Performed/Material Generated

A major category of inquiry involves the tasks the expert performed in completing their assignment. You can elicit the information either separately from finding out about the witness's opinions, or in conjunction with the witness explaining the basis of the opinions. Either way, depending on the case, the inquiry may include:

Q: What research did you or your assistants perform? What tests did you or your assistants conduct? What calculations did you make? Why?

Q: Did you investigate the scene? When? How long? Where? Why? What did you find? Notes? Photographs? Video?

Q: Did you examine the allegedly faulty equipment? When? How long? Where? Did you take it apart to examine it? Why? Where are the parts now? Notes? Photographs? Video? Witnesses?

Q: What documents did you generate in the course of your work (reports, timesheets, worksheets, to-do lists, correspondence, etc.)?[10]

Q: Were any writings, recordings, or photographs destroyed during the course of your work?

Q: What was the total time spent on your work in the case?

Work Left to Do

As alluded to previously, there is always some research, test, or investigation the expert could have done but did not do. The inference to be argued later to the court

---

9. The line between discoverable information and non-discoverable information in this context can be a bit murky. You may find it prudent to meet and confer with other counsel in the case and stipulate what types of information will be discoverable and what types will not. *See* Rule 29.
10. Under Rule 26(b)(4)(B), draft reports of the testifying expert are generally undiscoverable under Rule 26(b)(3)(A) and (B), except upon an adequate showing of need. Although the draft report is thus typically protected from disclosure under the federal rules, there is no protection for other written material the expert generates in formulating their opinion—e.g., the expert's worksheets, notes, calendar, memoranda, outlines, and to-do lists—except possibly to the extent they refer to the attorney's mental impressions. Similarly, a summary, chart, or timeline opposing counsel prepared and provided to the expert may be discoverable if the expert witness considered it in formulating the opinion, albeit perhaps in redacted form. At the very least, find out what material exists; you might be able to establish a basis for obtaining it.

or jurors is that the opposing expert did not conduct a sufficiently thorough analysis to be considered reliable. Questions may include:

Q: Have you now finished your work in this case?

Q: What more work do you need to do?

Q: What more work would you like to do?

Q: What more work could be useful?

Q: Why? How long would it take? Why haven't you done it?

In addition, you may know from your own expert some things that your expert did that the opposing expert did not do, or additional work that could be performed. Ask the expert if they did that work, why not, and whether it would be useful.

22.4.4 Expert's Report

There may be statements in the expert's report that are worth asking about, to the extent not covered in other topics at the deposition. Also important is how the report was drafted, whether it is the expert's own work and a finished product, and anything not reflected in the report. Again, subject to the rules of the jurisdiction,[11] questions could be along these lines:

Drafts

Q: Who participated in preparing this report?

Q: What did each of them do?

Q: How many drafts were prepared? Who prepared them? When?

Q: How did the drafts differ?

Q: What comments did counsel give you on the drafts?

Q: Where are the drafts now?

Ownership and Finality

Q: Did anyone ever suggest that you write something different than what now appears in your report? Who? When? What? How did you respond? Why?

---

11. As mentioned, under Rule 26(b)(4)(B), the expert's draft reports are usually not subject to production under the federal rules, although they might be upon a sufficient showing of need (*see* Rule 26(b)(3)(A), (B)). Notwithstanding, the existence of those draft reports should be discoverable; it is less clear whether the differences in content and the attorney's communications about them could be discovered, at least under the federal rules.

Q: Is there anything in the final report that is not in your own words?

Q: Is there anything you would like to change in the report?

Anything Missing

Q: Did you reach any conclusions not in the report?

Q: Were you asked for opinions not in the report?

Q: Have you done any work since the report?

22.4.5   *Expert's Preparation for the Deposition*

As mentioned, under the federal rules, communications between the attorney and the expert are generally not discoverable except to the extent the communications relate to the expert's compensation, identify facts or data the attorney provided and the expert considered, or identify assumptions the attorney provided and the expert relied on. Nonetheless, ask these questions: Who did you talk to in preparation for your deposition? How many times did you meet? When did you meet? For how long? Who was present? In some jurisdictions, you might also ask: What questions did you ask of the attorney during your preparation session? What did the attorney tell you in response? What else did you and the attorney discuss (as to facts or data you considered or assumptions you relied upon) during the preparation session? What documents or other material were you shown? What did you learn about answering questions in a deposition?

22.4.6   *Opinions*

The expert's opinions are of obvious and paramount importance. Your task is to confirm what opinions the expert is intending to give. Then, for each one, discover all the expert's bases for the opinion, including the methodologies (theories) and each and all assumptions.

Ask the opposing expert all the opinions they reached in the case. Yes, the opinions should have been disclosed already in expert disclosures and discovery, but confirm them anyway. Have the expert list them all before asking about the bases and details of any individual opinion. Some experts are savvy enough—or have been trained well enough—to start their list of opinions with the least significant, hoping to entrap the questioner into getting all the details on relatively unimportant opinions without exploring the bases of the more troublesome or important opinions. If you confirm the entire set of opinions first, you can choose which one to start with, and the inquiry into the most important opinions will get the time it deserves.

Q: Do you still maintain the opinions set forth in your expert report?

Q: What other opinions have you reached in this case?

Q: Have you now told me every opinion you have reached in this case?

Q: Do you have any intention of modifying any of your opinions?

Q: Do you have any intention of doing additional work in this case?

Q: Do you have any intention of forming or rendering any other opinion in this case? Do you have any reason to believe you might reach any other opinions in this case?

22.4.7 Basis for Opinions—Methodologies

Broadly speaking, the basis for an expert's opinion may include the witness's expertise (education and training, specialized knowledge); authorities the expert consulted; the *methodology the expert employed,* including any research, calculation, testing, or experimentation, and the results; *factual assumptions* in implementing the methodology; and the witness's interpretation of the results from the methodology or the reasoning applied in reaching the opinion.[12]

Some of these items—the ones not italicized in the foregoing paragraph—are easily covered with a few questions: How did your expertise in the field contribute to your opinion? What authorities did you consult in reaching your opinion? (The authorities may be outdated or criticized.) What inferences did you draw from the results of your research/calculations/testing? (The reasoning may be faulty.) Of course, there may be follow-up questions as well.

But two of the bases for the expert's opinion frequently demand in-depth inquiry: the expert's methodology, and the expert's factual assumptions. Faulty methodology can lead to exclusion of the expert's opinion; faulty factual assumptions can lead to the rejection of the opinion by the jurors. We address methodologies in this section and assumptions in the next.

The expert's methodology is the theory the expert applied to reach their opinion. Essentially, it is what the witness did to answer the question posed: conducted an autopsy; performed specified testing; evaluated records using accepted diagnostic criteria; applied a mathematical formula, capitalized cash flow and reduced the figure to present value; or employed a scientific technique or process. More specifically,

---

12. Or, more simply, the methodology (theory or formula), applied to the case by making factual assumptions, will yield a result (test results, for example), which will lead to and support the expert's opinion.

it is the method of conducting the autopsy, the particular type of testing, or the specific formula or approach used to value a business or calculate lost profits.

As mentioned at the outset of this chapter, the expert's methodology must be reliable for the expert witness's opinion to be admissible. The reliability of the methodology will generally turn on the *Daubert/Kumho* factors, as applied in the jurisdiction and adapted to the case; generally, whether the methodology can be tested, has been subjected to peer review, has standards and controls, and has been generally accepted in the scientific community (or other field), as well as similar criteria (e.g., derived from research independent of the litigation and from intellectual rigor).

Inquiry into the expert's methodology is therefore important. The expert may have used a theory that the industry has rejected. The expert may have failed to comply with standard industry procedures. Use of the methodology may be contrary to a treatise, textbook, or article that your consulting expert can point to. All of that can be used to discredit if not disqualify the opposing expert.

There is one exception to the need to inquire into methodology: if your expert witness is using the same methodology and has reached a different opinion only because of different factual assumptions or different interpretation of the data. In that case, you do not want to undermine the methodology, and you do not want to waste time asking about it. All you really want is to get the opposing expert to confirm it is the correct methodology and they are not relying on any other methodology.

Assuming that the expert witness's methodology is worth inquiring about, the exact wording of your questions will of course depend on the expert's field. Here is just a general idea of the types of questions you might ask.

Identifying Methodology

There are different ways to start off this topic. The easy way, but usually too broad, is simply to ask, "What is the basis for your opinion?" or "How did you reach that opinion?" With those questions, you could receive a response as curt as "the facts, standard theories, and my forty-seven years of experience," or you could get a hodgepodge of factual assumptions, theory, and deductions. Other times the question will work just fine—"I determined the three years of losses going forward and converted to present value using an 8 percent discount rate." It depends on the expert, but even more, it depends on the nature of the opinion.

A more formal approach would go something like this:

> Q: I want to talk to you about the methodology you used in forming each of those opinions you just stated. Now, not to get hung up on wording, by "methodology," I mean the theory, formula,

method, process, testing—what you did to reach your opinion. As an example, in your report you referred to the "market approach valuation method" to arrive at the value of the business.

So, with that in mind, let's take your first opinion. What methodology did you use in reaching your opinion?

You could also follow the lead of the expert's report or disclosures and use the nomenclature employed by the expert. It could go like this:

Q: I saw in your report that you reached your opinion by performing the [test, analysis, research, etc.]. Is that the only methodology you used in arriving at your opinion?

If you get any guff or pushback from the expert witness at this point, say something like the following to the witness and opposing counsel.

Look, we all know that your opinion isn't seeing the light of day unless your methodology is shown to be reliable. So that's what we're talking about here. What methodology you used, and was it reliable. Let's start with methodology. What methodology did you use to arrive at your opinion?

But usually, the expert knows exactly what you're looking for and is more than willing to tell you.

Choice of Methodology and Reliability

The goal of inquiring about methodology is to gain evidence that the methodology is not reliable. While an opposing expert is not going to admit to pushing a fringe theory, they may not have much to defend it. Here are some inquiries to consider.

Q: Why did you choose that methodology?

Q: Is that methodology generally accepted in your field for determining [opinion]? How do you know?

Q: Has the methodology been subject to peer review and publication? Which publications? How was the methodology received? Where can I find the publication?

Q: Is the methodology the subject of any books or other writings in your field? Which ones?

Q: Who in the field agrees with using that methodology under the specific circumstances here? Who in the field disagrees?

Q: Has the methodology been tested under real-world conditions or only in the laboratory?

Q: Do you know of any studies quantifying the rate of error of this methodology? What is the rate of error?

Q: What standards are followed for this methodology? Where are they recorded? Who requires them? Did you follow them? How?

Q: What controls did you employ in implementing the methodology?

Q: Have you ever employed a different methodology in reaching an opinion on the topic of _____?

Q: Did you consider any alternative methodology? What others? Why did you not pursue them here?

Q: You didn't consider _____ as a methodology, did you? Why not?

Details of Steps Taken Pursuant to the Methodology

Some methodologies have multiple steps. Start the inquiry with a broad question such as, "What steps did you take in using that methodology in this case?" Obtain a list of all the steps from the witness. Then, for each step, "funnel" what the step entailed: what it means, why it is performed, who performed it in this case, what the results were, were there any notes or other recordings (*see* Chapter Eight). This can take a substantial amount of time.

Results of Using the Methodology

After the expert performed all the steps in the methodology, there was some sort of result. That result was then used to form the expert's opinion. Ask about the results with questions like these, including a concluding question that wraps up the inquiry:

Q: After applying the methodology, what result did you get?

Q: How did that result lead to (support/refute) your conclusion?

Q: Have you now told me everything you did to reach your opinion?

22.4.8 Basis for Opinions—Assumptions

Not only must an expert witness choose a reliable methodology; the expert must plug reliable facts and data into the methodology to reach a conclusion. If the facts and data have not been established, the expert must make certain assumptions. Thus, in calculating lost profits using a standard methodological formula, the expert will have to make assumptions regarding the extent to which the wrong-doing resulted in losses in year one, the number of years those losses will continue, and the rate at which those losses will continue. Each of those factual assumptions will be based on subsidiary data and assumptions derived from treatises, the nature of the company, industry data, market trends, and the like. Once arriving at the amount of loss, the expert would need to reduce the figure to present value by applying a discount rate; the amount of the discount rate would be chosen based on other factual assumptions pertaining to the amount of return yielded by investments of similar risk.[13] If any of those assumptions are errant or unreliable, it can affect the entire opinion.

Under the federal rules, the facts and data on which the expert bases their opinion must be observed by the expert witness personally, provided to the expert witness before the trial, or provided to the expert at trial by way of a hypothetical.[14] The facts and data do not have to be admissible in evidence, as long as they are of a type reasonably relied upon by an expert in the field to form the same type of opinion.[15]

In the deposition, therefore, find out the expert's factual assumptions, how the facts and data on which the expert relied were observed or received, why the expert made the assumptions, and why the expert believes the assumptions are reliable, including whether the facts and data are of a type reasonably relied upon by an expert in the field. The expert witness's assumptions may be readily apparent from the expert's report or testimony regarding the methodology, in which case most of the inquiry will address where the expert found the facts and data and why the expert thinks they are reliable. (Later, you will get the witness to admit that if the assumptions are wrong, the opinion is wrong.)

Here are some ideas for questions.

> Q: In applying the [methodology] in this case, what facts did you assume about _____?
>
> Q: Why did you make that assumption?
>
> Q: What was the source of the facts and data that led to that assumption? (Attorney, opposing party, deposition transcript, witness statement, trade publication, government database, internet, etc.)

---

13. Other examples abound. A psychologist testifying in a case alleging sexual harassment depends to a large extent on the truthfulness of statements made by the alleged victim. The damages expert testifying for the plaintiff in a patent infringement case must accept as accurate the plaintiff's statements regarding the success with which they would have marketed the product if the infringement had not occurred.

14. Fed. R. Evid. 703.

15. *Id.*

Q: What did you do to investigate the facts and data?

Q: How do you know the assumption is reliable?

Q: Are the facts and data the type reasonably relied upon by an expert in the field to form this kind of opinion?

Q: Did you consider any alternative factual assumption?

Q: Why did you not go with the alternative?

Q: If you had used the alternative, what result would you get?

22.4.9 Attack and Change the Assumptions in Hypotheticals

Once the expert has identified and defended the assumptions underlying the expert's opinion, challenge the assumptions to see if the witness will acknowledge that, if their assumptions are incorrect, the opinion would change. This is where the fun starts. If the expert witness admits the possibility of alternative factual assumptions, and you establish the facts are as you say they are and not as the expert assumed, game over.

Alternative Factual Assumptions

Broadly speaking, there are two ways to challenge the expert's assumptions. The first way is to show that the assumption is false. It may be false simply because it is demonstrably untrue. It may be false because the person who informed the expert of the assumed fact is a liar, mistaken, unreliable, or biased (as where it came from the opposing party or opposing attorney, or from a disgruntled employee of the client). The assumption may be false because the document or ESI from which it was derived was incorrect, forged, or falsified. Or it could be that the assumption on which the expert relied was outdated or superseded by newer developments or research. Ask questions such as, "Did you know that the person who gave you that information had been convicted of perjury?" "Would it matter to your opinion if you learned that the information was false?" "If the patient did not tell you all the times she experienced dizziness, could your opinion be based on inaccurate facts?" "Would it matter if the conditions at the scene when you investigated were different than the conditions at the scene when the accident occurred?"

If the expert based their opinion on false assumptions, the opinion likely goes down the drain. More subtly, if the factual assumptions have a high probability of being false, the opposing expert's opinions may be based on assumptions upon which experts in the field would not rely. The more factual assumptions are based on speculation and subjectivity, the less reliable they are. The more factual assumptions are based on hard data from established sources or facts undisputed in the case, the more reliable they are. Showing reliance on facts not typically relied upon by experts in the field can lead to a successful motion precluding the expert's testimony.

A second way to challenge the expert's assumptions is to get the expert to admit that alternative assumptions would also be reasonable. For example, your client may have a different but reasonable view of the facts, or your expert may have a factual assumption different from what the opposing expert has used. It is not uncommon for two eyewitnesses to observe an event or conversation differently. If the jurors believe your client's version, it may follow that the jury must reject the opposing expert's opinion.

Acknowledging a Different Result, With or Without Hypotheticals

The further goal is to get the expert to acknowledge a different result would be obtained with different factual assumptions. The essential idea is to change the facts assumed by the opposing expert and ask how that change in the facts might affect the witness's opinion.

Ask the opposing expert a hypothetical. "Assume that the defendant was traveling forty-five miles per hour at the time of impact rather than thirty-five miles per hour. How would that affect your calculation of the time it took her to from Point A to Point B?" The expert witness will either admit the possibility of a different conclusion more favorable to your side or attempt to explain away the change in the facts.

Sometimes the witness will have to admit that a change in the factual assumptions will change the result. For example, changing the value of a variable in a formula will necessarily change the mathematical result. On other occasions, where the witness is evaluating data, the witness may claim that the change in the assumption would still yield a result consistent with the witness's opinion (e.g., the driver was still intoxicated, the part was still not suitable for consumers, etc.)

If the witness testifies that they would not change the opinion regardless of a change in the assumed facts, inquire if *any* change in the assumed facts would yield a different opinion. If not, it leaves the impression that the opposing expert is not an impartial professional dedicated to the truth, but a paid advocate for the other side who is not to be believed.[16]

22.4.10 *Limit the Certainty of the Expert's Opinion*

Experts know that they cannot be 100 percent certain in their opinions and typically opine to a degree of "reasonable certainty" in their field. Having the opposing expert admit that they cannot be certain in their opinion may not turn out to be all that helpful in the long run—since your experts would have to admit the same thing about their opinions—but there is usually no downside.

---

16. Sometimes a change in the assumed facts would require an entirely different analysis or methodology, rendering the expert's opinion unreliable.

Q: You cannot say to an absolute certainty that the arrow in the victim's arm caused their death?

Q: You cannot rule out every possibility based on the tests that you conducted, can you?

Q: What do you mean by, "a reasonable certainty"? It's less than 100 percent, right? More or less than 50 percent? What percent certainty is "reasonable certainty"?

Q: In reaching a conclusion regarding _____, have you ever been wrong?

22.4.11 Critique of Your Expert's Opinion

The opposing expert has been hired not only to generate an opinion, but also to explain why your expert's opinion is incorrect. Sometimes the opposing expert has furnished this critique in an expert report, or it has been disclosed through expert witness discovery. During the deposition, make it a topic of inquiry.

Start out broadly by asking the witness, "So where do you think my expert went wrong" or "Is there anything in my expert's report that you disagree with?" Ultimately, have the opposing expert identify each aspect of your expert's opinion, methodology, and assumptions that the opposing expert disagrees with, and why. This will not only help you prepare for the rest of the case; it will help your expert prepare as well.

22.4.12 Admissions and Points of Agreement

Often the opposing expert witness will have to admit matters that are helpful to your case. For example, the opposing expert might have to admit that your expert witness is an expert in the field due to their experience, academic credentials, or publications. The opposing witness might have to agree with your expert's methodology or factual assumptions, because they used the same ones. To this end, it is worth asking something to the effect of, "What parts of [your own expert's] analysis do you agree with?" Follow-up with more pointed questions as needed.

Other admissions are possible. The opposing expert may have to acknowledge that, even if the experts in the case used different methodologies or assumptions, reasonable experts can disagree on the methodology to use or the facts to assume. Sometimes the expert will have to admit substantive facts in the case, such as that the opponent violated an industry standard. Occasionally, your opponent will have more than one testifying expert; ask the witness whether they have any disagreement with the methodology, assumptions, or opinions of the other expert witness for the opposing party. (If the expert claims not to know what the other expert has said, be prepared to state it.)

More generally, attempt to obtain the opposing expert's confirmation that certain sources of information—sources that your expert is going to use—are reliable authorities:

Q: What written materials do you consult when you have a question in your field of expertise?

Q: Who do you consult when you have a question in your field of expertise or want a second opinion?

Q: What written materials do you use in the classes you teach?

Q: If you were asked a question on [topic], what steps would you take to find the answer?

Q: I noticed in your article on _____, you cited _____ article on _____. That authority you cited is reliable, isn't it?

Q: You'd agree that [name of publication] is an authority in the field?

22.5 Ordering the Examination

The preceding discussion presented the deposition topics in a logical order, starting with the expert's qualifications and progressing through the expert's retention, the work the expert performed, the opinions they reached, their bases for those opinions, how those opinions might be different if the facts were different, and ultimately any points of agreement. Many attorneys tackle the topics during the deposition in just this order.

It is important, however, to make the best use of precious deposition time, which is usually limited by rule, court order, litigation budgets, or all three.[17] Consider handling the topics in a different order.

Starting with a lengthy examination of the expert's qualifications wastes time. Check their qualifications before the deposition by investigating the CV and other sources. Ask about qualifications only when the pre-deposition investigation leads you to believe the expert is biased or unqualified in the relevant area. Even then, you do not have to start the deposition with the expert's qualifications. In most cases, it can wait until the end.

Attorneys also seem to spend a great deal of time taking the expert through a chronological recitation of how they were hired, what they are being paid, what

---

17. Where expert issues are complex, the parties often stipulate that an expert deposition will consume multiple days. The parties should discuss this in their conference pursuant to Rules 16 and 26.

they were shown, and what they were asked to do. This eats up valuable time and energy with relatively little return; it elicits no information that pins the expert down on their opinions, methodology and assumptions—which is what will support a challenge to the admissibility of the opinions.

Devotion to this background material not only misuses time; it is what everybody expects. The witness is likely anticipating the deposition will begin with qualifications, retention matters, and assignments due to their experience in prior depositions or because of what their counsel told them during a preparation session. If you behave as predicted, you increase the expert's confidence.

Instead, consider starting with the expert's opinions. Ask the expert to describe each opinion, methodology, and basis in detail and to articulate fully every purported indicia of reliability. You may catch the expert and their counsel off guard. At the very least, you will get through the most important parts of the deposition before time runs out.

Also consider addressing areas of potential agreement early on, rather than at the end of the deposition. It is easier to get opposing experts to agree to the reliability of treatises and aspects of your own expert's methodology and opinions before there has been too much attack on the opposing expert's methodology and opinions.

In light of all this, the deposition topics may be more effectively organized as follows:

- opinions;
- methodologies, details, and assumptions on which each opinion is based;
- points of agreement with your own expert;
- the certainty of the expert's opinion;
- changes to the assumptions and hypotheticals;
- work performed (other than what has already been testified to);
- work still to do;
- the expert's report (to the extent not already covered);
- the expert's preparation for the deposition (time permitting);
- the expert's qualifications (at least regarding red flags);
- the opponent's retention of the expert (time permitting).

22.6 Concluding Thoughts on Taking the Deposition

Deposing an expert witness can at first seem quite daunting. But most of your job is getting the expert witness to talk, which is usually something they are more than happy to do. And keep in mind that it does not take much to argue the insufficiency of the expert witness's opinions at summary judgment, to bring a motion in limine to exclude or limit the testimony at trial, or to cross-examine the witness in front of the jury. You do not need to show that the opposing expert is a dummy or a charlatan—and in fact the chances of you doing so are small. All you need to do is find some combination of the following: a sketchy record of publications or experience in the specific field in which the opinion is given; two or three additional tests or inquiries the expert did not perform; a questionable methodology; one or two areas in which the expert is unaware, mistaken, or poorly prepared on the facts; the existence of material alternative assumptions the expert could have reasonably made; a source of data the expert did not consult; or a learned treatise that supports your own expert's opinion. Some of this you can obtain outside the deposition; the remainder is within your reach during the deposition.

22.7 Preparing and Defending Expert Witnesses

Preparing and defending deposition witnesses is discussed at length in Chapters Sixteen through Eighteen. Preparing an expert witness generally follows the format described in Chapter Seventeen: during a check-in phase, let the witness vent any concerns about the deposition or the case, respond to them, and set the expectations for the preparation session; in a procedural phase, confirm the deposition process and familiarize the witness with the basic rules of testifying; and in a substantive phase, identify the issues, describe the expert witness's role, review substantive answers (in this case, the expert's opinions, methodologies, and assumptions primarily) in light of the testimonial and documentary evidence, and rehearse answers in a mock deposition that exposes the witness to an aggressive examination.

Without unduly repeating the information presented in our prior chapters, let's supplement it with some observations pertinent especially to expert witnesses.

22.7.1 *Confidentiality and Privilege*

Unlike the preparation of most lay witnesses, where the attorney-client privilege applies, preparation of a testifying expert witness is not privileged. There may be some protection for communications under Rule 26(b) or the attorney work product doctrine, but carefully consider the applicable law and generally assume that opposing counsel may find out what occurs during the preparation session.[18]

---

18. This brings up interesting and complex issues when other persons are present for discussions with the testifying expert. It is not always clear, for example, whether conversations among a testifying

22.7.2 Check-in and Venting

Some experts have testified scores of times. Others, never. Some will be over-confident, while others will be insecure about the process or opposing counsel. Even those with substantial public speaking experience—in the classroom, at professional meetings, or in the courtroom—may suffer some anxiety at the thought of giving a deposition in front of lawyers in a formal and foreign environment. Furthermore, the expert may be concerned about particular substantive issues (*see* "Areas of Difficulty and Biggest Fears," below) or burdened by other events in their life. As with lay witnesses, therefore, invite the expert witness to express any concerns at the outset of the preparation session, and ensure that those concerns are addressed during the session.

22.7.3 Procedural Preparation

The expert witness will be interested in learning the essentials: how long the deposition will last, who will be there (including, possibly, the opposing party's expert), whether the deposition will be videorecorded, and whether it will be conducted in person or by video conference. The expert witness may also need their role in the case clarified. In that regard, the expert should appear knowledgeable, intelligent, impartial (yes, impartial—as in not an advocate for one side or a "hired gun," just confident in their opinions), and willing to consider additional facts and points of view, without rashly reconsidering the opinions already reached.

The "one concept, three rules" advice about listening to and answering questions applies to expert witnesses as well as lay witnesses (*see* section 17.3.3). The overriding concept is to tell the truth; from that one concept derives three essential rules: make sure you understand the question; answer honestly; and that's it—don't answer anything more than what the question asked. (Or, as it's often expressed, give the "shortest honest answer" directly responsive to the question.) The expert should not volunteer explanations, analogies, cute stories, or anything else. Remind them to resist the urge to teach.

Some aspects of these rules must be emphasized to expert witnesses. In terms of understanding the question, stress the need for the expert to understand what the attorney is asking, not what the expert thinks the attorney should be asking or is trying to ask. If the expert is not sure what a question means, they should say so. If the question makes no sense, the expert should (politely) say so. The expert should not assume what the lawyer means, nor should the expert give in to the temptation to rephrase the question for opposing counsel.

---

expert, a consulting expert, counsel, and the client could be construed in some circumstances as privileged or protected as trial preparation or attorney work product. As a general rule, do not convey to the testifying expert anything privileged and assume that no privilege applies to a preparation session.

Answering the question honestly requires some explanation as well. If the expert does not know the answer to a question, or if the expert does not remember the answer, the honest answer is that the expert does not know or does not remember. (This can pose a hurdle for an expert, because experts are used to knowing things or figuring them out.) If the question is not within the expert's area of expertise, the expert should say so. If the expert needs to refer to a treatise or a document, they should say so. If they need more information to answer a hypothetical, they should say so. Most importantly, the expert should not ramble on; indeed, this is the number one challenge for expert witnesses.

Many expert witnesses are frustrated by the direction to abstain from volunteering additional information. You will hear statements like, "Why can't I just tell them what I know? Won't that shorten the whole process?" Or, "I know where they're going. Why don't I just tell our side of their case?" But in reality, the more the expert witness volunteers, the more the deposing attorney has to ask about, and the longer the deposition will be. The best advice for the expert witness is to let the deposing attorney do the work; make them ask the right questions.

On the other hand, tell the expert not to disparage or argue with deposing counsel—especially in video depositions—to avoid appearing as an advocate for the client. They must refrain from jokes or sarcasm.

Also inform an expert witness about objections. The expert should realize that you, as defending counsel, may object to some of the deposing attorney's questions, but the expert will still have to answer the question. As a general matter, there is no attorney-client privilege protection for communications between the expert witness and anybody; under the federal rules, communications between counsel and the expert may be protected under Rule 26(b), except to the extent they relate to compensation, identify facts or data that the expert witness considered, or identify assumptions on which the expert witness relied.

22.7.4 *Substantive Preparation*

Preparing the expert witness on substantive matters has a different dynamic than preparing a lay witness. This is due in part to the difference between a witness testifying to facts they perceived, and an expert testifying to opinions they have reached. In addition, you may have already worked with the expert on the substance of the opinions while preparing expert witness disclosures, reports, and discovery responses.

Not surprisingly, the expert witness should be familiar with the topics most likely covered in the deposition, all of which we have discussed in preceding sections of this chapter from the perspective of the deposing attorney.

Qualifications

The expert must be able to explain their relevant area of expertise clearly and concisely and back it up with training, experience, etc. Before the deposition, have the expert review their CV and prepare to describe how the listed expertise relates to the opinion provided in this case. Prepare the expert to address any issues of potential bias, such as testifying always for one side or repeatedly for a given law firm or client. Research your expert thoroughly—even though you vetted them before retaining them—to see what opposing counsel might have uncovered; experts sometimes forget to disclose all their past testimony or matters that could undermine their credibility.

Compensation and Retention

The expert should review on their own the dates of retention and details of compensation. The expert does not need to be vague or evasive in answering questions about these matters. They should testify to the hourly rate, amounts billed so far, and the like.

Work Performed

Prepare the expert to describe the assignment received from counsel; the work the expert performed to accomplish that assignment, including the materials reviewed and persons spoken to; the identity of those who performed the work (e.g., the expert or an assistant); how long the work took; when, where, why, and how it was performed; and if there was any recording of it. If the expert did not conduct a test, perform research, or consult a source that experts in the field would usually do, the expert should have a reason why. If asked if the expert has any work left to do, the expert should respond honestly; even if the expert has nothing in mind, a customary response is that additional work may be undertaken if something new arises.

Opinions

It goes without saying that the expert must be able to articulate each of their opinions well. The opinion must be the result of a reliable application of the methodology to the facts. If opposing counsel asks if the expert is going to prepare or testify to any other opinions, typical answers include "Not at this time" or "I don't have any plans to do so, but if provided with new information or developments, I may revise existing opinions or render new ones."

Methodology

Confirm that the expert is ready to name and describe the methodology used to reach each opinion and demonstrate that the theory, test, etc. is reliable—in other words, that it is testable, subjected to peer review and publication, has a low potential error rate, possesses standards and controls, and is generally accepted in the field, along with any other indications of reliability. The testimony should be clear, confident, and concise. Prepare the expert to address any contrary prior testimony or any contrary literature or other authorities, as well as alternative methodologies the witness did not employ and why.

Facts, Assumptions, and Hypotheticals

Make certain the expert can recite the facts of the case, at least as relevant to their opinion, including party names, dates, and events, and be able to identify the sources of that information. In addition, the expert should be able to justify their choice of facts assumed in applying the methodology.

Pay special attention to the handling of hypotheticals in the deposition. On the one hand, the expert should appear open to considering new facts and how they might affect the analysis, in line with the impartial professional who desires only to reach the correct result. If the hypothetical is simple and can be answered without qualification (e.g., changing a variable in a mathematical equation), the expert should respond accordingly. On the other hand, new facts may or may not compel a different result or require a modified opinion, and complicated hypotheticals may necessitate extensive consideration. The expert should not feel compelled to give a definitive answer to a hypothetical if they need time to consider the matter further.

Critique of Opposing Expert

The expert witness should be prepared to identify concisely where their analysis parts company with the opposing expert's analysis, and why the witness's approach is better. For example, the witness's methodology may be preferable under the circumstances of the case, the assumed facts may be better supported by the evidence or gleaned from more reliable sources in keeping with the practice in the field, or the witness's reasoning may just make more sense.

Certainty of Opinion

The expert witness must acknowledge that the opinion is stated to the degree of certainty customary in the field. The witness should be able to explain, for example, what a reasonable degree of certainty means, and address any margin of error inherent in the analysis. Discuss fully with the expert witness, in advance, the ramifications for the margin of error.

The Mock Examination

Holding a mock deposition, in which your colleague assumes the role of the opposing counsel and peppers the witness with questions as in a real deposition, is vital to the preparation process. To challenge the expert, the role of opposing counsel can be supplemented by the consulting expert asking follow-up questions. Provide feedback in terms of how credible the witness appears and how well the opinions and their bases are being communicated. If the deposition will be videorecorded, video—with your phone, if necessary—the mock examination for review.

Areas of Difficulty and Biggest Fears

Before and during the mock examination, find out the specific substantive areas that the expert is most concerned about. The ensuing discussion can turn out to be the most important part of the preparation session and the most time-consuming. If the concerns have not surfaced during the "check-in" phase of the preparation, ask the expert straight-on:

- What are the most difficult questions you can be asked?
- What do you hope the opposing counsel does not ask you?
- What do you think the opposing expert is telling counsel to ask?
- If you were going to cross-examine yourself, what would you ask?

Then go over these areas with the witness.

Final Instructions

Give the expert witness the usual tips on how to dress for a video deposition (*see* sections 17.5.2 and 23.7.1). As with lay witnesses, instruct the expert witness to meet you shortly before the deposition, at a location other than the deposing attorney's office, for final preparation. Tell the expert witness not to bring anything to the deposition (with the possible exception of expert materials already produced, to which the expert might need to refer in communicating opinions and their bases) and not to take notes before or during the deposition (because they will likely be discoverable).

22.7.5 *Defending the Expert Witness*

With good preparation, you may not have much to do during the deposition of an expert witness. Listen carefully to the questions, keep the record clear, make sure the witness has sufficient breaks, do not let the witness become hostile to the deposing attorney (especially on video), observe whether the witness is conceding too little or too much, evaluate whether the witness is volunteering too much, be alert to the potential disclosure of trade secrets and other confidential information (and the need to seal the transcript), and object to the deposing attorney's questions (including incomplete hypotheticals and questions exceeding the area of expertise) as needed to protect the client's interests. And again, assume that discussions with the expert witness during a break are likely discoverable.

CHECKLIST
EXPERT WITNESS DEPOSITIONS

✔ Study the law for admissibility of expert witness opinion.

✔ Prepare to take the deposition by

- ✓ Gathering information on the expert from the client and other experts;
- ✓ Reviewing the expert's report and expert witness discovery;
- ✓ Researching the expert, the field, and specifics of the law;
- ✓ Considering expert witness tendencies;
- ✓ Creating a deposition outline and timelines.

✔ Consider the following topics:

- ✓ Qualifications and experience as an expert;
- ✓ Retention of the expert;
- ✓ Work done, including materials reviewed, communications with others, research and tests on which the expert is not relying for the opinion;
- ✓ Work left to do;
- ✓ Expert's report;
- ✓ Expert's preparation for the deposition;
- ✓ Expert's opinions (and no further opinions);
- ✓ Methodology used to reach each opinion, including acceptance and reliability of the methodology;
- ✓ Assumptions made in applying the methodology;
- ✓ Attack on assumptions and hypotheticals with alternative assumptions;
- ✓ Limits on the certainty of the expert's opinion and margin for error;
- ✓ Critique of your expert's opinion;
- ✓ Favorable admissions to obtain and points of agreement with own expert;

✔ Select the topics and ask about them in the deposition in an order geared for maximum effect (including starting with the opinions and methodologies).

✔ Prepare the expert witness for the deposition by:

- ✓ Addressing confidentiality and privilege;
- ✓ Checking-in with the witness and making sure the witness knows how depositions work;
- ✓ Preparing the witness to answer questions on substantive matters, including the facts in the case and the topics listed above, with special attention to the expert's opinions and methodologies and dealing with hypotheticals;
- ✓ Conducting a mock examination;
- ✓ Working with the witness on the most difficult and feared questions.

CHAPTER TWENTY-THREE

VIDEO DEPOSITIONS

A picture may instantly present what a
book could set forth only in a hundred pages.

—Ivan Sergeyevich Turgenev

A deposition will generally be more effective if it is videorecorded. The presence of the camera puts the witness and the attorneys on their best behavior. The camera and microphone pick up the witness's vocal tone, facial expressions, body language, gestures, and demeanor, which are lost with a purely written record. The video allows for better evaluation of the witness as a potential trial witness. And at trial, playing video testimony has much greater impact than reading a written transcript. To ensure that the visual record conveys the desired impression of the witness, you must handle tasks beyond what is ordinarily required.

In this chapter, we consider the circumstances in which depositions should be videorecorded; the advantages and disadvantages of doing so; and matters for counsel to keep in mind about legal requirements, preparing for the video deposition, taking the deposition, presenting the video record at trial, and, for the defending attorney, preparing the witness.

23.1   When to Record the Deposition by Video

Prior editions of this book included a separate chapter on video depositions because video depositions were, at the time, a specialized option that would be beneficial in limited contexts given their cost and technical requirements. Today, video depositions are common and readily possible due to decreased costs and technological advances; in some practice areas, it seems that all depositions are recorded by audiovisual means unless there is a strategic or logistical reason not to. Accordingly, this edition of the book has incorporated insights relevant to video depositions throughout the preceding chapters that cover deposition practice generally; for clarity and ease of reference, however, we retain this separate chapter to discuss in one place the special concerns and considerations that video depositions present.

Before turning to the advantageous use of video depositions, we must first acknowledge that live testimony from an in-person witness at trial is almost always preferable to evidence presented by any other means, including by video. Not only does a witness answering questions from the witness stand hold the jury's attention and interest better, the trier of fact can also better gauge the credibility of an in-person witness and the testimony tends to be more persuasive. In addition, jurors expect that parties and key witnesses will testify in person (or at least live by remote feed). If the witness does not appear at the trial, jurors might assume that the witness does not care too much about the case.

In This Chapter:

- *When depositions should be videorecorded*

- *The advantages and disadvantages of videorecording*

- *Legal requirements*

- *Preparing for the video deposition*

- *Taking the deposition*

- *Presenting the video record at trial*

- *For the defending attorney, preparing the witness*

Nonetheless, there are instances when the witness cannot appear at the trial. Under Fed. R. Civ. P. 32(a)(4) and Fed. R. Evid. 804, the witness may be deemed unavailable due to circumstances such as the witness's death, infirmity, age, geographic distance from the courthouse, or refusal to testify (*see* sections 11.3, 15.3.2). In some cases, the court may find an expert witness unavailable due to the expert's schedule and the expense to the client of having the expert waiting around the courthouse to testify. If the witness is deemed unavailable, and the problem is not resolved by the witness appearing remotely, a party to the lawsuit may choose to present the witness's testimony by reading or showing the witness's deposition testimony.

Similarly, even if the witness *is* available for trial, the witness's deposition testimony can be presented for other limited purposes (*see* section 15.3), including impeaching the witness's trial testimony and as a statement of an adverse party.

If the witness's deposition testimony can be used at trial, the question becomes how to present that testimony in the courtroom—by reading the written transcript or by showing a video of the testimony. Of these two options, video is usually superior for the reasons set forth below. At the same time, the fact is that very few cases go to trial, and if there is no reasonable prospect for trial, much of the need for a video recording evaporates. Therefore, while video depositions have become common and relatively inexpensive, it is worth considering in greater detail the advantages and disadvantages of a video deposition for any given witness.

23.2 Advantages of Video Depositions

Consider the following advantages of recording a deposition by audiovisual means, which result in a video of the testimony, as compared to recording it (solely) as a written transcript.

23.2.1 *When Used as Evidence*

Video depositions permit jurors to see the witness's demeanor and assess credibility. Video allows jurors to evaluate a witness's sincerity and trustworthiness based on the witness's demeanor almost as well as they can with live testimony at trial. A confidently delivered response will enhance the witness's persuasiveness. A witness's evasion, fumbling, pausing, or smirking will undermine their believability. None of these things are recorded in a written transcript, so merely reading selected portions of a stenographic deposition to the jurors deprives the jury of this opportunity.

Some witnesses do not perform well in the deposition room, and their counsel may conclude that they will perform just as poorly in the courtroom. If the evasive or fidgety witness becomes unavailable for trial, the witness's counsel could present the witness's deposition testimony by merely reading the transcript, thus reducing the negative image the witness presented. The deposing attorney, however, could use the video recording so the jurors could observe the witness's lack of credibility.

Video depositions allow jurors to see the witness's frail physical condition. A video deposition can capture the physical condition of a witness who is terminally ill or who has become too infirm to testify at trial. For example, a video deposition of a plaintiff with asbestosis allows the jurors to see the effects of the disease on their health in a way the bare transcript of a stenographic deposition cannot.

Video deposition testimony is more likely to capture the jurors' attention and facilitate comprehension. Stenographic deposition testimony is usually presented by one or two lawyers reading the questions and answers to the jury. No matter how well it is presented, jurors repeatedly confirm that the reading of transcribed deposition testimony leaves them confused and bored. While not as easy to follow as live testimony, video depositions are vastly better than reading a transcript. Ample studies have shown that people recall much more of the information they have seen and heard than the information they have only heard.

Video depositions allow better presentation of exhibits. During a deposition, the witness may refer to an exhibit, as where a doctor refers to an anatomical diagram. The witness might say, "The fracture occurred here," and the lawyer will attempt to make the record clear by saying, "You are pointing to the upper portion of the ulna?" and so on. If the deposition is merely read at trial, a copy of the exhibit must be shown to the jurors with the hope they can comprehend from the deposition testimony the relevant portion of the exhibit. The procedure is cumbersome and risks that jurors will not understand what part of the exhibit the witness was referencing.

A video deposition better coordinates the testimony with the exhibit. The camera can zoom in and capture a close-up of the exhibit and show the viewer exactly where the witness is pointing while testifying, "The fracture occurred here." In fact, video of the exhibit could be taped separately by the videographer and inserted into the video of the witness's testimony at the appropriate point, subject to the opposing party's objection.

Video depositions allow the witness to demonstrate how equipment operates, describe a scene outside the courtroom, or conduct tests and experiments in a laboratory. Counsel in a products liability case may want the jurors to see how a piece of equipment was operated when an injury occurred, or how a consumer was using a product when, for instance, a piece of scaffolding collapsed. When the item is too large to bring into the courtroom or the witness is unavailable, the best way to help jurors understand the witness's account is through a video deposition. Similarly, a video deposition may be taken at the scene of an accident or construction site, with the witness pointing out where the events occurred in response to the deposing attorney's questions.[1] And where an expert witness has conducted experiments, but the expert is unavailable for trial or the experiments cannot be conducted in the courtroom for reasons of safety or practicality, a video deposition of the expert demonstrating the experiment will let the jurors see exactly what the expert did and what results the expert reached.

Video depositions can be more effective for impeachment and party admissions. The dramatic impact of impeaching a witness with the witness's prior inconsistent statement from their deposition is heightened when jurors can both hear and see the witness making the prior inconsistent statement.[2] Similarly, an admission by the opposing party is more powerful when jurors see the witness uttering the damaging words. When the testimony is presented by video, a bonus is that the video can refute any claim by the witness at trial that they did not understand the question or were too weary to know what they were saying.

---

1. *See* Roberts v. Homelite Div. of Textron, Inc., 109 F.R.D. 664 (D. Ind. 1986) (allowing video deposition of a reenactment of plaintiff attempting to start a lawn mower that had injured his hand); Gillen v. Nissan Motor Corp. in United States, 156 F.R.D. 120 (E.D. Pa. 1994) (allowing videotaped demonstration of the alleged defect of seatbelts); Bassily v. Louisville Ladder, 2:20-cv-01120-BHH, 2021 U.S. Dist. LEXIS 224563 (D.S.C. March 30, 2021) (allowing plaintiff's deposition to include video reenactment of the plaintiff's position and actions when he fell off a ladder at the accident scene).

2. If used for impeachment purposes, the video would constitute extrinsic evidence of a prior inconsistent statement, which need not be shown to the witness on the stand at trial but must be disclosed to counsel on request. The video itself would not be admissible unless the witness denied the statement and was shown the video, and opposing counsel had the chance to question the witness about it. Fed. R. Evid. 613. If offered as a statement of an opposing party (or its managing agent, officer, or director), video of the statement would be admissible as set forth in Rule 32(a)(3).

Video depositions can be edited for use during opening statement and closing argument. Courts are increasingly permitting the use in opening statement of video deposition excerpts that have been ruled admissible or that the proponent reasonably believes will be admitted during trial. Showing jurors a key deposition question and answer during opening—to introduce a theme or place the witness in the desired light even before testifying—has significant impact. Assuming the testimony is thereafter admitted into evidence during the trial, the video can be used in closing argument as well, awakening clear memories of important witness testimony just before the jurors deliberate.

23.2.2 To Make the Deposition More Efficient

Video depositions are more likely to control the behavior of disruptive opposing counsel. As noted earlier, lawyers who are willing to disrupt the deposition and act completely inappropriately are more reluctant to do so when their actions are captured on video. Coaching the witness—from hand signals to throat clearing to whispering in the witness's ear—miraculously vanishes. And even if the lawyer is undeterred by the eye of the camera, the recording will make it much easier to obtain sanctions for counsel's behavior, as the judge will be better able to evaluate obstreperous counsel and the effect of that behavior on the discovery process. This advantage itself is enough to convince many attorneys to choose video depositions even if the case is unlikely to make it to trial. And if the case does go to trial and the video of counsel coaching the witness is played for the jurors, the credibility of both the witness and counsel will be dealt a blow.

Video depositions reduce a witness's evasiveness. In a similar vein, it is harder for the witness to avoid answering the deposing attorney's questions with flippant assertions of "I don't know" and "I don't remember" when testifying in front of a camera. The witness knows just how foolish such answers will look to the judge or jurors. And if the witness's ignorance or amnesia persists notwithstanding the camera's presence, the evasiveness is captured in the recording for all to see at trial.

23.3 Disadvantages of Video Depositions

While video depositions offer many important advantages over stenographic depositions, they also have some drawbacks, such as the following.

Video depositions are more expensive than stenographic depositions. The expense of video depositions has declined substantially, but video depositions are still more expensive than stenographic depositions due to the added cost of the videographer and the need to edit the video before presentation at trial. You can try to save money by not hiring a court reporter to record the deposition stenographically—proceeding with a video record alone—but that has its downsides. Specifically, you still must arrange for a deposition officer to swear the witness (unless the videographer is qualified to do it) and, if you want to present the deposition testimony to the court later, you will most likely end up hiring someone to transcribe the audio portion of the video into written form (Rules 26(a)(3)(A)(iii), 32(c)). Attempts to save money by having a paralegal operate the recording equipment—or attempting to operate it yourself—are unwise, since self-generated video can result in inaccuracies that jeopardize the usefulness and admissibility of the video. And while some attorneys think they can circumvent the cost of a professional videographer by conducting the deposition remotely and simply pressing "record" on the Zoom platform, the resulting recording is not likely admissible under the federal rules.[3] Bottom line, recording the deposition by video will cost hundreds of dollars more per deposition.

Video depositions can be more difficult to use for trial preparation. One of the important uses for depositions is to help prepare for trial. As discussed in section 15.2, depositions can be reviewed to find evidence to support or oppose a position, plan a witness's cross-examination, and sketch out a closing argument. Using a stenographic deposition is more convenient than reviewing a video, at least for many attorneys. It takes more time to review the video than to skim the transcript, since reading the witness's words is faster than listening to the witness speak them. A paralegal can search the transcript by key words, speeding up the process, but it is still time-consuming. Furthermore, it has traditionally been cumbersome with video to go back to an earlier question and answer and navigate the testimony.

There are, however, ways to resolve these issues. Normally, a written transcript is prepared in addition to the video, so the pretrial review can be accomplished by reading the transcript if reviewing the video is too cumbersome. Moreover, the court reporting service can provide the written transcript in a MPEG-1 format that can be synchronized with the video recording, allowing the two to be viewed on the same computer screen (the transcript on one side, the corresponding video on the other). Simply scroll through the transcript or search for a particular word or phrase, highlight the desired section of the transcript, and then click to review the corresponding testimony on the video. (Or click to create a video clip of the testimony, which can be exported to presentation software to display the video and corresponding text of the excerpt at trial.)

Video depositions are less valuable if the case does not go to trial. The strength of video is in presenting evidence at trial or to a mediator or arbitrator. If there is no likelihood of a trial or similar proceeding, there is less reason to incur the expense of a video deposition. (Some reason remains, of course, if the fact of recording controls the behavior of an obstreperous defending attorney or uncooperative

---

3. Alcorn v. City of Chicago, 336 F.R.D. 440, 443–45 (N.D. Ill. 2020); *but see* Sanders v. Univ. of Idaho, College of Law, Case No. 3:19-cv-00225-BLW, 2022 U.S. Dist. LEXIS 184883 (D. Idaho, Oct. 8, 2022) (objection waived).

witness. In those instances, it is not the video that provides the advantage, but the presence of the camera, and it may well be worth the cost.)

Video depositions are more likely than stenographic depositions to have technical or mechanical problems. Occasionally, video equipment malfunctions. More rarely, the operator forgets to turn on the equipment at the proper time or no one notices the batteries have died. Such occurrences are unlikely with a professional videographer, but the results could be disastrous if the malfunction or error is not discovered until the deposition is completed and the witness has departed.

Video depositions require special equipment and extra arrangements when used in court. Video monitors or projection equipment need to be situated so they do not interfere with movement in the courtroom during the trial, yet capable of being moved into position and readied to promptly display important testimony or impeachment. Furthermore, you must allow for the possibility of equipment malfunction, maintaining backups of everything. Again, these concerns are greatly diminished with technological advances and modernized courtrooms, but some courtrooms are still not up to speed.

Some deposition witnesses do not speak or film well. This is more of a concern for the defending attorney, although it can plague a deposing attorney who is taking a preservation deposition of a friendly witness to use in lieu of live testimony at trial. A classic example is Richard Nixon in the 1960 presidential debate, in which poor preparation and hot lights made him look like a gangster and may have cost him the election. Decades later, the video of Bill Gates's deposition in *United States v. Microsoft* made him appear distracted, ill-informed, evasive, arrogant, and unpleasant.[4] The lesson? A witness's appearance on video can instill distrust and dislike in the viewer. So, if your witness will not testify at trial and a video deposition will be presented instead, consider how the witness will appear and sound on the recording and prepare the witness for the deposition with the audiovisual recording in mind. A stenographic deposition does not hint at a witness's halting answers, furtive looks, and nervous manner, but a video deposition reveals all these flaws and more.

Video depositions allow the opponent's witnesses to hone their performances if they later testify at trial. In contrast to the foregoing point, if you depose an opposing witness who is going to testify at trial, the video can end up helping the witness. The witness can watch the video of the deposition and realize the shortcomings of their presentation and delivery: poor eye contact, hesitations, fumbling with documents, appearing evasive when answering questions, slouching,

---

4. Dan Goodin, *Revisiting the spectacular failure that was the Bill Gates deposition*, Ars Technica, Sep. 9, 2020. Available at https://arstechnica.com/tech-policy/2020/09/revisiting-the-spectacular-failure-that-was-the-bill-gates-deposition/ (Last visited Apr. 10, 2023).

volunteering information, rambling on, and the like. The video will spur them to improve before they appear before the judge or jurors.

23.4 The Law

Rule 30(b)(3) states that video depositions may be taken as a matter of right unless the court orders otherwise. The only requirement is that the deposition notice disclose that the deposition will be recorded by audiovisual means. The taking party bears the cost of the video. If the deposing party has not opted to record the deposition by video, any other party may, as of right, require that the deposition be recorded on video; in that case, the requesting party will be responsible for arranging and paying for the video recording.

> *Video depositions cost more, but they produce more compelling trial evidence and may keep the witness and lawyers on their best behavior.*

Rule 30(b)(5)(B) specifically instructs that the appearance or demeanor of the deposition witness must not be distorted through camera or sound recording techniques. In other words, the recording must be fair and accurate. Professional videographers take this seriously, but always ask to see how your witness is being captured by the camera.

Other rules pertain to using the video deposition at the trial. Rule 26(a)(3) states that if a party intends to present a witness's testimony by deposition, it must disclose the intention to opposing counsel as part of the required pretrial disclosures and provide a transcript of the pertinent portions of the deposition if it was not recorded stenographically. Under Rule 32(c), if video deposition testimony is offered other than for impeachment (usually, as the testimony of an unavailable witness), it must be presented in nonstenographic form on the request of any party, unless the court orders otherwise for good cause. Whenever a video deposition is used at trial (or in support of a motion for summary judgment or other evidentiary motion), the offering party typically must provide the court with a transcript of the portions being offered.

23.5 Preparing to Take the Video Deposition

If you plan to use lengthier clips from the video depositions at trial—three minutes or more—make those video excerpts both interesting and persuasive. If the direct examination on video drags on, is poorly organized, or is filled with jargon, the jurors will not follow the story or chronology and the intended points will be lost. If the impeaching segments are not crisp, or take too long to set up the contradiction, the jurors will fail to see the inconsistency or appreciate its significance. Although some editing of the video may be possible before trial, effective video depositions must be carefully planned productions.

23.5.1 Hire a Professional Videographer

Using an experienced and capable video operator to conduct the deposition will avoid many of the difficulties that can occur with video. An experienced operator can provide guidance in setting up the room, positioning the camera, lighting, post-production editing, and many considerations that do not exist with a stenographic deposition, but which are crucial to taking an effective video deposition. The videographer will also be familiar with the requirements for certifying the recording so it can be admissible in the litigation. Most court-reporting firms can arrange for professional videography. Before deciding which outfit to use, disclose your intention of recording the deposition by video and find out what services they offer.

23.5.2 Arrange to Record Stenographically, Too

If the jurisdiction requires a written transcript of the deposition testimony to use the testimony at trial, either have a court reporter attend the deposition and create a stenographic record of the testimony or arrange for someone to transcribe the audio portion of the audiovisual recording after the fact. A stenographic transcription is useful to have even when it is not required, because it is easier to review and gives additional options for presenting the testimony at trial. Therefore, state in the deposition notice that the deposition will be recorded both stenographically and by audiovisual means.

23.5.3 Select a Suitable Location

Choose a deposition room large enough to seat all the participants comfortably and to hold all the necessary equipment. Give the videographer enough space to position the camera and to move around. Always check that the lighting is adequate and whether to open or close curtains or shades. Make sure the room is free of distracting noise from traffic outside, from air conditioning in the room, and from conversations out in the hall.[5]

23.5.4 Plan the Questions

The video deposition substitutes for live testimony at trial. Carefully organize the portions of deposition testimony that you think you might use at trial (as direct examination, impeachment, etc.) as you would if you were in front of a jury.

---

5. *See* Cal. Code Civ. P. § 2025.340(a) (the area for the video deposition shall be "suitably large, adequately lighted, and reasonably quiet").

A video deposition is not the place for stream-of-consciousness questioning or for asking questions on the fly. The goal is to present the factfinder a clear, persuasive, and memorable nugget of testimony. An orderly progression through the topics also reduces the cuts and splices in editing that can make the video look choppy and distract from the testimony.

Arrange exhibits so they are quickly accessible during the deposition and are in the order in which you will use them. Avoid delays during the deposition by premarking exhibits and having extra copies for opposing counsel and the court reporter.

Objections during the deposition can be edited out before the video is presented at trial, but such editing can take time and can give the video a choppy appearance. Therefore, review the plan of questioning and the expected answers before the deposition to avoid objections.

23.6   Taking the Video Deposition

For the most part, a video deposition proceeds in the same way as a deposition that is recorded only stenographically. Here are some additional considerations.

23.6.1   *Dealing with Microphones*

Aside from the presence of the camera, the most significant difference in equipment at the video deposition is the microphone—or, hopefully, microphones—used to capture the audio portion of the recording. Ideally, the videographer will have the witness and counsel wear lavalier microphones on the lapel of their shirts, with each microphone providing a dedicated audio that is less susceptible to background noise than the alternatives. These mics are, however, subject to muffling and static whenever a hand, paper, or clothing brushes against them. Also be aware that a microphone may have been left on during a break, even when no one else is in the room. If you are going to have a private conversation, go into another room and, depending on how the videographer instructs you, turn off the mic or cup your hand over it and take it off.

23.6.2   *Working with the Videographer*

Without cooperation between the deposing attorney and the videographer (and stenographer, assuming there is one), a video deposition can quickly turn into a disaster. The good news is that professional videographers are trained, skilled, and usually available from the same service that provides the court reporter.

A videographer may need an hour to set up in the deposition room, so make sure the room is available well before the scheduled start. Talk with the videographer about the lighting in the room. The videographer will know to frame a camera shot that does not include glare from windows or dark shadows on the deponent. Consider whether the light and shadows will change as the sun moves, necessitating an adjustment to the window coverings or shifting the camera location by mid-afternoon. Before the deposition, ask to test how well the exhibits, especially those like x-rays and photographs, will show on the video.

Also discuss the possibility of zooming in on exhibits. During the deposition, you can instruct the videographer to capture an exhibit at a specific point in the questioning. For example, when the witness points to an exhibit, it will appear quite natural for you to say, "Why don't we get a close-up of where you are pointing on Johnson Deposition Exhibit 17?" Keep in mind that it may take a few seconds for the zoom to occur.

23.6.3 Controlling the Tone

A video deposition captures not only the witness's voice, but your voice as well. Even if a nonresponsive witness is frustrating, remain polite, calm, and professional. It would be disappointing if your snarky or intimidating tone of voice ruined the effect of an admission you wrestled from the witness.

23.7 Defending a Video Deposition

Defending the witness at a video deposition requires the same techniques we discussed for defense of the witness in Chapters Sixteen through Eighteen. Here are some additional tips and things to keep in mind when preparing the witness for the deposition, defending the witness at the deposition, and assisting in post-deposition review.

23.7.1 Preparing the Witness—Attire and Demeanor

The video deposition reveals your witness's clothing, facial expressions, tone in answering questions, gestures, nervous habits, and other aspects of demeanor. To improve the impression the witness will make on the judge and jurors, explore the following items during the witness preparation session a day or more before the deposition.

In terms of attire, encourage a professional look that befits the witness's image. Generally, this will mean wearing the type of clothing that the witness would wear to court—a suit or something that passes as business casual. Usually, a dark suit jacket and a shirt or blouse in a pastel color—especially light blue—looks good on camera. Avoid checkered or striped tops, loud colors, and large or flashy jewelry, and "just say no" to tank tops, hoodies, sunglasses, and baseball caps.

In describing how to answer deposition questions, attorneys sometimes tell a witness to pause before answering—the idea being that a pause gives the witness a chance to make sure they understand the question and know the answer, and it gives the defending attorney a chance to interpose an objection if needed. In a video deposition, however, such a pause can make the witness look evasive or conniving. While the witness should make sure they understand the question, do not instruct most witnesses to pause before answering.[6]

Rehearse the witness's deposition testimony in a mock deposition. As explained in section 17.4.7, this gets the witness used to answering questions, allows you to work on the witness's substantive responses, and trains them to put into practice the "one concept, three rules" approach to answering questions. The mock examination is even more important in preparing for a video deposition, which captures the witness's demeanor when responding to counsel's

> *Telling your client to dress appropriately for a deposition is generally straightforward. Convincing a **witness** that they need to dress well requires tact and understanding. If the deponent has no "skin in the game"—if they are the witness to an accident or the mechanic who noticed a defect, for example—you have very little leverage for convincing them to pay attention to their personal presentation. Try building rapport with the deponent: show a personal interest in their story, listen with empathy and respect if they have complaints, and ask them to help you make their testimony persuasive by putting their best foot forward.*

queries. Instruct the witness to answer all the deposing counsel's questions in a courteous and responsive manner, even when pressed in an aggressive examination. Jousting with opposing counsel and displaying anger or irritation will come across negatively on the video. Work with the witness to avoid being drawn into such conduct. Simply put, encourage the witness to exercise the same manners and restraint at a video deposition that you would want the witness to display in front of the jurors and judge at trial.

Do not merely conduct a rehearsal, however; record the rehearsal on video with the same framing as the videographer will use, so that you and the witness can see the on-screen effect of looking down, wringing their hands, clicking a pen, shifting in a chair, rocking, swiveling, and various gestures. Remind the witness to sit upright, fold their hands on their lap or the conference table, be attentive to the question, and look at the deposing attorney when answering.

---

6. That said, if the witness displays a really bad habit of jumping on the attorney's questions and answering them before the questions are finished in the mock examination, the mandated "pause," along with an exhortation to focus on whether the witness understands the question, may help. Preferably the pause can be ingrained in the witness during the preparation session so that the witness appears naturally in the video deposition.

23.7.2   At the Deposition—Checking the Camera, Room, and Witness

The major additional concern in defending a video deposition is ensuring that the witness appears in a good light—figuratively and literally. This comes down to the camera view and the witness's demeanor.

In terms of the camera view, ensure the recording is fair and is not done in a way that would make the witness appear in an unflattering or deceptive light. Ask to see how the witness is going to be framed in the camera before the video deposition begins. Request correction—on the record if necessary—of any distorting camera angle, unflattering close-up that shows the pores of the nose and every drop of perspiration, backlighting (which makes the deponent look like a member of a witness protection program) or distracting background. Professional videographers know to avoid these things—and are required to avoid them by law—but check anyway. As the day wears on and the light in the room changes, check again.

Note also the temperature in the deposition room. If the room is too hot, the witness will sweat; the sweat on the witness's brow will show on the video and may cause jurors to think it is due to nervousness or lying. A room that is too warm also makes everyone, including counsel, drowsy by the time mid-afternoon rolls around.

As for the witness's demeanor, monitor how the witness is answering the questions. If the witness is clicking a pen, take it from them; if swiveling in their chair or making facial expressions, remind them not to in a break. Better yet, make sure they are not seated in a chair that swivels or rocks.

23.7.3   After the Deposition—Reviewing the Record

Upon a timely request under Rule 30(e), the witness has thirty days after notice of the preparation of the transcript to submit proposed changes and errata. For this task, the witness and you will review the transcript to catch any errors. Note, however, that the video can support or undermine a witness's assertion that the court reporter transcribed their words incorrectly. Also note that, if the witness wants to make a substantive change to answer a question differently (e.g., the witness misspoke or misunderstood the question), there is no way to correct the video of the deposition. In that circumstance, the deposing attorney has the advantage when introducing the opposing party's statements at trial—the deposing attorney can show the video as it was originally recorded, while you only have the written errata sheet to present to the jurors. The visual testimony will have more impact.

23.8   Preparing to Use the Video Deposition at Trial

The extent to which you can use deposition testimony at trial is discussed extensively in section 15.3. To prepare the testimony for such use is a little different when offering it by video rather than a transcript.

23.8.1   *Transcribing*

In those jurisdictions that require a written transcript of the deposition testimony when the testimony is to be used at trial (e.g., Rule 32(c)), have the audio portion of the audiovisual recording transcribed if the court reporter did not create a stenographic record.

23.8.2   *Editing*

While video is more entertaining than transcripts and holds the jurors' interest better, even the best video deposition can be tedious. Keep the jurors' exposure to all deposition testimony, both video and stenographic, as short as possible, consistent with the jurors hearing the necessary testimony and being persuaded of its truthfulness. Do this through prudent editing. Because so many more questions are asked at a deposition than are necessary for the effective presentation of the critical evidence at trial, examine each question and answer with an eye to deleting anything that does not advance the theory of the case.

Editing video, however, is trickier than editing a transcript. Although software has made the task so much easier and cheaper than it once was—allowing the selection of video clips with the click of a mouse—lumping together edited video clips can result in a jumpy and jarring presentation. Softening the transitions from clip to clip will help, but the whole process takes some effort. The takeaway is simply this: Allow plenty of time for the video excerpts to be prepared.

23.8.3   *Ruling on Objections*

The pretrial conference is the usual and best time for the court to rule on objections to exhibits and to deposition designations, but this is a matter of local practice and court rules. Whatever procedure is used, suggest that it be done sufficiently in advance of trial so that any portion of the video ruled inadmissible can be deleted or a new video clip can be created before trial begins—or at least before the clip is set to be used.

Having the judge watch the video to rule on objections is time-consuming and wasteful, and most judges will refuse to do so unless the objection is to the taping or to the attorney's or parties' conduct during the deposition. If the objection is to a question or answer, the court can much more conveniently examine the stenographic recording or a transcription of the video.

Once the court rules, any inadmissible portion must be edited out of the video excerpt. To preserve the matter for appeal, maintain a complete original of the testimony, without deletions. Once the excluded portions have been edited out, be sure to review the video to ensure that the editing was done correctly.

23.9   Using the Video Deposition at Trial

There are various ways a courtroom might be set up to display the video deposition to the jurors. One way is to position a monitor and playback unit in front of the jury box. Another method is to use monitors built into the jury box, or large screens mounted in the courtroom, connected to a master control unit under the ultimate control of the judge, counsel, or court personnel. Ideally, you should be able to connect a laptop into the courtroom audiovisual system and run the display from the laptop. Learn at least a couple of weeks ahead of trial what technology and connectivity is available in the courtroom, including the compatibility of the courtroom equipment and the required digital formats, as well as the extent to which you may supplement the court's equipment.

When jurors watch a video excerpt, they either receive a written transcript to accompany the video, or the words of the witness appear at the bottom of the video (like subtitles or closed-captions, but verbatim from the transcript). Determine if your trial judge has any requirements in this regard long enough before trial that you have time to prepare the video properly. Finally, if your video exhibit is choppy due to editing, ask the court to instruct the jurors that the video was pared down for relevance and to save time, not to hide anything the jurors should know.

Chapter Twenty-Three

CHECKLIST
VIDEO DEPOSITIONS

✔	Determine whether to record the deposition by audiovisual means (i.e., it is not cost-prohibitive, and the deposition is likely to be used at trial and/or the presence of the camera will put participants on their best behavior).
✔	Notice the deposition to be recorded by audiovisual as well as stenographic means.
✔	Retain a professional videographer.
✔	Arrange a suitable location.
✔	At the deposition, deal with the microphone, work with the videographer, and remain mindful of the tone of the questions.

Defending attorney

✔	Prepare the witness concerning appropriate attire and demeanor.
✔	At the deposition, be cognizant of the camera view of the witness and the witness's appearance.
✔	Coordinate the video with a review of the transcript after the deposition.

All counsel

✔	Prepare to use the video deposition at trial with appropriate edits and, if necessary, transcription of the audio.
✔	Know the equipment and technology available in the courtroom.

CHAPTER TWENTY-FOUR

REMOTE DEPOSITIONS

We are now connected by the internet, like
neurons in a giant brain.

—Stephen Hawking

A deposition will be more effective if you accomplish the purposes of the deposition in a proficient and cost-effective manner, conducting the deposition remotely when circumstances warrant. A deposition is deemed "remote" when one or more of the participants (witness, attorneys, court reporter) joins in the deposition from a different physical location by telephone or, more commonly, by videoconference. The remote deposition brings unique opportunities and challenges.

Remote depositions gained prominence during the COVID-19 pandemic that began in 2020, when stay-at-home orders, physical distancing requirements, and travel restrictions precluded in-person depositions. Some federal and state courts established protocols for holding depositions remotely, many state legislatures modified deposition laws to facilitate them, and remote depositions became recognized as "a necessary and regular occurrence in legal proceedings."[1]

> **In This Chapter:**
>
> - *Deciding whether a remote deposition is in the client's interest*
>
> - *Representing the client during a remote deposition*
>
> - *The advantages and disadvantages of remote depositions*
>
> - *Applicable laws and notice requirements*
>
> - *The deposition protocols and preparation needed to maximize the advantages and minimize the disadvantages*
>
> - *Best practices in taking and defending the deposition*

---

1. Raiser v. San Diego County, 2021 U.S. Dist. LEXIS 6819, 2021 WL 118901 at *16 (S.D. Cal. Jan. 13, 2021); *see* Swenson v. GEICO Cas. Co., 336 F.R.D. 206 (D. Nev. 2020).

In the post-pandemic world, remote depositions continue to play a vital role. Lawyers have grown accustomed to online platforms, and lawyers and clients alike have realized the efficiencies and cost-effectiveness remote depositions offer. Attorneys must therefore be familiar with remote depositions, both to advise their clients of a strategic option and to fulfill their ethical duty to keep reasonably abreast of relevant technological advances.[2]

In this chapter, we consider how to decide whether holding a deposition remotely will be in the client's interest and how to best represent the client when a remote deposition is selected or compelled. This requires understanding the advantages and disadvantages of remote depositions, the applicable laws and notice requirements, the deposition protocols and preparation needed to maximize the advantages and minimize the disadvantages, and best practices in taking and defending the deposition.

24.1   When to Take a Remote Deposition

Conducting depositions remotely is appropriate if the advantages outweigh the disadvantages, as outlined below. As we have seen, a remote deposition will be the only choice when public health regulations preclude in-person depositions during the discovery period. In other circumstances, remote depositions will generally be a better idea for relatively minor witnesses who are located at great distances from the proceeding; they may be less appropriate for critical witnesses in cases involving many parties, a great volume of confidential documents, and a suspicion that a witness or counsel will exploit aspects of a remote deposition unfairly.

24.2   Advantages of Remote Depositions

Remote depositions relieve participants from the burden of traveling to the deposition site. Depending on where the witness and counsel are located, not having to travel to the deposition can significantly reduce the time and cost associated with the deposition. It may also make the deposition easier to schedule for busy attorneys, clients, and expert witnesses. Cost savings and convenience are the primary benefits of holding a deposition remotely, both for counsel and for the witness.

Remote depositions facilitate the use of video and other digital services. On one computer screen, counsel can view all the other deposition participants and the exhibits as they are introduced. On that same screen, counsel can check the court reporter's real-time feed of the deposition transcript. An interpreter can be added to the proceeding if needed, with associated devices for simultaneous translation. A videographer can easily be added as well, offering the benefits of a video

---

2. ABA Model R. 1.1, Comment [8]; Cal. R. Prof. Conduct 1.1, Comment [1].

deposition (*see* section 23.2). On the same or different screen, the deposing attorney can maintain an electronic folder of potential exhibits, a deposition outline, evidentiary cheat sheets, timelines, notes, and more—out of view of the witness and opposing counsel.

Remote depositions allow witnesses to testify in their own environment. Some witnesses may be more at ease, and therefore more forthcoming, testifying from the comfort of their own home or office rather than in an unfamiliar conference room full of attorneys. This is not always the case, however, as other witnesses may be less inclined to disclose incriminating testimony and more likely to deceive if appearing in their own environment.

Remote depositions allow litigation to continue despite health concerns. In the event of health concerns of a witness or other participant—or at times an entire nation—a remote deposition allows discovery to go forward. Health issues may require or encourage people to stay at home or, if venturing somewhere else, to wear face masks indoors. If the deposition is conducted in-person with the witness wearing a mask, the deposing counsel may not be able to detect facial expressions that would provide clues to the witness's credibility. A video recording of a masked witness is not optimal either. Conducting the deposition online, with the witness isolated in their own home, allows the witness to appear unmasked.

24.3 Disadvantages of Remote Depositions

Remote depositions are more susceptible to interruptions and delays. Because remote depositions rely on multiple participants connecting to an online platform, the failure of any one of those connections can disrupt the deposition or even lead to its termination. For the deposition to run smoothly, each participant must possess adequate equipment, a suitable ethernet or wireless connection, and a minimum level of technological competence, including the ability to navigate the platform and access electronic files on their computer. Because of the time lag associated with the medium, the deposing attorney may find it more difficult to control the pace of the examination and the deposition may take longer to complete. Unless in the same physical room as the witness, it will be harder for defending counsel to interpose objections and communicate with the client. The court reporter may find it more difficult to take down what transpires. Screen fatigue requires shorter sessions or additional breaks. If there are many participants, these issues become more significant.

Remote depositions can give rise to privacy and security concerns. At an in-person deposition, each participant knows who is in the room and who has access to the confidential information that might be discussed. Remote depositions, on the other hand, are more susceptible to intrusion from outsiders and eavesdroppers. Therefore, think through the terms of protective orders and constraints on the disclosure of trade secrets and other confidential information. Take care that the deposition is accessed only by those who are supposed to attend. Determine if unidentified persons are lurking at a participant's location out of the view of the camera. Restrict who can record the deposition and how any recording will be disseminated.

Remote depositions may not provide an adequate basis for evaluating the witness's veracity and credibility. Not being in the same room as the witness may limit the effectiveness of the deposing attorney's inquiry of the witness. It may be more difficult to gauge whether the witness is being evasive or deceptive, especially if gestures and body language cannot be observed. It may be harder to control an uncooperative or lying witness. Rather than testifying from their personal recollection, the witness may surreptitiously refer to notes, electronic devices, documents open on a computer screen, or even texts or other electronic communications from their attorney.

Remote depositions require a different approach to presenting and using exhibits. At an in-person deposition, the attorney will usually hand the court reporter, witness, and opposing counsel a copy of each exhibit at the time the deposing attorney decides to use it. In a remote deposition, with participants in separate locations, counsel must find an alternative way of presenting exhibits to the witness, counsel, and the court reporter and examine the witness about the document. There are several ways to accomplish this, as discussed below, but the process may prove cumbersome in a document-intensive case.[3]

24.4 The Law

Under Rule 30(b)(4), a deposition may be held remotely only by stipulation of the parties or by court order. As a result, the parties may dispute the propriety of a remote deposition in various contexts—for example, when they confer on a discovery plan, when one party has noticed a remote deposition and another party objects, or when one party has noticed an in-person deposition and another party seeks a protective order requiring the deposition to be held remotely. In any of these situations, if the parties cannot reach agreement, the proponent of the remote deposition must convince the court that conducting the deposition remotely is appropriate.[4]

During the COVID-19 pandemic in 2020, some courts issued blanket orders requiring all depositions to be held remotely; other courts granted motions to compel

---

3. Furthermore, if the jurisdiction or court order requires the deposing attorney to give intended exhibits to the witness and counsel ahead of time, the inability to surprise a witness with a document at a remote deposition may weigh in favor of holding an in-person deposition.
4. Some states allow a remote deposition upon notice, without the need for a stipulation or court order. *E.g.*, Cal. Code Civ. P. § 2025.310(a); Cal. R. Court 3.1010(a); Ill. Sup. Ct. R. 206(h); Tex. R. Civ. P. 199.1. Others require a stipulation or order. E.g., NY Com. Rules 37.

remote depositions on a case-by-case basis, essentially concluding that pandemic conditions provided a legitimate reason to do so.[5]

Post-pandemic, it remains unclear how readily parties will stipulate to remote depositions and how likely courts will order them over a party's objection. Based on rulings issued before and during the pandemic, a court will consider the purported need to conduct the deposition remotely as well as any claim of prejudice to the other side.[6] As a general matter, courts are to interpret and apply Rule 30(b)(4) to secure the just, speedy, and inexpensive determination of a case, and the mere fact that the deposition will involve voluminous exhibits or that counsel will not be physically present with the witness has not been enough to establish undue prejudice.[7]

When the federal rules allow remote depositions, two issues may arise concerning the administration of the oath to the witness. Rule 28(a)(1) provides that a deposition must be taken before a person appointed by the court or an "officer authorized to administer oaths either by federal law or by the law in the place of examination." Because Rule 30(b)(3)(A) deems the place of examination to be where the witness is located, the rules could be interpreted to mean that a court reporter, if not authorized to administer oaths under federal law, must be authorized to administer an oath in the state from which the witness will be participating. This may be difficult in a remote deposition if the witness is participating from a different state than the court reporter. Make sure the court reporter is authorized to administer oaths under federal law or where the witness is located; alternatively, obtain a stipulation or waiver of the requirement from opposing counsel.

Another issue arises from Rule 28(a)(1)'s requirement that the deposition be "taken before" the officer. Rule 30(b)(5)(A) similarly states that, unless otherwise stipulated, the deposition "must be conducted before an officer appointed or designated under Rule 28." Some cases interpret these rules to mean the oath must be administered in the physical presence of the witness, which would pose a problem in a remote deposition.[8] Other courts have ruled it is sufficient if the court reporter

---

5. *E.g.*, Swenson, 336 F.R.D. at 211; Cavenaugh v. County of San Diego, 2020 U.S. Dist. LEXIS 80792, at *3 (S.D. Cal. May 7, 2020); Lee v. Dennison, 2020 U.S. Dist. LEXIS 149383, at *13 (D. Nev. Aug. 18, 2020).

6. Swenson, 336 F.R.D. at 209; *see* United States v. $160,066.98 from Bank of Am., 202 F.R.D. 624, 629 (S.D. Cal. 2001) (requiring in-person deposition); Jahr v. IU Int'l Corp., 109 F.R.D. 429, 432 (M.D.N.C. 1986) (allowing remote deposition).

7. Fed. R. Civ. P. 1; United States v. K.O.O. Constr., Inc., 106 Fed. R. Serv. 3d 1383, 2020 U.S. Dist. LEXIS 81866, at *4 (S.D. Cal. May 8, 2020) (voluminous and highly detailed exhibits are not a bar to remote videoconference depositions); Rouviere v. Depuy Orthopaedics, Inc., 471 F. Supp. 3d 571, 575 (S.D.N.Y. 2020) (a document-intensive examination is not an obstacle to a successful remote deposition). If the mere lack of being physically present with the witness were sufficient to preclude holding a deposition remotely, the authorization in Rule 30(b)(4) to conduct remote depositions would be meaningless. Id. at 575.

8. *E.g.*, Aquino v. Auto. Serv. Indus. Ass'n, 93 F. Supp. 2d 922, 923–24 (N.D. Ill. 2000); Jahr, 109 F.R.D. at 433.

attends the deposition by the same remote means as the witness (i.e., by videoconference) and all participants can clearly hear and be heard by all the other participants.[9] The oath may also be administered remotely by stipulation of the parties.

To the extent the deposition is recorded by video, Rule 30(b)(5)(B) requires that the "deponent's and attorney's appearance or demeanor must not be distorted through recording techniques." This proviso, and the fact that the video will not be admissible unless the deposition recording is certified pursuant to the rules, confirms the wisdom of using a qualified videographer to perform the video recording aspects of the remote deposition.

If state law applies, remote depositions are generally permitted by state rules of civil procedure.[10] In the wake of the pandemic, many jurisdictions enacted legislation that explicitly abolishes the requirement that the oath be administered in the presence of the witness.[11]

Whether proceeding in federal court or in state court, know the law and orders governing remote depositions in your jurisdiction, including the local rules or standing orders of the court in which the matter is pending, the courtroom rules of the judge presiding over the case, and any case-specific orders issued in the proceeding.

24.5 Scheduling the Remote Deposition

Schedule remote depositions using the same general form of notice as other depositions, albeit with modifications dictated by the law discussed in the preceding section. State in the notice that the deposition will be taken remotely. In accordance with Rule 30(b)(3), you may reserve the right to record the deposition by audiovisual as well as stenographic means (*see* section 25.7.3). Specify in the notice that the court reporter may administer the oath even if not in the presence of the witness, and the participants waive any objection in that regard. The notice may require the parties, through counsel, to contact you to obtain the information needed to access the deposition remotely.

Select the date for the remote deposition carefully. Because technical or connectivity problems may arise during the proceeding, schedule the deposition far enough ahead of trial (or the summary judgment deadline) to leave time to reschedule or continue it if needed. If you are videorecording the deposition

---

9. SAPS, LLCS v. Ezcare Clinic, Inc., 2020 U.S. Dist. LEXIS 69575, at *2 (E.D. La. Apr. 21, 2020); Sinceno v. Riverside Church in the City of New York, 2020 U.S. Dist. LEXIS 47859, at *1 (S.D.N.Y. Mar. 18, 2020).
10. Cal. R. of Court 3.1010(a); Colo. R. Civ. P. 30(b)(7); Ill. R. 206(h); N.Y. CPLR 3113(d).
11. *See, e.g.,* Cal. Code Civ. P. § 2025.310(a); Colo. Exec. Order D2020019; Ill. R. 206(h) (if parties agree); N.Y. CPLR 3113(d) (parties must stipulate).

National Institute for Trial Advocacy

with the aim of using it at trial, allow time for the video to be edited before the trial date.

Because remote depositions under the Federal Rules of Civil Procedure may proceed only by stipulation or court order, try to secure agreement to the remote deposition in advance or serve the notice of deposition early enough to obtain a court order compelling the deposition if needed.

24.6   Selecting the Platform and Court-Reporting Service

A remote deposition may be held using any online videoconferencing platform, such as Zoom, Webex, or Microsoft Teams. These platforms offer similar functions, although their interface and operation are somewhat different. Sometimes the choice of platform has already been made in a prior discovery order or the court's standing order, or it may be dictated by the general practice of your law firm or the court reporting service used for the deposition. Otherwise, choose the platform you know best.

Whatever online platform you select, confirm how to adjust the display, mute microphones, turn the camera on and off, view the list of participants, use the chat feature, share the user's screen, use the annotation feature to highlight or underscore shared documents, and switch audio inputs. Also learn how breakout rooms are created and how participants are assigned to those rooms and returned to the main session. Although a court reporting service will typically handle putting participants into the breakout rooms, be familiar with it.

Court reporting services often integrate the online platform with other aspects of the remote deposition. In addition to providing the videoconference on the platform and a court reporter to record the proceeding stenographically, the court reporting service may include an exhibit-sharing function for displaying exhibits remotely, real-time display of the court reporter's transcript, and a videographer for audiovisual recording. In selecting a court reporting service for this purpose, consider the platform the vendor uses, the vendor's experience with remote depositions, and its ability to maintain confidentiality and comply with protective orders.

24.7   Establishing a Remote Deposition Protocol

In addition to noticing the deposition and deciding on the platform, craft a protocol that addresses the unique challenges of remote depositions. The terms of this protocol may be dictated by a local rule, a standing order of the court in which the case is pending, or a pretrial order in the case. Otherwise, consider the topics set forth below, consult with the court reporting service, and strive to reach agreement with opposing counsel on these matters before the deposition begins. If the witness is not represented by counsel, communicate the protocol directly with the witness to the extent permitted by the applicable jurisdiction's rules of professional conduct.

(If you are the defending attorney, review the proposed protocol in light of the issues below, require revisions to the protocol if necessary to protect your witness, familiarize the witness with the protocol, and help the witness comply.)[12]

24.7.1   *Location and Connectivity of the Witness and Other Participants*

Clarify where the witness and other participants will be located during the deposition and, in particular, which participants will be connected to the deposition via remote videoconferencing technology. Each participant appearing remotely should have their own room, internet connection, camera, and microphone to ensure adequate privacy, connectivity, video, and audio. (As addressed in the next section, however, accommodation may be made if there is more than one person in a room.) Ask participants to select a quiet location that is well lit and free from background noises and distractions.

> *If the court or jurisdiction does not dictate the protocol, negotiate with counsel, keeping your client's interests in mind—and recognizing that the protocol for your depositions will be the protocol for the opponent's depositions too; consider if there should be exceptions for any of the potential witnesses.*

Ask the witness's attorney (or the witness if unrepresented) to confirm before the deposition that the witness's computer and internet connection are sufficient for the audio and video aspects of the deposition. Also confirm that the witness is adequately familiar with the online platform's essential functions by the time the deposition begins.[13]

---

12. As this book went to press, the American Bar Association House of Delegates was considering a resolution to adopt its Best Practices for Remote Depositions, dated February 2023. The practices embrace the principles set forth in this book—knowing the applicable rules; understanding the technology; preparing for the unique aspects of remote depositions regarding logistics and exhibits; distributing exhibits in advance or using platform tools or exhibit-sharing applications; addressing concerns about witnesses communicating with others during the deposition; attending the deposition with the witness; and avoiding potential problems by having the court reporter in the same location as the witness and reaching agreement on a protocol.

13. Can someone from your office talk an unrepresented witness through downloading the remote application, setting it up, and becoming familiar with the platform? Rule 4.3 of the ABA's Model Rules of Professional Conduct prohibits lawyers from giving legal advice to an unrepresented person if the lawyer "knows or reasonably should know that the interests of such a person are or have a reasonable possibility of being in conflict with the interests of the client." Helping a subpoenaed witness set up their computer does not constitute legal advice. But it might risk an accusation of witness interference. One solution is to have opposing counsel join you in the task; another is to inform counsel in writing of your intentions. Alternatively, if the case warrants the cost, arrange for the court reporter's office to walk the witness through the setup. Remember that any communication you have with the witness is not likely privileged. If you do assist the witness in this manner, clearly

The court reporting service may offer a pre-deposition diagnostic test with all participants to make sure each participant will have a stable connection and understands how to use the platform. If the participants agree, hold the test a couple of days before the deposition.

24.7.2 Persons in the Room with Witness

At the height of the pandemic, most participants in a deposition were at separate locations or at least in separate physical rooms. Post-pandemic, that is still the case for many remote depositions. But sometimes, the witness will be in a conference room with the court reporter (and videographer, if any), while others appear remotely. Another frequent option, barring undue travel expense, is for the witness's attorney or support person to attend in the same room as the witness. This may trouble the deposing attorney, who would prefer that the witness not be in a room with counsel and colleagues due to fears about security and the witness being "assisted" in their testimony. Subject to privacy concerns that would apply to depositions generally, however, courts have been reluctant to preclude the attendance of other persons without a showing that their presence has affected or will affect the integrity of the deposition.[14] In particular, the witness's attorney will not easily be barred from the witness's room and has a right to be there under the law of some jurisdictions.[15]

Work all this out before the deposition, for two reasons. First, all counsel need to understand who will be where, because it affects the manner of witness preparation and how the deposition will proceed, including how exhibits will be distributed and used. Second, it affects how the participants will join the deposition and how their

---

tell them who you represent and do not try to obtain privileged or confidential information. ABA Model R. 4.3. If you delegate the task to an office employee, take reasonable steps to ensure their conduct is consistent with a lawyer's professional obligations in the jurisdiction. ABA Model R. 5.3.

14. Stowe v. Alford, No. 19-cv-01652 KJM AC, 2021 U.S. Dist. LEXIS 98021 (E.D. Cal. May 24, 2021) (refusing to exclude the deponent's spouse from being physically present in the witness's room during the remote deposition, despite the argument that she could give nonverbal cues to the deponent, because the deposing attorney can instruct that nonverbal cues are not permitted; also refusing to require that all persons "present at the deposition should be on camera;" noting, however, that all individuals present must be identified under Rule 30(b)(5)).

15. Hall v. Wilmington Health PLLC, 872 S.E.2d 347 (N.C. Ct. App. 2022) (trial court's blanket order banning hospital's attorney from being physically present at the deposition of the hospital's employees and witnesses violated due process); Klein v. Facebook, Inc., No. 20-cv-09570-LHK (VKD), 2021 U.S. Dist. LEXIS 173434 (N.D. Cal. Sept. 13, 2021) (there is "no justification here for excluding counsel defending the witness from being physically present in the same room as the witness," although "[a]ny party may ask the Court to revisit this issue if circumstances warrant"); Cal. R. of Court 3.1010(a)(3) ("Any party or attorney of record may be physically present at the [remote] deposition at the location of the deponent with written notice of such appearance served by personal delivery, email, or fax, at least five court days before the deposition, and subject to Code of Civil Procedure section 2025.420 [protective orders]. An attorney for the deponent may be physically present with the deponent without notice."); Cal. Code Civ. P. § 2025.310(b).

voice and image will be captured. For example, if the defending attorney insists on being in the room with the witness, the camera could view just the witness with the attorney in the same room but off-camera; but then, only the witness sees the witness's attorney. Alternatively, the camera could view the witness and the attorney next to each other, but that reduces your view of the witness and can pose problems if the deposition is recorded audiovisually. As another option, the witness and the attorney can be set up next to (or near to) each other, with separate electronic devices, cameras, and mics. Unless there is microphone interference or a connectivity issue, this may be the best solution.

Whether or not the defending attorney is in the witness's room, try to have the court reporter with the witness if possible. This removes any concern about the reporter needing to be in the witness's physical presence when administering the oath (Rules 28(a), 30(b); *see* section 24.4). In addition, it ensures that the reporter hears the witness's testimony clearly. The reporter can facilitate delivering exhibits to the witness in either electronic or hard-copy form. And the presence of the reporter reduces the likelihood the witness clandestinely refers to documents or others when answering questions.

24.7.3 Administration of the Oath and Manner of Recording

If the court reporter (or deposition officer) is not going to be in the same room as the witness, address issues concerning the administration of the oath in the protocol as well as in the deposition notice.

Similarly, while your deposition notice identified whether the remote deposition will be recorded by "audio, audiovisual, or stenographic means" (Rule 30(b)(3)(A)), confirm this in the protocol as well. Your first impulse may be to think, of course a remote deposition will be videorecorded, but you cannot use a recording in court without giving proper notice. Nor can you simply record the proceedings using the remote platform and expect that recording to be accepted by the court—admissibility requires certification by a videographer in compliance with the federal rules.[16]

If the deposition is recorded stenographically, the court reporter's transcript constitutes the official record of the testimony.[17] If you provided notice that the deposition will be recorded audiovisually, hire a qualified person to handle the videorecording, and have the court reporter maintain a master copy of the recording. In any event, the protocol should allow the court reporting service to provide a video copy of the deposition to the court reporter to assist in the preparation of the transcript. To help the court reporter record the proceedings accurately, stipulate that each participant in the deposition will identify themselves by their full name as

---

16. Alcorn v. City of Chicago, 336 F.R.D. 440, 443–45 (N.D. Ill. 2020); Ryan v. eXp Realty LLC, Case No. CV-20-00325-PHX-GMS, 2022 U.S. Dist. LEXIS 28043 (N.D. Ariz. Feb. 16, 2022).
17. *See, e.g.*, Rule 32(c); Cal. Code Civ. P. § 2025.510(g).

it will appear in the transcript, and, when speaking, the participant will have their camera on and be unmasked.

24.7.4 *Security and Privacy*

Information elicited at the deposition, or exhibits presented to the witness, may be subject to protective orders, the Health Insurance Portability and Accountability Act (HIPAA), or another statutory or constitutional right to privacy. The protocol must therefore include a means of ensuring the security of the virtual deposition room.

Limit access to the remote deposition to those who have the right to attend. Send each participant a link to the platform, with a password unique to the deposition meeting. Have the link place participants in a virtual waiting room that requires the meeting host (court reporting service) to admit them into the deposition room, based on your list of approved attendees.

Stipulate that each participant will be alone in their room or that all persons in the room will be identified (Rule 30(b)(5)). Require participants to disclose at the start of the deposition and after every break if anyone else is in the room. Also confirm they will take steps to prevent others from entering and will promptly report if anyone does enter. Consider requiring all persons in a room to be on camera and that cameras always be on. (You will supplement these protocol stipulations with on-the-record inquiries of the witness and other participants at the deposition. *See* sections 24.10.1–24.10.2.)

Similarly, agree that no one is allowed to observe the deposition surreptitiously, even if not in a participant's room, such as by a video or audio feed from one of the participants. Both before and during the deposition, have all participants agree that they will not broadcast the deposition to anyone in any manner.

Stipulate that no one other than the court reporting service will record the deposition. A participant's use of the platform's recording feature, or a recording of the screen with a phone camera or other device, threatens security and confidentiality because the recorder may not be turned off when the parties go off the record, and because recordings of testimony can be edited, manipulated, uploaded to the internet, and otherwise disseminated. Usually, the court reporting service can disable the platform's recording feature for other participants. Nonetheless, have the witness and all counsel agree before and at the start of the deposition that they will not record the deposition by any means. (Alternatively, if you want an informal recording of a deposition to assess the witness for trial, consider stipulating that counsel may record the deposition only for purposes of the litigation, with advance notice, and shall not reproduce or distribute the recording except to designated persons for litigation-related reasons.)

24.7.5 Witness-Attorney Communications and Breakout Rooms

You must be confident that the witness is testifying from their recollection, without assistance or interference by the witness's attorney. At the same time, the witness and their attorney may need to discuss whether a question calls for information protected by a privilege. To accommodate these competing concerns, define the permissible extent of witness-attorney communications in the protocol.

First, place limitations on the ability of the witness's counsel to communicate with the witness while the witness is on the record. One approach is to agree that any communication between the witness and counsel while the witness is on the record will be spoken aloud, except for communications directed to deciding whether to assert a privilege. Alternatively, you may agree that no attorney shall initiate a private communication with a witness during questioning, including by text message, email, or the chat feature of the videoconferencing system, except that the witness's counsel may communicate privately with the witness to determine whether a privilege must be asserted. In either event, before the witness and counsel confer, they must first announce on the record their need and intention to do so.

Second, the witness's counsel needs a place to confer privately with the witness on matters of privilege and, to the extent allowed in the jurisdiction, to confer during a break. To that end, have the service provider establish a breakout room for each party and their respective counsel. The parties may use their assigned room during breaks in the deposition, with the service provider moving the parties into their respective rooms to the extent requested. To prevent disclosure of confidential information or privileged communications, do not record conversations in the breakout rooms. Instead of conferring in a breakout room, the witness and their attorney may seek a greater guarantee of confidentiality by instead muting their microphone, turning off their camera, and communicating with each other in another room by telephone or another device.

24.7.6 Notes and Electronic Devices

Take care that the witness testifies without the assistance of notes, documents, other material, or other persons. One option is for counsel to agree that the witness will not refer to any material without disclosing they are doing so, identifying the material, and providing it to the parties. A more stringent option is to agree that the witness will not refer to any notes, documents, displays, electronic communications, or anything else in answering the question at all, unless you specifically direct them to do so; provided, however, that the witness may consider an electronic communication from counsel for the purpose of determining whether to assert a privilege.

As a further precaution, the parties may agree that only the online platform window (and, if applicable, an e-file of deposition exhibits) can be open on the witness's computer screen. Closing all other browsers, programs, applications, and files not only minimizes the chance the witness will refer to improper material, it also helps ensure connectivity and privacy.

Some attorneys require the witness to turn off all electronic devices other than the device used for the deposition. That alternative may be particularly appropriate when you suspect the witness cannot be trusted to abide by a promise not to refer to those devices, as where the witness has already been caught testifying from a cheat sheet.

The witness may protest that they need their phone or other electronic device in case they receive an emergency call from an employer or family member. As a general matter, the time set for the deposition is the time for the deposition only, and there is rarely an instance in which a call cannot wait until a break or be directed to someone other than the witness. Sometimes a compromise may be appropriate, in which the phone or other electronic device remains silenced and outside the witness's reach.

24.7.7 Exhibits

There are three main approaches to providing deposition exhibits to the witness, to counsel, and to the court reporter. Identify one or more of them in the deposition protocol.[18]

Provide Documents in Advance

The first approach is to premark the exhibits and provide them to the witness, the witness's counsel, and the court reporter in advance of the deposition, either by mailing hard copies or sending an electronic file. This approach ensures that the participants have the documents available for the deposition. If the documents are sent in an electronic file, sending them in advance allows the witness or counsel to print them out if they prefer. Password protect the file to avoid inadvertently disclosing any confidential information contained in the documents.

A downside to this approach is that the witness and counsel will know before the deposition what documents you intend to use. While in some cases the exhibits for the witness are predictable anyway, in other cases you may want to preserve the element of surprise and not prematurely disclose a "smoking gun" document or give the witness's counsel time to prepare the witness on intended lines of inquiry.

To ameliorate this problem, arrange that the documents will be delivered, but not reviewed, before the deposition. If sending hard copies, deliver them in a sealed envelope with instructions that they remain sealed until the deposition, at which

---

18. Some jurisdictions have rules setting forth the procedure. *E.g.,* Ill. Sup. Ct. R. 206(h).

point the witness and witness's counsel unseal them on camera. If sending a password protected electronic file, withhold the password from the witness and the witness's counsel until the deposition begins.

Screenshare

A second approach is to present premarked exhibits to the participants during the deposition using the screenshare function of the online platform. This approach keeps the witness and defending counsel from knowing in advance what exhibits will be used, lets you introduce exhibits on the fly as they become relevant during the examination, and allows the witness to view the exhibit in the deposition window—an advantage over sending exhibits by electronic file, which requires the witness to open and view the documents in a window on the computer screen separate from the window used for the deposition. With the screensharing approach, you will usually have to send a copy of the exhibits separately to the court reporter after the deposition so the court reporter can attach them to the transcript.

Screensharing, however, presents its own issues. You must make sure, in the process of sharing a deposition exhibit from your computer screen, not to display other items you have open on your screen. You must have the intended exhibits ready for sharing, which means they must all be opened on the computer (presenting a challenge if the deposition involves a large number of exhibits), or tabbed and well-organized in a folder for that purpose. In addition, you may need to scroll through the entire document on the screen if the witness or other participant wants to review it. (Although sometimes the court reporting service allows a "tech" person to handle the screensharing and give control to the witness to scroll on their own.)

To avoid the shortcomings of these first two approaches, consider a hybrid method, sending obvious documents to the witness and counsel in advance while reserving the right to present other documents by screenshare during the deposition. Alternatively, provide the exhibits in advance to the court reporter only, and then at the deposition display (or request the court reporter to display) the exhibit to the witness and counsel using the screenshare function.

Use Specialized Software

A third approach uses specialized exhibit-sharing software that allows you to store potential exhibits in an electronic folder on your computer, mark each exhibit one at a time, and drop it into another folder that all other participants can view. This approach keeps the witness and the witness's attorney from seeing the exhibits in advance, eliminates the issues with screensharing, allows each participant to review the exhibit independently, and, unlike exhibits distributed in an electronic file, displays the exhibit in the same window as the deposition. Court reporting services may provide this software as part of their service.

In deciding which of these approaches to choose, consider the extent to which you need an element of surprise regarding the exhibits, the number of exhibits, the number of pages of any particular exhibit (such that it may be more efficient for each participant to have their own electronic or printed copy to review), the facility of the court reporter, and the witness's technological ability to open and view electronic files while participating in the deposition.

24.7.8   *Procedure If Connectivity or Technical Issues Arise*

Connectivity issues—ranging from short-term screen freezes to disconnection— may arise during the deposition. Lay out what steps to take if these issues occur. For example, if a participant's connection interferes with the ability to hear or see the proceeding, the participant should make that known immediately. If the participant is disconnected from the deposition altogether, they should check their internet connection and attempt to rejoin the proceeding by signing in again. If unsuccessful, the participant should contact the court reporter or counsel. The parties might also stipulate that the deposition will be suspended until the witness, the court reporter, and counsel can hear and see the proceedings.

24.8   Equipping the Virtual Deposition Room

Make sure the environment from which you will participate is conducive to a successful deposition. The room should be quiet and not subject to interruptions. In addition, maximize connectivity and audiovisual quality for strategic as well as aesthetic purposes.

Maintaining a stable connection is paramount. The remote deposition relies on the connection between the participant's laptop or personal computer (mobile phones are not recommended) and the online platform. In general, this connection is stronger with a hardwire connection—that is, a cable between the computer and the router—rather than a wireless connection. If a participant must use a wireless connection, they should minimize the distance between the device and the router and make sure no other devices are sharing the wireless signal.

Laptops and personal computers typically include a microphone and speaker, as well as a camera built into the monitor, enabling the transmission of the user's video image and voice. Obtain better video and audio quality by using an add-on webcam and microphone combination, which plugs into the computer's USB port. To further enhance audio quality—both the ability of others to hear you and your ability to hear them—consider a USB headset with a microphone. For adequate video quality, the environment should be sufficiently lit. Avoid seating any participant with a window or other light source behind them; instead, use a light source— such as a portable ring light—to illuminate the face. Adjust the camera angle and seating arrangement so that the camera is roughly at eye level and displays the subject's chest and shoulders—approximating the appearance of news anchors or commentators on television—so that hand gestures can be seen. Some deposing attorneys call for a broader view of the witness that allows the attorney to see the table in front of the witness and what the witness is doing with their hands, but that compromises the attorney's view of the witness's facial expressions. Finally, make sure that the area behind you looks professional and is not distracting. Online platforms typically allow the user to select a virtual background or blur effect that obscures the area behind the subject.

This is not merely to look good on camera; it all contributes to an effective deposition. The more professional the connection, audio, and video, the more professional the deposition. Good audio facilitates proper questioning pace. Good lighting and framing enhances the presence of the attorney—both the deposing attorney and the defending attorney—and allows you to view the witness's facial expressions, which can provide vital clues to the witness's veracity and state of mind.

24.9   Preparing to Take the Remote Deposition

24.9.1   Prepare Exhibits

Prepare and distribute exhibits consistent with the parties' remote deposition protocol and the rules of the jurisdiction. If sending the exhibits to the witness, defending counsel, and court reporter in advance, premark the exhibits with an exhibit number. To protect confidential information and to preclude the witness and counsel from knowing what documents will be used as exhibits, deliver hard copies in a sealed envelope that remains sealed until the witness and counsel open them on camera, or digital copies protected by a password you disclose only when the exhibits are used at the deposition. Make the file name for each digital exhibit reflect the document's exhibit number.

If you intend to introduce exhibits using the screensharing function of the online platform, name each digital exhibit and assemble them in a file that you can open on your screen. Familiarize yourself with the screen-sharing function of the online platform. If you want to mark on the documents or have the witness mark on them, learn to use the platform's annotation feature and be prepared to explain to the witness how to annotate the exhibit.

24.9.2   Anticipate Delays

Prepare your deposition outline and choose deposition topics (*see* Chapter Five) cognizant that remote depositions take longer than in-person depositions—small delays in loading exhibits and momentary lags in connectivity add up quickly; screen fatigue requires more breaks; the whole process is just slower. Where the applicable rules limit the duration of a deposition, organize and prioritize the areas of inquiry so you address critical subjects within the allotted time.

24.9.3 Perform a Test Run

By now, most attorneys are familiar with the online videoconferencing platforms (some would say all too familiar). But if you are new to remote depositions or unfamiliar with the platform or exhibit-sharing software, conduct a test run of the remote deposition. Create a pre-deposition meeting on the platform, and have colleagues connect from other locations to play the roles of witness, court reporter, and opposing counsel, so you can experience the differences in taking a deposition remotely and address any technical issues.

24.10   Taking the Remote Deposition

While on the record during the remote deposition, reiterate important aspects of the stipulated deposition protocol, gain additional commitments from the witness, and carefully note any technical issues and improper conduct as they arise.

24.10.1   Include Stipulated Deposition Protocol on the Record

At the outset of the deposition, the court reporter or videographer may set forth the parties' stipulations to various aspects of the deposition. Also note the other counsel's agreement to the deposition protocol. One option is to mark the protocol as an exhibit to the deposition and ask all other counsel to confirm their stipulation to it. Another option is to elicit an on-record agreement from counsel to key protocol provisions.

Key Protocol Provisions (see section 24.7):

- no one other than the court reporting service records the deposition;

- each participant's camera will be on at all times;

- no one is present in the room except persons on camera;

- except for the witness and deposing attorney, mute microphones when not speaking;

- counsel will not communicate with the witness while the witness is on the record, except as necessary to ascertain whether a privilege must be asserted; and

- in those instances, the witness or defending counsel must first state on the record the fact of that communication.

24.10.2   *Obtain Additional Commitments from the Witness*

In addition to the basic commitments obtained from the witness as described in section 6.3, obtain commitments germane to the remote nature of the deposition (*see* section 6.3.2). Some of the basic commitments mentioned previously—such as not speaking over one another and letting counsel know if a question was not heard or understood—can easily be modified to explain their importance in the online context. Other commitments described in section 6.3.2 are repeated here using a slightly different dialogue to address issues unique to the online environment.

Q: Other than the computer you are using to connect to the deposition right now, do you have any electronic devices within your view?

A: Just my phone.

Q: Is your phone on or off?

A: It's on, but it's turned to silent.

Q: It's important that there not be any distractions during the deposition and that you're focused on answering my questions. So please turn off the phone. You can, of course, check it during breaks.

A: Okay.

Q: Can you hold up your phone so I can see it's turned off?

A: Sure, here. (Holding up phone.)

Q: Great, thank you. What files and programs do you have open on your screen right now?

A: Just the deposition.

Q: Do you agree not to have any other file or program open on your computer screen while we're on the record?

A: Yes.

Q: And you understand that, after a break, I will ask you if you viewed anything on your computer screen or electronic devices or referred to any notes, documents, or other material?

A: Yes.

Q: Do you have, within your view, any notes, documents, or other material regarding this case or the underlying events?

A: Nope.

Q: Do you agree not to refer to any notes, documents, or other material or person or anything else unless I ask you to do so?

A: Sure.

Q: Are there any persons in the room with you today?

A: No.

Q: It's important that we all know who might be in the room to know who is listening, observing, or trying to communicate with you, especially since what we talk about today may include confidential information. Do you understand that?

A: Yeah, I get it.

Q: If anyone enters the room, will you tell me immediately?

A: I will.

Q: If at any time you're unable to hear or see me or your attorney, will you let us or the court reporter know?

A: Yes.

Revisit these commitments after breaks. At the end of the deposition, confirm that the witness followed them.

24.10.3   *Make a Good Record If Issues Arise*

During the deposition, a witness may appear to be reading something on their computer screen, referring to something in their lap, or looking off camera to another part of the room. Promptly call out the behavior for the record and inquire of the witness. You can even ask the witness to "show me your hands," to see if they are holding anything, or request a camera-sweep of the room to confirm that no one else is present and no notes or other documents are within the declarant's view.

Make a record of anything else that might lead to terminating the deposition or require a ruling from the court, including connection issues and improper communications between the witness and counsel.

24.11   Defending the Remote Deposition

When defending at a remote deposition, take these additional steps to protect the interests of your client and witness.

24.11.1   *Promptly Interpose Any Objections to the Notice*

Objections to the deposition notice are waived unless promptly served, and an objection to the officer's qualification must be made before the deposition begins or promptly after the basis for disqualification was known or, with reasonable diligence, could have been known (Rule 32(d)).

24.11.2   Confirm Protocol and Whether to Attend with Witness

Ascertain whether any remote deposition protocol exists by virtue of court order or the law of the jurisdiction. If not, negotiate the protocol with the deposing attorney (*see* section 24.7). Also determine whether you will attend the deposition in the same room as the witness. If possible, that is the better option.

24.11.3   Prepare the Witness

Conduct the witness preparation sessions, or at least the mock examination portion (*see* section 17.4.7), using the deposition platform. In addition to covering the usual witness preparation issues, work with the witness on answering questions in a way that accounts for the time lag for some participants in the proceeding (e.g., if necessary, taking a beat before answering to give time for objections), reviewing documents displayed on exhibit-sharing software, and accessing electronic files containing exhibits.

If you will not be physically present with the witness at the deposition, ensure that the witness has adequate technology and connectivity, is seated in front of a suitable background, and has front-facing lighting and favorable camera framing. As in video depositions, tell the witness not to sit in a chair that swivels. Emphasize that the witness's room should be quiet and free of distractions, and their attire should be appropriate for court or, at the least, business casual. Finally, coordinate with the witness on the best way to alert you if the witness has a concern about disclosing privileged information, as well as the best way to confer during breaks (assuming conferences are allowed in the jurisdiction).

24.11.4   Protect Your Witness During the Deposition

When an exhibit is delivered in an electronic file or shared on screen, your witness may need an extra moment to review the exhibit before answering questions about it. Make sure the witness is given ample time to review the entire document and that the witness uses that opportunity.

Be ready to object and, where necessary and appropriate, to instruct the witness not to answer, notwithstanding the online format. If your microphone is muted during the proceedings, be ready to unmute immediately to interpose the objection, particularly if you are not in the same room as the witness.

Because of "Zoom fatigue," pay extra attention to whether the witness needs a break. If the witness appears weary, call for a break when no question is pending (if allowed in the jurisdiction) or ask if the witness needs one.

During any type of break or recess, remain on guard. Even with their camera off and mic muted, opposing counsel is still able to hear everything that is said and see all that is done. Therefore, make sure that the witness does not confer with you in a manner that could disclose confidential or privileged information.

If you are in the same room as the witness, mute your mic(s), turn off your camera(s), and go out of the room for the break. If you and the witness are in different locations, you may confer in a virtual breakout room assigned for that purpose; better yet, before the deposition arrange with your witness that during breaks you will mute your mics, turn off your cameras, leave the physical rooms in which the cameras are set up, and confer by phone or some other means besides the deposition platform. If you must meet with the witness in a virtual breakout room, make sure there are no other participants and the recording function is off. Remember, also, that if the breakout rooms have been set to return the participants to the main room after a certain number of minutes, you both may be returned to the main room automatically or with a countdown you do not see.

24.12   Conclusion

The remote deposition brings together the skills and techniques discussed throughout this book for preparing and using exhibits, questioning the witness, preparing the witness, and defending the witness, and it prompts all counsel to adapt these skills and techniques to a videoconference format. As such, it is a fitting topic to close this book, leaving you simply with this: May all your depositions, whether held in person or held remotely, be effective.

Chapter Twenty-Four

CHECKLIST
REMOTE DEPOSITIONS

Deposing counsel

✔	Determine whether a remote deposition is prudent in light of reduced travel costs, the witness's role in the case, the number of potential exhibits, and other factors related to the litigation.
✔	Check all laws, rules, and orders applicable to remote depositions in the jurisdiction, including any standing orders or Rule 26 orders that provide a protocol for remote depositions.
✔	Select an online platform and court reporting service, considering whether to incorporate a videographer and specialized exhibit-sharing software.
✔	Serve notice of the deposition, specifying an intention to conduct the deposition remotely, the manner in which the deposition will be recorded, and how the oath shall be administered.
✔	Decide the best way to introduce exhibits at the deposition based on the particular witness and any specific security needs.
✔	Work with opposing counsel on a deposition protocol, covering the location and connectivity of each participant, who (if anyone) will attend with the witness, the administration of the oath and manner of recording, adequate security, limitations on witness-attorney communications, restrictions on notes and electronic devices, the introduction and use of exhibits, and measures to take in the event of connectivity and technical issues.
✔	Equip the virtual deposition room with an adequate computer, internet connection, camera, microphone, and headset as needed.
✔	Prepare the intended exhibits for use at the deposition.
✔	Organize the topics of inquiry to ensure that the most important ones are covered even if the deposition takes longer than anticipated.
✔	At the deposition, confirm agreement to the protocol and obtain additional commitments from the witness regarding electronic devices, materials in view, answering questions without assistance, and who is in the room.
✔	At the deposition, attend to any indication of improper conduct by the witness or counsel.

Defending counsel

✔	Object to the deposition notice and file a motion for a protective order, if needed.
✔	Prepare the witness for a remote deposition using the selected online platform, covering the handling of exhibits, the means of communicating with counsel, and the appearance of the witness and the deposition room.
✔	At the deposition, remain vigilant of witness fatigue, connectivity or technology issues, timely assertion of objections, and confidentiality during breaks.

APPENDICES

Example Commitments (see Chapter 6.3)

Q: My name is _____. I represent _____, and I am taking your deposition. Are you represented by _____ as your attorney today?

Q: Have you ever been to a deposition before?

Q: Have you ever testified under oath in any type of proceeding?

Q: Let's go over the ground rules for this deposition, so we all have the same understanding.

Q: In this deposition, I will be asking you questions and you will be answering them truthfully under oath. Do you understand that?

Q. My questions and your answers will be recorded by the court reporter, who is at the end of the table. For the court reporter to do that, you need to speak up and answer with words so you can be heard, rather than giving a nod or a shake of your head. Do you understand that?

Q. Will you do your best to give audible, oral answers?

Q: The court reporter also might have trouble if we talk over each other. I'll try not to cut you off while you're answering a question, and I ask you to wait until I finish my question before you begin to answer, even if you think you know what the rest of the question will be. Will you wait for me to finish my question before answering?

Q: You have just taken an oath that requires you to tell the truth, the whole truth, and nothing but the truth. Do you understand that?

Q: That's the same oath you would take if you were to testify in court, do you understand?

Q: We're interested in finding out everything you know about the events and facts that underlie this lawsuit. We are looking for full, complete, and accurate answers to my questions—the "whole truth" that you just took an oath to give. Will you tell me the whole truth today?

Q: If you don't understand any of my questions, please let me know.

Q. If you do answer, I'm going to assume that you do understand the question, alright?

Q: I intend to take one break in the morning, a break for lunch, and one break in the afternoon. If you need a break at another time, please let me know. I will finish my line of questioning, but then we'll break at the next appropriate time. Sound good?

Q: You see that we have water and coffee here for you. Feel free to get up and get whatever you need during the break, okay?

Q. I know I asked you before we started, but do you need any water or coffee now?

Q: If you need to talk to your attorney, let me know. I just ask that if I've asked you a question, you finish your answer before speaking to your lawyer, unless you need to talk to her about whether your answer would be privileged. Okay? [Check law of the jurisdiction.]

Q: Sometimes it happens that you'll give an answer as completely or as accurately as you can, but then later on you'll remember some additional information or a clarification to give to the earlier question. If that happens, will you tell us that you'd like to add to your answer?

Q: Now, because I'm entitled to your full, complete, and accurate answers, I have to ask you this. Are you taking any medication or drugs of any kind that make it difficult for you to understand and answer my questions today?

Q: Have you taken any cough syrup or anything containing alcohol that might make it difficult for you to understand and answer my questions?

Q: Are you at all sick today?

Q: Is there any reason why you cannot give full, complete, and accurate testimony today?

Additional Commitments for Remote Depositions (see section 24.10.2)

Q.   Other than the computer you are using to connect to the deposition right now, do you have any electronic devices within your view?

Q.   Is your phone on or off?

Q.   It's important that there are no distractions during the deposition and that you're focused on answering my questions. So please turn off the phone. You can check it during breaks.

Q.   Can you hold up your phone so I can see it's turned off?

Q.   What files and programs do you have open on your screen right now?

Q.   Please close any file or program open on your computer screen, other than what you are using to connect to the deposition [or view exhibits] and confirm for me that you've done that.

Q: Do you agree not to open any other file or program until we've completed the deposition [or while we're on the record]?

Q.   And you understand that, after a break, I will ask you if you viewed anything on your computer screen or electronic devices or referred to any notes, documents, or other material?

Q.   Do you have within your view any notes, documents, or other material regarding this case or the underlying events?

Q.   Do you agree not to refer to any notes, documents, or other material or person or anything else unless I ask you to do so?

Q.   Are there any other persons in the room with you today?

Q.   It's important that we all know who might be in the room to know who is listening, observing, or trying to communicate with you, especially since what we talk about today may include confidential information. Do you understand that?

Q.   If anyone enters the room, will you tell me immediately?

Q.   If at any time you're unable to hear or see me or your attorney, will you let me (or us) or the court reporter know?

Common Objections at a Deposition

Form Objections—Waived Unless Made at the Deposition

Leading (Fed. R. Evid. 611(c))

Ambiguous/Vague/Unintelligible/Complex/Confusing

Argumentative

Asked and Answered

Assumes Facts Not in Evidence

Compound Question

Misleading Question

Misquoting the Witness/Misstates Prior Testimony

Calls for a Narrative

Calls for Speculation

Calls for a Legal Conclusion

Calls for an Improper Lay Opinion

Calls for an Opinion Beyond an Expert's Qualifications

Calls for Hearsay (Possibly)

Calls for Privileged Information or Work Product

Foundation Objections—Waived Unless Made at the Deposition

No Authentication (Fed. R. Evid. 901–902)

Lack of Personal Knowledge (Fed. R. Evid. 602)

Not Best Evidence (Fed. R. Evid. 1001, et seq.)

No Foundation

Sole Bases for Instructing the Witness Not to Answer (Fed. R. Civ. P. 30(c)(2))

To preserve a privilege

To enforce a limitation ordered by the court

To present a motion under Fed. R. Civ. P. 30(d)(3)

National Institute for Trial Advocacy

INDEX